OVERTURE & BEGINNERS, PLEASE

by

John Toogood

© John Toogood 2014

A copy of this book has been deposited with the British Library

All rights reserved.

No part of this publication may be reproduced, stored in a retrieval system, or transmitted in any form by any means, mechanical, electronic, photocopying, recording or otherwise, without the written permission of the copyright holder.

ISBN 978-0-904327-21-2

Published by Ruddocks Publishing Ltd, 287 High Street, Lincoln LN2 1AW

Printed by Ruddocks, 56 Great Northern Terrace, Lincoln LN5 8HL

FOREWORD

It is a wonder to me that I didn't cross paths with John Toogood until he had semi-retired to Lincolnshire and I had moved to the county to work for, among others, the local BBC. It was only when reading his book that I realised that our careers have, on many occasions, come so close to converging, particularly during my periodic stints in the West End. We know many of the same people, have worked at most of the same theatres, even, at times, had a hand in the same productions, yet we never actually met. It was a shared love, not of the theatre, but of big-band and jazz music that finally put us in touch with one another when I moved to Lincolnshire and transferred by Big-Band music programme from BBC Radio Kent. One of the first people to contact the show was John, who was eager to fill me in on all the local and regional bands, venues and gigs. Over time we met at various events and he became, and I am pleased to say still is, a regular and valued contributor to our programme with his reviews and gig information.

People who are interested in entertainment and the lives of the people in the industry are well used to biographies of great actors, musicians, entertainers, comics and performers, but it is unusual to get a view from the front of house. For the "turns" like me, life is lived on the boards or back stage, with few of us having any real idea of the work going on at the other end of the building to get the house in, keep it happy, get it out and make a profit. John Toogood has had a remarkable career, not least because his was not a "steady" life. Indeed, in so many respects it was much like that of an actor – good jobs, bad jobs, great jobs and occasionally no jobs. The pressures to find work and keep working are no different. What is different is the extent to which a good theatre manager has to equip himself with practical skills, for the odd bit of hasty maintenance; people skills to, quite literally, be at ease with everyone from Royalty to rock fans, the operatti to all-in wrestlers; a thorough knowledge of showbusiness so that visiting "stars" will feel they are dealing with an expert; and a sharp business mind.

From John's story, you will quickly realise that a theatre manager's role is not simply a question of popping on the tuxedo and standing at the back watching the show. Fire drills, production meetings, crew wages, staff and customer complaints, stocking the bars and merchandise stalls, hosting VIP guests, placing advertising, PR and marketing and, most importantly, totting up the takings at each performance for the inevitable meeting with the producers and investors are all in almost every day's work.

This is a candid tale of the life, laughs, loves, frustrations, elations, injustices, and celebrations in a long career in the theatre. A career that took John Toogood around much of the world, soared at times to the heights of running the most prestigious theatres in the UK and interspersed with spells calling bingo or keeping order at the nude review venues of the 60s and 70s. All in all this is a fascinating view of the entertainment industry from a seldom-shared perspective and amply illustrates that crazy, desperate, thrilling, awful and wonderful world of showbusiness.

Howard Leader

Overture and Beginners, Please

CONTENTS

Prelude vii

Overture ix

Act 1 Scene 1	Lincoln 1958-63	15
Act 1 Scene 2	Bristol 1963-66	22
Act 1 Scene 3	Liverpool 1966-71	30
Act 1 Scene 4	Greenwich 1971-72	43
Act 2 Scene 1	Peter Pan Tour (Lulu) 1972-73	50
Act 2 Scene 2	Cheltenham 1973	57
Act 2 Scene 3	Margate 1973	61
Act 2 Scene 4	Revolution Club 1973	66
Act 2 Scene 5	Peter Pan Tour (Anita Harris) 1973-74	70
Act 3 Scene 1	Into the West End 1974	79
Act 3 Scene 2	Let's Get Laid 1974-76	83
Act 3 Scene 3	Happy as a Sandbag 1976	89
Act 3 Scene 4	Emu in Pantoland 1976-77	93
Act 3 Scene 5	Side by Side by Sondheim 1977-78	96
Act 3 Scene 6	The Unvarnished Truth 1978	102
Act 3 Scene 7	Peter Pan (Jane Asher) 1978-79	107
Act 4 Scene 1	The King & I (Pre-Production) 1979	111
Act 4 Scene 2	The King & I (The Palladium) 1979-80	121
Act 4 Scene 3	Hinge & Bracket 1980-81	129
Act 4 Scene 4	Rowan Atkinson in Revue 1981	133
Act 5 Scene 1	Johnny Zero 1981	136
Act 5 Scene 2	M.M.A. Presentations 1981-86	138
Act 5 Scene 3	Seven Brides 1986	151

Act 6 Scene 1	General Manager at P.E.T. 1986	157
Act 6 Scene 2	The Run of Chess 1987-89	162
Act 6 Scene 3	Anything Goes Opening 1989	174
Act 6 Scene 4	The Run of Anything Goes 1990	185
Act 6 Scene 5	Six Shows 1991	189
Act 6 Scene 6	Some Like It Hot 1992	196
Act 6 Scene 7	Refurbishment 1992-93	200
Act 6 Scene 8	Crazy For You 1993-96	205
Act 7 Scene 1	Courier 1996-97	214
Act 8 Scene 1	The Green Room Cabaret 1997	219
Act 9 Scene 1	The Old Vic 1999	225
Act 9 Scene 2	Atlanta Ballet 1999-2000	232
Act 9 Scene 3	Sheffield City Hall 2000	236
Act 10 Scene 1	Back to Lincoln 2001-07	242
Act 10 Scene 2	A Close Shave 2008-10	251
Act 10 Scene 3	The Lincoln Legend 2011-12	255
Act 10 Scene 4	Identity Fraud 2013	264
	Encore	269
	Acknowledgements & Thanks	272

PRELUDE

How is it that an impressionable young man from a humble upbringing in a small provincial city got involved in the theatre and entertainment business which resulted in over 50 years of enjoyable employment, where he was respected by his peers, artistes, and eminent stars from the world of show business? I will tell you all about it, but first of all you should know a little about me, my past, my lifestyle and what makes me tick.

Over the years, several remarks and observations have been made about me, that I intend to expand upon and explain to you in the following pages, and amongst them are some of the following.

I have an inherent motivation to get to the top and be the best at whatever I choose to do, or to overcome a challenge that presents itself, and feel at times that I am a man of fate, and am far more than the 'silver tongued Lounge Lizard' that I am often mistaken for.

I have always put pleasure and enjoyment on an equal footing with work and study, and relied on a good grounding in life, which I have obtained at The University of Life, and have become a popular and familiar figure for whom nothing is too much trouble.

I attempt to do everything in my own inimitable way, with a certain personal style and Chutzpah, and have an immaculate sense of dress which is much admired, judging by remarks I get from both sexes.

I have discovered over the years that I have the ability, charisma, leadership skills, willpower and ego to fulfil my own prophecy and have been told that my attention to detail would have made me an ideal candidate to mastermind The Great Train Robbery in 1963 or The Great Escape in World War Two.

I am often described as someone who is his own man, which I put down to the fact that I am someone who does not mind being in his own company and prefers at times to do his own thing rather than be with a group of friends who have no plan of action for their social evening. Looking back, many of my activities have also been solo things, and being in a Senior Management role for most of my career I have had to keep my distance from many people that I would like to have known better under different circumstances.

I have developed into a character that exudes confidence, which at times has spilled into arrogance, as I have been determined to get to the top and be the best at whatever I do. My word is my bond and I find unpunctuality unacceptable.

I have always been a night owl, and a good listener, and believe that a problem shared is a problem halved. I always live life to the full, burning the candle at both ends and sometimes in the middle as well, and believe that age is unimportant in life, except if you are a nice cheese or a vintage wine.

Employers have said to me during my career that: "I have no hesitation in offering you the position, as you are head and shoulders above the other applicants" and posted in my portfolio: "You are without doubt the finest Manager that we have ever employed".

I like to think that I am universally respected and liked by those who KNOW me, but unfortunately have attracted negative comments and a bad press from people who DON'T and get the wrong impression about my good intentions.

During the last three years, since 2011, I have found it to be a great privilege to be accepted by a large cross section of younger people, many at Lincoln University, who respect the fact that I still go out most nights to mix, make new friends, socialize, dance, advise them and listen to music of another generation, which all helps to keep me fit, young and active. I thank them here for creating what has become "JayJay the Lincoln Legend".

Dream...Believe and Succeed

OVERTURE

I was born in the Bromhead Nursing Home in Lincoln to Ray and Joan who were Antique Dealers. We lived at 44 Steep Hill, which is the site of the Roman South Gate to Lindum Colonia. I was joined by my sister Susan a year later and we lived a very happy life together as 'The Folks Who Live on The Hill'.

My parents were both social animals, from whom I have inherited my joy of life, and they could be found most weekends dancing the night away at The County Assembly Rooms in the Bail. Indeed on many a night we could hear the chattering outside on the Hill as a ladder was pitched up to the first floor window of the bedroom Susan and I were sleeping in, as Ray had lost his front door keys during the evening. Such was their joy of dancing that Dad had laid a parquet dance floor in the kitchen, and bought a Radiogram to play his collection of 78rpm dance and jazz records.

Both my parents enjoyed a good drink and their motto was 'Live for today as you don't know what tomorrow will bring'. I certainly inherited the taste having first woken up with a hangover on the morning following my 17th birthday and having to attend school as normal.

Susan and I first attended Eastgate School, where an afternoon nap on a camp bed was de rigueur, to be followed by high tea at 5pm in the kitchen of the house. This was a proper knife and fork high tea of cold meats and salads, or pork pie, and bread and butter, followed by cake and a cup of tea. Playtime in the kitchen followed whilst Ray and Joan cat-napped in front of the traditional coal fire before a wash. Bath night was once a week, and then off to bed. Most nights whilst we were having tea, Uncle Bill would call in for a cuppa on his way home from work as a Painter & Decorator and discuss where he and his wife Gazz would meet up with Mum and Dad over the weekend.

I next attended Westgate School and made many friends with whom I still keep in touch. Most of them shared my interest in Motor Cycle Racing and what was Scrambling in pre Moto Cross days. In order to emulate our heroes we used to race our road bikes on any off-road area we would find: a car park, a rough track leading to a set of garages or a strip of land next to the West Common. So keen were we to pursue our hobby that sometimes we would meet up at 7.30am to ride for an hour before school. The core of these lads, Colin Reed, Tim Pepper, Peter Watson, Clem Jarvis and Bob Lilley, formed 'The Hills & Hollows Gang' and we used to organise our own Cycle Trials & Scrambles with entry money, track markers, programme, a reporter and awards.

I first developed my organisational skills at these events. In addition to collecting the sixpence entry money and drawing up the race format, including a 'two on a bike pillion race', and even a sidecar race, I made the marker posts and direction signs to the track in Dad's

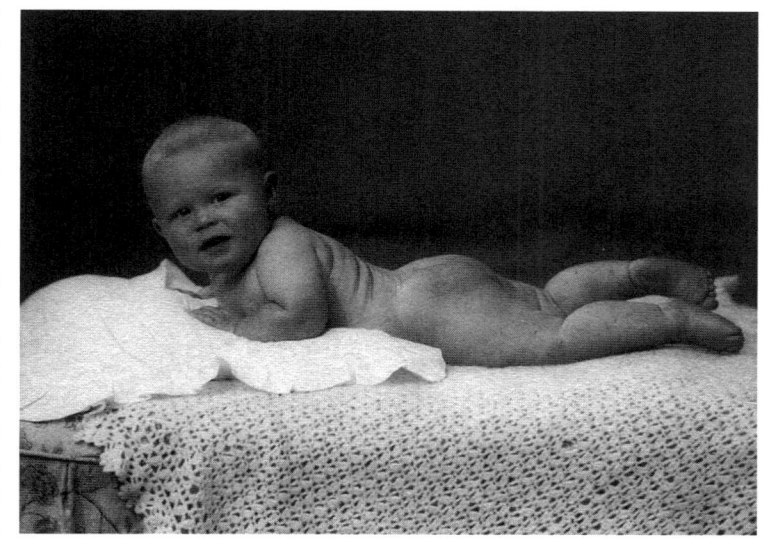

JT at 8 months 1945

workshop. The road bikes and frames were not up to such punishment and did not last long, so many of us built our own specials. Being somewhat of an individual, even then, I built a bike with front suspension, which was inherited by my cousin Steve, and a sidecar with a hinged wheel.

Not all of my spare time at Westgate was taken up with individual pursuits. I played Right Wing for the school football team, earning the nickname of 'Lightning'. I was no mean athlete in the sprint events in the 1954-56 seasons, representing the school at the annual interschool challenge held at Sincil Bank football ground. I had my photo published in The Echo attempting to clear the high jump bar at 3'2" with my scissor kick.

On a wet and gloomy day in 1956 the School organised an outing to London to attend The Royal Tournament at Earls Court, and as this was my first long steam journey to Kings Cross and back, I can recall it well. Those of us whose parents could afford the school uniform looked resplendent in our caps and gabardine macs, with a rucksack over our shoulders that contained sandwiches and drink to last the whole day. Six or eight of us crammed ourselves into one of the individual compartments off the coach corridor and I can remember sharing the compartment with Colin Reed, Dave Cullen, Tim Pepper, and Colin Mole, filling in our Ian Allan Train Spotting Book as we sped up and down the main East Coast Line. However I recall little of what went on in The Royal Tournament apart from the Naval field gun race.

Colin Mole was a very close friend. His Mother was the cook for the Dean of Lincoln Cathedral, and he lived in accommodation there, the gardens of which backed onto the upper parts of Steep Hill. The garden was huge and we spent most summer days playing cricket on the lush lawn, building a bonfire for Guy Fawkes night or slipping under the cover of the back wall to sneak a look at the nudes posing for the life drawing class on a Tuesday evening at the Arts School that overlooked the Deanery Garden.

We both had an interest in Meccano building and model railways. I had an 0-6-2 loco with lots of assorted mixed freight wagons and the L.M.S. The Duchess of Montrose, whilst he had the 60022 A4 Mallard 'Streak', the finest example of a piece of engineering you could find. One of our masters at Westgate, who had a gammy leg and used to ride a Vespa, encouraged us to become members of The Lincoln Model Engineering Society and assist in the building and running of a large table top track in the basement of a dank cellar off Long Leys Road, past the West Common.

Here again I showed early signs of being an individual and a leader, by arriving at the venue half an hour early, collecting the keys from the caretaker and putting the heating on prior to the arrival of others. It was always dark by the time we finished about 10.30 pm, and the walk or cycle along the side of West Common was not something I looked forward to, for despite being a good runner I was not one for fisticuffs, and I used to get a pillion lift back to Castle Square on the Vespa.

Weekends at home were dependent on the seasons, but always started with a roast 'Sunday Lunch' at 1pm on a Saturday to which my Grandmother Gertrude, or Big Mama as I called her, would join us. She and my Grandfather Arthur Albert, or Little Papa to me, owned the antique shop at 24 Steep Hill. This was a well-known part of Lincoln with its many antique shops, and as if to keep it in the family my Uncle Eric, my mother's brother, also ran one at number 46. Eric had been a Sapper in the War and met a Dutch Girl, Tannie, whom he brought

JT on bike doing wheelie 1959

over to Lincoln in 1945, and who was accepted as one of the family by Arthur and Gertie.

The Saturday dinner (we never referred to it as lunch), was the big social meal of the week and consisted of either a roast beef, lamb or pork joint, a variety of fresh vegetables from Arthur's allotment and of course a pan of mushy peas. The meal was frequently interrupted by what we called 'lookers round' who rang the bell at either 24 or 28 Steep Hill, which Dad had purchased as a second shop, with workshop and storage, to come in and browse, but without buying anything.

Our parents were out most weekends till the early hours to pubs in the Bail, where there were regular 'lock ins'. One of Ray's favourite tricks was to say to the landlord that it was his birthday and ask if there was any chance of 'one for the road', which under the circumstances there always was. He taught me this trick at a Theatre Pub in The West End years later, when I was Drinking for England, and it still worked.

Dad used to pop back during the evening to check that we were safe, and I remember one night when Susan had been sick in bed, getting her cleaned up and bringing her down to the kitchen to await the next visit by Dad, and put clean sheets on her bed. Sunday morning was usually a lie-in morning, when as a treat I would take my parents breakfast in bed, a meal taught to me by Little Mama, Grandma Florence, which was scrambled eggs with a tin of tomatoes, which Susan thought was similar to eating a bowl of sick.

Ray and Joan Toogood

We then went out as a family to the coast, a Motor Cycle Race Meeting, or visited a historic House like Chatsworth, which both my sister and I loathed. On our return journey we would always stop off at a pub in the countryside and our treat was a glass of lemonade and a packet of crisps with the salt in its little blue wrapper. This was in the days before the drink drive law came into being, but we always got home safe and sound.

I passed my eleven plus school exam, and whereas most of the gang went to The City School, I went to The Lincoln School, which was a boys' only Grammar School with 50 or so boarders in School House. This terrified me, as tales were rife of fagging by the Prefects and punishments such as having your head held in a toilet bowl as its contents were flushed.

On my first September morning I parked my bike in the bike shed resplendent in my brand new blazer and grey shorts with a shiny brown satchel slung round my neck to be allocated to Class 3C in the Prep School. The Prep was a wooden outbuilding situated at one side of the school playing field away from the main school buildings and necessitated a walk in all weathers to go anywhere else.

The Form Master was Mr. Grainger who also taught French and I found out later he was the Director of the Annual School Drama Production. I found this out after being called to the front of the class one day to be asked to take a letter home with me. This I imagined was a letter to my parents removing me from the school as I was not doing too well and found some subjects like French very difficult to get my head round.

I need not have worried as when the letter was opened that evening at home, Mr. Grainger was asking for some stage props for his forthcoming production of *The Importance of Being Earnest*. Being keen to help I suggested that a set of Snooker Cues at the back of the shop could be used as the 'stage props', not knowing what a stage prop was. He was in fact asking to borrow a Georgian silver tea set for the 'Cucumber Sandwiches' afternoon tea party scene, which my parents were unwilling to let him have because of its value and possible damage. I did however volunteer to be part of the stage crew for the scene changes on the show and this was my first involvement with anything theatrical.

As I was not an academic, I found the school work very challenging. The only subject I found at all easy to get on with was the Carpentry Class as I was quite at ease using tools that were to be found in Dad's workshop at home, and made items such as a bookcase, coffee table and rush mat stool which are still in use today some 60 years later.

I made many new friends in Class 3C, the most notable being Peter Upton or 'Uppey' as he was nicknamed, because as we sat at desks in alphabetical order 'U' was always behind 'T' and I found him a great character and a most talented musician. Rock and Roll Music was just beginning to take over the charts and Peter and our 'One Hand Gang' used to go along to The Regal Cinema to see Bill Haley in *Rock Around The Clock* or the latest Elvis film like *Jailhouse Rock* at The Ritz Cinema.

He was always late in the morning and his reasons for not being on time were legendary, such as: "The railway crossing gates were closed"; "All the traffic lights were on red"; "The chain came off my bike, and I had to push it up Lindum Hill". When the inevitable lines or detention were dished out his reply was always the same: "Frick me, Sir…that's not fair" and then burst into giggles with the rest of us. He was always up for a laugh, and one occasion put his hand up to stop the class, and when asked what the problem was announced: "Toogood has just stabbed me in the eye with his compass, Sir" which of course I hadn't and earned him more lines for wasting time in class.

Visits to his home in Sibthorpe Street were a joy as he could play and sing most of the tunes by Elvis, Buddy Holly, Chuck Berry and The Everly Brothers by ear on the family piano in their front room. Weekly family film visits were also taken to The Radion Cinema in Newport, which is now the home of Radio Lincolnshire. We did not have a television at home, but used to be taken to Carholme Road to visit my father's parents George Henry (Big Papa) and Florence Jemima (Little Mama) as a Sunday evening treat to watch *What's My Line*, if we had been good. They had purchased one of those new-fangled TVs to watch The Coronation in 1953 and we all sat around in the dark, as if you were at 'the pictures' to look at a nine inch screen, with a huge bulbous magnifying glass in front of it.

Following the dash over to the cloisters for the regulation third of a pint of milk from a mini milk bottle, much of the morning break ritual was for an Inter-Class pitched battle behind the Prep building where building rubble was dumped, and which provided ample items to be thrown at the other class. On one occasion I took half a brick slap on the forehead and Mr. Franklin the Headmaster was so concerned that he took me to The County Hospital to have my wound dressed and stitched, before taking me home to my parents. I still have the forehead scar.

Sue and I used to attend the Saturday Morning Minors' Club screenings at The Radion which cost us our weekly pocket money of sixpence. The programme comprised a couple of cartoons, a Laurel and Hardy short, a main Western with The Lone Ranger, and ended with another episode of an ongoing serial film that always ended with the hero or heroine just about to have a horrendous accident, which encouraged you to return the next week to discover the outcome.

Dad and Uncle Bill went to the Cinema on Monday nights, usually again to The Radion, and as we were now getting older were able to join them. It was on these visits that I began my interest in musicals as Sue's choice of what we went to see was usually a Doris Day film like *Calamity Jane* or a classic Fred Astaire & Ginger Rogers show like *Top Hat*. An additional treat on the walk back home was to call at the Fish and Chip Shop in Bailgate for a bag of chips with plenty of salt and vinegar.

My and my Uncle's choice would be a war film as Bill had been a Desert Rat in North Africa during the Second World War before being captured, and we both enjoyed films like *The Colditz Story*, *The*

Wooden Horse and *Sink The Bismarck*. Dad and Bill were very close and when he heard of Bill's release from capture, barrel rolled from the top of Hampton Street Hill to the bottom, such was his joy.

Whilst I was finding academic studies hard at The Lincoln School – my efforts are best summed up with comments by Mr. Grainger on my Report: "With the best will in the world, John will never become a linguist"; "We hope for much better results from John in the non dressing room future" - I regularly represented Bluecoat House in athletics. The 800 yards race proved to be my best distance as I was able to produce a sprint finish after hanging back in 3rd or 4th place for most of the time. I calculated that by saving my burst of speed till the final straight, I could save a few yards not going around the outside of my competitors on the final corner, as the yards saved would be enough to win the race. It worked on most occasions.

I did not enjoy Cross Country Running, but was successful enough at school level to be selected to represent The County one year at Grantham. Cricket, rugby, swimming and the Public School game fives were not my cup of tea, which again shows my early independent attitude to do things as an individual, rather than being a member of a team.

I used to stay for lunch at school and admired one of the Sixth Form Table Monitors who used to serve us as he had modified his regulation school uniform by wearing a black shirt and matching tie, which I admired. This was my first interest in attire, which I still have to this day and am frequently told by admirers that I am 'the smartest man in Lincoln', with my individual taste in what to wear on a night out to which I reply: "I am a fashion setter and not a follower".

Following our dinner, most of my fellow pupils went off to kick a ball around or play cricket in the playground whereas I would slip off to the fence at the side of the playing fields to meet a girl that I had my eye on and who used to come home from the Girls High School to have her mid-day meal. Sue came to the bottom of her garden, where a public footpath separated us from one another, and we used to chat for twenty minutes or so, before going our separate ways and back to lessons for the afternoon. In 2012 I invited her to be my partner in a charity 'Strictly Ballroom' competition held at The Lincoln Performing Arts Centre.

We were given homework daily which I hated as I had formed the opinion that I ought to be able to learn all I needed to know about what life held for me in school hours, without having to do further studies at home. This is again something that I carried forward into my working life, in that I never brought my work home with me, but arranged my workload to meet the deadlines. The only time this rule was broken was at the very end of my career, when one of my last employers issued me with a mobile phone to be able to contact me 24/7 which I regarded as an imposition, and used to 'forget' to put on charge, to ensure some quality social time away from work.

I continued to expand my interest in all forms of good music by listening to Dad's vast collection of 78rpm shellac records in our upstairs front room. I thoroughly enjoyed conducting Elgar's Pomp and Circumstance March, endeavouring to emulate Sir Malcolm Sergeant or 'Flash Harry' which I understood was his nickname. Also in the collection were original copies of recordings by the likes of Paul Whitman and other big bands of the '40s, which Humphrey Littleton described as one of the finest collections of period music he had seen when it became time for me to dispose of the collection, when Sue and I had to sell 44 Steep Hill in August 1999.

As a family we were also keen listeners of the BBC Light Programme and enjoyed *Two Way Family Favourites*. In addition to the modern Pop Songs that were requested I began to enjoy the musicals of the day, and singers like Sinatra, Ella, Sarah Vaughan, Bobby Darin, and the Big Bands of Count Basie, Duke Ellington, and Benny Goodman. This interest has lasted and developed over the past fifty years and led to me now being well informed enough to review bands for the Press and Radio.

In addition to traditional schoolwork and sports, I also joined the Debating Society and enjoyed the formal format of debate and sensible arguments, learning to put across a logical point of view, which has again stood me in good stead during my work in later years. On another occasion I attended a lecture on fire prevention, and was quite astounded to see a bundle of steel wire wool ignite when it came into contact with the positive and the negative terminals of a six-volt battery, which is something else that made a lasting impression on me.

It was during my final year at Lincoln School, in November 1961, that I had my only fight when I was cornered in the bike sheds one day on the way to collect my bike, by a group of lads who had taken objection to something that I had said earlier in the day. My normal reaction would have been to leg it away on the bike, but I was surrounded and outnumbered. With no option but to fight, I picked on one and said: "Hit me anywhere you like but not on the face as I have a show to do tonight" and I got away with bruising to the body.

I failed spectacularly in the end of term 'O' level exams and was advised to stay on for an extra year to re-take them, as I was only in possession of a 'Pass' in Carpentry. During this final formative school year I was left very much on my own devices to study in the School Library but in the exams fared no better the second time round, basically because I had already decided what career I intended to pursue, and did not need academic grades to start.

The Headmaster's (Mr. Martin, known affectionately as 'Nimrod') parting remarks to me were: "Best of luck, Toogood, in the world of the theatre, you will need it", a remark that showed, even in the early days, how misunderstood I was in my determination to get to the top of my chosen profession.

Act 1 Scene 1
LINCOLN
(1958-63)

It all began in December 1958 while I was still at Lincoln School. My sister was a member of a dance troupe with the Christine Orange School of Dance (they called themselves 'The Pippins') and they were in the local Pantomime, Aladdin. When I asked her how the dress rehearsal had gone, she replied: "It went very well, but we were short of the middle legs of the dragon." As I had my eye on one of the dancers, whom I hoped might be in the dragon costume, I said I would be the middle legs, and duly presented myself for the following day's rehearsal.

I enjoyed myself so much working in the theatrical environment that I immediately became hooked, and knew from that moment where I wanted to make my career. I returned the following year, this time working mainly backstage fulfilling any odd jobs that were required. I enjoyed the hard work and long hours, but mostly the social aspect of partying hard, which all theatricals do. Indeed the highlight was the New Year's Eve bash, which went on until the early hours of the morning.

In order to expand my knowledge of theatre techniques and etiquette, I too enrolled with the Christine Orange School of Dance. I began basic dance training, the discipline of which has stood me in good stead to the present day, taking my first Royal Academy of Dancing Exam in May 1959. I made my first appearance as a dancer in the County Amateur Operatic & Dramatic Society (CAODS) Production of the hit musical *The Pyjama Game* in November that year, which was great fun and good experience.

Of the two Amateur Groups based in Lincoln at the time, The Lincoln's and The County, the latter was the more forward looking as it had embraced the new wave of Musicals that people wanted to see. In 1955 they had presented *Oklahoma*, to be followed by *Carousel* in '56, *Annie Get Your Gun* in '57 and the relatively unknown show *Summer Song*, based on The New World Symphony by Dvorak in 1958. The Lincoln's meanwhile stuck with old favourites such as *The New Moon* and *White Horse Inn*.

At this time schoolwork was taking a back seat, and my Mother and Father, who had no theatrical background, gave me every encouragement to pursue my chosen career.

My Father was a skilled cabinetmaker and antique dealer, whilst my Mother ran our antique shops on Steep Hill. One contained the little known South Roman Arch to Lindum Colonia in our coal cellar, on which I used to break down the larger lumps of coal into more useful sizes. I inherited some of my Father's skills, as he was a most gifted engineer. I put them to good use when I was offered the position of Assistant Carpenter at the Theatre Royal, Lincoln, following the end of my full time education. I did finally manage an O level in carpentry, but have since earned Honours from 'The University of Life'.

In order to acquaint myself with the very different types of play that were presented weekly by the Lincoln company, I made it my Saturday night ritual to be first in the queue for the 'second house early doors' to obtain the best seat in the gallery, affectionately known as 'The Gods', where I enjoyed a huge cross section of classical and contemporary shows. By 1959, the Lincoln Theatre Association was in its fourth year, having been instrumental in saving the building from being demolished or used as a Bingo Hall following its closure as a number two touring house which had been run by The Butterworth Chain of theatres. A small group of people rightly thought the building was worth saving, and a Lincoln Repertory Company was established to present plays weekly. The Association's Patrons were Sir Laurence Olivier and Miss Vivien Leigh, the Chairman was Councillor Allan H. Briggs, with Mrs. Kay Darbyshire as Secretary.

The Manager and Licensee was Harold Lander with K.V. Moore as the Director of Productions. He directed the first production I saw from The Gods in February 1959, *The Remarkable Mr. Pennypacker* by Liam O'Brien. Regular members of the cast included Kristine Howarth, Sheila Price, Raymond Llewellyn, Clive Elliot, Audrey Barr and John Ronane.

By Autumn 1959 the Association, which received financial support from The Arts Council of Great Britain, was in its fifth year. I saw Arthur Miller's *A View from the Bridge* with a Stage Director now in the Company named Julian Oldfield. At this point it is worth remembering that in 1959 the Director of the show was traditionally known as 'The Producer' whilst the Stage Director was the most senior person in the backstage team. In the programme for *Two for the Seesaw* that year it was announced that the Pantomime for 1959-60 would be *Jack and the Beanstalk*. As Susan would again be one of The Pippins, I volunteered to work over Christmas doing whatever was required. Other shows listed for presentation included the Whitehall farce *Dry Rot*, *The Beaux Stratagem*, and Oscar Wilde's masterpiece *The Importance of Being Earnest*.

In 1960, its sixth year, the Chairmanship passed to Dr. C. A. Lillicrap, with that other eminent physician Mr. G. C. Wells-Cole as one of the Vice Chairmen. On 23rd May, Harold Lander was pleased to announce that 'The Theatre in Action' Youth group, of which I was the Treasurer, were forming themselves into a more permanent group and that we had set out our objectives, fixed conditions of membership, formed a committee, elected officers and were planning to go to London to see *West Side Story*. A notable addition to the Company for *The Potting Shed* by Graham Greene, and playing Mrs. Potter, was a young actress called Penelope Keith.

I was completely knocked out with *West Side Story* at Her Majesty's Theatre in The Haymarket. It was such a change from the traditional musicals I had seen before, and it has remained one of my favourite musicals of all time, as the show was the 'Star', not someone being a 'Star' in the show. The Theatre in Action Group followed this up the following year with a visit to The New Theatre (now The Noel Coward Theatre) to see Lionel Bart's *Oliver* with the two revolving sets by Sean Kenny and a remarkable performance by Ron Moody as Fagin.

Back in Lincoln, productions of note that Spring included Oscar Wilde's *The Importance of Being Earnest*, with Sheila Price as Lady Bracknell, Tennessee Williams' *The Glass Menagerie* with Clive Elliott as The Son, the Philip King farce *Sailor Beware*, a masterful *The Love of Four Colonels* with Freddy Jones as The Wicked Fairy and Penny Keith as Mrs. Rinder-Sparrow, Shaw's *Arms and the Man* and *The School for Scandal*.

On 29th February, Harold Lander announced the exciting news that The Civic Theatre in Rotherham had joined the unique partnership with The Civic Theatre Scunthorpe and The Stanford Hall Theatre near Loughborough, to enable productions to rehearse for two weeks by playing one week in Lincoln and one week on tour.

He also announced that Theatre in Action would be limited to just 50 youngsters aged 15-18, and a series of six practical demonstrations would be held to increase their interest in the dramatic arts. This age rule ensured that we did our own thing and did not impose on the excellent work done by The Lincoln Theatre Club so ably led by Kay Darbyshire.

By June Roger Winkley had been appointed as Master Carpenter - I will speak more of him later - and that masterful actor Freddy Jones played Claude Vole in *Who's Your Father?* In Autumn 1960 a new Manager & Licensee succeeded Mr. Lander, the formidable Kay Gardner who was to play a pivotal role in my later career.

In the programme notes for the mammoth production of *Romeo and Juliet* it was announced that the Pantomime for 1960-61 would be a three week run of *Puss In Boots* starting, as was the tradition then, on Christmas Eve. Prior to that I would appear as a dancer in my second show for the CAODS production of *The Dancing Years*, by Ivor Novello.

By the start of 1961 Kay Gardner had firmly established herself as leader of The Lincoln Theatre Partnership embracing Lincoln, Loughborough, Scunthorpe and Rotherham. There was a new programme format, with an exciting range of new works that commenced with Harold Pinter's *The Birthday Party* directed by K.V. Moore. Playing McCann was a young actor Roger Redfarn who would go on to direct *Underneath the Arches*, the life story of Flanagan & Allen, at The Prince of Wales Theatre in the West End. One of the ASMs was Christopher Hewis, a versatile young man who used to play percussion in the pit when required and assisted me in running Theatre in Action Sunday Jazz Nights in the Circle Bar. What trust the Licensee showed in my ability as a young seventeen year old, as I was responsible for the organisation, security and well-being of such a prestigious venue for one night a week.

Notable productions during that sixth year included the hugely popular Sandy Wilson musical *The Boy Friend*, memorable for an unforgettable performance by Frederick Hall as Lord Brockenhurst, and Dylan Thomas' *Under Milk Wood* with lighting by Kay Gardner. This was the most ambitious lighting plot that had ever been attempted on The Junior Sunset Switchboard, which was a smaller version of The Grand Master, but without the mechanical interlocking for mastering. The board was operated by John Edwards and me with an assortment of lengths of wood to push and pull the switchboard handles to the required level. It was great experience of working one of the last Junior manual boards in the provinces.

The very Camp Scenic Designer Bryan Graves designed many of the productions and was huge fun to be with at social gatherings.

In May 1961 the Production chosen to end the sixth year was an adaptation of Pickwick Papers entitled *Mr. Pickwick* with Fred Hall in the title role, ably supported by Ray Llewellyn as Sam Weller, Roger Redfarn as Winkle, and Brian Tully as a memorable Snodgrass. On the technical side Jolyon H. Coombs was now the Stage Director, whilst a close friend from Theatre in Action, Bill Fisher, was Assistant Carpenter, whom I would succeed a year later when I had finished at the Lincoln School.

One production of note during the Autumn Season of 1961 was *The Tiger and The Horse* by Robert Bolt with a cast which now included in the Company, Stephanie Cole (who was to advise me which Drama School to attend), and Euan Felton as Stage Manager, with whom I would work again in 1982 on 'Trade Shows' for Mitchell Monkhouse Associates (MMA). I was given a credit as 'Switchboard Operator' by Kay Gardner in the 5th September programme. I played the part of Ptolemy in *Caesar and Cleopatra* by Bernard Shaw at Lincoln and on tour that September.

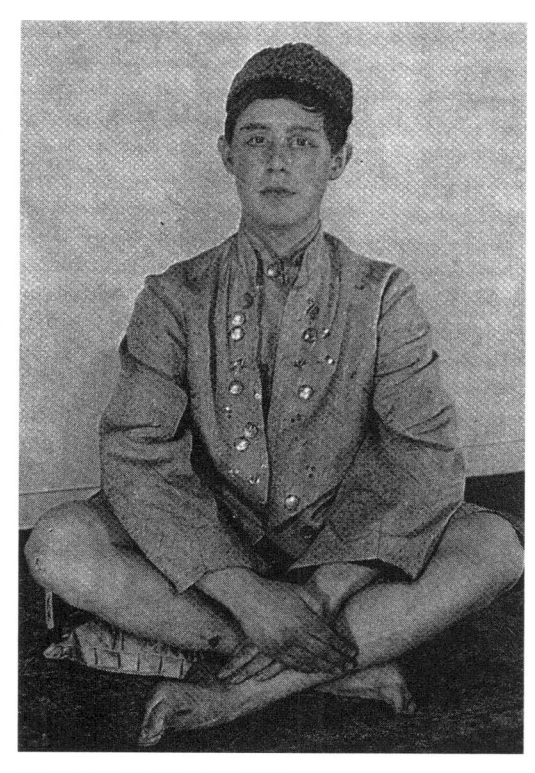

JT as Prince Chulalongkorn 1961

In November 1961 I played my biggest role to date as Prince Chulalongkorn in *The King and I* with Bob Bunn as The King, and doubled as King Simon in The Ballet. Little did I know at the time that I would be Production Manager at The London Palladium for a revival of the show with Yul Brynner in 1979.

The annual money earning Pantomime in 1961 was a production of *Dick Whittington and his Cat*, devised and directed by the ever faithful K.V. Moore, which broke with tradition and opened on Boxing Day for a four week run. Susan was again a Pippin along with Carol Bean, Elizabeth Best, Janette Freestone, June Cook, Barbara Thorpe, Stephanie Nicoll and Hilary Sladdin. I again volunteered my services for the fourth consecutive year as a general dogsbody but by now had experience of working on the Switchboard, on the Fly Floor, running a flat, throwing a cleat line, making props and even stoking the coke fired boiler.

The seventh season of plays commenced in January 1962 with a two week run of *Simple Spymen* by John Chapman, to be followed by a week of 'Opera for All'. This was one of the last occasions at Lincoln when a 'Station Job' was required to move the scenery from The Central Station to the Get In at The Theatre Royal.

It was not unusual back in the early '60s for Productions and Companies to tour by train as British Railways offered very favourable fares between venues. Dependent on the size of the Company, free scenery wagon(s) were provided to move sets, costumes, props and personal luggage. Indeed the size of flattage and length of rolled cloths were determined by the free wagon's dimensions, which were 40' long, 6' high along its side and 8' high in the centre. It was essential to double check with a station that they still had dead end platforms to facilitate a quick off load, as side doors were of little use when manoeuvring an 8' flat or a 40' cloth.

It was also vital to know which theatres were classed as 'Difficult Get Outs' as laid down by the NATKE Union agreement, as an additional payment of ten shillings (50p) per man was charged.

The May production was the Stratford East, Joan Littlewood inspired, show *Sparrers Can't Sing*, which featured music improvised and played by The Lincoln Jazz Club and designs by Suzanne Billings. I lost contact with Suzanne until she came to see a show at The Old Vic that I was managing, some 38 years later, and recognised me Front of House (FOH) in my dinner suit.

In the Spring of '62 the theatre created the role of Public Liaison Officer and the first person appointed was a man we now know as a much-respected Press Critic, Michael Billington. On the technical crew was a new Electrician Derek Drescher, who was later to work for BBC Radio and produced Desert Island Discs for a number of years.

For the Whitsun attraction in June 1962 the repertory season, now in its eighth year, was suspended whilst a couple of other attractions were presented in an attempt to widen the audience base. First were the Spanish Dancers Antonia Mena & Morino Morijo with a programme of songs and dances from Spain, and I attended one of their open classes where we were taught the basics of Flamenco and the Spanish way to hollow clap and click our fingers. In August, as we were at the height of the Trad Boom in Popular Music with Bilk, Ball & Barber getting records into the hit parade, the theatre presented a Holiday Season of Trad Jazz featuring *Ken Barton's 7 piece Oriole Jazz Band*, introduced and compèred by Brigit Forsyth and Paul Chapman from the Lincoln Theatre Company.

Changes were afoot for the start of the '62 August Season with Kay Gardner now firmly established as Director. She was joined by Alan Vaughan Williams as Producer, who again would play a pivotal role in my future, as I had been taken on full time to work as the Assistant Carpenter in the theatre workshops for 7 pounds 15 shillings per week and worked alongside new Scenic Designers Helen Dines and Sam Anderton.

I was also engaged to play as cast, and played Morgan in *Badger's Green* by R.C. Sherriff in August. I was also credited as ASM on *The White Sheep of the Family* in September, and as a Reporter in *Fit to Print* in the same season.

By Autumn '62 I was firmly established as a regular member of the Company. Alan Vaughan Williams had directed several shows, including *Billy Liar* by Keith Waterhouse & Willis Hall. The Company now employed a Production Manager, Steven Webber, to head the Backstage Technical Team, and a new position of House Manger was given to James Harpham to assist the ever-faithful Harry Whitworth. *Humpty Dumpty* was the choice for the 1962-63 Grand Family Pantomime, which ran for three weeks from Boxing Day.

Over Christmas and New Year the weather took a turn for the worse and touring in the early months of 1963 was horrendous. The winter became known as 'The Big Freeze'. It was the tradition for the Get In and Fit Up Crew to travel in the back of the Fred Hunt removal van with the sets, props and wardrobe. To try and keep ourselves warm during the journey, it was not uncommon for us to wrap ourselves into the Black Tabs or a Border, and the stop for a bacon buttie and a mug of tea en route was all we had to look forward to.

In the Panto cast were several people I got on well with, notably Anna Carteret, Penny Keith, Norman Jones, John Savident, Janet Saddleton and Pamela Miles.

I had been a regular patron of The City Club even during my school days. It was always amusing to me that the resident pianist at the Club, Arthur Maynall, who used to play a mean Errol Garner piano with the traditional strident left hand, was also one of my school teachers. As a result of my interest in Jazz we hit it off very well. I recall Dad at the Club ordering a tray full of Champagne to celebrate an occasion, and on his return to his table, slipping over with tray, glasses and contents going everywhere. In typical Toogood style he picked himself up, apologised to his guest and returned to the bar for another tray of drinks.

The Spring Season of the eighth year at the Royal continued post Panto with *As You Like It* directed by Kay Gardner with the relatively unknown Steven Berkoff playing Orlando. In March 1963 the Company toured with Alun Owen's play *The Rough and Ready Lot* to The Little Theatre, Stanley, the Town Hall, West Hartlepool, The Little Theatre, Middlesborough and The Civic, Rotherham in a co-presentation with The North Eastern Association for the Arts.

Following on from this was a Home Tour to the Lincoln Theatre Partnership with *All my Sons*, then another three week Home Tour of *Pyjama Tops*, which again was a show I would work on in the West End for The Paul Raymond Organisation some eleven years later. On the social side, The Theatre Association held its eighth birthday celebration with a May Ball at The Moor Lodge Hotel, Branston with tickets at thirty shillings (£1.50) available from Mike Billington in his role as Public Relations Officer. The evening Dress Ball included a Buffet Supper, Dancing from 9pm – 2am to the Basil Rose Quartet, and a Midnight Cabaret, which was attended by all the good folk of Lincoln.

During Spring 1963 I had decided, with advice from fellow members of the company, to leave Lincoln in the Autumn and pursue my career development at The Bristol Old Vic Theatre School (BOVTS) as it was the only Theatre School that offered both Acting and Technical Courses. I auditioned and was accepted, receiving a grant for my tuition fees from the local Council, thanks to glowing reports from Kay Gardner of my potential in this notoriously unreliable profession.

I continued with the Company into its ninth year of 1963, and worked on *Maria Marten* (or *The Murder in the Red Barn*), *Billy Liar* and *Two Stars for Comfort*, along with the Pantomime *Cinderella*, before I departed for Bristol. By the time of my departure I was sufficiently experienced and trusted to be sent to oversee a Show Fit Up. I had made my own 'Touring Box' of items I would need to ensure the opening of a show on time, something I have achieved on all the shows that I have ever been involved with, apart from one.

Many of the company used to enjoy the hospitality offered by my parents in their living room at Steep Hill, as access to free drinks for poorly paid actors was a godsend. On one occasion, one of the members of the Company over indulged, and as he was my guest, in our house, it befell upon me to sleep on the sofa that night ensuring his safety.

On another occasion, one of the female members of the company, who happened to live close by, invited me to go round for lunch. I duly purchased a bottle of what I thought would be a suitable beverage to take, a sweet Bordeaux Graves Sauternes. My mother Joan was very impressed that I had the courtesy to take such a gift on a lunch date, but collapsed in giggles when I returned half an hour later, with the bottle unopened, as my date had failed to appear.

Having been invited by the theatre director Kay Gardner to join the company full time, I found myself, when not on stage, working in the converted cottages adjacent to the Theatre Royal, which had been gutted and were used as the theatre carpentry shop and scenic studio.

The Master Carpenter was an ex magician called Roger 'Two Hammers' Winkley. He acquired this name as he used two hammers, one to use while the other (allegedly) cooled down. In addition to making the scenery for the weekly Rep shows, I also undertook any menial tasks which would broaden my backstage knowledge. This included working in the Fly's, on the Switchboard, doing Follow-spot, being a Stage Hand, mopping the wings prior to the show, playing small parts, and even being the boiler-man.

As the carpenters shared the area with the designers, who also undertook their own scenic painting, I became very familiar with a cross section of the habits and scenic techniques used by the various designers. Helen Dines acquired the nickname of 'Black Splash' because whatever she created on the flat was then flicked over with black paint. As this was very much a working scenic studio, all the paints were mixed with size on site in a galvanised bucket, which was then placed within a larger bucket, which acted as a water jacket. It was a familiar occurrence for the bucket of paint to overheat when all the water in the surrounding larger bucket had boiled dry, which filled not only the workshop area, but also the surrounding stage, and at times auditorium, with an obnoxious smell.

As well as playing productions at the Theatre Royal, Lincoln, the Company by now had a policy of weekly touring to other theatres in the Partnership. Playing a week at Lincoln and a week at one of the touring dates enabled a production to rehearse for two weeks, which was of great benefit to all concerned, as the ritual was to board a coach after rehearsals at tea-time in Lincoln, travel to the venue for an evening performance and then travel back after the show, traditionally stopping en route for a fish and chip supper. The etiquette was for the most senior member of the Company to be permitted the back seat, where they could lay down and have a cat nap. The hours were long and exhausting, the standard of productions was incredibly high and many eminent actors learnt their trade in this system.

Some of the notable artistes I worked with went on to greater acclaim later in their career and included Penelope Keith (*The Good Life*), John Savident (*Coronation Street*), Stephanie Cole (*Tenko*) and Freddie Jones (*Sir in The Dresser*). The week I was taking my O level exams at school, instead of cramming for my exam the following morning, I was working a follow-spot for the production of Brendan Behan's *The Hostage*. I was even given my own solo spot where a 'pin-spot' beam of light hopped slowly up the stairs, until it got to the bedroom door, where it was extinguished by the door slamming.

The highlight of the year was undoubtedly the annual Pantomime. One particular year, when Sunday Night at the London Palladium was a regular feature, the Pantomime Director decided, in his wisdom, that we should emulate the famous revolving stage, which was so much part of the finale at the Palladium. Unfortunately however, the theatre didn't have a revolve, so some bright spark came up with the idea of making a revolving rostrum on stage with yours truly providing the motive power, lying on my back inside the tomb. As the stage floor had a rake on it, propelling the revolve downhill was fine, though uphill was much harder work. I wonder what the Health and Safety Executive of today would have made of all this.

JT Gopak 1962

My dancing career achieved new heights when I was entered in numerous dance competitions during the summer months at local coastal resorts. My speciality was a Russian 'Gopak' dance, when I would jump as high as I could with my feet outstretched to meet my hands with a yell of delight. For this dance, I frequently achieved very good points and beat many of my fellow female contestants - male dancers at this time were a rare breed. I still possess the medals, cups and certificates I was awarded, and am still friends with many of my fellow competitors, who were much better dancers than I was, but didn't receive the same sympathy vote that I did.

As well as presenting Jazz on a Sunday at the theatre, I was also a member of the Lincoln Jazz club (now disbanded), which met weekly in the rehearsal rooms behind Ye Olde Crowne public house in Clasketgate. On several occasions coach trips to other cities to see eminent visiting American artistes were organised. Highlights were the trip to City Hall in Sheffield to see Ella Fitzgerald and a mystery trip to RAF Scampton in 1963 where the great Count Basie Band was performing on a stopover trip to Germany with singer, Mr 'Five by Five' Jimmy Rushing, so called because he was only five feet tall but had a girth of five feet. It was during this period, and following a visit to the huge Astoria Theatre in Finsbury Park to see The Woody Herman Band, that I wrote my first Jazz Review entitled 'The Best Herd ever Heard?'

My involvement with motor cycle racing continued when not working on a Sunday, but I was still reliant on my parents for transport to get me to and from any meeting I wished to attend, although on occasions I hitch-hiked to meetings. Once I had got myself over to a track near Bevercotes in Nottinghamshire, but could not get a lift or a train back to Lincoln. I had to resort to phoning Dad to see if he would collect me which thankfully of course he did.

I had achieved everything I had set out to do since leaving School, learned a great deal of basic theatre techniques, especially from the ever present and reliable Resident Stage Manager 'Art' Walker. I now knew exactly what I wanted from the course at Bristol as no other pupil, I discovered later, had work experience in a professional theatre, which was going to stand me in good stead for the next three years.

Act 1 Scene 2
BRISTOL
(1963-66)

I decided I should undertake some formal training as everything I had learnt so far had been very hands on. It was suggested I go to the Bristol Old Vic Theatre School (BOVTS), which was the only known training school that had a combined Acting and Technical course spread over a three year period. I auditioned at the age of 18, when I was far too inexperienced in life, and was told to re-apply the following year.

My audition piece was Jacques *Seven Ages of Man* speech from *As You Like It*, which they obviously liked as I was offered a three years' scholarship beginning in September 1963. This was the first time I lived away from home, like most of the other students who had not been to Boarding School, and I was allocated digs in Westbury-on-Trym, a suburb of Bristol. I was with a fellow student, Bill from Nottingham, who was quite a complex and tense person, whom I didn't feel fitted into the concept of a potential theatrical. He was rather immature, and shared very few of my interests. I wanted to go out and enjoy my freedom without the constraints of home life. My first tea away from home was a Melton Mowbray Pork Pie, a tin of Baked Beans and Cheddar Cheese all washed down with a jug of cider… oh the joys of student life!

The academic year was split into three sections: the first year basic acting techniques, second year technical work, and third year final productions at the historic Theatre Royal in Bristol. Unlike many of the students, I already had a good grounding in basic theatre and knew exactly what I wanted from the course, which was basically to find out what the actor does. My intention, after seeing how much better my fellow students were at performing than I was, was to move into management. In addition to basic speech, movement, singing, improvisation, and dancing classes, we undertook extra-curricular Saturday morning events, such as horse riding, judo, and fencing. The most respected tutor was the legendary Rudi Shelley, who insisted during his classes that we all "Squeezed our Lemons" which was his polite way of telling us to clench our bottom cheeks. He joined the BOVTS soon after it opened in 1946 and worked there into his nineties.

My social life revolved around fellow students, music, jazz, dancing, and enjoying myself. I continued my love of big band jazz by attending the Colston Hall to hear as many of the eminent American touring artistes who were visiting England at the time. An added bonus for me, being a student, and only able to afford the cheaper seats, was that I could sit in the choir stalls, where I would be onstage with such bands as Duke Ellington, Count Basie, and Stan Kenton with his 'Wall of Sound'. There were numerous weekly jazz and blues events in clubs and pubs around the city, which I frequented with fellow students. I worked for a time at The Iron Duke Pub in King Street, where Ted the landlord made the most delicious pork doorstep sandwiches I have ever tasted. I used to take these delicacies with me on the overnight milk train which came from the West Country via Bristol to the Midlands for my occasional trips home to Lincoln.

The main reason was to accompany my parents, who were still keen Motor Cycle Grasstrack fans, to major meetings in the north of England, as I did not have any transport of my own. The first of these visits was in September 1964 when I hitch-hiked from Lincoln to Sleaford where that year's National Championships were being held. The following year I hitch-hiked, which was not an uncommon thing for students to do in the sixties, to Braintree in Essex. In my final year in Bristol,

1966, the venue was Wetherby in Yorkshire. My mother was very proud to explain to the person sitting next to her by the ropes that I had travelled all the way up from Bristol to attend the meeting. It was a great time for a great sport which was having its Golden Age. It is now sadly in decline with bad leadership from the top brass and faceless idiots who post anonymously on its forum pages.

The first real love of my life was Maggie Richardson, a beautiful, tall, redheaded, fellow student from Torquay. While I was courting Maggie, my parents came to visit Bristol for a weekend and I took them out to dinner in Clifton with her. My taste in wine had progressed to ordering a bottle of Portuguese Mateus Rose, which impressed them. I was heartbroken when Maggie and I split up at the end of our training, but later went to her wedding in Hampstead to give her a token of our former love.

Maggie Richardson

During my years in Bristol, the much respected Old Vic Company was under the stewardship of Val May. I attended productions at both the Theatre Royal on King Street, and the Little Theatre within the Colston Hall on a regular basis to further my knowledge of authors and witness good acting. Amongst the shows I saw in that first term were *The Golden Rivet*, *Twelfth Night* and Peter Shaffer's *The Private Ear* and *The Public Eye*. As Bristol was a Three Weekly Rep the Company had a longer rehearsal period than I was used to at Lincoln and the quality of productions presented reflected this, along with the quality of actor.

One of the productions is etched in my mind, not because of its quality but because of the events surrounding it. On 22nd November I was walking across the main square in Bristol City Centre, on my way to The Theatre Royal to see *Ironhand* by John Arden, when I heard the cry from a newspaper vendor of "Stop Press Issue" and went over to investigate what this was all about

On reaching the vendor I read the headline **J.F.K. DEAD** and like the rest of the world wondered what would happen next. This is a moment in history I will never forget. Unfortunately I cannot remember a thing about the play.

One of the joys was to be seconded to the electrical department in the bowels of the ancient Theatre Royal, where the legendary Chief Engineer, Ernie Peppin, enthralled me with tales of his involvement at the theatre over numerous years, and how he had invented and manufactured the snout for a Pattern 23 lantern. I also had the opportunity of working in the carpentry shop under Master Carpenter Alf Gleason, making elementary pieces of scenery from a plan, which I found challenging yet enjoyable.

The Old Vic Company comprised many young artistes who were later to make a big name for themselves, including Nicholas Smith, Frank Middlemass, Dorothy Tutin, Peter Vaughan, Paul Eddington, Margaret Courteney, Michael Jayston, Richard Pasco, Barbara Leigh-Hunt, Russell Hunter, Gawn Granger and Patrick Stewart.

The Christmas show at The Theatre Royal in 1963-64 was *Around the World in Eighty Days*, with Christopher Benjamin as Phileas H. Fogg and Russell Hunter as Passepartout. I was asked to understudy several of the roles in addition to working as part of the crew on the show backstage led by Deputy Stage Manager (DSM) Gabriel Prendergast and ASM Richard York, with whom I would team up later when he was Chairman of The Association of British Theatre Technicians (ABTT). There was a running gag in the show where The Consul in Rangoon, Calcutta or Hong

Kong, always played by Frank Middlemass in a pith helmet, would make his entrance via one of the original Star Traps set into the stage. This gave me my first experience of working with original stage equipment, and I found it fascinating.

The quality of the casts that wanted to work with Val May at one of the country's leading Repertory Theatres with an International reputation, can best be illustrated by the cast who appeared in Sheridan's *The Rivals* for a three week run in October - William Lucas, Sheila Allen, Sarah Badel, Eithne Dunn, Christopher Benjamin, Peter Baldwin, Russell Hunter, and Terrence Hardiman, many of whom I would have the pleasure of working with again in later years.

My fellow students at BOVTS would also gain international recognition playing a variety of roles, amongst them being Christopher Cazenove, Norman Eschele, John McEnery, and Shane Connaughton. I had left my accommodation in Westbury and moved to a house in Redland, which I shared with several fellow students. Amongst them was Geoff Todd, who rode a motorbike and gave me pillion lifts to London on the back of his twin cylinder machine. The house had a reinforced cellar, as during the war Bristol had been subjected to heavy bombing by enemy aircraft. The cellar provided an ideal venue for student parties, which I hosted on numerous occasions.

The BOVTS was run in close association with the Department of Drama at Bristol University. We used their small in-house theatre for productions during term time in addition to being seconded to the BOV Company itself for any major productions. This enabled us to use the university refectory for meals when in town and away from the Clifton Area where the School was situated overlooking the Bristol Downs near the Zoo. The normal routine however was to go for lunch at the Terminus Café, where the owner knew us by name and provided us with student priced meals such as pasty, chips and beans for a shilling (5p).

On our way home to our digs we would buy bacon off cuts to make into a simple Spag Bol or buy some savoury faggots to cook up in a rich gravy. These early attempts of making something tasty out of nothing have influenced my way of cooking even to this day, when I still buy reduced items nightly from my local supermarket.

Mention of a supermarket reminds me of an incident in the Bristol Co-Op one lunchtime when I had gone in to buy some sliced cooked meats. As the revolving blade of the slicer was not cutting the meat very well, the assistant foolishly put her hand into the slicer to push the joint closer to the blade, but her hand slipped and she ended up slicing off bits of her fingers.

Most weeks the Stoll Moss Touring House in Bristol, the huge 1,991 seated Hippodrome, the fifth biggest in the provinces, would run a mid-week matinée. As many of the usual Stage Crew had other full time employment, I would be asked, because of my past experience, to go in and work the show as a casual for cash in hand. I was more than happy to do this as it gave me an opportunity to work in the light entertainment side of the business, which I had not experienced before.

I would usually be seconded to the Chief Electrician, Derek, who would ask me to work The Limes FOH, or onstage working the Dips. His private domain[1] was in the Bastard Side Prompt Wing up on a gantry where he maintained an immaculate fully working Grand Master. I was taught how to work The 'Strand Electric Pat. 501 Sunspot Arc Follow Spot' by Roger Jeffery. The knack was in keeping the carbon rods close enough together for the current to jump between the two and, via a system of reflectors and mirrors, produce a very bright intense light that could travel over 200 feet from the Limes Box to the Stage.

Working onstage, you were responsible for all the electrical equipment in the Wing to which you were allocated, and the plugging and unplugging of equipment into the stage floor Dip Traps, which were all colour coded to achieve an overall wash of the same colour light, if required.

---

1. Bastard side prompt (or Bastard side corner). Used when the prompt position is downstage right, opposite where it would normally be.

The venue presented a cross section of shows including ballet, variety, opera, ice shows, and musicals, but the highlight of the year was the annual Pantomime where all the big names from the light entertainment field came for a Season.

In 1963 I had the privilege to work on *Sleeping Beauty* with Morecambe & Wise, Ted Hockeridge, and Eddie Molloy. The following year it was *Merry King Cole* starring Harry Worth, and that great Dame from Dudley, Billy Dainty, with Pat Lancaster and the Cox Twins in supporting roles.

The Pantomime in 1965 was *Puss in Boots* starring The Bachelors, with Freddie (Parrot Face) Davies, Audrey Jeans and a young Mike Yarwood as support.

The Panto could be scheduled to run for anything up to 20 weeks, and one year I went to The Theatre Royal in Nottingham at Easter to see Danny La Rue in *Aladdin*. With a good long Summer Season at one of the major seaside resorts, like Blackpool, Great Yarmouth or Bournemouth, it was still possible for an Act, with a good booking agent, to survive on just doing Panto and a Summer Season. If you could also get a Cruise engagement on one of the Cunard liners for a few weeks, as many of the big names did, you were laughing all the way to the bank and could afford a new set of golf clubs for the next Summer Season.

In September '65, I travelled back to Bristol early as Marlene Dietrich was booked in at The Hippodrome for six performances only, and I was not going to miss the chance of seeing this legend perform live. The show was sensational and presented to the highest standards, with the lighting by Joe Davis. Something I still remember is the call for the orchestra, which began with two follow spots on the Musical Director standing in the centre of the pit. They then split, one to the left and one to the right, and traversed the length of the pit to return back again to the M.D. who took a second bow, so simple but oh so professional. I waited at the Stage Door that night to see her exit the theatre, escorted by Joe who took her to supper at Harvey's. When I worked with Joe a few years later, I recalled this story and he said that she had been a dream to work with.

Other visits of note to the Hippodrome were the occasions when the touring section of the Royal Ballet appeared, as the reputation that Master Carpenter John and Props Master Wally had were legendary. When they were in town you knew you were in for a few late nights at the Stage Door pub opposite. I have never known a crew who could sup like they did and still work so professionally on the show. I learnt the quickest way to lift a Stage Cloth during an interval change, by running a garden spade or hoe along the tack line, and folding it so the downstage edge was always along the 'Carpet Cut'[2] on the stage, for relaying next time. I also noticed that the regulars accustomed to touring, like Wayne Sleep, lived in camper vans which they parked by the Stage Door for the week, using the facilities within the theatre dressing rooms for most of their needs. I recall Wayne flying out down stage left on a Kirby Wire at the end of Act One of *La Fille Mal Gardee*, holding an inverted umbrella as if caught by the wind. Great lads, great shows and always fun to be with.

The touring section of Sadlers Wells Opera was not as much fun to spend a week with, but worked hard with tight schedules to meet. I had the same opinion when The D'Oyly Carte Opera Company was in residence. The shows and patter songs by John Reed, who was the last of the great comic actors to play and sing such songs as *I am the Very Model of a Modern Major-General* from *The Pirates of Penzance*, and the like, were superbly presented, but the crew was not as lively as The Royal Ballet on tour.

Back at The Little Theatre in May '64, I was a Soldier and Guard in *Edward II* by Christopher Marlow, for a week, which was the end of term show for the students in the year above me. It later played a week at The Theatre Royal in June with *The Caucasian Chalk Circle*, *Volpone*, and *Equality for Eve*.

---

2. *Carpet Cut*. A shallow recess along the front of the stage into which the downstage end of a stage cloth is placed. Hinged sections are dropped into the recess to secure the cloth and improve the visual appearance.

I had struggled during my first year at Bristol and was not at ease with myself or the outcome of my studies. In the second year (1964-65) however, I fully came in to my own and only really found tutorials on design difficult. Between 1963 and 1980 the Principal of the school was Nat Brenner, who was the ex General Manager of the BOV Company. He saw potential in me in theatre management, and helped groom me in such a way that I was able to flourish like a plant that had been given a gallon of fertilizer.

As the second year was the Technical Course year I was back on home ground, and felt much more at ease. Certain people had been spotted by Val May and asked to join the Company, amongst them the very talented bi-lingual Jane Lapotaire (she was half French) who had joined the Theatre School at the same time as me, and was later to make a huge name for herself in The West End playing the lead in *Piaf*.

I also enjoyed seeing Dorothy Tutin portray Queen Victoria in *Portrait of a Queen* by William Francis. I remembered how things had been staged in this production when I came to work it again at Liverpool some years later.

In April 1965 I worked on helping to build the settings for my first West End production, which was the World Premiere of *The Killing of Sister George* by Frank Marcus and starring that great comedy actress Beryl Reid, who I had listened to in *Educating Archie* on the wireless in the 1950s. Alf Gleason ran the workshops like a military operation and taught me many little tricks of the trade, which I found most useful in future years when I oversaw productions.

My over-riding memory, however, is the way they made the tea in the workshop using a tin of Carnation condensed milk instead of normal milk, which gave it a rather sickly taste. They were also in the process of restoring an old car in a corner of the large carpentry shop, and they used to spend much of their tea breaks and dinner time with a welding torch.

For the end of term productions at the Theatre Royal we presented *Pericles*, a selection of works by modern playwrights entitled *Theatre of the Absurd* and *An Italian Straw Hat*, which Nat Brenner asked me to stage manage.

Some of the cast and crew would later go on, like myself, to bigger and better things in their careers. I recall some who made a lasting impression on me, back in June 1965. I was in no doubt that Alan Dossor had the potential to be a great leading man, whilst Jeremy Child, with his Public School voice and looks, would never be out of work. Of the girls, I thought that Jane Lapotaire, Maggie Brown, Sylvia Brayshaw, Susan Sheers and Janet Key were all set for future stardom. I got on well with Peter Blayney as we shared an interest in Great Jazz Drummers such as Buddy Rich, Louis Belson and Gene Krupa, but did not think he had any acting potential. Allan Stirland, with whom I had first shared digs in Westbury-on-Trym, and Richard Frost who had a room in the digs in Redland, remained good friends. One of the Technical Assistants was Warren Smith who went on to be one of the longest serving General Managers ever in the provinces when he went to the Leeds Opera House. We met again when I was on tour with Peter Pan some years later. Peter Gregory and I shared a house in Hotwells with Ian Cowan. Peter was invited to join the BOV Company as an ASM at the end of my second year.

In the meantime Susan won the £60 Bursary Prize at the Scunthorpe Music Festival in 1963. She left home in 1964 to study dance with Andrew Hardie at his studios in Queensbury Mews in South Kensington. I used to go to London from Bristol to see West End Shows and stay with her and her dance friends, whose company I enjoyed, as they were all most attractive young ladies. By the summer of 1965 she had finished her training, joined The Pam Devis Dancers and was playing the Summer Season at the ABC Theatre in Great Yarmouth. This was a typical revue style variety show of the period, with a big name act who was Top of the Bill, supporting acts and a group of usually a dozen girl and boy dancers.

Most of these big provincial Summer Seasons and Pantomimes were presented by the Delfont Organisation, which was based in offices at The Prince of Wales Theatre in Coventry Street just off Piccadilly Circus. Little did I know that years later, in 1996, I would be part of this international organization.

The usual routine was for the big new show to spend its first Summer Season playing at The ABC Theatre in Blackpool, moving on to play Yarmouth the following year. In 1965 at Yarmouth playing the ABC were The Bachelors, Freddy (Parrot Face) Davies and Anita Harris, and a new band called The Rockin' Berries who had made the charts with *A Poor Man's Son*. This was too good an opportunity to miss, and I made my way over to Yarmouth, hoping to work on one of the Summer Shows which were there that year.

In addition to the show at the ABC, there were seven other venues in operation that season: The Britannia Pier, The Wellington Pier, The Pavilion, The Hippodrome, The Little Theatre, The Windmill and the Royal Aquarium. On arrival, I had a tip-off they were short of staff at The Aquarium where Lonnie Donegan was topping the bill, so I made my way to the 1,340-seat venue and met the resident Stage Manager, who offered me a job working on the fly floor, which was no problem for me, as it was a hemp house like Lincoln.

The rival big show to the ABC that year was on at the southernmost Wellington Pier and starred Jimmy Tarbuck, Mike & Bernie Winters and Matt Monroe. Such was Jimmy's interest in football that he used to organise inter-theatre matches at a weekend and his team, which I was lucky enough to play in, always wore the Liverpool home kit. The results did not really matter, as the intention was have a social gathering of the pros who were in town for the summer.

That Summer was blissfully happy as the shows were twice nightly, leaving the days free to sunbathe, while the social life at night was sensational with so many pros in town for the season.

On a Sunday many of the acts were booked to do a one-nighter at another seaside venue. I joined Terry Bond, who by now was dating Sue, and the rest of The Berries, for the long drive to Torquay for their Sunday gig.

I was back in Bristol in September 1965 to finish my last years' training at the BOVTS, and at The Theatre Royal they were presenting the usual high standard productions. It is interesting to recall that Jane Lapotaire and Jeremy Child from the school were now firmly established as regular members of the Company along with the likes of Gawn Grainger, Frank Barrie, Patrick Stewart, Frank Middlemass, Rowena Cooper, Eithne Dunne, and Thelma Barlow, who was married to Graham, one of the Designers.

Jane Asher joined the Company to play the title role in *Cleo* by Frank Marcus and ex DSM Gabriel Prendergast directed *Great Expectations*, in addition to being the Company & Stage Manager.

For Christmas 1965-66 the production was *The Happiest Days of Your Life* (which they weren't for me) about school life in Hilary Hall School for boys, with Jane Asher again as a guest playing Barbara Cahoun, a pupil at St. Swithins. I would work again with this charming actress in the West End doing *Peter Pan* in 1978 at the Shaftsbury Theatre.

I returned for my last Christmas Show in Lincoln that December, and to complete the circle it was back again in 1965-66 to *Aladdin* which opened on Boxing Day for three weeks. Major changes had happened that year while I had been away in Bristol. Brian Spiby had taken over as Administrator from Kay Gardner, who had moved to The Liverpool Playhouse (more of that later). Nicholas Barter had succeeded Alan Vaughn Williams as Director of Production, as he was now working at the Greenwich Theatre and more of that, as well, will follow.

Ray Dicks was now Public Liaison Officer, and Chairman of Theatre in Action, as Michael Billington was now a Press Critic, whilst Malcolm Fraser was the Production Manager. Of the regulars who had been with the theatre since its early days, Art Walker was still in the corner[3] running the shows, Harry Whitfield was now Manager with an Assistant, Bryan Newton, whilst Kay Darbyshire was still Secretary of The Theatre Association and the Theatre Club under Chairman J.H. 'Black Jack' Spence. How would the theatre have survived without the dedication of Kay, Art and Harry?

The Spring Season at BOV in Kings Street was a Bicentennial Festival of the opening of this most famous 1766 working theatre with much of its original stage equipment like the Star Traps and Thunder Run still in working order. Notable productions for this festival were to be seen with Paul Eddington as Elyot Chase in Coward's *Private Lives*, *The Critic* and *Harlequinade*, but the highlight for many of us was *Sixty Thousand Nights*, which someone had calculated was the number of nights there had been a show on in King Street since it opened on 30th May 1776. It opened for a four week run on 18th May 1966 and was a Val May epic of a show with Grant Hossack as the Musical Director, and music by Julian Slade. The cast was immense, even by BOV standards, with the penultimate number being *We Said We Wouldn't Look Back* from *Salad Days*, the royalties from which were still funding the school. All that remained for me to do in Bristol was to oversee the three end of term productions in June, which were by tradition always held at the Theatre Royal.

The three productions were *The Merry Wives of Windsor*, *Tiger at The Gates*, and *The Empty Chair*. Principal Nat Brenner asked me to be the Stage Director, scheduling Fit Ups and production time onstage for all three of them, as well as being Stage and Company Manager for each one. This was a great show of confidence in my ability to put into practice all that I had learnt, but I was confident I could do the job, to the highest possible standards.

In addition to these technical and management roles, I was also cast to play Rugby in *Wives*, so things were certainly going to be busy for my final weeks in Bristol. To assist me on *Wives* I had Patricia Martin as my DSM and we worked well as a team, so much so that we were to work together many times again in future years and I was her best man when she married Graham Phoenix on 17th August 1974. Whilst on *Tiger* I had David Hennessey as DSM, and on *Chair* Jacqueline Fisher filled that position.

At this point in my career I could not type or drive, so all my elaborate production schedules, of what should be happening where and when, were all hand written and colour-coded. They were much admired by Roger Jeffery and Ian Cowan, both of whom had guided me through the last three years of my development.

The cast, led by Richard Glyn Davis Lewis as Sir John Falstaff, also included many of the young actors who had been on the same course as me, including Norman Eshley, Janet Key, Sylvia Brayshaw, Gavin Richards (who would become a household name thanks to playing the flamboyant Italian Alberto Bertorelli in '*Allo 'Allo* on TV and stage), Maggie Steed and the suave, attractive Christopher Cazenove, who would later make it big time in *Dynasty* as Ben Carrington, playing opposite Joan Collins on TV in the 80s but who sadly died in 2010 aged just 66. I like to think they respected the management roles I was now undertaking, as having trained alongside them I was in a position to understand what they were doing, and hoping to achieve in the future, which was after all the reason I chose to go to Bristol in the first place.

Following the shows in Bristol, which were a huge success, especially *Wives*, we took them out on tour during the summer. One blistering hot summer's day, I was sunbathing on Plymouth Hoe without any sun protection thinking: "I don't need that stuff." I regretted it all evening while playing the part of *Rugby* where I had to wear a thick pair of woollen tights throughout. The highlight of that summer of 1966 was listening on a small portable radio to England win the world cup final against Germany, whilst quaffing cider overlooking Plymouth Hoe.

---

3. *Corner*. The position usually downstage left from where the show is run.

We also took the productions to minor West Country towns, like Blandford Forum and Falmouth, touring in a converted coach with the scenery in the back and the artistes in the front. As we could not afford accommodation, we were billeted with local arts lovers, who provided us with dinner, bed and breakfast. The Headmaster of the local boarding school, with whom I was billeted, could not understand why I was unable to leave at the end of the production with him. I had to ensure the safe removal of all the scenery and costumes etc. out of the theatre and into the coach before accompanying him back to the private dining room where his House Keeper had prepared a supper which should have been eaten two hours earlier. On another occasion, the coach broke down en route to Falmouth and I had to make the decision as to who and what went forward to keep our appointed date. Several actors within the Company, who obviously had a vested interest in their particular roles, suggested they should go forward with their costumes, which I as Stage Director did not agree with, and said to them: "If you make a mistake and it all goes wrong, I carry the blame. If I make a mistake, and it all goes wrong, I still carry the blame, so we'll do it my way." This was a policy I tried to follow in my career for many years and have gained the reputation of being firm but fair, which I think would be a nice epitaph.

Whilst I was on tour in the West Country, I sent several letters to the many friends I had made in the business during my days in Lincoln, including the ex Director of the Theatre Royal, Kay Gardner, who by now had moved to the Liverpool Playhouse. I received a very favourable reply from her to indicate that at the moment the Playhouse was closed for refurbishment, but would be opening in the autumn, and I should contact the Production Manager, which I duly did.

Act 1 Scene 3
LIVERPOOL
(1966-71)

I purchased a cheap day return from Euston to Lime Street Station in Liverpool in August 1966 to visit The Playhouse for my interview with Chris Bullock and have a look round the building. As the train passed through the suburbs of this great City, I was not impressed and thought that this would be a bit rough and ready for me. On arrival at the Theatre in Williamson Square I was directed to a nearby warehouse, which the theatre was using as a base whilst some of the works to the stage, including the installation of both a single and double purchase counterweight system to replace the old hemp system, were being carried out.

A tall person with jet black, swept back hair greeted me and introduced himself as Chris and said that he had heard a lot about me from Kay Gardner. Tossing me a roll of plans he said: "What do you think of these?" On inspecting them I found that they were the half-inch to the foot plans and cross section drawings of the proposed changes to be made to the building. These weren't a problem for me to understand, as I was quite used to working with plans to this imperial scale from my time in the workshops at Lincoln and Bristol.

The proposed changes were very impressive but what excited me most was the concept to build a set upon a wagon stage in the full size stage workshops on the OP side of the stage, raise the Fire Door that separated the stage from the workshop, and then winch the wagon stage into place. This was a simple idea but you needed the space and foresight to envisage the concept, and it was evident to me that Mr. Bullock had this in abundance.

He went on to explain that until all the work at the Theatre had been completed the workshop facilities, wardrobe, props store etc., would be at the Warehouse along with the technical and Stage Management offices. I was being interviewed for the post of Stage Manager. The DSM would be appointed by him to be compatible with the successful candidate and the team of ASMs would come from the ranks of the junior actors in the Company appointed by David Scase. The season was scheduled to open in late October and the successful team would be employed from early Autumn. I returned to London very impressed with what I had seen and heard, and liked Chris to whom I would be reporting, if successful.

A week or so later I got a letter from Chris saying that I was "head and shoulders above the others who had been short listed", which offered me the post of Stage Manager from Autumn 1966. The post would be reviewed annually and the emolument was £15 per week.

I accepted without hesitation, and knew that I would be able to learn much from Chris. No acting was required for this appointment, which would leave me free to concentrate on honing my new technical and management skills.

I returned to Lincoln to spend some time with my parents, bought a typewriter and taught myself to type, went off to Cromer to spend some time and have some fun with an old girlfriend who was doing a Summer Season there, and popped down to London to see Sue who was now working for Dougie Squires at the London Palladium in *London Laughs* with Harry Secombe, 'Tatty Ead' Jimmy Tarbuck, Anita Harris, Russ Conway and those very funny comedians Freddie Frinton and Thora

Hird. The show had been devised and produced by the prince of darkness himself, Robert Nesbit, with settings by Todd Kingman.

I knew Jimmy from the Summer Season in Yarmouth a couple of years before. I would work with Dougie in 1972 and tour with Anita in 1974. Mr. Nesbit would become a much respected friend when I was at the Prince Edward in 1986, whilst Todd and I would work together on several shows later in my career. Who said: "It's not what you know, but who you know" in this business?

Ray & Joan were horrified to see their daughter dressed in a tartan coat on the front page of The Daily Mail leading her fellow dancers out on strike following a disagreement with the Management of this most prestigious theatre over some issue or other.

As well as visiting the London Palladium and chatting to George the Stage Doorkeeper whilst waiting to see Sue after the show, and little knowing that I would have the honour of working there a few years later, I also continued to go and see other shows in the West End over the years, including *The Four Musketeers* at The Lane and *Maggie May* at the Adelphi Theatre. I began to spot the name of Peter Roberts in many of the programmes of shows that were produced or co-presented with other Managements by the Delfont Organisation, and noted his name as a possible future contact.

In the meantime Chris, at Liverpool, kept me informed of developments during the extended six months summer vacation to allow the stage and dressing room alterations that I had seen on the plans at my interview, of opening dates, the shows that were to be presented in the first Season up until Christmas, and the appointment of my DSM, Jill Fraser. She, like me, had just left a Drama School and we were due to meet prior to the opening of rehearsals of the first play, *A Family Man*, which was to open on 26th October 1966. As Liverpool was a three weekly rep, like Bristol, and attracted all the best repertory actors and actresses, I calculated that we would begin a three week rehearsal period in the first week of October. I duly made plans to travel over to Liverpool from Lincoln on the morning boat train which ran cross country direct from Harwich to Liverpool, in September.

I packed all my worldly goods into a cabin trunk and holdall, and set off to begin the next stage in my career. The taxi journey to the theatre digs I had booked out of town in one of the suburbs did not excite me, as Liverpool looked very dismal and down at heel in the autumn drizzle. I was warmly welcomed at the digs and discovered that all my fellow guests were working at 'The Clubs' which were slowly taking over from Variety shows in the theatres around the country, mainly in the North of England. There was good money to be made, especially if you could get two bookings for the same period which were within a reasonable driving distance. I met what I later discovered to be one of the top acts on the Club Circuit, Ronnie Dukes and Ricky Lee, who came to introduce themselves to me on my first night, when they returned to the digs. They were playing the week at Allison's Litherland Theatre Club and invited me to go along one night, as their guest, to see them. I was blown away with the energy in their act from comedian Ronnie, the superb singing of his wife Ricky and The Mother in Law, who was the butt of all Ronnie's jokes, sitting po-faced at the piano.

This was something new for me in Liverpool and I liked it so much, that over the next six years nightly visits to Entertainment Clubs such as The Cabaret Club in Duke Street, The Blue Angel nearby, Dino's, and what would turn out to be my favourite club, the Shakespeare Cabaret Theatre in Fraser Street, known to all Liverpudlians as 'de Shaky', were to become part of my new social life after work.

I met Jill and we got on fine, as I have always been a 'first impressions that count' man, and I told her how I wanted to run the Stage Management Team and what my priorities were. I wanted her to be on The Book[4] for rehearsals and run the shows as was the tradition for the DSM. I would

---

4. *The Book*. Short for 'Prompt Copy', the Book is the prompt script and also details everything that should happen during the performance. It is usually used by the DSM to run the show.

organise the Marking Out for rehearsals, the Fit Ups, under the control of Chris as Stage Director, and the work of the ASM's team, mainly on Propping. I would look after discipline, as all the ASMs were fresh out of Drama school and really wanted to act, rather than be part of the Stage Management. The ASM with the smallest part would be responsible for working the Sound Desk, still a Stage Management duty in 1966, whilst the others would be responsible for the counterweight flying, which thankfully was operated at stage level in the prompt wing, and running a side each during performances, as it was not envisaged that we would need to use or employ any casuals. My overall aim was to run a happy and efficient team that earned the respect of the Management and Company.

The first show was to be *A Family Man* by John Galsworthy, directed by David Scase with designs by Jonathan Porter, who incidentally had also worked at Lincoln Rep under Kay Gardner whilst I was away in Bristol, and for whom Mum had been a babysitter on occasions.

Rehearsals were held at the YMCA building in Mount Pleasant, a short walk from the Playhouse in Williamson Square. The Stage Management Team and I marked out the settings in coloured tape on the floor, prior to the commencement of the first rehearsal, which Davis Scase was impressed with.

This production was to be followed on 8th November by *The Little Mrs. Foster Show* by Henry Livings, and then a show that I had seen before at The Royal in Bristol, *Portrait of a Queen*, whilst the Christmas and New Year Show was *Brer Rabbit*. I particularly remember working on *Portrait*, which was directed by Kay Gardner, and I was so keen to show her that I was worthy of the trust she had showed in me that, one lunch break during rehearsals at the theatre, I hung a black Tab on one of the mid stage 'Double Purchase' counterweight sets, and did a reveal of Morag Hood as the young Queen Victoria. I recalled it had been done that way when Dorothy Tutin played the part at the Royal in Bristol during my student days. Kay liked the idea so much that it was kept as part of the show, much to my delight.

As I had expected the standards were high, and I was enjoying the new challenges that were coming my way. Most of the Company was new apart from one or two like Lynda Marchal who had been in the 1965 company with Anthony Hopkins, John Savident, who would later make his name in *Coronation Street*, Cynthia Grenville, and Jean Boht, who would later become a household name in *Bread*, and played a part in *Brer Rabbit* that Christmas.

I really looked forward to doing the run of *Around The World in Eighty Days* between 28th February and 18th March 1967, as I had enjoyed doing it so much at Christmas in '63-'64 when at Bristol. A guest artiste for this show was John Thaw, who would play alongside Clive Elliot (ex Lincoln again) as Phileas Fogg's French valet Passepartout. I suggested that we do the running gag of the Consul at each port being the same person and entering as a statue in a pith helmet via a Star Trap, but the expense of installing a new Star Trap was prohibitive. I did however have a spur of the moment idea kept in the show. When Fogg was announced as having safely landed on a steamer from New York to Liverpool, I sang: "Yeh, Yeh, Yeh" as the Beatles had done on the hit record of *She Loves You*, and Director David Scase kept it in.

As football is a way of life in Liverpool, during one of the Saturday matinées, when the local derby match between Liverpool and Everton was being played, Mr. Thaw in his role as Passepartout read from a newspaper whilst going around the world: "I see Liverpool beat Everton 3-2 in the Derby Game at Anfield" which got a round of applause and a cheer from all 'The Reds' in the audience that afternoon.

In May we staged *Black Comedy*, a very clever play by Peter Shaffer, which in my opinion is a real coup de theatre, which starred Maggie Smith and Derek Jacobi in the original 1965 West End production. The play starts off in total darkness and is only lit when the fuse, in the flat in which it is set, blows and the stage lights come on. During the ensuing farce one of the characters has to fall down a stage trap upstage of a sofa and disappear. We duly made the stage trap and it was yours truly that volunteered to be the first to see how safe it was. Fortunately, and much to my delight, it worked well and I landed under the stage unharmed.

That first season at Liverpool finished on 1st July and during it I had introduced my own style of social life to the company in that after an opening night on a Tuesday we would all go out clubbin' as a Company. We mainly patronised The Shakespeare Cabaret Theatre, as it itself was a converted Theatre. They had a fine restaurant, I knew the Doorman, who would let us all in for free, and the Acts were the best that would play in Liverpool. As the Wednesday was traditionally a read through of the new production during the afternoon, the Stage Management team would willingly stay on for half an hour after curtain down, to mark out the new floor plan.

The cabaret acts at the Shaky were top class with acts like my old friends Ronnie Dukes & Rickey Lee, and The Rockin' Berries filling the place along with new acts such as Lovelace Watkins. The compère was the very talented Pete Price, who I first met at the Cabaret Club in Duke Street and had moved across town. Everyone in Liverpool knew him as 'the fella who wears the newspaper suit' and he courted publicity like it was going out of fashion, but was totally charming with it.

In addition to working at The Playhouse, I had been introduced to Oscar, the Stage Manager at The Shaky by Billy Meall, who was a most talented scenic artist, and worked on the electrics. If they were short staffed, I would work their show after the Playhouse show, as The Top of The Bill was not on until 2300hrs, when patrons had finished their meal in the very good upmarket Circle Restaurant or their Scampi in a Basket meal in the stalls area. Part of the incentive to work the show was the fact that you were entitled to the staff meal which was provided for the acts and crew during every show.

I did not mind the long hours. If I wasn't working the show at the Shaky, I would be out somewhere like The Blue Angel Club drinking and dancing the night away till closing time, when I would stagger home to my new Flat at 13 Canning Street very near to the Anglican Cathedral. I would get six or seven hours sleep before rehearsals, which always began at 10am, and as The Stage Manager would always try to be in first.

During the summer closure in July and early August, and before rehearsals began for the opening show on 5th September, it was time for the annual maintenance to take place backstage. One job involved ensuring that the lantern light would work in the event of an emergency. Its purpose, over the top of the stage, was to open in the event of fire to vent the smoke and fumes through the roof. This was achieved by a fusible link melting, and the glass sections opening. All the Stage Management Team went onto the roof, roped together and to any convenient chimney, and were positioned in front of each of the sections of glass to break its fall should the winding system malfunction during the test.

We also checked all the ladders, steps and 'A' Frames for any loose rungs, or weak points, and I christened one of them 'The Clive Hornby Memorial 'A' Frame' in honour of one of the team who would go on to play Jack Sugden in Emmerdale Farm for 28 years. Clive sadly died in 2008. In addition we labelled all the black tabs and borders on the leading edge below the hanging tabs, and then refolded these so that the label was readable for easy and quick access. The same applied to drift wires, which were colour coded according to their length, and stage braces were all checked.

I mentioned The Blue Angel Club, which was run and owned by Alun Williams as being one of my drinking haunts. Alun was a real Scouse legend. Scouse is a local stew that is similar to a Scandinavian delicacy, which was brought over to Liverpool by Norwegian sailors and for which every family has its own recipe, which is always much better than anyone else's.

He had first met *The Beatles* when they used to frequent his Jacaranda Coffee Bar in Slater Street and had subsequently taken them over to Hamburg in 1960, at the beginning of their career. Foolishly (for him) he sold them to the owner of the NEMS Music Shop in Liverpool, Brian Epstein, who incidentally had studied Drama at RADA alongside Albert Finney, Peter O'Toole and Susannah York, but dropped out after a while as he decided he preferred to be a businessman. On one occasion Alun bought a young bull, and kept it shut up in the Club Beer Cellar all day and then announced to everyone that he was going to have a bullfight live in the club. As it happened the bull was more frightened of being let loose in a crowded club than Alun was of it, and showed so in the traditional manner.

We got on well together as I have always liked 'characters' being a bit of a one myself. When he invited me to go on holiday with him, and his delightful wife Beryl Chang, to Palma in Spain, I jumped at the opportunity. He was not only going over for a summer break, but also to open the first automated bowling alley in Palma. On arrival he took me to see his new club and the 'automated' alley. What he showed me was typical Alun. He had engaged two local pensioners to stand at the far end of the alley, with mattresses tied around their lower legs. They would roll the balls back to the bowlers, and re-set the pins.

He fell on hard times in later years, but still had an eye for making a bob or two. He bought a job lot of coffee mugs, had the inscription "I'm the Mug who sold The Beatles" printed on them and sold them in Camden Market on a Sunday for many years. The last I heard of him was in 2014, aged 84. He was in a Liverpool care home, and was saying to people: "You don't know who I am, do you?" In typical scouse humour the reply was: "No mate, YOU don't even know who you are!"

On Christmas Eve 1966 I met a girl at The Blue Angel and we stayed together for Christmas because, as we had a show on 24th December with an early call for the Matinée on Boxing Day, I was not able to spend Christmas in Lincoln. We shared a joint of pork and vegetables together for our festive lunch, which I cooked on the Baby Belling, accompanied by a bottle of wine.

The second half of my first season at The Playhouse went off without a hitch, and works on the new extension were going well and were on schedule from what I could gather from Chris Bullock. The 1967 Christmas show was *Treasure Island* with Clive Elliott as a memorable Long John Silver, and we got lots of local publicity in looking for and casting a suitable parrot to be Captain Flint. The show was directed by an Arts Council Trainee Director who insisted that a table was 'off its marks' onstage and was adamant that it had been set wrongly by the Stage Management. I asked him, in front of the Company how far upstage of the setting line it should be set, and he replied: "Four Foot". I was quite sure that we had set it correctly, so went to the 'Fit Up Tool Box' that was onstage in the prompt side wing, got out the plumb line and a tape measure, and proceeded to show him that the table was in the correct position when the plumb line bob came to rest exactly four feet from the setting line - one up to the Stage Management over the Arts Council trainee, who never questioned the correct setting of anything again.

I had always worked closely with Stage Manager Charlie O'Neil at Howard & Wyndam's Royal Court Theatre just up the road in Roe Street, managed by Terry Jones. I would tour to this theatre in 1974 with *Peter Pan*. Over at the Moss Empire Theatre on Lime Street, where the Manager was Neil Brooks, was to be found the legendary Jack Roach, the resident Stage Manager, who would oversee the Get In and Fit Up of a show or the break down and get out from the comfort of an armchair, in the prompt corner, because of his bad feet. He used to offer me casual work on shows when he was short staffed.

Built in 1925, the Empire was huge and was the largest two-tiered theatre in Britain, capable of seating 2,550 patrons, which is only surpassed by the 2,920 seats at the Blackpool Opera House.

The Beatles had played their Christmas show there in December 1965, but for the Christmas and New Year Season of 1967 it was to be the touring version of the musical *Hello Dolly* with Dora Bryan as Dolly Levi in the title role. Sue was in the chorus of the show, so I invited our parents over to Liverpool to spend their Christmas with us. Dad was reluctant, as usual, to leave his drinking mates in Lincoln, but was eventually persuaded to make the trip over the Snake Pass - no M62 then - to spend Christmas at the very posh Adelphi Hotel. I drew up a schedule for them each day and booked seats for all the shows in Liverpool. Ronnie Settle, the Musical Director, suggested a nice place for us all to have our Christmas Lunch over on the Wirral, which I remember was badly affected by an outbreak of Foot & Mouth Disease. The meal was below par and once we had come back through 'the tube' to Liverpool, headed up to The Philharmonic Hotel in Hope Street for the rest of the day.

I worked on the Get In and Fit Up of *Dolly*, and also on the shows when we did not have a Matinée at the Playhouse of *Treasure Island*, and loved every moment of it, so much so that I realised my heart was really in the light entertainment and musical side of the business, rather than the pure drama side.

The summer break at Liverpool was between July and September. Following the now traditional summer maintenance checks, I headed off to Bournemouth where Susan was doing summer season that year, dancing again for The Pam Devis Dancers. It was the Summer of 'Flower Power' and almost everyone wore a flower in their hair and the house that Susan and her fellow dancers had booked for the season had a summer house in the garden, which I was able to use as a base.

Her show was at the 1,519 seater Pavilion Theatre, which was immaculately run backstage by Tony Bond who did everything correctly and to the highest standard, even down to stacking the flats in the wings on 3 x 1 battens, to prevent them getting wet when the wings were mopped daily. The stars were Des O'Connor with his sidekick Jack Douglas (Mr. Ippititimus) and Scottish singer Kenneth McKenna. Tommy Cooper and *The Rockin' Berries* were providing alternative excellent entertainment at the new Winter Gardens in Exeter Road.

Tommy was one of the funniest men I ever saw onstage with a most original opening. He faced upstage, and all you could see were his hands trying to locate the rabbit to pull out of the hat - difficult to describe, but hilarious to watch. After the show all the Companies from all the local summer shows used to meet up to socialize, including Tommy who liked a drink. The first thing I noticed when I met him was the size of his feet in highly polished shoes. He used to be a Guardsman, and because of his sheer size, you could see why.

This was a blissfully happy summer season. Among the firsts were taking one of the dancers out after the show and ordering buttered corn on the cob, ordering a bottle of Sauternes, not knowing that it is a dessert wine, and having a wet shave, having previously been an electric razor man. It was thus with a heavy heart and fond memories that I made my way to the station in Bournemouth for the return to Liverpool for the new Autumn 1967 season.

Jill Fraser, my first DSM, had left the company in the July of '67 and I employed my old friend from the Bristol days Tricia Martin, now professionally known as Courtney Martin, as her replacement. The first show of that autumn was *Inadmissible Evidence* by John Osborne which, for some reason, was to be rehearsed in London at a pub in The Grays Inn Road used by The Grand Order of Water Rats. This may have been at the insistence of the Director Stuart Latham and the stars John Bancroft, Georgina Hale and John Ingram, but was most inconvenient for me as all of my working paraphernalia was up in Liverpool.

I found cheap digs in Kings Cross, which was a notorious red light area, and as evenings were free from rehearsals, it was an ideal opportunity to see West End shows and visit the clubs in Soho, where I would later work.

The designer was another ex-Lincoln person employed by Kay Gardner, the very talented John Page. The Wardrobe Mistress was Cathy Alger, who traditionally always had a Scouse New Year's Eve bash at her home in the suburbs, which was a nightmare to get to and from, as cabs were very hard to book or flag down. The Stage Management team now included Sid Livingston, who I would meet a year later when he was in the National Theatre's revival of Oklahoma at the Lyceum theatre in Covent Garden, local wag Sid Dunn, Chris Maudsley, the lovely Moira Hughes, the burly John Maynall and Fern Richardson.

The five productions leading up to Christmas were all good rep shows of high quality and the Stage Management and I were working well together, and knew our roles and responsibilities so well that I was able to introduce a night off routine that went down well with all concerned. It worked as follows: the most senior of the ASM's, who was not cast to play a part, would learn the Book after the first night and then run the show, supervised, at the Matinée/Early House on the Saturday. One of the other members would learn the sound and run the show, also supervised, until competent, whilst I would fill in as required. In addition to giving people a night off to go to the cinema or see another show in town, it meant that we were fully covered should an indisposition occur at short notice during the run.

In addition to my normal duties I had now become 'The First Night Party Social Secretary' and organised the first night Company outing to the nightlife in Liverpool. On one occasion I took them down to the famous Cavern Club. Amongst the Company was the eminent actress Eithne Dunne who was wearing a mink stole over her shoulders, as it was a chilly night and the wind was blowing straight off the Mersey and up into Mathew Street. I knocked on the Cavern door, and the admissions flap was opened by Billy, one of the heavies on the door, who said: "Now den John, how many to-night wacker?" I told him how many and the door was duly opened for us all to enter and go down the stairs. As Eithne entered she removed the stole, handed it Billy and said to him: "Would you look after this for me, young man?" and tipped him ten shillings. He was dumbfounded. Not only had he never seen a mink stole before, but no one had ever given him a tip either. Needless to say we had a memorable night in the sweaty underground Cavern Club.

The remainder of the 1967 season of productions at the Playhouse was pretty unmemorable, although still of a high standard, but the exciting thing was to watch and be involved with the development of the extension of the existing building on the OP Side where the workshop, paint frame, green room, wardrobe store, rehearsal room, administration offices and FOH restaurant and mezzanine levels were now taking shape and on schedule for opening the following year. This would mean that we would be able, at long last, to vacate the temporary warehouse building a short way from Williamson Square, we had been using since 1966. It had served us well, but was a nightmare to use on a wet, cold winter's night when doing a Get In or Get Out.

I used to continue my love of the light entertainment scene by vising the Royal Court or Empire on a Sunday evening, when we did not have a change over weekend, to see shows as the guest of The Manager. I was still very much a loner at times as I could not always find someone to accompany me to concerts, but was not going to let that stop me from going out and enjoying myself. I would sometimes meet a nice young lady at a club, provided I did not leave it too late by having another pint to give me enough Dutch courage to ask her for a dance. It was on these occasions that I learnt the hard way that 'he who hesitates is lost', an expression that I still abide by to this day.

Around this time Jon Swain, the Stage Manager from The Everyman Theatre in Hope Street, which was the newest theatre in Liverpool, moved into the flat above me and we immediately hit it off as we both liked having a good time and so formed the Thirteen Club. This was an exclusive key holders' only club, we told the girls, to impress them last thing at night, with the invitation: "Fancy going on to the Thirteen Club, luv?" although it was in reality our flats. This little trick worked very successfully for the whole time Jon and I lived at 13, Canning Street, in the Toxteth area.

Sunday afternoons were washing day, and I used to walk up to the corner of Upper Parliament Street (or Upper Parley as the locals called it) to where there was the nearest Launderette to do my all my washing, apart from the stiff white collars I used to wear and which were sent off weekly by Jack Kelly, the Stage Doorkeeper, to a dry cleaners. On the way I used to pass a church, which had a notice board outside with the service times on it and parish notices, one of which asked: "If God came to Liverpool, what would YOU do?" Some Scouse Liverpudlian had written across it in bold capitals: "Move St. John to inside forward". Football is a religion on Merseyside, so I had decided to support Liverpool Football Club - 'The Reds' - because for years I had heard on the radio talk about Everton Football Club, but had never known where Everton was. Following the fortunes of The Reds became a passion for me, and I went to matches at Anfield as often as I could, standing on the famous Kop, so named after the battle for the Spion Kop Hill in the Boer War of January 1900 during the campaign for the relief of Ladysmith, where many brave solders from Liverpool Regiments perished.

The deciding match of the season was usually over the Easter weekend when arch rivals for the title Leeds United (Don Revie) would play Liverpool (Bill Shankly) in a 'four pointer', the outcome of which would mean that you either had a good or bad weekend.

The last production of the David Scase reign was *The Birdwatcher* on 1st July 1967 after I had worked under him for some twelve productions. On one occasion I happened to go to the toilet immediately after him, soon after we had been paid. I saw that he had unsuccessfully tried to flush away his payslip, which was still floating in the bowl. Inquisitive as to what remuneration he was on, I fished it out to find that as the Director of Production, at one of the country's most prestigious reps, he was on £40 per week. I thought that when I earned that much, I should be in a position to get married and settle down, but it took me until 1973 to get there.

Moving on to 1968, we were working in the re-vamped Playhouse where there was a succession of special productions with guest artistes to tread the boards of the swish new theatre. There was a Royal Gala opening on 29th October, graced by the presence of HRH The Duchess of Kent, who came to see *Man and Superman*, by George Bernard Shaw. Finding a priceless 1903 car that someone was prepared to loan proved a big challenge for my powers of persuasion. This was the first of many Royal events that I have been honoured to work on since them, and my parents visited Liverpool again for the occasion and shared adjacent seats with Courtney Martin's parents in the rear of the stalls and got on like a house on fire as they too liked a bevy or two.

The Christmas show that year was *The Thirteen Clocks* and whilst this was playing over Christmas and the New Year, we prepared the following production, *A Kind of Loving*, in the adjacent workshop on the new wagon stage that was to be used for the first time. This proved to be a huge success and time saver as had been envisaged by Chris Bullock in his wisdom.

In January 1969 a new Artistic Director, Anthony (Dick) Tuckey, was appointed. Chris was promoted to General Manager, and I was asked to succeed him as Stage Director with an increase in salary to £22/10/- (£22.50) per week, a fortune for me then. With Dick's appointment came an influx of notable actors: Ian Talbot, later to be the Artistic Director of the Open Air Theatre in Regents Park; Barbara Ewing who would play the lead in *The Prime of Miss Jean Brodie*, and Ian McKellan, later to be knighted, who was to play the lead in *The Bacchae* by Euripides, and direct *Jean Brodie*. The productions were enormous and very challenging for me as the new Stage Director. Other productions included *The Servant of Two Masters*, the unmentionable Shakespeare play in which Dick played the title role himself, *In his Own Write* by John Lennon, Ibsen's *Peer Gynt* and comedy *Billy Liar* by the great Keith Waterhouse, with whom I would share many a glass of champagne in Gerry's Club in Soho in later years. To round his first season off, A Victorian Music Hall played, which included a memorable version of the George Formby song With My Little Piece of Blackpool Rock. Boy was it hard work, but at the same time good fun, with a Company that wanted to enjoy life in Liverpool as much as I did and come out to the local nightspots on a regular basis. The DSM Courtney Martin had now moved into the front room flat at 13, Canning Street and was the proud owner of a small television set. On the evening of 20th July I and several other members of the company crowded round this TV to see the first landing on the Moon, and wondered what lay next for space exploration in our lifetimes?

I continued to develop my interest in the light entertainment side of the business, as this was what I really enjoyed, but was mature enough to realise that a grounding in the classics, as I had found with my ballet training, would stand me in good stead. I was a regular at the Royal Court Theatre, where many of the big variety names would play, and got to know Ray Walker who used to run the shows for The Delfont Organisation for many years.

The remainder of the 1969 season at the Playhouse, between September and December, continued with another selection of fine shows with guest artistes, the highlights for me being *Spring and Port Wine*, another Shaw play, this time *Pygmalion* and the controversial play *Saved* by Edward Bond, which was Directed by a young Director Barry Kyle. I clashed with him over the stoning the baby to death pram scene as he wanted the pram to be down stage right which I, as the Stage Director, felt was dangerous for patrons sitting in the front stalls. The play had been heavily criticised by the national press when it opened at the Royal Court Theatre in Sloane Square in November 1965, but the Management there had used a loophole in the censorship clause that the Lord Chamberlain's office had invoked, by making the theatre into a 'Club Theatre' whereby patrons had to become members prior to admission. We eventually compromised and the pram was faced upstage, on safety grounds.

At Christmas I was promoted to be The Production Manager with a salary of £30 per week, and we presented a double bill of *The Snow Queen* for the matinées and *The Ghost Train* at night. The very quick daily changeovers from one show to the next were only possible thanks to the wagon stage being fully utilised. *Ghost Train* was great fun to work on as we set out to create all the train effects onstage, just as they would have been done in the original production of 1925, with milk churns in the wings, train door slam boxes, compressed air for the steam noise, a garden roller that ran over equally spaced batons screwed to the stage floor to create the noise of the ghost train arriving, and guards whistles to blow for the departure. Arnold Ridley had written the play in 1923 following his own experience of being stranded at the remote Mangotsfield Station, near Bristol one night.

By now my production schedules for the Get Out and Fit Ups had become legendary. On the last Saturday of the run of a show there would be a run through of the new production, followed by two shows of the current production. After the final performance of the current show at about 1030pm the Break Down and Get Out would commence. The Stage Management would clear away any props or set fixtures, such as pictures and window curtains, for safe keeping prior to going back into storage; the wardrobe staff and any dressers would collect costumes from the wings and dressing rooms, and put on one side for dry cleaning before going back unto the ever-growing wardrobe storeroom; the Electrical Department (Elex) would take away any onstage electrical equipment; the Carpentry Department (Chippies) would start to dismantle the settings.

Billy Meall (because he had a head for heights), would be dispatched to the loading gallery where all the counter weights were on or off loaded when the next stage of the break down began, for the removal of the flown pieces of scenery or soft drapes that were specific to the previous production.

Once the stage floor area was clear we could commence to drop things into waist height to be offloaded. The chief, Michael Williams, assisted by Brian Kendrick and Bill Gough handled the electrics, whilst possibly the most important role was handled by one of the SM Team on the hauling line brake at stage level. It was essential that the cradle be offloaded of most of its weights, thus making the load still on the bar heavier than the cradle, before the brake was released and the bar, light now, could be gridded.[5]

My schedule set a curfew time at 2am, so after sweeping the stage, and a general tidy up we would, time permitting, commence the Fit Up of the new production that would always open, and it did during my time there, at 7.30pm the following Tuesday evening. I was now the named driver of the

---

5. *Grid.* A structure well above the stage used to hoist (fly) scenery etc. out of sight.

theatre mini bus, and it was my last duty of the day to run the staff home, turning in after having a strip wash at the flat.

Sunday always commenced, like rehearsals traditionally did, at 10am, so at best we would all have had only about six hours sleep - thank goodness I was (and still am) a night owl. The fit up of the new production really began in earnest starting with the stage floor and working upward, until a dinner break which I would host at the Stage Door pub in Williamson Square, at 1pm for an hour, when each crew member was permitted a pint out of my petty cash float.

The Elex took an early break so that they could have the stage to themselves during the dinner break and work without having to fight for space. During the preceding week I had prepared a meticulous hanging plot and cross section, so that they knew exactly where to hang their lanterns and at what height, so to be in mask by the borders hanging downstage of these dedicated lines.

The show began to come together during the afternoon, with the design department dressing the set as we progressed from scene to scene. Meanwhile wardrobe would be finishing their final touches to the costumes and distributing them to the appropriate dressing rooms that I had delegated according to sex, personality, smokers or non-smokers.

The females of the SM Team prepared an in house evening supper for all us workers to eat at 6pm, usually fried chicken, in addition to setting out the hand props on wheeled prop trolleys that I had made for each wing. All being well we would commence lighting the show on schedule at 7 pm, scene by scene, or in some cases reverse order to finish up with the opening set at the end, in readiness for the Company's arrival the following morning. Depending on the complexity of the lighting plot and the demands of the lighting designer, this could involve over one hundred different settings and combinations of the equipment. We usually called it a day at 2am (although it had been known to go on later), when I would run everyone home again, as public transport had well finished running.

The Company was permitted onstage to walk the set, and try on their finished costumes from 10am Monday, prior to a photo call for the press and in-house photographer at noon, before a break and then a technical rehearsal from 2pm.

This was when the DSM, in the Corner and running the show, had to be on the ball despite her lack of sleep. The scene and interval changes were organised and overseen by myself to ensure that all the staff, having been briefed previously and given a job sheet, knew what their particular responsibility was, and how it would dovetail into what others were doing to ensure a smooth and quick change, that was acceptable to the demands of the Director.

If the technical had gone without a hitch, which was not always the case, following a short break the first full dress rehearsal was scheduled to start at show time of 7.30 pm, with me timing the show on the stop watch which my parents had bought for me as a twenty first birthday present in December 1965.

This information was vital to the FOH Manager, who needed it to inform the box office of the curtain downtime and set the 'Carriages At' sign in the foyer along with the interval times for the bars and for the usherettes to collect their supply of ice creams from the deep freezers in the cold store.

I would wander around the auditorium checking sight lines and masking from all three levels in the auditorium, and for each different scene making copious reminder notes on the clipboard that was always with me and became my trade mark as any note, request or demand was acted upon at the earliest opportunity. At the conclusion of the first Dress Rehearsal (DR) it was time to hold a post mortem with all the departments to find out what had gone wrong or not worked as I had planned, and delegate my notes to departments or individuals for action. These jobs were actioned, in order of priority, on the Tuesday morning, before the second and final DR commenced at 2pm. This by now, I hoped, would be the final definitive version of a tight show because there was only a short break following this DR, prior to the FOH Manager opening the house at 7pm to what was usually a full house of local VIPs and the Liverpool Echo reporter sent to review the show for his copy deadline later that evening.

My attention to detail in my pre-production schedule usually paid off, with the show running faultlessly, at least to the audience. Irrespective of how the first night had gone, and before we went out on the town to party at a club that I had made arrangements with, I and the SM team would clear the stage and mark out the floor plan of the next show in coloured tapes, with small marker dots at each major intersection, so that the tape could be taken up and put down again as and when required. The staff did not object to staying on for the extra half hour it took, as I had prepared this new ground plan in advance with all the measurements taken left or right of the tape measure on the centre line and taken from the 'carpet cut' as it meant that they could have a lie-in on Wednesday, and also give the Company thirty minutes to wind down and remove their slap.

The first night parties became legendary, with both cast and crew having a good knees up, consuming too much alcohol, and generally letting their hair down.

During the '69 season I had to lock up one of the Stage Management Team in a quick-change dressing room as he was too inebriated, after an afternoon on the batter going backwards and forwards to and from Wallasey on the local ferryboat, to work the show that night. The following day he was full of remorse, apologised and bought me a book as a peace offering, as he felt that his job was on the line, which it was. Tricia, my faithful DSM, left Liverpool to pursue her career elsewhere, and was later to become the Stage Director at the Salisbury Playhouse. After *Saved* closed at the end of November 1969 and during the preceding weeks, whilst she was working her notice, I had advertised in the theatre trade paper The Stage for a new deputy to work at what was now, along with the Bristol Old Vic, Nottingham Playhouse, and Oxford Playhouse, one of the most prestigious and modern theatres on the rep circuit.

I was inundated with applications, some much too long, some without a curriculum vitae attached, or even a resumé of previous employment, and eventually drew up a short list of six whom I would interview, aiming for a two from whom to make a choice. The interviews were held in the plush new boardroom on the top floor of the new office block and I laid on coffee and biscuits from the FOH catering department that ran the restaurant. I got down to my final two females who I thought would mix in well with the team, had sufficient experience, and were both happy with the remuneration of around £15 per week as a starting salary, dependent on their experience.

The girl, who was my first choice, turned the job down post interview as she had also been offered a similar position at Guilford and she preferred to stay in the south of England. Maris Sharp (of whom a lot more later) however was equally qualified having worked with Bill Kenwright at the English National Youth Theatre, and was happy to come up from London. She had impressed me with her openness, ability, interview technique, and personality and would, I hoped, be equal to her predecessor, who knew how I worked and what my foibles were. Her first show on the Book was, from memory, to be *A Christmas Carol* followed by *The Snow Queen* and *Ghost Train* as a Christmas & New Year double.

During the late '60s I had not let my interest in motor cycle racing diminish and as the Isle of Man ferries sailed from Liverpool, I went over to the island each June for the Tourist Trophy races. In 1967 I witnessed one of the greatest achievements ever over the mountain course, when Bill Ivy achieved the first ever 100mph lap on a 125cc machine. In my opinion this achievement was even more remarkable than the first 100mph lap set by Bob McIntyre ten years earlier, but on a motorcycle with an engine that was four times larger and had a full dustbin fairing attached. As I had wheels in the form of the Playhouse mini-bus I was able to attend motor cycle meetings at the Prestatyn Trotting Stadium, and at national meetings run by the Point of Ayr Club.

The opening season in 1970 offered another fine collection of quality productions ranging from *The Critic* and *Harlequinade* as another double bill, Michael Gambon playing the lead in *Coriolanus*, during which I took a spring week off, and left the Stage Manager Don Harly, an Oxford Rowing Blue in charge, and the wonderfully poignant piece of theatre that originated at Joan Littlewood's theatre workshop in Stratford East *Oh What a Lovely War* and a multi-talented company that included the delightful Brigit Forsyth. The latter was a very technical show with a ticker tape electronic board centre stage giving the running total of dead to date etc. on it, which required precise cueing from the corner by Maris, the new DSM. The way she ran this show convinced me that she was the right person for the post, as her prompt copy was perfect, so it could be taken over by someone else at a moment's notice in an emergency. To say that she and her work impressed me is an understatement.

During my years in Liverpool I had not let my interest in jazz, and especially big band swing jazz, diminish and was a regular at many local jazz club events in the City and the Royal Philharmonic Hall that used to attract all the big name bands that were touring the UK. On one occasion the great *Count Basie Band* was playing at the Phil and I found out they were staying at the prestigious Adelphi Hotel. I went there post concert to have a drink in the hotel bar, as I suspected that the band members would be having a nightcap, and it would be a golden opportunity to meet and chat to them. I waited in the bar for ten minutes or so and then asked the Bartender if he was expecting the band to come in for a drink. "Not until they get back from having a jam session at the so-and-so club" he replied, so I quickly downed my drink in one, and set off to find them playing at the aforementioned club. What a dream come true to hear the world-renowned Count Basie band having a jam session.

On some Sunday evenings the Syd Lawrence Orchestra came over to the Liverpool Adelphi to play a big band swing concert in the ballroom. This was an offshoot of the smaller 'Trad Lads' of the *Northern Dance Orchestra*, based in Manchester. Syd had started his own band in 1967, playing regularly at the Mersey Hotel in Manchester, until their reputation and popularity required larger venues. I had listened to the NDO and the Trad Lads on the portable radio that my parents had bought me for Christmas, so I knew I liked the sound, but to hear the full seventeen piece band play live was something else.

I also supported the local Traditional Jazz Band, *The Merseysippi Jazz Band*, whenever I could, as then they were the oldest two trumpet Jazz Band in the UK. They had formed in 1948 as *The Wallasey Rhythm Kings*, but as their gigs were usually on a night when I was doing a show, that was only occasionally. They had something of an international reputation and had played alongside Louis Armstrong at the Liverpool Stadium in 1956, with the ragtime piano playing of pianist Frank Robinson being second to none.

Amongst the other top flight American bands I saw in Liverpool were *The Stan Kenton Orchestra* and what was termed his 'wall of sound' which featured a booming brass section and percussion, and the more refined, but equally exciting, sound of *The Duke Ellington Orchestra*, with his sophisticated arrangements.

The spring and summer season ended on 25th July 1970 with a revue written by and starring Bob Harris and Ian Talbot entitled *Hello Everybody*, which I thoroughly enjoyed working on as it was more in the light entertainment field.

I used to borrow the company mini-bus regularly for a weekend and pop up to Blackpool to see a girlfriend I had met at a nightclub, and who was doing a summer season dancing in one of the many shows that used to be so plentiful at this resort. In 1968 there were over a dozen major shows at venues such as the Central Pier, the Grand Theatre, the huge Opera House (the largest in the UK), The Queens, the South Pier, the Winter Gardens complex and the Tower Circus, as well as numerous hotels on the front that had a cabaret room.

With careful planning it was possible to see three shows a day, as I frequently did. A 2.30 matinée at one show would give time to dash over to another venue for the first house at 5.15, before the second house of another show at 8.30 pm - exhausting but fun. I would then meet up with my girlfriend and her fellow dancers at The Town and Country Nightspot near the North Pier, which was the pros venue of choice during the season. Here you could meet up and chat with all the turns and artistes playing the town that summer. On one occasion Kathy Kirby was in the club and I was introduced to her Manager Bert Ambrose (but always called Mr. Ambrose to his face), who was also her mentor and lover.

What a thrill it was to meet and chat to the legendary dance band leader of the 1930/'40/'50s whose records from Dad's collection I had listened to many times, during my days living at home.

Back in Liverpool the autumn 1970 Season began with *The Boy Friend* by Sandy Wilson, with all the cast having a good old romp, continued with The Crucible, where we had to make a pan full of rabbit stew for each performance and *Taming of the Shrew*, starring Paul Shelley. The green room prop kitchen was now run full time by Norman Hurst, who had been with Gerry & The Pacemakers when they were at their height, and provided drinks and hot food during the day. I had met him and his brother Les at one of the nightclubs where they provided food as part of the licensing requirements, and asked them if they could help me out by making coffee during rehearsals as all of the SM Team were busy, and it had grown from there. Norman was later to meet and marry Ray Dawson from the Company, and they would become close friends of mine for many years until Norman's untimely passing in December 2013.

The Christmas show 1970-71 was *Old King Cole* by Ken Campbell, and a great production of *Hadrian The Seventh* with Neil Cunningham. In February, during the Council of Repertory Theatres conference, Ronnie Settle and Joan Ovens made their final appearance together playing the in-coming music to patrons as they had been doing since 1948, and it fell on my shoulders to remove the two grand pianos from the orchestra pit, where they had been for a quarter of a century.

Her Majesty the Queen officially opened the second Mersey tunnel on 24th June, and the Playhouse Company, led by Ian Talbot, was invited to perform an extract from *The Lancashire Twins* at the Empire Theatre alongside all the greats who had their roots in Liverpool like Frankie Vaughan, Arthur Askey, Tom O'Connor and Jimmy Tarbuck.

I was then informed that my contract would not be renewed after the summer break and that the pipe smoking Bindon Kinghorn was to succeed me. I was in a dilemma. What should I do next?

Act 1 Scene 4
GREENWICH THEATRE
(1971-72)

At the time I was devastated to be given the news, but on reflection it was what I needed to kick start my career onto another level, try different things and make new friends and contacts. I had worked on over seventy main house shows during my six happy years at Liverpool and learnt a lot about myself and how to behave in a senior management role that would stand me in good stead for many years to come.

Following the success of *Lancashire Twins* at The Royal Command at the end of June, I production managed my favourite Ayckbourn play *Relatively Speaking* prior to taking my final curtain call with *The Knack* by Anne Jellicoe. One of my final jobs was to look after Ken Dodd when he came to audition for the part of Malvolio in *Twelfth Night*, which was to be produced at The Playhouse in November. Like many other stand-up comedians, he had a desire to perform one of the great Shakespearean characters in his illustrious career, and was duly cast.

What had been the highs and what had been the lows of my years at Liverpool? Certainly to be offered the post of Stage Manager, and be told that I was head and shoulders above the other candidates, when straight out of Drama School, was a high, as well as having, mostly, a good tight team around me, with one or two exceptions. James Broadbent came as an ASM and was working the House Tabs in the Prompt Corner, and I instructed him to 'Stand By to Take the Tabs Out', which he interpreted as 'Take the Tabs Out'. The house lights were still on, and the Company was all lounging about, waiting for their cue. He in his naivety did not realise that he had done anything wrong, which we laugh about now when we meet, as we all know now that he turned out to be a very fine actor and film star, but one of my worst ASMs.

We also had Harry, a Duty Fireman, who claimed, with his vast experience in the Brigade, to be capable of dealing with any incident in the building, yet when called upon to deal with a prop fire that was overheating onstage, tripped over holding the CO_2 extinguisher whilst getting to the incident. Lesson: never trust someone who is an expert at anything because they know more and more about less and less. I had mastered the new decimal currency and was the first person at the Playhouse to present his weekly petty cash account in this new format where everything appeared to cost twice as much as it had done prior to its introduction.

I hoped that I had proved to possess all the qualities that a good leader should show both to my superiors and subordinates and that some would happily come and work with me again in a different arena in the future, which many did.

I had found the people of Liverpool to be good humored, always up for a laugh, and many have remained my friends to this day.

I have always believed that it is not 'what you know', but 'who you know' and 'being in the right place at the right time', and I relay this philosophy to the many University students that I now socialise with who are studying drama. I contacted some colleagues with whom I had worked and who knew what I was capable of, and the high standards I worked to, and one such person came up trumps for me.

Alan Vaughan Williams had been a Director of Productions at Lincoln in 1963 before I went to Bristol. He was now working with Ewan Hooper at The Greenwich Theatre, as Associate Director of Productions down on the river in SE10 and about 20 minutes by train from Charing Cross, and was looking for an experienced Production Manager to commence in mid July. This fitted in perfectly with my plans to work eventually in the West End as the theatre, at this time, was being used as a pre West End try out venue by leading West End Producers.

I had purchased my first car, an Austin A40 registration VFU 396 (funny how I can remember this number but not the one of my current car), loaded it up in Liverpool with all my worldly goods, which were a lot more than when I arrived, and headed south down to London on Sunday 4th July 1971, stopping off at Honeydon en route, where the Hunts Falcons Motor Cycle Club was running The National Grass Track Championships. The 500cc Champion was Brian Maxted, with whom I would later become close friends, as he lives at Brant Broughton, a charming village near Lincoln.

Arriving in London I began to look for accommodation as near to the theatre as I could and found a furnished flat in Royal Hill, which was a short walk to the theatre adjacent to Greenwich Park. It was more than I wanted to pay out of my new wage of £35 per week, but that is the price I had to pay to live in a nice part of London, near to my workplace. Once I was settled in I called to see Alan after some eight years and have a look round, and was engaged to start on Monday 19th July 1971. I would be sharing an office with Alan at the top of a house next to the theatre. I was introduced to Ewan, one of the old school Actor Managers and the Head of Design, Roger Butlin, who also lived in Royal Hill, a few doors from my flat.

The Venue, situated in Crooms Hill, had been The Greenwich Hippodrome in 1897 but was now an Open Thrust Stage Theatre with no flying, proscenium arch, or orchestra pit. It had a difficult Get In some twenty feet off the street level, and had opened in 1969, a couple of years before I went there. It had a single raked auditorium seating only 421 patrons, two dressing rooms, a restaurant and an art gallery. The stage sets were all constructed by outside contractors, and there was a resident electrician, who lit the shows if an outside lighting designer had not been engaged. This set up was not what I was used to at all and presented me with a new challenge to get to grips with.

I had inherited the Stage Management Team from my predecessor, Sean Hurst, headed by Stage Manager Gabby West. I was happy to start with them to see how they worked and see if we got on together during rehearsals, fit ups and the social side, which was, and still is, vital to my way of life. I was not that impressed with the way rehearsals were conducted at a nearby church hall, but was happy to see how things worked out during the forthcoming weeks. Robert Chetwyn, who had been responsible for many shows in the West End, directed the first show that I was fully involved with, and knew what standards he wanted from us.

The Theatre Bar, named Crowder's Bar after the Music Hall on the site many years earlier, was a local meeting place for the characters who lived in SE10 and surrounding areas, along with Vic's pub next door, *The Rose and Crown*, which had regular lock-ins mainly for off duty policemen from the local Police Station nearby.

I contracted out the first set to a local set maker who had a workshop in Greenwich, and part of the deal was that we would do the Get In during the actors' lunch break on the Friday preceding the Fit Up weekend. This did not go according to plan, as the Get In was far more difficult than I had envisaged and overran into the afternoon rehearsal time, which obviously did not go down well. I vowed that this would not happen again and began to draw up plans to make things easier and above all safer.

These included having a roller bar on the edge of the Get In lip, a rope hoist, and safety belts, which clipped to the Get In door side to prevent a fall into the street below. I also made a Fit Up tool box, which could be hung next to the Stage Management Prop Room, or moved around onstage as it had castors on its base.

This was in addition to a hardware cupboard, which contained assorted screws, nails, hinges, and screw eyes etc., in fact anything that might be required on a Sunday when the local hardware shop was closed.

During October we had a double bill of Greek tragedies by Sophocles, *Antigone and Electra*, which were not my cup of tea. The Director, Hovhanness Pilikian, wanted it staged on a bed of sand, which was impractical to get onto the theatre stage, so a compromise was found by using bags of Vermiculite insulation, which got everywhere and had to be kept hosed down and dampened with water from the onstage hose reel to prevent it being inhaled, and was a nightmare. The Director also refused to finish rehearsals or give out notes to the Company until way past the time they should have been on a break prior to the evening show, until I had a word with him about the regulations, which he claimed to 'know nothing about as he was Greek'.

By October I had made my mind up that the current Stage Management Team were too set in their old ways to change to the way of working that I wanted, and made enquiries about the availability of Trish Martin, and reasoned that 'the devil you know is better than the devil you don't know'. I knew what Maris was up to as we were seeing quite a bit of one another post Liverpool. After a spell in Oldham, she would move down to The Playhouse in Salisbury. Much to the chagrin of many, I appointed Trish as my Stage Manager, retaining the services of Dafydd ap Reece as her Deputy. Her first production was *Liberated Woman* in early November. This appointment did not go down at all well with some of the drinkers in Crowder's Bar, but I was determined to surround myself with a team that I could trust and would work to the standards that I demanded from them. John Roffey remained as Chief Electrician with Pete Stenning as his Assistant in the re-shuffle.

During the second weekend of November Mum and Dad came down to London, as Susan was due to appear with *The Young Generation* at The Royal Command Performance at The London Palladium on Monday 15th November, when traditionally the current Palladium show was suspended. They came to Greenwich on the Saturday night, saw the show there, and I then took them over the road to the Spread Eagle Restaurant in Stockwell Street, where I knew the owner Dick along with Chef and many of the staff. This was because over a working weekend we would often pop in to see if there was anything left over, which we could buy at a reduced rate, and on occasion we were sold pieces of roast duck and other fowl. Sue had somehow managed to get three seats for the Royal Command Show and Ray was over the moon when he met and chatted over a glass of red wine to legendary Jazz Guitarist Stéphane Grappelli in the stage door pub, before the show.

 I had gone to a very upmarket hairdresser in the afternoon to have a new style of haircut and thoroughly enjoyed the show, which was in the presence of H.M. The Queen and hosted by Bruce Forsyth. In addition to the Young Generation on the star-studded bill were Lovelace Watkins, who I knew from the Shaky Days in Liverpool, Norman Collier, Ned Sherrin, with whom I would work the following year, Mr. 'Settle Down' Ken Goodwin, Sacha Distel, who Mum loved, Shirley Bassey, and Tommy Cooper. It was the custom for a party to be held in Hanover Square, and tickets were limited to those appearing, agents, and VIP's only. Ray went up to the burly doorman, as soon as he saw that he was on his own, explained that he had inadvertently left his three party pass admission tickets in his hotel room, slipped him a tenner for a drink, and we were in. I danced the evening through with many of Sue's friends. It was a night to remember.

At the end of November, we presented a revival of the play *A Day In The Death of Joe Egg* by Peter Nichols, about a child who is unable to communicate and is wheelchair-bound as a result of having cerebral palsy, which was one of the most memorable and moving pieces of theatre I had been involved with for some time. I had established a new social life in London, but tried not to mix business with pleasure. I was also well into the fashions of the day buying hipster trousers in Carnaby Street (where else?), and I paid £35, a whole week's wages, on a pair of pure chamois leather trousers in the Kings Road. Talk about me being a trend setter.

I had now settled into a routine of getting up as late as possible to be at the theatre in time for the daily rehearsals or a meeting with contractors, going down to the Terminus Café near to the Cutty Sark for a spot of lunch, where they knew what I liked and would save one of the daily specials, like a stuffed heart, for me. At tea time I would call at one of the many local shops in Royal Hill for fresh produce. We had a proper greengrocer, who always wore a brown working overall like Arkwright in *Open all Hours*. He would say: "The watercress is fresh and peppery today, John", and it tasted fresh as it had not been kept in a plastic bag, but come up from Hampshire on the *Watercress Express* train to Covent Garden, or: "Got some new crop shallots in this morning, want half a pound?" The same would apply at the butcher who knew I liked the cheaper cuts of meat, such as lamb breast, and would cut me one as required, and similarly at the bakery, where they baked on the premises. It had a real village feel to it and I felt at home. Once back at the flat, I would rustle up a substantial meal that had not cost the earth, before getting dressed up for the show at night, retiring afterwards to the theatre bar or Vic's.

In January 1972, a boyfriend of Trisha's, Graham Phoenix joined the Company as a relief on the SM Team for *Never The Twain*, and would later return as Chief Electrician in 1973. Roger Butlin and I went over to have a look round the Ashcroft Theatre which was part of the Fairfield Hall complex in Croydon on the 6th January 1972, as we were going to be taking a show there in February. We found it well appointed, seating 750 with a green room bar backstage for the use of all the artistes playing in the complex. The play was to be *The Feydeau Farce Festival of Nineteen Nine*, a new work written by the Quizmaster of University Challenge, Bamber Gascoigne, who I first met in the production office when he was discussing casting with Alan, who was to direct the piece.

The cast was very strong and included the outrageous Gaye Brown, Andrew Ray, Donald Hewlett, Bill Wallis, Anna Dawson and Derek Smith. It was set a thousand miles up the Amazon in and around the Theatro Grande in Manaos, which apparently did exist and presented a Festival of Feydeau plays in 1909. It would be lit by Robert Bryan.

Greenwich had always been very strong with its Music Hall traditions, and between 30th May and 24th June 1972 we presented Music Hall, with several big names from the heyday of Variety and Music Hall topping the bill for a week as they had done in their prime.

Geoffrey Robinson was the eloquent, alliterative Chairman with the gavel and block, much as Leonard Sachs was in *The Good Old Days* from the Leeds City Varieties Theatre. Peter Spraggon was also an ever present member of the cast playing a tune on the rip saw or singing a little ditty or two, whilst John Gould, who lived in nearby New Cross, was the Musical Director prior to becoming one of the team on Esther Rantzen's *That's Life* the following year. I wanted to create a series of 'swags' onstage, much as the settings of the period would have been, but the lack of a flying system frustrated me, and we finished up with a plain black surround or nothing.

I found it a great honour and privilege to work with *Max Wall*, as Professor Wallofski, whom I had seen play Dame in Panto at the Theatre Royal Hanley in 1959. After his usual introduction about being a "brick in the Great Wall of China" and his trademark walk and comic dance in the black tights and circus boots, he would seat himself at the pianoforte to play a tune "with the aid of an AA Map and a spirit level". Not very funny when written, but hilarious to see! Max always enjoyed a pint of Guinness after the show, where he used to hold court in the Theatre Bar to those of us who were interested and fascinated by the career of the man who was, at heart, like Ken Dodd, a frustrated classical actor. He later went on to play the lead in a memorable production of *Waiting for Godot* in 1979.

Other top of the bill acts booked to appear for a week at a time were *Gert & Daisy* (Elsie and Doris Waters) who were the sisters of Jack Warner from Dixon of Dock Green, which was huge on TV at the time.

Another of the all-time great comedians to appear was the one and only Jimmy Wheeler, who was a burly man who worked with a violin, usually wore a trilby and sported a moustache when onstage. One night he was not in the theatre for his call, but I had an idea where he might be. I went round to Vic's, the Stage Door Pub, where I found him having a swift one. I explained that he was late arriving and that we were worried about him. "Don't you worry about me son" he replied and I escorted him back and into his dressing room. Once there he opened the violin case, took out the violin and bow along with a cork and a candle, lit the candle, blackened the end of the cork in the flame and with two swift movements applied the tash to his upper lip. It had only taken a couple of moments to prepare him and once the trilby was back on his head, announced: "I'm ready now son, where do you want me?" You knew when he had finished the act as his final lines were always "Aye Aye, that's yer lot". It was wonderful to work with this great comic genius, only a short time before he died.

In July 1972 we premiered the new musical by Ned Sherrin and Caryl Brahms, *Liberty Ranch*, which was booked in for a five week run prior to a West End transfer, we hoped. This was the first time I worked with Ned, a man I much admired. Our paths would cross again five years later on *Side by Side by Sondheim* and again at the Old Vic in 1999 with *Jeffrey Barnard is Unwell*. The piece was written by Dick Vosburgh and choreographed by Gillian Lynne, who during my Modern Dance lessons taught me that one of the greatest moves is stillness. I now pass that on to dance students at The Lincoln Performing Arts Centre who I meet socially.

The casting was a Who's Who of the world of the musical theatre and had Margaret Courtenay, Elizabeth Seal, Derek Griffith, David Kernan, Bob Sherman, Bill Kerr and Leslie Meadows in the cast - quite a line up for Greenwich. Bill frequently wore a coloured handkerchief in his breast pocket, which I discovered one day was actually a pair of ladies briefs, which he wore to match his tie, which is a trick that I still sometimes use today. However the show, despite doing excellent business, did not get the expected transfer into town, which was a shame as I had been looking forward to working on my first West End show.

Following this slight setback in my plans to work on bigger shows with names, I began to get itchy feet and attended an interview with Stephen Mitchell at London Pavilion Chamber, the offices of the legendary Tom Arnold, where he was the Production Manager. This firm had produced the Major Ice Show at Wembley Arena for years and co-produced many a show with the Delfont Organisation and other high class Producers. They were, to my mind, a slightly old fashioned Production House but this year, in association with Howard & Wyndhams, were trying something new. H & W were one of Britain's premier theatre circuits and owned many of the larger theatre touring houses, mainly in the North of England and Scotland, such as The Kings Edinburgh, The Alhambra Glasgow, the Theatre Royal Newcastle and The Opera House Manchester. Here they planned to stage *Peter Pan* starring *Lulu* for the Christmas and New Year Season, before a short tour. Rehearsals were due to start in late November in London and I was offered and accepted the position of Company Manager at £37 per week.

Meanwhile back in Greenwich I informed Ewan and Alan of my plans and agreed to stay on and work the final two shows of that season. *Gymnasium* by Robin Chapman was a challenging setting as the Designer wanted authentic wall bars, climbing ropes and the like, which we managed to obtain from a school in Poplar that was being demolished. My final play was to be *Brussels* by Jonathan Hale in October. This again was a huge challenge as the stage had to be covered with grass, and have a tree growing with a stream running. All very idyllic for a play about Boy Scouts out on a camping weekend and what they got up to. The performance by John Ringham as the Scout Master in charge was memorable, as was the running stream effect conjured up by Ant Peters, who could turn his hand to anything. He even welded my car to get it through its annual MOT at a local garage. He set the dashboard alight, and I was thankful that I had an extinguisher in the car, which is something that I have always carried.

During my time at Greenwich, what had I learnt? I now knew for certain that I was not an Open Thrust Stage man, but preferred the safety of the Proscenium Arch, with a flying system and a Plush & Gold Matcham's Style auditorium. I had confirmed my belief that I was admired by my superiors and was still the romantic type, and in many ways slightly old fashioned, but remained an inspirational leader, with a great sense of fairness towards those I worked with, and inspired great loyalty from them. For example for the Get In of *Brussels* I made a wooden pallet with wire strops attached to each corner, which could be lifted by a rope and hoist, which was attached to the outside wall above the Get In door. All the turfs of grass that were to be taken up on to the stage floor, with a peat underlay, could be hoisted into the theatre in groups of 20 or so at a time, thus alleviating the need to carry them all up by hand through the FOH stairs, one at a time. This would not only speed up the Get In and shorten the Fit Up time, but would also prevent soil being trodden into the stair carpets.

When Alan Vaughan Williams enquired: "What are you making now, John?" and I told him, he replied: "That's an inspirational idea, and going to save so much time over the weekend".

I had it confirmed on several occasions that I was developing and honing my personal charm skills, and had an enormous capacity for work and play being able, quite easily, to mix with and understand people from all walks of life, from the arty-crafty leading artiste to the humble cleaner, which was a skill that I had developed from my Mother. I had sometimes shown a ruthless streak, and was confident that I had developed a flair for organisation and planning, and the ability to foresee any possible problems, at the same time giving confidence to my subordinates that they were doing things the correct way.

I had enjoyed a wonderful social life whilst based in Greenwich, especially as Sue was now the youngest dancer in Dougie Squires Dance Group *The Young Generation* who were on the box most Saturday nights with the likes of Lulu, Rolf Harris, Engelbert Humperdinck and Dame Vera Lynn. These television shows were always pre-recorded and put in the can at the BBC Theatre, which was formerly the Shepherd's Bush Empire, and on the Sundays when I was not doing a Fit Up I went to watch the show and socialise afterwards over a nice bottle of wine with the most attractive girl dancers of their era. How I wished that I had not given up my dancing career, and could partner the likes of Kay Korda, Miranda Willis, Denise Fone, Wei Wei Wong, Terrie Robinson, and Liz Robertson, who was later to become Mrs. Alan Jay Lerner.

I was so convinced I could still dance to the standards of Nigel Lythgoe, Roger Finch, Trevor Willis and Richard Gough, who popularised the wearing of spectacles as much as Eric Morecambe, that following reading an advert in *The Stage* for male dancers to join *Young Generation*, I packed a bag one night to attend the audition but wisely, in retrospect, decided against it the following morning.

My sister's big break came on 18th July 1972, when she was asked to play opposite Gerry Marsden (of *Gerry & The Pacemakers*) in *Pull Both Ends,* the new musical at the Piccadilly Theatre in Denman Street, just off Piccadilly Circus. Set in a Christmas cracker factory, it was really a stage vehicle for the Younger Generation Dancers, but did not do justice to their known talents. Sadly it ran for only 36 performances because of bad press and lack of support. I was proud for her, after attending her opening West End performance, that one of the Toogoods from Lincoln had appeared in the West End by the age of twenty six, as she would soon emigrate to Australia, and we had only worked together once on a Trade Show for MMA at The Theatre Royal Drury Lane.

This 'who you know, NOT what you know' was again relevant for my new job as Company Manager and Stage Director on *Peter Pan* with *Lulu*, as the Director was to be Dougie Squires, who I knew from having seen him at work, was very organised, and planned each show like a military operation, which suited me fine.

What would this new stage in my career, working in commercial theatre where bums on seats mattered more than artistic content be like? I couldn't wait to find out.

Act 2 Scene 1
PETER PAN TOUR WITH LULU
(1972-73)

As soon as I had finished at Greenwich I began my preparations for Peter Pan. It was announced that I would be succeeded at Greenwich by David Adams from the Mermaid Theatre at Puddle Dock, in January 1973, and by a strange quirk of fate it had been David who had lit Pull Both Ends in July.

We had been booked in to rehearse at the Sundown Cinema in Brixton, which had closed on 29th July 1972, and which was an ideal rehearsal venue because of its sheer size. It was formerly The Astoria Theatre/Cinema, built by Edward Stone in 1929 at the height of the pre-war cinema building boom. The following year he was to design the Casino in Old Compton Street, where I would spend ten happy years as General Manager between 1986-1996, and was the largest venue south of the river at the time, seating an awesome 4,750 patrons.

Situated in Stockwell Road in SW9 the venue was a most ornate barn featuring statues, which created the impression of an atmospheric auditorium set in an Italian Garden. The stage was more than adequate with clear flying facilities for *Kirby's Flying Ballet* to perfect the many flights that Peter, Wendy, John and Michael had to make to and from The Never Never Land. My contact was Chief Engineer Don Dansie who had been there, I think, since it first opened, and knew every nook and cranny of this once proud building. It was being considered for demolition, but thankfully survives to this day as the O2 Academy.

We were contracted to commence rehearsals on Monday 27th November for three weeks prior to a Fit Up weekend on 17th-18th December (my birthday!), opening at 7pm on Tuesday 19th December at Howard & Wyndham's flagship north west venue The Opera House Manchester, for a run until Saturday 13th January 1973, playing twice daily for most of the run. We were then booked into another Howard & Wyndham's theatre, His Majesty's in Aberdeen, for a further two weeks terminating on Saturday 27th January.

I visited The Astoria (as I knew it) the week before on Wednesday 22nd November to introduce myself to The Chief - Don Dansie, have a look round, and mark out the settings from the half-inch to the foot ground plan that I had received from Reg Allen (Production Manager for Howard & Wyndham) who had built and painted the scenery at the Howard & Wyndham Roseburn Studio Workshops (an old sugar factory) up in the Murrayfield Area of Edinburgh. He would come down to supervise the Fit Up in Manchester with Sandy McFarlane, the Opera House Resident Stage Manager, who would be Master Carpenter for Tom Arnold Presentations on tour. Jean Onions was to be the Wardrobe Mistress, whilst on the Strand D/C Board were to be the Chief Electrician/Engineer Wally Tompkins assisted by Eve or Ray Walker. Lulu's costumes were to be made by Anthony Holland, whilst the remainder would come from the extensive H & W wardrobe collection.

I was given the cast list by Production Manager Stephen Mitchell and was amazed at the quality of the cast that Mr. Squires had contracted. I was also introduced at Pavilion Chambers to 'Young Tom' who was now running Tom Arnold Presentations with his Mother Mrs. Helen Arnold, who came up from her home on the south coast for meetings as required, and their faithful accountant Edward Lake. Mr Arnold Jnr. was the prospective candidate for the Conservative Member of Parliament for the Hazel Grove constituency in Cheshire, and thus very keen for *Peter Pan* to be a huge success in Manchester over the Christmas and New Year, when he would be bringing many of his party workers to see the show. He would be elected on 10th October at the 1974 general election and serve the same constituency until 1997. Tom Senior had been an institution since the '30s when he presented Ivor Novello as Henry V at Drury Lane in 1938, but was much better known as *The King of Pantos* having produced some 400 shows by the time of his death in 1969. I was also led to believe that one of Tom Junior's godfathers was Ivor Novello. Edward Lake ('Lakey') would be instrumental in teaching me the money side of the business, at which I was new. This included organising the weekly Payroll Call, which was traditionally held at lunchtime on a Thursday; the Petty Cash Account; Settling the weekly Contra Account with the Resident Theatre General Manager & Licensee, who in this case at The Opera House was the legendary 'Tommy' Francis Appleby, and setting out a weekly spreadsheet as Mr. Lake required.

In addition to *Lulu* being cast as Peter Pan, the boy who never grows up, Anthony Sharp who was then 58 years old, and twice my age, who usually played aristocratic, middle class roles, had been cast to play the usual double of Mr. Darling and Captain Hook. Comedy duo *Freeman & Paige* provided the laughs playing Gentleman Starkey (Al Paige) and Smee (Brian Freeman), with Prue Clarke as Wendy and Susan Hannay as Mrs. Darling and Mother Mermaid.

Other things I learnt about the cast at the first rehearsal, always a nervous moment for anyone but especially for me as this was to be the first of many shows that I would be Company Manager for over the next twenty five years or so, were that Malcolm Dixon was a charming 4' 1" dwarf, and would be Nana the Darling's household pet dog. He would later find fame in the Star Wars films of 1981-83. Peter Duncan, then only 18 years old, later to be a presenter on Blue Peter and the ninth Chief Scout from 2004-09, was to play Noodler, in addition to the Crocodile and a stunt man for all the fights onstage which were arranged by Ian McKay. Alan Bone was cast to play an assortment of roles including Bill Dukes, and he would also be on the hauling rope for all of the flights that Lulu undertook. This was to ensure consistency for what can be quite a hazardous element of the show and was insisted on by Lulu's demanding Manager and Agent Marion Massey who was naturally very protective of the young girl she had discovered in 1962 at a Glasgow discothèque. It was she who changed Marie Lawrie into the phenomena that was then, and still is, *Lulu*.

Dougie's idea was that this J.M. Barrrie Play for Children, which still gives its royalties to The Hospital for Sick Children in Great Ormond Street in London, would have music composed by Grant Foster and John Crook interwoven into it, but the production was not conceived or presented as a Pantomime, and Scotsman John Forsyth was engaged as the Touring Musical Director, picking up good session men locally in Manchester and Aberdeen when we were out of town.

I knew the Stage Management Team I had surrounded myself with could cope with my being away for a day, but I felt it was vital for Manchester to put a face to the name John Toogood. In addition to engaging Maris Sharp from my Liverpool Playhouse days (no relation to Anthony) as my SM to run the show, I had Frank S. Robinson as Sound ASM, Tony Ryan and Dafydd ap Reece from Greenwich.

During rehearsals I went to Manchester on the train to introduce myself to the Management and Crew at The Opera House and to choose some accommodation from the digs list for Maris and me, with whom I was now living in East Dulwich with friends of hers.

I looked though the theatre digs list and went to view a small but comfortable flat in Moss Side on recommendation from Sandy, which I liked and booked for the run, paying up front. We would only be sleeping there, as twice daily performances, understudy rehearsals and payroll calls would mean I was at the theatre for a 12 hour day and sometimes longer. I would be working 72 hours per week for £37 remuneration, or to be realistic less than £2 per hour, but it was what I wanted to do, and no one forced me into doing it.

I soon mastered the art of running a Pay Call and would tot up the total amount required to pay out according to the contracts and give that figure to Lakey to issue a cheque made out for 'Cash to John Toogood ONLY'. In the meantime, now that we were working with decimal currency, I would draw up a master sheet of what notes and coins were to be put into their envelopes, and given to them at The Payroll Call held during the lunchtime Rehearsal Break on a Thursday, in my Company Office, which was one of the Dressing Rooms at The Astoria, nearest to the stage. A typical example would be for myself shown as 3 x £10 notes, 1 x £5 note, and 2 x £1 coins, and once this had been done each week, for each member of Cast and Crew on my payroll list, by cross checking I could ensure it all balanced out. This time consuming task was all done in my head as calculators were not in common use then. I would get the cash cheque delivered to me or collect it from London Pavilion Chambers last thing on a Wednesday and go unescorted to the bank in Brixton to cash the cheque first thing on a Thursday morning for a figure that was usually around the £1,500 mark. That was not an insubstantial amount for a single person to walk out of a bank with in Brixton and wait on the busy street with, until a vacant black cab came into view for the short journey back to my office at the Astoria. All of this was quite new to me. I did not check with the office what the limit was for cash in transit for a single unescorted person to have in his briefcase, but later in my career I insisted that the amount of payroll cash carried by a single person must not exceed the insurance ceiling figure, as we would not have been covered by insurance in the event of an attack on the person with £1,500 in his briefcase….ME!

Because my office did not have a direct line, I had no option but to use the Stage Door coin box to make calls and receive messages, always ensuring that I had plenty of the right coins in the petty cash box to make them, often long distance calls to Reg or Sandy. In order not to disclose the amount of cash I was requesting from the office for the payroll run and to enable me to send nightly, weekly and advance figures when on tour and having to use a public call box in the theatre again, as mobiles and computers were unheard of, I devised a ten letter code to send this delicate information to Head Office. The word I chose was CAMBRIDGE, because it contained nine different letters, so for example if I was requesting £1,355.60 pence I would give the code CMRR.IO as C was 1, M was 3, RR was 55, and I was 6 with O being 0. This was simple and only I and Head Office knew what gibberish we were talking to each other about. I also used a similar code to send greeting telegrams to lovers, using the 26 letters of the alphabet allocated to numbers, but now you all know this, that's blown that.

Rehearsals finished in Brixton on Friday 15th December, and we all made our own way up to Manchester for the Fit Up and Technical weekend over the next three days. However, I did not feel that I was in charge of the Fit Up despite being credited as the Stage Director, as I had delegated this aspect of responsibility to Reg Allen from Edinburgh and Sandy McFarlane from the Opera House. I was concerned not only with ensuring that Dougie Squires was kept happy, as Director and Choreographer, and that we were on schedule for the Tuesday opening, and all the FOH Billing contractual agreements had been met by all parties concerned, and I could only be in one place at any one time. All billings are expressed as a percentage of something else, for example Lulu was shown as 100% of Peter Pan i.e. the same size but in a different font, whilst Anthony Sharp was 75% of the aformentioned and Douglas Squires as Director, again 100% but in a box and so on, and it was not unknown for an artiste to go to the FOH Bill Board armed with a ruler and notepad to check his billing was as per the Contract, and you had to be ready with an answer if you discovered an error on arrival. I usually made this my first job.

The show was in a much rougher state than I would have liked come the Tuesday afternoon DR. We had a problem with Freeman & Paige, who were trying to make their comedy spots into Pantomime, which was not what we wanted at all. They were asked to come to The Company Office by Dougie for a formal dressing down and told in no uncertain terms that if they did not comply with the request to change and persisted in doing the Panto stuff, they would be in breach of contract and the understudies would go on. In the end they both agreed to change and stayed on for the rest of the run, but it was a close call, and the first time that I had asserted my power as The Company Manager.

The opening performance went well, and the haunting song sung by Peter at the end of the show *To Live Must be an Awfully Big Adventure* was a fitting tribute to a great show and really showed those present that Lulu was much, much, more than just a girl who sings pop songs, but an accomplished actress as well. We then launched into the exhausting routine of performing twice daily at 2.30 & 7pm, but I still found some energy to go out and enjoy the nightlife of Manchester where the undoubted star was George Best who was in his prime playing for Manchester United. At one club I saw him flick a succession of 50p pieces into an empty brandy goblet from the toe of his shoe. No trick, just young raw talent showing off to the crowd of adoring females.

One night post show Lulu and a group of us went to see Dusty Springfield in cabaret at Bernard Manning's Embassy Club. The management wanted to move people at the front to make room for her, but she was having none of it, and we sat at the rear.

Between shows, I used to invite all the Heads of Department (HODs) to open house in the Company Office where I had a couple of bottles of wine either chilled or at room temperature to offer to them. This was not only an opportunity to resolve any problems that had occurred and socialise away from the Cast and Crew, but also to help us bond as a team and be ready for the tour up to Aberdeen, which was due after the second house in Manchester on Saturday 13th January 1973. In the meantime I had to start planning what I was going to do after the end of Peter Pan on Saturday 27th January, and began to scout the pages of The Stage and use my contacts for possible work.

On this occasion my contacts, which had been so useful in the past, let me down and the only thing I spotted that was available when I would be free was Production Manager at The Everyman Theatre in Cheltenham. I rang them, explained that I was working twice daily Monday to Saturdays on Peter Pan up in Manchester, and asked for an interview on a Sunday, which was my only day off. They understood my position and I arranged to attend an interview at 2pm on Sunday 7th January 1973 at the theatre in Cheltenham as it was vital for me to see what I was letting myself in for, as I was not familiar with The Everyman and did not know anyone who worked there. I did my research prior to attending my interview, as I always have done, and found that it was a very ornate 700 seat venue, which had been built by my favourite theatre architect Frank Matcham on three levels. It opened as The Opera House (Good Omen as I was at the Manchester Opera House?) in 1891, in Regent Street in the quaint historic spa town of Cheltenham. It had been operating as a three weekly rep since 1960, when it was re-named The Everyman Theatre. It did not figure in my list of the top six Rep Companies, but sounded interesting, if only for a short time. The Artistic Director was Malcolm Farquhar, whom I vaguely knew, and the General Manager was Rae Hammond, who I later found out was a star in one of the *Concert Party Revues* run by ENSA during the war. This formed the basis of Peter Nichols's Play *Privates on Parade*. Rae had also been a magician and member of the Magic Circle for many years, but above all he was still a character in the business. He claimed he could drink anyone under the table and to make his point used to drink whiskey from his own pint pot at the first night parties.

On my arrival at The Stage Door I was greeted by the Production Manager and shown round backstage as they were in mid performance of their Pantomime, which starred Cyril Fletcher as Dame. What I saw, I liked, and was most impressed by the assisted hemp fly floor lines which had sandbags attached to the hauling line as a counterweight aid, similar in principle to Lincoln with a beer keg filled with water and suspended on a line from the grid to just below the working fly floor. A simple but cheap way to assist the fly-men haul out a French Flat or Heavy Drape that it would not be possible to fly out or grid without the assistance of a dead weight suspended on the hauling lines.

I was duly offered the post, but had to take a pay cut down from the £37 per week I was currently earning, to £28 per week, which I reluctantly agreed to as it meant that I would only be unemployed for a week, as I would start on Monday 5th February 1973, which again suited me.

Having now sorted my immediate future out, it was back to finish the tour of Pan which ended the following Saturday 13th January. We had contracted the scenery removal firm of G.H. Lucking (motto 'Keep on truckin' with G.H. Lucking') because they had recently added to their fleet of scenery trailers. They were 40' long and because they ran on a series of triple bogies were able to use 16 inch wheels, which meant there was no wheel arch box in the trailer which made packing them easier. Units were named after well-known theatres in the West End, and it provided an early form of tractor unit spotting that still exists today with Eddie Stobart naming their units after wives and girlfriends.

You can only imagine the excitement of some anorak when he spotted *Prince of Wales* and *London Palladium* on the same job, as we had at Manchester that cold winter night. The only firm that ever came close or even surpassed G.H. Lucking, with its unique approach to advertising how good it was at what it did, was Edwin Shirley Trucking, who were contracted to provide 30 identical tractor units and trailers, including generators, for a Rolling Stones World Tour some years later.

During the week leading up to our final pay call in Manchester, I had been to Victoria Station and purchased a single train ticket from Manchester to Aberdeen for every member of the Company and Crew who were not going to make their own way there. As the Train Call was to be at 10am on Sunday 14th January and there was no direct train, it meant a change at Crewe, which used to be one of the main meeting stations for Variety Acts who were changing venues on a Sunday, before road transport became fashionable and available to the masses, and I handed out these precious tickets with the pay packet on the Thursday lunchtime. I had typed out a sheet for them to sign, as if they lost their ticket the onus was then on them to be in Aberdeen for the DR. Those who had elected to make their own way there, and there were very few, received the equivalent of the train fare in cash to cover their costs.

The Final Performance, breakdown, Get Out and load had all gone according to plan, and fitted nicely into the two special trailers that I described earlier, and departed, with Reg going in *The Prince of Wales* and Sandy in *London Palladium* at 0200 for the 250 mile trip to our second venue. They travelled with the load in tandem to ensure that the Get In was supervised at 10am, as the main party of us would only just be departing.

Having settled my last Contra Account with Tommy Appleby, who I had found most helpful in showing me the ropes FOH, and representing The Visiting Promoting Management for the Incoming, Interval and Outgoing, a practice that I was to follow every night I was on duty for the next thirty years. You would never see Mr. Appleby on duty for a Saturday Matinée however - this was delegated to his Assistant Manager David Liddy - as Tommy had a box at Old Trafford which he religiously attended. On one occasion he offered to run me back to my flat in Moss Side, in his black Hackney, as it was on his way, and before we departed Quay Street, where the theatre is situated, he instructed the driver to "drive round the block please". When I asked him why we had driven round the block before departing, he said: "To check if any Dressing Room lights have been left on or any signs of smoke or fire", a practice which again I remembered, and followed, when I became a Theatre General Manager myself in 1986.

Having cleared my office, and packed my touring office boxes in the Lucking's Trailer I was able to catch a few hours' sleep prior to ticking off the Company on the 'Checking In List' as they arrived at the station for the first part of our eight hour journey northward. Some left it to the very last minute to arrive, but all of the underage 'Lost Boys' arrived with their chaperone in plenty of time. It was a requirement of the The Children (Performance) Regulations that either in Rehearsal, Performance or Travelling, a detailed log had to be kept of what time they did this, that or the other, again a very time consuming job, which I learnt on future occasions, when working with children who came within the Children in Entertainment Regulations, it was best to delegate.

All went well until the train change at Crewe, which was very tight, as we had to get to where the Aberdeen train was waiting via a bridge. At this point one of the Lost Boys needed to use the station toilet, and I could see out of the corner of my eye the hands on the big face of station clock slowly creeping up to departure time. I ushered the others on to the train to find seats, as they could not be reserved, and it was not unusual to have to stand for much of your journey on a Sunday. A minute before departure the Lost Boy was indeed lost and I had no option but to yell at the top of my voice: "Hold the Train" (like 'Sir' did in the play *The Dresser* eight years later) to the Guard who was poised to wave the green flag and blow the Acme Thunderer whistle. Thankfully he heard me shout and waited, for which the petty cash gave him a drink and we all caught the express a couple of minutes late.

We arrived in Aberdeen at about 6pm and after checking into our digs I went along to the 1,820 seated His Majesty's Theatre on Rosemount Viaduct, where the first thing I noticed was a sign that announced "In The Event of Inclement Weather The Matinée Performances May be Cancelled". That's a good start, I thought. The sets had arrived on time, and as HM's (as we called it) was classed by the Technical Union NATKE as a 'Difficult Get In' because items had to be handled twice, with a full width stage trap being set half way between the Ground Get In and The Stage, it had taken longer than anticipated. My next job was to check the billing FOH, before any of the Company were permitted into the venue, with their rulers and clipboards, for any errors. I was happy to find that the Manager and Licensee, James Donald, had done everything correctly.

As HM's was a Hemp House, where each piece of flown scenery, drape or lighting bar is hauled out manually by a team of well built and strong Fly-men (the Opera House had a counterweight system and each flown item could be moved by one man), we knew we were going to struggle as several of the pieces were known to be very heavy. Fortunately for us, HM's used the same system of sandbag counterweights attached to the hauling line as I had seen during my tour backstage at Cheltenham, but this one was on a much larger scale, as the weight of some pieces was not conducive to flying on hemps. Thankfully the SM was a master at calculating the number of sandbags to attach, using a special bit of kit he had made and which worked surprisingly well.

The show opened successfully for the two week run, and we even managed to have some time off to explore 'The Granite City' as we did not have a matinée on some days. The Understudies were by now well-rehearsed, although they were not required, and thankfully we did not have to cancel any shows because of inclement weather.

We had a wild party in Aberdeen on 25th January. Lulu's husband Maurice Gibb came to see the show with his entourage, and I entertained them. John Paul Jones and John Bonham of Led Zeppelin, who had been playing at the Music Hall that night, also came to join us.

The run went smoothly until the last night when I went outside, on a cold wet windy Scottish night during the Get Out. To my dismay, I discovered that G.H. Lucking, who were based on the South Coast, had sub-contacted the job of return journey from Aberdeen to the H & W stores in Edinburgh to a local firm and instead of what I was expecting - two very low, wheel arch box free trailers - discovered to my horror two soft sided trailers which although admittedly were wheel arch box free, had a loading height about five feet off the road!

What could I do? I rang Lucking's Office, but of course at 11pm on a Saturday night it was unmanned, and the local firm did not have any other lower or even hard-sided trailers, so I was well and truly snookered on my last night. We had to use the trailers provided, as we were contracted to vacate the theatre after the Get Out as a new show was booked in for later on the Sunday, but it took far longer to stack than it should have done.

On Sunday 28th January 1973 I caught the mid-morning train to London, diverting to Lincoln to stay with Mum and Dad for a couple of days, and to pick up my car. I planned to drive to Cheltenham to start my new job on Monday 5th February. What had I learnt about myself and how had I coped with being a Company Manager for the first time? I loved it, and felt I had coped well under pressure to resolve the problems as they had occurred.

Lulu had been the perfect Leading Lady, Anthony Sharp had been difficult at times, as had Reg Allen, but I had a lot of respect for Sandy McFarlane who was my sort of Master Carpenter, as when he said: "No problem, it will be done" you knew it would. My Stage Management Team headed by Maris Sharp as SM had performed well and coped with everything that had been thrown at them. Her Prompt Corner Copy was, as usual, immaculate and a perfect example of how the Book should look and be set out. I was vindicated in my opinion as when I last visited the Theatre Museum in Covent Garden it was on display in a section on touring and Tommy Appleby.

I had picked up in Manchester how to interpret correctly the advance, daily and weekly Box Office Returns and my code for sending them to head office had not been cracked. I was now happy to have the traditional gin & tonic with the Resident Manager during the final show on a Saturday, and discuss and eventually agree the final settlement, according to the contract, and sign off the contra account for the stay at the venue. These were all essential things that would be of vital use in the future and would help expand my cv and develop my experience. Would The Everyman Cheltenham be as exciting and as challenging or a backward step?

Act 2 Scene 2
CHELTENHAM
(1973)

I drove to Cheltenham, taking the scenic route on the A40 road in my A40 car, passing Stokenchurch Top where the 1961 National Grass Track Championships had been held at Wheelers Farm, run by The Wycombe & District Motor Cycle Club on Sunday 3rd September. The winners were Alfie Hagon (500cc) and Dennys Goodacre (350cc) both of whom I would get to know when I organised 'Riders' Reunions' many years later.

I had not had spare time or transport to attend meetings since leaving Liverpool, and was hoping that I would now be able to attend race meetings once more.

On arrival in the spa, on Sunday 4th February, I went to check out the flat I had booked on spec over the phone beforehand and found it in the Pittville area of the town, near an old brewery which was quite close to the theatre and city centre amenities. I had a pint (or three) in a Berni Inn close to the theatre in Regent Street, had my prawn cocktail, scampi & chips, and black forest gateau (that was Gourmet food in 1973!) and studied the list of productions planned for the Season. These included *Northanger Abbey*, *The Tempest*, *Conduct Unbecoming*, *The Imaginary Invalid*, *Butley*, and the local Am-Drams in *The Gondoliers*, which was the only one that I had worked on or seen before. I knew a little about some of them. *Abbey* was a period piece by Jane Austen, *Conduct* was a military play about a kangaroo court that premiered at Bristol Old Vic and then transferred to the West End in July '69, whilst *Invalid* was a period play by Molière, and would I suspect require music from a harpsichord. *Butley* was a very dark piece by Simon Gray, which had starred Alan Bates, and won Best Play & Best Actor Awards in 1971. It was all going to be different to the commercial theatre I had just grown to love, and I couldn't wait to get cracking again after a week out.

I met my Stage Management team headed by Carol Evans, who would run the show and who (I would discover, much to my dismay) always had a lap dog with her during rehearsals and on-stage. Roger Hendry was ASM, Donald Crosby the Designer and the Chief Electrician was ex Theatre Royal Bristol Keith McLaren. Things were very much 'but we have always done it this way in the past' when I suggested what I considered was a better way to do things, and what I wanted to be done in future, but it was hard going. They were also not used to the Senior Member of the Backstage Team being there during showtime but that was the way I worked to keep my finger on the pulse of a show. They were quite put out when they saw the detail in my first Production Weekend Schedule, and remarked 'we have never done that then' etc., but it worked and so at least I was happy.

I was now able to begin a new social life, mix with the Company in The Stage Door Pub post show, and do a bit of clubbin' again. The town was not awash with nightclubs, but I sniffed out one or two in the main drag, The Promenade, up towards Montpellier and the elegant Regency Queens Hotel which was always full to overflowing during Gold Cup Week each Spring. The big hit at the time, at least in the nightspots of Cheltenham, was *Tie a Yellow Ribbon Round the Old Oak Tree* by Dawn and featuring Tony Orlando.

I was not feeling happy at having moved back into subsidised theatre, as many of the jobs that I was used to delegating over the past three years, such as finding furniture and dressings for the shows, were expected to be undertaken by me. I clashed on several occasions as I firmly believed that I should be organising this that and the other, rather than doing it, as they expected. However I did not mind being the nominated driver of the theatre van, and going on trips to pick up swords from Bristol for *The Tempest* or *Conduct Unbecoming*, or going to London to collect a harpsichord, which was required for the Molière (as expected), as it got me away from what was becoming a rather drab experience at work and out into the beautiful Cotswolds, which was and still is one of my favourite parts of England.

In addition to the Main House shows, on every Monday which was not part of the working weekend we had one night shows and performers which really only required me to organise and run them, which I quite enjoyed doing. Highlights for me were Ken Campbell's one man show on 19th March, as I had not seen or met him since Panto in Liverpool, an evening of nostalgia with Jack Hulbert and Cicely Courtneidge, and a visit by The Sooty Show for a week commencing 23rd April 1973. It was an immense honour to be able to say that one had worked with the great Jack & Cicely in the twilight of their illustrious careers as Jack was over 80, and they had been husband and wife since 1916. He had been voted the UK's most popular man in 1934, and their last West End appearance together had been a couple of years earlier in 1971. It was a sheer pleasure to chat to them both, as they were some of the nicest old pros I ever met and they had me spellbound all evening with their anecdotal tales and stories.

I also knew Harry & Marjorie Corbett very well, as I had worked *The Sooty Show* previously both in Liverpool and even back in Lincoln where they had become personal friends of my parents. Rumour had it that they were staying at The White Hart Hotel during their week in Lincoln, and they got into conversation with Ray & Joan in the front bar where they only served halves in silver tankards (Dad had his own hanging from a hook above the bar) and they had hit it off. They were introduced to the late night drinking holes and Ray signed Harry into the male only Castle Hill Club as his guest, to satisfy the pipe smoking Steward Jack, whilst Marjorie and Mum stayed at the hotel. At some point my name and occupation came into the conversation, and from then on I was always well looked after when the 'thanks for a good week' tips were handed out at the end of the run of Sooty, which was unusual as Harry hailed from Yorkshire. Incidentally, he was the nephew of the Guiseley fish & chip shop owner, and later entrepreneur, Harry Ramsden. The glove puppet Sooty had been bought by Harry for his son Matthew in Blackpool in 1948, and he never failed to end his shows either on stage or on the box with those immortal words: "Bye bye everybody, bye bye", an institution if ever there was one for children of many generations to remember.

I was not enjoying my work in Cheltenham which on reflection had been a backward step, although the social side of my life was enjoyable, so I started to make enquiries about doing a Summer Season. Most decent Summer Seasons I knew ran from June for four or five months, or if Blackpool, to the end of 'the lights', so time was of the essence when I began to look in The Stage during late May 1973. Two possible shows caught my eye and I duly contacted the Managements to express an interest and find out more about them, as the adverts were only very brief, like 'Company Manager for Summer Season'. I noted a number to ring on one of the adverts, which was Bernard Delfont Ltd, one of the, if not the, biggest presenters of Summer Shows in England. I spoke to a gentleman who would have a profound effect on my career some thirteen years later, Peter H. Roberts. He explained that they were looking for a person to work Johnnie Hamp's *The Comedians* show on the North Pier Blackpool for the season. I was asked to send them my C.V. with a covering letter and let them know if I was still interested in working for them the following week, and if so we would discuss terms.

I was familiar with the show as it had been a big hit on television since 1971, and the format was so simple, but worked like a dream. Six or so comedians, mainly from the Northern Working Men's Clubs, were all put together on the same bill, and each did their own twenty minute spot. Some of the new names, to those who did not patronise the club circuit, were Mike Reid, Charlie Williams, Colin Crompton, George Roper, Stan Boardman and Bernard Manning, who I had met and seen at work over Christmas and New Year at his world famous Embassy Club, when I went out one night with some of the Company from Peter Pan to see the show and experience one of England's most talented stand-up comedians perform.

Bernard was a real larger than life character, and had been singing and telling gags to his chums in the army, who were for many years the guards of Nazi criminals Hess, Speer and Donitz in Berlin's Spandau Prison. Following his army discharge he joined the *Oscar Rabin Band* as vocalist when they had a residency at The Lyceum in The Strand. Notable names in the Rabin Band of the early '50s were Oscar himself, originally a violinist but later bass sax, Jack Deucher on trumpet, Kenny Clare who would become one of the world's great drummers playing with John Dankworth and Cleo Lane, and visiting American superstars such as Ella Fitzgerald and Tony Bennett. The highlight of his career was in 1971 when he played at Queen Elizabeth Hall with Buddy Rich and Louis Belson. Bernard did not like it in the south however so returned to his native Manchester where he and his family re-opened the rather dilapidated Embassy Club, hosted by the ebullient Bernard telling a few risqué jokes and singing popular ballads. Would I have the confidence to work with this group of multi-talented performers or should I go for something else?

The other Management that I had on my list to contact was the Paul Raymond Organisation, who was looking for a Company Stage Manager to work on *The Bed* for the Summer Season in Margate. I spoke to Production Manager Janet Chapman and arranged to visit The West End for an interview at The Whitehall Theatre, just off Trafalgar Square.

I did my usual pre interview checks on who I knew or thought would be interviewing me. I found out very little about Janet, apart from the fact that she had worked on *A Tale of Two Cities* recently with Edward Woodward in the West End in 1969, was a leading Member of the Stage Management Association, and lived in Catford SE6. Mr. Raymond's history was legendary even then. He was born in Liverpool (another link) as Geoffrey Quinn in 1925, and following his National Service as a bandsman drummer with the Royal Air Force, went on to begin his entertainment career as a mind reading act on Clacton Pier. He changed his name to Paul Raymond, moved to London, bought the old Doric Ballroom at Walkers Court in Soho in 1958, and turned it into The Raymond Revue Bar. In order to circumvent the rigid Licensing Requirements of Westminster Council he made it a Members only Club which by 1960 had 45,000 registered members. His mind was out for publicity, and he was developing an interest in presenting shows at other venues, and adding theatre freeholds to his property portfolio, which was why I found myself at The Whitehall Theatre, which he owned. His also owned the new Royalty Theatre in Portugal Street (built to replace the old Stoll Theatre in Kingsway), The Revuebar and soon the Windmill. He was also a member of the theatrical charity organisation The Water Rats.

Following my initial interview with Janet, which went well, I was introduced to General Manager George Richardson, also Mr. Raymond's right hand man. Contrary to the informality of theatre folk, who usually address each other using their Christian or nickname (e.g. 'Binkie' for Hugh Beaumont of H.M. Tennent), Mr. Raymond was always addressed by his surname, or between Company Members as 'P.R.', but never as 'Paul' unless you were very special. I was shown into his palatial office on the first floor overlooking Whitehall, where he was sitting behind a huge desk with my C.V. on it.

Following polite chit chat during which I noticed he had a slight stutter, he said: "My shows are not Shakespeare you know", a reference to my time at Bristol Old Vic, which showed that he had at least read my C.V. We then went on to discuss his show which was a 'light hearted romp that was intended to entertain not educate' and personal terms, should I be offered the post. "What are you on at the m..m..moment then John?" I replied and told the truth: "£28 per week Mr. Raymond." "Not e..n..nough if you are going to work for me John, what about £40 per week for the Season?" I wanted to snatch his hands off, but played it cool asking for time to consider the offer. "Let Janet know w..w..within seven days" was his reply, we shook hands and I was shown out of the office. This was the only time in my long career that a Producer offered me more money than I was asking for as you usually have to haggle, and it is usually only the Equity minimum that you are offered.

Once downstairs I was given a copy of the Script by Sam Cree to peruse back in Cheltenham and was overjoyed to have cracked the £40 per week barrier that I had set myself back in Liverpool some five years earlier. There was no real decision to be made and at the earliest opportunity I wrote to P.R. to accept his offer which was to commence rehearsals in London on 11th June 1973. My appointment as Company & Stage Manager for *The Bed* was confirmed by Janet, so I gave my notice to finish at the Everyman on Saturday 2nd June which would give me a week off prior to rehearsals for the new Summer Show.

What had I gleaned from my relatively short fifteen week stay at The Everyman Rep in Cheltenham? Quite a bit when I look back, and I vowed never to take a backward step in my career and return to something I had done in the past. I had not been very happy at the Everyman, although I had enjoyed the town and people. I had not been challenged at work, and knew that my future lay in commercial entertainment and not in subsidised theatre, a decision I do not regret one little bit. I still firmly believe that whatever art form you choose, be it dance, acting, jazz, painting, singing or, in my case, theatre management, a good grounding in the 'Classics' of that genre is always going to stand you in good stead, and this is something I willingly pass on to the many students I now socialise with in Lincoln on a regular basis.

Act 2 Scene 3
MARGATE
(1973)

I received my contract for *The Bed* as Company Manager in the post and noted that it was with Debward Limited, which was based at Jersey International House, in the Channel Islands. Strange, I thought at the time, but discovered that this was an offshore company named after P.R.'s two children DEBbie and HowWARD and used because of the laxer tax laws in Jersey.

I also received a cast list with contact details and knew of the two stars John Inman and Barry Howard, but nothing about anyone else. John & Barry were not only known as the best Ugly Sisters in Panto, but John had worked in the past with Albert Modley, Charlie Chester, Terry Scott, Hugh Lloyd, Harry Worth, Hattie Jaques, Richard Wattis, Freddie Frinton, and Jimmy Logan. John had appeared in West End shows such as the David Croft & Cyril Ornadel Musical *Anne Veronica*, at the Cambridge Theatre in 1969, Lionel Bart's *Oliver* and Julian Slade's *Salad Days*. Barry had recently played Sir Andrew Aguecheek in Twelfth Night at the Comedy Theatre and John had just finished recording a Comedy Playhouse series of a new sit-com entitled *Are You Being Served?*, where he played Wilberforce Claybourne Humphries, which suited him perfectly, as he had worked in retail at Austin Reed's Menswear shop in Regent Street between the Panto/Summer Season and theatre work. Here were two pros that could hold a show together and get a laugh out of anything. John was also a leading light in The Water Rats and would never be seen without his lapel badge, for which you could be fined if spotted by a fellow Rat.

The Director was Alexander Dore who had directed *See How They Run* at The Vaudeville, *Big Bad Mouse* at The Shaftsbury and *Mixed Doubles* at The Comedy Theatre in the West End, again a vastly experienced man of the theatre. My Deputy Stage Manager Frank Warwick had been engaged by Janet Chapman and was to understudy Berwick Kaler (later to find fame as a Panto Dame at The Theatre Royal in York). Delightful Carole Saulsbury was my ASM and engaged to understudy all six of the females.

The design was by John Halle, and was built by Michael O'Flaherty to just fit in the very limited stage of The New Dreamland Theatre, which until we went there for the Summer in 1973 had been a cinema and did not have the required safety curtain. Costumes, such as they were, mainly lingerie, were overseen by Fiona Richmond, who at the time was the leading lady in *Pyjama Tops* (more about that later) and a favourite of Mr Raymond's. The six girls were Andee Cromarty, Caroline Grenville, Helli Louise, Patricia Ford, Deborah Brayshaw and Polly Trickett. Whether these were their true names or stage names I know not.

They had all come from different backgrounds. Helli had been one of The Benny Hill Girls, Caroline had been in *Hamlet* and *The Dirtiest Show in Town* at The Duchess, where incidentally Maris was working, Deborah had been in *Applause* at Her Majesty's whilst Andree was in constant demand as a cabaret singer and dancer. Patricia appeared in the rock musical *Hair*, where there was a nude scene, and Polly was a contemporary dance trained performer and was born, so she said, within the sound of Bow bells. The other member of the cast was Charlie Stewart who had done Panto with fellow Scot Ronnie Corbett and been a member of *The Fol De Rols*.

Rehearsals commenced after the traditional marking out of the set with tape at The Royalty Theatre, off the Kingsway, which PR owned, at 10am on Monday 11th July 1973 and were scheduled for two weeks. We then went down to Margate for rehearsals on Monday 25th June and an opening night on Friday 29th June, followed by a twice nightly run to Saturday 8th September. Not the longest Summer Show ever, but ten weeks was acceptable especially if the Summer was going to be a hot one, and the prospects looked good for that. Bill Denis, who had once been half of the *Denis Brothers Variety Act*, managed the Royalty, and was in a relationship with Janet, so we all got on well and we were made most welcome there. Rehearsals went smoothly and Frank, Carole and I proved to be a good team. Few props were required for the show: maple syrup, assorted underwear to fall out of a suitcase and imitation fruit. I used to leave Frank and Carole, who were also understudies and needed to know the part(s) as well as the cast artiste, to run rehearsals whilst I popped out to buy or obtain the items required.

Over the weekend of 16th-17th June, when there were no rehearsals, I took a drive down to the Thanet Coast to find some accommodation, as the New Dreamland did not have a digs list for us to use. Although there was an abundance of Bed and Breakfast establishments and a nice hotel on the cliff at Westcliff, what we as a Company wanted was a place that we could call home for the ten weeks we were away from London, as not everyone wanted to commute daily.

I drove around town and eventually came upon a guest house off the Westcliff Road, overlooking and within walking distance of the sea and with unrestricted parking for those of us that drove. There was a self-contained flat at the top and half a dozen bedrooms with a communal kitchen, bathroom/shower room and living/dining area. I thought this too good an opportunity to let go, and thought quickly. If I could offer John and Barry the top floor flat, and Frank, Carole and I had a room each, that would leave only three rooms vacant, which I was sure some girls in the show would be keen to take. I duly paid the landlord a holding deposit of one week's rent and put my proposal to the Company at rehearsals on the Monday when I was back at The Royalty. Needless to say they were all delighted with the plan, and I subsequently contacted the landlord to say that I would take the whole house for the Summer from Sunday 24th June until 9th September. He was equally delighted, as he had a secure income for ten weeks and as a thank you I got a special rate for my room.

Before I departed for Margate I met the 'two Georges' who ran the accounts department most efficiently for the many different strings that were part of The Paul Raymond Organisation, be it *The Golden Glitter Girl Revue* twice nightly at The Revuebar, the magazines such as *Men Only*, the property empire where P.R. was buying Soho freeholds, at a rate of knots that would soon have him in the list of the ten richest men in England. I arranged with them to have the Treasury Call on a Thursday lunchtime, for those who wanted it, because as there were no Matinée performances, many of the artistes would only come into the theatre for the shows, but as usual there were always those who had spent up and needed cash.

We always paid cash - no cheques to bounce or credit transfers to be activated - and all I required from them was their National Insurance card to be stamped weekly. It was assumed, unless I was told otherwise, that everyone was self employed and had a Schedule D tax code, and a theatre accountant to sort it all out at the end of the financial year. I had engaged Michael Henshaw as mine back in Liverpool when I switched from PAYE to self employed, and found him to be very good as there were so many things on the Equity list that could be claimed as legitimate expenses, such as accommodation whilst away from home, photographs, hair styling, a percentage of travel expensed plus of course his accountancy fee.

Arrangements were made for me to collect the cash first thing on a Thursday morning so the packets were all made up and ready for the Treasury Call, from a local Barclays in Margate Town, which was a short distance from the Dreamland complex, but I still took a cab for security and Frank usually came along as well to ride shotgun for me. To maximise the time, Thursday mornings were nominated by me as the Understudy Rehearsal Call time, and ensured that I was not alone in the building with cash, as security was minimal.

I had very little to do with the Get In and Fit Up in my role as Company Manager as Janet was the Production Manager and did things her way as that was her area of responsibility. Dressing Room allocation was easy as there were only four rooms and there was nothing contractual for me to observe, so John and Barry had one room, Berwick and Charlie had another, the six girls had the third whilst I, Frank and Carole used one as the Company office, and should they be required at some point to go on and play a part, they would use the room which had the costumes for that character.

I checked the billing FOH and all was correct. The technical rehearsals went according to play with Frank on the Book and in the Corner, myself seeing the House in and then working a pair of Ferrograph 632 tape recorders for the incidental music and sound effects. Carole was the floater and looked after prop settings and day to day items that were required like tea, coffee, sugar and milk. I covered the Corner, should Frank be required to go on, and Carole covered me, so we could mix and match as necessary.

The Box Office advance sales, for the 550 seat venue, were disappointing when I looked at the plan and got figures from the Box Office Manager. We were hopeful that once we had opened, and with the excellent publicity John was getting from *Are You Being Served?*, which was going out weekly, along with good word of mouth, things would improve. Before leaving London, where Maris and I were staying with friends of hers in a room at 15, Oxonian Street, in East Dulwich, I had gone to Carnaby Street, which was where every fashion conscious young man bought his clothes in those days, and purchased a lightweight suit, shirt, bow tie and snazzy shoes to wear as my office attire for the Summer. When I look back at the photos, what a right little bobby dazzler I was.

Mr. Raymond (I forget if Fiona was with him, but probably not as she was the star of *Pyjama Tops* at the time), came down on Wednesday 27th June to oversee the opening, and drum up some publicity for the show with interviews to local Press and media in Margate and the surrounding area, like Ramsgate.

During one break in rehearsals he went to the Dress Circle Bar for refreshments and got talking to the mature lady who was behind the bar serving him. During their conversation, she mentioned she had been a showgirl in the past, and he immediately opened his wallet and took out a £10 note which, I remind you, was a quarter of my weekly salary, and said to the barmaid: "If you c..c..can still do the splits, you can have the note."… at which she got up onto the bar, cleared the glasses to one side, and performed the splits like she had done years before.

That evening after rehearsals had finished we were all invited to go with him to Hades, a local nightclub on the front, but I had to decline the invitation, much to my chagrin, as it was the first time we had all been out as a Company. I still had the cash breakdown list to complete for the first Treasury Call the following morning. He tried to persuade me otherwise, but I thought that the first Treasury Call was more important than the get together. Was I right? …Time would tell. We opened on schedule on the Friday, and all went well, even though the attendance was disappointing. The laughs were plentiful, and the girls looked stunning on stage.

We then settled into a daily routine that went something like this: up about ten, depending on what time I had got to bed, as there was quite a bit of nightlife in Margate; on with the swimming trunks, grab a towel and a portable radio; walk across the road and down the short flight of steps leading from The Promenade to the beach; slap on some sun block and sunbathe all day. There were quite often six or so of us in our circle and life was fun frolicking in the sea and drying off in the hot sun afterwards. The big Summer hit tune that year was Garry Glitter's *Do You Want to be in My gang*, which Radio One played constantly.

We all left the beach at about 1600hrs to shower, dress and grab a bite to eat, before walking the short distance along the Promenade to the theatre from the digs, all aglow from a day in the sunshine. We soon all developed a nice deep tan as Helli was a firm believer in using coconut oil, which we all borrowed and seemed to work well, as no one was sunburnt for the whole Summer. Twice nightly was hard work, as sometimes you would think: "But have I already done this or that? … But that was at the First House, two hours ago." Post show a gang of us would go down to Hades Club and it was here I first heard the sound of *The O'Jays*. I have always found music to be one of if not the most evocative of all the memory jerkers, like a particular perfume that you associate with a special lover, and every time I hear their recording of *Love Train*, I am taken back to Margate and the sunny summer of '73. Why I particularly like this R & B recording by them, who were previously known as the Triumphs, is hard to put my finger on, but the fact that it has been a big hit for them since January '73 may have something to do with it. Who knows?

If we did not go out to a club, and the tide was out, we would come back home and go skinny dipping for mussels, put them in a bucket of sea water and when we had collected enough, return to the digs and make a huge bowl of Moules Marinière with copious amounts of white wine. No wonder it is still one of my favourite starters.

I also used to mix socially with the other pros in Margate that Summer. There were shows at the 1,312 seat Lido in Clintonville, the Winter Gardens where Larry Grayson was packing them in at this large 2,026 seat venue, with his High Camp Music Hall style of comedy in *Shut That Door*, along with *Slack Alice*, *Pop it in Postman Pete* and *Everard*, some five years before he became a household name hosting *The Generation Game* in 1978. In addition there was a season of plays at The Theatre Royal in the old part of town, which is the oldest un-restored theatre with an original stage in the UK, and I was fortunate enough to be able to have a good look round this piece of working history in the company of owner Jolyon Jackley (son of comic Nat Jackley), later to be Assistant Theatre Manager to the legendary George Hoare at the Theatre Royal in Drury Lane in 1988, before selling the Theatre Royal (Margate, not Drury Lane I hasten to add.)

As mentioned before, the venue had been a cinema prior to *The Bed* being presented so did not have a Safety Curtain, and it was necessary to install one to comply with the licensing regulations. A team from a local scaffolding firm came in during the week prior to installation, and built towers in the downstage left and downstage right Corners, as the Safety Curtain was to be of the roller type because of the lack of a Fly Tower on the building.

I was most insistent that all the scaffolding clips and open ends to the scaffolding tubes were well covered to protect the girls who would have to push past them to get on and off stage. "We have never been asked to do all this before" was a remark I got from the Foreman, "and I don't expect you have had scantily dressed girls pushing past them before either" was my reply.

When I returned to the Theatre on Monday for the shows that evening, there was an eerie silence on stage and the scaffolding was still in place. Looking round, I spotted an open builders boot, almost cut in half covered in blood, in the Down Stage Right Wing near to the scaffolding tower. I asked what had happened and why was the scaffolding still there? I was told by one of the staff that there had been a terrible accident while the half-ton Safety Curtain was being lifted into place at the top of the towers. Apparently one of the shackles linking the roller to the chain hoist had snapped, causing the roller to crash back down onto the stage, where it unfortunately landed on and partially severed the foot of the poor lad who was working the hoist. Naturally we decided to cancel the show. The lad in question came to the final night of the show, sat on the front row as our guest and was in good spirits considering his ordeal. The medical team at the local hospital to which he was rushed had, I am pleased to say, managed to save his foot, but it was still heavily bandaged.

During that summer my other interests in life took a bit of a back seat, as I was having such a good time and enjoying the show and the Margate nightlife. There was no Jazz to speak of in that corner of Kent, but I did manage to attend a Motor Cycle Race Meeting or two at weekends. On 5th August I went to watch racing at Brands Hatch as it was the Hutchinson Hundred Meeting, where racing was in the reverse direction to normal, and on the Sunday of the Bank Holiday weekend drove up through the night after the show to Spilsby in Lincolnshire to watch the annual Inter Centre Championships, where my old centre the East Midlands, on home soil won the 500cc Class with Brian Maxted, who was four times National Champion, and later a close personal friend, leading the team home. Mum and Dad were also there, so it was an ideal opportunity to tell them that Maris and I planned to get married later in the year.

During the first week of September, I spoke to the office in London about the Get Out of the show, and was told to forget about it as the intention was to leave it all there - set, furniture, costumes the lot - and let Dreamland deal with getting rid of it. My mind again went into overdrive, as there was a lot of good stuff that was just going to be left there and as I was furnishing a new flat in London, much of it would be of use. I hired a Luton van from Hertz in preparation for the final performance and the Get Out on Saturday 8th September. I selected what was going to be of use and loaded it into the van. I finished up with a good van full consisting of all the furniture and the super King Sized Quilt, which had been specially made for the show.

I also began to think about what I was going to do next and for the first and only time in my career, rang Vincent Shaw, an Agent who specialised in work for Stage Management in London, who also had Harry Corbett and Sooty on his books, who I knew from my times working with them in the past. He did not have anything suitable, but told me he was sure he could get me something in the near future, for a commission of ten per cent, which was normal and was what I had expected to hear, so I agreed to go on his books.

The weekend of Sunday 9th September was quite a sad one as we all packed our bags and left Margate. It had been the happiest show I had worked on, the weather had been idyllic, I had made lots of new female (and male) friends, and contacts, always important as I was finding out more and more. I knew for certain now that the Commercial Theatre was for me, and that Margate was not ready for nudity in 1973, as the business had not been as good as we had expected. The only Full House was the final one, when all those who had seen *The Bed* and enjoyed it before, came back for one last time.

Act 2 Scene 4
REVOLUTION CLUB
(1973)

I had been back in London for a few days when Vincent Shaw, now my Agent and 'Mr. 10%' rang me to tell me about a job he thought I could do in the West End. He told me that he had been approached by Jim Carter-Fea, who was the owner of the Revolution Club in Bruton Place, and who was looking for a Stage Manager for the Floor show, who was also expected to double as the Disc Jockey. As I had patronised nightclubs for the past few years and enjoyed the lifestyle, the opportunity to work my first nightclub was a dream come true, so I said I was interested, provided I could have Friday 26th October off, to get married. He did not think would be a problem, provided that I found a suitable deputy to cover for me.

We duly arranged to meet that night at The Guinea, a very up-market restaurant with a small bar in Bruton Place, just off Berkley Square in Mayfair, for a drink before going on to look around The Revolution Club, which had previously been known as Le Prince, and was open from 11pm- 4am, Monday to Saturday.

I was very impressed with what I saw, as it was on a par with, but more modern than, its rival establishments like The Pigalle, Stork Room, Astor, Gargoyle or the Latin Quarter, with plush décor and a small stage. The fee was acceptable at £50 per week, less 10% as an Agents fee, and I accepted the offer to start immediately.

For the first night, Monday 17th September 1973, I was just an observer and was introduced to the Head Barman Pino, a jovial Italian, and to the dancers who were also hostesses when not onstage doing their act to a 45rpm disc played at the open DJ booth, from where the stage could be seen. There was a nice relaxed atmosphere in the club where the idea, I soon discovered, was for the girls to encourage their clients to buy them bottles of champagne, as they were on a commission for every bottle that was put on the tab for their booth. Come 4am some of the bills were astronomical.

It was "Cash only, Sir" when the time came to settle the tab, as cheques were not accepted, nor were these new American Express Cards that some clients wanted to use on the expense account. A couple of heavies would appear if the client refused or could not settle his account for the night, but usually there was no need for further encouragement as the punters all knew the score. I was asked, before I left in the early hours, what my signature tune was going to be and I thought that the 1971 Soul Funk theme from *Shaft* by Isaac Hayes on the yellow Stax Label was appropriate.

The following night (Tuesday) was my first night in charge and I soon got into the swing of things, playing background music early in the evening, introducing the acts, and building up to playing quality dance music. As the evening progressed the clients and hostesses got more inebriated and ordered more champagne. I managed to play a few of my favourite Jazz tracks, such as the Dave Brubeck Quartet playing *Take Five* and The Count Basie Band playing Wild Bill Davis' arrangement of *April in Paris*, which I enjoyed even if the clients didn't.

The Revolution was mostly frequented by business executives who had to 'work late at the office' and was busiest Monday-Thursday before they went home to their families for the weekend.

In order to comply with the licensing requirements then, 'food of a substantial nature' had to be served to the clients with any beverage. This requirement was circumvented by serving a piece of pork pie and a smear of coleslaw on a disposable paper plate.

When the club was quiet, and over a cup of coffee, I used to chat to the dancers while they waited patiently for the punters to arrive, when they could start the show.

I was quite enjoying the work, and got on very well with Pino behind the bar. I liked the Night Club lifestyle and hours, as I have always been a night owl, but soon began to crave the live theatre environment again. But first there was my marriage to Maris to take care of. We had booked Caxton Hall, for the ceremony with the reception at the St. James Hotel in Buckingham Gate SW1 for 2pm on Friday 26th October 1973, and had invited our respective families and close friends to join us. I purchased a new three piece suit from Take Six, which I wore with a blue shirt and polka dot tie with my grandfathers 'Albert and Half Hunter Pocket Watch' which I had inherited in his will, hanging from the waistcoat pockets. I had asked Jon Swain, from *The 13 Club* in Liverpool to be my Best Man, and Graham Phoenix, who was now an item with Tricia Martin, to cover for me at The Revolution for the night of the 26th, which he agreed to do. I thought it wise for him to come in and see what was required the night before. I would be hosting a 'meet the family' dinner at the nearby *Guinea Grill* at 30 Bruton Place, just a few doors up from *The Revolution*, where I had arranged for those attending the dinner to visit after we had dined. *The Guinea* had a reputation for providing simple English fare, but of the highest quality, and was renowned for its steaks. When Americans used to stop over in London, before doing Europe, they marked the size of the steak they required with a sharp knife before it was cooked to their liking. It was also the haunt of John Wayne when in London, and in need of a good steak.

I booked a table easily as they knew me because I would pop in for a pint of Young's most evenings, and perused the menu with my family from Lincoln and my new family from London, and was most impressed. We ordered a bottle of Lanson Black Label Champagne to start with and then moved on to select our starters from the simple à la carte menu, which was a choice of either smoked salmon (London cured), crayfish & crab cocktail or globe artichoke with Hollandaise sauce. After consulting the Sommelier we chose a bottle of Pouilly-Fumé, which was a Toogood family favourite. We all went for the steak as it was well marbled and had been hung for 28 days, and chose either a fillet, sirloin or rib eye, with goose fat fried pommes frites and gravy boats full of freshly made horseradish sauce and English mustard, along with a bottle of Chateau Lanande Mèdoc to accompany the mains, which were out of this world. After a brief rest to aid our digestion, we had a communal English cheese board with celery sticks, grapes and a glass or two of Warres 1977 Vintage Port to finish.

When Dad and I went to the Gents at the end of the meal I said to him: "I don't think I have enough money with me to pay for this" to which his reply was: "Don't worry …… I'll look after it" and when the final bill arrived he took out a wedge and paid for the lot, plus a good tip for the staff, who always looked after me for the rest of the time I worked in Bruton Place.

The whole party came to see the Floor Show at *The Revolution* and for the most part enjoyed what they saw. Ray was very impressed with the ballet dancer Suzette, so much so that he bought her a drink.

I had thoroughly enjoyed my taste of gourmet dining, as the last time I had been to an upmarket restaurant it had been a bit of a disaster. I took Maris out for dinner on her birthday when working in Liverpool in the '60s, and as I am a big seafood fan, chose Lobster (either Mornay or Thermidor), which was marked as 'M.P.' (which I now know stands for Market Price). In my desire to impress I hadn't asked what the Market Price was that day. Silly me, as when the bill arrived I went ashen. "What's wrong?" she asked. "Nothing" I replied, lying through my teeth, because the bill for our meal of £30 had come to the same amount as my salary for the whole week.

The experience at *The Guinea* had reinforced what I already suspected, that 'you only get what you pay for', and I had a 'Rolls Royce taste on a Morris Minor budget'. I had learnt from my mistake the hard way, which was to benefit me in years to come when I entertained clients, organised swish events, or just went out to dine myself with a friend or family to places like Rules, The Savoy, La Caprice, The Café Royal, Bentley's and Overton's Oyster Bars, Sheekeys, or The Dorchester.

I had booked a room at St. James Hotel to stay after work, as it was tradition not to sleep with your bride before getting married then - how things have changed - and most of the Lincoln crowd was staying there anyway. Following a hearty breakfast (Is it just me, or does everyone always have a huge and unusual breakfast when they are staying in a nice hotel and it is prepared for you? - I had the kedgeree as a change from the traditional fry-up), I got dressed and as I had no intention of driving that day, started mid-morning on the Bloody Mary's to give me courage for what lay ahead. I had had a good innings as a single man, with a fair share of girlfriends, been adventurous, and burnt the candle at both ends, something I still do now. As I had now reached my target figure of earning £40+ per week, which I had set myself back in the 1960s, it was time to settle down, buy a flat (if I could - we were still living in a room in Oxonian Street with friends), and start a family. One of the owners of Oxonian Street worked in the wine trade and had secured us a good deal on an acceptable wine from Coleman's in Norwich (of mustard fame) on sale or return. Maris's Uncle I. B. was a baker by profession, and made us a cake, whilst Mickey, Maris's Mother was very supportive and, I think, liked me as a son-in-law who was suitable for her daughter.

Maris drove to a nearby multi storey car park in Greycoat Place during the morning in the Austin A40, to prevent the honeymoon vehicle being got at - daubed with paint and old tin cans etc. - as I had booked to stay my night off from The Revolution at The Bell at Aston Clinton, about a 90 minute drive from London, near Aylesbury and nestling in the Chiltern Hills. It had been recommended to me by my sister, who had stayed there with her husband-to-be Tony Cumming on a previous occasion. It was a delightful old coaching inn, with individual en-suite apartments around the stables on two levels. The ceremony and reception went without a hitch, as you would expect from two Stage Managers. Jon Swain, who had flown from Scotland where he was on tour as Company Manager with *Cats*, read the greetings telegrams, and proposed the toast, before dashing off for his return flight to Scotland.

We left the reception about 4pm for Aston Clinton, where we had an apartment on the first floor overlooking the cobbled courtyard, and as the room had its own fridge with chilled wine in it, we soon opened a bottle of German Piesporter Michelsberg, which we enjoyed and consumed before dinner. We had a haunch of venison, with the traditional Cumberland sauce, made with plenty of cowberries, port, mustard, pepper, orange, ginger and vinegar and all the trimmings, with another bottle of Piesporter …. delicious. We then had breakfast in bed, followed by a short walk, before heading back to London, where I had arranged to meet Mum and Dad and take them to watch a meeting at *Brands Hatch* Race Track, as they had never been before.

Walking down the start and finish straight, who should I bump into but Art Walker from the Theatre Royal in Lincoln. He had driven down to Kent in his modified rally car to see the racing as well… small world.

It was back to work at the Revolution Club for the Saturday night Floor Show, and I was told that Graham Phoenix, who I had asked to cover for me, had done a faultless job the previous night, for which I was thankful.

On Monday 29th October, Tom Arnold Presentations contacted Maris and me to find out if we had availability and were interested in taking *Peter Pan* out again, over Christmas and into 1974, with Anita Harris as Peter and Alan Curtis as Hook.

We discussed it and as I had itchy feet and was ready for commercial theatre again, and even though it would be out of town and not where we really wanted to work, agreed that we would do Pan again if the terms were right. We felt that we had both been underpaid the previous year, and that a bird in the hand was worth two in the bush in work terms. Following discussions with Production Manager Stephen Mitchell and with the approval of Head of Accounts Edward Lake, we secured a pay rise of £13 each over what we had been paid the year before, and felt reasonably happy as we knew the show backwards and what to expect, or so we thought.

Act 2 Scene 5
PETER PAN TOUR WITH ANITA HARRIS
(1973-74)

I was happy that all these jobs were dovetailing into place so well, and that my periods of unemployment had been so few (so far), and felt fortunate that the gods were smiling down on me. As soon as I had the deal done with Tom Arnold Presentations, I gave my notice to Vincent Shaw and planned to leave The Revolution Club on Saturday 10th November, as Pan rehearsals were to commence in London on Monday 26th November at a rehearsal room in Victoria.

The Director this year was to be Pauline Grant who was a respected Director of Opera, Musicals, Ballet and Panto especially at The Coventry Theatre which was operated and run by her husband, the impresario S. H. (Sam) Newsome. He was also on the Board of Directors for Moss Empires in addition to running a Jaguar Car dealership in the city, where they had gained a good reputation for the annual *Birthday Show* each Spring.

She was anxious to meet us and get on with pre-production planning and a meeting was arranged by Head Office to meet her at The Coliseum Theatre where she was the Director of Ballet for The Sadler's Wells Opera Company, at 1730hrs on Friday 2nd November 1973. I found her to be a typical Ballet Mistress type, very disciplined, but quite arty and on first impression, a little disorganised, but we got on well, and were able to tell her what we knew, having worked on the show the previous year. Armed with this information, a pre-rehearsal meeting was arranged for Wednesday 14th November, but this time at her mews flat, in the evening.

My last night at the Club went well and Pino gave me, as a farewell gift, a Moet & Chandon 'Top Hat' Ice Bucket, which I had admired and lusted after during my time working there. In the meantime Maris and I went up to Lincoln as it was Mum's 56th birthday on Remembrance Day, and as we knew now that we were going to be on tour over Christmas quickly did some Christmas shopping to take with us, returning to London on Monday in readiness for our next meeting with Pauline Grant, on the Wednesday.

We now knew what dates we were going to be playing, and one of the deciding factors in my decision to take the job was opening at *The Royal Court Theatre* in Liverpool on my 29th birthday, 17th December, prior to going on a six date tour of the Number One Provincial Theatres, which had been booked by the associate Production Company Howard & Wyndham Ltd, to finish on Saturday 23rd March 1974. We were booked to play a mixture of single week and fortnightly stays at the following theatres, some of which were known to me: *Royal Court Liverpool* (five weeks); *Mayflower Southampton* (single week); *Congress Eastbourne* (single week); *ABC Stockton on Tees* (single week); *Kings Glasgow* (2 weeks); *Opera House Leeds* (2 weeks) and the *Grand Wolverhampton* (2 weeks).

The second meeting went well with Ms. Grant, and I had also managed to get some work on a Trade Show for Mitchell Monkhouse Associates (MMA) as 'Show caller' for their client Rank Xerox. There were several reasons I was so keen to do the job. This was a relatively new form of Industrial Theatre and was pushing the bounds of technology forward, the Company worked to high standards, they paid well, this early morning show was to be held at *The Theatre Royal Drury*

Lane (TRDL), which was currently dark between, *Gone with The Wind* and *Billy* and just doing the odd one nighters, and Susan was dancing in the show. The date for the MMA show was Sunday 25th November, after only four rehearsals. Rehearsals for *Peter Pan* were due to start the following day, so things were going to be tight, but again all dovetailed into place nicely.

During the meeting with Pauline, I had been given a cast list, and began my research to find out a little more about those I did not know.

Anita Harris (Peter Pan) was one of the country's few international singing stars. I had met her when she had been in *London Laughs* with Harry Secombe and Jimmy Tarbuck at The London Palladium. Susie, as my sister was known professionally, had introduced us when she was dancing for Pam Devis in 1966. I knew that she was an accomplished ice figure skater, and had also seen her when she was the assistant for magician David Nixon on *Magic Box*, and of course in the films *Carry on Doctor* and *Follow that Camel*. She had recently married songwriter Michael Margolis, who was now her Manager.

Alan Curtis (Hook & Mr. Darling) was perhaps best known as one of Panto's top villains having played that role for five seasons at The London Palladium, with all the big name stars, and so had been well cast as the dastardly Captain Hook by Helen Arnold. He had been married to the stunning Yana (Pamela Guard) and was equally well known for his love of cricket, as he was Chairman of the Lord Taverners Cricket Committee, and a regular commentator on Test Matches for the Test and County Cricket Board. He had been around the business since 1948 and although fourteen years my senior, we were to get on well together during the run.

Holly Doone (Wendy) was a Panto regular and I had seen her play *Cinders* at The Bristol Hippodrome. Mercia Glossop (Mrs. Darling) had been in the West End Musicals, *Man of La Mancha*, *My Fair Lady* and *The Great Waltz*. Michael Harding was cast as Smee with Christopher Robb as his sidekick Gentleman Starkey. Wisely, in my opinion for this production, the Producers had not gone for a comedy duo to play these important characters.

The Director had said from the outset that she wanted to remain faithful to J.M. Barrie's enduring 'Play for Children' but with incidental music and original songs by John Taylor, and John Forsythe was to return again as Musical Director.

It had been agreed that this year I would have some control over the Stage Management Team of four, and in addition to having Maris as my Stage Manager (I was to be Company Manager & Stage Director again), the girlfriend of Jack Forsyth, Alex Alec-Smith joined us as one of the ASMs, along with Peter Kinley and Richarde Mascall.

This year we would also have Michael Saddington as our Lighting Designer as for some of the tour we were contracted to be opening on a Monday, and the Royal Court still used one of the last working 96 way 'Grand Master' switchboards. Other senior appointments made by Head Office were Reg Clark as Master Carpenter, his wife Jean Clark as Wardrobe Mistress, Les Latner as Property Master and Robert Roberts as Chief Electrical Engineer, with the touring lighting equipment supplied from Howard & Wyndham's Stores and Concord Theatre Services. So at least on paper we had more staff with the show this year, but the openings were bound to be tight at some theatres, because of the distance involved between dates such as Liverpool to Southampton, and Glasgow to Leeds for a Monday opening. Who drew this schedule up? Another unknown quantity was the switch from *Kirby's Flying Ballet* to a new firm *HI-FLI*.

Meanwhile back in London I was not happy with my performance in the Corner of the TRDL on the MMA show, as I felt under rehearsed and show calling was not my forte. I thought I had blown my chances of ever working for MMA again, but how wrong could I have been? On the positive side I had enjoyed working as a professional with Sue for the first and, as it would turn out, the only time, because she went to live in Australia in the Summer of the following year after her marriage, and started a family. At least I could say I had run a show at the world famous Theatre Royal Drury Lane, but I was now anxious to get started on rehearsals for *Peter Pan* on the Monday.

Rehearsals this year were to be held in a room above a Westminster City Council Cleaning Depot close to Victoria Train and Coach Stations, with very limited parking facilities. The SM team arrived early for the first call, which was to be a meet and greet session, followed by a read through from scripts, with John Forsythe at the piano playing the original music for most of us to hear for the first time. This more relaxed first call also gave us time to Mark Out more accurately, without being under pressure to be ready for a 10am start. Rehearsals went according to schedule, and I soon fell back into the routine that I had used successfully the previous year, with the Treasury Call on a Thursday, using my ten letter code for secret information as I again had to use a public call box as there was not a dedicated office line. There wasn't a dedicated office either, just a small room off the main rehearsal room which I used as 'The Company Office'. I had made some touring notice boards on which were details of the tour dates, digs, and travel arrangements, as this year we were to travel by coach and not by train, which I was much happier about.

Our final London rehearsal was on Friday 7th December, which gave us all a day to pack for fifteen weeks, prior to travelling to Liverpool on Sunday 9th December 1973. I parked the car up at Maris' Uncle I.B.'s in South London as I had no intention of driving up and down the country in the middle of Winter, when I could maybe have a cat nap whilst travelling in the coach as I, as usual, would be first in and last out at each of the seven venues. The trip up to Liverpool was uneventful, and we had arranged to stay in a room at Norman & Ray Hurst's flat in Huskinson Street, as they were old friends from the Playhouse days. They were just round the corner from the infamous *13 Club*, which I had last seen in 1971.

It was great to be back in 'de pool' again but it looked to me that the developers had ripped the heart out of the City around St. Georges Hall and The Royal Court Theatre.

The Royal Court was H & W's flagship venue in Liverpool and was built in the Art Deco Style of 1938. Our main rival was the 2,550 seat Empire which was a Moss Empires House, but we only had 1,608 seats and very limited onstage storage facilities. I knew from my experience of working shows there as a casual from 1966 to 1971 that for many of the big shows (Pan had six major scenes) much of the dead scenery had to be kept demurrage in empty scenery trailers parked outside and adjacent to the Get In door for an interval changeover, which was inconvenient on a cold Winter's day as the stage temperature would plummet when the huge dock doors were open.

We had a week of technical and Dress Rehearsals from Monday 10th December, prior to an opening night on my 29th birthday. The main problem was sound, as Pauline wanted a natural acoustic sound, whereas Anita was more accustomed to using radio microphones, then a relatively new bit of kit, and thus expensive. Things came to a head on the Friday, when there was a Tannoy call from the Stage Doorkeeper: "Mr. Toogood required immediately at the Stage Door." and I wondered, as I made my way there, what this was all about.

The Stage Doorkeeper explained that there was a courier who had driven from London with a radio microphone 'from Mr. Margolis' (who was Anita's Manager and husband) and required a signature of acceptance, which he was not authorised or prepared to do. I told him that was the correct action to take as even I, in my role of Company Manager, was not aware that this had been ordered and asked the courier to wait while I rang the London office to try and find out what was going on. The office also expressed their surprise, but said to me if it was from Mr. Margolis for Ms. Harris, I was authorised to sign for it, and they would sort it out later. I signed for it, and took it to Anita in her Dressing Room, who said that she had been expecting it from Mike, and apologised for the embarrassment caused, as she was under the impression that Head Office had agreed to hire a radio microphone for her, which they certainly hadn't. I was therefore rather apprehensive about meeting Mr. Margolis, who was due in Liverpool for the opening night.

I had arranged the first night party at the *Old Shakey* nightclub in Fraser Street, as I still had very fond memories of it from my previous time in Liverpool. I thought that it would be an ideal venue as it had opened as a four level theatre in 1888 and still retained many original features, despite a devastating fire on 15th November 1963, when press pictures showed that the Safety Curtain had not been dropped in. It had subsequently been acquired by the multi-millionaire George Silver and turned into 'the most elegant nightclub in Britain' with an American Bar behind the tables in the Stalls Area, and a plush French Restaurant at Dress Circle level, and a Polynesian Bar. There was a dance floor that could be raised up to Stage level for the show, which attracted all the top name stars. From 1969 it had been compèred by 'Mr. Personality' Peter Price, with whom I became close friends when working the Switchboard or Follow Spot at the club.

It saddened me to hear that it had gone bust and closed in April 1975, and was then demolished in 1976 following a second major fire that was its death knell.

The Company found it a most congenial club and I dined with friends in The French Restaurant before going downstairs for a boogie until the early hours, as thankfully we did not have a matinée the next day. We were soon into a routine of matinée, understudy call, treasury call, evening show and then out clubbin' like in my old Liverpool days, at places I already knew like the Mardi Gras Club in Mount Pleasant, where I had first heard Motown and *Don't Walk Away Renée* by the Four Tops in 1968, and The Zanzibar. For Christmas that year most of the Company stayed in Liverpool as we had a matinée on 24th December and one again on the 26th, with just Christmas day off, so we had a bit of a do at Huskinson Street, where we were staying.

New Year 1973-74 was also a bit of a non-event as we had two shows on New Year's Eve and two again on New Year's Day. Still we made the most of it.

As we got into 1974, accommodation for the Company on tour became a priority, as not all of the venues had a digs list they could post to me (no email then) and it was vital to get in first otherwise you could be struggling to find somewhere. It was also impractical for me to go and visit each of the six tour dates, because of my involvement with the show in Liverpool, but at least I had a Company office to work from, and organise things for the first date in Southampton.

Mayflower Theatre Southampton

We closed in Liverpool on Saturday 19th January and had the Coach Call at 10am on the Sunday for the 200 mile drive to the South Coast. I had made it clear to everyone that we would depart at 10am sharp and anyone who missed the call would have to make their own way there and bear the cost involved, as I did not want any misunderstanding for this first call, that I was not prepared to wait for latecomers. I had estimated the journey would take up to six hours, as it was not all motorways then and we would need to stop at least once for a meal break, in addition to any loo stops. We duly arrived about 4pm at the theatre in Commercial Road and close to the City Centre.

My research had told me that the venue had been opened in 1928 by Moss Empires, seated 2,300, and had had a chequered history both as The Rank owned Gaumont and had almost closed before being Grade 2 listed and re-named The Mayflower Theatre.

I had a quick look in this barn to ensure that the wagons had arrived safely after their overnight drive, and that the Get In and Fit Up were progressing on schedule, before getting a cab to the digs, which I had booked on spec before we left, as we were only in town for the week. We had a technical run through on Monday evening, which went well, and a Press Call organised by John Watts (the Press Rep on the show) at noon the following day, with an opening performance at 7pm on the Tuesday. We subsequently played twice daily for the remainder of the week, and did good business as Anita was a South Coast Girl from Bournemouth. I met and looked after her parents when they came to see the show during the week, and as she was only two years older than me, we got on and worked well together. We closed on Saturday 26th January and loaded up for the relatively short move of 75 miles along the coast to Eastbourne, which I estimated should take two hours.

The Congress Theatre Eastbourne

The Congress was a new theatre which had only been open for ten years, and seated 1,700 people. It had a ramp up to stage level to facilitate the easy loading and unloading of scenery, which was going to be handy as we opened at 7pm on the Monday, which was going to be tight, but OK if it all went according to my plan. I had booked a self-catering flat near to the theatre for the week, we played twice daily which went uneventfully, and it was nice to do some home cooking again, as I can rustle up an acceptable meal out of almost anything.

The ABC Theatre Stockton on Tees

What did I know about this venue as we set off on the 250+ mile journey north that I estimated would take seven hours even with just the one meal stop en route? In truth very little, apart from the fact that they had not been able to supply me with a digs list and that it was not a very popular or well frequented venue for weekly runs, like ours. It opened in 1913 and was in Art Deco style, with seats for 2,372 patrons. It had previously been known as The Globe but was mainly used as a cinema on the ABC circuit and had the occasional Rock Show in for a one-night stand, which was not promising for quite a demanding and heavy show like Peter Pan, with its flying scenes, and other technical demands.

The accommodation I had booked in advance turned out to be a tatty commercial hotel, but at least it would only be for the week, but what a week.

Things got off to a bad start as the Get In crew was not used to handling scenery, and it took an age. We had to push on as best we could because we had a Press Call at 4.45 before a technical that Monday evening, as we were to open with a Matinée at 2.15 on the Tuesday, 5th February. There were no notice boards to be found, but thankfully I had brought those used at the rehearsal rooms, for such an eventuality. The Dressing Rooms were not up to standard and when we fired the maroon at the technical, to simulate the bomb being thrown from the Pirate Ship in Act 3, the explosion dislodged years of dust that had accumulated in the Grid, which covered everything. I felt that we were totally unprepared and under rehearsed for the opening and wondered if things could possibly get worse. I was soon to find out, as at the first big scene change in Act One from The Nursery to The Never Never Land, things came to a grinding halt with my SM Maris tearing her hair out in the Corner. Musical Director Jack Forsyth, played the scene change covering music again, but to no avail as the crew had still not done the change and there was nothing left but for me to go on and stop the show. "Ladies and Gentlemen, Boys & Girls I have to crave your indulgence, as because of a technical problem onstage, we are unable to continue with this performance at the moment, but please remain seated, as we will continue as soon as possible. Thank you". This was something I had been prepared for, and kept a crib card with the announcement in the Corner, but this was a first for me.

At the post mortem, which I held with the resident staff, and with their Manager in attendance, I told them in no uncertain terms that this must not happen again, as it had turned out that the afternoon crew were not the same as those who had worked the technical call on the Monday evening, as most of them were working days at the Billingham ICI Chemical Works nearby. Thankfully this was the last major incident that week, and I could not wait to get away from Stockton after the final show on Saturday 9th February, and get on the coach the following morning at 10am for the 150 mile trip to a proper touring theatre in Glasgow, which I estimated would take us in excess of three hours. The Stage Doorkeeper did not get my usual £5 tip as 'thanks for looking after us' that week.

Kings Theatre Glasgow

I had not been to Glasgow before but knew of the reputation that the old Empire Theatre in Sauchiehall Street (closed in 1963) had as the 'English Comic's Graveyard', so we were to play the second biggest venue in town, the 1,841 seat Kings (the largest was The Alhambra which could seat 2,265) and found it around 2pm in Bath Street in the City Centre. It had been built for Howard & Wyndham's, our associate Producers, in 1904 to a design by the greatest of all theatre architects, Frank Matcham, and was on four levels. It was a well-established Receiving House, which had been sold by H & W in 1967 to Glasgow Corporation, and was renowned for the annual Panto, which had top Scottish names to head the bill each year, such as Stanley Baxter, Rikki Fulton and Jimmy Logan.

The trailers had arrived safely after their drive through the night, the Get In had happened, the hanging of equipment was well under way by mid afternoon, so I went to check out where we were going to be staying for the two week run and, as it happened, Maris had relations in the City, so we would stay with them. We rehearsed on Monday, before our opening matinée at 2.30 on Tuesday afternoon, followed by an evening show.

For some bizarre reason, the Press Call was not arranged until the afternoon of Friday 15th February, when we did not have a matinée.

It was my customary practice to begin discussions with the NATKE Union Representative about the Get Out as soon as the show opened. The Head Flyman was the Steward at The Kings. The regulations are quite clear and state that 'the number of men employed for the Get Out shall not be less than the number of men called for the Fit Up' so this was not a sticking point, but the remuneration per man was open to negotiation, depending on whether it was classed as a difficult Get Out, and this again was in the agreement. We were a 'Two Load' show, so the minimum call was for four men at £8 each, but we had exceeded that for the Fit Up, so were contractually bound to employ the same number again. It is worth remembering that back in 1974 the Get Out fee was paid in cash by the visiting Management and did not go through the books at all. Anyway, I offered £10 per man, which received a scowl from the wily old Scot of a Steward. "But you paid £12 per man in Liverpool" he pointed out, having phoned them to find out. "Ah yes" I replied "but we were there for five weeks and the Royal Court is listed as a 'Schedule A' venue in the London Suburban and Provincial Agreement." "We are 'Schedule A' listed in the Scottish Theatrical 'Proprietors and Managers Association' agreement." he replied, and after checking on page 435, I had to agree with him, and £12 per man, cash in hand, was agreed. Lesson … always know the small print in the relevant agreements as well as the Union Steward does.

One Treasury Call is memorable as it could have all gone so wrong, and been expensive for me. I had received the salary cheque from Head Office for the correct amount on Wednesday, ready to take to the bank on Thursday morning, with my breakdown of how I wanted the cash. At the time it was custom and practice for Scottish Banks to count the coins into large 'egg cups' then emptied into a money bag, with the notes in a separate cloth bag. Halfway through making up the pay packets, I realised I was running low on coins, and on checking found the coin bag was short of several pounds. Should I take all the money back to have it re-counted? I decided not to, as I could have been accused of theft, so rang and asked them if they would close the till down that I had used, and perform a tally check of coinage that they still had, against what they should have, if I had been paid correctly. After an agonising wait, they confirmed, thank goodness, that I had indeed been short changed by the agreed amount, which was subsequently brought to the theatre in time for a slightly delayed Treasury Call. After that experience I always insisted that the coins and notes were counted out in front of me.

Whilst I was up in Glasgow, I had a bit of free time as we did not have a matinée performance every day. I purchased a grey Ford Anglia van, which was to prove invaluable when I took up cycle speedway racing a few years later. It needed a few things doing to pass the MOT, and meant that for the last two dates of the tour I would make my own way there, as the tried and trusted travelling routine could be overseen by one of the ASMs now, without too much trouble. The next leg was to The Grand Theatre and Opera House in Leeds, and what a great time we were to have there.

Leeds Grand Theatre

On Saturday 23rd February we packed the two Edward's Trailers (motto 'The Importance of Getting Edwards') who we were using this year for all our transport to travel the 170 miles to Leeds overnight. The Company followed on Sunday and I had estimated that the journey would take about four hours from Stage Door to Stage Door. I would drive there, once I had checked that the coach departed on time, leaving Alex Alec-Smith in charge for the journey. I arrived mid-afternoon in Briggate to check that all was well before going off to the digs.

One of the joys about playing Leeds Grand was that not only was it a well-run number one touring house (it is now home to Opera North & Northern Ballet), but is steeped in history. It had opened in 1878 with a Romanesque, Gothic, Baronial style from the local Leeds based architects George Corson, seated 1,600 patrons, and had a unique cloth chute that many thought was to get the beer barrels up to the backstage Green Room Bar, but was in fact to get backcloths easily up from street level to the stage floor. It was also full of characters, for example the Chief Electrician Mr. F.W.S.P. Kay or 'Billy' as he was known to everyone. He would arrive at work in his three-piece suit, a fresh carnation in the lapel buttonhole of his jacket, a silk handkerchief in the top pocket, wearing a bowler hat or straw boater, carrying a shellac cane, wearing thick horn rimmed spectacles or a monocle and the ends of his moustache waxed to a point. He didn't use a wristwatch, preferring to use a pocket watch, hanging from an Albert chain in his waistcoat pocket, and took snuff and smoked endlessly, with ash from the cigarettes mixing with spilt snuff, landing all down the front of the waistcoat, and was partial to the odd gin & tonic, but it had to be Gordon's. He was a stickler for doing things 'The Grand' way, since his arrival from the Leeds Empire when it closed in 1961, and when he saw some of the female members of my SM team wearing trousers onstage, said to me in his broad Yorkshire accent: "They won't be wearing them on first night will they … 'cos females don't wear trousers on a first night at Leeds Grand ye know." When the S.M. Team heard about it, they decided to wear long evening gowns or dinner suits for the scene changes on the opening night.

Anyone who ever lit a show there when Billy was plotting on the board will recall this conversation. "Stand by Billy for Q eight" to which the reply would come: "Standing by for Q Eight, where the oil comes from". He worked at his beloved Grand for twenty five years, until his retirement in 1986 through ill

Billy Kay

health, lived all his life with his devoted mother, and was by then driving a swish sports car. It is an overused expression to say that anyone is a legend in his own lifetime, but one that does justice to Mr. F.W.S.P. Kay, I feel, and it was a real privilege to work with him.

The Managing Director and licensee was John Beaumont, and an old friend of mine Warren Smith, with whom I had worked both at Lincoln and Bristol, was the Manager. Indeed Warren would spend the next 36 years of his career working at Leeds Grand until his retirement in 2007. It was a real pleasure to share a last night drink with him and chat about our previous careers, as we settled the Contra Account, which was always immaculately presented, with no mistakes to argue about. We had opened on Monday 25th February with an evening show at 7 pm followed by a Matinée and evening shows on the Tuesday, and things progressed nicely for the whole run as all the staff knew what they were doing and were used to handling multi-scene shows like Peter Pan.

One night after the show, many of us decided to go over to the *Batley Variety Club*, as it was only seven miles away, as *Lulu* was topping the bill. James Corrigan owned the Club, which had opened in 1966, as Theatre Clubs were now replacing the Variety Theatres, which were suffering badly because of television, and people were no longer going to sit in the same seats in the Stalls on a Tuesday evening as they had done formerly. They would however have a night out at a Theatre/Variety Club and see a top international star, and have a meal for six shillings and six pence (33 pence now), which was the all in price when it first opened its doors. Your only other expense was the bus to and from the venue (late night buses were the norm), a bottle of Blue Nun with the meal, as many Cherry B's or Babychams as your wife or girlfriend could handle, and as much beer as you could drink.

Batley was not your usual Northern Working Men's Club, but the 'Talk of the Town' of the north, where international stars would come to perform. Louis Armstrong (paid a staggering £20,000, plus expenses, for two weeks in 1968), Jayne Mansfield, Johnny Mathis, Tina Turner, Tony Hancock, Eartha Kitt, Gracie Fields, Roy Orbison, Vera Lynn, Gene Pitney, Buddy Greco and the Bee Gees, would all fly over to play Batley, along with the cream of our own British talent, who took second spot on the billing.

The Club could accommodate 1,600 people, who sat in plush velvet covered booth pods, facing the stage, with waitress service all night long. It was best summed up by some wag who described a night out there as 'Chicken in a Basket, the World's Top Performers, as much beer as you could drink to get Kay-Lied, and a good fight in the Bus Queue'. Sadly the club closed in 1977 when some artistes got greedy and began demanding extortionate fees for a week's work. My lasting memory of going there in Winter 1974 is my smart new Crombie overcoat was missing when I went to collect it from the cloakroom, and I had to make a claim for it to be replaced, on their insurance.

We finished a very happy two week run in Leeds on Saturday 9th March, and headed south again for our final venue of the tour.

Grand Theatre Wolverhampton

I estimated the 100 mile journey from Leeds to Staffordshire would take about two and a half hours to complete for the coach, but it would be quicker for me now that I had wheels of my own. My pre-visit research had informed me that the building in Lichfield Street opened in 1894 and had been designed by architect Charles J. Phipps, with seating for 1,410 in the Stalls, Circle and Upper Circle. It had recently been re-painted from its original Wedgwood Blue in Spanish chestnut red, white, and gold, and had a new stage floor installed the year before we were to play there.

Things had been delivered on time by Edwards, and the crew were hard at work on my arrival, because we had a Monday evening opening on 11th March to aim for which, being the seventh Fit Up, we would be able to achieve if all went to plan, which it did, for the opening and subsequent two week stay.

We were now a well-oiled machine, and held a party on the final Thursday to celebrate the success of the tour, as we didn't have a Matinée on the Friday. I had given everyone a breakdown of their remuneration whilst employed with the Company (the equivalent of a P60 if you were on PAYE) to hand to their accountants at the final Treasury Call, and many said to me "What's this?" as no Company Manager had ever given them anything like it before. Another first for me, and demonstrated again that I knew, by now, what I was doing. The final performance was an emotional one on Saturday 23rd March, as there had been many friendships and romantic flings during our time on the road and there were a few tears as we all went our separate ways on the Sunday. I had decided to travel cross-country to visit my parents in Lincoln, prior to going back to London, where a new flat beckoned.

So what had this tour been like for me as a career move? If asked again, which I was, to take the show out for a third year, I would have to be out of work to contemplate it, as I was now more determined than ever to work in the West End. I began to work towards achieving that dream.

Act 3 Scene 1
THE WEST END
(1974)

I returned to Lincoln quite late on Sunday 24th March as it had been a difficult 80 mile journey from Wolverhampton, via Derby and Nottingham, to find that whilst Mum had been preparing a meal for us all, Dad had gone to the Castle Hill Club in Castle Square where we were to join him. Mum was reluctant, and couldn't be bothered to go and get togged up - she would never go out on a Sunday in her working clothes - but was eventually persuaded to come. One welcome drink turned into two or three as we each bought a round and we did not return to Steep Hill until much later than anticipated.

It had been my intention to sign on for the first time in thirty years, but I did not feel bad about it as I had been paying my National Insurance contributions on and off for over ten years. However I had over indulged at the club with Dad on an empty stomach, and did not feel up to it on Monday, so I signed on the Tuesday. There was some sort of problem, as Lincoln was not my permanent address and it was my intention to move down to London, where there was a possibility of work. I was told that this was not acceptable

I phoned Mike Wilson at MMA to see if they had any Trade Show work going, which they didn't, so I had a holiday with my parents and Maris till moving to London on Monday 8th April to begin to look for work intensely, as I was getting bored.

The Anglia van took us uneventfully back to 15, Oxonion Street, and as the A40 was now surplus to needs, offered it to Jon Swain, who was without wheels at the time, at a knock down price, which he was happy with as I had modified it a bit and installed seat belts whilst working at Greenwich.

As Easter was approaching fast, and the Motor Cycle Racing Season was about to start with the traditional *Trans Atlantic Races* over three days: Good Friday, at Brands Hatch, Easter Sunday at Mallory Park and Easter Monday at Oulton Park, I had time on my hands to go to watch them from 12th-15th April. An American newcomer, Kenny Roberts, making his racing debut in England stole the show, winning three of the six races, and coming second in the rest, to be top scorer on 93 points which was 5 more that the great Barry Sheen scored with his tally of 88. Roberts had well and truly arrived on the Motor Cycle Road Racing scene and proved that the 'Yankee Flat Trackers' could ride conventional road tracks as well as the Brits.

The other avenue I pursued was to get in touch with Janet Chapman again, who was The Production, Company and Stage Manager for the Paul Raymond Organisation, and for whom I had worked the Season at Margate the previous Summer. I was under the impression that the big boss Paul Raymond had been more than happy with what I had done on that show, and whatever anyone else thought, if he liked me, he would give the OK for Janet to re-employ me. She told me: "There might be something that I would be interested in" coming up in May, which was only two weeks away.

In the meantime, to tide me over, as funds were getting short, I hired a ladder, put a roof rack on the van, and started work as a window cleaner, because as everyone knows, you cannot get a reliable window cleaner in London for love or money, and it was the latter I was more interested in for once in my life. This was a big mistake as I do not have a good head for heights and balancing at the top of the ladder in the wind, thirty feet in the air, and hanging on for dear life with one wet and frozen hand, was not my idea of a job, even if it was to be a cash in hand, give you a receipt next week, job. Thanks but no thanks and I packed it in and returned the ladder after two weeks, as I had now heard from Janet.

She told me, in confidence, that she was going to be taking maternity leave from 13th May to have her first child, and asked if I would be interested in covering for her as Company Manager, on a temporary basis, at *The Whitehall Theatre* on *Pyjama Tops*? Without a second thought, I accepted, as not only was I known to the PR Organisation, but they knew the standard of Management I worked to, and that I was used to semi-nude shows. Most importantly for me, it was a good career move, as it was working in the West End.

The contract arrived on 1st May and I would be on the same money as I had been for *The Bed* in Margate, £40 per week with a four week get out clause for both parties.

I waited till the Saturday (4th May) to celebrate properly as it was F.A. Cup Final day and Liverpool (still the team I supported) were playing Newcastle United at Wembley. Liverpool thrashed Newcastle 3-0 in what was described as the most one sided Cup Final ever seen, and I went out to celebrate 'Up West' with the scousers that night. In the early hours I phoned my best mate Jon Swain, who by now was driving the A40, to see if he would pick me up and take me home from Macready's Club as I was legless. The club was an after-hours drinking club for those working on West End shows (I got in by showing my Actors Equity Card) and named after the Classical Actor. It was situated by the Stage Door to the Cambridge Theatre in Seven Dials, and Jon found me hanging round a lamppost, awaiting his arrival and singing Liverpool songs, as I was always happy, not melancholy, when drunk. I had arrived at last in The West End and it had taken me sixteen years to get this far in my chosen career.

Pyjama Tops at the Whitehall Theatre (1974)

I began my West End career on Monday 13th May 1974. As I was taking over from Janet Chapman, I had a week shadowing her to find out what normally happened, as the last thing I wanted to do was rock the boat and change things in what was a successful show. There was no rehearsal period thank goodness, my least favourite part of theatre management, as I prefer working to a routine. Although the show had opened to mixed reviews on 22nd September 1969, its 1000th performance had been celebrated on 23rd February 1972, despite what the press had said. We played the traditional West End eight evening shows a week with an early at 6.15 on the Wednesday and Saturday.

It quickly became clear that my main role as Company Manager on this show was to ensure that Fiona Richmond, playing Fiona Lovell, was happy as she was being nurtured by Mr. Raymond into being a star both in live shows and in his publications *Men Only* and *Club International*, both of which were on sale to customers in the theatre at 40 pence.

One of the many unique aspects of *Pyjama Tops*, which was based on the French comedy success *Moumou* by Jean De Letraz and directed by Alexander Dore, was a small swimming pool at the front of the stage in which the girls swam during the show.

The character Leonard Jolly provided the comedy in the show, and was played by David Konyot, who I found out came from a famous Hungarian circus family and had a successful nightclub act. The delightful Carole Saulsbury, with whom I had worked at Margate, had joined the Company. Others in the cast were Jenny Cox, Roger Avon, Jenny Kenna, Tony Bateman, Mervyn Pascoe, Judith Hepburn and Zoe Hendry. The DSM was Keith Morris, who was also an understudy, whilst the Wardrobe Master was Mr. Vicky, who I never saw in the Green Room without a cigarette in his mouth or fingers. Within the ranks of the Senior Management were General Manager George Richardson, another smoker, and the Senior Group Engineer Ronald Edbrooke, who held overall responsibility for anything technical at the Whitehall and also at the Royalty and Revuebar.

The Revuebar was still going strong in its sixteenth year and known as *The World Centre of Erotic Entertainment*, playing twice nightly at 8.30 and 11pm.

Having been taught the ropes by Janet for a week, she departed for maternity leave with the instruction: "Don't forget to include a pint of milk for each show on the petty cash", which was not required in the show, but had been claimed for since the opening, and was used by the Company and Staff for drinks in the Green Room. Things went smoothly and I soon got the hang of what to do.

I had a bit of a run in with Roger Avon, playing Inspector Grindle, who was an old pro of many years standing and never took his trouser bike clips off. When I gave him his pay envelope, he examined the pay slip advice note and asked: "What's this?" The two Mr. Georges in Accounts made them up in cash, weekly, as they were based at the Whitehall, so I replied that as far as I knew he had been paid correctly, but was happy to check with the Accounts Department the following day. "I'm only doing this crap play to pay to send my family to Public School" he retorted, and stormed off.

When I signed the contract it had been agreed I could have both shows of Saturday 25th May off, as Susan was to marry Tony Cumming on that day in Lincoln. It was a grand do, with all the family and many friends in attendance, and following the service, Dad had paid for The Cathedral bell ringers to ring a toll on the great Minster bells as we moved to the formal reception that was held in The Richard the Second Suite at the White Hart Hotel next door. The centrepiece of the wedding breakfast was a roast suckling pig, with an orange in its mouth and Dad had put £40 (the same as my weekly wage in London) behind the front bar for everyone to have a drink, in addition to the Champagne for the toast and wine with the food. I had purchased a new three-piece suit from Take Six in Carnaby Street, still THE fashion Street in London, and looked the bee's knees.

One of my first duties when I was back in London was to meet the Company at The Savoy Chapel, where The Reverend Edwin Young, was holding one of his regular parties. He was Chaplain to most of the shows in the West End, and the girls at The Revuebar thought so highly of him that they purchased a beautiful punch bowl for him. He was about six feet tall and had a head of pure white hair, looked a striking figure and was utterly charming to all, and we got on famously. The Managements respected him as well, and he was permitted to visit artistes in their Dressing Rooms during the show, where they could discuss any spiritual problems at length, as he was a great listener.

Janet expected to be on leave for about three months which meant there would be a cast change before she returned. The changes took place with Carole getting a part as she replaced Jenny, Berwick Kaler (who had been with my Summer show in Margate) taking over from Tony, the DSM Keith was now to play Mervyns's role as Jack and we had three new swimmers Jandy Millar, Cleo Moran, and Nina West-Sadler. The two major changes however were that Fiona was leaving to open in a new show at *The Windmill Theatre* and was replaced by Judith her understudy, and Chubby Oates was now to play Leonard and replace David.

Mr. Oates was a short 5' 4", pipe smoking, fifteen stone funster who proved quite hard work to manage as he had a flatulence problem, which I attributed to the copious amounts of Guinness that this ex-journalist consumed. One thing I had learnt when working with artistes was to be respectful, and the frequent breaking of wind onstage, which he thought was funny, did not go down well with les girls and was reported on more than one occasion in the nightly show report to Head Office. Eventually it came to the attention of Mr. Raymond, and Chubby was given an official warning.

I too had been asked if I would like to move over and re-open the *Windmill Theatre* in the heart of Soho, which Mr. Raymond had recently added to his portfolio, when Janet returned in February, which I accepted as I thought that it would be a good move for a variety of reasons. The Windmill was a legendary theatre as during the War the Manager Vivian Van Damm, appointed by owner Mrs. Laura Henderson, had used the slogan *We Never Closed*, which some wag had changed to *We're*

Never Clothed to promote the continuous Revudeville show that was presented daily between 2.30 – 11pm and featured most of the top comics of the day.

In addition to comics who played there such as Jimmy Edwards, Tony Hancock, Peter Sellers, Michael Bentine, Bruce Forsyth, Tommy Cooper and Barry Cryer, Mr. Van Damm had also introduced The Windmill Girls who posed nude in a number of Tableaux Vivants, with the rule: "If You Move It's Rude" imposed by the Lord Chamberlain.

The Windmill soon gained a reputation not only for the shows, but the fact that it remained open throughout the War (apart from the Government's compulsory closure 4th-16th September 1939), and it was not unknown for fans to remain in the building for the whole day, gradually moving forward into a seat that had become vacant to be closer to the stage. There were two pianos in the pit to provide music and it was argued that many of the young men in uniform, who had waited patiently in line past the Lyric Stage Door, under the supervision of the uniformed Commissionaire, would only ever see one nude female in their life before they were killed in action, and this was it.

It was very much a family theatre where the Management and Staff remained loyal for many years, like Stage Director Johnny Gale, General Director Anne Mitelle and Maintenance Engineer Cyril Sadler (all 25 years); House Manager Ernest Horton (23 years), Chief Electrician Dickie Grout and Stage Doorkeeper Ben Fuller, all 22 years. During the worst of the air raids many of the girls used to sleep in the basement, and take their chance of a direct hit, as it was safer than venturing outside.

When Vivian died in 1960 the building was taken over by his daughter, the rally driver Sheila Van Damm, but continued as a live venue for only another four years, until closing on 1st October 1964, to become yet another seedy Soho cinema, known as *The Palais de Luxe*. Now, thanks to Paul Raymond, it was to present live shows once again.

The new show was to be called *Let's Get Laid* and was to be a re-vamp of *The Bed* by Sam Cree, which I had worked on during the Margate Summer Season the previous year. It was to star Fiona Richmond as 'Fiona' and John Inman again playing Gordon Hardcastle, both of whom I had worked with, and liked. I had also been offered a pay rise of 25%, the engagement was from 12th August and the new show was due to open on Monday 2nd September 1974 following extensive building works to bring it up to standard. This was too good to turn down and again showed that as well as luck in the business, you also have to be in the right place at the right time, and this had happened to me.

Act 3 Scene 2
LET'S GET LAID
(1974-76)

I worked out my time at The Whitehall Theatre, which I had enjoyed in the main, and made many new friends, some of whom still remain in contact with me forty years later. I spent quite a bit of time working between the two theatres, as there were Production Meetings to attend with Director Victor Spinetti and Designer Tod Kingman, of whom much more later. In addition Mr. Raymond was spending £200,000 on refurbishment of the FOH, Stage and Dressing Rooms and was intending to move his offices into the new building when it was ready. I wanted to have some involvement with the refurbishment after my experience at The Liverpool Playhouse.

On one memorable occasion I was given a lift between the Whitehall and the Windmill by Fiona. I felt I had really been accepted.

Welsh comedy actor Victor brought with him a wealth of experience, and had recently shot to fame as the obnoxious Drill Sergeant in Joan Littlewood's masterpiece *Oh What a Lovely War* both in the West End and on Broadway where he won a 'Tony'. He had also worked with The Beatles on *A Hard Day's Night*, *Help* and *Magical Mystery Tour*, as well as directing the musical *Hair*. We got on well from our first meeting and I would frequently meet him when he was on tour with shows in the twilight of his career. He was to remain a friend right up to his death.

In addition to casting Fiona and John as the two leads we also had the delightful Jenny Kenna playing Vera Dunwoody, who was transferring over from *Pyjama Tops*. Veteran comic actor Jack Haig, affectionately known as 'The Mayor of Solihull', specialised in playing supporting roles and had recently finished a two year stint playing *Steward* in *Canterbury Tales* at The Phoenix Theatre. He was later to find fame playing *Monsieur LeClerc* in the TV hit show *'Allo 'Allo*.

Other new members of the Company to me were Kevan Sheehan (Tony), Terry Denton (Harry 'Goldie' Locke) previously played by Barry Howard in Margate, Lynda Rae (Suzie), Kate Harper (Nancy), Andrea Godfrey (Judy), Carla Duncan (Britt) whilst Jean Watson was the female Understudy. My Deputy was Tom Cockrell, who was also the male understudy, whilst Annette Sharville, who I knew from my Tom Arnold days, was the Wardrobe Mistress.

I had met many of the new Company when they came to The Whitehall to audition for small supporting roles in the show. Carla Duncan arrived wearing very fashionable culottes for her audition and was offered the part of Britt.

Tod Kingman's design used every inch of the small stage, and was built in his workshops in Flitcroft Street, where I met Eddie Ryan and Phil Stelling, who would be in charge of the Fit Up. Chris King had been transferred over as Theatre Manager from The Revuebar, while Pyjama Tops would still be at The Whitehall. Ray Cooney's *The Bed Winner* played The Royalty, with the Eros Theatre to open soon, making P.R. one of the biggest theatre owners in London, with five theatres to his name.

We began rehearsals on Monday 12th August, with three Preview Performances planned for 29-31st August. The main problem was not the show, but the refurbishments, which were, as usual, running behind schedule.

The Previews were advertised, and in true theatre tradition - the show must go on - we were going to make it happen and the contractors achieved this, by the skin of their teeth, by introducing overnight working. The plot of the show was that a couple of friends, played by John Inman & Terry Denton, were flat sitting for a James Bond type character who was frequently visited by a galaxy of stunning girlfriends.

The show had a budget of £20,000, but in order to keep wardrobe costs down Fiona (who was also credited as being the shows costumier) had used many exclusive costumes, strings of pearls, diamante chokers and feather boas, from the drag show *Birds of a Feather* starring Larry Grayson at The Royalty Theatre, which had folded.

As a publicity stunt Fiona staged a 'Lady Godiva' horse ride down Great Windmill Street, and into Piccadilly Circus, where she was stopped and arrested by a Police Inspector outside Swan & Edgar's store. She was fined £20, but the press coverage was worth much more than that.

The first night, when the theatre was hardly ready, saw a galaxy of celebrities in attendance including Ernie Wise and Elizabeth Taylor, who went to visit Fiona back stage post show.

The following day there was a letter for me at The Stage Door, from DebWard Ltd., my employer, to state that my contract with them had been converted from a 'two week notice contract' to 'run of the play', and if this show was as successful as *Pyjama Tops*, I could look forward to four or five year's work. Things looked secure for a while to pay the mortgage on the flat I had purchased at Morley Court in Lewisham for £8,000, and start a family with Maris.

There were two camps of fans at this time, and you were either in the Fiona Richmond camp or the Mary Millington camp. Mary had been born out of wedlock in Kenton in 1945, worked for The David Sullivan Empire as a model, and behind the counter of his Whitehouse shop in Norbury. Fiona, on the other hand, was the daughter of The Reverend John Harrison, and was born on 2nd March 1945 (incidentally the same day that Mr. Raymond died in 2008) near Swaffham in Norfolk. She had first worked for the P.R. Organisation as a swimmer on *Pyjama Tops*, having auditioned on 22nd July 1970, because she had finished at The Penthouse Club, thought that it would be fun and had quickly become the leading lady in the shows. So apart from being born in the same year of 1945, they had little in common.

As the run progressed we had such fun as a Company, with many famous thespians coming to see the show and have a look round the revamped theatre. Kenneth More came round one night and Ronnie Fraser was a regular, as he was close friends with Andrea (Andi) Godfrey, and we would all meet up in *The Lyric Tavern* most nights after the show. Mr. Raymond was renowned for his parties and one night after fruits de mer, with Champagne of course, at *Bentley's Oyster Bar* in Swallow Street, we were all invited back to his elegant, exclusive flat in Portman Square, to continue into the early hours as he was notorious for not going to bed till dawn, like me. The master bedroom had a ceiling that could be removed somehow, so that whilst on the bed you looked up at the twinkling stars. If you were very lucky, you were invited to visit *Veste Demitte*, his yacht moored on the Thames at Chelsea Embankment, where P.R. would be the Captain dressed in his navy blazer, white trousers and cap.

In order to comply with the licensing regulations at any West End theatre, a Duty or Full Time Fireman had to be employed and (pardon the pun) I got on like a house on fire with ours, Norman Johns. He was a quiet spoken man, who did voluntary work with the Boy Scouts and grew vegetables on his allotment, something that I had now begun to do in the communal garden at the flat, and anything surplus to his needs he brought in for les girls in the show. He was very fair and understanding of the needs of the show, but insisted that we comply with all the relevant regulations and, like all other firemen I have worked with, are real human beings.

As we were playing twice nightly at seven and nine o'clock, I felt that it was only fair to run the Corner for one of the Acts each night to give Tom a bit of time off to watch *The Sweeney* on the small black & white portable television set I had brought into the theatre. Dressing Room space was at a premium with two individual rooms, one for Fiona and one for John, and two communal rooms, one for the males and one for the females, so I had set up office at the far end of the male Dressing room. This was not ideal by any means as any business or disciplinary matters had to be conducted elsewhere and on that floor there was only the unisex shower and the FOH bar.

One night when sitting on my own running the show from the Corner, I had a surprise when one of the girls came up behind me and put her hands over my eyes. "Guess who?" she purred, and on looking round found that it was Carla Duncan, who I had first met when she came to audition for the show at The Windmill. She told me that she had come down from the dressing room to share some time with me, which I was very flattered to hear from her. She had trained as a classical ballet dancer, had worked at both The Raymond Revuebar & The Royalty Theatre, hailed from Belfast and now lived with her mother in a flat off the A4 Great West Road, near Hammersmith.

I went out with Terry Denton on a fishing trip to somewhere in Kent that Terry knew. Not my scene, but a pleasant day socialising with some of the Company, who by now I was beginning to like.

On the corner of Archer Street and Great Windmill Street, between the theatre Stage Door and FOH, you would find on most days an old plastic milk crate and large cardboard box that were used by the 'find the lady' three card tricksters, who I used to watch when I was not on duty, to find out how it was done before the cry of "Coppers" went up from the lookouts. They would melt into the background with the wedge of notes they had won from unsuspecting tourists, but I never did work out how it was done.

On a Wednesday I read the Motor Cycle News, which was worth buying then, as it covered most off-road motor cycle race meetings, and I noticed a piece about the forthcoming final round of the British Grass Track Championships which were to be run by the Evesham Club at Aston Somerville, near Broadway in the Cotswolds, on Sunday 29th September. A coach trip from the South East was being planned to go, if there was enough support, so I rang the number and spoke to a Mr. Humphries in Folkestone about joining it, as the coach price was cheaper than it would cost me to drive there in the van. It was arranged that the coach would stop in Lewisham at 7.30 am and then continue up to the Cotswolds, arriving there in plenty of time to soak up the atmosphere at this one really big and important date in the calendar. The other passengers were real fanatics from the hotbed of this type of racing in Kent, were all very knowledgeable, and good company on the three-hour trip. Mr. Humphries and his brothers (Brian & Des) proved to be real characters and Brian was famous for having the most bulldog clips on a programme board in the South Eastern Centre, which he was very proud of. The racing was good and the tension electric, particularly in the 1000cc Sidecar Class, which had a first bend pile up in the first race involving Steve Smith and his passenger Roy French, the reigning champions, who were catapulted over the handlebars as soon as they hit the loose dirt. The return journey back to London was a nightmare.

The coach driver noticed a red warning light on the dashboard when we were leaving the track, and proceed at a gentle pace to see if the problem rectified itself. When it hadn't by the time we got to the outskirts of Worcester, he stopped on a garage forecourt to investigate prior to joining the M5. We waited patiently for the driver to complete his checks but the warning light still glowed brightly, and it was only when he walked round to the back of the coach, that he spotted that the rear emergency exit door was just slightly open. A quick slam to close it properly extinguished the warning light, and we were on our way again after an hour. Many years later when Sue had returned from Australia, she lived in Pershore and I frequently used to pass this garage when on my way into Worcester.

The show had now settled into a nice run, and Mr. Raymond paid regular visits to see the show and have a bottle of his favourite Champagne in the bar.

I also had a bit of a run in with Jack Haig as he was quite a strong willed character and objected to doing one piece of business in the show. A hairpiece he wore had to fall off and as it was quite a problem for us to keep it in place with wig tape, I resorted to something stronger and used Duct tape which solved the problem. I was passing him in the communal Dressing Room to go to the office section soon after the stronger tape was used, and he said to me in a very aggressive manner: "If I get alopecia from using this tape, expect to hear from my Solicitors." but he didn't and that was the end of the matter.

The months leading up to Christmas were pretty uneventful, and I was enjoying myself both at the flat where I was doing many odd jobs, and the work at The Windmill. I asked Chris King (the Theatre Manager) who also ran VIP Boxes at Epsom Racecourse for Lords & Ladies, if we could have a Company Christmas Party in the Theatre Bar which, after checking, was agreed and the evening of Sunday 22nd December was selected. I asked him how much we should charge per head, and was told "Just leave it to me" which I was happy to do. We all came togged up in our finery, and waiting for us on arrival was the perfect Champagne cocktail, which he had made by using a sugar cube, soaked with Angostura Bitters, before adding a shot of brandy to the flute, and topping up with chilled Champagne and a garnish of orange slice and Maraschino Cherry. Simple but perfect and delicious. I have never made mine any other way since.

We all had a great time and what a way to start the Christmas festivities as we had shows right over Christmas and New Year apart from Christmas Day. In the New Year of 1975, I began to think about cast changes as some artistes were only booked for six months, and their replacements had to be rehearsed so there would be a seamless take over. The big change was Fiona leaving, John Inman as the star turn with Jenny Kenna, Kate Harper getting bigger billing and Danny O'Dea coming in to take over from Jack Haig as Lionel Wills. Unlike Jack, Danny was a real sweetie and later to find fame as the long sighted bumbler Eli Ducker in *Last of the Summer Wine* between 1986 – 2002, when he was 90 years old. Although he had appeared in plays, done Pantos, Summer Seasons, musical comedy, worked on radio, TV, and films, he told me he was very nervous as he had never appeared in the West End, which he was quite excited about. The Girls changed parts in the re-shuffle, with Tony Sweeney replacing Kevan Sheehan as Tony Scott, and Maria St. Clare taking over as Suzie. If you didn't know any of the cast, apart from Fiona who was by now a major star touring the world doing research for the magazine *Men Only*, and as a recording artiste with Frankly Fiona, you wouldn't have known the difference, which was how Mr. Raymond liked it to be done.

The weeks settled into a nice routine, with me doing jobs at the flat or working in the vegetable plot during the day, cycling to work for the two performances, drinks in the pub with the Company, then cycle back to Lewisham and have supper, which was my main meal of the day. Cycling for seventy five miles a week was keeping me at a trim eleven and a half stone (Middleweight if I were a boxer) which was good, as I felt fit and was toned and tanned. I bought a new dinner suit to wear with some yellow frilly front shirts, and was feeling and looking on top of the word, working in the West End.

Pyjama Tops ended its run at The Whitehall on Saturday 3rd May 1975 after a run of five and a half years, and was turned into *The Theatre of War* which Westminster Council were unhappy about, and I felt lucky that I had been offered the move from The Whitehall to The Windmill, or I would have been out of a job.

After the *Lyric Tavern* had closed at 11 pm, some of us would go out clubbin' to one of the theatrical clubs such as *The Buxton* by the *Haymarket Theatre* Stage Door, *Macready's* in Covent Garden, *Gerry's* near China Town, *The Arts Club* or to one of the new discos that were starting to spring up in London. We were always made most welcome, and danced till the early hours to The Hues Corporation, ABBA, Donna Summer, KC & The Sunshine Band, The Tramps, Gloria Gaynor, and The Jackson's. Great artistes and songs that still evoke happy memories.

I now had time during the day to go to meetings that were organised by *The Stage Management Association* (SMA) in the first floor room of *The White Swan* public house in New Row, once a month at 11am on a Monday. Here matters of common interest to the Stage Management working on a variety of shows in the West End could be discussed openly as employers were not members. The Chairman was Griff James, and David Ayliffe, a founder member in 1954, was Secretary, ably assisted by his wife Jean, who would take the minutes and circulate them. One of the main advantages of being a member of the SMA was that if you were resting you were entitled to put your name on the 'Free List', which was circulated to most Managements. Little did I realise at the time that I would be asked by my peers to be their Chairman from 1984-93, a position that I was proud and privileged to hold.

Janet Chapman, who I had taken over from on *Pyjama Tops*, gave birth to a little girl, named Jody, in Bromley Hospital on 20th June 1975, and her father Bill Denis moved in with her to share a house in the Lee Green - Catford area, very close to my flat in Morley Road. I would work with Bill in a number of roles later on in my career, both in The West End and Provinces, and used to love to chat to him about his days as part of a tap dancing act in the Variety Theatre of the late '50s, and his time working at *The Talk of the Town* with the legendary impresario Robert Nesbitt, **'The Prince of Darkness'**, who brought real class to the West End for a quarter of a century with his sumptuous shows there.

At the end of July Terry Denton left the show and the search was on for a replacement Harry (Goldie) Locke. After auditions were held Brian Godfrey was given the role. The replacement show at the Whitehall was *Snatch 69* directed again by Victor Spinetti and written by the prolific Bryan Blackburn. It opened in April '75 but was a flop and closed on Saturday 9th August.

With more free time on my hands, and Sundays free to take up a sport that would keep me at a good fighting weight, I approached Ron Johnson about joining my local Cycle Speedway team in South East London. He called me on Tuesday 12th August about the track and Club, *The Beckenham Monarchs*, which he personally controlled, and invited me to go for a trial one Sunday in late August or early September, which I did. I joined them straight away as part of the second team, which was good grounding for someone new at the sport. The next thing I had to do was buy a purpose track racing cycle with straight front forks, north road bend handlebars, low gearing of 32 x 18, with Avon Skidway Gripster Tyres on it. I found one in a specialist shop near to Wimbledon and bought it for £25, but as it was finished in an all-over black only colour scheme, stripped it down and repainted it in my traditional racing colours of pillar box red with black lugs.

From the fixture list Ron had sent me, I saw that Beckenham were going to be riding at home on Sunday 28th September against Tottenham, and the following Sunday 5th October, again at home, against Hawkinge from near Folkstone in Kent. I went to meet the Club Manager Bernie Vickers from Dagenham in Essex, liked what I saw, and this became my regular Sunday sport for the next five years. Soon I made the First Team, was then made Captain, rode as Number One and won the prestigious *Bud Flanagan Trophy*. This meant a great deal to me, as Bud was a great star of Variety Theatre and a leading member of *The Crazy Gang*.

We celebrated the first anniversary of *Let's Get Laid*, which incidentally was also Victor's forty-sixth birthday, with drinks in the bar on Tuesday 2nd September. On Wednesday I had dinner with friends at *Rules* traditional English restaurant in Maiden Lane, where Lillie Langtry had been entertained by The Prince of Wales (Edward VII) in a private first floor room, and ate sublime jugged hare, whilst on Saturday 6th September Terry Denton and Andrea Godfrey did their final shows. All in all, quite a week.

The next piece of news was to make a dramatic change to my life, as Maris was now pregnant, and expecting a child in April 1976. For the time being I had to concentrate on getting Brian Marshal rehearsed and ready to take over from John Inman as Gordon Hardcastle. John's character of Mr.

Humphries in the BBC TV series *Are You Being Served?* had made him a huge household name, and he was much in demand. Brian began his week's rehearsals on 20th October for an opening night on Monday 3rd November, which went well. Brian was an up and coming young comedian, but had been in the business for a while as he came from theatre stock (his father was the Music Hall Comic Larry Dene) and we got on well together, and had a laugh or two, over a drink or two in *The Lyric Tavern* or at a club, post show. The Principals in the show were now Brian Marshall, Jenny Kenna, Kate Harper, Brian Godfrey, Danny O'Dea, and Tony Sweeny. Les Girls all swapped round a bit or had their character name changed for some unknown reason, and Jan Demiller joined us from *Pyjama Tops* to play Carla's role of Britt. This cast would remain unchanged for the rest of the run of the show.

Mr. Raymond celebrated his fiftieth birthday on Saturday 15th November, which none of us in the present Company were invited to, but I suspect Fiona and John were. November rolled over into December and the New Year without any dramatic differences to note, except without John and or Fiona the mid-week houses, especially the first house, looked down in attendance, which was confirmed by Box Office Manager Philip Guthrie. We all began to wonder how much longer we would be at The Windmill?

We still had some VIPs come to see the show, especially at weekends, and on one occasion Mr. & Mrs. Billy Smart (of the circus family dynasty) who were personal friends of P.R. came to see the show, and as it was a cold Winter night Mrs. Smart wore a tiger skin coat, which she asked us to look after during the show. It weighed a ton in my arms as I took it from her for safe keeping, and on closer examination I noticed that it was made of real tiger, I presume from some of the animals that once appeared in their circus.

One of the joys of working in the multi-cultural Soho of the '70s was the huge variety of trades, eating establishments, snack bars and clubs that flourished in the pre pink pound era. If I was peckish I would pop over the road to The *Nosh Salt Beef Bar* just opposite in Great Windmill Street for a hot sandwich with several slices of brisket and lashings of English mustard and a gherkin served on thick rye bread. This Bar was a Soho Institution, and open till 2am. What a late night treat.

During January 1976, we had both Kate Harper and Tony Sweeney on holiday, returning on Friday 6th February, but we struggled through and were thankful that no one went off sick during this period. Les Girls were susceptible to colds because they were flimsily dressed at times, and the actors union Equity was insistent that we maintained a temperature of 68 degrees during show time, which was difficult during a cold snap.

Maris was heavily pregnant, and from scans we knew it would be a boy, with his arrival expected over the weekend of 11th April. When he had not made an appearance on my arrival home after the show on Monday, arrangements were made for Maris to be admitted to University College Hospital the following day, to be induced.

I drove her to the hospital in the Ford Van and waited, and waited for baby to arrive and Julian Frank Toogood made a belated appearance at about 6pm on 13th April 1976, with mother, father and son, all fine. Naturally I had to take the night off from the show, the first time I had EVER missed a show. When my Deputy, Tom Cockrell rang me to see how things were, he informed me that the Notice had been posted to close the show, and I would be unemployed very soon. What a time to find yourself out of work, I thought to myself.

Act 3 Scene 3
HAPPY AS A SANDBAG
(1976)

I had celebrated the arrival of my son and heir to the Toogood dynasty in Greenwich, as the rest of my family were kept in Kings College overnight for observation and to ensure there were no after effects from the epidural. I met up with Tricia Courtney Martin who was living with Graham Phoenix in a comfortable flat near the indoor market. I got sloshed and Tricia had to drive me back home in the van as I needed it to pick Maris & Julian up the following morning. I had made a conversion in the back of the van to enable me to strap the top part of the pram we had bought to the van floor. Mission completed, I cycled into work to see what had been going on when I was away for just one night, and was pleasantly surprised to learn, when I read the full text of the Notice, that we had not been given the minimum two weeks, but were to close after the second show on Saturday 5th June 1976. I had hoped that I might be kept on for the new show, a dance show that was going to be called *Rip Off*, but that was not to be.

I began the search for a new job in the West End, as with a son to support touring was not the way of life I desired. I began to make contact with friends and colleagues who might know of something coming up, and answered advertisements in *The Stage*. Things were slow in town, as it was turning into the hottest, driest summer for years and shows were closing, not opening. "Just my luck" I thought as I worked the last eight weeks of *Let's Get Laid*. I was in for another shock when my last pay packet was given to me as it did not contain any redundancy money, which I was due having been in their employ for over two years. I was told by Accounts this was an oversight but did not believe them, as I think they were trying to get away with it as they assumed I was unaware of my rights. I was quite prepared to get Equity involved, as I had been engaged on an Esher Standard Contract, which had been converted to 'Run of the Play' engagement on 3rd September 1974. I had nothing to lose in pressing them for redundancy money, as they could have kept me on for the next show, but chose not to, and eventually they coughed up the money without me having to resort to a court case. I think I was the only person ever to be paid redundancy from the PR Organisation.

The first interview I attended was on Thursday 10th June, for the post of Production Manager at the newly built Churchill Theatre in Bromley. It turned out to be with the full Board of Directors, including the Labour Party activist, playwright and novelist, Lord Ted Willis, and was a bit of a disaster. Doing my pre-interview research I gleaned that this new theatre, built by the Council to replace the Little Theatre in North Street and run by David Poulson, was to seat 785 patrons on two levels, be very up to date technically with three separate stages that could be manoeuvred into place as required (very similar to Liverpool Playhouse) and was due to open the following year. I had decided I would record the interview on a portable tape recorder hidden in my large briefcase, which I took into the Boardroom, as I was keen to have some sort of record of the proceedings to help improve my interview technique. The questions were concentrated and fast, about what I had done and what I thought I could bring with me to this new theatre, when suddenly a loud 'buzzzzzzz' came from within the briefcase, as the tape had run out. I though very quickly, and apologised for my alarm clock going off during the interview, and like to think that I got away with it, but who knows? The questions continued and David, who knew Chris Bullock at Liverpool, had rung him to find out a bit about me, said: " So you don't suffer fools gladly I hear?", which took me completely off guard as it was not a phrase with which I was familiar. "Can you please explain the question to me again?" I asked, which he did, and again I fumbled out some sort of answer to the board, who were not impressed that I did not understand the initial question. After about 90 minutes of intense interview I was asked if I had any questions. I had prepared twenty or so in advance, and hoped that this section would save the day for me. I asked questions like: "Was it proposed to be a single or double purchase counterweight system with how many lines?" and "Where is the Get In going to be situated?" along with similar technical information that I wanted to know about as I have always believed an interview is a two way exchange of information to see if I like you, and you like me. These questions all fell on deaf ears as no one on the interview board could answer them and I was told to "Ask someone who knows about these things, as we don't know". I was not offered the post, and would have thought very hard about accepting it, if I had been, but at least the interview was useful experience.

Rip Off opened at the Windmill on 21st June 1975, but I did not expect to be invited, and wasn't. Friends who saw it was a larger version of what you could see at the *Revuebar*. I heard from a mutual friend I met in the bar of *The Buxton Club* that Griffith James, who was currently working on *Happy as a Sandbag* at the *Ambassadors Theatre*, was about to retire. I knew Griff because he was the current Chairman of the SMA and had been on the show since it opened on 10th September 1975, and was a most experienced West End Company Stage Manager of the old school, most polite, efficient and charming. I contacted The Producers London Plays Ltd., in Clifford Street about an interview to take over when Griff left. I received a favourable reply from their General Manager Anne Rawsthorne, and was invited to go and see the show on Wednesday 21st July.

I liked what I saw, met the staff and indicated that I would be interested in accepting the post, should I be offered it, which I was. I began a familiarisation week on Monday 26th July, received a letter confirming my appointment on 28th July from the Director of London Plays, Roger Clifford, stating that I would be on a run of the show standard Esher Contract and that my emolument was £60 per week, and that I would take over the show as Company Manager on Saturday 31st July 1976. This was a drop of £4 per week from my final salary at The Windmill, but on the plus side, it was for eight shows a week, not twelve.

I had been resting for eight weeks, and enjoying the Summer heat wave, which brought a few problems because of the subsequent drought. A hose pipe ban was imposed, and watering the allotment I had started in the communal garden, complete with a greenhouse, became a problem.

As the flat was on the third floor of a small block, I siphoned off all the used bath, sink, and washing machine water down a hundred foot long hosepipe and into a water butt at ground level. It was obvious that the ground was parched, as the only green showing in the back garden, leading down to the Lewisham to Hither Green railway line, was a straight line of lush grass below the washing line. I also constructed a hook ladder that would act as a means of escape in the event of fire, from the living room balcony up to the flat roof area where we could seek refuge.

Little Julian was putting on weight and was for the most part a good baby, but had to endure a disturbing religious practice very early in his life. Maris was Jewish, and offspring inherit the religion of their mother, so he had to be circumcised, by a Mohel in a ceremony called the Bris on his eighth day. I found it difficult to watch and grimaced throughout.

The new show was a 'Compilation Music Revue' of 54 songs from the war years which I was really looking forward to. On the front of the programme, under the ash from Churchill's cigar, it stated that it was 'all the fun of the forties', an era of music and comedy that I knew well.

The Author was Ken Lee whom I vaguely knew as he lived quite near my parents in uphill Lincoln with his wife Marie and their three children. The piece had first been produced at the Theatre Royal Lincoln in May 1972 where it had been directed by Clare Venables, so yet another connection with my home town. The Director was Philip Headley, who had also been at Lincoln between 1968-71, before becoming Artistic Director of Joan Littlewood's Theatre Royal Stratford East for twenty-five years. This particular production was presented by arrangement with The Watford Palace Theatre, from where it had transferred. David Fisher had designed the Scenery and Costumes, with lighting from the doyen of lighting designers Michael Northern, Choreography by Patricia Adams and the Musical Director was Nigel Hess, the great nephew of Dame Myra Hess (1890 – 1965).

I was hooked on the show as soon as I heard the opening number *Chattanooga Choo Choo*, with the ten members of the company in ranks onstage playing toy musical instruments to simulate the Glenn Miller Orchestra of 1941, and featured in his film Sun Valley Serenade, with members of the company taking the vocals of Tex Beneche, Marion Hutton, the Moderaires and Andrews Sisters, with Nigel playing leader and Trombonist Glenn.

We were also treated to a sketch from *It's That Man Again* (ITMA) with Tommy Handley, Colonel Chinstrap, Mrs. Mopp and the rest of the gang. Alvar Liddell, The Western Brothers, Lord Haw Haw, The Cheeky Chappie Max Miller (gags from the 'white book' not the 'blue one' of course), George Formby and that great Liverpool comic Robb Wilton and his *The Day War Broke Out* monologue were not forgotten.

Herr Hitler, Neville Chamberlain, Winston Churchill, Field Marshal Montgomery and Rommel also made cameo appearances and we were taught how to make a Molotov cocktail. Excerpts from the Terence Rattigan play *Flare Path*, and Noel Coward's *In Which We Serve* were also included, along with Moira Heath's song *Room 504*, the royalties from which had helped form the great Ted Heath Band in 1945. The highlight for many however, was to hear Mr. Hess re-create Dame Myra playing The Warsaw Concerto, a tribute to the many Polish forces fighting with the British, played in the style of Rachmaninoff, which she had made her own in the lunchtime concerts in The City of London to boost morale at the height of the Blitz in 1940.

All the Company were relatively unknown, and some would go on to better things, they were so talented, switching from one character to the next with the change of a hat, or costume. A recording of the whole show was made by Decca Records, which I still have and play. This was very much an ensemble piece of theatre with no one getting star billing, in fact it was done alphabetically. This fast moving and technical show was run immaculately by my DSM Richard Andrews, with whom I would remain friends for many years, assisted by ASMs Judy Hopton and Clive Flint, who would later be replaced in the run by Bill Stirland (but now working as Alan), with whom I had first shared my student digs in Westbury-on-Trym in September 1963, another connection from the past.

I brought Julian Frank (he was named after the first Stage Director I worked with in 1958, Julian Oldfield and his late Grandfather Frank Sharp) in to meet the Company after the mid-week matinée in mid August when he was about four months old, to discover that one of the Wardrobe Staff was an ex-midwife and she confirmed that his cranium was settling into place nicely. I knew The General Manager of The Ambassadors, George Cross, quite well as he had been the Touring Company Manager when Maris had been on tour with Bill Kenwright's production of *No Trams to Lime Street* by the Welsh playwright Alun Owen earlier in her career. He was kind enough to teach me one or two things about being a Theatre General Manager, which I hoped to become one day, and it was always a pleasure to share a glass or two of G & T with him on a Saturday night as we settled the Contra Account for the week. Never once did I have to write at the bottom 'agreed and signed under duress' which I had known happen to other Company Managers in the past. The Box Office Manager, Peggy Easton, was a sweetie in her small compact Box Office in the Foyer, and could get a 'doors house' in far faster with her pens and books of tickets than they can these days with computers and printers. Nor were there the dreaded 'doubles' as there is only one valid ticket, the one that you got from the box office, and if the seat was occupied on entry into the auditorium, then it was almost a foregone conclusion that the person was there on the wrong day, and thus easily rectified by Peggy.

We had a few small cast changes to deal with during September, and as the very hot Summer drifted into Autumn, the business began to drop off, so much so that we dropped below the break-even figure on two consecutive weeks, thus triggering the clause in the Contract permitting the bricks and mortar Management (the Ambassadors Theatre) to give the visiting management (London Plays Ltd.) notice to terminate the run of the show, which they did. We closed on Saturday 16th October 1976.

In the meantime however, prior to us having to vacate, Roger Clifford and all of the Company who still believed passionately in the show, were convinced that it still had life, and agreed they would all be willing to transfer, if a suitable venue in London could be found in time.

The plush seated but very underused *Westminster Theatre* in Palace Street SW1, close to Buckingham Palace, was found to be available and a transfer was immediately organised for an opening there on the Monday after we closed in The West End.

I immediately set about drawing up one of my very detailed transfer schedules, as it was going to be a tight call to be ready to open on the Monday 18th October. General Manager Anne Rawsthorne was most impressed, and said that she had never before seen such a comprehensive schedule and it was much admired and appreciated by everyone concerned. I was delighted when it all worked like clockwork, thanks to the experience that I had gained doing numerous Fit Up weekends in the past. The stay of execution was short lived however, as business did not pick up after the transfer, and we were there for only four weeks before the Notice went up again on Saturday 13th November to close two weeks later. The show was to tour, which I was invited to manage, but declined as we were planning to visit Canada early in 1977 to visit Julian's Grandma in Calgary, as she had not yet seen him.

The Theatre Chaplain, Edwin Young, came to see the show on the last Thursday and stayed on for our farewell party. I was given a beautiful handwritten letter from Roger, in copper plate calligraphy, saying how much he and Anne had appreciated the splendid way I had managed the production, and that the ease of the transfer to The Westminster was entirely due to the way I had co-ordinated the changeover. This letter concluded with the sentiment that I would be sadly missed on the tour, and a hope that I would work for them again. Sadly that never came to pass, but I retain the letter in my portfolio, should I ever need to accept the offer.

I sensed during November that I would be out of work again before Christmas, and thought that if you are ever going to get work, it had to be over Christmas. I had put out a few feelers to prospective Managements about Christmas work and received a favourable reply form David Gordon Productions, based in The Strand, on 24th November, just three days before we closed, offering me work at The Shaftsbury Theatre on their Christmas Panto. This meant I would be out of work for only a week, yet again proving that in this business in addition to 'it's not what you know but who you know' you also have to be available in the right place at the tight time, which I had been on this occasion, thank God.

Act 3 Scene 4
EMU IN PANTOLAND
(1976-77)

Initially I was rather reluctant to work for David Gordon Productions, which was the Production Company set up by Bill Kenwright, who had found fame playing Gordon Clegg in Coronation Street on TV in 1968-69, as he was regarded as a bit of a maverick in the business. However the dates of his Christmas Show at The Shaftesbury Theatre, *Emu in Pantoland*, dovetailed exactly with my plans, and when I saw the cast list I soon changed my mind, as it was quite mind blowing. I received my letter of appointment from General Manager Rod H. Coton, but it did not constitute a run of the show Contract between us, which would have implications later. Shortly after that the stars *Rod Hull & Emu* appeared on *The Parkinson Show* on Saturday 27th November with, amongst others, Billy Connolly. The 'Parkey Show' was at its height of popularity, and must see viewing on a Saturday night. An appearance on the show was regarded as a huge honour. Rod & his Emu took every opportunity to attack or annoy Michael and create as much havoc on the non-rehearsed show as possible, and thus boost interest at the box office for the Christmas show which was to open in three weeks' time on Saturday 18th December, scheduled for a run of eight weeks. Emu had attacked Parky because he had refused to stroke him, knocking him to the floor where they wrestled with each other and Emu pulled off one of Michael's shoes. It all ended with Michael getting back up onto his feet and muttering "that bloody Emu", but it worked wonders and David White, the Box Office Manager and his staff at the Shaftesbury were inundated on the Monday morning. We were able to open with a healthy advance at the Box Office for once.

The cast that was to support Rod & Emu read like a Who's Who of stars. That well-loved Cockney comedienne Irene Handl was to play Madam Purvis with Pat Coombs being thrilled to be reunited with Irene again as her daughter Nola. They had kept millions of us laughing on radio and TV in the fifties and sixties. Bob Todd, the star from countless comedy series, notably *The Benny Hill Show* on TV, was cast to play Dame Dotty Trott, whilst my old friend from *Lets Get Laid*, Victor Spinetti, would play the evil Wizard, and double as The Sheriff of Nottingham. It didn't end there either, as singing starlet Susan Maughan (of *Bobby's Girl* number one single fame) was to be Sleeping Beauty and Carl Wayne, the former lead singer with The Move, would play Prince Jack. The guest stars were to be the new TV Dance Group *New Edition*, with a number of stunning girl dancers, choreographed by Geoffrey Richer, who had started his career with The Young Generation, and they were now the resident dance group on TV's Seaside Special. A cast list to savour.

The show was to be directed by Brian Rawlinson, with settings from Saxon Lucas, costumes from Kay Gallwey and sound design by Dick Lock. Susan's Musical Director Danny Sandige was engaged to front the band in the pit. The team at the Shaftesbury was headed by Richard Schulman, with House Manager Robin Alexandar, Master Carpenter Jim Bragginton and Chief Engineer Stewart Grey, whilst Neville Humphreys was the Production Manager. We began rehearsals for a week in a room at the corner of Upper St. Martin's Lane and Long Acre at 10am. I arrived in plenty of time to mark out, thank goodness, as the room was a tip, and I was barely ready to greet them when the Company arrived. Alan Wallace, who I knew from my days at Lincoln, was now the West End Organiser for the Actors Union Equity, and it was his duty to check that members of the Company and Stage Management were all paid up members, and to deal with any problems that there were or likely to be. After the usual pleasantries he asked me about the Stage Management team that had been appointed for me by Neville and there was an immediate problem, as I had suspected there would be.

The minimum team under the Standard Esher Contract, which I was still to receive, for a show of this size was deemed to be three persons unless prior dispensation had been granted. Alan told me it hadn't been sought or given, so we were one short. I had met my ASM Vanessa Gee, but not a DSM who I would expect to run the show from the prompt corner. Alan decided that he had no option but to suspend rehearsals forthwith until a DSM had been appointed, which did not please the Director or the Company, who wanted to get on with it, but Alan's decision was firm and final. Lo and behold a DSM, Edmund Harris, arrived at lunchtime and rehearsals were able to commence that afternoon. During the week I attended a Production Meeting at The Shaftesbury to meet the staff and discuss the staffing requirement that was needed to run the show efficiently, and we immediately hit another problem. Jim's (Master Carpenter) proposals for Stage & Flys were acceptable, but Mr. Kenwright objected strongly to what Stewart (Chief Engineer) was proposing for the electrical department, although I thought it was in line with accepted West End custom and practice. Stewart proposed that he should have a floating role and thus be free as Chief Engineer to deal with any non-show related problems, such as the heating going off, or a major black out, but Bill was adamant he did not want that saying: "I'm not paying for someone to sit in their office and do nothing" which I thought was unreasonable and said so. In the end Bill reluctantly agreed to the proposal. This represented the second problem to come to a head and be solved in the first week and I hoped that this was not going to be a trend for the whole Christmas period, as I was working hard for my £67.50 per week salary.

As Production Manager Neville oversaw the arrangement for the Get In and Fit Up, whilst I was happy to concentrate all my efforts, as Company & Stage Manager, on the Treasury Call, dressing room allocation, time sheets, daily calls, and the Children in Entertainment paperwork - we were using children from The Barbara Speake Stage School - along with the hundred and one other things that needed to be done prior to opening night. We moved into the theatre which is situated at the far end of Shaftesbury Avenue from Eros, and seats 1,300, on Monday 13th December for the opening on the Saturday.

I did have a rather delicate matter to deal with, as soon as the rest of the Company arrived at the theatre. It concerned the delightfully dizzy Irene Handl who had a lap dog with her throughout rehearsals. In the Company Rules I had prepared and posted on the Stage Door notice board next to the Dressing Room list, it clearly stated that 'animals are not permitted backstage or in dressing rooms'. I had to tell her: "I'm sorry Miss Handl, but if I permit you to come into the theatre with your dog, then I am duty bound to permit others to do the same, which is not practical and could annoy others, I'm afraid to say." She claimed not to have seen the Company Rules, which I could understand, so I permitted the dog backstage and in her dressing room for the remainder of that day, on condition that it wasn't brought in again, which thankfully it wasn't.

As was becoming the custom now, my birthday on 17th December went uncelebrated, apart from a pint in the Stage Door local, where they played Julie Covington's pre show recording of *Don't Cry for me Argentina* constantly, and we opened to great acclaim the following day. Soon after we had opened yet another problem arose, this time with Carl Wayne who was constantly late for the half hour call which is traditionally made 35 minutes before Curtain up and half an hour prior to the Act One Overture and Beginners call. It is done to ensure that once the show starts all the Company have arrived, are safely in the theatre, and no understudy was needed for that show. With his limited stage experience (as far as I knew he had only done a short season with Josephine Baker at the London Palladium), he was under the impression that as long as he was there in time to go onstage for his first appearance, then that was acceptable, which it wasn't and I explained why. He was late again on 21st and 24th December, and I decided that enough was enough and reported the matter to his agent. He then began to arrive on time for the 'half' and twenty five years later, when we were doing a show together in Sheffield, he said to me over the footlights: "You were right, you know, to take me to task about arriving late for the half all those years ago" which was some consolation, even after 25 years.

On New Year's Eve afternoon, Bill asked me to try and organise a Company party at the Stage Door pub or hire a room at a nearby hotel, but they were not interested at such short notice. The lack of forethought summed up the Management in a nutshell.

I, like the rest of the Company, made our own arrangements to celebrate the arrival of 1977, but what would it bring I wondered? I knew for a fact that the show was due to close on Saturday 12th February, and I had a flight booked to Canada on holiday until 10th March, although after that my diary was blank. Then came the first problem of the New Year. Business had been so good that an extension to the run was announced and it would not now close as planned but go on till the end of the month. I explained that as I had still not been issued with a Contract, I was under no obligation to stay, especially as I had plane tickets booked, and intended to leave as planned. Bill said that he would get John Spradbury to come in and run the extra two weeks, which was fine by me, and I duly worked out the last few weeks of the show.

Before the curtain went up on one show towards the end of the run, I found Victor peeping through the house tabs and into the stalls: "Paul and Linda are in you know" he said, "Paul and Linda who?" I enquired. "Paul and Linda McCartney" he replied "They are my guests and sitting in the middle of G row. Look after them and bring then to the dressing room after will you please?"

"My pleasure Victor" I replied and did as I was asked. Victor knew The Beatles well as he had appeared in all their films over the years and they greeted each other like old mates when I eventually got them out of the auditorium and up to his dressing room.

This was a good way to end what had not been a very easy show to manage, and I got a very nice personal thank you letter from Susan Maughan who said 'Many thanks for your assistance during our lovely show, your tolerance has been unforgettable! Love Susan x" which again I have kept in my portfolio for employers to peruse.

This wasn't the end of the *Emu in Pantoland* saga however, as on my return from Canada, I was told that my replacement for the final two weeks John Spadbury, had paid the whole Company holiday money, to which they were not entitled!

Act 3 Scene 5
SIDE BY SIDE BY SONDHEIM
(1977-78)

I enjoyed my three week holiday in Canada, which wasn't too cold, thanks to the Chinook Winds. We made a trip up to the Scottish style baronial castle in the Rockies, the Banff Springs Hotel, which has graced the hillside for over one hundred and twenty five years, did a bit if cross country skiing, and drove up the boring Atlanta Highway for three hours to stay in Edmonton, where my old friend from the Lincoln Rep days Bill Fisher was now living.

I came back with a pair of Canadian snow boots, with the felt inner lining, which I wore to keep my feet warm and dry on the allotment for many years, as well as a rear wheel for my Cycle Speedway racing bike, as it had a Westrix Rim on it, which I had been after for ages. All the time I had been worried about where the next job was going to come from, as I was totally out of touch with things in the West End while I was in Calgary.

I returned to London on Wednesday 9th March and immediately began to look for a job in the West End as I had decided that touring the Number Ones was not for me anymore. At first prospects were slow coming, but then, as it sometimes happens, I found out about two possible jobs at the same time.

Richard Schulman, who ran the Shaftesbury Theatre for Chartergate Estates, and with whom I had got on well while working on Emu, had been so impressed with the way that I had handled the trickier parts of Management that he contacted me about *Rolls Hyphen Royce* (of Rolls-Royce Fame), a new show that would soon start at his theatre and starring Wilfrid Hyde-White in the title role. The play had been written by William Douglas-Home and was scheduled to open on Tuesday 10th May for an unlimited run, which sounded interesting, however I was not sure about a play being presented at The Shaftesbury, as I thought the venue was too big, and wondered how much of a draw Mr. Hyde-White would be since he last shot to fame as Colonel Pickering in the 1964 film *My Fair Lady*?

Almost a year before, in May 1976, my friend Helen Dufeu, who worked sound on many shows, had invited me to The Mermaid Theatre in Puddle Dock, where she was working on a new revue called *Side by Side by Sondheim*, which it was hoped would transfer to The West End.

It had started life when Cleo Laine and John Dankworth had approached David Kernan with the original title of *A Sondheim Songbook*. David was a well-respected actor/singer in West End shows including *1776*, *A Little Night Music* (where he played Count Carl-Magnus Malcolm), the film *Zulu* and the TV hit show, *That Was The Week That Was* (TW3). They wanted him to put on a musical revue and support their annual fund raising festival in The Stables at Wavendon, near Milton Keynes. David contacted Stephen Sondheim about the idea of a compilation revue of his songs, who said he could not think of anything more boring. David also got in touch with Ned Sherrin from TW3 who liked the idea, and Millicent Martin (again TW3) and with Julia McKenzie the show was born. A relatively unknown young Producer, Cameron Mackintosh, went to see the show, liked what he saw, thought it had potential and put it on (after several try outs) for eight weeks at The Mermaid, where I saw it.

I went backstage after the show with Helen and introduced myself to Mr. Sherrin (who I thought at the time was the Producer as well as the Narrator) and asked him if they might require a Company Manager when the show went to The West End. He advised me to get in touch with Cameron, which I did. The 'musical entertainment' *Side By Side by Sondheim* as it was now billed, had been a huge success at The Mermaid, and transferred to the West End at Wyndham's Theatre, opening on 7th July 1976. The co-producer was H.M. Tennent Ltd, which was now run by the ebullient West End producer Helen Montague, who had succeeded Hugh 'Binkie' Beaumont following his death in 1973, and with whom Cameron became close friends. Robert West (known to all as Uncle Bob) was promoted to become the Production Supervisor of the show. We met, got on well, and I was offered his former position of Company Stage Manager.

So here I was in the classic position of having two offers on the table, but which one should I choose? Should I go back to The Shaftesbury, where I was known, or go with this relatively unknown young Producer, whom I knew little about?

I pondered long and hard and drew up a sheet of advantages and disadvantages of each offer. After consideration, I chose to join up with Cameron Mackintosh on *Side By Side by Sondheim*, commencing on Monday 18th April.

I immediately informed Richard Schulman of my predicament and subsequent decision, which he understood, and wished me well with the show I had chosen instead of *Rolls Hyphen Royce*, but boy had I made the correct choice, because *Rolls* closed within a month of opening, and SBSBS was to become Cameron's first hit show. Had my instincts been right or was I just lucky? In retrospect I like to think the former.

My contract from H.M. Tennent Director Bernard Gordon was dated 18th April 1977, and was for run of the play at a salary of £75 per week for eight performances a week. There had been a compete cast change when I joined the show, as the original four of Millie, Julia, David and Ned had gone to Broadway to present the show at The Music Box Theatre. Hal Prince had persuaded British Actors Equity to allow the original West End Cast to transfer to Broadway, where they began Preview performances on the previous Wednesday 13th April with a Broadway opening night on the same day I joined the London show. The cast now comprised Maggie Fitzgibbon, Gay Soper, David Firth and Robin Ray, but the thirty classic Sondheim numbers remained the same as had been performed by the original cast.

Maggie was from Australia, where she had done a great deal of work and, as I was to discover on my nightly chats to her in her dressing room after the half, was a keen gardener. Gay had appeared in many shows in town, such as *Canterbury Tales*, *Godspell*, and *Billy* (starring Michael Crawford) at the Lane in 1974, where she played Barbara, one of Billy's girlfriends, alongside Diana Quick and Elaine Paige. David was a well-respected actor and performer having played three seasons with the Royal Shakespeare Company and two at The National. He had recently played Nicholas Nickleby in the Ned Sherrin/Caryl Brahms Musical *Nickleby and Me* at The Theatre Royal Stratford East, where it was well received but did not move on, much like Liberty Ranch (by the same authors) had done during my time at Greenwich in 1972. Robin was the eldest son of Liverpool comedian Ted Ray and had trained at The Royal Academy of Dramatic Art (RADA) before going into *Beyond the Fringe* at The Fortune Theatre. He presented the popular BBC TV Show *Face The Music* and had just had his first book *Time for Lovers* published.

The concept of the 'The Musical Entertainment' was simple, and had been proved to work. The Narrator Robin would introduce a series of numbers from a Sondheim show, for example *A Funny Thing Happened on the Way to the Forum*, *Gypsy*, *A Little Night Music*, *Company* or *Follies*, which were performed in turn by Maggie, Gay and David. Two pianists sitting at grand pianos onstage would accompany them. The only other things onstage in Peter Docherty's simple setting were four bar stools for the singers to perch on during the introduction. Simple, but elegant costumes were supplied by Gina Fratini (later Jane Caitlin) and John Wood had lit the show. The Musical Director was Ray Cook, who had been Musical Director for *A Little Night Music* at The Adelphi and thus knew David Kernan and Mr. Sondheim, whilst my Stage Management team consisted of Tim Spence Brown as DSM and Magda Taylor as ASM. Helen Dufeu was still on sound and Ros Bailey looked after the Wardrobe. Notable members of the staff at Wyndham's, which was owned by Sir Donald Albery (knighted earlier in the year) with his very efficient son Ian Albery as the Deputy Managing Director, were Harry Pegg (Supervisory Master Carpenter) and Stan Coppin (Chief Engineer).

Harry's favourite test was to place a used cigarette butt in the space where the Safety Curtain would drop into and so be just out of sight. "Stage been swept?" he would ask the Chargehand. "Yes Harry" would come the reply. "What's this then?" he would inquire as he walked to where he knew he had hidden the butt. "Sorry Harry, must have missed it earlier", would come the reply.

I was soon into the routine I liked, mornings and afternoons working the allotment, tinkering with the bikes (I now had an Eddy Merckx replica road bike for my daily commute to and from the show), a bite to eat before I left at 6pm to be showered and in the dinner suit for the half at 6.55 pm. After the show, unless I was going out to dinner, most of us would go to the nearby Round Table pub to meet up with fellow thespians. Mine host Des Tate, with his charming wife and son, who also supported Liverpool FC, were most hospitable. The General Manager from The Strand Theatre, John Hollingshead and his wife, could be found there most evenings, as they lived in a flat just round the corner in Charing Cross Road. *No Sex Please We're British* was the resident show at the Strand and David Jason, who had taken over from Michael Crawford in the lead role, would often accompany him. I spoke to David about a new TV show he was doing in which he was going to be riding a Motor Cycle and Sidecar, and we shared our common interest.

SBSBS was about as far removed as you can imagine from many of the shows I had been managing for the past few years as not only was it a quality show of the highest order, but with a payroll of only eleven people it was a piece of cake compared to the payrolls of fifty I had experienced on *Peter Pan* for example. We did not have understudy calls to worry about either as Garthe Bandell was engaged as Standby, which was a first for me, but he never had to go on.

I was not a huge fan of Sondheim's work when I joined the show, although I did know several of the songs, for example *Comedy Tonight*, *If Momma Was Married*, *Send in the Clowns*, *You Gotta Have a Gimmick*, and the duet from *West Side Story*, but soon got to know and admire his genius with songs from shows that were new to me like *Evening Primrose*, *The 7% Solution*, *Anyone Can Whistle*, *The Mad Show*, *Pacific Overtures*, *Company* and *Do I Hear a Waltz?*

Follies became my favourite show without doubt, and most performances I would come down from my office (which was a large Dressing Room) to stand in the Prompt Corner and enjoy *Broadway Baby*, *Losing My Mind*, *I'm Still Here*, and *Could I Leave You?*

These are songs I still love to hear, and request them on a regular basis when I get in touch with Jonathan Parker who co-hosts the Musicals Request Show *Westenders* every Sunday evening on BBC Radio Lincolnshire.

Mr. Sondheim himself came to see the show one night soon after I had joined to see how the new cast had settled in now the show was firmly established on Broadway, and I naturally met up with him at the interval. "Ten o'clock call tomorrow morning please John", he requested in an off-putting way. "Can I tell the Company why please, Stephen?" I asked. "Sure" he replied. "[name of artiste] changed an 'and' to a 'but' in [name of song] in Act One. When I wrote that song it took me half an hour to decide to use 'and' not 'but' so we need to rehearse it and get it right." That was how meticulous and protective the man was.

Side by Side by Sondheim (1977-78) Act 3 Scene 5

On the evening of Wednesday 25th May, Liverpool was playing in the final of The European Cup for the first time in the Stadio Olimpico Rome and won the match 3-1. Liverpool played in their all red strip, whilst the opposition Borussia Monchengladback wore all white. Goals from number 11 Central Midfielder Terry McDermott, number 4 Centre Back Tommy Smith and number 2 Right Back Phil Neal, put the smile on Captain Emlyn Hughes's face as he held the trophy aloft for the first of five victories in this, the biggest Club Match of the year.

We had about six pianists who played onstage with the Company including Neil Rhoden, Michael Hyatt, Tim Higgs, Stuart Pedlar and an old friend of mine Bunny Thompson who I had employed as a rehearsal/audition pianist many times in the past. As we were such a small, intimate Company, they too became part of the family. They gathered in the Green Room during the Saturday interval, and discussed what was on the menu for Sunday lunch or play party games, whilst I was FOH taking comments from members of the public, or dealing with a problem. Robin, who was a great leader, instigated most of the games, many of which began life at Highgate School where he had been a pupil.

On occasions he would pose music questions, and once we were talking about the Jazz Singer Etta James and her recording of the song *At Last* and he asked who had composed it? With my interest in Jazz, I said: "I am pretty sure it was the great Harry Warren." Impressed, he asked: "How do you know that?" I explained about my lifelong interest in Jazz, and from that day forward, we got on like a house on fire.

Sundays were taken up with driving to Cycle Speedway meetings all over the Southern Counties, as I was now Captain of the First Team. I had converted a roof rack into a bike rack holder to take my two racing bikes with me, keeping the inside of the van free for all my emergency tools etc. If I didn't have a Cycle Speedway meeting, I would go to a Grass Track meeting somewhere, work on the vegetable plot, where I was growing up to thirty different types of vegetables or visit friends. Life was full but above all fun.

In mid July we found out that Maris was pregnant again, due in March 1978. As the current flat had only two bedrooms, I had to think about moving into a bigger property, a three bed roomed house this time, and began a search. I eventually found Mount Pleasant Lodge on the borders of Hither Green SE13, which needed a lot of work doing before we could move in.

We also had some cast changes with Jill Martin and Julia Sutton replacing Maggie and Gay along with Eric Flynn who replaced David. Robin remained as the Narrator and anchor man, but was now given 'box billing'. When he had the odd night off Russell Harty would cover for him.

The ASM Magna Taylor also moved on and I invited my old friend from the Peter Pan tour Alex Alec-Smith to replace her, from Monday 7th November, which she was delighted to do.

The work on 104, Mount Pleasant Road was extensive, and the first problem occurred when the Surveyor couldn't get into the loft to inspect the roof purlins and other support timbers. I duly opened an access hatch near the bathroom and found out why. It became obvious that the house had been involved in a fire, as many of the timbers were charred. Well at least that solves any woodworm problems, I thought.

I also wanted a chimney breast removed from a room I planned to make into the kitchen, which went right up through the bathroom, and exited the roof at the rear of the triangular site.

The two main living rooms were divided by a brick wall that I wanted removed, to make one large ground floor area, but was the wall load bearing and would an RSJ be required, I wondered? I took up floorboards at first floor level to check which way the joists ran, and thankfully they did not rest on this wall, so it wasn't load bearing, so no need for an RSJ.

The house was devoid of any heating and hot water came via an Ascot heater, so I got an estimate for full central heating, which when it arrived was way beyond my budget. How could I do the job for a lot less? I decided I would set about designing and installing a system myself, and raided the local library for any books on DIY central heating and how to go about it. The first thing was to work out the volume of each room and how many thermal units would be need to heat them to seventy degrees, and also fill a hot water cistern. By adding all these room thermal units together, plus what was needed for the cistern, I was able to determine what size boiler would be required. I then worked out what size radiator I wanted for each room, bearing in mind things like the height from floor to window sill, doors, party walls etc. The large ground floor Living Room was a headache, because of its huge volume and triple bay windows to the front and conservatory doors on one side, so I opted for a fan heater, which ran off the main boiler system, which was to be in micro bore for ease of installation and speed.

The outside garden was a rubbish tip and the garage was roofless. What had I let myself in for? And these were just the big jobs. Fortunately I found and purchased some second hand radiators from a block of flats that was being demolished nearby, and brought them back in my van, but getting the old rusted on valves out was a nightmare. After soaking them overnight in penetrating oil, I found the best way was to fit a large King Dick adjustable wrench onto the nut, and with a four foot long scaffolding pole extension for extra leverage, tighten the nut a little to break the seal then lever it back and forth a bit, then a bit more, and so on until the old fitting was out of the radiator.

I was, of course, still working the eight shows on SBSBS to pay for all this, from my earnings of £75 per week, and was thankful for all the builders, engineers, and carpentry tools that I had inherited from Dad to work with, but there was also a venue move to contend with on SBSBS.

The run at Wyndham's Theatre ended after the second show on Saturday 1st October 1977 after 518 performances and moved just a few hundred yards down Charing Cross Road to The Garrick Theatre, which had a slightly smaller capacity. We opened on Tuesday 4th October.

The General Manager at the Garrick was James Lytton, the Box Office Manager was John Cliff, the Master Carpenter was Ian Hesketh and the House Electrician was Colin Whilier, who dabbled in politics in his home town, from where he commuted.

We had several VIP visitors come to see the show at the new venue. There was an incident one evening in November which resulted in the General Manager having a heart attack and needing to be replaced by John Adrian on 5th December.

Meanwhile we had exchanged contracts on the house and I was able to start work proper on 6th November. I drew up a list of things to be done before the arrival of the new baby in five months. To meet this deadline I engaged a local builder, George Dashper, to take the old chimney down, as I do not have a good head for heights, along with Bill Whitnell to do the odd carpentry job, which I could not tackle, and Steve Smith a local painter and decorator. Meanwhile I removed the dividing wall downstairs and spent hours in the loft, with a facemask on, clearing out charred debris from the fire. This was before the days of mobiles, so for safety, I used to leave a message on the van windscreen that said: "If this van is still parked here at 5pm then I am trapped inside the loft at 104 Mount Pleasant Road", but luckily that never happened.

There was no way that I could work eight shows a week, deal with problems at The Garrick (fortunately there were few), and install a new heating/hot water system by March, when baby was due. I therefore made the executive decision that we would keep the house warm with a number of strategically placed paraffin heaters for the first few months. Once the chimney breast had been removed, I was able to plaster the wall, a job I hate as I always want to do just one more finishing stroke with the float when I should just leave it. I could also start making a kitchen as the gas stove was connected so we could now cook. We moved from the Morley Road flat to Mount Pleasant Road on Monday 19th December, and I had planned it like a Fit Up weekend so that I could work the show on the evening of the move, which happened according to plan. James (Jimmy) Lytton sadly never recovered from the heart attack he had suffered, and I attended his funeral, on behalf of the visiting management, on Friday 23rd December. Christmas was a rather quiet affair, as was the New Year, but I wondered what 1978 would bring in both my domestic and working life, and I didn't have to wait long to find out.

SBSBS closed in New York on Sunday 19th March at The Morosco Theatre where it had transferred to, and Maris went into labour nine days later. I took her to Kings again and stayed with her all night, grabbing a bit of sleep on the floor, wrapped in the winter jacket I had brought back from Canada, and she gave birth to a girl the following day, Wednesday 29th March, who we named Rachel Louise. Her mother chose her first name, as it is a good old-fashioned Hebrew name, whilst I chose Louise, after the character I had seen in a recent production of Carousel.

I took them both to Mount Pleasant Lodge, to join my mother who had come to look after Julian, and went into work as usual, only to find that the Notice had gone up and the show was due to close on Saturday 8th April. It had happened again. I take a night off for the birth of one of my offspring, and the closure Notice goes up.

Act 3 Scene 6
THE UNVARNISHED TRUTH
(1978)

I was now a big Stephen Sondheim fan after my time on SBSBS and I realised that this young producer Cameron Mackintosh had a good eye for a quality show, and should go far. I didn't have time to reflect further as we were now a family of four with a mortgage to pay and a half habitable house, so I began working on my contacts and getting in touch with new Production Companies which might need the services of an experienced West End Company Manager. Fortunately, I was in luck.

The Cambridge Theatre Company (CTC) had been on tour with a new farce, *The Unvarnished Truth*, and it was coming into town at The Phoenix Theatre. The Producer was to be Michael Codron, one of the many people I had contacted, and I met Production Manager Joe Scott Parkinson, who offered me the post of Company Stage Manager commencing on Monday 10th April. I received my Contract from General Manager David Sutton on 3rd April and read that I was employed on the new Equity minimum rate of £90 per week, which was the same rate I had been on before. That meant I would go from one show to the next without a break. How lucky was that, or being in the right place at the right time again? Joe introduced me to Michael, who at the time was the Senior Impresario in town and one of the old school, who told me that he had checked me out with Cameron and that I was OK. The deal was that the current Stage Management Team would run in the show in at The Phoenix, as they knew it backwards before I, my DSM and two ASM's took over.

The CTC Deputy Stage Manager was Fern Britton, whom I vaguely knew as she was the daughter of that wonderful actor Tony Britton, who just happened to be working at The Comedy Theatre on *Murder Amongst Friends* at the same time. I got on well with her and fifteen years later, when she was a presenter for a London Television Company, came to cover the weekly developments of the refurbishment at The Prince Edward Theatre. She dubbed me 'Mr. One-take' as I would relate to her what had happened since her last visit, in just the one take.

Fern, who was to be replaced at the end of the opening period by my DSM Pauline Gaunt, ran the show from the Corner on the opening night, Thursday 13th April (which was Julian's second birthday) and had a major moment just prior to the Interval. At the end of Act One the stage had several bodies lying all over it, and a very quick House Curtain drop was required to end the Act, and let the actors get off the stage. Despite Fern cueing the Fly-man as required, nothing happened and the Tabs did not come in, so she did what every experienced DSM does, she called for a blackout which did happen thank goodness. This upset her so much, being her West End debut, that I understand she went straight round to see her father in his dressing room at The Comedy after the show had finished, and broke down in tears fearing that she had let the family name down and that her career would be in ruins because of an error, albeit not of her doing.

A rather eccentric thespian Royce Ryton, who also played the part of Bill Carlisle, had written the play, but the two leads were Tim Brooke-Taylor and Graeme Garden, who with Bill Oddie were collectively known as *The Goodies*, along with fellow actress from the Cambridge Footlights Revue Jo Kendall. The plot of the piece revolved around Tom (Tim) and Annabel (Jo) who are a happily married couple living in Tom's Cottage in Thames Ditton. One evening, in the present, they discuss who loves who the most, a rough and tumble ensues, and Tom discovers to his horror that Annabel is dead. So begins an evening of farce with all the traditional chasing up and down stairs, people coming in and out of numerous doors, but with the added twist that anyone who comes to this cottage, finishes up accidentally dead. This gives the lead character every excuse to throw copious numbers of buckets over these bodies in an attempt to revive them. All this may sound fun, and certainly was for the audience, but it was a major headache for us on the SM Team, as after each performance all the water on the stage carpets had to be removed with the aid of mops, buckets and a carpet cleaner, which when operated in reverse would suck up most of the water. Also, as everyone was soaking at the end a second set of costumes was required, especially on a Matinée day, when there was no time for them to be dried out.

Jonathan Lynn, who would later go on to find fame with Anthony Jay, writing for *Yes Minister* two years later in 1980, directed the play in a setting by Robin Archer with lighting by Michael J. Ryan, none of whom I knew. I did however know some of my SM Team and some of the Phoenix Staff, as my two ASMs were Tricia Martin, ex Bristol, Liverpool and Greenwich, and John Guest, ex Liverpool, whilst Master Carpenter Jack Tripp had also trained at BOVTS, so my ways of working, and playing, were known to some.

The take-over happened smoothly and we said our farewells to the CTC Team, who went their different ways, and we all settled into our new daily/nightly routines. Unlike SBSBS there were Matinées that interrupted my daily work on the house, but I pressed ahead installing the central heating, which was proceeding according to plan.

Mr. Codron was very specific about how he wanted the figures each day, and I would ring him at home to inform him, or the call would be taken by a telephone answering service if he was unavailable.

It had to be given in a certain order: 'nightly' or 'daily' take, 'advance' taken on that day, and the 'carry forward' figure, along with a word or expression to relate to how the show had been received. I drew up a list of about half a dozen of these words or expressions, which varied from 'Disappointing' or 'Well Received' up to 'Ecstatic' to summarise the show for him. As I was still cycling into work most days, I would hand deliver the returns to his office in Regent Street. I had to climb over the metal railings by standing on the cross bar of my bicycle, as they were six feet high and securely padlocked, and post them in the letterbox to ensure they were there first thing in the morning. This West End detour was a bit of an inconvenience, but I like to think it put me in his good books as the other Company Managers he employed would post the Return and show report to him. That meant it did not usually arrive the following day, unless one caught the midnight post from Trafalgar Square Post Office. On the odd occasion I used it, the Post Office was full of Showmen taxing their multi trailer show trains for their move the next day before the licence expired.

We were a happy Company at The Phoenix. It was a typical '30s theatre which had opened with Noel Coward's *Private Lives* on 7th September 1930, and had seen many successful shows over the past forty eight years. Since 1967 it had been run by ex ballet dancer Veronica Flint-Shipman, the wife of owner Gerald, who was Chairman of Impact Quadrant Films. Their General Manager was John Sykes. During the run, there was an incident which necessitated the show being stopped, and Mr. Sykes came sheepishly onstage to make the announcement: "Ladies and Gentlemen, owing to circumstances beyond our control we unfortunately have to stop the show at this point. Please remain seated and we will re-commence as soon as it is practical and safe to do so." I vowed that if I ever had to stop a show I would not make a sheepish entrance, but make the announcement with some authority to indicate that I was in charge and everything was under control.

Another member of the Staff was the backstage cat Gus (Asparagus was too long for him) and like his companions Beerbohm (Globe now Gielgud), Ambrose (Theatre Royal Drury Lane), Bouncer (Garrick), along with Goomey & Percy (Aldwych) knew every nook and cranny in their respective theatres. Goomey & Percy had been brought in to work as a pair following the closure of the market in Covent Garden, causing an influx of mice. Most backstage felines are frustrated Thespians, and love to make an appearance, but woe betide you if you do. A visit to the bar in the interval is usually permitted, but Percy regarded it as one of his duties to be in the Circle Bar of the Aldwych at 6.30pm to welcome playgoers to his theatre. These essential members of any theatre are held in such high esteem that when poor Beerbohm passed on to the big theatre in the sky, it warranted a front-page obituary in The Stage, with many mourners at the wake in the Stage Door local.

I had my office at the Phoenix near to the Stage Door, and in addition to the usual office paraphernalia I had invested in a small portable television to watch before and after the show while I was changing in or out of my cycle gear. The weekly Kenny Everett Video Show broadcast by Thames Television was essential viewing. Kenny's fertile mind created such characters as Sid Snott, the lecherous Frenchman Marcel Wave and Mr. Angry of Mayfair, all played in 'the best possible taste', as Mr.E. would say. The real reason to watch the Kenny Everett show was to see the raunchiest dance troupe ever, *Hot Gossip,* dance to the latest pop record release and push the boundaries of respectability to new limits with their risqué routines.

Sundays were mostly taken up with Cycle Speedway Racing travelling all over Kent, Essex, Sussex and the Home Counties, when away meetings came up in the fixture list. Now the weather was improving, I felt able to get started on some work outside, rebuilding the garage, putting down a lawn, making a gazebo, planting shrubs, making a sandpit, laying a new concrete floor, which I adorned with the Prince of Wales feathers motif before it set and building a brick wood burner and barbeque.

To help with the food budget, because the garden was in no state to grow vegetables, I agreed to maintain the garden of an elderly neighbour in exchange for the use of part of her garden as an allotment and her large greenhouse. This was a lot of additional hard work, but free, and I kept all that I grew, and any surplus I would blanch and then deep freeze until it was required. It did not go down too well with her however, when I cut back her vine that had been trained to run into the greenhouse and bear fruit, to make extra room for my vegetable growing in the greenhouse, but we settled our differences when I gave her a box or two of fresh produce, straight from the ground.

On 21st June there was great excitement on the other side of Charing Cross Road in Soho, where the new Musical by Andrew Lloyd-Webber and Tim Rice was opening at the newly named Prince Edward Theatre. It was of course Evita, which made a star out of the relatively unknown Elaine Paige overnight, and little did I know that I would be the General Manager of that theatre in Old Compton Street only eight years later. We were now well and truly into the routine of mopping up after each show. The original Wardrobe Mistress Irene Hardman, a good old fashioned trooper from Manchester who lived in a nice flat in Soho, where she and her husband were most hospitable for a nightcap, had left the show on Saturday 17th June to be replaced on the Monday by Eve Barnes.

On Sunday 25th June there was a four-a-side Cycle Speedway meeting at Thurrock, which I was not involved in, so we had a housewarming party at Mount Pleasant Lodge with the many friends that we had made over the years. We listened to some big band Jazz on the new record system that I had installed, with speakers in both the front room and the much larger living room with the conservatory and kitchen adjacent. It was the perfect house for entertaining as it allowed movement between rooms, into the garden via the conservatory and back into the house through the kitchen door. Perfect.

I had by now put a new roof on the garage, cut a side entrance into it with a hired brick saw, and installed an up and over drive in door onto the street. For added security along the side street wall, which could have been easily climbed, I erected a six-foot high link fence, which ivy was by now growing through.

We celebrated our hundredth performance of *Unvarnished Truth* in the West End on Saturday 8th July and were all invited to a reception given by Royce and his wife Morar Kennedy, whom he adored. Susan and Tony had returned to this country with Joanna and Katy the day before and had gone to the Cotswolds to find a house near to Tony's work with British Leyland in the Midlands. We would catch up with each other soon after.

We were a very sociable Company and on Sunday 20th August, Jo Kendall (who played Annabel) and her husband David Collings had an open house party at their well-appointed home. In addition to the Company many of her, Tim's and Graeme's Cambridge Footlights Revue friends were in attendance and it was here I first met Barry Cryer. Leeds born Barry had worked with Tim and John Junkin on *Hello Cheeky!* and we had a long chat about some of the great Northern Comics such as Norman Evans, Arthur Askey, Ted Ray and the living legend Ken Dodd. He also knew what Liverpool 'keks' were!

On Sunday 3rd September I had the opportunity to hear some live big band Jazz again, which I had missed as I had been so preoccupied with work and making the house habitable. The *Crissy Lee All Girls Big Band* was playing at a pub in Blackfen, and as I had heard a lot about them, I went along to see and hear them. Crissy had been playing drums since the age of four, and was recognised as one of the top female drummers in Europe, having supported The Beatles on the Spanish leg of their tour. She had been praised by 'Traps' himself, the 'king showman' drummer Buddy Rich. She had joined *Ivy Benson's All Girl Band* in 1960 in The Isle of Man, where they had a residency, but left to form her own band as The Beatles and Rolling Stones were storming into the charts. In later years she was to find TV fame as the drummer of the *Skinnerettes* when she took over from Ronnie Verrel on the Frank Skinner Chat Show. The sound from this seventeen piece band was nothing short of sensational from the moment they began with Sammy Nestico's fine arrangement of Gershwin's *Strike Up The Band* to their closing number. Crissy was a fine leader and dynamic driving force behind her Pearl kit. I supported the band for many years, and tried to persuade the Producer of *Some Like it Hot* (when I worked on it at The Prince Edward Theatre in 1992) that this band, comprised as it was of only female musicians as in *Some Like it Hot*, would be ideal to play at the Opening Night Party, but in the end Mark Furness opted for a trio. The band contained many multi-talented soloists, among them Annette 'Sox' Brown on the trumpet and flugelhorn, who could blow a mean horn like Harry James. Along with many of the other band members, she had joined the band via The National Youth Jazz Orchestra (NYJO) which was, and still is, such a fertile breeding ground for young musicians. It is reassuring to know that the future of Big Band Swing is safe in their hands.

A night of listening to live big band Jazz again revived my interest, not that it had ever been far removed, and I began to seek out other Jazz Bands and Venues in South East London that were relatively easy to get to on my Sunday night off, but they were few and far between. Meanwhile, back in the West End, I noticed from the returns I received from Box Office Manager Derek Bessey that the show was in decline, and I wondered how much longer we would be at The Phoenix. Lo and behold on Saturday 21st October the dreaded Termination of Run Notice was posted. A transfer to another venue was mooted, but nothing came of it, and we closed on Saturday 4th November after a run of 30 weeks and 236 performances.

On the Thursday before the final show Michael invited us all as a thank you to a meal at Mon Plaisir, a French Restaurant in Monmouth Street which I knew well, as I had dined there before when entertaining. It had a wonderful reputation then, and I believe still does, and is the oldest French Restaurant in London. It serves the very best of traditional fare and wines, nothing fancy, just French cuisine at its best, which I love. They offer a simple menu with choice from either Gratinée à l'Oingon or Escargot au Beurre, followed by Cuisse de Canard or Filet de Plie Florentine finishing with either Crème Brûlée or Fromage.

I had been the last to arrive, making sure that the Company and Staff, all of whom had been invited, had left the theatre and The Stage Door pub, to be met by a rather stern looking Mr. Codron. He said that when he threw a party everyone was expected to be there. It was obvious from some empty chairs that some people had just gone home without telling me, which was most embarrassing, and had put me in Michael's bad books. I never allowed this to happen to me again on the subsequent shows I managed for him. We parted on good terms after the meal and he said: "I had heard that you were rather too business-like to have a good time, but I am pleased to see that you can let your hair down." I replied: "Michael, there is a business and a playful side to me, depending on the circumstances."

I felt that on the whole I had acquitted myself well working for the, at times, very demanding Michael Codron, but as it was to prove later, I was good enough to be invited to manage other shows for him in 1980 and 1981, but what was I to do now that we were a family of four with a still unfinished house to live in, and a crippling mortgage to pay?

Act 3 Scene 7

PETER PAN WITH JANE ASHER

(1978-79)

No sooner had the notice been posted on 21st October, confirming my worst fears that I would soon be out of work again, than I was in touch with my old friends at Tom Arnold Presentations, as I had heard that *Peter Pan* was going into The Shaftesbury Theatre for the Christmas Season. I asked if they required the services of an experienced Company Manager, and I was told that they did. This was a good move as I knew both the Management and show from the previous tours that I had done with them in '72-73 and '73-74, as well as the Theatre Staff and Management at The Shaftesbury from '76-'77 when I had managed Emu there. It looked like things were falling nicely into place again, being in the right place at the right time, and on 3rd November 1978, the day before I finished at The Phoenix, I received a Contract from Production Manager Stephen Mitchell confirming my appointment for seven weeks, at £115 per week. The show would commence on Monday 27th November for twelve shows a week (which was above the Equity minimum), with an opening night scheduled for Wednesday 20th December. I was happy with the deal as I had at last broken the £100 per week barrier. I had three weeks off before rehearsals commenced in which I planned to visit Susan and her new family and introduce her children to mine, as they were nieces and nephews after all.

We set off to visit Susan and her girls on the Tuesday after the show closed, with the Anglia piled to the gunwales with the hundred and one things which a young family needs to survive. We arrived at the Goodwell Poultry Farm near Stratford upon Avon, which was their temporary home until they found something they liked in Worcestershire. The youngsters got on well together, we all got to know each other, and had a pleasant time.

Following our stay at Susan's all eight of us, Tony, Susan, Joanna, Katy, Julian, Rachel, Maris and me set off to visit Mum and Dad in Lincoln, as it was her sixty first birthday on 11th November, and this was their first opportunity to meet all four of their Grandchildren. Where everyone slept I have no idea, but I do recall Julian splashing around in the enamel bath with the three girls and we all had an enjoyable, if at times hectic, break.

I returned to London to continue with work on the house and to prepare for what would be my third, but not last, production of *Peter Pan*. There were a few changes to contend with, both with the producing management and at the receiving theatre. The co-producers with Tom Arnold Presentations were Howard & Wyndham and Elyot Beaumont.

At The Shaftesbury the new owners were Cooney-Marsh under the direction of Brian Rix, and Richard Schulman was retained as General Manager. I had worked on Emu with him but turned down his offer to work on the Wilfrid Hyde-White show *Rolls Hyphen Royce* in 1977. Jim Braggington was still Master Carpenter and Stuart Grey was Chief Engineer, both of whom I got on well with.

The cast was headed by Jane Asher as Peter and Nigel Patrick as Mr. Darling/Hook, supported by Sheila Mathews as Mrs. Darling and Tony Sympson as Smee. Jane was the fiftieth actress to play Peter on the London stage, following in the footsteps of Fay Crompton, Phyllis Calvert, Pat

Kirkwood, Sylvia Syms, Millicent Martin, Dorothy Tutin, Maggie Smith and Susannah York. Nigel was in equally esteemed company as previous Captain Hooks since 1904 had included Gerald du Maurier, Ralph Richardson, Charles Laughton, Alastair Sim, Donald Wolfit, Donald Sinden, and Ron Moody.

The SM Team were all new to me, and consisted of DSM Janet Seager with Sarah Whiting and Alyson Green as my ASMs. Bob Williams was our Master Carpenter, who organised and supervised the Get In and Fit Up along with my old friend Rene Hardman as Wardrobe Mistress, a team I was happy with. Alan Pinniger was to direct this Robert Helpmann Production, as he had been Robert's assistant on the original show, along with Choreography by Aubrey Budd, Lighting by Brian Harris, with Derek Taverner in the pit. It was a good experienced team.

Rehearsals started for the dancers and pirates at The Concert Artistes Association in Bedford Street on Monday 4th December, whilst the Get In took place at The Shaftesbury, and all went smoothly according to plan. We moved into the theatre the following Monday ready for a Press Call, organised by Rosa Heppner on Wednesday 13th, leading up to technical rehearsals on Monday 18th followed by a full Dress Rehearsal the following day for an opening on Wednesday 20th December, as per schedule. I felt fully in control of things, with the Treasury Call, understudy calls, time sheets, all well within my capabilities, but there is always something that you have no control over.

I spent Sunday 17th (my thirty fourth birthday) at home with the family and a few friends, and heard on the news that an IRA car bomb had exploded at 01.22 hrs on the Monday morning in Central London, which I thought no more about, as these were, unfortunately, regular occurrences, and went to bed. In the morning however, more details were released and to my horror I discovered that the car had been parked outside the Shaftesbury Theatre and I wondered what damage had been caused. Additional information from Reuters and ITN indicated that the yellow car used was a hire car, which had been completely demolished to twisted metal by a thirty pound bomb, intended to damage a nearby government building.

I cycled into the West End as quickly as I could, as we had a technical rehearsal scheduled for 10am, and I needed to know what the situation was. On my arrival in Endell Street (I used to cut through Covent Garden once over Waterloo Bridge) there was a Police cordon preventing access to the bomb damaged area. Somehow, dressed as I was in full cycling gear, and wearing a helmet, I managed to convince the officer who I was, and the urgency of my visit to The Shaftesbury.

On my arrival in High Holborn I saw for myself the remains of what had once been the car, and was deeply shocked. I met General Manager Richard Schulman and asked if we were going to be able to open on time? "Of course dear boy" was his reassuring reply. I went inside and up to my office, which looked out over High Holborn, to change into my lounge suit and on opening the office door found broken glass on the floor and a large piece of yellow metal embedded in my desk, obviously part of what had been the metal bodywork of the hire car. Had I been sitting at my desk at the time of the explosion, I would have suffered a severe shrapnel wound or even been decapitated. How lucky I had been to survive this incident, which I regarded as a great birthday present. We managed to muddle through the scheduled technical and dress rehearsals and open on time, thank goodness,

As I knew I was only in this job for seven weeks up to 13th January, I kept my ear to the ground for any snippets of information going around about new shows or possible take overs. One evening after rehearsals I popped in to see my old friends at The Round Table pub next to Sheekey's fish restaurant, where I loved dining, in St. Martins Court near to Leicester Square. Here, whilst I enjoyed a libation or two, I gleaned that the next show at The Palladium was to be *The King and I* with Yul Brynner, no less. This sounds interesting I thought, having been involved with the show in Lincoln in the 1960s, and made a mental note to find out more, which was closer at hand than I thought.

Peter Pan was running like clockwork and the Stage Management were astounded to receive overtime in their packets one week as I had calculated they were due this additional payment because of infringed breaks and lack of time off as a result of the car bomb. They all said they had never been paid overtime, ever, on any show. I had always believed that it was necessary to tread a very tight line as Company Manager, being both loyal and fair to the Management you represented and the Company and Staff you served. If it was justified, in my book, they were paid the overtime.

Mark Deamer was one of the Lost Boys, and I got chatting to his mother Carole Deamer. I discovered that she was an ex Ice Dance Champion, and was soon to be working with another ex-skater and choreographer, turned Producer, Ross Taylor, as his PA on *The King and I*. I already knew this was going into The London Palladium after the Panto Aladdin, which starred Danny La Rue, Alfred Marks, Wayne Sleep and Wei Wei Wong. Carole told me that Tom Arnold had set up a new Company Tom Arnold Associates to present the show with Ross Taylor, and as I was already known to them, would put in a good word about me to Ross who was in charge of the day to day organisation of the show. This she did, and a meeting was arranged for me to meet Mr. Taylor at noon on 4th January. Little did I realise that this initial meeting would have lasting consequences for my career.

It was a rather strange first meeting as it was not clear what Mr. Taylor, who went on about this and that, was interviewing me for. Eventually I deduced that he was looking for what he described as a lieutenant to be his right hand man, but was not specific about what that would entail, and I was none the wiser as the term lieutenant is a non theatre term. I left the meeting assuming that the interview had been for The Production Manager, but with added responsibilities, which were unclear. A second meeting was arranged for the following week, which I attended, armed with a list of questions, as although I was keen to work on such a prestigious show at the world renowned London Palladium, did not want to accept something I was unhappy with. This second meeting was more successful as far as I was concerned and I managed to pin Mr. Taylor down about one or two points, but it was hard work as again he would go off at a tangent about irrelevant things that I did not need to know about at this stage. I got the impression that he thought I was already working for him, which was not the case, as I had not finished on *Peter Pan* or agreed to work on *The King and I*.

As I was about to leave the building in Great Windmill Street, Edward Lake, who was the well established and much respected Accountant for Tom Arnold, and who had taught me the correct way to lay out a weekly spread sheet and other things when I first worked for them in 1972, took me to one side and into his office, where he closed the door to have a private conversation with me. In hushed tones, so as not to be overheard, he said to me: "Do you know what you might be letting yourself in for, if you work for Ross?" "No, but I have a rough idea, Edward." "Well, I advise you to think about it very carefully, and good luck." he replied.

I met Ross for the third time the following day, and bearing in mind what Edward had said to me in confidence, was determined that it would have to be a good deal to make it worth my while, but as usual the sticking point was money. If what I was being offered was the position of Production Manager as well as being Ross's lieutenant then a substantial emolument had to be on the table, but it wasn't. A compromise was suggested by Ross who was obviously keen to secure my services, and what he proposed was a £100 per week for six months, until the show opened in June, when it would double to £200 per week.

This was not ideal from a cash flow point of view, but as I have always believed that a bird in the hand is worth two in the bush I accepted, provided I could have a week off after *Peter Pan* closed, to start on Monday 22nd January, which was agreed. For once I had done a deal for a new job before the old one had finished, as *Pan* closed the following day Saturday 13th January….what a relief.

I reflected on what had happened to me over the past seven weeks. I had successfully managed my third Peter Pan in six years, I was lucky to be alive, which I might well not have been had I been sitting at my desk when the car bomb exploded, and I had landed a new and exciting job I was looking forward to immensely.

Act 4 Scene 1
THE KING AND I (PRE PRODUCTION)
(1979)

During the week I had off after finishing on Peter Pan and prior to what I expected to be an intense six months preparing for the opening of *The King and I* on 12th June 1979, in addition to doing some urgent, essential work on the house, I thought it vital to do some research into some of the new people with whom I was going to be working. With the aid of friends, work colleagues and press cuttings I gathered as much information as possible about them, their background, traits and habits, and I detail what I found that was of interest.

The Executive Directors of Tom Arnold Associates Ltd were Tom Arnold (Chairman) known as 'young Tom' to save any confusion with his late father Tom Arnold (dubbed as 'The King of Pantomime') and his mother Mrs. Helen Arnold, who had jointly taken over the interests of the traditional family entertainment business following her husband's death in 1969. 'Young Tom' had been elected to The House of Commons as the Member of Parliament for Hazel Grove in Cheshire in 1974. At only 27 years of age he was one of the youngest MPs in the Commons and was an up and coming star in the Conservative Party. In addition to having presented *Peter Pan* for a number of years, their portfolio included *Pickwick* starring Harry Secombe, which was composed by Cyril Ornadel, Pantos with Danny La Rue, *The Sunshine Boys* by Neil Simon and *The Water Babies*, which had been directed by Ross Taylor, who was now working in association with them.

In addition to what I had hurriedly found out about Ross Taylor prior to my interviews with him, I discovered that he had conceived the flippant Musical *Charlie Girl*, which I had seen during its record-breaking run at the Adelphi Theatre where it played 2,202 performances between 1965-71 staring Joe Brown (replaced by Gerry Marsden) and Anna Negal. The show had music by David Heneker and John Taylor (no relation) and Derek Nimmo and Hy Hazell in the cast. Settings were by Tod Kingman but the show did not transfer to Broadway, as had been hoped.

He had also conceived and directed the Musical *Mr. & Mrs.* which was based on Noel Coward's one act plays *Tonight at Eight Thirty*, and had created and directed the highly successful *John Curry's Theatre of Skating* at The London Palladium, following John's 1976 Olympic and World Championship triumphs.

The story was that he had gone to see Louis Benjamin (Managing Director of The London Palladium) about putting on a Pantomime, but the suggestion had been declined. However Mr. Benjamin added: "Bring me Yul Brynner in The King and I, and then you can have The Palladium." All credit to Ross, he did just that.

The King and I had originally opened at St. James' Theatre on Broadway on 29th March 1951 where it ran for three years clocking up 1,246 performances. It starred Gertrude Lawrence as Mrs. Anna Leonowens, and she had top billing over a young actor named Yul Brynner who had been cast as King Mongkut, because the Producer's first choice, Rex Harrison, was unavailable at the time. It is also worthy of note that the first Tuptim in 1951 was Dorretta Morrow. Brynner did eventually get equal billing with Deborah Kerr as Mrs. Anna in the 1956 film, which cemented his association with the role for years to come, and again it is interesting to note that in the film Tuptim was played by Rita Moreno, who would later find fame in West Side Story.

Twenty years later in 1977 Producers Lee Guber and Shelly Gross thought that it was time for a revival of the show. Brynner agreed and he was booked into the Uris Theatre (now The George Gershwin Theatre, the biggest on Broadway seating 1,933 patrons) but Y.B. insisted on major refurbishment to what he called 'a public toilet' before he would open there on 2nd May 1977. Ross Taylor flew over to see the production, with Constant Towers playing Anna. A deal was done to transfer to London after it closed on Broadway on 30th December 1978, subject again to the world famous London Palladium being refurbished backstage to his requirements. This was as much as I could find out about Ross, Yul and the show before I started work on it.

Tom Arnold had done a deal with British Actors Equity to permit Mr. Brynner and June Angela (Tuptim), Hye-Young Choi (Lady Thiang), Susan Kikuchi (Eliza), Gene Profanto (Prince Chulalongkorn) along with Director Yuriko to work on the show in an exchange deal that would permit British Equity Members to work in the USA. A rough ball park budget was scribbled in the Playbill from the Uris Theatre by Ross, which estimated the costs to be about £3,000.

Prior to commencing the job, as I had not received a contract, I wrote to Ross on 13th January, outlining my understanding of the terms of my employment and remuneration as follows. A: To start on 22nd January 1979 for a trial period of four weeks at £100 per week. B: If at the conclusion of this period on 19th February we both agreed to continue, then my salary would rise from £100 to £150 per week in three instalments. As from 1st March £120 per week, 1st April £140 pw, from 1st May £150 pw, rising to £200 pw after opening night with a change of title to General Manager from Production Manager once we had opened. A signed copy was returned from Ross dated 16th February.

I have always made it my policy to have my understanding of my terms of employment in writing, in the absence of a formal contract, as at least then, if there is a dispute and things go sour you have some sort of redress from the other party. This is something that I pass onto the many Drama students who I now meet.

During the week prior to my starting work at London Pavilion Chambers, in Great Windmill Street, just off Piccadilly Circus, I took my working suit into the Office with a towel and a hair dryer as it was my intention to cycle into the office daily from Lewisham, change in the toilet (which had no heating) and return home in the evening. Cycle gear was not the image I wanted to present at meetings which were to become a frequent feature of my new job.

I arrived early for my first day, feeling like I was at a new school, and very

JT taking names at King & I auditions 1979

apprehensive about the new job, as there was so much to do in such a short time over the next twenty weeks. I felt I would have enough on my plate as Production Manager without the added workload of being Mr. Taylor's lieutenant, but that was what I had agreed and had to honour. I soon decided it all boiled down to prioritising, as certain deadlines had to be met, and people's availability known. I shared an office at the back of London Pavilion Chambers with Carole Deamer (Ross's PA) who I knew from Peter Pan at The Shaftesbury. We got on well with each other, which I was very happy about. I spent the first day compiling a contacts List of all the people so far involved on the show and what their role was going to be.

On the first Wednesday I went to the Theatrical Costumiers Bermans & Nathans and met one of the Directors, Noel Howard who was to be the Costume Co-Coordinator and would be responsible for recreating all the costumes for the world famous *Irene Sharaff*. She had worked on over sixty Broadway Shows, and had designed the costumes for the original production, for which she had won a Tony award. He was organised, as you would expect, and we again got on well together. In the afternoon Ross asked me to assess the resident staff at the Palladium during the matinée performance of *Aladdin*, staring Danny La Rue. I first visited Cranbourne Mansions (Head office of Moss Empires who owned The Palladium) to meet General Manager Ronnie Swift. I explained to him what Ross had asked me to do, which like me, he found rather unusual, but reluctantly agreed, saying he would inform his Production Manager Tommy Elliot, who in turn would let the Company and Staff know that I would be in the Prompt Corner making notes

I met Stage Manager Fred Pearson, Chief Electrician Bill Platt, Property Master Ronnie Harris and Tony Pinhorn who was running the show, who all eyed me with some suspicion, as they did not really know why I was there, only that I was P.M. on *The King and I*.

I knew some of the *Aladdin* Company as I had either worked with them or met them through Susan. Wei Wei Wong from the *Younger Generation* was in the show, directed by Dougie Squires, and said "hello" along with Ros Cole from *New Edition* who had been in *Emu in Pantoland* in 1976. Brian Marshall was playing Wishee Washee (he had taken over from John Inman at The Windmill) and asked how I was, but the warmest welcome came from Linda Johns, who was the dancer I knew from Emu and had given me the bottle of Champagne on my last night.

Tony Pinhorn ran the show very well, but it was very much a variety show, and I wasn't sure he would be the right person to be my DSM on a book show like *The King and I*, and be able to cope with, what I was beginning to hear, could be a very demanding Mr. Brynner. I reported as much back to Ross on my return to the office. He suggested I should find my own Stage Management Team and forget about using Tony on the show.

The following morning I had another meeting with the staff at The Palladium and met Manager John Avery (from whom I was to learn so much), Box Office Manager Edwin Shaw, Wardrobe Supervisor Dawn Thesiger, House Manager Ken Rowcliffe, Moss Advertising Manager Brenda Thomas, and the legend that was number one, lead follow spot operator Linford Hudson. Tod Kingman, Scenic Consultant, joined us at noon, as he was responsible for the reproduction of Peter Wolf's setting and props from the Broadway show. He had to build, make and paint them at his Brunskill & Kingman Scenic Workshops in Flitcroft Street, just behind the Phoenix Theatre Stage Door. Tod had flown over to Broadway to see for himself what was involved, and taken a multitude of photographs and measurements to enable him to adapt the setting to the size of the Palladium Stage, and make working drawings for its construction. Following our meeting I accompanied him back to Flitcroft Street to meet some of his staff who would be responsible for the Fit Up, supervised by Eddie Ryan.

Things were looking good. We had the three magic things that make a successful show: an international Star above the Title, a universally respected Matcham's Theatre, and a much loved show. The theatre would soon be improved, once *Aladdin* had closed and works on the major backstage refurbishment had begun, which was a requirement of Brynner's to appear in the show in London. At the end of the first week I knew what I had let myself in for, but felt quite capable of handling the workload, and only wished that I could be at my desk more.

The Association of Theatre Technicians (ABTT) used to meet monthly for Production Manager's meetings at their office in Great Pultney Street in Soho, under the Chairmanship of Technical Officer Ken Smalley. The ABTT had been formed in 1961 to provide a forum for discussion and exchange of ideas amongst like-minded individuals with a common interest, and I was a regular attendee, time permitting, which was now at a premium for me. They were usually open meetings with no agenda and a carton or two of red wine and a lump of cheese on hand. This I found a nice way to relax after 'a hard day at the office' and popped in on Monday 29th January to meet colleagues and let them all know what I was now doing. We got around to discussing budgets, and it turned out that I and another PM both had a ten per cent shortfall in our respective budgets, but his was a £500 shortfall and mine was £5,000.

During week two of the pre-production period I continued to have meetings with Tod Kingman, with whom I was getting on really well, as he had designed the set for *Let's Get Laid* and shoehorned it onto The Windmill stage for its reopening in 1974, and I respected the quality of his work. It was a big secret who was to play Mrs. Anna, but I and Carole knew, and were sworn to secrecy by Ross. Costume fittings had to be arranged for the lady in question who would wear the ball gown when she was revealed at a Press Conference to the International Press. A secret final fitting was held at Bermans on 5th February, prior to a reveal onstage at The Palladium with Yul on Monday 12th February, which was exactly four months prior to our opening night.

I met Mrs. Helen Arnold for the first time when she came up to town from the South Coast, where she lived, at 3pm on 8th February. I was ushered in to meet her by Ross to see her sitting at her desk in front of the bay window of the Great Windmill Street offices, overlooking the statue of Eros, in the very room that had once been the office of Ivor Novello. Tom (senior) had produced shows for Ivor from 1938 right up to Ivor's death in 1951, including his big hit musicals *Perchance to Dream*, *Kings Rhapsody*, *Gay's the Word*, and *The Dancing Years*, which I had danced in 1960. She was a sprightly lady for her years, with a mischievous twinkle in her eye, and I liked her as soon as we met.

Mr. Brynner flew in from the US via Concord, of course, on Sunday 11th February, and I met him for the first time in the back of his Austin Princess Limousine, which was parked in Great Marlborough Street, by The Palladium Stage Door. We did no more than exchange pleasantries to each other before he was driven off to his luxury five star hotel, The Connaught in Mayfair, where he was planning to stay for the run of the show. It was a 9am Press Call on the Monday morning, organised by Press Representative Jason Pollack, and as the stage at The Palladium was available, auditions held from 9.30-11.15. These auditions were for those artistes who had written in on spec about being in the show, and preceded the moment all the press had come to see, the noon presentation of who had been cast to play Mrs. Anna.

The whole thing was Stage Managed by Mr. Taylor with the famous Palladium swag house tabs down and Mrs. Anna and Brynner waiting onstage. Precisely at noon the house lights dimmed, the house tabs were taken out to their top dead and from the back of the stage, out came Y.B. (wearing his customary all black trousers and shirt) to the music *Getting to Know You* revealing Virginia McKenna wearing the full ball gown, as his Mrs. Anna. The flashlights popped and the BIG secret was out. It had gone sensationally well for all concerned.

Virginia was ideal casting for the role and was very experienced both on the stage, appearing with Sir John Gielgud and Flora Robson in 1952, and with Jack Hawkins in *The Cruel Sea* in 1953 playing Julie Hallam. She had won the coveted British Academy Best Actress Award for her role in *A Town Like Alice*, but was perhaps best known for her work in the films *Carve Her Name With Pride* and *Born Free*. Another consideration was that she could look after herself.

The King and I (Pre Production) (1979) Act 4 Scene 1

There was one vital role in the production team that still needed to be filled, prior to the announcement of who was to play Mrs. Anna, that of Musical Director. Mr. Arnold arranged for Ross to meet Cyril Ornadel for lunch at L'Ecu de France in Jermyn Street. Cyril was under the impression that he was having lunch to discuss a forthcoming revival of *The Dancing Years*, and was absolutely stunned when Ross said that he and The Arnolds would very much like Cyril to be in charge of the music on *The King and I* at The Palladium.

Cyril discussed it with his agent Richard Stone, who drew up what Cyril regarded as a sensational contract, which was accepted, and the great Cyril Ornadel was now part of the team.

Cyril Ornadel

Cyril was an ideal choice to be our Musical Director as he knew the Palladium well. He was the face of 'the most famous back on TV' during the overture (*Startime* by Eric Rogers) for *Sunday Night at the London Palladium*. He had worked with all of the big superstars who topped the bill for those legendary television shows. He had also been the original Musical Director on *My Fair Lady* at TRDL in 1958 with Rex Harrison.

He had also been The West End M.D. on *Kismet*, *Call Me Madam*, *Pal Joey* and *Wonderful Town* to name but a few of his credits. In 1963 at The Saville Theatre, he had written the music for the big hit show *Pickwick* with Harry Secombe in the lead role, and what a joy it was for him to now to be on board with us.

Also present at the Press Launch was Gayna Ramsey who had replaced Edward Lake as the Production Company Accountant, and it soon became clear as to why we all got on so well together. Gayna, Cyril and I were all Sagittarians.

Following the Press Launch, the Box Office advance, already quite healthy, really took off. The pricing of the show tickets had been carefully thought out and was based on Mr. & Mrs. Average, travelling by train from Guildford, paying for a babysitter, buying two tickets, a programme or a brochure, having an interval drink, a post show meal at a steak house or similar, and needing a taxi once back in Guildford. The tickets were priced so that this evening out would cost no more than £100, and it worked. The Box Office was inundated with phone calls and there was a queue waiting to buy tickets in the Box Office Annexe, next door to the theatre in Argyll Street.

Yul flew back later that day to rejoin the show in Los Angeles to where it had transferred for a limited ten week run. It opened on 15th February, and on Monday 19th I completed my month's trial and decided to continue with what was turning out to be a very demanding, but rewarding job. Ross flew to LA week commencing the 26th and was joined by Cyril on 2nd March. There they went to see the show at the huge 2,703 seat Pantages Theatre on Hollywood Boulevard, and met Milton Rosenstock who was the American Musical Director, and the cast, some of whom would be coming over to London with Brynner. Milton had as good a pedigree as Cyril, having been Musical Director on such Broadway shows as *Gentlemen Prefer Blondes*, *Finian's Rainbow*, *Can Can*, *Gypsy*, *Funny Girl* and *Fiddler on the Roof*, and taught Cyril all the little tricks to help him take care of Yul in the West End. All this was nothing new to Cyril, as he had been in the same position with the legendary Franz Allers on *My Fair Lady*, twenty-one years before.

Cyril also sat in the pit for a couple of the shows to get a feel for the show and the wonderful orchestrations that had been penned by Robert Russell Bennett, and Cyril's lovely, charming wife Soo joined him on 5th March as they planned to have a holiday in the US, before he got bogged down back in London.

Whilst Ross was away in the States, it gave me an ideal opportunity to interview the people I wanted to be part of my Stage Management team of three. The first person I interviewed was Dot Tenham who was teaching Stage Management students at RADA in Gower Street. She was vastly experienced and mature, which I thought would be a good thing, as I was beginning to hear more and more that Yul could be a handful at times. After a long and detailed interview, when I explained what I expected from her, should she take the position, she decided that she didn't want to return to the Corner again for just the one show when she had a secure position at RADA, so I looked again.

This time I decided to look for someone who I thought could be charming to Yul whilst still be efficient, and keep the show tight, and such a young lady was Mollie Kirkland, who had an excellent reputation and whom I knew from my work with trade shows in the past. She again was not interested when I told her more about it, and felt her future lay as a show caller on Trade Shows rather than returning to the theatre. In the end I found the perfect trio who were loyal, trustworthy and efficient, so it had been worth waiting for.

As my Company SM, I chose Willie Cameron, and Caroline Hughes was the ideal DSM to cope with YB and in ex-dancer Ian Bunday I had a reliable ASM.

It was time to hold auditions for the Royal Dancers, Wives, Nurses, Amazons, Priests and Slaves. I placed an advert in *The Stage* for auditions at the Palladium the following week, as the Director Yuriko was able to be in London between Tuesday 13th and Saturday 17th March.

Yuriko had been Eliza in the Ballet *The Small House of Uncle Thomas* in the original Broadway show which had been choreographed by Jerome Robins. She had taught her daughter Susan Kikuchi the role, as well as reproducing Mr. Robin's choreography, and as such would be one of the American cast to perform in London. On the first day we auditioned those people we had on file, and Yuriko knew exactly what she was looking for, as only those who looked oriental and were capable of holding their hands up to at least ninety degrees at the wrist, would be successful. This soon eliminated many. I then took details of all those who had been approved by Yuriko to keep on file for a re-call. The second day Thursday 15th March was an open call and we were inundated with people from all over the country, so much so that I had to ask Manager John Avery if we could use the stalls bar as an overflow changing area.

The final day was just as hectic and at the end Yuriko had whittled the numbers down to the dozen or so Royal Dancers and Wives plus two swing dancers, who would be trained to learn all the dance parts and provide cover during any indisposition. I then prepared myself for the auditions week commencing 19th March for the six female singing Nurses and Amazons along with the six male Priests and Slaves.

For the children, we would be looking for three groups of eleven Royal Princesses and Princes, who were such an integral part of the show's success and appeal, along with three Prince Chulalongkorn, the eldest Prince who takes over as the new King at the end of the show and Louis, who is Mrs. Anna's son. Initially the Prince was to be played by Gene Profanato, who would be coming over from the USA, but we needed to be ready for when he left after three months. This was where Carole Deamer was in her element. A contact of hers was Gladys Farmer, who had been the children's chaperone on the film *The Inn of The Sixth Happiness* in 1958 and as she was oriental herself, was an ideal choice as our head Chaperone. She was an enterprising person, having opened London's first Chinese Restaurant, appropriately called Chinatown, on the Commercial Road, in Limehouse, many years before. It was the heart of Chinatown then, and served the very best oriental buffet meal I ever had.

To help us find the right sort of young men (we needed three, one to play Monday and Tuesday, another Wednesday and Saturday and the third Thursday and Friday) to play Chulalongkorn, our

Press Representative Jason Pollack had approached Biddy Baxter of *Blue Peter* fame to assist us with our search, and at the same time give us some added free publicity. After weeks of searching we eventually got down to a final three, but they had to be approved by our American visitors, and one of the boys that we had short listed did not meet their demanding standards, and he was rejected. Unfortunately I was selected to go to the BBC Studios in White City and give him the bad news. There he was, waiting in the dressing room, full of happiness, and I had to tell him that he had not got the part and would not go on Blue Peter later where they were to be introduced to the nation. There was no easy way to break the news to him, and he was devastated. This was one part of the job that I hated in the extreme.

The second week of auditions was taken up with Virginia working with the three different groups of Royal Princesses and Princes, to see who was best with whom, as they were all involved in *The March of The Siamese Children* and *Getting to Know You*, two of Rodgers & Hammerstein's most loved tunes. When performed correctly, they proved to be show stoppers. Yuriko left after her twelve day visit on Saturday 24th March, which was the same day that the Pantomime *Aladdin* closed at The Palladium. What an inspiration she had been to us all.

Now back in England, after his holiday with Soo in the States, Cyril was setting out to select the players for his twenty five piece orchestra, and they had to be quality players. He had a meeting with Victor Slaymark whom he asked to form the orchestra, and selected Tony Stenson to be his Associate Musical Director, and Rosemary Roberts, who had been a soloist with the world renowned Paul Whiteman Orchestra, as the leader. It was vital that we had an associate MD for Cyril as the sensational contract drawn up by Richard Stone stipulated that he be permitted to have certain Jewish holidays off. Also he didn't have to conduct the show for the whole of the limited run, once his associate had been taught the ropes and, most important, been approved by The King. He would however retain the status and title of Musical Director throughout the entire run, which was scheduled to terminate in October 1980.

It was now time for me as Production Manager to approach some of the top Lighting Designers and Sound Engineers to join our ever growing team of quality people. On Thursday 29th March I met David Collison, my first choice for this prestigious job, from Theatre Projects to tell him about the show, and to see if he had availability to work with us. David had worked with Richard Pilbrow at Theatre Projects since 1959 and had been the first man to be credited with 'Sound Design by David Collison' on *Pickwick* at The Saville Theatre in 1963. This had also been a big hit for Cyril as he composed the music for it. Our meeting lasted for an hour before I had another appointment about the sets with Tod Kingman, and David said he was interested and would get back to me, once he had checked his availability with the Theatre Projects Office.

This was quite a significant day, as twenty-eight years ago it had been the opening night with Gertrude Lawrence and a young Yul Brynner on Broadway in 1951, and Yul was still The King…. quite an achievement. It was also my daughter Rachel's birthday, and quite a lot had happened to me during the first year of her life.

Whilst I was waiting to hear back from David I got in touch with the leading Lighting Designer of the day David Hersey, who in addition to being a member of the National Theatre Company, worked freelance and had founded his own Company David Hersey Associates in 1973, which manufactured and designed specialised lighting and projection equipment

David came over to the UK from New York in 1968. His reputation had increased considerably following his sensational design concepts for *Evita*, which had opened at The Prince Edward Theatre in June 1978, with the first use of a 'curtain of light' effect. I offered him a substantial deal with a deadline for him to get back to me by 14th April, which he did, accepting the offer.

On Easter Monday (16th April) I received a hand written letter from Tom Arnold, saying "how delighted he was with the way that I was tackling things" and "how impressed others have been when dealing with me" on the many aspects of the show that I was now handling. He went on to say that Ross, whom he had known for most of his life, was now at "his most creative" but that it was "down to the ability of his personnel" to ensure that matters were attended to promptly and efficiently. He concluded by saying: "In this your role has proved crucial", and that "he was deeply grateful and obliged to me." This cheered me up, as at last all my efforts over the previous twelve weeks had been appreciated.

David Collison found that he was unavailable for *The King & I*, so my dream of the ideal team on Sound and Lighting had to be rethought. However I was put in touch with Bruce Elliot, who had worked extensively in Great Britain and the USA with artistes as diverse as Tony Bennett, Herb Alpert, and Chicago and had been responsible for the installation of the new Palladium Sound System, as a director of SHE Audio. I had not worked with him, but his credentials on paper looked impressive, and if anyone could make the recently installed system work, it must be him, so I took a punt and offered him the job, which he accepted.

We now had in place a very strong Technical Team with Tod, David and Bruce and as the world famous, sensational photographer Ernst Haas, was part of the US contingent, I felt that things were in good shape with eight weeks to opening night.

Now that the Palladium was dark the mammoth refurbishment of the backstage dressing rooms for Mr. Brynner could commence. The requirements were explicitly set out in the Rider to his Contract and were most specific. It all centered on what had been a set of Quick Change Dressing Rooms off the 'Donkey Run' (so named because it was where the Ponies were kept when doing Cinderella) on the Prompt side of the stage, and entailed their alteration and re-decoration to make a 'Star Dressing Room' for Yul. His Personal Assistant Clare Howard, would have an adjacent office. The cost of the work would be split 50/50 between Tom Arnold Associates and The Palladium management. Some of the many specific requirements included a TV link from a camera on the Circle Front to a monitor in the dressing room to enable him to watch the show when not onstage, the colour of the room and its temperature, the number of wheels on the dressing room stool, the size and shape of his bath and the dressing room mirror lights, and the pressure of water to be pumped though a specific shower head. This had to be imported from the States, and to achieve the required pressure a new header tank was put on the roof. This all took time to organise and install and to my knowledge was never used at all during the run of the show.

I received my pay increase to £140 a week on 1st April and got away a bit early on 13th April as it was Julian's third birthday. Irene Sharaff flew in to supervise the costumes being made at Berman & Nathan's. She came into the Palladium during her visit and demanded that some of the children have new underwear bought for them, which was not in the budget, but was done anyway, as she was quite a demanding lady with years of experience behind her, and knew how to get what she wanted.

I had booked the two large Dance Studios in Jay's Mews, normally used by The Festival Ballet, for our rehearsal period and they proved to be ideal as we could have two rehearsal sessions running at the same time.

On one occasion Michael Cowie, who was an ex-dancer and had joined us as a Production Assistant, rang me at the office one afternoon from a the communal coin box, as it was pre mobile phone days, and said to me in hushed tones: "John, we have a problem here at rehearsals, but I can't talk." "OK" I replied "just answer these questions Yes or No." (JT): "Is it to do with Sir?" (MC): "Yes." (JT): "Is it concerning rehearsals?" (MC): "Yes, he won't." (JT): "If Cyril is there, put him on the line please." …. Cyril comes on line (JT): "What do you suggest we do then Cyril?" (CO): "Rehearse with the understudy." was his immediate reply. (JT): "Great idea, let's do it" and so Standby Nick Burnell (who played the small part of Captain Orton) got a chance to rehearse with Virginia and the cast before opening night, which was unheard of.

The King and I (Pre Production) (1979)   *Act 4 Scene 1*

The run in L.A. at The Pantages Theatre had ended on 22nd April, five weeks before our Technical Rehearsals began in London and two week before the Rehearsal period began with the American contingent of Hye-Young Choi (Lady Thiang), June Angela (Tuptim), her brother Gene Profanto (Prince Chulalongkorn), and Susan Kikuchi (Eliza) joined us in London.

A newcomer to the West End from his native Australia was Marty Rhone (Lun Tha). I had protracted telephone conversations with the agent of John Bennett, who we wanted to play The Kralahome, as this was my first experience of negotiating a contract with an artiste of some standing, as Mr. Bennett was. The rest of the cast were Kevin Heuston (Louis Leonowens), Maurice Chong (The Interpreter) and Paul Williamson (Sir Edward Ramsay). We were complete.

The workload for Carole Collins was extreme, as in addition to being Ross's Personal Assistant, she was in charge of Children's Casting which was ongoing, as the children used up their permitted working days under The Children (Performances) Regulations Act which we religiously adhered to. Julie Layton was engaged to assist her as the Children's Coach along with Dorothy Yates as another Chaperone to assist Mrs. Farmer.

Other appointments that had to be made were Company Hairdresser, Janice Barnes, Rehearsal Pianist (mainly for all the children's rehearsals) Paul McGuire, a Personal Dresser for Virginia, Anne Parry and for Yul, the unflappable Rae Cotes.

I now set about preparing the most comprehensive and detailed Production Schedule that I had ever done, as I was, and still am, a firm believer that an hour spent in preparation is worth three hours onstage during a Fit Up and technical period. This I duly circulated to all departments, in order that each of them knew what the other was doing at any given moment, and the old hands at The Palladium, Fred Pearson (Stage Manager), Ronnie Harris (Property Master), Linford Hudson (Head of Follow Spots), Keith Barnes (Sound Engineer) and Bill Platt (Chief Electrician & Lighting Console Operator) said in amazement "We have never been given anything like this before" which was proof that I had learnt my trade from numerous productions during the previous twenty years.

Production Assistant Michael Cowie was given the task of seeking out accommodation for our American guests, and found suitable flats and a small house in the Waterloo area, and in Balcombe Street Marylebone, which had been the Street involved in an IRA siege four years earlier in 1975. Obviously if the Americans did not like these apartments they were at liberty to move, but at least they had a base to start from, and get to know London.

Despite numerous problems with the dressing room refurbishments, we were on schedule for the Company to move into the theatre for a week of technical rehearsals commencing Monday 28th May. There was much anticipation to hear the orchestra play that magnificent score for the first time in the theatre, when we hit our first major problem. Prior to the first seating of the twenty five members of the carefully selected musicians in the Orchestra Pit, it became obvious that the Sound Designer Bruce Elliott, had completely misunderstood his brief as he had set the pit out with twenty nine microphones and covered the pit walls with sound proofing material. It looked like a recording studio would, and his intentions were that he would balance the sound from his console at the rear of the stalls. This might have been all well and good if there had been enough room in the cramped pit for the twenty-five members of the orchestra to sit down, but there wasn't.

The Resident Palladium Production Manager Tommy Elliot, who knew Cyril very well from his days in the Pit during *Sunday Night at The London Palladium*, took one look at the chaos and asked what we wanted to do about it? "Remove all the microphones and strip the walls of all that stuff" was the reply, and we went back to what had always been the intention of a natural acoustic sound that had been good enough for hundreds of shows since the Frank Matcham designed venue had opened on 26th December 1910, and now enabled the orchestra to sit with their music stands in the confines of the pit.

I began to liaise more with The Palladium Manager John Avery, and Box Office Manager Edwin Shaw, as several of the Preview Performances during the week commencing 4th June were to be Charity Performances, culminating with a Royal Gala prior to opening night.

The daily advance figure and carry forward was now huge and in excess of one million pounds. That was then the largest advance ever on a West End Musical, which Yul took great delight in announcing: "It's not a play, it's a happening." It was agreed that we could use The Royal Retiring Room and Toilet, behind the Royal Box, to entertain our VIP Gusts, and facilities for keeping the bar stocked with Champagne were made with the Cellar Man, along with triangular smoked salmon sandwiches from a nearby caterer recommended by Mr. Avery who ran the theatre like an ocean liner crossing the Atlantic, where nothing was too much trouble.

We were now firmly established in our new surroundings and, as was the tradition at The London Palladium, Ross had decided that some of us were to have brass door plates put on our Dressing Room Doors with an inscription etched on it: 'John Toogood, The King and I, London Palladium, 1979'. These are known as 'Getting an Oscar' in the business. At the end of the run they are removed overnight and mounted on a polished wooden stand as a keepsake of your time at The World's Most Famous Theatre. Mine has pride of place in my living room.

Mr. Brynner had initially asked for two armed guards to be on duty outside his dressing room, but when it was explained that this was impossible in this country, he settled for the brother of 'The World's Strongest Man', Geoff Capes, as his bodyguard. Standing at six foot five and weighing twenty three stones was an ideal choice, I thought.

On Saturday 2nd June we had a Final Technical Call in the morning to iron out any lingering problems, followed by our last full DR. Ross and I sat at the Production Desk, with a telephone, bottle of champagne on ice and chicken sandwiches, feeling very much like the charming Robert Nesbitt (The Prince of Darkness) behaved during The Royal Variety Performance rehearsals. The first Royal Gala Evening on Saturday 2nd June, was to be attended by H.M. Queen Elizabeth, The Queen Mother and Princess Alexandra, The Honourable Lady Ogilivy, for The Alexandra Rose Day Charity.

The following week we performed eight Charity and Public performances and Virginia celebrated her forty eighth birthday on 7th June before the opening night on Tuesday 12th June 1979. We had done it and opened on time.

Act 4 Scene 2
THE KING AND I (THE PALLADIUM)
(1979-80)

To help celebrate what I hoped would be the pinnacle of my career so far, I invited Mum and Dad to come to the opening night on 12th June, along with my old dance teacher Christine Orange, who had taught me so much in my formative years, and her partner Canadian Bev Richardson, both close friends of Ray and Joan. They were all booked into a smart West End Hotel, as Mount Pleasant Lodge was too small to accommodate another four adults. There was much excitement and anticipation, as none of them had been to a West End Opening Night, and this one promised to be a mammoth event for all those invited. It was, of course, a full house and anyone who was anyone wanted to be there.

To say that the opening night was sensational and well received would be an understatement. Yul gave a tour de force performance of a lifetime and the standing ovation at the end was well deserved, not only by Brynner, but Virginia and the entire company. The press reviews were outstanding in their praise.

Maris looked radiant and a rare photo taken at the reception following the performance shows her glowing with pride on the arm of her husband. I also received a personal letter from Tom Arnold, thanking me "so much for everything" and inviting me to take a holiday for two anywhere in the World as a first night gift from Tom Arnold Associates. His letter concluded by stating: "He was fully aware of the tremendous burden which I had been carrying, and wanted me to know how much it had been appreciated." There was another pleasant thank you surprise, as for the first time in my career I was given a title page credit in the programme alongside, and in the same size lettering as David Hersey, Ernst Haas, Susan Kikuci, Tod Kingman and Noel Howard, along with a third of a page biography. In it I mentioned Maris, Julian, Rachel along with the fact that I was Captain of the Beckenham Cycle Speedway Team, and enjoyed growing thirty different types of vegetable. Ross was very good at coming up with these little surprises that made one feel special.

Merchandise and T-shirts went on sale on the Friday after the opening with, it was rumoured, YB on ten per cent of anything sold with his face on it, and they sold well. Fuji Film had a deal with Yul, and as a result we had to keep them happy, and regularly supply them with the best available seats. Yuriko was to leave London on 18th June and what an inspiration she had been to us all. She left the show in good shape and safe hands as we all settled into the eight-show weekly routine.

Having spent the last six months working damned hard to get the show on by opening night, and appreciated by Mrs. Arnold in a hand written letter to me on 14th June I felt it was time to reap some rewards, and share in the success of what was the most successful show in town. To that end I met Ross two days after we had opened, and as per my letter contract of 24th April, it was confirmed that my weekly salary would rise to £200 pw from 18th June, for the run of the show based on an eight show week.

My first priority was to get the allotment into shape, as it was looking like a rubbish tip, and the sowing season was marching on apace. This took longer than I anticipated, and I was already

JT & Maris at King & I Opening Night 1979

shattered some nights as I cycled up the Old Kent Road and into the West End to start work on the show. The adrenalin soon kicked in however, once I heard Cyril and the orchestra start to play The Overture. Oh how I had missed this magic moment at seven thirty each evening.

My show routine was like clockwork every performance. After a wash, shave and hair dry to freshen up, I put on my new evening suit, or if it was a matinée, the lounge suit Ross had kindly bought me. Then I would check with the senior members of the Stage Management, Willie Cameron, and Caroline Hughes, to find out if there were any indispositions etc. at that performance, before going to see Yul in his luxury Dressing Room. The bodyguards all knew me, as admission to his dressing room was strictly controlled and you were only admitted on production of a laminated Security Pass with his face on it. Once inside the ritual was the same on each day, "Good evening Mr. Brynner, how are you to-night? This will be performance number so and so, and we have the sixth full house this week." I would then go on to tell him of any Royalty or VIP's that were in for that show, and ask him if they could come round and meet him in the dressing room afterwards. Depending on who this was, or their status in life or the entertainment world, approval would be given or refused.

I would then go FOH and meet up with John Avery in the top marble office and see the house in with him and House Manager Ken Rowcliffe. John ran the Palladium immaculately and as I saw how he dealt with the trickier aspects of the job, vowed that if I were ever in a position to run a theatre as General Manager, then I would have no hesitation in doing it the Avery way. Ken was a loyal, dedicated man and was the perfect right hand man for John. Together they worked as a perfect team

The King and I (The Palladium) (1979 -80)   *Act 4 Scene 2*

Box Office Manager Edwin Shaw would come FOH from the Annexe next door, once he had closed, and give us the figures which were mind blowing in size, and still healthy. I would greet any VIPs on arrival and ensure that one of the liveried Palladium staff would escort them to their seats and report back immediately if it had doubled.

On Sunday 8th July we held a party in the Cinderella Bar for all the children in the show, both those playing, and being rehearsed by Julie Layton & Michael Cowie during the day. Yul and Virginia were present, and those of us with children of our own were invited to bring them along and Julian (now three) was given a T-Shirt by The King.

We knew that Cyril would be leaving at the end of August to compose the music for a new series of *Sapphire and Steele*, so it was imperative that Tony Stenson was up to speed and confident to take over conducting the show at every performance. After he came back from a two week holiday we arranged for him to conduct a rehearsal with the Understudies playing their respective roles, on Thursday 2nd August.

Nick Burnell covered Yul whilst Eileen Battye covered Virginia, with seven other members of the Company swapping parts to provide cover in an emergency and keep the show running to its very high standard. Nothing was ever left to chance. This rehearsal proved to us all that Tony was ready to take over on Monday 3rd September, and The King himself had also approved him.

I arranged for Champagne to be delivered to Cyril's Dressing Room after his final regular show (it had been agreed that he would still come in and conduct the occasional show) and we said a fond farewell to each other with the phrase *Ever the Best of Friends*, which I remained with him and Soo, his wife, until his death on 22nd June 2011.

On the following Wednesday, Ross went away, and two days later Mr. Arnold went away as well thus leaving me as the senior management person on the show. I was not daunted by this responsibility, as I knew I could rely on the excellent team I had surrounded myself with, to help me through any problems that arose during their absence.

The first American to leave the show was Gene Profanato (Prince Chulalongkorn) on Saturday 25th August as he had completed his run of permitted performances under The Children (Performance) Regulations. He was to be replaced by three young men who would split the performances between them, which was the same arrangement for the part of Mrs. Anna's son, Louis.

We celebrated the hundredth performance on Friday 7th September, which was Mr. Brynner's 2,609th as King Mongkut, and a few of us were invited to the inner sanctum to celebrate the success of the show with him. Many of those who visited his reception room for the first time were surprised at its opulence, as it was extremely luxurious and had cost a small fortune. In addition to the wall chart in the make up area, where he meticulously logged the takings for each performance, and closed-circuit television showing him the stage and auditorium at the touch of a button, was the lounge area with a comfortable settee and big armchairs, a twenty-six-inch colour television, video recorder and audio play back facilities. Only a few of us knew that every conversation in the Dressing Room area was recorded and kept on file.

He had a collection of fine wines flown in from his Chateau in France, which he often visited on a Sunday to see his wife Jacqueline de Croisset, whom he had married in 1971, but later divorced, before marrying Kathy Lee. He was generous to an extreme and knew how to enjoy the fruits of many hard years' work. He would only offer you a glass of Lafite Rothchild '47 (which is universally known as The Kings' Wine) or Dom Perignon Champagne. At the end of his tour de force performance, which he delivered every show, he was often in great pain from a brutal fall he had suffered whilst working as a circus acrobat and flying trapeze clown when he was just seventeen years old, but never showed his discomfort to his guests.

This discomfort often led him to be tetchy and discourteous to his legions of fans that used to wait outside the Stage Door, clutching their programmes and brochures for him to sign. On one occasion a disabled girl, who was a big fan of his and had been to see the show several times, was waiting in line when he just ignored her and went to the next person in the line. At this, she did no more than give Brynner a whack across his bald head with her rolled up brochure. The Stage Door Keeper was to remark afterwards: "It was the first time that he had ever seen the fan hit the shit."

The second of our American friends, who had brought so much class to the show, to leave us was Susan Kikuchi, who brilliantly danced the part of Eliza in the ballet *The Small House of Uncle Thomas*. She departed after the second show on Saturday 15th September to be replaced by Diana Choy, whom we had auditioned in London, and who previously had been The Ballet Mistress with the British Dance Drama Theatre. If you hadn't come to the show to see Ms. Kikuchi dance Eliza, you would have found it very hard to notice any difference, such was the quality of the take over artistes we had engaged.

Mr. Arnold returned from his summer holiday, which had to be taken when The Commons was not sitting, and rumour had it that he and Ross had been seeking permission from the Richard Rodgers and Oscar Hammerstein Estate to present a revival of *The Sound of Music* when *The King and I* closed. To compound this rumour William Hammerstein, the son and eldest child of Oscar, flew in to see the show on Thursday 27th September. It looked like the rumours were true, and I wondered if I would be asked to be involved with it, as I thought I was held in high esteem by Tom Arnold Associates.

On 8th October Ross celebrated his fiftieth birthday, with closest friends Lonnie Donegan and Marti Caine, which was also the anniversary of *The King and I* opening at TRDL in 1953, with Herbert Lom (King) and Valerie Hobson (Mrs. Anna). Valerie was also the wife of John Profumo MP, whose affair with Christine Keeler, and the subsequent scandal, may have helped to topple Macmillan's Conservative Government of the day. Ross then went away again on the following Thursday for two and a half weeks, fuelling more rumours about the new show. The hundred and fiftieth show at The Palladium was clocked up at the evening performance on Saturday 20th October, and things were still in fine shape apart from one or two seasonal colds.

Cyril returned to conduct for the first time since he had departed the show on 1st September, and Eileen Battye went on to cover for Ms. McKenna, the first person to suffer. Eileen was a triumph and all her hard work and dedication to the show, waiting patiently and being prepared as she was, paid off handsomely, especially when she had the approval of The King, as she was a most elegant, stylish Mrs. Anna and she and Yul got on famously thereafter.

Soon after there came the day we all dreaded when Yul was ill, but despite advice from Doctor Rossdale he insisted on performing. I made the following announcement just prior to Curtain Up.

"Ladies and Gentlemen, I regret to inform you that Mr. Brynner is unwell." (audible moans from the Auditorium … pause for a moment) "however he insists on performing for you, provided that he may omit singing *A Puzzlement* at this performance" (Applause and cheering from the Auditorium) "Thank You." The song was The King's only song in the whole show, but Yul being Yul, he could not give anything less than a hundred and ten per cent. This announcement ensured that he received an ovation the first time he appeared. This was an announcement technique I would use on other shows later in my career, and it worked every time.

On 1st November, the six months' original agreement for the visiting Americans expired, and others who had agreed to a limited time left. Some major cast changes took place with Paul Williamson moving up from playing Sir Edward to replace John Bennett as The Kralahome, Kathy Lee had replaced Susan Kikuchi as 'Court Dancer' after she had left on 15th September and Richard Frost, an old friend of mine from the Bristol days, joined the show as Sir Edward Ramsay. We also lost some of our original and best Royal Dancers Ran Hamilton, Claire Lutter and Seeta Indrani who departed on 12th December. Seeta would dance Cassandra in Cats, before finding national fame playing WPC Datta in *The Bill*.

June Angela (Tuptim) and Australian Marty Rhone (Lun Tha) were proving to be a huge success as the two young lovers, especially when they were singing *I have Dreamed* at the beginning of Act Two. June celebrated playing the role for the thousandth time on 23rd November. The Society of West End Theatre Awards (which in 1984 became The Laurence Olivier Awards) for 1979 were held at The Café Royal in Regent Street, and Ms. McKenna won the award for 'Best Actress in a Musical,' beating Carol Channing for *Hello Dolly* at TRDL, Liz Roberson (who was to become the eighth Mrs. Alan Jay Lerner in 1981) for *My Fair Lady* at The Adelphi, and Antonia Ellis for *Chicago* at The Cambridge. Neither Mr. Brynner nor the show received any nominations, which was a disappointment, but it was a huge recognition of the sensational performance that Virginia was giving day after day. On Monday 26th November we did not give a show at The Palladium because we were honoured to be invited to be part of the fifty second Royal Variety Performance held at TRDL in the presence of H.M. Queen Elizabeth and Prince Phillip. On the same bill that evening were Elaine Stritch (who was sensational), Jim Davidson, veteran comedian, award winning actor Red Buttons, Ned, David, Millie & Julia from *Side by Side*, Marti Caine and *Hinge & Bracket* (with whom I would soon be working, but didn't know it at the time). Louis Benjamin, who in addition to being the Managing Director of The London Palladium was also a co-producer on the show, presented the 1979 show.

I celebrated my thirty fifth birthday at home with family and friends on Sunday 16th December and was invited for lunchtime drinks with Edwin Shaw in the Box Office Manager's office on the actual day following. There was no performance on Christmas Eve, and with Christmas Day off as well, all eight of that week's shows were played twice daily.

The following week we played a matinée as well as the usual evening show on New Year's Eve and had New Year's Day off in lieu. Would 1980 be a good year working with Tom Arnold Associates on their new show that was now known to be *The Sound of Music*, or would I be going back to work with other Producers? I didn't have long to wait before the writing was on the wall. During January and February we continued to hold auditions for replacement artistes, but by now we had seen the cream of the crop and in some respects standards were beginning to fall below what we all expected.

Following a report to me that some of the new artistes were going out between shows still wearing their full stage make up, I was prompted to post a notice on The Company Stage Door notice board, asking them to cease this unprofessional habit, which many were unaware of as they were quite new to the business. I posted the notice before the matinée on Wednesday 27th February, and went out for a bite to eat. On my return I discovered it had been taken down on Mr. Brynner's instructions and later that afternoon, once the show had commenced, I was summoned to the Company Solicitor's office in Soho Square, where I met Barry Shaw of Wright & Webb, Syrett & Sons. Following a short interview with Mr. Shaw I was basically relieved of my duties and returned to the theatre in a complete state of shock and told those that were close to me like Carole Collins, Willie Cameron, John Avery and Edwin Shaw, what had just happened. They, like me, found it hard to believe after all the sterling work, effort and commitment I had shown to the show.

I thought the quickest solution was to seek a personal meeting with Tom Arnold, who had been glowing in his praise for me and, as a Member of Parliament, could be trusted.

I spoke to Maris's Uncle and arranged for him to accompany me when I went to see Mr. Arnold, as he was quite knowledgeable on employment law. Mr Arnold agreed to see us on his sick bed at his parliamentary flat near the House of Commons. After I had introduced I.B. and told him why we were there, he said: "Of course you must be reinstated as Production Manager on The King and I" which really meant that there was not much more to say.

In order to let things settle down a bit, I took some time off and returned on 4th March for a meeting with Ross when it was agreed I should carry on with my duties as Production Manager as I had previously been doing, but 'avoid meeting Mr. Brynner'. I said I would 'do so to the best of my ability.' Matters continued to rumble along, but this was beginning to look like constructive dismissal.

I began to wonder if it had been a wise move to accept the offer of a first night present of a holiday for two 'anywhere in the world' which Maris and I had taken the previous November. We chose to visit Egypt and sail on the Nile, visit Luxor, the Pyramids and many other delights, but it was water under the bridge now, and sometimes we have to learn about our mistakes in life the hard way.

I settled into continuing my role, albeit with restrictions and a heavy heart, for the next six months. I had been re-instated and had much sympathy from the many close associates at The Palladium, and on the show, but things could never be the same again, and I regarded my position now as 'just another job' to pay the bills.

In April, Virginia took a well deserved week off between the 14th and the 19th to re-charge her batteries, and Eileen Battye gave eight scintillating performances, to full houses still.

Also crucial to the team was Linford Hudson. Linford had worked at The Palladium since 1961 after moving to live in the UK with his family from Jamaica. He had replied to an advert for a liveried Page Boy, at the then Variety Theatre. When he grew too big to be a Page Boy, he was asked by the management what he would like to do, and he replied "The Spotlights" and so began a career as the most respected follow spot operator in the UK and, some would argue, the world. He had been working the Stelmar Carbon Arc Follow Spots from high up at the back of the theatre since 1963, and in addition to working on 395 shows including 41 Royal Variety performances before he retired in 2011, was always asked to work 'the limes' by such international stars as Frank Sinatra and Sammy Davis Jr., who recognised his unique talent to be able to 'see in the dark' and 'pick them up in a pin spot' following a dead black out. The Limes Box became his home and his attendance record showed that he had never missed a show. We didn't know how lucky we were to have such a man, as lead follow spot operator, and it was a privilege and honour to work with him.

It was during this period of the run that I learnt the art of entertaining VIPs in the Royal Retiring Room, because it is an art. I had the best tutor in John Avery, who was not only most sympathetic about the way that I had been treated, but was also very 'anti-Brynner' and we got on well together. What he didn't know about entertaining VIPs could be written on the back of a postage stamp, and I vowed that some day in the future, when I would hopefully be in a position to run my own theatre, I would entertain guests in the way I had learnt from John.

Ross still continued to go away to work on his new project, as was his prerogative, and I continued to work on this mammoth money making machine that continued to break West End Box Office records. It was at this time that I entertained, and spoke to coach parties that came to see the show, on the recommendation of my ex-ballet teacher Christine Orange. She had loved the quality of the show when she saw it on the opening night with Bev Richardson, Mum and Dad. Bev, who was a loud and at times obnoxious Canadian, had upset me on the opening night when, as I was taking him up to my office for a celebratory glass of Champagne, he had knocked on Ms. McKenna's Dressing Room Door, and when Virginia had inquired who it was, had replied "Richardson of Lincoln." I hurriedly pushed him away and tore a strip off him, saying, "If you ever do that again Bev, you and I will no longer be friends." He got the message and apologised.

Virginia celebrated her 49th birthday on Saturday 7th June, and I attended the party that she hosted as she had invited me personally, and was sympathetic to the shabby way that I had been treated, as some referred to my 'troubles' in the past few months. The first anniversary was celebrated on Thursday 12th June 1980 and I reflected back on how happy I had been a year ago to be working on the most successful show that London had seen for years, and how it had gone so sour a year later. But I still had a job.

In order to protect the quality of the show a Deputy Musical Director called Gordon Kember was appointed to cover Tony Stenson in an emergency, and he took up his position on Monday 16th June. We had made it a condition from the very start that only one 'dep' was permitted to play in the pit at any performance, as it had been known on other shows for the whole orchestra to be made up of deputies who were there to cover for a mate who had gone off to do a recording session or something equally rewarding. Our insistence had paid off handsomely, as the quality sound from the pit at every performance was still as good as it had been a year ago, on the opening night.

On Wednesday 30th July, after the Matinée, I had a meeting with all The Palladium HODs Fred, Ronnie, and Bill about the inevitable 'Break Down and Get Out' of the show, once we knew for certain the date of the final performance, which was looking like it would be Saturday 27th September, and how we would go about it. The set was going to be kept in store at Tod Kingman's workshops in Flitcroft Street, and I proposed that I would engage two freelance crews, which would be made up of respected West End HODs selected by Tony Ramsay (The Master Carpenter at The Globe, now The Gielgud Theatre). One would help load at The Palladium, whilst the other would be based at Flitcroft Street to offload. I told them I would engage a Theatrical Removal firm like G.P. Radcliffe to provide two tractor and trailers and run a 'shuttle service' between the theatre and the store. To save time on packing, once the empty trailer returned, the freshly loaded trailer would be dispatched, even if it was only a part load. The same principle would apply to the Costumes that were to go back to Berman & Nathan's, and for any hired electrical equipment, during the week after the final performance. As a 'thank you' for all their hard work and dedication to the show, I further proposed that I would engage an outside catering firm to provide hot food and drinks for the Crew throughout the night. They were more than happy about this, so I then set about getting in touch with two or three firms to tender for the transport and Tony to get a couple of crews together, for the usual 'cash in hand' arrangement. I knew about a caterer called Jack King, as he used to have a van and stall at The Derby each year, and after chatting to him about what was to be a new venture for him, a deal was done, and all we needed to know now, was the date for it all to happen.

Brynner clocked up his 3,000th performance as The King on Tuesday 19th August. If there was a celebration party, I wasn't invited, and began to write to some of my old contacts about work, as the closing performance was confirmed as being 27th September. I would have a further week's work doing all the tidying up of loose ends, which meant that I was free for new work from 6th October. Even if I were offered a position working with Ross again on *The Sound of Music*, I doubted that I would take it after what I had been through, and it was mooted that Caroline's boyfriend Max was in line to do the job that I had done on *King and I*.

I received a favourable reply from my old friend Joe Scott Parkinson (Production Manager for Michael Codron, who was now the General Manager) as he had been impressed with what I had done at The Palladium, when he came to see the show, and I had entertained him. They were bringing *Hinge and Bracket* into The Globe Theatre opening on Wednesday 22nd October, and were looking for an experienced Company & Stage Manager, which suited me fine as it would mean only a couple of weeks being out of work. The stumbling block was the money on offer, as even with all my experience, they were still only prepared to pay the Equity minimum of £127.50 per week, which was a hell of a come down from my current £200 per week. I reasoned however, yet again, that 'a bird in the hand is worth two in the bush' and accepted their offer. I could now see out the final weeks at The Palladium, with the confidence that I knew I had a job to go to.

The final weeks dragged on as far as I was concerned, and I couldn't wait for 27th September to arrive and be free again. I kept myself busy with the final arrangements for the Get Out, which were all in place now, and had a meeting at Michael Codron's office about the *Hinge & Bracket* show and the staffing on Thursday 18th September, where I was told that the legendary Lighting Designer Joe Davis had agreed to light the show, and could I be free to go down to Bristol on Saturday 18th October to see the show with him? This was a bonus, to have the opportunity to work with the greatest Lighting Designer this country has ever produced, and without hesitation I said yes.

On the Sunday before the show closed Virginia held a party for a select few at her home near Dorking and I was invited to attend during the afternoon, with my family. We had always got on well together during the whole run and I had done little jobs for her like moving her car during a matinée, so that she didn't get a ticket, which she had appreciated. I spent time during the final week buying 'thank you' presents for the stage management team who had supported me and served me well during the run. At last the magic day arrived, which happened to be Maris' 32nd birthday and Mum and Dad's Wedding Anniversary as well. I received a surprise letter from Ross "thanking me from the bottom of his heart for all the love and devotion I had paid to his production of *The King and I*." This from a man who had done his best to get me sacked earlier in the year.

All my pre-planning on the Get Out worked like clockwork, and the staff were very happy with the catering I had arranged for them, I had been to hell and back on this show, but I was now my own man again.

Dad & Sue on her wedding day 1974

JT with Bud Flanagan Shield 1979

Caroline Hughes, Gayna Ramsay, Ross Taylor, JT and June Angela 1980

JT and HRH the Princess Royal at Anything Goes, PET, 11th July 1989

JT & Rachel on her wedding day 2007  *Art Walker receiving his Life Time Achievement Award 2013*

John's got the legs for theatre. I bet if you come back in 50 years, he'll be doing the <u>front</u> of the dragon!

Cartoon to celebrate 50 years in the entertainment business December 2008

Shape Up and Slim 2011

Sue Jones with JT 2012

Act 4 Scene 3
HINGE & BRACKET
(1980-81)

No sooner had I finished working on *The King & I* on 4th October than I received a personal letter from Mrs. Arnold. In it she said that she had just returned from Cannes and wanted to say "how much she had appreciated my splendid contributions to the success of *The King and I* and that it would always be a pleasure to ask me to run any future productions of theirs." Of course I was very flattered to receive such a nice letter, which only endorsed my gut feeling that the work I had done on *The King & I* had been very much appreciated by The Arnolds although not by some others.

That was water under the bridge however, but I would still keep in contact with Carole Collins, as we had become close friends by now, and almost knew what the other was thinking. I also had a new show to prepare for.

I began by trying to find out as much as I could about the two 'ladies' who I had seen perform at The Royal Variety back in December '79 at the TRDL. I found out that 'Dame Hilda Nemone Bracket' was Patrick Fyffe and 'Dr. Evadne Mona Montpellier Hinge P.T.H.' was George Logan, and that they had appeared in many productions in the lovely Suffolk market town of Stackton Tressle, which was situated seventeen miles from Bury St. Edmunds 'as the crow flies.'

Evadne always wore half-moon spectacles, with a hanging chain round her neck, and neither lady would be seen without a handbag, the contents of which were regularly discussed and often shown to the audience. They had worked together as H & B since 1974, and could often be found with their showbiz chums in the Toucan and Piano Bar in Soho, where they held court. They had both trained at The Rosa Charles Opera Company and loved the music of Gilbert & Sullivan, Noel Coward and Ivor Novello, or 'Dear Ivor' as they would refer to him. Dame Hilda was 'driven around in her open topped Rolls Royce' whilst Dr. Hinge preferred to use her faithful old tricycle and trailer. Both were accomplished musicians and if a comparison of their style of humour were made it would be similar to an Ealing Comedy or Joyce Grenfell.

As their show was more or less self-contained there would only be myself and a Deputy to run it. Roger Hendry, whom I knew from my days working in Cheltenham seven years earlier, came with the show as my DSM. The staff at The Globe Theatre were all first class and in John Causebrook they had a fine Manager who was ably supported by Sean Lennon (Box Office Manager), Tony Ramsey (Master Carpenter) and Ronnie Martin (Chief Electrician). All in all it was a tight ship and I looked forward to having a happy time there.

As I now had a few evenings off I was able to attend Lewisham Council's Awards Ceremony night on Thursday 9th October. I had been nominated for 'Best Kept Allotment' and surprise, surprise, I won. This was quite an achievement as I had been very late with sowing, but had managed, even with the pressure I was experiencing at work, to pull through in the end, as it was often quite relaxing to get away and just concentrate on growing vegetables. We had such a good crop of Purple Sprouting Broccoli that I had to buy a chest deep freezer to keep it in after blanching.

H & B were to play week commencing 13th October at The Bristol Hippodrome, which I had not visited since 1966, and was looking forward to seeing the show there with Joe Davis who was going to light the show in the West End. I arranged to stay overnight with my close friends Graham Phoenix and Trish Martin as they now lived in Clifton. I had worked with them at Bristol, Liverpool and Greenwich and had been Graham's Best Man when they got married in 1974. I had always felt rather bad about the way I had conducted myself in this role six years earlier, as I had bottled making the traditional humorous Best Man's Speech and had just stuck to thanking the bridesmaids, and reading out the 'Good Luck Telegrams' that were traditionally sent then.

I drove down the M4 on Saturday afternoon, 18th October, from London to Bristol at a steady pace and found Trish & Graham's flat quite easily. I remembered the streets of Bristol well, once I returned to the City that I had spent three very happy years in as a student between 1963-66. I got a taxi to the Hippodrome as I thought that Joe and I would have a drink or two together during and after the show. I collected my ticket that had been arranged by the Codron Office and met up with Joe Davis in the Auditorium, where we watched a very funny show together. He was immaculately dressed as usual, with his familiar tash neatly trimmed, and I was glad that I had bought a new lounge suit to wear. After the show we went round to introduce ourselves to George, Patrick and Roger, who was running the show for Triumph Productions. Joe, who was staying at a City Centre Hotel within walking distance, suggested that we should retire to the Residents Bar and chat there about the show and theatre in general.

What followed was one of the most enjoyable evenings of my life, as Joe and I chatted on into the early hours of Sunday. I told Joe that I had been to see Marlene Dietrich when she had played there when I was a student, and had admired the way that he had lit the orchestra and Musical Director for their call that night. I had seen him leave the Stage Door with her and escort her to dinner at Harvey's Restaurant nearby, and asked him how he became her personal lighting designer for twenty two years? He told me that Ms. Dietrich had asked Noel Coward "Who is the best lighting man in London?" and he told her "Joe Davis" and thus their friendship began, with him lighting her shows throughout the world. Alexander H. Cohen asked him to recreate his stage lighting for her 1973 Television Special. Joe described her as "the most beautiful woman I've ever seen". We then went on to discuss his career from him joining Strand Electric in 1926 and then lighting almost six hundred shows over a forty-year period. Joe told me as we chatted, that he had joined H.M. Tennent in 1935 and spent the next thirty-five years as their lighting designer. He had served in The Royal Air Force as a reserve stationed at Gatwick Airport, and served in Burma, Assam and India prior to demobilisation, during WW2.

The first show he lit had been *Blackbirds* in 1936, and since then his lighting credits were remarkable as he had been responsible for such major shows as *West Side Story*, back in 1958, *The World of Suzie Wong*, *A Man for All Seasons*, and *Gypsy*, amongst many others, and I kicked myself for not having asked him to light The King, as we were getting on so well together.

He had joined The ABTT in 1961 and co-founded the British Lighting Designers (BLD) with Michael Northern (whom I would work with in 1986) and was now a Director of Theatre Sound and Lighting (TSL). He knew so much about the business and was utterly charming.

I told him that I had just finished working on *The King and I* at The Palladium, and he was very sympathetic when I briefly told him what I had been through. It turned out that his birthday on 18th December was the day after mine, which explained why we were getting along so famously. We then got talking about Stage Equipment, and I asked him "Which of the many lanterns he had used over the years had made the biggest difference to the way he approached lighting on major Musicals?" Without hesitation he replied "The Pattern 23 Profile Spot, without a doubt, as it was so compact and powerful when it was introduced, compared with the old Pattern 43's that were the staple unit on the number one bar before then." We gossiped and chatted on, buying each other glasses of wine, until we were the last two patrons in the Residents' bar. What a night it had been, having the privilege to chat, on my own, to a man that was a legend in his own lifetime. Joe died following a heart attack when he was working on *42nd Street* at The TRDL, and I am reminded of something he once said to a group of young Lighting Designers: "Don't you boys ever forget that it was Michael Northern and me who started this lighting racket." It is comforting to know that all his diaries, account books, press cuttings and lighting plots were given to The University of Bristol Theatre Collection in 2012, to help keep the memory of this uniquely talented man alive for future generations.

I slept soundly that night in Clifton and went for brunch with Trish and Graham, who as a Theatre Electrician was so envious of the previous night that I had spent with Joe, before heading down the M4 and back to London. The simple Get In and Fit Up at The Globe was supervised by that legend of the West End and Touring, Billy Jay, and I re-met Joe after lunch on stage. "Have you tried the set lunch at the stage door local?" he asked me, "I've just had a nice pork chop there, and very reasonable" he continued. This from a man who had eaten with Marlene at some of the finest restaurants in the world, was indeed a compliment. It was only a two-day lead up to the opening night on Wednesday 22nd October, and as Roger was very familiar with the show, it all went according to plan, apart from an accident during the DR which involved a member of the electrical crew having to go to hospital following a blow to the head.

The show opened on time however and I got back into the nightly ritual of telephoning the figures to Mr. Codron every night, and dropping the show report off at his office as I cycled home.

I got on very well with Brendon the Stage Doorkeeper as he was a Liverpudlian, and we chatted about 'de pool' and of course our interest in football. He was one of the custodians of the theatre cat Beerbohm. I regret to say he disgraced himself at one performance, by making an appearance during the show when Patrick was in the middle of a G & S song. Patrick, being a seasoned pro was not flustered by it at all, as some others would have been. He simply took Beerbohm in his lap and sat down on the chaise longue with him purring away gently. An improvised story was then concocted, before Patrick took the cat over to Roger sitting in the corner at the prompt desk, and said, "Go and find some mice" as he said farewell to him.

I got on well with my DSM Roger Hendry, who knew the show inside out, and had been employed by The Noel Gay Agency on the show for some time. One night when I was cycling home and he was driving his van, we had a mock argument at a Soho junction, where I accused him of cutting me up in his bloody van with no concern for my safety. Voices were raised and I banged on the van side with my clenched fist, which must have been convincing, as a crowd of visiting tourists began to gather. We kept this charade going for a while, until we both were fed up with it so I told him to "Get on your way mate, and show some respect for us cyclists in future." Roger gave me a toot on the horn, waved and disappeared, much to the astonishment of the onlookers who asked: "Why didn't you call the police? We would have supported you."

Trish and Graham, with whom I had stayed in Bristol, came to see the show on the first Saturday, and afterwards they took me for dinner Chez Victor, a lovely French Restaurant in Wardour Street. The show was one of the easiest that I could have wished to work on, as apart from arranging a regular visit of the piano tuner, the show ran like clockwork. I spent much time FOH with John Causebrook, who I got on very well with, and honed the front of house skills I had picked up at The Palladium. Billy Jay came to see the show on Wednesday 5th November and I entertained him during the interval. Billy was a good laugh and fun to gossip with, as he had his finger firmly on the pulse of things.

Meanwhile, I had the pleasure of entertaining my old friend John Avery from the Palladium on the evening of 1st December, which was also the day when it was announced that Petula Clark would star in the revival of *The Sound of Music*. It was to open in August 1981 at The Apollo Victoria Cinema after major alterations, like building an Orchestra Pit and Dressing Rooms. Maris went away with the kids to visit her sister, who lived on a Kibbutz in Israel, and had something like seven children, for two weeks 9th – 23rd December. I was able to get on uninterrupted with some major works at the house. We had a Christmas party at The Queens Theatre, next door to us, on Tuesday 23rd December, and Christmas and New Year were unspectacular.

To keep myself busy I was elected as an Equity West End Deputy, and attended regular meetings at the Equity Office in Harley Street, where my old friend from the Lincoln Rep days Alan Wallace was now the West End Organiser. As money was still tight, having taken a substantial salary drop to work on *Hinge & Bracket*, I went for an interview as a Bingo Caller at the local Mecca in Lewisham, and got the job which paid £2 per hour, for every hour I wanted to work. I could work there on non-matinée days and the extra money would be useful. I did my first shift as Johnny Zero (because I did not want it known that I worked in the West End) on the afternoon of Monday 19th January. Knowing that *H & B* was to going to close on 31st January, I received an offer from Codron's to stay on at The Globe managing a Revue with a new comedian who had been doing well at The Edinburgh Festival called Rowan Atkinson. I received my new contract, with a pay rise to £142.50 per week, on Thursday 22nd January, to start rehearsals on 9th February, which meant I only had one week resting. This suited me very well, and I wondered what it was going to be like managing a young new comedian. I did not have long to wait to find out.

Act 4 Scene 4
ROWAN ATKINSON IN REVUE
(1981)

Following the last night of Hinge and Bracket, I did not have to clear out my office as is normal at the end of a run, because I knew that I would be back in a couple of weeks, so all I took with me was what I would require during the rehearsal period, which was due to commence on 9th February.

I had a week off and first checked out our rehearsal room which was The Notre Dame Hall, Leicester Place. I had been given the contact sheet by the office, which contained the telephone numbers for everyone who was connected with the show, and from this I set about finding out a bit about the people that I would be managing. As it was a bit too early to do any sowing on the allotment, which was more or less keeping us in fresh fruit and vegetables throughout the year, we all went to Lincoln to spend a couple of days with Mum and Dad, and for them to see Julian and Rachel growing up.

Rowan Atkinson, who was twenty-six years old, had been brought up outside Newcastle where his father was a farmer, and educated at Durham School and St. Bees in Cumbria, before getting an Honours in Electrical & Electronic Engineering at Newcastle University. He went up to Oxford in 1975, and was widely reviewed when playing in the *Oxford Revue* in 1977. After the *Hampstead Revue* in 1979, he had gone on to work for the BBC on *Not The Nine O'clock News*, recording six episodes in 1979, seven in the Spring of 1980 and a further eight later that year. I hadn't seen any of these television shows as they were usually broadcast when I was working, but had heard they were pushing the boundaries with their sketches, and very funny.

Twenty five year old Richard Curtis was to receive equal billing with twenty two year old Howard Goodall, and that was the cast. Richard hailed from Wellington in New Zealand and had been educated in Manila, Sweden and England before going to Oxford. He was primarily a writer and had co-written the show that I was going to be working on with Rowan. Howard, on the other hand, was born in South Bromley, just down the road from where I was living, and had won a scholarship to Stowe School. He had then gone on to study music, which was his forte, at Oxford.

The Revue was to be directed by Mel Smith, who was also a part of the *Not the Nine O'clock News* team, was the son of a London bookmaker, and had attended New College in Oxford, before working with Lindsay Anderson as Assistant Director at The Royal Court Theatre in Slone Square. Christopher Richardson was the Designer, Howard Eaton, who had done some specialist work on *The King & I*, was in charge of lighting and Ian Gibson was looking after the sound. My DSM was Deborah O'Brien, and my ASM was Angus Reid, the son of legendary Lighting Designer Francis Reid, with whom I would become a personal friend.

My conclusions after this break down of the people I was going to be working with in a few days' time were that I was, for once, about ten years older than most of them. I was far less well educated, not having been to Oxford, but knew more about life in general and the business than they did.

Rehearsals went well at Notre Dame, and my DSM Deborah was not only attractive but most efficient, and seemed to quite enjoy all the attention she was getting from the University boys from Oxford, who were naturally very bright, humorous and charming. One day, after a liquid lunch in Soho ably led by Mel, they had been quaffing Champagne and Vodka, and all returned to the Rehearsal Room rather the worse for wear. I let it pass on this occasion, but vowed if it ever happened again, words would have to be said.

Howard was never far from his Yamaha CS 60 Synthesizer, which was a new instrument to me, but appeared to be very versatile in his hands. We all moved into The Globe over the weekend of 14th - 15th February, before a technical and DR on the Monday. Two Previews followed before the opening performance, brought forward from 8pm to 7pm for the benefit of the Critics, on Thursday 19th February 1981. The Revue was well received, and box office business boomed. I was overjoyed to be involved again with another show that was hot property in town, with people clamouring to see it.

The familiar routine kicked in again and I was able to spend quite a bit of time at home in the mornings and doing the afternoon sessions as Johnny Zero at Mecca. There were a couple of sketches I used to watch nightly from the wings as they were so funny. One was based on who would carry The Kendal Mint Cake, when a group of hikers were out walking in The Lake District, and Rowan's interpretation of Richard Spark's Schoolmasters morning roll call using names like Carthorse, Dint, Ellsworth Beast Major and Minor, Loud Hailer, Nancy Boy Possum and Plectrum was hilarious. All were guaranteed to be well received by the full house.

I went to see my Accountant Michael Henshaw, with an envelope full of receipts on Thursday 26th, as I had been with him since relinquishing my Schedule E status to go onto Schedule D, back in Liverpool in the late sixties. He was most creative in claiming expenses which were permitted as a member of Equity, such as photographs, hair dressing, work clothing (in my case a dinner suit) and theatrical publications like *Plays & Players* and the weekly *Stage* newspaper, where jobs were advertised and reviews of shows printed. His fee was tax deductible too.

I continued to attend meetings of The Stage Management Association, and was now confident enough to speak up about matters I felt strongly about. On Sunday 15th March, my old friends *Hinge and Bracket* were playing at The Wimbledon Theatre, and Patrick, George and Roger, were most happy to see me when I went backstage afterwards and recalled the incident when Beerbohm, the theatre cat, had come onstage during a show at The Globe, at the point where Dame Hilda had just finished singing *The Cats Duet* by Rossini, and had said "I hope for your sake Evadane that it has been neutered" or words to that effect, which had caused George to face upstage to try and mask his laughter, a real show stopper, if ever there was one.

The hours on the show really suited me as there wasn't a mid-week Matinée (it wasn't a kids show) and in addition to getting ahead with planting on the allotment, I was able to fit in five afternoon sessions as Johnny Zero which was helping to boost the weekly take home pay, which was much needed at this time. My friends Des Tate, and his wife (the landlords of the Round Table Pub) came to see the show on Thursday 19th March, and I was able to return some of the hospitality they had showed me over the years we had known each other since I worked on *Sondheim* at Wyndham's in 1977.

As was my custom, I visited each artiste in their dressing room after the half to find out if they were having any problems on the show, which I could resolve, and to chat in general about a variety of things. Like all geniuses, I found Rowan could be quite dizzy at times and was quite amazed when he told me that he held an HGV Licence, and liked nothing better than getting behind the wheel of a Volvo Big Rig. Richard, a cyclist like me, used to ride into the show every day, and we discussed the merits of such diverse subjects as the benefits of wearing a full yellow oilskin cycling cape or alternative items that gave you a bit more freedom, and how nice it would be if the Greater London Council (GLC) were to introduce dedicated cycle lanes all over the Capital, similar to the one alongside the A40 which had opened in 1934. Deborah O'Brien, was proving to be a most efficient DSM, and a real asset to the company, whilst Angus Reid was a real chip off the block of father Francis, with his mixing of Ian Gibson's sound design.

I got on very well with Manager John Causebrook, and after I had done my pre-show Dressing Room visits, used to go FOH to see the incoming of the full house at each performance. Feedback from the audience during the interval would be relayed back to Rowan on my next Dressing Room visit, as after the show he usually had many guests to see and entertain as he was fast becoming hot property. On a Saturday night, once the Box Office Manager Sean Lennon had collated the weekly figure of takings, we would sit down with a Gin and Tonic to go through and agree the weekly Contra Account which was never a problem, and only occasionally needed clarification about an item that had been deducted from The Producer's Share.

Master Carpenter Tony Ramsey was a gentleman, and a real gem as he represented one of the last of a dying breed of West End Master Carpenters who would go out each weekend for a Producer (in his case Michael Codron) and oversee the Fit Up of one of the shows on a pre London try out Tour. What I particularly liked about Tony was his insistence that everything was Ship Shape and Bristol Fashion prior to a DR and the opening performance, a practice that showed true professionalism in my book, and I rated him the best around. Rachel had her third Birthday, which fortunately fell on a Sunday (29th March), and as we didn't have a show, I was able to help organise a party for her at Mount Pleasant Lodge. I found it difficult to understand what was a new practice for me, where YOU give gifts to those who have come to eat lashings of sandwiches, twiglets, crisps, jelly etc., as her guests….why…what's the logic? We held a similar gathering for Julian's fifth birthday on the day before the actual day (13th April) as it was again a Sunday, and I had spruced up an orange pedal-racing car for him, with many appropriate racing car stickers, which he loved.

Easter came and went, with the show running like clockwork, and doing fantastic business, with the House Full notice board on display for most performances, so it was with some surprise that I went to the Codron Office on Thursday 30th April to collect 'The Notice of Termination of Run'. This was posted on the following Saturday, giving the traditional two weeks' notice, to close on Saturday 16th May. During the final two weeks I had the pleasure of entertaining Doctor Rossdale, who was the doctor who had looked after the Company so well on *The King & I* at The Palladium. I also went to the opening party of *Cats* at The New London Theatre, which was to remain in residence there for twenty-one years, clocking up a total of almost nine thousand performances.

"That's what I want" I mused to myself, as for once I did not have another theatre show to move on to and would have to rely on being Bingo Caller Johnny Zero for a while, until I secured another show.

Act 5 Scene 1
JOHNNY ZERO
(1981)

I had really enjoyed working for Michael Codron at The Globe on *Hinge & Bracket* and *Rowan Atkinson in Revue* over the past eight months, as I regarded Mr. Codron as a fair and honest man, with impeccable standards and a good eye for a potential hit. I was particularly flattered when I discovered that the overworked Stage Manager, Timothy Allgood, in Michael Frayn's brilliant award winning play *Noises Off,* which had been commissioned by Mr. Codron to be expanded from a one-act play by Mr. Frayn in 1977, was allegedly based on me!

However I had to face the daunting task of being a married man with two young children to support, and the only money coming in was from the number of Bingo Sessions I could fit in during a week. Previously when I had been working on an evening show, I had only worked as Johnny Zero during the afternoon, but as I had now been accepted as one of the team, and had met the approval of all the old dears who frequented the Mecca Club in Lewisham High Street, I asked for, and was given, evening spots as well including the link up sessions. Let me explain to those of you who have never had the pleasure of playing bingo, the etiquette of participating in this gamble, which many are hooked on and is their only social activity, and almost takes over their lives.

First you always arrive with a collection of multi-coloured pens to mark off, but not make illegible, your card or book, for what you hope will be the call over and winning line, when you have called out "Bingo" to stop the session. Several of these coloured markers are necessary as the more advanced players would be playing and marking off in more than one book. You always sat in your lucky seat and God help anyone who had the audacity to sit there prior to your arrival….if looks could kill, wasn't in it. The same gang of four would always sit together, and mind each other's property when they went to spend a penny or buy a cup of brown liquid from an urn, that was sold as tea. The link up session was once a week. Many of the Mecca Clubs in the South East of London and Kent got together and pooled the prize money from each club to make a Jackpot prize fund that everyone wanted to win, as it could be several hundreds of pounds. The locals in Lewisham knew that when I was calling the number nought, I would announce it as "Number 10, Downing Street, one zero" which was if you like my little trade mark idiosyncrasy, and linked in with my caller's name of Johnny Zero.

The other clubs on the link up were however not familiar with this, and on one occasion one of the punters claimed that she had missed the jackpot prize because of mishearing my call. There was uproar, with threats, and the Manager, who usually kept a low profile, and avoided the customers whenever he could, was called to sort it all out. The outcome was I was asked not to call zero in future.

As the television show *Hi-de-Hi* was very popular at the time - it was first aired the previous year in 1980 - I began my session by introducing myself as "Johnny Zero, your caller for this session", welcome them to The Mecca Lewisham, wish them Good Luck before I went into "Hi-de-hidy-hidy-Hi" to which they replied "Ho-di-hodey-hodey-Ho" and off we went into the first session of the day. How I hated it, but it was a job, certainly the worst so far, that I had ever done, but "hey" it was work, of sorts, paid the bills and kept a roof over our heads.

The Club was not being run to the standards I was used to and, as an employee, I questioned their evacuation procedure, or lack of it, and why we had not been trained in the use of fire extinguishers and other equipment. I requested that the management call a meeting of fellow employees, some of whom worked in the bar, box office, or were the floor walkers, and the outcome was that I was asked by the staff members to put in writing to the management a vote of no confidence as they said to me "You know what you are doing and can write a nice letter." I got the impression, when I gave this letter to The Manager, with a copy for the Head Office that nothing like this had ever been received before and it sent shock waves throughout the organisation. I felt more than justified in sending this letter, on behalf of my fellow employees, as I was the only one who had experience of being involved in an IRA car bomb in the past, and knew that pre-planning and knowing what to do in an emergency was essential. I can report that soon after, a mock evacuation was rehearsed, and we received basic training in the use of the first aid equipment on hand.

By mid-June I was getting more and more fed up with being Johnny Zero, and doing a job I did not enjoy. On Wednesday 24th I sent a letter to MMA asking if there were any trade show work in the offing. The following day I received a call from Euan Felton, with whom I had worked at Lincoln twenty years earlier, and he remembered me. He now held the position of Technical Director with MMA, and invited me for an interview to catch up with what I had been doing since I left Lincoln in 1963, and to discuss a proposal that he would like to make to me.

This all sounded most interesting as Trade Shows were the latest thing for large companies to hold and they paid well, if what I had received when doing the show for Rank Xerox at The TRDL was anything to go by. A meeting was arranged for the following Tuesday 30th June at 1030 am.

Anyone who knows me knows that I am a night owl and not at my best at 10:30 on a Tuesday morning, well any morning to be honest, and if I had my way, they would be abolished, but I wanted to attend despite that. The MMA office was situated in Neal's Yard off Monmouth Street in the heart of Covent Garden, which was now being taken over by small companies since the fruit and vegetable wholesale market had moved to Nine Elms in 1974.

We chatted about what I had been doing and the experience I had gained since we had last worked together, which appeared to impress him. He then told me about MMA's future plans, and the fact that he was looking for an Assistant Technical Director to work under him on a show by show basis, commencing, if I was free and agreed to the terms, in August, at a starting salary of £200 per week. I was secretly overjoyed to be offered it, but played it cool, and said that as I was married with a family, could I please discuss it with my wife and family and get back to him within the week. I did, accepting of course. On the positive side I was back in regular employment again with a job that offered me potential to develop, on decent money, and able to ditch Johnny Zero for good. The downside was that for the majority of the time the work would be office hours, except when I was on a show which, I had been told, would not be very often. I duly finished my last Bingo calling session on Sunday 19th July, and took two weeks off to prepare for my new life in Trade Shows and Conferences, starting with MMA on Monday 3rd August.

Act 5 Scene 2
M.M.A. PRESENTATIONS
(1981-86)

During my two week break between jobs I endeavoured to find out as much as I could about the people I was going to be working with, but apart from the names of the ten Directors listed at the bottom of a letter, I had little to go on. I knew Euan Felton from my Lincoln days when we had worked together on *Caesar & Cleopatra*, *Passage to India*, *Any Moment Now* and *Dick Whittington* and had vaguely heard about The Managing Director Malcolm Mitchell, who was the leader of The Malcolm Mitchell Trio in the late '40s. My Jazz History knowledge told me that he was the first Englishman to play with The Duke Ellington Band in 1948. He had also accompanied Hoagy Carmichael & Maxine Sullivan, and had been responsible for the musical content of Kenneth Horne's very funny radio show *Round the Horne*, 1966-68. He had started MMA with the scriptwriter/comedian Bob Monkhouse, and the current Chairman of The Board of Directors, Henry Howard in the 1960s and it was the pioneer company in the Corporate Conference field, commonly known as Trade Shows in the business.

The other seven Directors were Jeff Inman (Creative), Howard Burbridge, Gina Vanning, and actors Michael Ingrams, Gordon Clyde, Peter Reeves and Denis Norden. Michael was the half brother of Richard Ingrams (of Private Eye fame), and in addition to being an actor of note - he was Ivor Novello's Understudy in *The Dancing Years* in 1939 - was also a film maker and documentary presenter, who had joined MMA in 1970. Gordon had written scripts for Ronnie Corbett and Harry Secombe. He appeared with Dick Emery and Morecambe & Wise in the 1960s. Peter had first come to fame on Jack Hylton's Music Show in 1957, had worked with The Goodies and Tommy Cooper, and had recorded *The Way I See It* for Decca. Denis was Denis, and was a familiar face on television because of his regular appearances on *My Word* and *My Music* and *It'll Be All Right On The Night* since 1977. He had worked with Frank Muir for much of his career, first working on *Take It From Here* with Jimmy Edwards, Dick Bentley & Joy Nichols (who was replaced by singer Alma Cogan and then June Whitfield in 1953) which I used to listen to on the BBC *Light Programme* between 1948 and 1959.

As you can see I was joining a group of people most, if not all, of whom were my seniors and had been around a bit. I took a packed lunch with me on that first Monday of August, not knowing what the etiquette was, and travelled in by train, as I was unsure about the facilities that were on hand for changing out of my cycling gear and into my work suit, but knew that I would not have the luxury of a Dressing Room, as space was at a premium in Neal's Yard. I was shown round the building by Euan, and introduced to people in each department, as we moved from floor to floor.

The building had been built, and until 1974 used, as a Fruit & Vegetable Warehouse and the loading gallery and hoist were still visible on the top floor, which featured an open plan office layout.

In the basement there was a small viewing theatre equipped to show projected audio visual (AV) presentations to clients, with a small kitchen, with the Technical Office situated on the ground floor. I was given a spot on a raised corner area, overlooking Neal's Yard, to make my base. On the first floor was Jeff Inman's Creative Department, whilst the Administration Offices were across the road in Shorts Garden. In the same building, near to Seven Dials, was the Prompting Company QTV, and an AV hire department service, wardrobe store etc. It was all self-contained, and well thought out.

As we went round I was introduced to people, but almost blew it on my first day when Henry (The Chairman) asked me if I spoke any languages. "Yes" I replied "English, Yiddish, and Rubbish" to try and be humorous, but not knowing that he was Jewish. I went to a nearby park to eat my sandwiches, and contemplate the first day so far, wondering what the afternoon would bring. My main duties were to prepare budgets for forthcoming shows, and once they had been confirmed, staff them with Lighting Designers, Fit Up Electricians, Carpenters, Sound Engineers, AV Engineers, Show callers, Assistant Stage Managers, Choreographers, Dancers, Riggers, Rehearsal Pianists and Transport Firms.

These people were engaged on a freelance basis, and hired just for the job. Along with the people they had used in the past, I would bring new people in to work on shows where their particular skill would be an asset. The first pitch to the client that I attended (where MMA would present their proposals) was on 7th August when Michael Ingrams was pitching to I.B.M. for a conference in Monte Carlo, to coincide with the Monaco Grand Prix. We showed them aerial shots of the track, the hours of preparation that were required, such as the welding down of the street man hole covers to prevent them being displaced by the aerodynamic forces of the F1 car, and how quickly it was all put back to normal. At the end the client said they would be in touch but I don't think we got the job. We were more successful with eight other clients such as Iveco Trucks, Whitbread, Data General, Leyland, and Avon, for whom we organized shows up to Christmas. The venues used hotels both in the UK and abroad, including The Skyline Hotel Heathrow, The Metropole Birmingham, The Imperial Hotel Torquay, The Mayfair Theatre, and The Casino in Monte Carlo.

I was asked not only to work on the Pre-Production of the Whitbread show, but also to go on site and look after it personally. The Producer was Judy Littler, daughter of the theatre Impresario, Emile Littler, who had produced over two hundred pantomimes, and with his brother Prince Littler had presented numerous big West End Musicals such as *Love from Judy*, *Guys and Dolls*, *The Pyjama Game* and *Can Can*, during their careers. The show was to be at The Metropole Hotel Birmingham in early October, and I would be there in my capacity as Assistant Technical Director.

The Metropole was next to The National Exhibition Centre, and had impressive conference and catering facilities for up to 2,000 delegates. I would get to know the building well during the next six years. I had my first meeting with the client on 10th August, which was eight weeks before the show.

On Sunday 20th September I tried my hand at the new sport of BMX Racing at the Eastway Track in London. During the evenings of the previous week I had built a BMX racing bike from some spare parts I had in the garage. I had equipped the garage with a workbench, vice, shelving and, most important, electricity, which I had run underground from the house on a fused spur, beneath the concrete flooring, before it was laid. Sadly my home made bike was no match for the imported American BMX bikes and I did not make the final. I decided that next time I went BMX Racing it would be on a purpose built bike, which I bought a few weeks later, and this was the very first new cycle that I owned.

I was on site at The Metropole for the three days 1st – 3rd October to oversee the presentation and cabaret for Whitbread, who were very happy with the way it all went. I received a letter from the Producer, Judy Littler, the Tuesday after, "Thanking me very much for all my hard work", and adding that she did appreciate it, which helped make up for the time I had spent working away from home. I was also sent a copy of a letter she had received from Andrew Steel (Marketing Development Manager) for Whitbread Take Home Division, in which he asked for his "sincere thanks to be passed on to me, as I had always been there when needed and had covered every eventuality". I felt at last that all my hard work, commitment and twenty one years of experience were being recognised in this new field.

My friend Des Tate had a party on Friday 16th as he was leaving The Round Table Pub, where Dad had once pulled one of his favourite tricks, claiming that it was his birthday, and could he buy a round for the staff after drinking up time, which always worked and of course one for the staff turned into a session until the early hours. I still somehow managed to fit in a visit to one of the best Track Racing events of the year - The Lydden Speedtrack International - in Kent on Sunday 18th and took Julian with me as he was getting on for six years old now.

I first met Philip Spalding from IBM at the office in early November, as The UK Data Processing Division had a presentation booked in for the Congress Centre in Vienna in April '82. As it was an overseas event for a prestigious client, time was of the essence, and as he liked the way I worked and dressed, asked for me personally to look after this conference in the Ballroom of The Hofburg Palace. I flew out with him to do a recce a month later. We were booked into The Vienna Hilton and Philip arranged to meet me for a night out in Vienna. As anyone who has stayed in a Hilton knows, once inside you could be in Amsterdam, Budapest or Berlin, as they are anonymous places, but IBM were paying, so it was their choice. Philip was a typical IBM type in a grey suit and beige mackintosh and his idea of a good night out was very different to mine. He suggested that we start off in a Beer Keller for a meal. I made the excuse that I was not hungry after the flight, and sat in polite conversation with him whilst he ate and had a beer, before I left him for an early night. On our way to the Keller I had spotted a Cabaret Bar that looked interesting, paid the entrance fee and settled down with a large glass of lager, which cost the earth. One drink led to another. I left about midnight and headed for another late bar nearby, and got chatting, as you do when you are having a good night out, to some of the locals, but I was spent up by now, so I made my way back to The Hilton. At one point I had to cross a busy four lane inner city ring road and forgot to look the opposite way to normal, and was almost run down.

I was slightly hung over in the morning when I met Mr. Spalding to get a cab to the Hofburg Palace, which was where the conference was to be held. Fortunately I had brought with me my standard recce form which was divided into twelve sections which covered everything that I could think of. The 12 headings were Venue Details (phone numbers etc.); Get in (door size/stairs/local labour etc.); The Room (dimensions/weight loading/nature of the floor etc.); Electrical (total power & phase availability/cable run from generator if inadequate mains supply/ house light control position etc.); Sound (normal operating position/and assessment of in house equipment etc.); Projection (number of 35mm slide projectors, and assessment); Catering (tea/coffee/canteen for the crew/possibility of kitchen noise in the room); Dressing Rooms (location/size/numbers/costume rails/cheval mirrors/house relay system etc); Charges (heating/electricity used/security staff/overtime etc); General (local fire regulations/smoke detectors/availability of a piano/can we screw into the floor etc); Details (who is the contract with/get in date & time/get out curfew etc); Specials (any local public holidays during our stay/local regulations re driving on weekends/public holidays etc). There was a total of one hundred and twenty questions I wanted answers to.

This took most of the morning, and the worst part was having to go up into the grid over the room to get an accurate measurement of the distance from the room floor. I haven't got a head for heights anyway and being hung over didn't help. The flight back to Heathrow was booked for a 5pm check in, so I went back to the Hilton for an afternoon nap, before joining Philip on the airport bus. All the information was vital for my pre-planning and brief to lighting designer, set builder, sound and AV engineers etc. On my return to the office and armed with the knowledge I had gleaned on site, I set about staffing the show, as I wanted a top rate team to work with me. I engaged Spike Gaden and John Tosh on Electrics and Sound, and phoned Diana Fraser, who was on holiday in New Zealand, as the show caller, because she was bi-lingual and reliable. A full detailed technical report of the show was published in the ABTT News, of June '82.

Spike was not only a good lighting man, but also a real character amongst his peers. It is rumoured that once he was engaged by a lighting designer to re-light his show on tour, as he was unavailable.

Spike got the train from his home near Chichester up to Newcastle where he had been told that the show he was to work on was playing. He got off the train, looked round for a taxi and spotted a billboard for the Theatre Royal where the musical was playing and noticed to his chagrin that he had got the date wrong. He was a week early and had endured a wasted 700 mile round trip train journey.

On 19th December we celebrated four years of living at Mount Pleasant Lodge, and felt well pleased with the £12,500 it had cost to buy, bearing in mind that we had sold the flat in Morley Court for £10,500. With all the work and improvements I had done, I estimated that it was worth about £70,000, which was a good profit, but had been very hard work during the uncertain times I had been through. This was important as Maris was now three months pregnant with our third child, due in June 1982, and a move to a larger house loomed.

In contrast to theatre work, where Christmas and New Year are peak periods, in the world of Trade Shows it is a very quiet period with up to ten days off. As I was employed freelance on a show by show basis I could not legitimately present my weekly invoice for £200, so things were tight again.

The first show of 1982 was back at The Metropole for Iveco Trucks and the, by now, well-oiled machine was up and running, much like one of their trucks. February was a quiet month, but in March I worked for Fiat on a show at The Old Vic, and Halfords back at the Metropole in Birmingham at the NEC.

March was busy with last minute pre-production preparations for the IBM Show in Vienna, with detailed talks with set builders, and a scaffolding firm to provide us with a quick-rig kit that was brand new, as it would be on view, to house the multitude of High Powered Kodak Carousel Projectors that were required with 300mm long lenses on them. I found a firm in Yorkshire who would hire us what we needed which was The Youngman's Easi-Build 800 Tower System, and would deliver it to us in London. I needed the projectors to be 4.80m up from the ground, which was Centre Screen height, and the main worry was that once they were all lined up, when the 850 delegates sat down on the sprung floor, the rig would dip and go below the centre of the screen. Short of me hiring a crowd there was little we could do. As a precaution I insisted that we have screw jacks at the bottom of the system to quickly adjust, if it should happen, once the delegates all arrived and sat down.

The Festsaal also had an echo like being in the dome of Saint Paul's and we hoped that the presence of 850 bodies would help absorb this.

We loaded the 40-foot artic trailer early on Tuesday 6th April and Tony Ramsay (Master Carpenter from The Globe) came up with a loading crew for me. This gave us a week to travel to Austria but we had to bear in mind that there were three days when we could not travel because of Good Friday, Easter Sunday and Easter Monday restrictions on the Continent. The technical office secretary handed over the detailed Carnet to the co-driver, and they set off for Dover and Europe. The crew and I flew out on Tuesday 13th April (Julian's sixth birthday) and thankfully the truck and trailer were parked up on our arrival.

The Get In, Fit Up and technical all went well and we waited with bated breath for the 850 men in identical grey suits and macs to sit down. My concerns were unfounded, thank goodness, and the opening sequence of the show and conference was very funny, and went like this: "Good Morning Ladies & Gentlemen and welcome to the Hofburg Palace here in Vienna. It gives me great pleasure to introduce to you your host for the day Mr. Leslie Crowther"…..huge audible moans…and on walked John Cleese doing his Monty Python Silly Walk.…..huge cheers from all. John had only agreed to do the show as he had studied Sigmund Freud and wanted to visit the city where Freud had studied medicine in 1881.

We packed up after the show on Thursday 22nd April and the offload was at 10am the following Monday, again with a crew provided by Tony Ramsay. I had now done my first Trade Show abroad, and felt proud that all the pre-planning had again paid off handsomely.

On the first Monday in May I went to Harrogate to do a detailed recce for a Lever Brothers Show, and took a detour on the way home to pay my first visit to The National Railway Museum in York, not realising that I would not be returning there again until 2013 when I attended The Great Gathering of all six of the last remaining Gresley A4's. June involved another show in Monte Carlo for Hertz, whilst at home in Kings College Hospital on 25th June, a second baby girl joined our family. We named her Rebecca Sarah. I had broken the curse that had happened twice before, when an addition to the family coincided with The Notice going up.

On 15th July Agfa Open Reel Audio Tapes held an early morning conference at The Savoy Hotel. As it was a local in town job I took it on personally, and what a wise choice I made. Not only did it feature the English Singer/Song Writer Judy Tzuke, best known for her 1979 hit single *Stay With Me Till Dawn* (and what hot blooded man wouldn't), but the maestro of the Trumpet Humphrey Littleton. It was a low-key affair designed to show off the superior quality of the Agfa tape, and at the end of the short presentation a few of us were invited to have breakfast at The Savoy, and I was lucky enough to be seated at a table with Humph. I ordered Omelette Arnold Bennett, a concoction of Eggs, Smoked Haddock and Parmesan, that has been a standard dish at the Savoy for many years, whilst Humph had the Kedgeree. This was 'toogood' a moment to miss out on, so I asked him what, in his opinion, was the difference between the Count Basie Band and the Duke Ellington Orchestra? Without hesitation he replied that Duke had surrounded himself with the very best soloists he could find, whilst Basie was an ensemble Band. This simple break down of two of the most renowned Big Bands that ever played has remained with me for the last thirty-two years… thank you Humph.

In 1982 a new form of National Grass Track Championship was introduced to find the three champions: solo, sidecar & passenger. Called The Masters, the first of the two legs was held on Sunday 15th August 1982 at Condover and was organised by The Shropshire M/C Cub, with the second and final leg to be run at the end of September. As I now had both Saturdays and Sundays off, and had more or less given up Cycle Speedway Racing, I went up to Susan's house, as she was now living in a beautiful period town house on the High Street in Pershore. It was nice to spend time with her, Tony, Joanna, who was now six and Katy who was four, and for them to meet Rebecca, prior to my going to the meeting on the Sunday. A new and most exciting rider Simon Wigg won the first Masters Title in the Solo Class, whist the crew of Ted Tucker & Dave Ward, from the Lincoln area, won the Masters Sidecar Title. I would attend the majority of these Championship meetings, each year, for the next thirty years.

Meanwhile I was enjoying my work at MMA, constantly adding names of experienced and, most important, reliable people to crew the numerous shows that we had coming in, and firms that could provide the quality service that we and the clients demanded, both in the UK and abroad.

One of the most demanding of my many duties was the preparation of the initial budget to present to the client at the pitch and like the recce form was divided into twenty-five sections. I had to complete the technical sections. The headings were Pre Production (with fifteen sub-sections); Live Action (13); Slide Projection (5); Video & Film Production (9); Music Production (11); Tape Preparation (9); Video/film/slide programming (8); Pre-Viewing & Rehearsals (8); Wardrobe (4); Staging (11); Lighting (6); Sound (6); Slide (7); Cine (5); Video (5); Prompting Services (3); Simultaneous Translation (4); Equipment (5); Transport (6); Travel & Subsistence (4); Venue Charges (3); Printing (8); Exhibition Space (5); Insurance (4); Sundries (2); and finally Ex-Budget Items (9); which totalled 175 separate sections to be filled in.

As you can imagine, this was very time consuming, and had to be justified. For example, the Technical Department fee was 2% of the bottom line, Dancers were budgeted @ £200 per week, Models @ £40 per day, Wardrobe @ £25 per costume required, Carpenters @ £60 per day, Electricians @ £70 per day, Sound Operators @ £75 per day, Projection Engineer @ £85 per day, and Cast & Crew 'Per Diems' @ £20 per day, minimum, and rising for away expensive dates, such as Paris or Monte Carlo.

The budgeting process for the Transport Costs for example, would be to ring Ronnie Fielding, who was our regular contractor, for a price. We used Ronnie, as it was a family run business based in Essex, with his son Tony Fielding being one of his main drivers. They were reliable, punctual, friendly and had been involved with Trade Show and Conference work since 1976 when Ron had a conversation in a pub with a local Scenery Builder, Dave Hoffman of *Light & Shade*, about moving a Set for him. Their drivers were familiar with the procedures and Carnet requirements at Customs, and had an extensive knowledge of continental driving regulations. They could supply us with Rigid Trucks, with up to a ten-ton payload, or one of their purpose built forty-foot step frame trailers, which had no wheel arch box, because they used a triple small wheel boogie set and air ride suspension, which was desirable for sophisticated electronic equipment, with a twenty ton payload, and were hauled by reliable Volvo or Scania Tractor Units. The conversation would go something like this: "Morning Ronnie, I need a price by 2pm please, for two trailers to pick up in London and be in Estoril to off-load at the Casino there on 14th April next year, and return to London to drop off in London week commencing 25th April, bearing in mind the Easter HGV transport restrictions." Pause… "By 2pm you say?"…." Yeah I am sorry Ron, but it's a rush job, and when would you have to leave by?"…. "I'll work something out and get back to you"… which he did without fail. That was why we used him, and not some cowboy firm, who were cheaper, but could let us down.

The next show I went on site for was to launch the 1983 Lamb's Navy Rum Calendar, and the selected venue was the Xenon Night Club in Piccadilly. This was a hugely popular establishment that was the Night Club of choice for many, and when I had been there, was populated with the fashion crowd. The Club was based on its sister club, with the same name in Manhattan that tried to rival Studio 54, but never quite made its mark in the same way, when it became known as 'the most famous club of all time'. The main problem I faced, after I had visited the plush club, was where to site the projectors, as the main basement room, which we were to use, was littered with support columns which prevented a straight projection onto the screen, vital to show the beautiful half-naked models sipping Lamb's Navy Rum on exotic beaches. It was only after many hours of painstaking drawing, and calculations of what lenses would be required to project the size of image onto the hanging front projection screen, that I found a solution.

In September, we all went on a family holiday to Normandy, with Maris's mother Mickey, and I had a wonderful time visiting all the D Day Landing spots, like Pegasus Bridge, Gold, Sword, Juno, Omaha and Utah beaches, along with the Point du Hoc. It was very moving to see the remains of Mulberry Harbour, and some of the Sherman Tanks that survived 6th June 1944, which were still in situ as a reminder of the terrible price many paid on that historic day. We enjoyed the beaches, and fresh seafood, and I found that the local Normandy Cider and Calvados were most palatable, and brought a bottle or two home.

The final show I worked on in 1982 was at the Café Royal, on my birthday, Friday 17th December. Little did I know it at the time, but fifteen years later I would be General Manager for the Cabaret Room at this prestigious venue, working with international stars. The show was held in one of the larger reception rooms, on the third floor, with the only access for equipment being the catering lift, which was constantly held at particular floors for pig swill waste dustbins to be loaded and offloaded. I therefore looked for another access route using the Emergency Evacuation Staircase that ran from top to bottom, exiting at Street level. As I set about finding if this was a practical route to carry equipment, I was horrified to find that the Emergency Stairs were completely blocked at one point with all the equipment that was associated with the frequent Boxing Tournaments that were held there.

I raised my concerns with the Manager, and he told me that the staircase was the only available space nearby where it could be stored and would not be moved. I was outraged that a venue with an international reputation could breach fire safety regulations, which require that 'any exit route must be clearly signed, lit and unobstructed,' in such a blatant manner and informed him that I wanted a formal complaint logged, and that I would be taking the matter further. I prayed that we would not have an incident that evening, which required us to evacuate. Thank goodness we didn't, and the show went without a hitch. After the Get Out, I went on to celebrate my thirty eighth birthday at The Xenon Club, where I was made most welcome as they all remembered me from the Lamb's calendar job. When I returned to the MMA office on the Monday, I composed a very concise letter of complaint to The General Manager of the Café Royal, and sent a copy to Lord Forte, who owned the venue. The following day I went into work wearing casual attire as I was going to see a Christmas show with the two eldest children at The Barbican that afternoon, when soon after 10 am I got an internal call from the Managing Director, Malcolm Mitchell, asking me to come to his office as he had Lord Forte with him. I was complemented on the concise nature of my formal letter, which His Lordship told us "would be investigated fully, acted upon, and that heads would roll," and he ended by thanking me for bringing this safety breach, to his attention. I felt that I had proved yet again that if you want something done about something then it is best to go straight to the top and not waste time with subordinates, who will just try to fob you off.

As was the custom MMA closed down for a week over Christmas. I did not set foot in the building again until Thursday 30th when I had a meeting booked in my diary with one of our most regular Production Managers John Bayliss, who lived in Brighton. He had been engaged to work on a show early the next year. John was another character who liked nothing better than to drink with his mates in The Crown at Seven Dials, which was a real techies pub, and when he was there, he smoked cigarettes one after the other. We always got on well together, and shared a mutual interest in the delightful fish restaurant, English's of Brighton, in East Street, near to the pier. This unique Edwardian restaurant had been serving seafood for over a hundred years, had been in the Leigh Jones family since 1945, and was famed for its marble topped Oyster Bar, where you could enjoy half a dozen natives with a glass of Champagne or dine on King Scallops St. Jacques, or a Plateau de Fruits de Mer with a bottle of Picpoul de Pinet in the plush red velvet room next to it, all at a very reasonable price. We chatted for a couple of hours. It was as much a social as a business meeting, and about 5 pm we wished each other a "Happy New Year" and went our separate ways to spend New Year's Eve with our friends and family.

1983 started quietly, as January was not a popular month for conferences, and the only one I went on site for was for Watneys at The Portman Hotel, in Portman Square. Every time I went there I was reminded of the party in Paul Raymond's flat nearby and what fun it had been. The following month there was only a show for Johnson & Johnson at the very nice Imperial Hotel in Torquay to worry about, and whilst I was there I tried to find the house that the parents of Maggie Richardson (my first student girlfriend) lived in, and which I had visited in 1965, to ask them where she was now, as the last I had heard she was working for The Royal Shakespeare Company in Stratford. When I eventually found the house, they had moved, and to this day I still don't know what happened to her.

March picked up as usual, and I began to prepare for my next overseas show for IBM at The Casino in Estoril, and was especially looking forward to working with Director & Choreographer Dougie Squires again. I had not seen him since the end of Peter Pan with Lulu in 1972-73. I was still constantly adding new people to my ever-growing contact list, and amongst them was Alan Jacobi from Unusual Rigging, which was a specialist firm of highly trained individuals who possessed skills that enabled them to work at any height, and provide safe and secure fixing points to suspend things like advance lighting bars or speaker stacks. They did not come cheap, but were essential on some of the jobs and many of these people went on to help build The Millennium Dome.

We loaded for the IBM job on Friday 8th April, again using Ronnie Fielding for transport. They - his son Tony would again be the co-driver and crew the show for me at The Casino - would travel by ferry from the south coast overnight to Santander or Bilboa, to cut down on road time, and then drive into Portugal, arriving there by Monday 13th, when the crew and I would fly out and join them. The trip through the Bay of Biscay had been very rough, and one of the trailer securing rings which were supposed to stop the trailer from moving about in the swell had snapped off during the night. Rather than opening the back doors to find the neat load they had left London with, things were now all over the place. Despite being in flight cases we were not sure whether any of the electric and projection gear had been damaged. The crew and I flew out to Porto on 13th April, which was Julian's seventh birthday, and then got a mini bus for the trip to Estoril. The Casino was set in a lush Mediterranean garden and was huge. In fact it was one of the largest Casinos in Europe, with an international reputation for its floorshow cabaret. When we offloaded, thank goodness we found only superficial damage had been sustained en route, and the carpenters from Light & Shade, who were notorious for being very laid back, set about repairing the damage outside, as it was pleasantly warm even in mid-April.

The Cabaret Dougie had devised was magnificent, and both client and delegates were thrilled with the quality of the show and the artistes. After the show, while the Get Out took place, all the Company went out for dinner with Dougie. We took over a local restaurant and shared huge platters of Paella, which contained some of the largest King Prawns I had ever seen. The Vinho Verde and Mateus Rose flowed, as we danced until the early hours, much to the chagrin of the crew, who had not been invited to the party.

As I had been away for Julian's birthday I went to a local toy shop and bought a fully working yellow tower crane for him to enjoy. For Rachel I found a super little Summer dress that I thought would suit her and for Becky, who was still not two years old, a selection of nice baby-gro things and a mobile to hang over her cot.

The next away day came the following month when I went down to Portsmouth to recce the historic 1890 neo classical Guildhall for the Admin division of IBM. Despite some misgivings, I thought we could put on a good show for them there, as they were accustomed to presenting live entertainment. Whilst I was in Pompey, and before I got a train back to London, I paid a visit to look around Nelson's flagship HMS Victory, which is maintained as a visitor attraction in the City, and was most impressed with what I saw and how cramped some of the areas were for the sailors to live and work in.

It was around June when Euan Felton, who I reported to, asked me to undertake the duties of what we would now call The Health & Safety Officer for the Company. I was happy to undertake this and trained the office staff in the use of fire extinguishers, introduced an assembly point for a roll call, and planned what to do in the event of a bomb threat. This was particularly important for the Production Manager on a prestige show for a prominent world company like IBM, who took security and the safety of their employees very seriously. I devised a basic check list for people to remember or keep by their telephone, and it was based on the letter 'W' for ease of memory. Anyone receiving a suspicious call was encouraged to try and ask the following questions: When will it go off? /Where is it? /What does it look like? /Why are you doing this? /Who are you? /Where are you? They were also told to listen for any background noise (such as a railway station train announcement), whether it came from a coin box (as mobiles were rarely used in the '80s) and to write down the exact text of what was said, and if in any doubt to take the call as genuine, because it is better to be safe than sorry.

It was also pointed out that it is not the job of the police to make the decision to evacuate a venue. This is down to the owner of the building, who should also look out for anything unusual. The inside of a toilet cistern was known to have been used in the past. The trainees were told that the sense of smell was a useful tool and to identify petrol, or marzipan, which would identify the presence of a possible explosive or incendiary device. A few years later I was able to invest in a hand held smelling device that was programmed to identify such suspicious odours, and would bleep an audible warning as the suspect item was approached. On one occasion I was required to use this device as a carrier bag had been left in an unusual place. As I approached it, the device did not bleep so I felt confident enough to look inside the carrier bag that had been left unattended. I found it contained a selection of adult magazines, which the person had obviously had second thoughts about taking home with him.

I had a very good working relationship with Jane Grecian, as she was responsible for dealing with all the room bookings for the staff and crew who went onsite. It was company policy that one didn't have to double up if at all possible, which everyone hated if it happened. On occasions we would slip off for a business lunch at one of the many fine restaurants in Covent Garden, and she was fun to be with, and very efficient at what she did. If I did not go out to lunch, I sometimes went and had a pint and a pork pie with the many technical and theatre people who frequented The Crown at Seven Dials, as there was always someone in there I knew to chat to. If I didn't visit The Crown, I used to take a late lunch and go along to the public gallery at the famous Bow Street Magistrates court opposite The Royal Opera House, to listen to the cases on the list for the day. On occasions I saw people in the dock to answer the charge of being drunk and disorderly in a public place, who I knew. I very soon came to the conclusion that every sixth-former should be taken, as part of their school work, to a Magistrates Court, to see what the procedure is, who sits where, and to appreciate the role of the Legal Clark who assisted The Stipendiary or Lay Bench of Magistrates, who would decide your fate or fine. I also learnt that you could be given free legal advice from The Duty Solicitor, and he was engaged to represent you if asked.

I was in a packed public gallery on the day that George Best was up before the court to answer the charge of assaulting a police officer in the execution of his duty. The brief that George had engaged rose to address the Court of the mitigating circumstances surrounding the case. No sooner had he got to his feet than the Stipendiary, who had a reputation as being of the old school and doing things by the book interrupted him and said: "Excuse me Mr. so and so, but in my Court anyone who assaults a Police Officer is going to receive a custodial sentence" and that was the end of any mitigating circumstances for Mr. Best, who went down for three months at Ford Open Prison.

I now had evenings to work on the allotment as I was insistent that I left the office at 5.30 pm each night, which gave me time see the kids before they went to bed. After all I was always first in the office as I used to set off for the ten mile cycle ride to Covent Garden as soon as I had got back from taking the children to their respective schools. I had by now been elected by my fellow plot holders as their Chairman and liaised with the Council over problems that arose, and the annual inspection on the thirty or so plots that comprised our site.

July saw me preparing a budget for a Volvo and IBM show in Monte Carlo, Rumbelows at The Night Out Club in Birmingham, and Peugeot Talbot in Hall One at the National Exhibition Centre. My main concern was making arrangements for the family holiday, which I planned to take in late August to early September.

I paid my annual homage to the Grass Track Masters Championships on Sunday 7th August and this year the second and final of the two legs Final was promoted by the Evesham MCC Club at their Long Marston Aerodrome near Stratford-on-Avon. Simon Wigg retained his National Solo title scoring 92 points, whilst Steve Smith & Trevor Pye took the Sidecar Title on overall points (61) despite the second leg being won overall by Roger & Jeff Measor on 59 which was the same as defending Champion Ted Tucker & Dave Ward.

As we had all enjoyed Normandy so much the previous year we decided to go along the French coast a bit further and visit Brittany, which was idyllic, with the beguiling crinkle-cut coastline and pink granite rocks. The children grew to love the variety of crepes, whilst Maris and I loved nothing more than to sit on a terrace, eating fresh seafood, watching the sunset, and enjoying the odd glass or two of the local calvados, but I was never quite sure if Mont-St-Michel was part of Normandy or Brittany.

Two new Production Managers began to work on shows during the autumn, Douglas Bullock and Max Chowen, and although both had worked on theatre shows in the past, they were virgins in our field. I helped them to adjust as much as I could, as by now I had over thirty shows, both in the UK and in Europe, under my belt. Douglas was a family man like me and rather laid back, but good company. I bought a Morris Traveller from him for spares for the one that I was now running, for which I had replaced the whole of the ash timber frame during the Summer evenings. Max was married to a dancer and I found him less approachable than Douglas. By now I was quite familiar with most of the AV and Projection equipment we regularly used on the shows, as much of it was kept in the subsidiary firm of TAV in Shorts Gardens, managed by John White. I took time when things were quiet in the Technical Office to sort, label and file all the drapes and costumes that had been used in the past, that few knew about, including I discovered, a whole bin liner full of dance attire as worn by Hot Gossip.

Chef and Brewer chose to use The Royal Albert Hall for their event in November, and I made a detailed floor plan, in the scale of a quarter inch to the foot, of the main arena following a visit in October. It was huge and much bigger than I had imagined from seeing it during The Last Night of the Proms each year. The following month I did the same for The Dominion Theatre, where IBM Area One was to hold a conference and show the following April.

I had a very rare sick day on 11th November, but had recovered to have a real treat on Saturday 26th as I went to see the legendary *Ted Heath Band* play a concert at the recently opened Barbican Centre. It was great to meet some of the band in the King's Head pub on the corner of Chiswell Street and Silk Street before the concert, and talk to Don Lusher among others. Don had led the Ted Heath Tribute Band since Ted's retirement in 1964 and untimely death in 1969 on Lead Trombone, which had been Ted's instrument. The band had been formed on D-Day, and funded in the early days by the royalties that Ted's wife Moria received from the 1941 composition *I Haven't Said Thanks For That Lovely Weekend*. Two members of that original band, Jack Parnell and Tommy Whittle, were to play at this concert.

On entering the bar I could hear the Yorkshire tones of trumpeter Kenny Baker in animated conversation with the clown in the band, fellow trumpeter Scotsman Duncan Campbell (who also performed falsetto vocals on tunes such as *Tequila*). They were as usual, and like any other horn players, discussing their teeth. The band was still regarded by many as The Greatest British Swing Band ever, and the Full House board was proof that they were still regarded as such. Big Band fans like me had come along to hear them play the famous signature tunes *Listen to my Music* (first set) and *Opus One* (second set) that we had listened to on the wireless or records, many times before. We were not disappointed either to hear such tunes as *Hot Toddy*, *The Swinging Shepherd Blues*, or vocals from Mr. Smooth himself, Dennis Lotus, who I knew from my days working on *Pyjama Tops* ten years earlier. This was a night to remember, for all the right reasons, and I remained a huge fan of the band until their final concert at The Royal Festival Hall in December 2000. A recording of that very last concert has pride of place in my collection of Big Band Music.

Wandering around FOH during the interval at The Barbican, I noticed hanging in the Duty Manager's room a Bull Horn amplified loud hailer which I presumed was to direct the public if the PA System had gone down. I thought it was such a good idea that I would invest in one, which I did. It would come into its own on a IBM event in London's Docklands, in 1985.

It was Euan's birthday on Friday 2nd December, the same day as my great friend Cyril Ornadel's. I suddenly realised why I got on so well with him - he was a Sagittarian like me. I celebrated my birthday at home with the family on the 17th and went out to Tokyo Joe's Club, just off Piccadilly, with friends, on the Sunday, where we had a celebration.

The Christmas office party was on 22nd December between 5 and 9 pm and we all went our separate ways until 2nd January 1985. Things started at work in the usual, by now, slow fashion, with conferences and shows for the Alliance Building Society in Brighton at The Metropolis, and Sealink at the Night Out in Birmingham. I had made good contacts with Sealink for my summer holiday, cross-channel ferry bookings for this year's holiday in The Dordogne.

I had been asked to look after the entertainment for IBM Germany in the spring. Their brief was quite a simple, but mammoth, one as they wanted to provide a typical English Pub for their 2,500 delegates for two social evenings, after attending a conference which was to be held at The Barbican. They wanted to provide eating, drinking and entertainment. The usual venues that we had on file that could accommodate these numbers were unavailable on the dates in May when this was all supposed to happen, so a suggestion was put to the German contact Herr Faller that we convert one of the semi-derelict dock-side sheds at The Royal Victoria Docks into a 1910 period Street Scene with a central square, bandstand, and various themed pubs off it. Ironically this would not have been possible if the Luftwaffe had not almost obliterated the Silvertown area of the docks forty-five years earlier. This was to be the biggest event for MMA since the launch of the Ford Sierra car.

I had my first meeting with Bill Harkin, the Designer for the project, in the middle of January, and he was hugely experienced having designed shows for the the Rolling Stones, and the Pyramid Stage at Glastonbury. His company specialised in providing architecturally based theatrical solutions for unique projects, and had been the leading company in this type of work for many years. I had been upgraded to Technical Director for this project, and Bill and I began to draw up our first budget based on using a shed that we had found, with the dimensions of 700' x 200' x 50' high, which gave us in excess of five and a half million cubic feet to play with.

The first design using most of the area was rejected on cost grounds (yes we did have a budget) and a revised plan using a 200'x 200' square was accepted by IBM on 15th March. The first night was on 8th May, only seven weeks away.

The idea was to make the basic walls from exhibition panels (1m x 2.75m) then apply vacuum formed sheets and a paint finish, with the detailed work for the bandstand, bars etc., to follow. We costed for a crew comprising 30 carpenters, 10 electricians, 5 sound engineers, 4 set dressers, 8 riggers, 6 painters. With onsite caterers and cleaners, it was mind blowing. I engaged Jeff Kitto, who I knew from his work at The Birmingham Rep as Production Manager with an assistant Tereesa Joselyn, as they were going to be in charge of over a hundred artistes and musicians who were to perform during the evening.

The shed was devoid of basic facilities, and just to sweep the floor before we could go onsite I had to engage a Road Sweeper to go up and down all day. We were going to have to install toilets, running water, dressing rooms, a catering area, offices, and a generator to supply enough power, as what was onsite was totally inadequate.

Several permutations of how much beer a German could/would consume and subsequently relieve himself of, were put forward to help us calculate just how many toilets would be required, and several hours of research in The Crown were carried out on this particular problem, as we did not want to have too few.

Lighting Designer Robert Stanbury estimated that he would require a thousand lanterns for the outside areas and interiors, but in the end this came down to 734 units mainly comprising 90 Vari lights, 40 Berkley's, 80 pat 743's assorted Lekos and 200 Par cans.

The whole lot was to be controlled via a 72 way zero desk with a 64-way memory, and powered from a 1000 KvA generator parked outside. The three phase 300 amp shed supply was split up to (a) supply the multitude of pub practical, and street lights, (b) be the domestic supply for catering, dressing rooms, loos etc., and (c) to give the sound boys a clean supply for their systems.

The brief given to Sound Designer Dave Hunt was equally onerous. We asked him to provide equipment and manpower to work a PA system throughout the interior and exterior of the building, along with five individual systems for the pubs and bandstand areas. These were to be independent, and not impose on each other when all on together. The main control selected was via a 16 – 8 Soundcraft 800B desk, plus Soundcraft 200's and Alice 1248's looking after each of the pubs and the main Bandstand, where Acker Bilk was to play, and an operator was assigned to each area.

Each pub was given its own name and identity such as Fisherman's Arms and The Shakespeare and dressed accordingly with all the bar and catering staff also dressed in period costumes. We even managed to get the crew to enter into the spirit of things and don flat caps and waistcoats. Crew travel to and from the venue caused quite a headache as public transport to the Royal Victoria Docks was not good, and with crew coming from all points of the compass a central pick up point was arranged. I provided a mini bus to run to and from the venue and credit must go to Neil McGrath for getting all concerned safely to and from the East End during the rush hours. Many of the crew could not face the daily commute, and a small caravan village grew up on one side of the shed.

Internal communications were handled by 16 handsets with the technical crew being on one channel, and the emergency services Doctor, First Aid, Fire Marshals and Security on the other. Three security men were employed to patrol the Emergency Exits and the fourth, who was a trained lifesaver, was to be on the deep-water side.

I used my contacts to find people with the right skills for this job and settled on Ronnie McKewan as the Overall Chief Production Electrician, with Phil Abbot as the ground-crew chief and Gerry Amies as the off-ground chief in charge of all the suspended gear and the maintenance of the generator. They were in charge of the six experienced electricians like Bill Wardroper, Angus Stewart, and Brian Hunt, who got the rig up on time. Most of the crew were used to being on a job for only a day or two so the thought that they would be submitting their invoices for £1,500 made them all willing to put in the hours, but I was a little put out as my weekly Invoice was still only £300 per week. The first night on Thursday 9th May went well and to everyone's satisfaction, apart from the arrival of a Transit Van full of Police in riot gear to find out what was going on. When they found out that it was not a rave, they left rather sheepishly, much to the amusement of the men in grey from IBM.

The next Gala Evening was on the Monday. The events at Valley Parade Football ground, during a match between Bradford City and my hometown of Lincoln City on Saturday the 11th, when the main stand caught fire and 56 fans died and over 250 were injured, caused me to re-evaluate the Emergency Procedures we had in place down at the docks. After talking to The Chairman, I was put in overall control of Evacuation, should it be needed, at the second show on the Monday.

To improve on what I thought was already a reliable, foolproof system I went to a local ships chandlers and bough two Air Horns (one as a back up) to sound as follows: three blasts to indicate to the staff that I, as The Incident Officer, had received a report of an incident and that it was being investigated; two blasts to say that it had been investigated and all was all now clear, and one continuous blast to indicate that I had decided to evacuate the building and delegates and crew should proceed to their assembly points for a Roll Check.

I would wear a florescent high vis waistcoat, to be easily identifiable, and meet the first attendance Crew from Silvertown Fire Station nearby based in North Woolwich Road, and brief them. I had visited the station in advance to introduce myself to the Red Watch Station Officer on the risks and numbers involved in the event, as his watch was scheduled to be on duty on these nights.

As further back up I seconded a German speaker to make any Emergency Announcements, and provided him with a Bull Horn Loud Hailer to use in the event of us losing our PA system for whatever unforeseen reason. The Chairman and I were both happy with this pre planning, and before the arrival on site of the 2,500 delegates, in a fleet of fifty coaches, I held a rehearsal with all of the crew and performers and explained the system, and what the respective air horn blasts indicated. Thankfully the system never needed to be used that night, but the lessons I had learnt and the detailed pre-planning would prove vital when I had to deal with an explosive oxy-acetylene cylinder at the fifth biggest theatre in London, a few years later. As a thank you Herr Faller presented me with an engraved barometer, which hangs in my hallway. The Get Out took longer than expected, but Shed 4 was given back to its owners, no worse for wear and much cleaner, to await its next adventure.

Herr Faller was heard to remark on the final night: "I don't know who was the crazier - MMA for suggesting the idea, or IBM for accepting it."

This huge adventure and challenge had been the highlight of my career with MMA and I could not see it being bettered. With Max Chowen having taken over from Euan Felton as my boss, I began to look for a return to my first love, the theatre, if only I could find a job that paid as well. I did not hit it off with Max as much as I had done with Euan, partly I think because I felt that I should have been offered Euan's postion, as I had been working on a show by show basis for almost five years and had contributed in no small way to the success of about sixty shows in that time.

I had been engaged as far back as 1983 by the ABTT as their assessor for the City and Guilds Theatre Electricians Project 181-1-03. I enjoyed passing on some of my vast experience to the forty youngsters who were making their first inroads and about to hopefully get work in their chosen profession, and I began to consider this as a new career. I started to undertake Part Time Freelance lectures to the Technical Students for David Ayliff at RADA and Steven Webber at Mountview Theatre School, but this employment was rather sparse. I applied to The Rose Bruford Theatre School in Sidcup to join their training school as a full time member of staff, got an interview, only to withdraw my application when I was told more about the job on offer.

The event that bought matters to a head occurred one morning when I arrived at The MMA Technical Office at my usual time of 9.30 to find Max already at his desk which was unusually early for him. After I had changed out of my cycling attire and into the work suit, he got up from his desk, closed the office door, and said that he wanted to talk to me. He basically told me that the rolling show by show arrangement that I had been engaged under since 3rd August 1981, was to be terminated because of my inflexibility and desire to leave at 5.30 each evening. I was rather put out to hear this, as I had been most flexible with my hours on the IBM Docklands Show in April and May, working well in excess of my usual forty hours. I explained to him that my working arrangements, being a family man, had been agreed with Euan and although I had not been given a contract by MMA I had, as was my usual practice, set out in a letter to him, the details of my understanding of the terms of my employment, and had not had a reply to the contrary. To my certain knowledge this letter was still on file in the office. However he was having none of it and I put it down to a clash of personalities and a lack of understanding of being a family man. I was offered a move to the QTV Prompting Division to work as Assistant to Managing Director Avril Voller, as a thank you transfer move for my loyalty until I could find something more suitable, however my weekly salary would be reduced from £300 to £200.

I reluctantly accepted the offer, as I did not want to be out of work, finishing with the Technical Department on Friday 28th February, when a farewell party was held for me at lunchtime, with gifts, a big card and a few surprising people offering me their support and good wishes. I started with QTV Prompting the following Monday 3rd March 1986, and hated the job even more than being a Bingo Caller. I stayed for two months before I got back into Musical Theatre with *Seven Brides for Seven Brothers* at The Prince of Wales Theatre, a move that would shape my career for the next ten years.

Act 5 Scene 3
SEVEN BRIDES FOR SEVEN BROTHERS
(1986)

If ever I was ready for a job it was this one. Although I had enjoyed most of my time working on Trade Shows and Conferences for MMA, and learnt a great deal about new equipment, I really had missed the buzz that one only gets in a theatre at seven thirty, when the orchestra strikes up and begins the overture to a full house. It became abundantly clear, and confirmed what I had known all along, that I am a people person and interact well with fellow thespians, not a technician.

During my (what would turn out to be) final year with MMA, in addition to taking some theatre lecture work, I began to write reviews of shows and technical reports on the trade shows that I had worked on. They were published in Theatre Trade periodicals, as very few people in the business were writing them at the time. It was something I enjoyed and found quite easy to do from the few notes I made during and after the shows. Where this ability suddenly came from I do not know, as at school most of my essays only received average marks. The exception was when I chose to write an essay on Jazz Music whilst the other members of the class went for Pop Music, and I received nine out of ten from Mr. Phillips.

In 1985 I wrote a review on J.B. Priestley's *When We Are Married*, which Maris and I saw at the new Churchill Theatre in Bromley (where I had that embarrassing interview for a job years before) as it was twenty five years since I had first seen it in Lincoln with Freddie Jones playing a delightful Henry Ormonroyd. Roger Redfarn, who was also in the Repertory Company with me at Lincoln, directed it, as he was now working at The Theatre Royal in Plymouth from where this production originated. All in all it was a nostalgic evening and we stayed on to partake of the post show dinner, at the theatre restaurant.

I changed the title of my review from 'A View from the Stalls' to 'A View from the Upper Circle' when I went to see The Royal Variety Performance, which that year was at TRDL, and was staged around the resident show at the time, *42nd Street* which starred Frankie Vaughan. I was rather critical of the whole show, as by now the Royal Variety was aimed not so much at the people in the Auditorium watching the show live, but the television audience who would see a pre-recorded version later. I recall Stephanie Lawrence having trouble with the long dress that she wore during her Marilyn Monroe routine, and Norman Wisdom doing an act that most of us had seen before. I went backstage after the show for some additional technical information, and discovered that those performers who 'worked live' (some were on a 'click' track) were using a battery of eight Micron Radio Microphones, which had been swapped from person to person, as required, which must have been a nightmare for the artiste's dressers.

The ABTT celebrated its Silver Jubilee in 1985 and I wrote a long article for them entitled "How it was done in '61" looking back at working conditions, customs and practices that prevailed when the Association was born, which received critical acclaim.

Since leaving MMA in March 1986, I had been on the lookout for something, with a better salary, as things were difficult with five mouths to feed. A good lead came from The SMA of which I had been Chairman since 1984. I was given a tip off that John Newman of Newpalm Productions was looking for an experienced West End Musical Company Manager to take over on *Seven Brides for Seven Brothers* at The Prince of Wales Theatre, and was I interested? Of course I was interested, as it was exactly what I had been looking for, and went to see John for an interview on 24th April, where I also met General Manager Philip Compton, who knew me by reputation.

They explained to me that the show had originated at The Theatre Royal York in April 1984, had toured round the UK, and visited Canada before moving into the POW a few weeks ago. The present Company Manager Peter Kemp had been with the show whilst on tour but was not familiar with West End Customs and procedures, and wanted to move on as soon as possible. I told them I felt obliged to give QTV at least a week's notice, and could be free to start on Tuesday 6th May, as the Monday was a Bank Holiday, and they weren't doing a show because of the overtime charges. I asked about remuneration, and was informed that it was £300 per week, based on the Standard Esher Contract, which meant that overtime would be paid, when applicable. This was exactly what I had hoped for, and the deal was done.

My duties would be those of a traditional Company Manager in the West End, to ensure that the standard was maintained, company discipline, the payroll, entertaining VIP's and other matters as and when they occurred. There was nothing there to faze me, and the post encompassed all that I had done successfully in the past. The Director was Michael Winter, who at the time was The Artistic Director of the Mercury Theatre in Colchester. The Choreography was created by Stephanie Carter, who was vastly experienced and a tutor in Jazz /Musical Comedy at The Italia Conti School. Martin Yates as Musical Director looked after the fourteen-piece orchestra, whilst Bill Pinner was the Sound Designer. The jewel in the crown however on the production side was legendary Lighting Designer Michael Northern, whom I regarded as highly as Joe Davis as one of the old school of lighting designers. Like Joe he was a legend in his own lifetime and deservedly so. He was the first person to be credited with 'Lighting Design by' in 1952, and had that unique skill to be able to paint with light. He had begun his distinguished career in Stage Management in 1938, and not unlike me, had come up through the ranks, was utterly charming, professional, a pioneer in his field, and knew the business. Over lunch at Rules Restaurant in Maiden Lane, he and his peers had formed The Society of Lighting Designers in 1961, which would become The Association of Lighting Designers in about 1982, and he served as its Chairman to 1995 and President until his death in 2001 aged 79. I was now to work with another of my heroes.

The cast of over thirty was headed by Ronnie Page (Milly) and Steve Devereaux (Adam). In addition to the other six brides Alice, Dorcas, Ruth, Liza, Martha, Sarah and alphabetically named brothers Benjamin, Caleb, Daniel, Ephraim, Frank and Gideon, there were six Suitors, and eleven Townspeople. The majority of the cast were my junior in terms of age and West End experience, and I was happy in their company and felt respected. Once again I had to deal with children and animals for the *Spring Spring Spring* number in Act Two, but by now this wasn't a big problem for me as I had drawn up a The Children (Performances) Regulations Form to keep all their movements logged and up to date, should we get an inspection from their licensing authority.

This Newpalm Production (so named after Managing Director John Newman & Executive Director Daphne Palmer) was presented in association with Mark Furness, with whom I would work on *Some Like it Hot* in 1992, and Sherwood Productions, which had Robert Mackintosh (the younger brother of Cameron) as one of its directors. The Art Deco POW Theatre was designed by Robert Cromie, opened in 1937, and seated 1,100 on two levels. I had seen the shows *Round About Piccadilly*, *Funny Girl*, *Sweet Charity*, *Catch My Soul*, and the play *Harvey*, with James Stewart, amongst others there, so was at least quite familiar with the FOH, if not backstage.

The venue had been owned by George Black and then by Moss Empires Ltd., but was now part of The First Leisure Corporation (FLC). The Chairman & Chief Executive of FLC was Lord Delfont, and Prime Presentations ran the Theatre with Richard M. Mills as Chairman & Chief Executive. The General Manager Michael Churchill was assisted by House Manager Neil Major, whilst the Master Carpenter was Dave Pedersen, Chief Engineer Douglas Grice, and the Property Master was Jimmy Hinchliffe. Jimmy was one of the last two people to hold such a position in the West End, the other being Ronnie Pearson at The Palladium. I had the honour of working with these two legends, both of whom who could talk the hind legs off a donkey.

There were some outstanding dancers from within the ranks of the seven brides and brothers, notably Simon Howe, Martyn Knight, Jackie Crawford and Debra Robinson, but the one that really stood out was Michaela Strachan (Liza). Michaela had that particular style you associate with those who have trained at the Arts Educational School, and soon got television work on The *Wide Awake Club* before sampling the club life all over the country with Pete Waterman in *The Hit Man and Her*.

It had always been my custom to visit artistes in their dressing rooms after the half call had been made, to chat with them and listen to and deal with any problems that were on their minds. This helped to break down the 'them and us' feeling between the Management and Company, as I was very conscious of the tight line every Company Manager treads to serve both parties fairly. More than that, I made a point of joining the Company onstage for the warm up session while my muscles were still warm and I was quite flexible after I had cycled into work. Being an ex-dancer I knew the importance of such a session and, much to my delight, found that not only did I enjoy it, but it improved relations with the Company. Once they saw that I could dance as well as manage, all the barriers were down.

The two leads, Roni and Steve, were most charming but in very different ways. Roni was petite and had originally trained with the Royal Ballet School, and later had gone on to play Liesl in *The Sound of Music*, Rosie in *Strike a Light*, Maria in *West Side Story*, and back to her roots as a dancer playing Maggie in *A Chorus Line* at The TRDL. She was a real professional through and through. Steve on the other hand was a tall man's man and was ideally suited to play Adam with his rugged good looks. He had worked on *Tommy*, *The Rocky Horror Show*, *Joseph*, and *J C Superstar* in his career to date. We could chat about who was off at that performance, their cover, general gossip, other shows and life in general.

Peter Kemp was to stay on for a short changeover period whilst I accustomed myself with the way things were done at the moment. I didn't want to come in like a new broom and ruffle feathers. That could come later, when I was accepted more by the Management and Staff who hardly knew me. The other members of the Stage Management Team and Staff would remain with me, including David Norris (DSM) who knew the show backwards having run the Corner for the whole tour, whilst I brought in Teresa Joselyn (who had worked for me on the IBM Germany Docks Show) as my new ASM. Rodney Worth looked after the Supervision of the Wardrobe, whilst Graham Robinson operated the sound desk for Paul Farrah Sound.

There were in excess of fifty people on the contact list, to be paid weekly in cash, as bank transfers were yet to come and cheques were not trusted. For the first week Peter showed me how he did the Treasury Call and paid the company, staff and musicians, and how the office liked it done. Alarm bells rang when he went alone to collect what was a considerable sum in a carrier bag from a bank in The Haymarket. I inquired what the limit was with Newpalm's insurance company for cash in transit by a single person, to which he replied: "I have no idea." So before I organised my first run, I phoned the General Manager Phil Compton to ask the same question, and his reply was just as non-committal: "No one has ever asked that before, but I will find out for you." It turned out that Peter had been carrying four times the amount covered by insurance, so I set about organising a safe system that fell within the maximum limit. It worked like this. Once I had calculated the total cash required, let's say £19,877.25 and I had received the cheque to present to the bank, I broke it down into limits that were covered, should one be attacked. £10,000 in £20 notes to be carried by two people, half each, £5,000 in £10 (one person) and £4877.25 in £5 notes and coins again for one person to collect. I asked Jimmy Hinchliffe if he and three others would be prepared to do the bank run, adding there would be a drink in it for them. He agreed, and I called them persons A/B/C/D. I then drew up four separate and differing routes to and from the theatre to the bank, keeping to main busy streets, and avoiding back alleys and potential hiding spots that might be used by a robber who had been given a tip off, leaving and entering the POW via different doors, at different times. These I called routes W/X/Y/Z. An hour or so before I needed the cash, and to make up the pay packets, the four on the run, A/B/C/D would come to my office and pick out of a hat the route that they were to use, either W/X/Y/Z. By using this random selection, I hoped that should they be so minded, which I doubted, then they could not predict in advance what route they would be using that day, and give any accomplices a tip off. I walked the four routes, timed them on a stopwatch, and could only see two weak spots in the system. There was only one door into and out of the bank, but CCTV covered that, and the doors to be used at the theatre were also covered by a comprehensive system that relayed images to Mike Churchill's office. I would set off first, with the cheque to be cashed, and wait in line. The boys would arrive separately and wait for me to be served, when I would call them forward with a nod to indicate at random again who was to depart first via his route, and so on until the transaction had been completed. I would then follow one of the routes to ride shotgun, and as a further back up, on some weeks, I would carry one of the amounts myself and one of the boys would go back light. They never knew if this was going to happen, as it was a spur of the moment decision by me. Once safely back inside the confines of the building they would come to my office individually, where I would count the money out in front of them, and give them a drink from the petty cash account. I was happy with the system, the Management were happy that in the unfortunate event of anyone being robbed, all necessary precautions had been put in place and any loss would be covered, and the four boys were happy. It all worked like clockwork, again thanks to detailed planning and trying to prepare for any eventuality.

I was still very mindful of the tragic events that surrounded the Bradford City Fire disaster at Valley Parade the previous year, and with Mike Churchill's approval drew up an evacuation plan and nominated assembly points for a roll call, should this ever become necessary because of a fire or bomb threat. I was very disturbed that the seven brides company, which had been together since April 1984, had never received such training before and so organised an evacuation rehearsal for them to all take part in. I planned it with two incidents in mind, either a fire within the building or a bomb threat. I went to see the landlord of the local pub, and he agreed that his basement bar could be used for a roll call, if it was not in the blast area from a device as well. Should this not be safe, and bearing in mind that the artistes would almost certainly be in costume, I went to the FLC owned Empire Ballroom in Leicester Square and they agreed to be my number two assembly point.

One evening, and prior to the warm up session, which most of the company attended either for the vocal or dance class session, I told them I had been informed of an incident and that we needed to evacuate (they did not know if it was true or not) for their own safety, and hold a roll call in the basement of the local stage door pub in Oxendon Street. They all trooped out and across to the pub where all the locals supping their pints were delighted to see a dozen or so dancers appear in lycra and skimpy tops at the door, only to go down to the basement. Dave Norris was responsible for the roll call and reported back to me anyone who was missing. If this had been for real I would have informed The Station Officer on the first appliance of anyone missing and a search would be undertaken to locate them. This again worked like clockwork and several of the Company said that they now felt reassured of what to do in an emergency and thanked me for organising the drill, which after all was for their safety, and peace of mind.

I was soon back in my familiar role, enjoying the job tremendously, and felt on top of the world as nothing so far was beyond my capabilities. We did not play a show on 26th May, because it was the Spring Bank Holiday, and would mean paying overtime. I had an extra day at home and on the allotment, which was in fine shape as I had acquired an adjacent plot to mine, which had a greenhouse on it.

On 13th June I went back to The Palladium, as in my capacity as Chairman of the SMA I had introduced a policy of holding meetings at West End Theatres in an attempt to attract more members to attend. The meeting was always followed by a visit backstage, which was proving very popular, and this one had been agreed with John Avery and Ronnie Pearson. We were dealing with matters arising when into the Cinderella Bar came the legend that was Linford Hudson, regarded by many as the best follow spot operator in the country. I immediately suspended the official business and introduced Linford to those who did not know him, and he was most complimentary about the way I had organised things on *The King and I* six years earlier. I asked him why he was in the theatre so early on a non-matinée day and he told the meeting that he had come in especially to see me again. He invited those who wished to go up to his domain in the sky and have a go on one of his follow spots. Such is the magic of that building that he was inundated with people.

One evening, during the run of *The King & I*, when family solicitor Jon Carter, who was a close friend, and a leading member of The CAODS was in London representing a client, and had come to see the show with his secretary. Jon's party piece was to sing *Mountain Greenery* and he did not take much persuading during his post show backstage visit to sing it on the Palladium Stage. Whenever I came back to Lincoln and met him in his Saturday night haunt, The Castle Hill Club, with Bob Bunn, he would announce to everyone: "This is the man for whom I sang on the Palladium stage."

During the run, on non-matinée days, I continued to lecture to the technical students at RADA, and mainly explained to them the meaning of the different theatre phrases that they would come across when working in the business. A Clacker for example is a plant who sits in the auditorium to encourage laughter and audience participation. 'Drop in the Blacks' is a request for the flyman to lower a black surround to stage level. It is common practice, and believed to bring luck, if an actor puts his left shoe on first. One that I got caught out on early in my career was a request from the Master Carpenter to get a long weight from the local ironmongers. I went along to Musgraves, our regular ironmongers, where they knew me, and when asked what I wanted I replied: "I've been sent for a long weight please"…Ok they said, we'll get you one. Half an hour later one of the shop assistants asked me why I was still there and I repeated that I had come for a long weight…."Well you've had your long WAIT now haven't you…. best get back to work."

In mid June, Michaela was suffering with symptoms of flu, and not at all well, but insisted upon going on. However, I thought she was being foolish and obviously in no fit state to perform exhausting routines without some sort of medication. Newpalm did not have a Company Doctor on standby so I phoned Doctor Rossdale, who had been the Company Doctor at The Palladium, and he agreed to see her, if she came to his home, as he was unable to visit the theatre. I told Michaela to get changed and took her in a black cab to see Doctor Rossdale, where he examined her and gave her some medication to get her through the show. As a small thank you I invited him to come and see the show on 3rd July and the Office settled his invoice without question.

The July SMA meeting was held in the large stalls bar of the POW Theatre with the kind permission of Mike Churchill, followed by a backstage tour of *Seven Brides*. I got on well with Mike who was gadget mad and his office, off the stalls bar, was full of TV monitors, showing images from all areas FOH, and he could observe what was happening, say, in the Vestibule, at The Stage Door or in The Circle Bar, without moving from the confines of his office. He could compare ticket sales against the same week the previous year, and could predict a bumper week during the Motor Show or Boat Show each year. In addition to the usual weekly contra account he would calculate the spend per head figure, which one normally associated with the cinema industry. I learnt a lot from Mike, which would stand me in good stead for my next job, but I didn't know it at the time.

In mid July Mike invited me to represent the visiting management at the Lunchtime Retirement Reception to honour Dougie Grice who was about to retire after a long and distinguished career. The Chairman & Chief Executive of Bernard Delfont Ltd, Richard M. Mills was to present Dougie with several gifts, and he was accompanied by Peter H. Roberts (Technical Director) and Leslie M. Desmond the Financial Director. There was a small buffet, with a glass of wine and several speeches as the various gifts were presented, and I proposed a vote of thanks from all the many previous visiting managements, who had worked with him over the years. I thought no more about it but now, in retrospect, wonder if this little vote of thanks had any bearing on the events that would soon follow. I knew that the show was only on a limited run at The POW, so when an advertisement appeared in The Stage for a West End General Manager I applied to the Box Number shown, as I felt that I was now sufficiently experienced, and just about at the right age to make a major career move, as I was now in my early '40s.

I carried on with my normal duties and on Friday 11th July made arrangements for the monthly SMA meeting to be held in the large Stalls Bar at the Theatre, with the now traditional backstage tour at the end. I was enjoying my role as Chairman, and was proud to be following in the footsteps of Hal D. Stewart, who had held the post between 1945-1959, Douglas Cornelissen (1964) and Griffith James (1970-84). He had first encouraged me to join the Committee, when I took over from him on

Sandbag by saying: "When are some of you youngsters going to come on the Committee as we old 'uns are not going to be around for ever." I had now been Chairman for two years, and had set about putting the association on a more professional footing by moving the office from David Ayliff's house in Chiswick, to an office in The West End. In addition, instead of holding the monthly meetings in the upstairs room of a pub in New Row at 11.05 am on a Monday, I moved them to afternoons at West End Theatres. When I enquired about the traditional starting time of 11.05, I was told it was arranged that way to enable SMA member Mervyn Gould to have time to buy his first pint of the day.

Meanwhile back on the show I thought several younger members of the Company were malingering, as they knew there were swings (dancers trained to cover any part) and understudies, who would be only too keen to go on and do a show for them. One of the brides left a message to say that she was sick and could not perform at the matinée. I was anxious to find out if she would be well enough to come in for the evening show, so I rang her.

Her flat mate answered the call, and when I asked to speak to her the flatmate told me I couldn't because "She was at the BBC Television Centre at White City recording a show." Keeping cool, I asked if she knew which studio, and she told me, much to my surprise, although she didn't know who she was talking to. I rang the studio and asked to speak to the girl in question, and when she said "Hello" I just said curtly: "If you value your job on Seven Brides, I want to see you in my office at seven o clock sharp." and put the phone down. She arrived as arranged, and was most apologetic, but I felt I had to give her an official warning as to her future conduct, and put it in writing to her and Head Office, to send a warning to others who might wish to try such a thing.

This warning however, did not deter one of the brothers. He was working on his first West End show having spent the previous twenty-nine years in Australia, and was one of the older of the main dancers. I had found him to be undisciplined, which is most unusual for a dancer, and when he phoned in sick for one show, I did not believe him. I decided that I would go round to his flat after the show, as he only lived in Shepherd Street in Mayfair, and deliver a letter to him, as he wasn't answering his telephone. I cycled into Shepherd's Market to deliver the letter to his flat, and there he was, with a few other people, sitting at an open-air table with a drink in his hand, and obviously not at all sick. I reported this to the Head Office, and with their approval he was dismissed for gross misconduct and left the show on 12th August.

During the matinée on Thursday 14th August, I was asked to go and see The Technical Director of BDL Peter Roberts in his office on the top floor of the theatre. I presumed that it was regarding a complaint that the theatre may have received about us using live animals onstage during the *Spring Spring Spring* number in Act Two, so I prepared myself for a grilling as I went up the flight of stairs to his office. He welcomed me with a warm handshake and I reminded him that he had offered me the Company Manager's position on *The Comedians*, in Blackpool, for the Summer Season in 1973 and that I still had his office number on file. We sat down and quite out of the blue, he said: "So you want to be a General Manager, do you?" which took me completely by surprise. It turned out that the Box Number that I had applied to earlier came from The Delfont Organisation, and the letter of application, which I had written in my office at the POW, had gone into the postal system, and back to the POW.

He went on to explain that they were looking for a new General Manager for The Prince Edward Theatre (formally The Casino & Cinerama) in Old Compton Street, and was I interested? Interested? This was just what I was looking for as a career move, and it was with such a prestigious Management. He explained further that Chess had opened there in May and the Benny Andersson / Bjorn Ulvaeus / Tim Rice show was the hit of the season and doing fantastic business. They wanted someone to start on 1st September, which was a problem as I was on a run of the show contract with Newpalm, but Peter said that something could be sorted out if I accepted. I did not need time to think and told him that provided thing were OK with Newpalm, then I would be happy to take over the position at the Prince Edward. The deal was done for me to start on Monday 1st September 1986, and I couldn't wait.

Act 6 Scene 1
GENERAL MANAGER, PRINCE EDWARD THEATRE
(1986)

The two Managements agreed that I would continue to the end of the run of *Seven Brides for Seven Brothers* on 25th October at The POW Theatre, but start with Bernard Delfont Ltd (BDL) on 1st September, as General Manager at The Prince Edward where *Chess* was playing. I would therefore be responsible for both positions at the same time.

I hoped that at last I would be able to put my personal stamp on this prestigious venue, as I had promised myself and John Avery to do, if I were ever lucky enough to run a West End Theatre. I set out to run the PET as well as he ran The London Palladium. I wisely decided to make no major changes to the way things were being done for the first six months, until I had got my knees well and truly under the desk and felt confident and accepted.

It would be a daunting task for the first eight weeks, but on the bright side I would be receiving two salary packets each week. I had been encouraged to bite the bullet and take a drop in salary at the PET (down to a £288 basic with add on emoluments), to lose my Schedule D status, and revert to PAYE.

During the final weeks at the POW (which was the sister theatre to the PET) I had few problems to deal with. As we did not play on the August Bank Holiday Monday, because of the usual overtime charges, I went off to Eastbourne for the weekend. My old friend John Inman was doing a Summer Season there and welcomed me with open arms when we all met up for a drink after the show, with his long term partner Ron Lynch.

I also set about finding out as much as I could about the PET, its staff, and *Chess* prior to my first day. The Company Manager of the show, Ken Grant, who I knew as one of the SMA members, was kind enough to put me in the picture about many things. We arranged to meet between shows at a neutral pub in Soho, where he told me lots about the current Management, Staff, and the show which had now been running for twelve weeks to phenomenal business. He thought that I was an ideal choice to take over as General Manager, and I felt confident that I had the support of at least one person from the visiting Management, as I was now part of the bricks and mortar management. I also made a point of going over to the PET and introducing myself to as many of the staff as I could, so that they knew who I was, prior to my first official day on Monday 1st September.

In the rooftop general office, which was once the flat above the shop for The General Manager, I met the current outgoing GM Paul Goldsworthy, The Assistant Manageress Maureen Poole, the part time performance FOH Manager Peter Russell, the office secretary Carolyn Godfrey and Catering Manager Julia Glenn. I was introduced to the Box Office Manager Jeannie McTavish, The Chief Electrician Alasdair Clement, and Master Carpenter Alan McCall by Paul, as all these would be my main points of contact whilst I established myself. There were a number of other Companies involved with the show, such as The Production Staff for *Chess*, Three Knights Ltd., Robert Fox

Ltd., The Production Office, The Video for Stage Company, and the day-to-day staff and Stage Management at the Theatre - another sixty or so people to get to know.

After some painstaking research I found the history of the PET was most interesting. It had been built by Edward Stone on three levels (Stalls, Dress Circle and Upper Circle) as a dual purpose Theatre & Cinema. It had an Italian Palace exterior, and was the first of four West End Theatres to open in 1930, the others being The Cambridge, the Phoenix and the Whitehall. This now made it a hat trick for me, as I had worked at The Phoenix and Whitehall already. The Art Deco interior was by Messrs Marc Henri & Laverdet, and featured a Proscenium Arch formed with a series of Lalique glass coves, which were tinted in amber. The stage was the third largest in London, and the auditorium had seating for 1,650 patrons, which made it the fifth biggest in the West End. It had been specially designed as a house for musicals, with almost forty dressing rooms, and occupied an inverted 'L' shaped site, which fronted Old Compton Street and Greek Street up to Au Jardin Des Gourmets French Restaurant, which had opened a year later. The Dressing Room block was to the left of the inverted 'L' side with the Stage Door entrance and emergency exit in Frith Street, opposite Ronnie Scott's Jazz Club (which was a bonus for me) and next to the bustling twenty-four hour Bar Italia, where in 1926 John Logie Baird had first demonstrated Television. It was named after Prince Edward, the then Prince of Wales. The first few years were not a huge success for this new theatre, so much so that in 1936 it changed to a cabaret-restaurant and changed its name to the London Casino which coincided with the abdication a year later. The first new show was Folies Parisiennes and the original idea was for an interchange of shows between itself, The French Casino in New York and the Casino in Miami. This venture was short lived however, as the New York Casino went bankrupt, but the London Casino boasted that it was taking more money than any other place of entertainment in London, and the shows continued until 1940.

During the war it became The Queensbury All Services Club, and regular radio broadcasts were made, including the last known broadcast by Major Glenn Miller and his Orchestra, on 12th December 1944, with guest vocalist Anne Shelton, who was asked to join Glenn on his fateful trip across the Channel to France on 15th December, but declined as she had a recording session with Ambrose already booked.

Major Miller is still officially missing in action some seventy years later, however recent publications indicate he landed in France on a peace mission arranged by Eisenhower to try and shorten the war, although this cannot be verified.

After the end of the war, in 1946, the building was taken over by Tom Arnold and Emile Littler, and live shows with the traditional Pantomime occupied the venue until 1949 when The Latin Quarter was introduced. This was the brainchild of Impresario Robert Nesbitt, which became an established success. Several versions of these most lavish of Revues were presented by a man I much admired, and would get to know and respect over the next few years. In 1954 came another name change, this time to The Casino Cinerama Theatre, with a huge sixty-four foot wrap around screen and it remained in this format for twenty years. In 1974 the EMI Corporation bought the theatre and spent £150,000 on refurbishments prior to presenting Stage Shows and an annual Pantomime again, with Bernard Delfont and Richard M. Mills at the helm. The last name change came in 1978, to honour the new Prince Edward, when it was announced that the Andrew Lloyd-Webber / Tim Rice Musical *Evita* was to open. It ran from 21st June for 3,173 performances and closed on 8th February 1986. The new PET had been dark for three months, for the very technically challenging *Chess* to Fit Up with its hydraulically revolving and tilting stage.

The cast of *Chess* was fantastic. Elaine Paige, now firmly established as a West End leading lady, following her triumph in *Evita*, headed the line up, which also included Murray Head, Tommy Korberg, John Turner, Tom Jobe, Kevin Colson and Siobhan McCarthy. There were a further thirty-five in the Company with an orchestra of twenty-seven conducted initially by Anders Eljas and subsequently by John Owen Edwards. It was a BIG show. The basic plot was based on a

General Manager, Prince Edward Theatre (1986)   Act 6 Scene 1

chess game between the American World Chess Champion Frederick Trumper (Murray Head) and the Soviet Challenger, Anatoly Sergievsky (Tommy Korberg) who had defected from the USSR. The involvement of Trumper's Second, and Mistress, Florence Vassy (Elaine Paige) and Anatoly's estranged wife Svetlana (Siobhan McCarthy) complicated matters, and there were several well-known numbers in the show. Just as Julie Covington had recorded *Don't Cry For Me Argentina* prior to the opening of *Evita*, so Elaine and Barbara Dixon (who Andrew & Tim, like me, had seen and admired in *John, Paul, George, Ringo and Bert*) had recorded an advance of *I Know Him So Well* in December 1984. It had been in the charts for four weeks the following year, thus creating much interest for the forthcoming show. At the time it was a little known fact that the two girls had laid down their respective tracks separately, and that Barbara was never in the show. Murray had also released *One Night In Bangkok* from The Concept Album of the show, which peaked at number twelve in the charts in May 1985, a whole year prior to the opening in the West End.

Having now found out much about the show, the staff, the cast and the theatre, I was ready for my first official day at The Prince Edward. My plan of action was to keep my base office at The Prince of Wales, cycle there, park up, change and then walk over to Old Compton Street. I entered via the Stage Door soon after 9.30 on the big day and met the Stage Doorkeeper Barry Nelson, who was expecting me. I went down and across the deserted stage into the Stalls where I introduced myself to a Filipino Cleaner, who was not expecting me, and didn't know who I was. Richard Mills had posted a letter addressed To All Staff the previous Thursday 28th August informing them that Mr. Goldsworthy would be leaving on the 6th September to pursue a career in the cinema industry, and that I would be starting on 1st September for a one week overlap with Paul and wishing him every success in his new position. Mondays were always busy with lots of paperwork to clear up relating to The Contra Account, which I would soon be responsible for making up on a Saturday night. Peter Roberts came over from the POW mid morning and told me that one of my first tasks would be to chair a disciplinary hearing very soon. He briefed me about the case, which involved one of the Flymen, who had drawn up a schedule that would enable one of the staff on the fly floor to get away early each night, and that the case would be conducted in accordance with the FLC Disciplinary Code, with which I was unfamiliar. The person concerned was entitled to have a representative, work colleague or Union Steward, with him and it was suggested that Carolyn was also present to take notes. I duly studied the paperwork and drew up a list of questions, most of which could be answered 'Yes' or 'No' and were along these lines: "Did you draw up a schedule?" "Why?" "Was it ever implemented?" and so forth, to help me make my mind up and what, if any action would follow.

The day of the hearing arrived and after listening to the answers to the questions, and considering any mitigating circumstances, I came to the conclusion that it was not a case of gross misconduct, but a desire to get to the pub early for an extra pint. I issued a first warning, which was accepted. I had just a week to pick up the vast amount of detailed information before Paul left, so time at home was very limited. Fortunately there were no major issues on Seven Brides which, I remind you, I was still Company Manager for as well.

Three weeks after I started at the PET on 22nd September, and still within my trial period, I received a copy letter from John Newman in reply to a letter from Peter Roberts, which requested a reference for me, which he had sent to Newpalm on 10th September. He was kind enough to say (and I quote): "I am very happy to say that John is by far the finest Company Manager ever employed by this Management, and we can vouchsafe one hundred per cent for his honesty, sobriety, ability and character, and it is our opinion that John is suitable for any post for which he would be considered. Our loss is your gain." Mr. Newman also thanked Mr. Roberts for being so understanding in allowing me to continue my duties on Seven Brides, whilst the takeover was happening. That was praise indeed, and I hoped would help when my trial period was over, and a permanent position was being considered by BDL.

I had been much too occupied this year to attend the National Grass Track Masters Championships in Yarm, near Northallerton or Greendale Barton in Devon, but I had read in Motor Cycle News that Simon Cross was the new solo champion and Roger Measor & Dave Heath had retained their sidecar title. I did however manage to pop down to The Woodman in Blackfen on some Sunday evenings to hear the Crissy Lee all female orchestra play some Big Swing Band music for a couple of hours. It was nice to meet up with some of the band members like trumpet player 'Sox' Brown and I found it quite relaxing to be away from theatre, if only for a short time.

On 10th October I held the monthly SMA meeting in the Stalls Bar of the theatre I now managed, and arranged the traditional backstage tour, which Ken Grant organised with the help of his Stage Manager Sam Hunter, and DSM Debbie Cronshaw. I was quite sad to see *Seven Brides* close on Saturday 25th, as I had got to know the very talented and gifted Company so well, especially at the daily warm up dance sessions on stage before the show. During the final warm up, the dancers had devised a short routine for me to join in with them, which was a nice surprise, and good fun, with kisses and handshakes all round at the end. The following day was our thirteenth wedding anniversary, and as the family was growing up fast, now aged ten, eight and four years old, we had a family day at home instead of going out somewhere to celebrate. With each of them now requiring a bedroom of their own, we began to start looking for a larger house with at least four bedrooms and which was within our price range, but still in South East London, which had good secondary schools in its catchment area.

One of my duties was to greet VIPs who came to see the show and entertain them in The Royal Retiring room. I received a memo, via the interval post from Mr. Mills, asking me to entertain Danny La Rue at one performance. Danny was no stranger to the PET having played Pantomime there in *The Exciting Adventures of Queen Danniella* for the Delfont Organisation in 1975, when it was still called The Casino Theatre. Danny lived in a flat in Manette Street off Greek Street and to save him exiting the theatre, after a performance of *Queen Danniella* via the Stage Door in Frith Street, and having to walk all the way round the block, he had been permitted to leave via the Stage Fire Exit route into Greek Street. Thereafter, this exit was always referred to as The Danny La Rue Exit.

I intended it to be my custom to offer VIP guests Smoked Salmon Triangles with a glass of Champagne, in the same way that my mentor John Avery had done at The Palladium when I worked there. I asked around but could not find anyone at a local pub or restaurant who was interested in making them for us, so asked one of the usherettes to come in early and make some for me to offer Danny. When I saw what she had made I was horrified, because the brown bread was too thick, had crusts on, and instead of being open had a top layer of bread. I thanked her and set about making them presentable, and with the addition of a damask napkin, some lemon triangles, parsley and black pepper, the plate looked quite appetising in the end. For the next ten years, unless an outside caterer was supplying food at the interval, I always made the plate of nibbles up myself.

Usually on the second Friday of each month I would represent the PET at a meeting with all the Directors, and answered relevant questions that were asked of me. The routine was always the same, with Mike Churchill, who was still the General Manager of The Prince of Wales going into bat first, whilst I waited patiently outside. These formal meetings were held in Mr. Mills' plush office that was formally used by Bernard, now Baron, Delfont of Stepney.

These two meetings lasted most of the morning, and it was my policy to then use the afternoon to meet people and attend to business that I could not do during an evening, as I was expected to be on duty on five of the six days each week. I set about drawing up an office rota that would enable myself, Maureen & Julia to have a long weekend off every three weeks. All the office staff were happy to have long weekends and the rest of the week was worked to make up a forty-hour week.

It was traditional at the PET for all the Management and Staff to have a slap up Christmas lunch on the Friday before Christmas Day, in the Private Eye Room on the first floor of The Coach and

Horses Pub in Greek Street. Selected members of the visiting management were invited to join us, along with a Director, usually Peter Roberts. The Coach was famed for its bohemian characters that used to prop the bar up from opening time till Norman Balon, who thrived on being known as the rudest landlord in London, threw them out at closing time. You would quite often find George Melly, Francis Bacon, Jeffrey Barnard, Beryl Bainbridge, Daniel Farson or Soho Pam putting the world to rights on most days and nights of the week. Once a non-regular came into the Shallow End, as the Greek Street end was known (the Deep End was the Romilly Street end) and asked Norman for Snakebite. "We don't do cocktails, and you're barred for asking for one" was his reply.

The female cook (she never wanted be called chef) cooked us a fine turkey lunch with all the trimmings. Also present was Three Knights Executive Producer Judy Cramer, who would later achieve fame with another big Abba based show, *Mama Mia*. Several of the Senior International Production people like Director Trevor Nunn, Lighting Designers David Hersey, Sound Designer Andrew Bruce and Scenic Designer Robin Wagner, were also invited, but most were working on new projects and unavailable.

Every Christmas without fail that *Chess* was in residence at the PET, a huge hamper full of cuddly toys would be delivered from Harrods Toy Department. The hamper was so big that it only just fitted into the office lift, and took two people to move it. It was addressed to Agntha Faltskog and Anni-Frid Lyngstad (the two females in ABBA) from an anonymous person who obviously thought that they were in the show. Benny Andersson and Bjorn Ulvaeus, who co-created the show with Tim Rice, only came to see the show two or three times a year, when they were in London or on an anniversary, so passing the hamper over to them to take back to Sweden was impractical. After discussions with all interested parties, it was decided to send the hamper with its contents to The Great Ormond Street Hospital for Sick Children. I often think back to an unknown child, who was in Great Ormond Street over Christmas 1986, and the fact that they were possibly cuddling a Teddy Bear that was intended as a gift for one of the ABBA girls. I had a long weekend before Christmas and went with the family to Lincoln to see Grandma & Grandpa. I agreed with Maureen (who had to be the senior person in the theatre in my absence) that I would work Boxing Day, thus enabling her to go to Coventry to spend Christmas with her family, and have New Year's Eve off, and that we would reverse the arrangement in 1987. So ended a good year for me. What would 1987 hold?

Act 6 Scene 2
THE RUN OF CHESS
(1987-89)

As the New Year dawned, I reflected that after just a few months in the job I was really enjoying the challenges that were being presented to me on a regular basis, but I still found time to write articles for Theatre Publications. One that I penned for the ABTT was a description of an average day from the alarm going off at 630am to my turning in at 130am, on a good night. In it I spoke about the pre-theatre school runs, and my twelve mile cycle ride, to be at the PET by 0930, the Box Office opening at 10am and the computerised BOCS system that we used. I posed the question, and still do, why is it that an experienced Box Office Manager with a plan, marker pen and a book of tickets can move a waiting queue and dress the house twice as fast as anyone with a VDU and printer? I bemoaned the fact that more and more patrons were choosing to buy tickets on a credit card rather than cash, which again took twice as long to process. With both these slowing down sales it was no surprise that sometimes we did not go up on time.

As Act One ran for almost ninety minutes, I had time to do office work prior to the interval, when I would walk the floor and chat to patrons and show numerous American ladies who lunch the way to the 'bathroom' before giving clearance to the Corner for Act Two. The outgoing of the house was always our busiest time for sales of merchandising from the small kiosk in the foyer. I did not mind hanging on for them to finish their purchases however, as one of my emoluments was a small percentage of the kiosk weekly take. I would then change out of my dinner suit into my cycling attire and drop the nightly returns off at the POW by 2315 hrs.

The journey home was not always without incident, because as a trained First Aider I was often the first on the scene of an accident, as I could cut through the traffic on my cycle, with my Acne Thunderer Audible Warning being blown hard. On hot Summer evenings I would stop off to water my allotment, before getting home after midnight. I would then cook my main meal of the day, and watch some late night television, before going upstairs to sleep for five hours.

On the odd occasion I did not go straight home, for example if I had the following day off, I would pop into The French in Dean Street for a last orders drink, as this hostelry was also full of Soho Characters, like Norman's. In addition to being closely associated with Charles de Gaulle in his Free French days during WW2, it had also been used regularly by Irish Playwright Brendan Behan, and Welsh Poet Dylan Thomas, when they had been in their prime. On one occasion when *The French* was being re-decorated, Gaston the landlord was asked what colour he would like the bar re-painted? His reply is typical of the humour that was associated with Soho: "Nicotine Brown, as it is now" was his immediate reply. After closing time, many of the regulars would move on to meet up with the crowd from The Coach and Horses at Gerry's Club, with mine host Michael Dillon. Gerry's was named after Gerald Campion who played Billy Bunter in the 1950 TV show. Here one could chat into the early hours to the likes of TV presenter Michael Parkinson, playwright Keith Waterhouse or Noel Botham. Noel was a most humorous man with a twinkle in his eye and could out-drink most others. He was a Journalist, Author, Publican, Raconteur and Bon Viveur, who enjoyed the good things in life. He had founded AAA - Anti-Alcoholics-Anonymous - and we often sat together listening to Petula Clark's Musical Director, Kenny Clayton, tinkling at the piano.

During the first month of the New Year I had a most unusual incident to deal with that no amount of training can prepare you for. Between the Matinée and Evening show one day I got a phone call in the office to inform me that a naked man was running berserk backstage. I set off to investigate, telling someone in the office to call the police to attend the theatre. In the under stage area, by the Master Carpenter's office, I was indeed confronted by a naked male, who became very agitated if anyone approached him. He was unable to talk in a comprehensive manner, or explain to me why he was behaving in this rather strange way. A group of us were in a circle around him, but keeping our distance from him. Once the police arrived, we all rushed the man, and despite a struggle he was handcuffed and taken away, to be sectioned.

One of the ongoing problems in the first year of the show was the dreaded double where two people have tickets for the same seat. This usually happened when an agent, who had an allocation from us to sell seats with a booking fee, either got his allocation mixed up with another venue or sold a voucher ticket to a client, knowing full well that by the time the double became apparent, he would not be in his office to explain, thus passing the buck onto the theatre to sort out. If the house was not sold out (which was very rare) you could just re-seat one of the parties, but usually someone had to be disappointed and leave. Invariably the wrong ticket holder got sat first, usually in the middle of a row, and would often refuse to move. In that case, I would have no option but to call the police and eject him or her that way. All this delayed the advertised start time, and caused much resentment to other patrons, who overhearing the conversation, very often gave the unfortunate offenders verbal abuse.

On one occasion a young couple had come down from Aberdeen to see the show as a wedding anniversary weekend treat and their seats had doubled and were the wrong ones. As they left the theatre heartbroken they asked if they could get seats for another show. As it was a Saturday, I said it was doubtful, but I would see what I could do for them. I duly rang Mike at the POW, but he had a full house with *'Allo 'Allo* so I took them over the road to Wheelers Restaurant, where I knew the Manager. I explained the situation to him, and despite being fully booked, he said that if they would like to have a drink at the Oyster Bar, they could have the next table that became available. The couple were so grateful for what I had done to try and salvage their wedding anniversary visit, that on their return to Scotland, the sent me the most charming letter of thanks.

We had many Scandinavian patrons, because of the ABBA connection, and they were very partial to the cheap spirits that were on sale at the theatre, so much so that a 'Quick Doubles' trolley was introduced to sell during the interval, to try and ease the load on the four other bars. These 'Quick Doubles' were sold in a small can with a mixer, and a choice of only three or four drinks, all at the same price, for speed of service. They proved so popular that it was not uncommon for one of our new friends from Sweden, to buy half a dozen unopened cans and take then back to their hotel to consume.

I was also introduced to The Annual FLC Conference, which was a two-day event at a suitable venue, like The Belfry, The Hilton at Stratford upon Avon or at one of their many venues in Blackpool. The format never changed with a get together of all the General Managers from the various divisions within the Corporation, of which the Theatre Division, which was only comprised of two venues (The PET & The POW) was the smallest. There were key point meetings, most of which were about non-theatre matters, a Black Tie Gala Dinner, usually with a Cabaret, and a free bar till about 2am. The highlight for many was the presentation of the 'Millionaires Lapel Badge', which was given by the Top Brass to those whose annual turnover at their particular venue, whether it was The Blackpool Tower or a Caravan Park in Wales, had exceeded £1m, and fortunately, one year, I was presented with one.

If the chosen location was Blackpool, then there was an opportunity to visit one of the many nightspots that were open, even in the winter months. Basil Newby's *Funnygirls* Burlesque Cabaret Showbar near to the North Pier was always worth a visit. Betty 'Legs' Diamond, and others, would get up onto the Stage Bar and mime to "*I Am What I Am*" or a Shirley Bassey number. The resident 'Follies', as they liked to be known, would serve you drinks at your table, and you risked a right old telling off from them if they did not consider your tip enough. It was all done 'in the best possible taste' as Kenny Everett would say, very funny at times, and was always full with a cross section of people from all walks of life.

These Conferences usually fell on Burns Night somehow, with the traditional Scottish Piper preceding the Haggis into the Gala Dinner. Now I like most food, don't get me wrong, but I must confess that Haggis & Neeps are very near to the bottom of my favourites, as I find it very dry to the taste. Tables were set with a mix of people from all the different divisions, but many I sat with never went to see a show, so conversation was hard work at times.

In February, I had my first experience of entertaining a member of The Royal Family at the PET, when HRH Princess Margaret attended the show in a private capacity, as a guest of Tim Rice. He greeted her at the main entrance and I escorted them both to The Royal Retiring Room, which was at the top of a flight of stairs, above the Royal Box on the Greek Street side of the building. I knew that she liked a cigarette, as Victor Spinetti had told me that on one occasion when he had escorted her to a function, there was no ash tray available for her to use, so I had made sure that there was one laid out, along with a bottle of Famous Grouse whisky, which I knew was her favoured brand. A programme and brochure were also laid out for her, and I waited until the rest of the audience was seated before asking her to take her seat. The whole evening went well, and I gained confidence with members of the Royal Family, which would become part of my life in the next few years. I felt privileged that the son of an antique dealer in Lincoln was now hosting members of the Royal Family.

One of the main duties I had at The PET was to liaise with Peter Roberts over maintenance, and hazard spotting to prevent potential accidents which, if serious enough, could possibly lead to a court case. I made it a point, when I was on my nightly walk round inspection, prior to the audience being admitted, to note in my pocket book any signs of loose handrails, lights not working, or carpets with frayed edges. These potential hazards were then brought to the attention of the Maintenance Team at the theatre, and they reported directly to Mr. Roberts. One constantly re-occurring problem was that of loose seats in the Auditorium, and as these were very often not discovered until a rather large patron took his seat, I kept an emergency tool bag in the foyer kiosk, which contained a hammer, a screwdriver, a pair of pliers and assorted plugs and screws. Chief of Staff, Ian Clark, would be asked to do most jobs, and saved the day on more than one occasion re-fixing the seat as the patron waited anxiously in the aisle.

If I was lucky, and the dates coincided, on the Friday when I had the morning meeting with the Directors, I was then able to attend the monthly Theatre Managers Luncheon Club for a three-course lunch. The events were organised by David Alexander, who was a Theatre Manager of the old school, and who lived in a block of flats in Maiden Lane next to Rules Restaurant. David had worked at many West End Theatres, but unfortunately his budget for the Theatre Management Liaison Committee (TMLC) did not run to us using Rules, and we had to settle for other non name establishments. As the name suggests, the club was set up initially for West End Theatre Managers to meet socially, to discuss common problems that were affecting all of us. It was not, as many thought, a Trade Union, in fact quite the opposite. Of late however it had been taken over by many of the cinema folk from Wardour Street, and only a few had experience of live theatre management, but most were good company.

David also acted as my standby Relief Duty Manager when Peter Russell was indisposed. He was perfect for the role, and most charming to patrons, being polite and knowledgeable. He shared the role with Fred Perryment, who had been a Manager at the PET during the Cinerama days, and he used to relate a most amusing story about his time there. Fred was in the habit of taking his daughter Mandy into the theatre with him on a Sunday, as she worked in the business, and would later play

Sugar in *Some like it Hot* at the theatre in 1992. One Sunday Fred, with Mandy at his side, was standing in the main foyer talking to one of the Directors, when Mandy, quite out of the blue said: "Look Daddy, they have the same carpet as we do in the lounge" much to Fred's embarrassment. He had done a deal with the carpet layers to save any large offcuts for him, from when the foyer had been re-carpeted, and the off cuts were laid in his home. Mandy was quickly ushered away before she could embarrass her father again.

One of the frequent visitors to the theatre, usually during the show, was an old friend of mine, Canon Edwyn Young, whom I had known since his days in Liverpool 1964-73, when I was at The Playhouse. His titles were numerous and impressive, being Chaplain to The Queen, Chaplain of the Royal Victorian Order, Chaplain of The Queens Chapel of the Savoy, as well as our Theatre Chaplain. He had told me on one of his many visits to see the artistes at the Revuebar or Windmill Theatre, who adored and respected him, that he began his Theatre Chaplain's work at The Collins Music Hall in the late '50s. In addition to looking after the spiritual need of us thespians. He was also Chaplain to many of London's leading five star hotels. We got on well together and he always found time to enjoy a glass of wine in the office before he left.

Mr. Mills would frequently ring me about nine o'clock to be told the nightly figures for the day, and ask about any problems that I had, which were infrequent as the show was by now running like a well oiled machine. It was not unusual for Lord Delfont to call me on some nights for the figures as well as Mr. Mills, and you really had to be on the ball when he, for example, asked for a comparison of the figures on the same day the previous year, which were not readily to hand. He was an utterly charming man with knowledge of the business that was second to none, and I always felt so proud when I picked up the receiver and heard: "Good Evening Mr. Toogood, Lord Delfont here, could I have the figures please."

I got on very well with several members of the Company, for example Australian actor Kevin Colson (Walter de Courcey) whom I had seen in several West End shows, for example *Cabaret*, *Two Cities*, *Robert and Elizabeth*, and John Turner, who played Sergievsky's second, Alexander Molokov. John was married to Shakespearian Actress Barbara Jefford, and was a very keen Jazz fan, like myself, and a keen Big Joe Turner fan.

Big Joe was known as *The Boss of the Blues* and was a legendary shouter from Kansas City. His name came from the fact that he was six foot two tall, and weighed in at twenty two stones. In addition to singing the blues he was also a recognised Rock & Roll and Swing singer, having performed with Duke Ellington, Count Basie and Meade Lux Lewis in his time. He was inducted into the Blues Hall of Fame in 1983, just two years prior to his death aged seventy-four. John could perform a more than passable blues number in the style of his great namesake, and could be found down at Ronnie Scott's Jazz Club on many a night, as it was directly opposite the PET Stage Door in Frith Street.

On one of my long weekends off in March, I took the train up to Lincoln, as Mum and Dad were now becoming rather frail, and their Austin Maxi Car was hardly ever being used. This was the only new car they had owned, and of late, just to keep it roadworthy, Dad had started taking a book down to the garage that he rented in Michaelgate, sitting in the driver's seat, and running the engine for an hour. As my family was growing, and with school runs and the usual kids taxi service, a second car to work alongside the Morris Traveller would be very useful to us, and it was agreed I could borrow it. On the Sunday morning my Uncle Bill, Ray's younger brother, came to give it the once over, and help bump start the underused car down Michaelgate hill. Once warmed up it purred and after filling her up I set off to drive the hundred and forty-five miles to London. The power of the Maxi was much superior to that of the Traveller, and I felt confident enough to use the fast lane for the first time, and completed the journey in record time.

Rachel's ninth birthday fell on a Sunday so we had a party for her at home. This would be her last birthday at Mount Pleasant Lodge, as we had found a five bedroomed house in Arran Road, just off the Bromley Road, about five minutes away. We had put a deposit down, and were waiting for the searches to be completed, expecting to move in May. Julian was eleven on 13th April and we had his name down to attend Colfe's Senior School starting in September. The school had been founded in 1568 and was now independent, situated in Horn Park, in The Royal Borough of Greenwich. I was delighted to find when looking at the list of former members of the school that the Comedy Club Promoter and Owner of Up The Creek in Greenwich, Malcolm Hardee, was an old boy.

The first anniversary of *Chess* playing at the PET was Thursday 14th May, which happened to be my day off that week. The move would be on Wednesday 27th May, and was planned like a military operation or a Production weekend, as I intended to work that evening. I had negotiated the price of the new house down to £98,000 and we sold The Lodge for a handsome £74,500, thanks to all the major work I had done in improving it. The last major problem I had to deal with was one of subsidence, which this was put down to the London clay subsoil being deprived of water by a large tree in a neighbour's garden. Lewisham Council's tree expert came to this conclusion after visiting the property dressed in jeans, a tatty T-shirt and bearing a carrier bag. There was no alternative prior to selling other than to have the property underpinned by experts, but we had to pay the first £500 of the claim against our Building Insurers. When the work began, our neighbours thought we were having a swimming pool installed from the amount of sub-soil that the hard working Irish navvies dug out. Once completed, the sale was agreed and we pressed ahead to obtain a £30,000 mortgage, which was the maximum I could borrow on my salary.

I reflected how we had progressed up the property ladder from buying the two bedroomed flat at Morley Court for £8,250 in 1974, selling it for £10,500 three years later, buying the three bedroomed Mount Pleasant Lodge for £12,500 in 1977, selling it for £74,500 ten years later, and now purchasing a five bed roomed semi-detached house for £98,000.

As I was now on Schedule E Tax status, with only an inflation matched salary rise each year to look forward to, things were going to be tight financially at the new property, which I liked, but was keen to improve. We talked about Maris going back to work and engaging a live in Au Pair to stay with us and use the fifth bedroom. The move went according to my detailed schedule. I had engaged one of the Theatrical Removal firms I knew for the move in the morning, with an offload in the early afternoon prior to my cooking the evening meal, before I set off for work on the bike as usual, and on time. The following morning the gas man visited to relocate the cooker to the other side of the kitchen, as I had drawn up comprehensive plans for the new kitchen layout we had planned, but for the time being, we muddled through as best we could.

I took the following week as holiday, but had to be back for the monthly meeting with the Directors on Friday 5th June. I started some of the basic works I had planned on the Ground Floor. The entrance hallway and lounge would remain the same, but a non-load bearing brick wall would be coming down to make a big open plan kitchen diner. I also wanted an archway making between the kitchen diner and the large dining room, which looked out through double patio doors onto a paved area. I planned to do most of the work myself, because of labour charges, which I felt confident I could undertake, based on experience gained at the previous two properties. Life was very full now with a forty-hour week at The PET, improvements to be undertaken at the house to make it how we envisaged and time tending the allotment to keep us in fresh fruit and vegetables.

The allotment now had to take a bit of a back seat, but on Saturday morning 11th July, and before I had to set off for the matinée show, we had an Inspection of Plots and I again, much to my surprise, was awarded the Best Plot Award, despite having spent less time down there than in previous years.

Whilst on duty in the Foyer on Saturday 25th July, I had spotted a familiar face in the foyer looking a little lost. I recognised His Honour Judge Alan King-Hamilton, not from having been in a case with him at The Old Bailey, but from the Channel Four Television programme *Case on Camera* in which he acted as Arbitrator. His Honour was a well known figure in judicial circles and I knew from press reports that he had presided over several very high profile cases during his distinguished career at the Bar. He had, I recalled, been the Old Bailey Judge in the Janie Jones case, when he had described her as "the most evil woman that I have ever met" following her conviction in 1973. He had also been the Judge in *The Love That Dares To Speak Its Name* blasphemy case brought by Mary Whitehouse in 1976. He was known to have given a floral nosegay to a female member of the jury on one occasion, but looked ill at ease in the Foyer, so I approached him and introduced myself to him.

He was utterly charming and when I escorted him to his seat asked if he would like to join me for an interval drink, as he was alone. He graciously accepted and I arranged with Phil Course, who was our regular Corp of Commissionaires Linkman to meet him at his seat and bring him up to the Royal Retiring Room, where he would have some privacy. We chatted and he told me that he had been a Squadron Leader with the RAF Intelligence Unit during the War and was staying overnight at The RAF Club in Piccadilly, and not travelling back home to Radlett in Hertfordshire. I had instructed Phil to have a taxi waiting for him at curtain down, and he thanked me as we shook hands and said goodnight. I thought no more about it until the following week when a hand written letter on RAF Club paper arrived expressing his thanks again for the way that I had looked after him. I hoped that if ever I was in really serious trouble in life, I could ask Judge Alan King-Hamilton for advice, but I never needed to make that phone call before he died, in 2010, aged a hundred and five years old.

It was now becoming a regular event to entertain guests of Lord Delfont, Mr. Mills and others, and I enjoyed not only meeting a cross section of very nice people, some of whom asked me to join them for dinner after the show at Le Caprice or Wheelers. I was able to put into practice all I had learnt from John Avery whilst at The Palladium, as there was no manual to refer to, or how to address members of the Royal Family.

I found time however on Sunday 2nd August to attend the first leg of the Masters Grass Track Championships that were held at Ashington in Sussex off the A24, and as the two eldest children were now old enough, being eleven and nine, I would make it a family day out with a barbeque supper before we left the field. I also encouraged Rachel to map read us to the venue asking her to get us there by the quickest route, but she was hopeless and I spent more time turning round and backtracking. In the end I gave up and planned my own route. Julian was entrusted to keep the programme up to date, and after the Solo 'A' Final, Martin Hagon beat Trevor Banks and Gerald Short, whilst in the sidecars the result was a win for Roger Measor & Dave Harris from Steve Dewison & Dave Ward, with the surprise of the meeting being Dave Manning & Paul Blanke in third place.

I was also continuing to keep my interest in big Band Swing Music alive. When Crissy Lee told me that she and her All Female Band had a gig booked on a Thames Riverboat sailing from Westminster to Greenwich and back, I offered to help her stage it. I hired a very basic Lighting Rig from the Robert Luff stores, as they were local, and loaded it aboard the moored vessel. The stage was small and the best I could do was to provide a colour wash for the band, and pick out the soloists with a follow spot. I did the voice over introductions live and stage managed the entrance of each section of the band by means of name tags displayed on the stairs from the dressing room below. The Gig went well, I enjoyed it and Crissy and the Girls were most appreciative of my efforts to help present the band in a professional manner.

Around this time Maris had got a job with an old friend of ours Ian Talbot, with whom we had both worked at Liverpool in the early 1970s. He was now the Artistic Director of The Open Air Theatre in Regents Park and Maris was his Stage Manager for the season. Bill Denis, with whom I had worked in the Paul Raymond days, was the FOH Manager there as well. The outcome was that she was working on some Sundays, which fortunately was my regular day off, so I was able to spend time with Julian, Rachel and Rebecca, despite the pressing need to get on with the alterations to Arran Road. Maris' employment was not the way I saw our marriage proceeding.

I had also been elected to The Executive Council of The ABTT, with a special assignment from the Chairman, Richard York, to organise and arrange Members' Meetings in London. I found that the most popular of these Members' Meetings involved going to a West End Theatre, where one of the Major Musicals was playing, talking to the Staff involved and having a backstage tour. I used many of the contacts that I knew in the West End to achieve this, and the ABTT Council and Members were delighted.

The ABTT also ran a Trade Show each year and another task the Chairman asked me to undertake was organising the Annual Awards Ceremony. This involved asking eminent people in their specialist field to be members of The Judging Panel that would walk round the various stands individually and assess them. We were looking for The Best Stand Display, The New Product of the Year, and deliberate on the nominations that had been received for The Technician of the Year. It was traditional for the winners to receive The Hook Clamp Award, which I made in my workshop at home. Event Organiser Roger Fox had a supply of Chrome plated Strand Hook Clamps which he gave me, and I would mount them on a polished piece of flooring from The TRDL and fix an engraved plaque to the base. They looked very impressive when finished. I further used my VIP contact book and asked big names in the industry to make the presentations and say a few words at the lunch on the first day. Very few of the VIPs I asked refused, and only then if they had a prior appointment or were abroad.

Looking back I don't know how I found the time to do the above, be Chairman of the SMA, hold down a full time job at the PET, bring up a family, undertake major improvements to the new house, be self sufficient in produce from the allotment and pursue my interest in Jazz and Grass Track Racing. Something had to give, and it did.

The first anniversary of my taking over full time at the PET was on the 1st September, and Maris celebrated it in style by pranging the Traveller. I felt I could not undertake the replacement of a front wing, as I could not weld or braze, or re-wire the headlights etc., so had no option but to make my first insurance claim in twenty-one years. Bang went my No Claims Bonus. Thereafter I had that protected and thank goodness we had a second car to use while the Traveller was indisposed.

The Andover Club ran the second and final deciding leg of The Grass Track Masters Championships at their excellent Winterbourne Gunner track on Sunday 13th September with Martin Hagon (son of the legendary Alf Hagon) winning his second title from Trevor Banks (son of the equally legendary Monty Banks) with Nigel De'Arth in third place. In the sidecars Steve Dewison & Dave Ward finished up as the winners, from Roger Measor & Dave Harris with Dave Manning & Peter Blake in third place.

In late September I took a week's holiday and managed to extend it to nine days by adding on lieu days to which I was entitled. This gave the opportunity to press ahead with the improvements that were in hand. The dividing wall was down, the arch had been made, radiators re-sited before the onset of winter, and the cabinets for the new fitted kitchen that I had designed, ordered. I also wanted to lay the black and white floor tiles in the main entrance hall and check that all the original fires were pulling a good draught, as we planned to heat by open fires whenever we could. All did not go according to plan, as some items in the self-assembly cabinets and base units I collected unseen were wrong or missing vital fittings, but hey ho….we got there in the end and I went back to work for a rest.

I had made close friends with the Manager of The Lewisham Concert Hall, Chris Hare and his wife Denise, while I had been living in South East London, as it was the only live venue of any size in the area. I had made an arrangement with him that I would look after him and get him good seats at any of the West End Theatres, where I had any influence, if he did the same for me when I had a night off, and he was presenting a show that I wanted to see. This arrangement worked well as he and Denise, along with Paul Davis and his charming wife the musical leading lady Jacquie

Toye, came to see many shows, and I likewise went to The Concert Hall on several occasions. Paul was a great jazz pianist and well-respected Musical Director and most years would play Interval incidental jazz during the annual Lewisham Jazz Festival. Saturday 31st October was no exception. Topping the bill was the great *Ted Heath Band*, led now by Don Lusher, and still containing many of the British greats of latter years like Duncan Campbell, Tommy Whittle and vocalist Denis Lotus. The programme that night contained all of the notable tunes the band had recorded like *Swingin' Shepherd Blues*, *Hot Toddy*, *Opus One* and a special treat for me *The Lincolnshire Poacher*.

One of the many things that I was desperate for at the new house was a large shed which I could use as a workshop, as I was garage-less now. I also needed a place to store my vast collection of varied tools. I had inherited all Dad's carpentry tools when he sold his last workshop in Lincoln, but had also accumulated builders, plumbers, mechanics and engineers tools which I stored in different wooden ammunition boxes. I made a pull down spanner board with metric & imperial spanners hanging in sizes, and used old coffee jars and tins to store nuts, bolts, nails, washers, hinges and a hundred and one other things I thought I might need one day. I knew exactly what I wanted, designed one, and had it built to order by a local shed maker. Once delivered and erected, I ran a fused spur extension from the house down to the workshop at the bottom of the garden, about one hundred and fifty feet away, and installed a ring main, working lights and outside floodlights for security. I was well pleased.

As an early Christmas treat for Julian and a couple of his friends, I arranged for them to have the house seats (which are kept back and retained by the theatre management and never put on sale until the day, if not allocated) in the Front Stalls at The Palladium to see Lulu recreate her role as *Peter Pan*, but with the legendary Ron Moody as Captain Hook and Mr. Darling. They thought it was great fun to be given the VIP Treatment.

Benny Andersson made a surprise Christmas visit from Sweden to see the show, now in its second year, on 16th December. We invited a select few up to the General Office for drinks & nibbles on Wednesday the 23rd following and had an early Treasury Call for Christmas week, which everyone appreciated. I had drawn up the rota for Christmas and New Year, and had put myself down to work the two shows on Boxing Day, so the big day in our new home was a quiet one, eating, drinking and watching Eric & Ernie with guests Leonard Rossiter, Eamon Andrews, Frank Finlay and former Prime Minister Harold Wilson no less.

The cycle ride in at 8.30am on Boxing Day was always quiet and I manned the office on my own until Peter Russell came on duty for the Matinée. Carolyn was off for four days. The festivities passed, and 1988 dawned with new challenges and prospects of another year of *Chess*, as business was still very good.

As was traditional on 1st Januaryst each year the TV Licence for the theatre was renewed, as we had numerous televisions throughout the building, including my small portable in the office. On my days off, I still did the odd lecture on backstage customs and practices to RADA students in Gower Street. Maris was now working at the Garrick Theatre, as we had an au pair called Nurten from Turkey, which was not to my liking.

The 1988 FLC Conference was held at The Moat House Hotel in Stratford upon Avon. I travelled to Pershore by coach on Sunday 24th January to stay the night with Sue and her two girls, Joanna who was now almost twelve and Katy, my Goddaughter, who had just celebrated her tenth birthday. She drove me to The Moat House after lunch, where I checked in and went for a swim in the indoor heated pool. I have never been a keen swimmer, which I think goes back to the early 1950s when Dad used to take us swimming at 7am in the open air Boultham Baths which were decidedly chilly. The two-day conference followed the usual format, and Mike Churchill (GM from the POW) kindly gave me a lift back to London.

I had regular meetings with Eric Young who ran the contract cleaning firm we used, and quite often he would take me to a Middle Eastern restaurant in Wardour Street for lunch, where the origins of the food on offer were dubious, but it was his choice.

Over the meal we would discuss additional cleaning work I wanted doing, over and above his normal duties. I drew up a rolling schedule of additional jobs, such as an annual steam clean of seats, a monthly high level clean and a six monthly drapes clean, which he would quote for, and usually be asked to carry out.

Another of my duties as General Manager was Chairman of The Health & Safety Committee. The FLC was very much a belt and braces Company, and I kept meticulous files and recorded our deliberations in a manual for inspection, should I ever have to back anything up. One re-occurring issue at regular meetings with the representatives of each department was that of First Aiders. As a trained person I knew the importance of this role, and so began negotiations with the Directors to train permanent members of staff, both FOH and Backstage, to take a course. I also proposed that a selected few should go on a training course run by the London Fire Brigade to be shown the correct extinguisher to be used on a particular fire: paper, wood, oil, or electric for example. This was also given the go ahead.

As a tenth birthday treat for Rachel, I invited her and three friends to come and see the show at the Saturday Matinée, before her birthday on the Tuesday. They all sat in the Royal Box and I gave them a large box of chocolates to share, but the highlight was using the Royal Loo.

In mid April, I again organised the Awards Ceremony for the ABTT Show, and Maureen ran the London Marathon on Sunday 17th April raising lots of money for worthy charities. The following day Mr. Mills and Mr. Roberts had one of their regular inspections, where things that needed attention were jotted down by Sue Fowler, Mr Mills' Secretary. Later in the month Maris began another Summer Season at the Open Air Theatre in Regents Park, which meant that for a while longer we didn't see much of each other.

As a vacancy had occurred, I started interviews for the post of Catering Manager, who would be mainly responsible for looking after merchandise, the four main bars in the theatre and the 'Quick Doubles' bar in the Foyer. I was looking for a person who was experienced, keen, honest, had good references and a love of the Theatre and entertainment. I was not doing very well until a young man from Kent stepped through the office door. I am a great believer in first impressions, and Rupert Bielby was the first applicant to make me sit up and take notice. He did a very good interview, and impressed me with his general attitude to life, and his willingness to learn about the West End, as he was currently working at The Marlow Theatre in Canterbury. Here I thought was someone we could all get on with and I offered him the post. His references were impeccable, and after working his notice he started on Friday 20th May. This proved to be one of the best appointments I ever made, as he is now the Manager at the TRDL.

The first anniversary of the move to Arran Road was a week later, and I was very pleased with the work that I had done so far to improve the house.

It was traditional for the Open Air Theatre to present *The Dream* on Midsummer's Eve and I went to see it on one of my nights off. Maris was working on the show, with my old friend Ian Talbot playing Bottom. I spent much of the incoming and interval with Bill Denis, whose company I enjoyed. We talked about the good old days when he had been on the road around the number one touring dates, as half of the Denis Brothers Variety Act. I learnt the meaning of many of the terms and phrases that were in use then, and felt it was a crying shame that they were not preserved and committed to paper, or they would be lost forever. I vowed that when I had the time I would compile a full list, and have them published. This was finished and published in 2013 as *Traditional Theatre Jargon* in the *Miscellany of Lighting and Stagecraft*, and I cite just one example. DECK: A term for the stage floor that dates back to when sailors worked backstage, because of their knowledge of ropes and knots.

I also included some of my favourite theatrical quotes, such as: "An actor is a guy who if you ain't talking about him, he ain't listening" (Marlon Brando); "Women are meant to be loved, not understood" (Oscar Wilde); "I used to be a Tour-de-Force, but now I am forced to tour" (Sybil Thorndike); "Acting is merely the art of keeping a large group of people from coughing" (Ralph Richardson); and "A woman is only a woman, but a good cigar is a smoke." (Kipling)

Five VIP Russians came to see the show on Saturday 18th June. As a security precaution I made a note in my pocket book of the seats they were to occupy in H row of the stalls, should there be an incident during the show. Fortunately there wasn't and the only slight problem was caused by their big limousine waiting outside at the end which caused a huge tailback along Old Compton Street. There was nothing for it but to act as a traffic policeman to get things moving, and I was thankful for my trusty Acme referee's whistle on my keyring, to give me some authority. I normally used to blow this to signal the opening of the house before each performance, and to alert members of the staff on duty in the Foyer when a known or suspected pickpocket had entered. On one occasion, I spotted a man with a raincoat draped over his shoulder, which looked out of place, even though his hands were showing out of the bottom of the sleeves of the raincoat. I watched him as he moved slowly around the Foyer looking down all the time, which was unusual, and brushing into people. Then I saw a third hand appear and realised straight away that the raincoat draped over his shoulders was to disguise the fact that his real hands were free to dip an unsuspecting patron, and the ones in the raincoat sleeves were false. As soon as this became obvious I gave a blast on the Acme and alerted the staff with: "Pickpocket operating in Foyer – be vigilant" and on hearing this, our friend made a very quick exit.

The first leg of The Grass Track Masters Championships was held at the boarded track at Collier Street in Kent. It was very akin to the type of track which you would find on the Continent, and this was the only one of its type in this country. It was unique because the perimeter of the six hundred yard oval grass raceway was defined not by ropes and stakes as usual, but by 8' x 4' boards held upright by scaffolding poles driven hard into the ground every four feet. This eliminated a run off area and spectators were much closer to the action. Both the riders and the paying public liked the set up, and it usually provided close, fast racing. As it was a fairly local meeting Julian and Rachel came with me and I planned a barbeque at the end. Being just the first of the two legs, the points accumulated were carried forward to the final round in September, so all eyes were on who would win the big 'A' Finals at the end of the day. In the Solos it was a win for Trevor Banks from Steve Schofield with Jeremy Doncaster in third place. In the Sidecar Class Roger Measor & Dave Harris scored a victory from the surprise of the meeting Mike Baxter & Danny Tully, with father and son Alan and John Blewitt in third.

The musical that was part of the 1988 season at the Open Air Theatre was *Babes in Arms* by Rodgers & Hart, which is one I love as it contains such classic songs as *Where or When*, *My Funny Valentine*, *Johnny One Note* and *The Lady is a Tramp*, all of which are show stopping numbers. The 1939 film by Busby Berkeley also confirmed Mickey Rooney and Judy Garland as superstars, so I had to see what The Park's version was all about, and very acceptable it was too.

One of the Police Officers assigned to the theatre from West End Central, when we had Royal or VIP visitors in to see the show, was Sergeant John Wall. He and I would liaise about security implications and arrangements. We would often lunch together or meet socially, as we shared many interests. Over the ten year period I was in office we never had a cross word, and I grew to respect him much as he could always be relied upon to do what he said.

The second anniversary of my starting at The PET came and went, and I went out to lunch with Eric Young, at the usual restaurant. Maris finished the 1988 Season at The Park on 10th September.

The second and final leg of The Grass Track Championships took place at Eaton near Abingdon on Sunday the 11th, and I attended to witness Steve Schofield win his first and only Masters Solo title from Trevor Banks and Jeremy Doncaster. In the sidecar class, Steve Dewison & Dave Ward retained their Masters title for a second year, with local crew Roger Measor & Dave Harris in second place and up and coming crew Richard (Sid) Piggott & Tony Angelico in third - a cracking day's racing all round.

The Chess Company Manager Ken Grant became very ill and was unable to continue in his role, which was upsetting, as he had been instrumental in persuading me to take the General Manager's job in the first place. He had been a vital link between the visiting show's management and us, the bricks & mortar management, and his replacement was the very efficient Annie Partridge.

One evening in late September I went to hear some late night Jazz in a bar in Covent Garden. I chained my cycle securely to some stout wooden barriers set into the road. On my return two hours later the cycle had disappeared, and on close inspection of the area I found two half links of my chain lying on the ground. They had obviously been cut through with a bolt cutter, and I reported the theft to Bow Street Police Station, just round the corner. They said that this was not the first theft of a cycle from the area at night, and suspected an inside job which they were investigating. It eventually turned out that the night security staff in Covent Garden had been in the habit of removing cycles and storing them for re-sale later, so it was goodbye and thanks to my faithful Eddy Merckx and hello to a new cycle I bought a few days later.

My mother Joan was now suffering the effect of having been a smoker for most of her life and in late September was referred to see a throat specialist at Lincoln County Hospital. The prognosis was not good, in that there were early signs of cancer. She was told it could be treated, but it would involve the removal of her voice box, which was devastating news for us all, but I knew she was a fighter and would be brave and cope. Her relationship with Dad had been unstable for a few years, but he was most supportive and told me that they would "fight this thing together" which was encouraging.

Norman Johns, the Duty Fireman during my time at The Windmill some fourteen years earlier, was now a Station Officer and attached to the Entertainment Section of the London Fire Brigade. Part of his duties was to visit places of public entertainment when they were open to members of the public, to check that all the requirements of the licence were in order. His visits were always unannounced, and following his inspection to ensure panic bolts were unchained and fire exits were not blocked (as I had found at The Café Royal), he would come up to the office and tell me his findings. Whilst there he would ask to see the log of the weekly fire drills that were required and details of fire extinguisher replacements etc. He was usually quite happy with what he found, making one or two small comments that needed attention, which I put on my to do list. We got on like a house on fire(!) as he knew that on his next visit, the points he had brought to my attention would have been dealt with.

The First Aid courses to train selected staff in Emergency First Aid at Work that had been requested at an earlier Health & Safety Meeting were held in the Dress Circle Bar at the PET, for both staff from the PET, and our sister theatre The POW. I had engaged the services of the Paremedico Organisation, as they had a good reputation and had been the First Aid Team to rescue the mortally wounded P.C. Keith Blakelock (the first officer to be killed in a riot since 1833) at Broadwater Farm in Tottenham three years earlier. We had split the training into two sections, the first two of the five days in early December with the final three days the following week. As we began our training on Monday 12th December, our tutor received a message on her pager to inform her that a major rail incident had happened at Clapham, with many injuries and could she attend? We would of course have perfectly well understood if she had left, but as re-booking another mutually convenient date was impossible she stayed, and everyone who took part was awarded a certificate of competence for three years.

I went to Lincoln for a long weekend on my birthday, which happened to fall on a Saturday, to see how Mum and Dad were coping, which was upsetting for me. I returned on Tuesday the 20th, for the traditional Christmas meeting at noon of all the West End Managers who sold Walls Ice Cream in their theatres, which was held in their plush offices in Jermyn Street. I did not stay long, as it was also the day of the annual Christmas lunch at the Coach and Horses, which was a must attend event.

Maureen, Carolyn and Rupert all had Christmas Eve and Boxing Day off (Christmas day fell on a Sunday) and Peter and I worked both days, although I had both New Year's Eve and New Year's day off. I had a feeling that *Chess* would not be playing at the PET in a year's time, but I would have to wait and see what developed in 1989 to find out.

I did not have to wait long as it turned out. Bookings for our next show, which was to be a revival of Cole Porter's *Anything Goes*, opened on 30th January. I could now start to plan major jobs that could be undertaken during the dark period between the end of *Chess* (which would close on 8th April) and *Anything Goes*, which was scheduled to open on 4th July. One of these was the cleaning of the main Auditorium chandelier. We contacted a specialist firm, Lynton's of Leytonstone, to visit on 22nd February to look at what was involved and quote to remove, wash and polish all the pieces. The first meeting to discuss the breakdown and Get Out of *Chess* was held in early March, with Production Manager Richard Bullimore organising things, including removing the huge bank of television screens that were flown, and the under stage hydraulic system that controlled the tilting and moving chequered, illuminated Chessboard Stage.

I decided that as I was still due some holiday I would take a week off in mid March. *Maureen* also decided it would be wise to have time off, whilst we were still in a routine, and she would take the week after. During my week I installed a loft ladder, and got ahead with preparing the allotment for another year. On my return to work, I was informed that Auditions were being held that afternoon for a leading role in the new show, and that this would be behind closed doors as it involved a big name television star. It transpired that Les Dawson was interested in playing Moonface Martin in the show, if American Director Jerry Zaks (who did not know his work) thought that he was suitable for the role. Les was very funny at his audition, as only Les can be, but did not get the part.

During the summer of 1988 Rachel had been away from home and spent some of her holidays with Joanna & Katy in Pershore. Rachel and Katy were like sisters and one afternoon Sue had taken them all over to Kidderminster for a swim in the pool there. One of the attractions dotted around for children to climb, was a whale, which became very slippery when wet. Unfortunately Rachel fell off it and cut her lip quite badly with blood spouting everywhere. Sue took her to the local hospital and on their arrival in A & E with Rachel still in her swimsuit, the receiving nurse said "Not the Whale again!" It transpired that this happened quite regularly, and nothing had been done about it. I rang Solicitor Jon Carter of Burton & Co as I knew he specialised in this type of accident and subsequent compensation. We had photographs taken of the scar and Jon pursued a claim which we won, and although it took until the Spring of the following year to settle, Rachel received the sum of £1,450 in compensation.

We were all sad to see *Chess* close after 1,209 performances. *Chess* was the second longest run at The PET after the 3,173 performances of *Evita*, and I felt that the theatre had at long last shaken off the unlucky theatre tag line, but who could tell in this fickle world of showbiz?

Act 6 Scene 3
ANYTHING GOES OPENING
(1989)

There could not have been a better show to look forward to than this Cole Porter classic, as I had always been a big fan of his shows and consider him to be one of the finest lyricists of all time, along with Sammy Cahn. Anyone who can think of rhyming Mahatma Ghandi with Napoleon Brandy must be a genius. It was also a record that the same leading lady, Elaine Paige, would be appearing at the same theatre for a third consecutive show, following triumphs in *Evita* and *Chess* over the previous eleven years.

This revival had originated at The Lincoln Centre in New York in 1987, and was to be produced in London by Robert Fox Ltd. and Anchorage Productions Ltd., a company set up by Elaine and Tim Rice. Many of the original American Production Team would be coming over to London to set up this new production, headed by Jerry Zaks (Director), Michael Smuin (Choreographer), Paul Gallo (Lighting), and Tony Walton (Set and Costume Designer).

The break down and Get Out of *Chess* began on the Sunday after we closed. It went according to plan until Friday 14th April when contractors were working under stage to remove the base unit that had supported the Chess Board stage for the show. This required the use of Oxy-Acetylene Gas Cylinders and cutting torches. Late in the afternoon, as it was quiet in the office, I thought I would get changed early to facilitate a quick get away at six o'clock, as it had been Julian's thirteenth birthday the previous day. No sooner was I back in the office in my cycling gear than the announcement came over the tannoy: "Mr. Sands is under stage" which was a coded message to say: "There is a fire under the stage" and I knew it was for real, by the tone in Barry's (the Stage Doorkeeper) voice. The pre-determined plan was that the Stage Doorkeeper would call the brigade to attend, and that I would investigate the incident. I shot down the stairs to the foyer, not using the lift, should there be a power cut, and collected the Incident Officer florescent bib from the kiosk where it was kept. I went onstage, looked down into the under stage area from where I could hear a very loud hissing of gas being released under great pressure and see flame issuing from the end of a flexible delivery hose. The situation was very serious, because if the cylinder exploded, it would be like a five hundred pound bomb exploding in the middle of Soho. I knew from attending an incident as a first aider back in 1983, that the usual procedure with an incident involving cylinders was for a hundred yard exclusion zone to be imposed by the Emergency Services. I returned to the Foyer to await the arrival of the first appliance, which would normally come from Station A24 Soho in Shaftsbury Avenue, only two minutes away, but from the time delay I suspected that they must be on another shout and would not be the first to arrive. It just so happened that a Police Car was passing down Old Compton Street at that moment, so I flagged it down and explained to the two officers that there was an incident inside the building involving gas cylinders.

They radioed for back up to assist them in setting up an exclusion zone and the first of the four appliances that was our predetermined turn out arrived. This turn out usually consisted of the two pumps and turntable ladders from A24 plus a third pump from Euston or Westminster. On this occasion however, the first attendance was from Euston, hence the slight delay, and I explained the situation to the Officer in Charge that cylinders were involved and he instructed his watch to set up cooling baths in the Foyer.

I led him down to the Stalls, took him to the under stage pass door, where he could hear and see what was happening, and he advised me to make myself scarce which I was happy to do. I found out later that a red-hot piece of metal had fallen onto the flexible pipe burning through it, and instead of turning the off key to stop the gas from leaving the cylinder, the contractor had panicked and legged it. A cooling jet had been played onto the cylinder and a fireman had then turned the key to the off position. Whilst all this was going on under stage, I rang Peter Roberts and informed him of the situation, and a member of the LFB Entertainment section arrived, as he had heard about the incident via the brigade radio system. As soon as the cylinders were safe we opened the dock doors in Greek Street to vent the building and I began to write my incident report, which took me way past six o'clock, so I did not get my early night.

I had the following day off, which was the FA Cup Semi Final Saturday. I still supported Liverpool FC from my days there, who were playing Nottingham Forest for a place at Wembley. It was the tradition that the two Semi Finals were played at neutral grounds and in 1989 they were Villa Park in Birmingham for the Norwich v Everton match and Hillsborough in Sheffield for the other one. I settled down at home to listen to the match live on the radio and at 1506 hrs the game was stopped by the match referee and he took the players off the field of play. The BBC commentator Peter Jones was describing what looked like a crowd invasion at the time, but we all know now that it was far more serious than that resulting in the deaths of ninety-six Liverpool Fans and injury to seven hundred and sixty six. Who was to blame on the day is still a matter of conjecture, even as I write in 2014 some twenty-five years later, but the truth will be told about that terrible day eventually. Little did it matter, but Everton won the other Semi that day, and an all Merseyside final was assured when Liverpool won the replay staged at Old Trafford, then went on to beat their rivals from across Stanley Park three goals to two in the final on 20th May in London.

As the theatre was dark and I had evenings free, I made the most of going out to see concerts and shows as often as I could. On Monday 17th April I was invited to attend the Opening Night and World Premiere of *Aspects of Love* at the POW. The cast was headed by Michael Ball and Kevin Colson who had been in *Chess*, inheriting the part of George when Roger Moore withdrew only two weeks prior to the opening night. As she was not working, I took Maris along with me, but sadly, after a fraught evening, she didn't want to go to the after show party, so we went home.

From the billboards and posters we at the PET got to know who would be in the cast of the new show with Elaine, who we all knew by now. Howard McGillin was to play Billy Crocker, the part that he created in New York, and this was to be his West End debut. Bernard Cribbins had been cast as Moonface Martin, with Kathryn Evans, Ursula Smith, Martin Turner, Ashleigh Sendin and Harry Towb in leading supporting roles. The Musical Director was to be an old friend of the theatres, John Owen Edwards, who had worked on *Chess*, who would be in charge of the sixteen-piece orchestra. The resident Director who would be responsible for the show when the Production Team left was the hugely experienced Larry Oaks.

In late April Maris started work on another Season at The Open Air Theatre in Regents Park. On 1st May *Anything Goes* Rehearsals began for a seven week period, leading up to the first Preview Performance scheduled for Monday 19th June. Rupert Bielby took advantage of us being dark by taking three weeks' holiday before the Catering Department swung into action again on 22nd May. I meanwhile took advantage of having nights and weekends off by going to The Berks Bonanza Grass Track meeting at Dalton Barracks Airfield near Abingdon on May Day where Kelvin Tatum won the Solos and Steve Dewison & Dave Ward triumphed in the Sidecar Class.

The following Saturday I had the rare opportunity to go and hear the legendary RAF Squadronaires Band (more commonly known as The Squads) play a live concert at The Imperial War Museum. The band had originally been formed in 1939 as The Royal Air Force Dance Orchestra with the mission to boost morale, and included the finest musicians of the day. It had amongst its members Ronnie Aldrich as arranger and co-pianist, George Chisholm (Trombone), Harry Lewis (Saxophone), who was Vera Lynn's husband, and Joan Regan on Vocals. In 1950 Ronnie had been promoted to Bandleader, and they played eleven Summer Seasons as the resident band at the Palace Ballroom on the Isle of Man. The New Squadronaires had been formed in 1985, and kicked off their set with their well-known signature tune *Something In The Air* by Harold Adamson & Jimmy McHugh played, as usual, as a slow fox trot. All the other tunes like *In The Mood* followed and it was pure delight to hear them play in such surroundings.

In May I again organised the Awards Ceremony at The ABTT Show, and took a week off at the end of May to prepare myself for the challenges that lay ahead. My return to work on 5th June coincided with the first arrival of the new company at the PET. During my absence I had arranged with Zoonie, the Housekeeper, and Eric Young, our Cleaning Contractor, for all the Dressing Rooms to have a deep clean in readiness for our new guests, and close liaison with The Company Manager Peter Roper followed. Peter had retained the services of the Production Stage Manager Sam Hunter, and Camilla Clutterbuck was Stage Manager with Lorna McLean as her Deputy.

Martin Hayes Associates was the Production Company responsible and Simon Robertson was their on site Manager who dealt with daily matters. Meanwhile at the PET Neil Franklin was now the Box Office Manager and Kevin Burgess Chief Electrician. Several of the freelance crew who came in to work on the Fit Up were familiar to me, like Bob Fitzsimmons & Mike Odam, from my MMA days and Madeline Loftin, who had been a dancer in *Chess*, was now the Dance Captain.

I was too busy working to have the time to go to Chetton in Shropshire for the first leg of this year's Masters, but read in the Motor Cycle News on 14th June that Simon Wigg was unbeaten all day in the Solos, and Steve Dewison & Dave Ward on their lightweight Miller Drifter outfit had won the sidecar class, dropping just two points during the meeting, so things were looking good for the final leg on 10th September.

The Preview period looked as if it would be hectic as several Royal Galas were planned to take place prior to the official First Night on 4th July. The first of these was on 27th June when their Royal Highnesses The Duke and Duchess of York attended a charity evening. They were entertained in The Royal Box at the interval, and the audience was prevented from leaving via the main Foyer until I had escorted them down from their Circle seats to the pass door to meet the Company who had all assembled onstage. Whilst this presentation took place the Auditorium was cleared and I was then able to escort the Royal Party to their waiting car parked in Old Compton Street, prior to them driving off with Police outriders.

The following day I had a de-brief with Police liaison officer Sergeant Wall about how we might improve arrangements for the next Royal evening which was the following Monday 3rd July. HRH Princess Margaret would be attending and we decided that as everything had gone so smoothly last time, we would stick with what had worked best for both the Police and Security and had the minimum disruption to our paying patrons. As HRH was a personal friend of Tim Rice he hosted her in The Royal Box and I ensured that she was escorted to and from her seat. The evening was a huge success for all concerned.

The Opening Night was a huge success, and I was responsible for making sure that Richard Mills and his FLC Guests, including our Chairman Lord Delfont and Chief Executive John Conlan, were properly looked after. I made sure there were Programmes, Brochures, and a full Bar available and asked Rupert Bielby to look after this for me, should I be called away to deal with an incident. This again went without a hitch.

Our third Royal visitor was a week after the Opening Night, and would be a benefit evening for The Variety Club. The Variety Club evening was a formal affair on Tuesday 11th July, and the

Guest of Honour was HRH Anne, The Princess Royal. I had a briefing the previous day with her personal bodyguard to discuss arrangements and patrons were to be asked to take their seats early as the Foyer would be needed for a Royal Line up 'Meet and Greet' handshake session and posy presentation at 1925 hrs. I was kept informed about the progress of the Royal Party and was able to update the waiting line up with comments such as: "Car passing through Trafalgar Square estimated time of arrival three minutes." My role as General Manager of the host venue was to meet HRH after she had got out of the car, shake her hand, and then hand her over to the Varity Club Personnel, who would do their introductions. I then escorted her to her Circle seat, and with a pre-arranged signal gave the clearance for the overture to commence. At the interval and again at the end of the show it was my duty to see her safely to and from her seat. At the end of the show there was another backstage visit. I led the way up the stairs from the stalls with HRH and was seeing her to the waiting car, when a member of the authorised Press Pack snapped a shot of us both, which hangs in my living room.

I was beginning to get used to these Royal Visits, but nothing could have prepared me for what occurred when His Majesty King Hussein and Queen Noor of Jordan attended the theatre in a private capacity on Friday 14th July.

The Royal Couple were to sit in Stalls seats H 23 & 24 and their Bodyguard insisted that he and a colleague sit in the two seats immediately behind them. I checked the seating plan with Neil Franklin, to discover what I had expected: the two seats behind, J 24-25 had already been sold as a pair. The only solution was to put a stop on these at the Stalls entrance and explain the situation to the ticket holders. I had in mind to offer them two equally good seats instead, and if that was agreeable a complimentary Programme, brochure and drink at the Interval with my compliments. Thankfully they were a most understanding couple and were more than happy to accept my offer.

I received news that the Royal Flight from Jordan to Northolt had been delayed, and the King & Queen might be late arriving at the theatre, and I was asked whether we could hold the curtain for them. I said under the circumstances we would delay the Overture for five minutes, out of courtesy, but no longer, which was acceptable. With the aid of 'twos and blues' and Police Outriders holding traffic up at junctions, the Royal Party just made it in time, and I quickly showed them to their seats.

I had arranged to entertain the Royal Couple in the Stalls Retiring Room, and once in the privacy of the room The King informed me that the Queen had something in her eye and would like to clean her contact lenses with water and tissues. As usual there was a long queue to use the Ladies during the interval, and it would not be courteous to ask her to use a public convenience, so another solution had to be found. I thought quickly on my feet and dashed back up to the General Office, stopping briefly in The Foyer to ask Aida Casela, the Head Usherette, to get one of her girls to go to the corner shop and buy a small sealed packet of tissues and bring them up to the office as quickly as she could. Once in the office I found a small round tea tray and a damask napkin to cover it with. I then emptied the sugar out of a small chrome sugar bowl into a cup, and washed and dried the bowl into which I put some cold water. I found a small square mirror in the emergency box of various items that I had in one of the drawers in a metal cabinet in my office, and polished that. Once the tissues had arrived I fanned them out on the tray and carefully took the tray, with its 'contact lenses cleaning kit' down to the retiring room.

Queen Noor thanked me and asked where I had got the tray from so quickly, to which I replied: "It is something we keep for such eventualities your Majesty" and chatted to The King. He explained that as a trained pilot he had been at the controls on the flight to RAF Northolt, and apologised for their late arrival. After this episode the rest of the evening was incident free, and on the following Monday, when I arrived at the Theatre for work, there was a small package waiting for me. On opening it I found a set of pens in a box tied up with Black, White and Green Ribbons which are the colours of the Jordanian flag, along with a note from King Hussein thanking me for my kindness. This was a treasured possession of mine until it was stolen during a burglary some years later.

I was beginning to think that this run of Royal Visitors must soon come to an end, but fate had another and even bigger surprise in store for me. On 1st August, I was asked to meet Producer Robert Fox in the Dress Circle as he wanted to introduce someone to me. This person was Sir Martin Guiliat, who was an Equerry to the Royal Family. He introduced himself and told me that a Senior Member of the Royal Family would be attending the theatre on her birthday in three days' time on 4th August.

Sir Martin gave me his personal phone number at Clarence House, and explained that he had been the Private Secretary to Her Majesty Queen Elizabeth The Queen Mother since 1956. He was making the final arrangements for her to attend the show, with other senior members of her family on her eighty ninth birthday. I had never met Sir Martin before, but knew that he had an abiding interest in the theatre and was a most generous angel when it came to backing a show. I suspected that he might have invested in *Anything Goes*.

He asked if the bar was open, and over a snorter he said that most things were in hand already. However he told me I would be expected to escort Her Majesty from her arrival outside the theatre and up the stairs to her seat in The Royal Box, adding: "Don't be afraid to take her arm as she is getting on a bit now and finds climbing stairs difficult sometimes." What a responsibility! He said that Superintendent Kirchin from The Royalty Diplomatic Protection Department would contact me to discuss security and that RDPD out-riders would be doing a stopwatch timed dummy run at the same time of day in the next forty eight hours, and on arrival would make themselves known to me. I was also in touch with Chief Inspector Maria Wallis, who was in charge of operations from West End Central who reported to Chief Superintendent Golding along with my usual liaison officer, Sergeant John Wall.

I was told that as this was an Official Visit on a special occasion, crowds were expected. As a precaution crowd barriers would be set up along Old Compton Street, the arrival and departure route. I thought it only courteous to inform the businesses in the affected area, such as Wheelers Restaurant, that there would be some disruption on the day, and asked them to be discrete about what I had told them. This evening was going to be a real test of my organisational skills, and an ideal opportunity to put into practice all I had learnt during the previous four Royal Visits I had overseen, since we had opened exactly a month before.

As my Mother Joan had by now had her operation to remove her cancerous voice box, I thought it would be a huge pick me up for her to be there on the night in question. I invited her along with my Mother in Law Mickey, who was delighted to accept and Mum came to stay with us for a week.

The big day arrived, the crowd barriers were in place outside and the theatre was searched by specially trained sniffer dogs before we opened to the public, with a sterile area set up around the Royal Box. There was a huge crowd of people outside by 1900 hrs as it had been announced at the traditional lunchtime Clarence House walkabout that Her Majesty would attend a West End Show that evening, and from the crowd barriers set up outside the PET from early morning, it was not difficult to work out which one.

Again I was kept informed of the progress of the Royal car from Clarence House, and patrons were asked to be in their seats by 1925 hrs, so that the Foyer was clear for the Royal arrival at 1927 hrs. The Royal limousine drew up, the bodyguard opened the door and I shook hands with the great lady I escorted her into the Theatre where one of the Press Pack took a photo, which I treasure. As we passed through the now empty Foyer, the Commissionaires all saluted, and I wished her a Happy Birthday on behalf of the Company and Staff. "Do they all know that it's my Birthday?" she asked, as huge crowds cheering and waving flags must have been a normal day for her.

She did need a helping hand up the stairs to the Dress Circle and I remember catching a glimpse of my mother, wearing a brand new pink evening gown, giving a polite curtsey as H.M. passed with me at her side. There was a spontaneous round of applause as patrons in the Dress Circle recognised who had just entered the Auditorium, and those in the front stalls turned round and looked up to see what was going on. Once in the Royal Box, the audience stood whilst the National Anthem was played, then on with the show, which was a huge success, and went like clockwork. I and all the staff had worked hard to make the evening the success it had been, learning Royal Etiquette, who to address as "Your Majesty", who to address as "Your Royal Highness" and when to use "Ma'am" which is always pronounced as in "Jam", not "Marme."

I was totally overwhelmed with the letters of congratulations that arrived the following day and for the next four days. The first franked at 1115 am was a hand written letter from Sir Martin, who had been asked by The Queen Mother to write me a thank you letter saying how much she appreciated all I had done to make her visit a happy and enjoyable one. This was followed by another hand written letter from The Lord St John of Fawsley,

JT and HM the Queen Mother 4th August 1989 © PA/PA Archive

who had been a part of the Royal Party on the night, and he too said that the evening had been a triumph and had been perfect. Peter H. Roberts, the BDL Technical Director, in a letter of 7th August, also endorsed this.

The Metropolitan Police were also most complimentary about the way the event had gone, and Chief Inspector Wallis commented that: "The success of the evening was in no small measure due to the assistance that the staff and I had given to them" and that "She had learnt from my expertise." Chief Superintendent Golding said that all the officers had been most impressed with the co-operation they had received and would trust that the close liaison would continue. What a triumph for the PET. I felt on top of the world and that I had achieved what I set out to do when I took the job on, which was to run a Theatre and Royal Event as well as my mentor John Avery had done at The Palladium.

Mum stayed with us in Arran Road and could not stop talking about the show and the events she had witnessed on the very special night. She kept telling me how proud she was of me and what I had achieved in my chosen career.

The following week The Ambassador of the United States came to see the show and the style of VIP protection was completely different to the way us Brits do things.

The Morris Traveller failed the MOT and the welding I had been taught at night classes, when I had evenings free during the MMA days, was insufficient for what was required. I contacted

Giovanni Villa, who was an expert with a welding torch, and he did what was required to get it through the re-test.

On my third anniversary of starting at the PET I reflected on how much I had learnt about being the General Manager of the fifth largest musical theatre in the West End, and the numerous problems I had overcome in eleven hundred days, and looked forward to what the future would present.

As Julian was now thirteen and a Jew, by tradition he was at the age to have his Bar Mitzvah. At the meeting with the Directors on 8th September, I asked if I could hire the large stalls bar at the POW on Sunday 26th November for the traditional celebration party. They were a bit confused about the ceremony until it was explained that the child inherits the religion of the mother. They agreed I could use the POW Bar, free of charge, provided I paid for the staff that would need to be on duty. We needed to send out the invites, hire tables and chairs, and find a Kosher catering company which would prepare the food and wine to take to the POW on the morning of the event. The only way was to plan the occasion like a production weekend, and this was put into motion along with all my other duties. At the same Director's meeting it was confirmed that Zoonie, our Housekeeper, would leave on compassionate grounds, and that the Head Usherette Aida Casla would take over these daytime duties in addition to her show responsibilities, which she was most happy to do. Aida was from The Philippines, a very hard worker, and above all reliable and honest. She had surrounded herself with her family and friends from the Philippines, who I had reservations about initially, but I soon grew to like and respect them. They were all most courteous to our patrons who often complemented me on their efficiency and politeness. I made it a rule that if addressing me in public I was to be referred to as Mr. Toogood, but in private they could call me John. They were uncomfortable with this, I found, and most would use the address 'Mr. John' in private, which I found utterly charming.

The Head of Staff, Ian Clark, was married to a lady from the Philippines, so he too surrounded himself mainly with these charming people as well, and they all got on like one big happy family. On the other hand our Linkman, Phil Course, was as English as Roast Beef, for as well as being a member of The Corp of Commissionaires he was an ex Military Band Big Bass Drum player and carried the size to match such an instrument. He did not mind standing outside the main entrance doors in the rain, with a cape over his smart black uniform, and opening cab doors for patrons whilst sheltering them with a huge umbrella. He insisted on calling me "Guv" or "Boss" which again was OK with me.

Sunday 10th September was the second leg of The Grass Track Masters Championship organised by The Andover Club at their undulating Winterbourne Gunner Track in Wiltshire. As things had now settled down on the show, I found time to go to this one. The great Simon Wigg came back to claim his fourth title, having won three on the trot between 1981-83 from Clayton Williams and Paul Fry. Steve Dewison & Dave Ward added a third consecutive Sidecar Masters title to their list of achievements, with the equally exciting crew of Richard Piggott & Tony Angelico second and the father and son Alan & John Blewitt in third place. It was an expertly run meeting by Ian Barclay and his loyal henchmen Dickie & Grubby.

The VIP entertaining continued the following week with a visit by The Admiral of the United States Mediterranean Fleet, based in Naples, with Admiral Howe and his family attending. If I thought that Security had been ultra tight for a member of our Royal Family, that was nothing compared to what the Admiral's protection officers did in their line of duty. They were constantly talking into the cuffs of the jackets they were wearing and tilting their heads to their lapels to hear messages. I could overhear things like: "Seal intends to go to base for dinner after the show". Despite all this Admiral Howe and his family were charming when I entertained them at the interval and they were most thankful for the courteous way in which they had been received.

My day off that week was Friday. By coincidence George Melly, one of the greatest British Blues Singers of all times, was performing at Lewisham Concert Hall with *John Chiltern and his Feetwarmers*. I decided to pop along as I knew George, having shared a libation or two with him when we were both in The Coach at the same time.

When I arrived he was holding court in an armchair in the main bar, as only he could. "Good evening George" I said, "would you like a drink?" "That's most kind of you, dear boy" he replied: "I'll have a small Double Brandy" and that was that. Great concert with Good Time George belting the blues out like his idol Bessie Smith with the subtle undertones of John Chilton's muted trumpet, fronting the Feetwarmers Band. This was not quite as enjoyable for me as when George used to perform with the Alex Welsh Band, with the outrageous Lennie Hastings on drums, who had died in 1978. I last heard Lennie play when I popped into a bar in Saint Martin's Lane after working a show at The Phoenix Theatre, in the year not long before his untimely death, and he was still a great showman then.

During the last few months I had been entertaining my friend Bill Denis a great deal, as he had moved on to be a Producer. He wanted to impress Angels (people with a keen interest in theatre who wished to invest in shows) with his proposals for a revival of *Stop The World, I Want to Get Off*. He had secured the services of Anthony Newley to recreate the role of *Littlechap* that he originally played at The Queens Theatre in 1961, where it ran for 485 performances. It was scheduled to have a pre-West End try out at The Churchill Theatre in Bromley on 21st September. This was the day following the opening of what would prove to be the major hit of the season, Cameron Mackintosh's *Miss Saigon* at TRDL, where it would play for 4,264 performances, and remain in residence there until 1999. Having scheduled my day off for the Thursday to go and show my support for Bill, I had to miss the opening at The Lane. The Bromley try-out was a huge hit and I found out later from Bill that he had been offered a transfer to The Lyric Theatre, with a gala opening on 19th October, which I put onto my wall-chart. Incidentally, these fifteen thousand wall-chart entries have been invaluable while writing this book, as events and dates can accurately be identified. Why I kept them I have no idea, but I am forever thankful that I did.

Anything Goes was a pure delight to be associated with. Every night without fail I would stand at the back of the auditorium and listen to *I Get a Kick Out of You* and *You're the Top*. The lyrics to these tunes show what a truly gifted man 'Coley' was and thank goodness he changed his mind, whilst studying Law at Harvard, to transfer to the music department, as the Law's loss was undoubtedly Theatre's gain.

One of the re-occurring problems leaving the theatre via the stage door, invariably being the last one out, was the faulty key mechanism on the stage door panic bolt lock. It would sometimes take me a couple of minutes to engage and throw the lock into its closed position, which disengaged the outside turning knob. Despite my checking the dressing rooms and closing windows, the importance of which Tommy Appleby had taught me about in Manchester in 1972, I was convinced that someone had secreted themselves backstage before I left on more than one occasion, and then exited via the panic bolt exit, to the stage door, which was the only one not chained overnight. No thefts were ever reported, apart from a pair of very expensive sunglasses, which I called the Police in to investigate. Fortunately we never had anyone take advantage of this, despite the many vagrants in the area looking for somewhere to sleep.

In early October Fred Perryment, my Relief Duty Manager, informed me that he was moving house and would not be available to cover the odd performances when Peter Russell was away. Peter was a well-respected layman in Police circles, visiting prisoners in his local Police Station, the High Security one at Paddington Green, manning the lost children's playroom during The Notting Hill Carnival each August Bank Holiday Monday, and being Chairman of several Police Liaison Committees. With Fred's unavailability I required a second stand-by and invited Tommy Turner, whom I knew as a fellow member of the TMLC, to come and see me during the show one evening. I explained what was required, and showed him round, but he wasn't interested, so I began to look elsewhere. I then thought about asking the Chairman and Organiser of the TMLC David Alexander if he might be interested, which he was. David was a very experienced Theatre Manager in semi-retirement but still enjoyed being involved in the business. He was an Angel and had invested a small amount as one of the original investors in *Phantom of the Opera* at Her Majesty's, which had opened in 1986. He is still receiving returns some twenty-eight years later in 2014. He had been Theatre Manager at The Metropole Theatre in Edgware Road during its final days before being closed on Good Friday in 1963. The stage at this prestigious Matcham's Theatre on three levels was unique in that it was triangular, which must have presented Stage Manager Ted Bigley with many a problem of storage and presentation. It was also the only theatre that I know of when you could watch the show live from a seat in the stalls bar situated on Auditorium Right. David recalled during Irish Week one year when the crowd from County Kilburn were in every night, they sold a hundred crates of Guinness. Many old Music Hall and Variety artistes loved to play The Met and the bill on that final night read like a Who's Who of the big names of the day, with Tommy Trinder compering a show that included male impersonator Hetty King, Issy Bonn, drag act Mrs. Shufflewick, Wyn Calvin, Liverpool Comedian Ted Ray and vocalist Dickie Valentine.

The one person missing onstage that sad night was Max Miller, better known as 'the cheeky chappie' and once described as "the pure gold of the Music Hall" by a critic after seeing him in Pantomime at the Casino Theatre, where I was now working. Max was regarded by many as the greatest stand-up comedian of his generation and was so popular that in 1957 his act was recorded live at the theatre. The LP is appropriately titled "Max at The Met" and has proved to be a collector's item. His act was full of innuendo and the audience had to choose if they wanted to hear gags from the 'white book' which few did or the 'blue book', which was far more popular. Following The Met David had managed the Savoy Theatre for a number of years and I knew him to be charming, polite and immaculately dressed. Of equal importance was that he lived within walking distance and could be with us, in an emergency, in half an hour. The remuneration was to his satisfaction and it was agreed that he would start whenever we needed him. He would turn out to be a great asset to the team and we all liked him, which was equally important, as I was trying for forge a family around me who respected each other.

Aida took over officially as Housekeeper on 7th October. The following Thursday I once again was awarded a prize for my allotment. The opening night of *Stop The World* at The Lyric was a huge success and the post show party was held at The Savoy with Joan Collins (ex Mrs. Newley 1963-71) in attendance with the paparazzi all after getting that one shot of them together again.

I had more Jazzy nights out when I went to see that great vibes player 'Mr. Showmanship' Lionel Hampton and his Orchestra top the bill at the 1989 Lewisham Jazz Festival. He gave his all, as usual, with a virtuoso performance on drums and vibes, including his big hit of 1942, *Flying Home*. I went to the Albert Hall two days later to hear The Syd Lawrence Band. They were much better than when I had last heard them at The Adelphi Hotel in Liverpool and were now a fine, tight ensemble playing all the Big Band Classics, not just The Glenn Miller repertoire.

I took Julian to The International Ace of Aces Meeting on the last Sunday in October which was won by Steve Schofield from Trevor Banks in the solo class, whilst Steve Smith & Keith Wall took the sidecar honours. One of the attractions at this end of season meeting, in addition to a funfair, Firework Display and Bonfire, was the guest appearance of a Sun Page 3 Girl, flown in by helicopter. This year it was the delightful Gail McKenna, who I chatted to whilst she was sheltering from the cold wind in a caravan.

The following night was the annual Awards Ceremony for Beckenham Monarch Cycle Speedway team, of which I was the Captain and rode wearing the Number One race jacket. I was presented with The Bud Flanagan Shield, and in my acceptance speech explained who Bud was, and that he had been part of The *Flanagan & Allen* comedy double act that found fame as part of the *Crazy*

Gang, hence the theatre connection with me. 'The Gang' was made up of three double acts working together on sketches. They were Flanagan & Allen (in which Bud was the comic in a long fur coat and battered straw boater, and Chesney was the straight man); Nervo & Knox, Naughton & Gold and Monsewer Eddie Gray. Bud was born and bred in Whitechapel, where Cycle Speedway had its origins on the bombsites around the East End, and from where his love of the sport had derived. He had died in 1968 and this shield was in his honour. Much respected as one of the greats in the post Music Hall and Vaudeville era, many of his songs such as *Underneath The Arches* were national favourites and he had recently found fame again when he recorded *Who Do You Think You Are Kidding Mr. Hitler*, the theme tune for *Dad's Army*.

In November I went to see *Cats*, now in its eighth year, and thought that it was still sensational. I then took a week off to prepare for Julian's Bar Mitzvah on Sunday 25th when we had invited around one hundred people to join us for the party in the Stalls Bar at The POW. We set the room up with the required number of tables and chairs, and the Kosher food arrived from the caterers Blooms in the East End. Robin Jackson, a friend of mine from the PET, had agreed to be official photographer for the day, and he captured the mood of the event perfectly.

As December dawned, the show entered its fifth month. It showed no signs of flagging with business at the Box Office still healthy and full houses for most performances. I had the evening of 6th December off-duty as Ken Dodd was appearing at the Lewisham Concert Hall. Now Mr. Dodd is akin to Marmite: you either love him or loathe him, and I am firmly in the former camp. I had last met him at The Liverpool Playhouse, when he came to audition for Malvolio in 1971, and had been a big admirer of his work in the intervening eighteen years. I am not so keen on his singing, but as a stand-up comedian, with his rapid delivery of one-liners, he is supreme. The energy that this sixty-two year old showed was remarkable, and he literally had members of the audience begging for him to give it a rest in order that they could compose themselves. He had begun his career at the old Nottingham Empire in 1954, and was always good value for money. The length of his shows is legendary. On this occasion the management, being wary of him running past public transport time, had begun the show at 7pm, but it was still after midnight when he eventually let us go. The packed house had been warned when he came back onstage for the second half at 9.30 pm with a flask of coffee and sandwiches, saying to a stout lady on the front row: "Haven't you brought yours then? You're going to be sorry about midnight." A regular part of his routine came at about 11 pm when he looked into the wings and said: "What do you mean come off? These people have paid good money to see me, just leave the keys and I'll lock up." The Stage Manager then threw a bunch of keys onstage, and it always got a round. It has always surprised me that he is only ranked at number thirty-six in the 'Comedian's Comedian' top fifty, as I would have expected him to have been in the top five.

The Christmas meeting for ABTT Members was held in their West End offices on 19th December. As the organiser I had asked the last two working Property Masters in the West End to come along and talk about their respective careers in an informal atmosphere with a carton or two of wine, and some bread and cheese. During the last ten years, I had worked with both Ronnie Harris on *The King & I* at The Palladium, and Jimmy Hinchliffe on *Seven Brides* at The Prince of Wales. I knew them quite well, and respected what they had achieved over the years. I knew that they could both talk the hind legs off a donkey, so it was arranged with Ken Smalley of the ABTT that the whole session would be recorded, edited and published in the first newsletter of 1990. I was delighted to see some old friendly faces there as well to support the two speakers, including Bill Platt and Linford Hudson, both from The Palladium.

I introduced them to the few members in attendance that didn't know them, and we started off by talking about their early days at venues like The Finsbury Park Empire and the Get Outs in those days. This led onto the art of 'pageing the tabs' (the practice where the centre overlap in a set of House Curtains is held back to give a clean, unobstructed entrance for a star to take their solo call or receive flowers from a flunkey) before moving on to talk about Follow Spot Operators, and inevitably Linford of course. It was agreed by all there that Follow Spot Operators were born not made and Mr. Hudson was the best example of that, which was why he was in such demand by TV companies recording live shows.

We then somehow, as you do, got on to talking about administration in the theatre and Ronnie began by saying: "I am going to say something truthful here, that might embarrass him, and I have got seven people here who will bear me out." He continued to say that: "The best Production Manager I have ever worked with is a guy called John Toogood." He went on to say: "We had a very difficult star in Yul Brynner and a very fussy Producer, but all the staff knew exactly what they were doing, as a result of one of the best schedules I have ever come across." He concluded: "This is the art of theatre. The man comes in, knows what he is telling you, organises you, sits down and discusses things with you, then comes back to say that is what we will do. That is exactly what happened on *The King and I*". To hear this from Ronnie was a true compliment indeed, and I thanked him before moving on to chat about other topics such as a member of staff at The POW who was 'the number one wood turner for British Rail' and would make the most fantastic props for Jimmy. We touched on the problems that the Palladium staff had overcome in presenting *Singing In The Rain* recently with its 38ft x 16ft rain street floor that had to be suspended upstage by the back wall. All those that attended agreed that this had been one of the best members meetings for some time, and I felt ten feet tall as I left having received such comments from my peers.

The following day was the traditional Christmas lunch day at The Coach with The Rudest Landlord in London, Norman as mine host. I worked on Saturday 23rd. Monday was Christmas day, so it was all hands on deck on Boxing Day, as we were a day late with the Contra Account. I took a long weekend off over the New Year, and with my batteries re-charged returned to work in Tuesday 2nd January 1990.

Act 6 Scene 4
THE RUN OF ANYTHING GOES
(1990)

I picked up 1990 with the same routine I had left in 1989, with a regular Emergency Training Drill each week on a rolling cycle of four weeks, to familiarise staff with the numerous hazards that could present themselves when we were open to the public, and at our most vulnerable. On week one, I would hold an Evacuation Drill, with a scenario of why we had to evacuate. This could be because of an imagined Fire incident in a public or private area, or a staged Bomb alert either in the building or outside that affected the safety of patrons or staff. I would make a prepared announcement which could be varied according to circumstances: "Ladies & Gentlemen, owing to circumstances beyond our control, I must ask you to vacate the building, for your own safety, using all available exits, as indicated by the staff. Please do not collect items from the cloakroom, or return to the building until you are told that the building is safe. Carry on Please."

"Carry on Please" was the signal for the staff who were at their pre-determined doors to say "This way out please" if their exit route was a safe one, or "That way out please" (with an arm indication) if it was not a safe route. This could be because their exit route discharged patrons into an area where the imagined explosive device was reported for example. When the auditorium was clear, staff then had designated areas to check, like the public toilets and bars, should the evacuation need to happen during the interval or the incoming. When these areas were given the All Clear staff would go to their designated Assembly Point for a Roll Call by the HOD, who knew who was on duty that performance. The HOD would then in turn report back to me, as the Incident Officer in the Foyer (if a safe area), any members of staff who had not been accounted for, and I would then report 'Persons Reported Missing' to the LFB Station Officer in Charge.

The second week was training in 'Searching for Explosive Devices' within the building, and each member of the FOH Staff had a certain block of seats in the Stalls, Dress or Upper Circle to individually check, and public areas such as the toilets. All the cistern lids had been sealed, and a broken seal would indicate that the top had been lifted, as it was not unknown for a device to be hidden there. To make it realistic, I used to sometimes plant a device down the side of a seat to be found during the seat check. If it were found, it would be reported to me as 'Suspect Package Stalls seat H 12' and checked out by The Duty Fireman using the Explosive Smell Indicator Device that the Management had invested in. Should the plant not be found, and the 'Auditorium Clear' signal indicated, I would ask "Who checked Stalls Seat H 12 this evening?" and ask the person who identified themselves to re-check it with the Fireman. I have to say on most occasions, however devious I thought that I was, the plant was usually found and reported in the correct manner.

The Training Session on the third Thursday between shows was on the use of the Fire Extinguishers, Hose Reels, their uses and locations. To try and keep it simple, but still provide the required cover, we limited extinguishers in the Public Areas to four main types. These were the basic Water Extinguisher, the AFFF General purpose, the CO_2 Carbon Dioxide Gas Cylinder for Electrical Risks, and Fire Blankets to smoother a person whose clothes were alight or deprive something of air, to extinguish it.

A hundred foot hose reel was situated on each of the three auditorium levels; the Stalls and Upper Circle ones on the Auditorium right hand side, with the Dress Circle one on the Auditorium left hand side. To permit these to be raised or lowered to another level, I provided a hauling line by the on/off valve that could be used for this purpose, and the staff practised the art of raising and lowering this vital piece of equipment and shouting "Water On" when they were ready for the valve to be opened. In this way, should it ever be necessary, we could bring three hoses into action to contain an incident prior to the arrival of the Fire Brigade. Additional special extinguishers such as Foam and Dry Powder were provided where cover for this type of risk was required, but only known to those who had received specialist training.

I organised a quiz on the last session of the month to combine all the elements that had been taught previously, and divided the staff into four teams: Stalls, Dress, Upper, and Bars to give it a bit of rivalry for a small trophy that was awarded to the winning team for the month. Typical questions were "In the Upper Circle where would you find the AFFF Extinguisher situated?" or "Which Stalls Exits would you indicate to use, if 'Mr. Jet' was in the Foyer Box Office?" which made them all think about a potential situation.

In addition the Visiting Company Manager Peter Roper was asked for his co-operation, and every six months the cast and Backstage Crew were given their own Drill and Evacuation with their two Assembly Points made clear to them. In the event of it being a Fire Incident assembly was outside the Stage Door by The Arts Theatre Club, where they could shelter if the weather was inclement, for the roll call. If it were a Bomb Incident Mike Churchill and I had come to an agreement that we could use the POW Stalls Bar, and he could use the PET Stalls Bar for the respective roll calls and a place of safety until the all clear was given, which could take several hours.

All my staff had been advised to have their house keys with them, along with sufficient funds to get home, when on duty and in uniform and not to leave these basics in a locker, where they could not access them. Annually I organised a Full Evacuation involving both FOH and Backstage, to ensure that everyone was familiar with what to do and where to go for roll calls. At the conclusion of each session, staff were required to sign a form to say that they had received training on such a date, and had understood it, which was then stored in the Emergency Training File and kept in the office for inspection by visiting LFB Officers, during their regular visits.

Most of the visiting LFB Officers were very impressed with the detailed planning and monthly training cycle I had implemented, so much so that on one occasion Station Officer Coward brought along a group of visitors from abroad to the theatre to attend a Training Session one Thursday, to show them how we do it in London. The staff were applauded for their competence in dealing with the imaginary incident that I had set for that session. I am pleased to report that during my stewardship, no major incident occurred, but the basic training the staff had received was put the test when the Admiral Duncan pub was bombed, which affected the whole of Old Compton Street, ten minutes before the house was due to open in April 1999, but by then I was working at The Old Vic Theatre.

The show was still doing good business, and we had some cast changes, which had not affected the Box Office. Most notable amongst these was our American friend Howard McGillin who left the show after three months and was replaced by a young man who was taking a short break from his studies in the States to study Shakespeare over here, and had seen the show with his parents. He auditioned and was offered the part of Billy Crocker within forty-eight hours. John Barrowman had been discovered, took over on 3rd October 1989, and was to stay with the show for six months.

Two of the most difficult jobs to find reliable staff to fill were that of Cellarman and Fireman. Both were vital roles for the smooth running of the building. Westminster City Council, as the licensing organisation, required a Fireman to be on duty whenever the theatre was open to the public for a performance. Fire in theatres is an old enemy that goes back to the days of lighting by candles, with the TRDL having been a victim three times since 1613, and both the Theatre Royal in Exeter and the Exeter Theatre in New York both burning down on the same day, 5th September 1887, with great loss of life.

As a result it is not uncommon for The Duty Fireman to stay overnight until relieved by the Stage Doorkeeper at 7am. At The PET his duties commenced with unchaining all the exit panic bolts at least an hour before we opened to the public, and locking them onto a numbered 'chains board' to ensure that they were not mischievously replaced before the public had left the building. Once he had chained all the Fire Exits, apart from the Stage Door, which was the final point of exit, and completed his daily log, his duties were over.

During my time I employed retired members of the Brigade, men who had served on the River Fireboat 'Massey Shaw' (which had been one of the little ships during the Dunkirk evacuation of 1940) and men who had been retired early as a result of an injury sustained whilst on active duty. I found them all to be a great bunch of men and admired their bravery, as they were the people who would go into a burning building, when everyone else is coming out. I got to know from chatting to them where the local stations were situated: A24 Soho, A25 Westminster, A23 Euston and A21 in Paddington, and which appliances were usually 'on the run' from them. A21 had earned the nickname 'Hollywood' because whenever there was a film unit attached to the Brigade it was usually allocated to Station A21. I had never forgotten the moving scenes in Shaftsbury Avenue in November 1987 when the cortege of Station Officer Colin Townsley, who had lost his life whilst on duty at The Kings Cross fire disaster, passed silently with his coffin on the turntable ladder from our local station A24 with the floral tribute 'Guv' on the front of the turntable ladder.

You did not need to be brave however to be the Cellarman, just very fit. Applicants were shown round and told what was expected of them, which involved every item of bar stock to be taken as ordered to each of the four bars, the furthest being the Upper Circle bar. There was no lift. They would all say that it would not be a problem for them to carry crates up to that level, but very few stayed for any length of time to justify their claim.

The 1990 FLC Conference was held in Blackpool at the end of January and followed the usual format of speeches, Gala Dinner, presentations, and more speeches. The highlight for many was Richard M. Mills' address and the showing of *There is Nothing Like a Dame* from the film *South Pacific*, which had played at the POW the previous year. I remained a close friend of Carole Collins from *The King & I* days of ten years ago, and she and her husband Bob Deamer invited the family round in early February. Despite the rather chilly day, we had a barbeque.

As an ongoing safety procedure we carried out a smoke test on 8th February to ensure that all the smoke detectors were functioning as they should be, and this successful test was logged in The Fire Manual for inspection.

Three of my old friends came to see the show on the same night in mid March. Des & Hazel Tate from the Round Table Pub happened to be there on the same night as Comedy Star Bob Todd who had been in *Emu*. I entertained them and they all enjoyed the show. I continued to entertain friends who had come to see the show on a regular basis and I enjoyed meeting Anita Harris and her husband again, before going to Gerry's Club with them to listen to Kenny Clayton play some Jazz. My old friend from the Lincoln Rep days, and then the MMA period Euan Felton, came to see the show with his wife Ginny a few days before John Barrowman left on 28th April. Another regular visitor who always came to see the show two or three times a year was Mr. Uttley from Halifax. He used to phone me a couple of days before his next visit to London and tell me that he would be in again on a certain night, and ask whether I would be on duty. If I were, he would bring me 'something from the White Rose County' such as Parkin, Pomfret Cake or a bunch of forced rhubarb from the 'Yorkshire Triangle' near Wakefield. He never expected or received anything in return, and was quite happy just to chat to me about his favourite Theatre, The Leeds Grand, and tell me how my old friend, and fellow General Manager, Warren Smith was getting on.

My Mother's health was not improving, and in June she went into a rest home in Lincoln. As it so happened, Kay Darbyshire (secretary of the Lincoln Theatre Club) had invited me to be their speaker at The Ladies Luncheon Club, which was held occasionaly at The Green Room Club. I thought that this would be a great pick me up for her and she was most proud to hear me talk about my work in the entertainment field. A couple of days later on 29th June Mum and Dad celebrated their Golden Wedding Anniversary and we had a celebration at 44 Steep Hill with all their friends and family.

A new cast for *Anything Goes* began rehearsals during June and their Dress Rehearsal was onstage on Monday 2nd July, before opening that night. The business at the Box Office had peaked however and one felt that it would not be long before the Notice was posted.

Indeed it was not long, as on Saturday evening 11th August Peter Roper posted the Notice giving the traditional two weeks' notice of termination. I posted the one for all PET Performance staff at the same time. There was no pre-planning to undertake for a new show as nothing was booked in for the remainder of 1990. The show closed on Saturday 25th August and it looked like we were in for a quiet few months, but who could tell?

Act 6 Scene 5
SIX SHOWS
(1991)

Following the closure of *Anything Goes*, which I had enjoyed being part of for 476 performances, it was time to reflect and enjoy evenings off again. Maris had worked another season at The Open Air Theatre during the Summer, and I felt we were slowly drifting apart.

As weekends off were now no longer a problem, I had no hesitation in going to Chetton in Shropshire on Sunday 9th September to watch the second and final leg of the Masters Championships. I stayed over with Susie and the girls in Pershore as it was not far from the venue, where Simon Wigg retained his solo title and Steve Smith won his fifth title in the sidecar class with Keith Wall now as his passenger.

With a blank evening to fill on 25th September, I went to Lewisham Concert Hall to see some Professional Wrestling for the first time in many years. I was inquisitive to see if things had changed much since the days of Dale Martin Presentations' Kent Walton, and the likes of Big Daddy and Giant Haystacks. I was not surprised to see a mature lady lashing out at the wrestlers as they made their way into the ring, or see her shouting from ringside at the referee that 'So & So' was cheating, which was just as it had been when I last saw wrestling. What happened next however was not expected, and happened during a four-man tag-team contest. After about a quarter of an hour of the two falls, two submissions or a knock out contest, one of the wrestlers went down in a corner after a forearm smash to his face, and looked as if he had been knocked out. His tag partner was shouting at him to get up, but the bulky eighteen-stone man just lay there motionless. I sensed that something was wrong and darted out to alert the Manager, whom I knew, in the Foyer. Wrestling continued in the ring whilst other wrestlers manhandled him to a side corridor where I and another First Aider attempted to administer mouth-to-mouth resuscitation to him as he had stopped breathing. An Ambulance was called, but they also failed to revive him and I read in the local press the following week that he had died following a heart attack when he had collapsed in the ring.

The following day Sergeant John Wall (the liaison officer for Royal Events) had invited me to visit The Black Museum at New Scotland Yard, which you can only visit by invitation from a Police Officer. The Museum is a collection of criminal memorabilia since 1874 and contains some very disturbing and upsetting displays. In it are items relating to the crimes of Ruth Ellis, the last female to be hanged in the UK, serial killer John Christie, The 'Kindly Killer' Dennis Nilsen, who murdered 15 young men, and the overalls worn by PC Keith Blakelock, showing the 40 stab wound entry points, when he was murdered during the Broadwater Farm riots in 1985.

On Saturday 6th October, I was working alone in the office when I received a phone call from Dad to tell me that my dear Mother had died that morning. I quickly informed my immediate superior Peter Roberts, who was at home, and told him the circumstances. He was most sympathetic, and told me to take immediate compassionate leave until after the funeral had taken place. I phoned Peter Russell, who again was at home, thankfully, and asked him to come in and cover for me, which he kindly did. As I had come to work on the bike, I had to travel up to Lincoln on the train and rang home to tell Maris and the children, what had happened and my plans. The journey from Kings Cross to Lincoln Central was the longest of my life, with numerous memories and plans for the funeral.

Overture and Beginners, Please

Sue had driven over from Pershore and we set about informing close relations of our bereavement and contacting a Funeral Director, and the vicar of our family church St. Mary Magdalene in the Bail. The nearest day that could be arranged for the funeral service and burial at Newport Cemetery was Friday 12th October.

We arranged with the Funeral Director that he would precede the hearse, wearing a top hat and carrying a cane, and that it would pause outside number 44 Steep Hill, where she had lived for almost 50 years. Sue and I arranged with the Vicar the hymns and reading we would like, and we requested that as the coffin was carried from the church Peggy Lee would sing *The Folks Who Live On The Hill* which was our family tune and for which we would supply a portable cassette player. This was all agreed and proved to be a tear jerking moment for us all. There were numerous floral tributes at the graveside from her many friends and one very special one that had been sent by Lord Delfont and all the staff at The PET, which I found very moving. We held the wake at The Tower Hotel in Westgate and Julian now aged 14 had travelled up on his own, to pay his last respects, as Maris did not want to attend, which upset me. I made a short speech of thanks and an A to Z list of all the things associated with Mum, which I struggle to deliver, without breaking down. Overall it had all gone smoothly, but it was a sad day for us all.

I reluctantly returned to London and went back to work on the Monday following the funeral, not knowing how Dad would cope on his own, to find that a new show had been announced and would open on 8th January 1991. It was a musical by Steven Schwartz, of *Godspell* fame, and was entitled *Children of Eden*. It was based on the Book of Genesis, and apart from that basic information I knew little more until nearer the time and saw the posters.

The big name at The Lewisham Jazz Festival during October was *The Woody Herman Band*, with guests Alan Randall on vibes and hoofer Will Gaines on the bill as well. A visit on Wednesday 24th October was a must, and turned out to be one of the luckiest days of my life. I was especially looking forward to hearing the band again, as I had done my first Jazz Review ever for this band, when I was still living in Lincoln. The review was entitled 'The Best Herd ever Heard'? In the meantime Woody had died in 1987, and the band leader was now Frank Tiben, who had vowed to keep on playing the music of the two 'herds', as they were known, and which had made this band such a favourite.

The first herd between 1936-46 was also known as 'the band that played the blues' but it was the second herd between 1947-87 that really made its mark. The outstanding composition was the 1947 tune *Four Brothers* which unusually featured three tenors and one baritone sax, with the original four players being Stan Getz, Zoot Simms, Herbie Steward and Serge Chaloff.

Alan Randall was perhaps best known for his George Formby impressions, but was also a brilliant jazz player on the Vibraphone and could play equally well with four hammers as two. Will Gaines was a Jazz Tap Dancer with a reputation only overshadowed by 'The Grandfather' of American Jazz Tap Dance Bill 'Bojangles' Robinson, who had created his own unique sound by using wooded taps on his dance shoes. Will was 50 years younger than the legendary Mr. Bojangles, was born in Baltimore and worked the Cotton Club with the likes of Duke Ellington and Count Basie, but was still capable of mixing it with the best even though he was now 62 years old.

On paper this looked like it would be a fantastic evening of pure Jazz, and it was, but what was not predicted was meeting Darcy Harris. She had gone to the concert with Bill O'Hagan who was a journalist on the Daily Telegraph and usually worked the night shift till 4am on the News Desk. I discovered that he was also a virtuoso in making top quality sausages, which he allegedly made at home in his bath using long lost English country recipes. He was the same age as me, was a larger than life character, who lived for booze and bangers and Darcy was helping Bill promote his sausages. She first caught my eye in the Theatre Bar at the interval, when she sang a song from *The King & I*, *Getting to Know You*, which was a most delightful pick up line. Bill had a most original way of avoiding getting stopped by the Police on the way home from a good night out. He drove his own second hand Black Cab as they are rarely stopped by the Police, and it worked every time. I gave Darcy my business card and she called me the following week to join her at a Bonfire Night party at the Coach and Horses in Greenwich Market, which was her local.

I would often meet up with Darcy & Bill in Gordon's Wine Bar in Villiers Street, near Charing Cross Station, as it was a unique, little known gem of a place, which was steeped in history and joie de vivre having opened as one of London's first wine bars in 1890.

It had been the home of Samuel Pepys in the 1680s and Rudyard Kipling had also made it his abode in the 1890s and the arched cellars had changed very little since. In fact the owner's policy was 'no change' - leave it as the customers love it.

By November the posters for *Children of Eden* (or *Children of Neasden* as it was known by the staff) were up, and it was to be a combined Production by Children of Eden (UK) Ltd. & Atlantic Overtures. The cast was a mixture of a respected top line cast and newcomers, all backed up by an impressive Production Team.

Names in the cast I recognised were Ken Page, Shezwae Powell, Kevin Colson, Ruthie Henshall, Frances Ruffelle, Anna-Jane Casey, Vanessa Leigh-Hicks and Sonia Swaby, a cast in total of around forty people. The Production Team was headed by John Caird (Director), Matthew Bourne (Choreography), John Napier (Designer), David Hersey (Lighting), Andrew Bruce (Sound) and Richard Sharples (Costumes), with Trevor Williamson heading the Stage Management Team of six people. Altogether an impressive list, and things looked good for another long run.

During Rehearsals it was envisaged that several members of the Company, dressed as animals to go into Noah's Ark, would walk along the Dress Circle front rail, which I was not happy about, because of the possibility that someone would fall into the stalls. The Council gave a ruling that if the walk were to happen, each of the artistes would have to wear a safety harness. This was obviously impractical, and the idea was cut,

The Previews for *Children of Eden* began on Wednesday 19th December and continued, with a Christmas break, into the New Year, with opening night on Tuesday 8th January 1991. Several friends, whose opinion I respect, came to see a Preview performance, and were not that enamoured with the piece and the Box Office advance was mediocre. It was announced that there would be a Royal Gala Performance on the 15th January, and that HRH Diana, Princess of Wales would be attending the show. Swiss Chef Anton Mosimann was to prepare the interval refreshments, to be served in the Circle Bar and not the Royal Retiring Room which was quite small. Anton had very high standards having been The Maitre Chef de Cuisine at the Dorchester for 13 years. We had no kitchen within the theatre, and the best we could offer was to build a small screen, which covered half the length of the bar, to create a discrete area for him to work in.

Royal Visits usually went without a hitch, but despite my usual meticulous planning, on this evening it did go horribly wrong. All the usual Police security arrangements were put in hand, and the sniffer dog search was completed to create the usual sterile area in the Dress Circle where HRH was to sit on an aisle seat with her bodyguard behind her. We had received a phone call in the morning asking us to ensure that the theatre was warm, as she would be wearing an elegant outfit. The crowds were out in force, along with the paparazzi, and as the limousine drew to a stop, I stepped forward and greeted her on behalf of the theatre. I was taken aback when she knew my name, saying: "Good evening, Mr. Toogood" and I then handed her over for the VIP line up and handshakes, before taking her up the stairs to her seat which we had marked with an antimacassar to identify it for her.

I then got the news that I did not want to hear that night: "John the heating has broken down and we can't fix it." There was nothing I could do, and just hoped that the heat given off by the stage lighting and body heat would be sufficient to keep the chill air off the patrons, especially our Royal

Guest. At the interval I went to collect The Princess from her seat and show her to the Dress Circle bar where Mr. Mosimann was waiting to entertain her. "I must congratulate you on the efficiency of your air conditioning Mr. Toogood" she said as we climbed the stairs, and all I could do was apologise profusely.

At the end of the interval when all the other patrons had taken their seats, I escorted Her Royal Highness back to her seat where a lady in waiting was holding a rug for her, which she had obtained from the Royal Car during the interval. The Royal rug had been enough to keep her warm, I presume, as there was no further remark made as I showed her out of the theatre, and back to her car. A night to forget I think.

By now I was seeing a Divorce Solicitor, Colin Marsh, as things at home were difficult, and he was giving me good advice, albeit at a price. Following the disaster of the last Royal visit, when the heating went AWOL, although all other arrangements had gone according to plan, Chief Inspector of Operations Maria Wallis invited me to join her for lunch at New Scotland Yard on 19th March. This was most enjoyable, as she had been very complimentary about the organisation that had gone into the visit of HM Queen Elizabeth The Queen Mother in August 1989.

Two days later Operation Desert Storm began and the writing was on the wall for the show as people, especially from the United States, cancelled their visits to Europe and London. The Desert Storm offensive lasted for six weeks until 28th February, but the show carried on with at times quite dismal audiences. I was reminded of what one of the First Night Critics had said in his review: "Where is the nearest Exodus?"

It was no surprise to most of us therefore that the Notice went up four days later with the last performance on Saturday 6th April after just twelve weeks and a hundred and one performances. It had not been the run that was expected, and the general consensus of opinion was that it would have run for longer were it not for the Gulf War. I am not sure that it was everyone's cup of tea, but we will never know. It had been a nice Company to work with, and I am sure that the two production companies took a big loss, but that's showbiz - some you win, some you lose.

We were dark for just five weeks before Sarah Brightman came into the theatre with her compilation show *The Music of Andrew Lloyd-Webber* on 13th May. Although Sarah and Andrew had divorced in January the previous year, she sang songs from all of his hit shows, including *Evita, Phantom, Cats, JC Superstar*, and *Aspects of Love*. As it was a one person show, she performed only six shows a week. The show had lavish costumes and a huge orchestra to back her and looked and sounded tremendous for the twelve performances that she played, closing on 25th May. During the two week run I had the pleasure of entertaining Impresario Robert Nesbit and his wife, Jazz legend Stan Tracey, old friend actor Victor Spinetti, and a charming lady, Deborah Davis from The South African Gold Coin Exchange, who was visiting London on her own. We chatted in the bar about the show and the theatre. She said she was on her own and asked if I would like to have dinner with her after the show, which of course I did, and had a most pleasant evening with her.

The next booking in 1991 was The Cole Porter Centenary Gala evening on Sunday 16th June. This was another compilation show featuring many of the great songs composed by 'Coley' during his troubled lifetime. The show was devised and produced by Barry Mishon with staging and direction by Peter Walker. The cast was international with many stars flying in from the States to pay homage to the great man, one hundred years after he had been born in India on 9th June 1891.

There were three Musical Directors, amongst them the flamboyant Jae Alexander, who would be back at the PET later in the year on another show. In addition to the American stars, the Brits gave a good account of themselves in what was to be a real Gala evening. Lorna Dallas performed *After You, Who?* whilst John Barrowman gave us *I Happen to Like New York* as his contribution. That great star Margaret Whiting performed *I Get a Kick Out of You* with the one and only Adelaide Hall singing a wonderful version of *What is This Thing Called Love* to critical acclaim. It just went on and on, getting better and better, with Alice Faye & Van Johnson giving us a memorable *You're the Top* (and they were), along with Lorna Luff who sang another *Anything Goes* song *Blow Gabriel Blow*.

The highlight for many of us present was to hear the new lyrics to *You're the Top* changed to *He's The Top* by Sammy Cahn, sung by him and Michael Feinstein which was just such a fitting tribute from one of the world's greatest lyricists to another. Other notable highlights in the show came from Elisabeth Welch (*Love for Sale*) Elaine Delmar (*Ev'ry Time we say Goodbye*) Dave Willet & Claire More (*All Through the Night*) Dolores Gray (*It's All Right With Me*) and Sian Phillips spoken version of *Just One of Those Things*.

I have a personal highlight however as at one point during the day I had the opportunity to chat to one of my great idols, Sammy Cahn. I asked him which of the many songs for which he had written the lyrics he was most proud of. Without hesitation he replied *Call Me Irresponsible*, so I asked him why. "Because John, I amazed myself at just how many five-syllable words I could find to rhyme with Irresponsible" and went on "Unreliable, undependable, unpredictable, irresponsibly, undeniably… I got all of them in it." Since then I have always been reminded of this conversation with the great man whenever I heard the song. This one night Gala Concert was one of the highlights of my career, working with so many great stars.

On 20th June I had an appointment to keep at Bromley County Court where Maris and I divorced after almost eighteen years of marriage. There had been some fun times, but there had been some troubled times of late. The most rewarding outcome was the three fantastic children, Julian, Rachel and Rebecca, who we brought into this world, all of whom have shown great love and loyalty to me throughout the years.

Just a week later yet another big star from the States came to the theatre to record a live concert, 'the singers singer Tony Bennett. His schedule involved him arriving in a limousine at the main entrance, already dressed in his immaculate dinner suit, where I would greet him, then take him to the stage where the Ralph Sharon Trio were waiting for him. Then the concert proper would begin. The ex-Brit Mr. Sharon, who had played in the great Ted Heath Band in 1946 before moving to the States in 1953, had been the Musical Director for Tony since 1958. The concert featured many of the songs that he had made his own over the years. These included *S'wonderful*, *Just in Time*, *When Joanna Loved Me*, *Sunny Side of the Street*, *Fly me to the Moon* and of course *I left my Heart in San Francisco*, which had been a chart hit for him in 1962. What a great occasion and such a thrill for me to be part of this concert, recorded live, featuring two of the greats of the Jazz World.

By coincidence I went to another concert at The Barbican to hear the *Ted Heath Band* that Ralph Sharon had played in forty-five years earlier, and one of his fellow band members from those days was playing in the band still. On reeds that night and still playing as well as ever was Tommy Whittle, who along with Jack Parnell (who occasionally still played in the band) had been one of the founding members of what many consider to be Britain's most dynamic post-war Big Swing Band.

One of my regular late night clubs, which I now attended on a more regular basis as I was officially divorced and single again, was the Limelight Club on the corner of Shaftsbury Avenue and Cambridge Circus. The club used to attract a good cross section of the in crowd, all dressed in their designer gear, along with a few others, many of whom had a reputation for one thing or another. On one occasion I was introduced to Lenny McLean (aka The Gov'nor) who was well known as an East End bare-knuckle fighter, bouncer, criminal, bodyguard, enforcer, weightlifter, TV Presenter, author and actor. He thrived on his reputation as 'the hardest man in Britain' and was a well-known associate of many of the country's most notorious criminals. He was charming to me and after we had chatted, and he knew my line of business, asked if I needed any good doormen for the PET. I explained I was quite happy with the set up I had in place, and we parted with him saying "If you ever need anything sorting out John, just get in touch" ringing in my ears. A couple of years later when I went to the 'Old Talk of the Town' London Hippodrome for a night out, which was now owned and run by Peter Stringfellow, Lenny was the head doorman, and he had the cheek to search the documents case that I had with me, but I did not argue!

Our next one-nighter was the up and coming American Jazz Singer Dianne Reeves in concert on Friday 19th July. It got off to a bad start when her support act, Cleveland Watkiss, was not ready to start at the advertised time of 7.30 and refused to go on. He was known as a rock, jazz, nu-jazz, funk, soul, and reggae singer and composer, and I suspected he was more used to the relaxed environment of a jazz venue, where people drift in and out with a bottle of beer, than the disciplined environment of a West End Theatre. I kept my superior Peter Roberts informed, as he quite rightly wanted an assurance that it had been Mr. Watkiss who had refused to appear and not a theatre decision, which I was able to give him. I duly made an announcement that unfortunately Mr. Watkiss would not be appearing, but the bars were open.

Dianne was an American Jazz singer from Detroit and had come to fame as a singer in the 1980s as a superior interpreter of lyrics and a skilful scat singer. Her mother was a Jazz Trumpeter and Dianne's big influence had been the velvet voiced Sarah Vaughan. Between 1983-86 she had been the lead singer touring with Harry Bellafonte. She presented a classic performance to end our short season of concerts.

During the previous year Lord Delfont had approached Cameron Mackintosh about joining him in running both The PET and POW theatres as a Delfont-Mackintosh venture. Cameron agreed provided there was a commitment to a major renovation and refurbishment to both venues, which was agreed. Therefore we knew we would be closing for a considerable length of time for this to happen, but not before *The Hunting Of The Snark* opened on 24th October.

The show was the idea of Mike Batt, perhaps best known for his Wimbledon Wombles, and was based on Lewis Carroll's mysterious, fantasy, nonsense poem. It tells the tale of seven characters in search of The Snark, which is something different to each of them. The first Snark album had been recorded in 1984 and featured Art Garfunkel, Cliff Richard, Deneice Williams, Captain Sensible, John Hurt, Sir John Gielgud, Roger Daltrey, Julian Lennon, Stéphane Grappelli and George Harrison. This was the first step towards a full dramatic treatment of the concept.

A try-out concert had been presented on April Fool's Day in 1987 at The Royal Albert Hall, with comedian Billy Connolly as The Bellman, and had been repeated three years later in Australia, this time with Singer Philip Quast as The Bellman.

The logistics of the show were unprecedented. A huge bridge was lowered from out of sight with many of the cast on it, and a fifty-piece orchestra was onstage. The design of the show was created by 1,200 slides projected from 152 high-resolution projectors, housed in a purpose built projection booth at the rear of the Dress Circle. Chris Slingsby was AV Supervisor from Imagination Ltd., who were the Production Consultants, and the back up team of fellow technicians was outstanding.

David McCallum and Kenny Everett headed the cast with Philip Quast and Mark McCann, David Firth, Veronica Hart, Allan Love and John Partridge in supporting roles. Mike himself wrote the Book, the music and the lyrics. He also directed and designed the whole show, with lighting from Andrew Bridge, Choreography by Jo-Anne Robinson, and Sound by John Del Nero. In addition Mike conducted many of the shows but was more than ably covered by the enthusiastic and exuberant Jae Alexander in his absence.

It was hoped that by having the much loved, outrageous Maurice Cole (aka Kenny Everett) in the cast as The Billiard Marker, and making his West End Stage debut, the Producers had hit upon the gem to capture the fickle West End Audiences, and lots of pre-publicity was aimed in this direction. Incidentally I found out he was eight days my junior having been born on Christmas Day.

Much work was done during September in removing the rear centre block of seats in the Dress Circle, and subsequently reducing the theatre's seating capacity, to provide the space for the

Projection booth. This had to meet the stringent Westminster City Council's regulations and was regularly inspected by them and the LFB to ensure that everything was built in accordance with the approved plans.

It was planned to have two weeks of Preview Performances prior to the opening night on Friday 24th October, to iron out all the many technical challenges. Lining up 152 projectors with the correct sized lenses onto the same area, as several overlapped each other, was very time consuming and required much detailed scheduling from the General & Production Company M.H.A.

The sound from the huge orchestra onstage was fantastic with several memorable tunes in the well-composed catchy score. The one that everyone came out singing was The Snooker Song *Snookering To-night*, which was later used as the theme tune for TV's *Big Break* shows featuring John Virgo and Jim Davidson.

The first night went well and Mike and his delightful wife Julianne presented everyone with a *Hunting Of The Snark* wristwatch in a case, before a lavish party at Imagination's plush Head Office. I had invited Darcy to attend as my guest, but somehow we got separated from each other during the evening.

The show received critical acclaim from the press for Mike's visual concept and Quast's performance as The Bellman, but the writing was soon on the wall for a short run. Several of the contractors had not been paid for their work on the show, which was estimated to have cost £2 million. Heated meetings were held between contractors and The Producers, before the Notice, not unexpectedly, went up on Saturday 30th November.

The last performance two weeks later on 14th December was sensational, and the only Full House of the run, as those who loved the show came to pay their last respects. The show had been a Marmite show - you either loved it or hated it. I was in the former camp and was sorry to see it close before Christmas, as it could have been a big Christmas show, but we will never know now will we?

Act 6 Scene 6
SOME LIKE IT HOT
(1992)

Following the closure of *Snark* it was time to take stock both at the PET and in my domestic life. A major refurbishment was still planned, which we expected would be after the run of the next show and sometime in 1992. Although I was still living at Arran Road, the current family home, I was talking to my solicitor Colin Marsh about selling it to raise funds for Maris and the children to move into a smaller property. I started looking for a flat so I could move into my own place. This of course was all time consuming and costing money. It looked like things would not be sorted until late in 1992, so there was a great deal to think about over Christmas that year.

The PET Christmas lunch still took place on December 19th at Normans as usual, despite the fact we had no show running, so it was basically an in-house event that year. I was seeing more of Darcy and she held a party on Boxing Day. She was the complete opposite of me, being disorganised, unpunctual, zany, and acted on impulse. Maybe it was this that attracted me, but most of all she and her friends were great company and we always had a laugh and a great time.

With no show schedule to worry about I went to Lincoln for New Year, as it was Dad's 78th birthday on New Year's Eve. I spent time with the Pantomime Company *Goldilocks and the Three Bears* at The Theatre Royal, meeting old friends like Art Walker and Chris Olney. Back in London in the New Year of 1992, I continued to socialize and often listened to the *Crissy Lee All Female Big Band* at The Woodman Pub in Blackfen, as it was close to Darcy's house. One night, when I was out clubbing, I met Elaine Hill who lived just off the South Circular, and got on well with her as we had a lot in common, and I used to pop round to her place whenever I could. Unfortunately I began to realise that I needed a stiff drink or two to give me the confidence to meet all these new people, and this worried me.

In January the new show was announced as being *Some Like It Hot* starring Tommy Steele with previews from 2nd March. The show was being premiered first at The Churchill Theatre in Bromley and as I knew many of the staff there, I was invited to an onstage technical rehearsal before the opening night to see what it was like.

The Producer was Mark Furness, and the Musical was based on the show *Sugar*, but it had been decided to revert back to the Billy Wilder Film title of *Some Like It Hot*, and of course retain that most famous of last lines "well nobody's perfect" as Jerry revels to *Osgood Bickertalk III*, that he is a man in drag. The pedigree of the piece was so strong that the American Film Academy named it as The Greatest Comedy Film in 2000.

The cast was outstanding with Billy Boyle (Jerry), Royce Mills (Osgood), Mandy Perryment (daughter of our Relief Manager) playing Sugar, immortalised by Marilyn Monroe in the film, along with a Company of forty dancers and singers. Musical Staging & Choreography were in the very capable hands of Norman Maen, whilst an old friend Terry Parsons looked after the complex Settings and designed the Costumes. Mr. Steele directed himself and the whole show.

Following the run at Bromley the show went on the road to play The Theatre Royal in Plymouth, prior to commencing the West End Get In and Fit Up on 24th February. In the meantime, with no show to worry about in the evenings, I and the office staff of Maureen, Carolyn and Rupert, just worked the day shift 10am – 6pm and enjoyed our evenings off.

During this quiet period I went to the opening night of *'Allo 'Allo* at The Dominion Theatre, as this was another production in the Mark Furness portfolio and I knew some of the cast. This was another Marmite show but as it was now playing in its third London venue, having previously had successful runs at The POW and London Palladium, as well as a tour to New Zealand and a Summer Season in Blackpool, most people were in the love it camp.

I also went to see a Big Band Concert featuring one of England's least known but most respected drummers, Lloyd Ryan. If you did not know about Lloyd as a drummer you might have recognised him from *World Of Sport* on a Saturday afternoon, as he was the Manager and spokesman for the masked wrestler Kendo Nagasaki (Peter Thornley).

Prior to the Get In I had arranged with our cleaning contractor Eric Young to do a builder's clean of the Auditorium especially in the area where the projection booth for *Snark* had been built, now removed. The full complement of seating had been reinstated, making it the sixth largest capacity for Musicals in the West End after the Palladium, TRDL, Apollo Victoria, Dominion and Lyceum.

I was now a regular at the weekly Jazz Evenings held at The Bob Hope Theatre in Eltham, and soon made friends with the bandleader and pianist Paul Davis, and his charming wife Jaquie Toye. She was a well-known West End leading lady, who had played Velma Kelly in the first ever production of *Chicago* at The Cambridge Theatre in 1979. The music was good, the atmosphere was congenial, and it was handy being close to home.

There was a week's Fit Up and rehearsal in the theatre. One afternoon Maureen and I were asked to go and see Mr. Steele in his Dressing Room, which we both thought was most unusual. We duly arrived and after a brief 'Hello' he told us that someone had to be in The Royal Box for every performance. I tried to explain that it was not the most popular of seats as the sightlines were bad from there and it was more of a box to be seen in than to see from, but he insisted. At the opening night we found out why the box had to have people in it. Part of his well-rehearsed solo call routine involved his turning to the Royal Box, as if a member of the Royal Family were there, to make a bow. Box Office Manager Neil Franklin confirmed that the four seats in the Royal Box were only booked occasionally, so we decided that on the day we would invite people to move to The Royal Box as a treat, but if they did not accept the offer there was little we could do, apart from sit there ourselves to comply with his wishes.

The first of the Preview Performances went smoothly, as you would expect from a show that had been on the road previously. The show is about Joe & Jerry, who have witnessed the St. Valentine's Day Massacre, then dress as girls and join an all female band to escape the Mob hunting them. I therefore suggested to Mark Furness that an all girl band would be ideal for the first night party, and spoke to Crissy Lee. She was most keen to be involved and her fee was not excessive, but Mark was not interested and booked a trio.

Mr. Mills entertained his VIP Guests in the stalls Private Room on the Opening Night (Thursday 19th March) and I made sure there were enough Brochures and Programmes available on arrival. A full bar was prepared by Catering Manager Rupert Bielby, with Champagne on ice, and known favourite brands of spirits set out.

Rachel celebrated her 14th Birthday on 29th March. She was enjoying her time at Prendergast School in Rushey Green and her Saturday morning Ballet Lessons in Blackheath. She had no idea what she wanted to do after finishing school, unlike me.

The good Box Office business was not affected unduly by the result of the General Election on 9th April, when the Conservative Party won for a fourth consecutive term of office. It was now led by Prime Minister John Major, who had succeeded Margaret Thatcher, following her resignation in

1990. On my nights off, or on a Sunday, if I was not doing anything with Julian, now 16, Rachel 14 and Becky who was now almost 10, I would go and see as many shows, concerts and motor cycle meetings as I could. I was thoroughly enjoying life and was meeting lots of new friends through Darcy, as she was into jazz, entertainment, and having a good time. We would often go and hear Glen Tilbrooke of Squeeze sing, or Jules Holland play piano as they were both friends of hers.

Most evenings in Greenwich would invariably finish at the Up the Creek Comedy Club, hosted by the quite unique Malcolm Hardee. If you were lucky, you might see him perform as *The Greatest Show on Legs*, where he would dance naked, using an inflated balloon to protect his modesty, which never stayed in place till the end of the act. The Club was renowned for the quality of the hecklers who attended regularly. I recall one evening when a comic came on and said: "Good Evening, I'm a schizophrenic" and as quick as a flash received the reply from the audience: "Well you can BOTH sod off then!"

In addition to being a well-respected Stand Up Comic (I never saw him without a cigarette in his mouth) he was a great talent spotter, compère and above all a character without equal. At the 1987 Greenwich by-election he stood on The Rainbow Dream Ticket as the 'Beer, Fags and Skittles Party' and got 174 votes. The people he first gave a break to and nurtured reads like a Who's Who of Stand Up comedy talent and includes, Alan Davis, Harry Enfield, Harry Hill, Paul Merton, Vic Reeves, Frank Skinner, Jo Brand, Jim Tavare and Jenny Eclair. I was lucky enough to see them all perform there before they became the household names they now are. On one occasion Malcolm was giving an 'Open Mic' spot to an act he had discovered at the Edinburgh Festival that year. The act was very visual and at one point a paving slab was put onto the naked torso of the act and smashed with blows from a sledge hammer, He came up to me as the act was preparing for the big moment, and said: "Don't heckle him, 'cos if he gets it wrong we've got a corpse on our hands, John" so I kept quiet.

At other London venues I also saw Norman Wisdom, Ken Dodd and Freddie Starr perform; went to the '100 Club' in Oxford Street for their Jazz Nights, went to see Lloyd Ryan again, a much underrated jazz drummer, and was a regular at the weekly Jazz Sessions at The Tigers Head in Lee Green.

Back in Lincoln my Father was not coping very well on his own and Sue spent many hours searching out a suitable Care Home for him in the City. We eventually chose Hartsholme House in the south of the City, where my Mother had been for a time, so we knew the staff, and he began his residency there on 22nd April. With Raymond George now in a Care Home, I decided to make regular trips up to Lincoln to see him, and deal with any problems at the now vacant Steep Hill house and shop, on my long weekends off work, roughly every three weeks. Sue and I both felt that the property was very vulnerable, being in such a well-used area (which did not have CCTV then) and she would also visit as often as she could. As a precaution we had all the ground floor windows covered in black painted block board and I put a grill over the shop door, as there was still several thousand pounds worth of family heirlooms and stock inside. I also put additional security grills and locks on the two back-yard doors, as these could be accessed from property on either side.

My routine was usually the same on each visit. I would drive up from work on the Friday evening, meet up with friends in a local bar, and stay at Steep Hill. On the Saturday I would visit Dad and take him out for the day, usually visiting a hostelry that he used to frequent when in his prime, before cooking myself a meal and going out, usually to The Theatre Royal where Manager Mary Bull, whom I had known for years, would always find me a seat somewhere. Lincoln nightlife finished at closing time unless you went to one of the two late-night clubs in the City. As it was just at the back of the Theatre, The City Club was my first choice, as I usually knew someone to chat to, whilst we ate the compulsory food that had to be served as a condition of the licence, usually pie and mushy peas. I was still fit enough to jump over the handrails as I made my way home up Steep Hill.

Sunday was a different car trip for Dad and then a visit to The William the Fourth Pub on the Brayford, where there was a band playing, before a night out at The International Club. This was a Singles Club and I had to produce my divorce papers to the organisers, Brenda and Tony, to get in. It was generally known as 'grab a granny' night by the Yellowbellies that came from all over the county looking for love and was usually packed. Being Lincoln however, the City Fathers had made it a condition of the Sunday Licence, that although The Club stayed open until midnight, drinks could not be served after 1030pm. The solution that I and others found was to buy four pints of whatever at 1030, and then hide them around the club behind curtains or sofas.

I was at The International Club on Sunday 17th May, when I saw a tall, elegant girl dancing and we looked at each other in that special way that is usually a good sign. I bought her and her friend a drink and introduced myself, giving her my business card. She looked at it and said: "Oh no, not another theatrical" so I asked her what she meant. It turned out that she had recently divorced from a singer, had a young family, lived in East Retford and was called Louise Brackenbury. She was going back to Retford after the Club, but she gave me her number, and we agreed to stay in touch and meet up again when I was next up from London. I am pleased to say that we did as she was such a nice girl and good company.

I would take Dad out again on the Monday afternoon, before going up the Bail to join my cousin Steve Toogood and his mates at the Quiz Night at the Duke William Pub. This was a general knowledge quiz and Steve was red hot on music as he restored juke boxes. Each week there was a roll over Jackpot, which currently stood at £700. When the Jackpot question: "Who was the first English Actor to be knighted?" was asked, I said quietly to Steve: "I know this." "What's the answer?" he asked. "Sir Henry Irving" I said. "Great, let's go for it." We did, but what I did not know was that you also had to have your correct answer paper drawn out from the hat, where it was mixed up with all the other answers, right or wrong. My paper was not drawn, so we didn't win. What a disappointment. The journey back the following day for the show that night, was a long one as a result of what could have been a nice treat for me, but at least I had met Louise.

Back in London, Relief Manager Fred Perryment organised a birthday celebration at The Savoy for daughter Mandy, and I was delighted to be invited. I went with one of the dancers from the Company, but little did I know at the time that Susan Freebury was at the same party, whom I would meet again in Lincoln some twenty years later when we were both on the same Shape Up & Slim Course, and she would be the singer with The Monsonaires Big Band.

I was back in Lincoln at the end of the month and went over to see Louise in Retford, and met her two girls, Alice and Bertie, who were both delightful. We had a take away and got to know each other better as we shared the bottle of wine that I had taken over with me. What I especially liked about Louise was her openness and lack of inhibition. She was a great giggler and loved them to death, telling me that she would kill anyone who harmed them. I could have quite easily spent the whole of the weekend with Louise, as we were getting on so well, but tore myself away to see Dad and take him out as this was the main point of my visit.

The show was not doing the business that was expected. Many people put it down to the fact that they expected to hear songs from the Billy Wilder Film and not ones from *Sugar*. It was of little surprise then that the Notice was posted on Saturday 6th June. There was a party the following Saturday night, and the show closed after just 108 performances on 20th June, and one hoped that this was the end of our run of bad luck, and short runs at the theatre.

Act 6 Scene 7
REFURBISHMENT
(1992-93)

With the closing of *Some Like it Hot* plans could swing into place for the major refurbishments that had been talked about for some time and would take, it was estimated, six months to complete. The plan was to refurbish the entire FOH of the Theatre and take it back to the art deco style of how it looked when opened on 3rd April 1930. Over the years several not so elegant features had been added, to what at the opening was described by The Times as a 'pretty theatre' decorated in broken fuchsia and gold. The Loges at Dress Circle front were to be added, and the seating in the Upper Circle was redesigned to prevent the domino effect whenever anyone leant forward. Access to this Circle was to be improved via a side entrance off the Foyer, with new entrance doors to Old Compton Street. All the bars would be upgraded and a new VIP Room created at Stalls level. The toilet capacity was increased, especially for the females, in an attempt to reduce queuing at the interval.

The architects chosen to oversee this enormous task were Renton Howard Wood Levine who were vastly experienced in this type of work, having been involved with projects at The Crucible Theatre in Sheffield, The Nottingham Concert Hall, The Derngate in Northampton and the Old Vic in London.

I had a meeting with the Directors to discuss redundancies as obviously we would not require the full complement of staff during the period we were to be closed. it was most distressing to have to make most of the loyal staff redundant, as only a basic team of HODs would be retained. I was asked to act as Project Manager and look after the daily needs of the theatre. I had undertaken a similar role at The Liverpool Playhouse in 1968 and again at The Windmill in 1974, but nothing on this scale, and I was looking forward to the challenge.

Work was scheduled to commence on 7th September with the contractors being a firm of quality shop fitters, who were used to working to tight schedules. We therefore had ten weeks to prepare for this and with evenings off, I was determined to make the most of it at all costs as I expected lead up time would be very hectic.

I first met Diana Davies having dinner one night on a riverboat on The Thames with friends. I began to meet her on a regular basis that summer as she was good fun to be with and liked to come to West End Shows and concerts with me. We went to the opening night of *Grand Hotel* at The Dominion on 9th July, as I was looking forward to seeing Tommy Tune's award winning Choreography for the show, which sadly only ran for four months.

The following week we went to The Royal Festival Hall to hear the legend B.B. King at one of his fantastic live concerts to a Full House. What this sixty-seven year old could do with a guitar was unbelievable, and he had us all spellbound for the whole of the two-hour set, just him, a chair and Lucille. Although he borrows from Blind Lemon Jefferson and T-Bone Walker, his own sound is uniquely identifiable. His guitar Lucille always has a seat to herself on any plane journey that BB makes, and the story of how she got her name is worth recalling. In 1949 on a cold Winter's night, BB was playing in a draughty wooden shack in Twist, Arkansas, and to help keep the building warm, a metal barrel was half filled with kerosene and lit. During the course of the evening a fight broke out and the barrel was knocked over causing a river of fire. Everyone ran for the door, including

BB, but once outside, he remembered that his guitar was still inside, and foolishly went back to get it. Two people died in the fire that night and the following morning BB asked what had caused the fight. "That fight was all about Lucille" he was told by one of the men involved. As a reminder to himself, never to fight over a woman, or re-enter a burning building, every guitar he has owned since then has been called Lucille.

Now I had Saturdays free, I made a long weekend of it in Dorset for the first leg of the Grass Track Masters Championships on 19th July. I slept at the track at Uddens in Dad's old Maxi that I was now using, as the seats folded down flat to make a bed. I had a day in Weymouth on the Saturday and met a friend in the trackside beer tent that night where there was a live band. After years in London I loved Dorset, as it is so rural, but I can never decide whether I prefer it to north Suffolk. In the finals on the Sunday, Steve Schofield won, beating newcomer Joe Screen in the solos, whilst Russell Ing & Paul Urycz held off Ken Lane & Mark Edwards in the sidecars.

All bar stock at the theatre was passed over to the POW, whilst all the seats were removed to be reupholstered off site, and to make way for the scaffolding in the Auditorium. An unusual discovery was made when a large mirror was taken down in the Foyer. It had not been touched for fifty years, and I spotted something fall to the ground from behind it. It was a membership card for The Queensbury's All Services Club, which is what the PET had been used for during the war years. The name and rank of the owner was still legible on the card, and as a TV Crew was following the refurbishment, an appeal was made for Private So & So to make contact with me to reclaim it. I was intrigued to know how it had come to be where it was and why, but that still remains a mystery, as he never came forward. The card is now on display in the refurbished building.

The documentary was being hosted by an old ASM of mine, Fern Britton, who had worked with me on *The Unvarnished Truth* in 1978. The idea was that once the building work started a camera would roll at normal speed to capture what was happening, and then be replayed at speed in a weekly update on her regular show. She would interview me in the office regarding progress, and used to refer to me as 'Mr. One-Take Toogood' as I could usually be relied upon to get it right first time.

During the Summer months there was an open-air concert every Sunday night at The Crystal Palace Bowl. A whole gang of us used to meet up there and have a picnic, listen to the music and share a bottle of wine or two. One of the regulars was Annette Sharville whom I had first met when she ran the wardrobe stores for Tom Arnold. She had been my Wardrobe Mistress on several other shows and was now Head of Wardrobe at The Churchill Theatre. Annette would pull all the stops out with a huge feast from her hamper, set up a table, light the chandelier, open the wine and be the perfect hostess. The music was, more often than not, a popular classical piece, film score, or songs from the shows, which we all joined in with.

I continued to see Colin Marsh about selling the family home and moving to a flat of my own, and with more free time on my hands, I began the search in earnest. I saw some terrible places that were available, but this sale and move had to coincide with Maris finding a property near to the schools that would be suitable for the children's needs as well. It all had to dovetail in together.

My regular visits to Lincoln to see Dad and Louise were beginning to become a nice break from London, and on the last weekend of August Cousin Steve held a fancy dress birthday party in The Assembly Rooms for 120 people to celebrate his fortieth birthday.

The theatre was handed over to the contactors on Monday 7th September and soon looked like a building site. Scaffolding was going up, carpenters were running around and there were electricians in every nook and cranny. Temporary lighting was from low voltage working lights on yellow stands placed at strategic intervals throughout the FOH area, as backstage was to remain as it was.

The second leg of the Masters was organised by the North Berks Club at their Eaton venue on Sunday 20th September and resulted in a Solo win for Joe Screen, whilst Ken Lane & Mark Edwards won their first and only Masters Sidecar title.

I had been a big fan of *The Four Tops* ever since I first heard *Don't Walk Away Renée* blasting out from a cellar club in Liverpool back in the '60s. When I got the opportunity to hear them play live, I jumped at it. Deborah, who I was seeing quite a bit of now, and I went to The Hammersmith Odeon Theatre on 21st September to hear this legendary group perform live. They sang all their big Holand-Dozier-Holand hits, and included *I'll Be There, I Can't Help Myself, Baby I Need Your Loving*, and *It's The Same Old Song* to critical acclaim, with us all singing and swinging along: a real night out to remember.

I attended the regular Wednesday morning site meeting, which monitored the progress of what had happened and what was the next stage. A project of this magnitude, estimated to cost £3 million, was far bigger than any previous theatre refurbishment programme I had been involved with, and I was most anxious to get it right.

During my next visit to Lincoln, Louise and I went to spend the night with some friends of hers in Harrogate, which sounded fun, as it was a town that I had not visited before. We began the evening in some of the more lively pubs, before we all went off to the local nightclub, where we stayed till the early hours.

24th October was a memorable day, as not only was it the second anniversary of my meeting Darcy at The Lewisham Jazz Festival, but The Crissy Lee Band, for whom I did everything I could to support, had a gig at the world famous 100 Club.

This was a big break for the band as the inconspicuous doorway on Oxford Street had seen the likes of Glenn Miller, Benny Goodman, Louis Armstrong, Ronnie Scott and Johnny Dankworth pass through, since it had opened as The Feldman Swing Club back in 1942. Crissy and her band did themselves proud, and I think were the first all female band to play the venue since The Ivy Benson Band, in which Crissy had been the drummer.

With my free evenings, I was fortunate enough to go to The Royal Festival Hall again to see and listen to another visiting Jazz Legend, little realising that a few years later I would work there. On 3rd November the *Lionel Hampton Band* was top of the bill, and rightly so, as over the years this American Jazz Vibraphonist, Pianist, Percussionist, Bandleader and Actor, had worked with some of the all time greats. As I listened to him weave his magic on the vibes I wondered how much the likes of Benny Goodman, Buddy Rich, Charlie Parker, Quincy Jones and Teddy Wilson had influenced him as he was a real virtuoso, and gave us fans a wonderful evening of Jazz at its best.

Work on the theatre refurbishment was progressing on schedule, and we were especially pleased with the re-rake in the Upper Circle and the construction of the Loges at Dress Circle level. On a personal note, one of the saddest days of my life happened on 25th November, when I packed my bags and moved out of the family home that I loved, to a small one-bed roomed flat in Abingdon Close, just off the Old Kent Road. This was part of a new complex of variously sized accommodation that had been built on the site of the former British Railways Bricklayers Arms Marshalling Yard. It suited my needs, and I made room under the stairs to store my cycle, as this was still my main means of transport around the congested West End. The semi furnished flat at ground level consisted of a large lounge, with open plan kitchen attached, bathroom & toilet, and a bedroom that I had some trouble getting a double bed into. I made myself known to my neighbours, many of whom were single or divorced like me.

As the Pantomime Season approached I paid my annual visit to The Churchill Theatre Bromley to see their seasonal offering. The previous year I had the pleasure of sitting with Anne Hart (Mrs. Ronnie Corbett) as a member of their family was dancing as part of the Company with Ronnie, and Barry Howard, with whom I had done the Summer Season in Margate in 1973. This year I took Darcy along as my guest. Knowing several of the resident staff, and some of the Pantomime Company, we were invited to the post-show opening night party in the large stalls bar, where a Jazz Trio was playing. As the evening progressed, Darcy who was rather partial to a glass or two of 'Screaming Orgasm' decided that it would be fun to ask the trio if I could sing a number with them. This request was unknown to me until the pianist asked me over the PA to join them to sing *Route 66*. Despite having some singing training at drama school, I would not call myself a solo singer, and it was the shortest trip along *Route 66 that* has ever been taken.

I went out with Darcy and friends in Greenwich to celebrate my 48th birthday, and we all finished at the *Up The Creek Comedy Club* as usual. Amongst the gang was Sarah Truscott, who was a teacher in the Greenwich area and good fun, so I took her out on a couple of occasions.

For Christmas I took the three children up to Lincoln to stay with Grandpa, as I did not want Dad to spend his first Christmas alone. I took them to see the pantomime at the Theatre Royal, which I reviewed as 'A view from the Gods' for publication in a Theatrical Trade Magazine.

The tempo of work at the theatre in the New Year of 1993 increased apace when I returned to work. The Fit Up for the new show *Crazy For You* was due to commence on 17th January, and there was still lots to do for me and the team.

Paramount on my list was the recruitment of a new team of Management to work with me in the office. I was quite certain I wanted Rupert Bielby as Theatre Manager, but one of the Directors suggested *Tracy Silverwood,* who had been working at the POW. Once this nucleus of people was in place, I could organise interviews for the new FOH Team of Usherettes, Checktakers, Linkman, and Bar Staff, which was a daunting task. It had been decided that everyone, once appointed, would be fitted out with a new stylish uniform that was in keeping with the plush new décor of the theatre, which looked stunning as the scaffolding came down.

Tracy Silverwood, who had been working with Mike Churchill at the POW, was however appointed as The Theatre Manager rather than Rupert. She replaced Maureen Poole who had moved on to a new career in the Prison Service. We decided that she would interview the males, who had replied to the Open Interview advertisement in *The Stage*, whilst I would interview the females. We were looking for people with personalities and commitment who would be prepared to work a minimum of six of the eight shows a week. I realised that many already had day jobs. This condition was intended to ensure consistency of trained staff, who knew the building and, equally important, the show. I did not want people who would just check your ticket, sell you a programme and show you to your seat, but bright theatrical people with whom patrons could converse.

It had also been decided that as the first impression is so important, whether it be at a quality hotel or a West End Theatre, we would dispense with a uniformed Sergeant from The Corps of Commissionaires (Phil Course who had been with me since the beginning) and train someone who looked the part, and was as charming. In John Fitzsimmons we found the perfect person to be the Linkman and a new image was created with him being dressed in an elegant long grey topcoat. He proved his worth, and went on to be The Manager at Her Majesty's Theatre for 18 years. Aida Casel was still to be Head Usherette and Ian Clark was still Chief of Staff with Anthony Lawrence as his Deputy. I knew Anthony's father Peter Lawrence who was attempting to break Yul Brynner's record of 4,625 performances in the same show, by appearing all over the country in *Joseph*.

The final two senior management appointments prior to opening were Ann Wells as Catering Manager to replace Rupert Bielby, and Adele Johnson to replace Carolyn Godfrey.

Adele was a close friend of Tracy Silverwood, the new Theatre Manager. Tracy wanted Adele to be known as The Assistant Theatre Manager, which was not how I saw her role as the office secretary. I was happy for her to be known as The Assistant To The Theatre Manager, but was overruled.

This turned out to be the first of many disagreements I had with Ms. Silverwood. The final piece of the jigsaw was filled by Peter Austin (FOH Duty Performances Manager) as Peter Russell, and dear old Fred Perryment, who had been such loyal servants at the Edward for many, many years, both retired, and I am forever grateful to them for the advice and counsel they afforded to me. The retained HODs were Alan McCall (Master Carpenter), Kevin Burgess (Chief Electrician), and Neil Franklin (Box Office Manager). I was happy with that, as there was consistency at, for example, the Health & Safety Meetings I chaired.

Prior to the first preview on Thursday 18th February, I had a meeting with a member of the Royal Protection Group about a visit by HRH Diana, Princess of Wales who was coming to see the show with the Brazilian Ambassador. This was, if possible, supposed to be a low key private visit, and provisional plans were put in hand.

The new FOH Staff began duties on the Monday prior to the first Preview for Uniform fittings, initiation, and Emergency Procedures, which all went well. We hoped this time that things were looking good for a long and successful run.

Act 6 Scene 8
CRAZY FOR YOU
(1993-96)

With just a few days to go before the grand re-opening, I needed to walk round the theatre and check that all the new direction signs were correct and in a visible position. Most of them were, but it was a good exercise to familiarise myself with the new route to the Upper Circle for example. The theatre looked quite beautiful, the staff looked immaculate and I bought a new dinner suit to mark the occasion.

There had been some discussions about the senior management on duty wearing name tags, which I strongly felt would give this plush new Theatre the 'McDonald's' look. "But how will people know who you are?" I was asked, and the reply was quite simple: "They will know who I am by my very presence in the building. As General Manager I do not require a label to show my authority." This was agreed and never discussed again.

The full house for the first preview on Wednesday 3rd March was most enthusiastic not only about the new look PET but also about *Crazy For You*, which fitted in perfectly. The show penned by George and his brother Ira Gershwin was based on their 1930 Musical *Girl Crazy*, which had helped to make Ethel Merman the star she is. This new concept of the show, with a Book by Ken Ludwig, still contained five of the original numbers, with the other fourteen borrowed from other Gershwin shows.

The London Producer was Michael White in association with Roger Horchow and Elizabeth Williams. Roger and Elizabeth had co-produced the Tony Award Winning show on Broadway in 1992. It starred Ruthie Henshall as Polly Baker (the Ethel Merman role in 1930), and Kirby Ward as Bobby Child. It was directed by Mike Ockrent with Choreography by the little known (in the UK) Susan Stroman.

There was some fine casting in the major supporting roles with Chris Langham as the bearded Hungarian Bela Zangler, Avril Angers (Mother) who was once a Tiller Girl, Don Fellows (Everett Baker) who had married an old friend of mine and my sister's, Miranda Willis, who had been a Pam Devis dancer in Yarmouth and danced with Susan in *Hello Dolly* in Liverpool.

I had heard the twenty seven piece orchestra in rehearsal and they sounded sensational. The orchestrations were by William D. Brohn, with the legendary Paul Gemignani (veteran of over twenty Broadway musicals) as Production Musical Director. The very talented Jae Alexander, who had conducted the fifty piece orchestra and sung the opening number in *Hunting Of The Snark*, returned with his baton to take control of the musicians, but this time in the pit, and not onstage.

Another person making a welcome return to the theatre was Scenic Designer Robin Wagner, who had designed *Chess* some seven years earlier. The Broadway Lighting Designer Paul Gallo came over from the States to repeat his designs for the show.

The main talking points during the interval and after the show from the public were, in addition to the performances of Ruthie and Kirby, the surprise entrance of dancing girl after dancing girl from the Rolls Royce, the tap routine with the 'click click' of the telephone being replicated by the taps on the pink dressed ensemble, and the Catherine wheel fan revolve by the girls with showgirl feather fans. However the main praise was for the finale to Act One, where farming implements are imaginatively used in *I Got Rhythm*, and the girls in 'down lighters' being used as an instrument in *Slap that Bass*. There was also a general consensus of opinion that Jae Alexander was leading the best pit band in the West End, that William D. Brohn's Orchestrations were sublime, and that Susan Stroman's Choreography was the most imaginative and original since Jerome Robbins had burst on the scene with West Side Story in 1958. People were also quick to say what a refreshing change it was to see dancers who were not in the usual mould and I was repeatedly asked: "Who is the more mature dancer with the beard?" "That is David Shelmerdine who has been dancing for years" was my reply.

The Princess of Wales' visit started off well. She was accompanied as expected by the Brazilian Ambassador, as H.R.H. was a close friend of his wife, Lucia Flecha de Lima. When the limousine arrived several photos were taken by the public, but some kind soul must have phoned the Press, as by the end of the interval, after I had finished entertaining them in the VIP Room, the area outside the theatre in Old Compton Street was awash with Paparazzi, several of whom I knew. "Is she in tonight?" was the question they all wanted an answer to, but I remained silent. At the end of the show, I met them at their seats and showed them the quickest way out. The limousine was parked outside ready for a swift getaway and the Ambassador went round to the far side of the car, whilst I went to open the nearside door for Princess Diana. I had just got to the door to open it, when a hot cup of coffee was thrown in my face and naturally I jumped back. That was the moment they had all been waiting for, just that one exclusive photo of Princess Diana out on the town. If published it could earn them thousands of pounds. I was left in a state of shock with a coffee stained dress shirt that was ruined. HRH was to return to see the show again with Lucia, but I was ready for the hot coffee trick that time.

Princess Margaret came to see the show with eight of her friends on Tuesday 9th March. By now the VIP entertaining routine was well rehearsed, and could swing into action at a moment's notice. Other VIPs who came to see what was regarded as the best show in town by many included Shirley Bassey, who would have liked to poach our Linkman John Fitzsimmons to join her staff, until I explained that he was such an asset to us, I could not possibly let him go.

There had been a thank you party for everyone who had worked so tirelessly to meet the deadline for the opening of *Crazy* after the second preview. Tracy and I and all the FOH Staff had received a communal letter of thanks from Directors Leslie Desmond and Peter H. Roberts, which was most gratefully received, as at times it had seemed an impossible task to complete on time.

On one of the last walk round inspections with Cameron Mackintosh, he had looked down at the Continental style seating in the Stalls, whilst inspecting the new seat tiers in the Upper Circle. He noticed there was a centre aisle running for about eight rows in the middle of the stalls. "How many top price seats are we missing there?" was his relevant question. When told he quickly calculated the money that would be lost by having this centre gangway. The seats were reinstated before the opening.

My social life was quite hectic as well as my work schedule. I was still meeting Louise whenever I went to Lincoln for a long weekend to see how Dad was coping, going out with Darcy whenever she was free, and occasionally seeing Diana Davis, whom I had met over dinner on a Thames Riverboat trip. She was my guest when I went to the Olivier Awards at The Dominion.

On 8th April Prime Minister John Major with his wife Norma and two other guests came to see the show. It was my pleasant duty to entertain them. Security and protocol were as tight for them as any member of the Royal Family, and they insisted that I had a glass of Champagne with them as we chatted. High on the list of conversation was his late father the Music Hall Performer & Circus artiste Tom Major-Ball who he thought may have performed at the PET. Unfortunately I had no record of him from the past history of the theatre, despite extensive research which I had undertaken while the theatre was closed. They both told me the theatre now looked most impressive and were astounded at the energy of the Company, especially in the seven minute finale to the First Act, *I Got Rhythm*. A few days later I received a hand written letter from Mrs. Major thanking me for looking after them so well and to expect their daughter Elizabeth to come and see the show, with friends.

In the office we had engaged Stephen King as a payroll clerk as it was envisaged to go all computerised in the general office as soon as possible. I was not keen on the idea as I had never been trained to use a computer, and would lose control of matters, but was assured I would soon get the hang of it as I could already type. Tracy, the new Theatre Manager, was all for it as working on computer was second nature to her, and she could not wait for all the kit to arrive. I was completely out of my depth, and doing the weekly Contra Account became a nightmare for me, as I had not been shown what to press to get this and that, which was very frustrating and I was constantly asking how to do things.

When I had calculated the Contra Account by hand I was able to cross check it and assure myself it was correct before I left on a Saturday Night, but now I found I had to trust the computer to be correct. Often when I did a manual double check it was out by small amounts in several sections, and trying to alter the figures that the machine had calculated was a nightmare, and took hours. The same applied when I received the nightly Box Office Return, which instead of being presented to me as a two page summary, was now twelve pages or more of every transaction to double check for accuracy, which I found was taking up more and more of my time, which could be put to much better use. My conclusion was that instead of being a help to me in running the office efficiently, it was no asset at all, and most difficult for an un-trained novice like me to be expected to use, without any formal coaching.

Tracy on the other hand was completely in her element. A loyal member of staff later warned me that "the knives are out for you John, she's after your job" as they had heard snippets of conversation during the day, when I was not there. This was brought to a head when, after eight years of unblemished service, I was summoned by the Directors to attend a meeting on 7th May to discuss and investigate matters concerning my conduct at The Arts Club on May Day.

I had no idea who had made the alleged complaint, and although my memory was hazy about the evening, I was sure in my own mind that I had not done anything I had not done before, when out clubbin' and could only assume that someone had misinterpreted something that I had said or done, or was it an attempt by those who wanted me out, to discredit me? Following the meeting I was given a formal warning. It became obvious that I had to watch my back from now on, as the knives were out and poised to deliver the fatal blow, to eliminate me to make way for Ms. Silverwood.

Meanwhile life had to go on. One night in May, at The Bob Hope Theatre in Eltham, whilst listening to Jazz played by The Paul Davis Trio, I met Carlene Pence, who lived in the Sidcup area, and worked freelance in wardrobe. We got on, had mutual interests and she was quite happy to take some of my clothes away and alter them for me.

During May I was given notice by my landlady that she wanted the flat in Abingdon Close for her own use, and I began to look again for somewhere in the SE Area, and planned a leaving party with as many friends as could attend.

I was sad to leave the Abingdon Close flat but found a new one on the site of the old Millwall Football Ground, 'The Den', near to Surrey Quays shopping centre. It was a little further out than the previous one, but larger, and I had no trouble getting my king size bed in. Myers Court was again a block of new flats and houses, built on the old Stadium site with plenty of off road parking for my Volvo Estate. I had bought this second hand on a visit to Lincoln. My cousin Steve came on a test run with me, declaring it to be "OK as far as I can tell" as it had recently been re-sprayed and looked clean and tidy for the £1,300 asked.

I had been forced to get a new vehicle as Maris had run the Maxi, which my parents had given me, whilst the oil warning light was on and completely ruined it. Even Roy Wooley, the mechanic who had looked after all my cars since my first Austin A40 back in 1966 and would always fix a problem for me if he could, was beaten.

Although I did not require a car during the week, because I still cycled to and from work covering about 125 miles a week, I had been attracted to the Volvo Estate 240 series as the back seats and tailgate area all folded down to give a clear six feet which was just what I wanted to sleep in as required, or on away trips.

One Saturday night in late May I was a guest of the owners Mick Parker and his charming partner Sandy at their Limelight Club, when in walked the American actor who had been the voice of 'Tweety Pie' in the cartoon films with an elegant, striking blonde on his arm. Heads turned as this 5'6" female walked in with an hourglass figure many girls would die for, in a figure hugging long blue gown and short bolero jacket. She went to the bar with the American who was paying no attention to her at all, so I walked over and introduced myself to her. She told me her name was Pandora, and she was a professional model in California over here on a promotional trip with her manager, who was elsewhere that night. Pandora joined me at my table with her drink and we started chatting about what we both did work wise. She told me she had worked a great deal with Russ Meyers who had learnt his trade as a cameraman during World War Two.

Russ had also worked for Hugh Hefner in the early days of *Playboy*, on which Pandora had worked, she told me. We had been in each other's company for about an hour when she suddenly said out of the blue: "Show me some exciting places in London, I've got the car outside, and you come along as well, as my guest."

I asked what she would like to do: eat, dance, go to a bar or something else? "Somewhere in the West End that's naughty, exciting and different" was her reply. The only places I could think of were run by my old employer Paul Raymond. It was too late to go the The Revuebar but PR had recently opened a new club close by at the corner of Brewer Street and Walker's Court called Madame Jojo's. Pandora's Minders went in to check the place out whilst we sat in the car blocking the road. The boys gave the basement club the OK and I helped Pandora down the stairs as she could hardly move in her long gown.

Once inside the busy club she was immediately impressed with the plush red seating areas, and stylish retro décor. The clientele impressed her as well, with everyone waiting in anticipation of the kitsch cabaret that was about to start. We ordered a bottle of champagne from one of the waitresses and sat down to see the show. I had done a bit of name-dropping on arrival and we were given the best seats in the house.

The star of the Cabaret was Ruby Venezuela, whom I knew from a club in Gerrard Street where I had first seen her with a group of girls after a first night party. They, like Pandora, thought she was the 'grand dame' and was quite outrageous at times. She adored some of the headdresses worn by Ruby, and the costumes had more glitter on them than those sold in any of the big shops on Oxford Street. Once the music began Pandora slipped off her bolero top, and we took to the dance floor till the club closed.

As we left to get the car back to her hotel, she invited me in for a nightcap, so I invited her and her Manager to come and see Crazy the following Monday, which she accepted on condition that they took me out to have dinner at Wheelers Seafood Restaurant, post show. Pandora, and her Manager Roger Schick arrived in good time for the show, which they enjoyed, as we did the dinner of Champagne, Oysters and Lobster. We kept in touch for many years and used to send each other birthday wishes as we had got on famously. Despite her looks, which could be misinterpreted, I found her to be most charming and she knew exactly what she was doing with her life and career. The last I heard of her she had retired from modelling, and was living in France, but what a tonic she had been to end the very turbulent month of May.

The show was doing sensational business, and everyone loved it. Many people complimented me on the efficiency of the staff, and said they were the best FOH Staff they had come across in the West End. I found only one of them to be untrustworthy. A member of staff had tried to ghost a person into the stalls to see the show without a ticket or my authority. The attempt was unsuccessful and he was given a warning that any repetition would be regarded as Gross Misconduct attracting instant dismissal. Word soon got round about this incident, and there wasn't a problem for the rest of the run.

The middle of June was a busy time socially with the birthdays of Carole, my ASM from Margate in 1974, Deborah, from South Africa, whom I had entertained during the Sarah Brightman Show in 1991; Carlene from Sidcup and Crissy all celebrating their birthdays on the same day of 17th June. Crissy's was a big one with a nought at the end, so I decided to go to her party at a restaurant in the Kings Road organised by her partner as a surprise. We would all be waiting in a room out of sight and burst out singing the traditional song. All the girls from the band were there, some with partners, some on their own, and we all had a great time after the meal until the early hours.

My two years of being a single man again was celebrated on the 20th June. Youngest daughter Becky was eleven on the 25th and was to join her sister at Prendergast School in September.

In late July we had a semi-official visit from The Lord Mayor of Melbourne, Desmond M. Clark, and his wife Irene, who invited me to contact them if I ever found myself in their City. Three days later my old boss Paul Raymond came to see the show. In his thank you letter to me the following day he was most complimentary about the new look theatre and the Staff, saying that it must be "One of the, if not the, most beautiful theatres in England" and that the "Whole of the front of house staff were the most polite and efficient in the West End and a great credit to you". He concluded by saying that the show was "absolutely fantastic" and that he could see it playing at the PET for many years to come. This from a man I much respected, who had certainly made his mark on the West End, particularly Soho, where it was common knowledge that he held the freehold for countless buildings of importance.

When I worked for him, he would always ask: "Have all the staff had their hands and fingers checked this evening?" as he was a stickler for cleanliness. PR knew that the hand check used to be carried out by most Theatre Managements in the heyday of Variety, when he was touring with his mind reading act. This was the first time since I had met him twenty years earlier that I had felt on equal terms with him. He asked me to get in touch with him if ever I wanted to leave my current position at the PET. Following this meeting, whenever he was out with Carl Snitcher (his Chief Executive) at Soho House opposite, he would beckon me over to join then, to ask me if I was ready for a move yet.

Wednesday 4th August 1993 was another momentous day in my career as HM Queen Elizabeth The Queen Mother had selected *Crazy for You* as the show she would like to attend on her 93rd birthday. This time she would be accompanied by HM The Queen. As was the custom by now, I had a pre-planning meeting with The Metropolitan Police at both Royal Protection and local level to discuss arrangements. As Her Majesty was now in her 93rd year, she was finding stairs difficult to climb, so it was agreed that the side exit door to the Dress Circle in Greek Street would be used for her arrival and departure. This was given a lick of paint by Kevin Millist and Mike Day from the theatre maintenance department, and a roll of red carpet was run out to the Royal limousine door. The Met Police outriders, guided the Royal Car the 'wrong' way into Greek Street, where I was waiting to greet The Queen Mother and her daughters Her Majesty The Queen, HRH Princess Margaret, and other members of the Royal Party.

JT with HM the Queen and the Queen Mother 4th August 1993

The crowds were out in force again to try and catch a glimpse of the Royals, as it had been announced at the lunchtime Clarence House walkabout with The Queen, Princess Margaret, The Duke of York, Prince Edward and the Princess Royal, that she would be attending the show with some of her family that evening, and they wanted to share her birthday with her.

As the lead limousine pulled up outside the entrance, the crowd bust into *Happy Birthday* and she carefully stepped out wearing a lavender beaded long evening gown, followed by The Queen and Princess Margaret. After the handshakes and my birthday greeting to her from everyone at the theatre, I showed our special guests to their Dress Circle seats. We had removed the usual tip up seats from the largest Loge, and replaced them with four armchairs. As we entered the auditorium, those patrons who could see the Royal Party go to their seats, burst into spontaneous applause, and those in the Stalls and Upper Circle looked round to see what was going on. Once all the Royal Party were standing in the Loge, I gave the nod to Musical Director Jae Alexander to play The National Anthem. The show was faultless and as the curtain calls were being taken Ruthie and Kirby quickly came FOH to be presented. As the Royal Party went to leave the theatre, The Queen accorded precedence to her Mother at the doorway and was overheard to say: "Mummy, shall I get into the car first?" and those of us within earshot formed the 'Mummy shall I get into the car first?' club to remind us of that very special day. As I went down into the vestibule to see the house out, an excited American visitor came up to me and said in a broad Texas drawl: "Every time I come to London, I go to Buckingham Palace and hope to catch sight of one of the Royal Family. God damn it, tonight your Queen Mother was sat just in front of me. It has made my night, son." Another happy customer.

In late August I took a couple of weeks' holiday and spent quite a bit of time in Lincoln with Dad who was now wheelchair bound, and in need of constant attention. As a special treat, I took him to The Lincolnshire Poacher Grass Track Meeting, organised by the Wainfleet Club at Irby-in-the-Marsh. This was a big meeting for Lincolnshire, in its second year, and had attracted a cracking sidecar entry, as the Club Chairman Reg Blackbourn was a driver himself with his son Colin as passenger. We could only stay for part of the meeting however as Dad needed to use a Disabled Toilet and there wasn't one provided. All I could do was complain, and take him to Spilsby where there was a public Disabled Toilet. Thereafter I was pleased to see Disabled Toilet facilities, not just at the Wainfleet Club's meetings, but others as well.

As I had the weekend of 12th September off, I decided to go to Bournemouth and sleep in the back of the Volvo for the first time. I made curtains from old sheets and put a two-inch foam mattress in the back, which fitted perfectly. The initial plan was to spend the Saturday in Bournemouth, take in a show or two, go out clubbin' and then take in the second leg of the Masters Championship on the Sunday at Motcombe. Unfortunately the weather was atrocious, and the meeting was called off, with the Masters Champions being decided on the results from the first leg at Tonbridge in July.

Then Mark Loram had scored a maximum 40 points in the Solo class, and Ivor Mathews & Peter Jones only dropped 2 points to claim their only Masters Sidecar Champion title. It was a long, wet drive home that afternoon and a big disappointment to all involved.

Later in September old friends Alan Curtis, from the Peter Pan Tour in 1973, and John Inman came to see Crazy. John had worked the Summer Season in Margate followed by two happy years at The Windmill on *Let's Get Laid*. Both were very complementary about the theatre and show. Alan said in his thank you letter: "What a great joy it must be to you, to be in charge of one of the top theatres in town" and concluded "They are lucky to have you". As a postscript he said that if I fancied a day at the Cricket Test next Summer, he would fix me some tickets. Unfortunately, because of circumstances, I was unable to accept them myself but arranged for Julian to go in my place.

The FLC Annual get-together Conference, Gala Dinner and Awards Ceremony was again held in Blackpool at the end of the lights and followed pretty much the same pattern as in previous years. Even though I have good communication skills, and can mix with all types of people, from the humble hard working man to Film Stars and members of the Royal Family, I found it hard at times to get on with some of the other Managers there as apart from those that worked in the nightclub division, I found I had little in common with most of them.

As General Manager I was on the call out list with our alarm company, should it be activated when the theatre was unoccupied. The system covered all the most vulnerable areas in the building such as the Box Office and Strong Room, but had a tendency to be activated by the wind or other things. I had instigated a system whereby the safe keys and its long holder were always kept separate for security purposes. Within the alarmed Strong Room was a key safe with all the principal keys numbered, and a list of what number key was for what purpose kept separately, also under lock and key.

I had reasoned that even if an intruder activated the alarm, he would only have a short period to find the safe key holder, which was useless without the nib, as it was never left in the theatre, or to break into the key safe to find over one hundred keys, and not know what Key 79 opened for example, before I and the Police arrived. On a number of occasions I had trouble setting the system as it was very temperamental, and had on occasions slept at the Stage Door to guard the building and await the attendance of the Alarm Engineer to resolve the problem. One night I got an 'Alarm activating in silent mode' call at about 3am and as time was of the essence, drove into Frith Street expecting to find the usual False Alarm I had attended many times in the past eight years. As I walked round to investigate the possible cause, with just a torch for company, I felt very vulnerable. On these visits I never carried the safe nib for fear of an ambush, and then being forced to open the safes and divulge the four digit clock settings. Entering the Stage door, the backstage area looked undisturbed, and the box office was secure, so it could only be the Office Safe and Strong room, I surmised. I always walked up the stairs when attending these incidents, for fear of being stranded in the lift. I found that the door to the strong room had been forced and the door to the key safe levered open. Fearful that the intruder(s) could still be in the building, and waiting to ambush me, I retraced my steps quickly back to the Stage Door, via a different route. Once there with an exit door to use in an emergency, I telephoned 999, and reported a 'Burglary in progress with suspects still on premises' and requested the immediate attendance of a police unit, at the Stage Door Entrance in Frith Street, to conduct a more thorough search, with a Police Dog if possible.

When no one had arrived after ten minutes, I went outside to look for them, and found four burly policemen at the Front Doors in Old Compton Street. They came round to the Stage Door with me and we conducted a more extensive search. I felt far less vulnerable walking round the building that I knew so well, in their company than I had done when on my own.

On another occasion I was away on holiday, and therefore not on call out duty, when someone managed to get on the theatre roof and smashed one of the office windows to gain entry. Not being able to access the strong room, they had forced open the metal cabinet that was on my desk and searched through the contents for anything of value. On my return I noted my Halifax Building Society Book had been stolen and went to see the Manager at the branch. He told me that an attempt to withdraw cash had been made, as the person wanted to purchase an expensive watch. They were suspicious of the attempt from the outset as the signature provided was nothing like mine. This was due to the person claiming that he could not write properly, as he had a broken finger, and no money had been passed over.

I also checked with the Jewellery shop staff who had been equally suspicious of the person. He had enquired about the purchase and asked for the transaction to be made on a street corner in Soho, which they rightly refused to do. I did not recognise anyone on the CCTV footage I was shown and how the person got to be on the roof remains a mystery.

Christmas and New Year came and went without incident, but the following years of 1994-5 would prove to be the most traumatic ones for a long time.

I was now seeing a couple of regular girlfriends, and we always met up and went to a Club which was not frequented by the Mafia members of the staff. I had an arrangement with one of the many Soho Mini Cab Firms, who used to insist on calling me 'Mr. John', who would pick us up and take me home at short notice, without having to wait in line, and be seen together. Anne and Navarah were both good company, fun to be with, up for a laugh, and many happy hours were spent together socialising.

As I was Chairman of the theatre Health & Safety Committee, which was now taking up more of my time, I enrolled on a 'Control Of Substances Hazardous to Health' (COSHH) training course with The Royal National Theatre on 18th January. The Maintenance department used various acids and other noxious substances, for various tasks.

I purchased 'HazChem' warning signs to display where they were kept, as by law the storage and safe use of such chemicals, and the precise details of what treatment to undertake in an emergency, are mandatory. I obtained these details from the manufacturer for every substance, and they were kept in the COSHH file in my office.

The *Crazy For You* Christmas party was held over to the New Year and as usual there was a cabaret performed by the cast and crew. Don Fellows sang *Mr Cellophane* from *Chicago* and a staff member came on in a dress suit and shirt, similar to what I always wore, and sang *Master of the House* from *Les Miserables*, much to my embarrassment.

I had made contact again with Pete Upton from my school days, and he and his wife came to see the show. He remarked: "I see you are still a hands-on sort of person, Tooey" which was my school nickname. During the course of the conversation that night, he told me that his group *The Sultans* were to perform a show at Lincoln School on Saturday 12th March, and would I like to come along? As it had been donkey's years since I had heard the group play, I said: "I'll do more than just come along Pete. I will be your FOH Manager if you like." It was great to hear what was regarded as the BEST group in Lincoln play again, and I met lots of old friends that night.

I was still seeing Diana Davis. She came to see the show when *Tim Flavin*, who had been the Standby for Kirby Ward, took over playing Bobby on 7th March. At the same time Helen Way, who had been playing Patsy for the past year, replaced Ruthie as Polly, and Janet Fowler took over as Patsy. Also in the Company was Peter Bishop whom I had disciplined on *Seven Brides*. Janet Chapman, who had given me my first West End break twenty one years earlier, was now desperately ill in Lewisham Hospital, and passed away on the 2nd May which was a sad loss to Bill, and Jody, her daughter, whom I had known since her birth.

One afternoon in June I was sorting out the display board in the Foyer when I heard a voice at the box office which I recognised. Looking round, I could hear a broad Liverpool accent and see the back of a tall female with blonde hair chatting to the staff. As I suspected the voice belonged to Lily Savage (Paul O'Grady) whom I had seen in a Sunday show at Lewisham on 5th June, and she had been to hairdressers in Soho to get 'the Barnet' fixed. I recalled the hilarious Lili Marlene send up I had seen him do. Whenever she moved downstage, the street light would follow her move for move.

I went to see the musical *The Card* at the Open Air Theatre on opening night, and was warmly greeted by Cameron Mackintosh, who had produced the show in 1973. This revival starred my old friend Peter Duncan, who had been in the *Peter Pan* Company with Lulu at Manchester back in 1972, and was to prove a great triumph for him.

Julian was now 18, and finishing his schooling. He was hoping to go to university in Sheffield, depending on exam results. A huge tragedy for the family happened on 23rd August, when the family home on Steep Hill was burgled and many precious heirlooms were stolen. I wonder if it would have happened if the CCTV system that now covers that narrow part of Steep Hill had been up and running then, and somehow doubt it.

I was invited to taste the first Oysters of the Season on 1st September by my friends over the road at Wheelers Seafood Restaurant, and what a delight it was to sample the new season's catch brought up from Whitstable. I also met Aldo Zilli for the first time as he was interested in promoting his new Soho Restaurant in the Crazy programme, and invited me to join him as his guest at the annual Festival of Soho Food at The Café Royal. There on display were all the delights from the many varied shops and restaurants that abounded in the Soho Village - a gourmet's heaven.

In September I met up with Peter Tate from the Round Table pub to discuss arrangement for my big 'Five-0' birthday at Christmas. As 17th December fell on a Saturday, venues were hard to find. However he came up with a brilliant solution to the problem, by suggesting we book Cauthen's Bar in the City, which was deserted on a Saturday. This we did and he agreed to look after the food side of things for me.

I thought it would be appropriate to invite 50 close friends and family to join me and I met up again with some old girlfriends who I had not seen for over twenty years, but still looked delightful. I wanted it to be casual and wore leather trousers and an open neck shirt. We all drank, ate and danced till the wee small hours, and it was a fine ending to what had been a rather troubled year for me.

If I thought that 1994 had been a bad year then 1995 proved to be even worse with just one or two highlights and one very major decision that would change my life. Briefly, Julian started university in Sheffield, Sue and I decided to convert Steep Hill into a London style sandwich bar, and on 17th June I met a new lady in my life. I was quite serious about Jeanne Maltby, who lived near Lincoln.

Tony, Susan's husband, died on 24th November, and his loss was felt by us all.

As I felt that after ten years loyal service I was now under extreme pressure, and I wanted to spend more time on the Southgate Sandwich Bar Project in Lincoln, I chose to resign on 14th December giving three months' notice, which was accepted. I handed my keys over to Tracy on 17th February 1996, just a week prior to Crazy closing after 840 performances. Tracy Silverwood, with a little help, had got what she had always wanted and was now The General Manager of The PET, a venue that I had put my stamp on, during the past ten years and made one of the best run in The West End.

Act 7 Scene 1
COURIER
(1996-97)

I reflected long and hard on what had gone wrong after ten happy years at the PET. I had risen to all the challenges set me, and learnt a great deal more about the business I loved, and about myself. Did I want to be involved again, after what I had been through in the last year? Of course I did.

With Julian now studying Politics and Economics at Sheffield University, the big Volvo came into its own as a removal van. I would make a weekend of being away to take him or bring him back to London, by stopping the weekend in Lincoln and overseeing our plans to turn number 44 into The South Gate Sandwich Bar. I had envisaged this name, as the property was at the exact point when the Roman South Gate to Lindum Colonia was built around AD 80, and as such attracted a lot of attention. I had engaged a firm of architects to design a re-use of the building and at every stage historians, and the local Council, had to be consulted as the site was of international standing and little was known about the arch. Dad had covered over most of the Roman stonework to hide it in the early 1940s when he converted the property into an antique shop, with living accommodation.

During these weekend visits, to see Dad and check on developments at Steep Hill, I used to meet friends in the new Magna Carta pub in Castle Square, or at The Lawn. The nightly routine was for people to start off a pub-crawl at The Duke William, and call into most of the pubs in Bailgate, prior to walking down Steep Hill to the only nightclub in town, Ritz's in Silver Street. When I was next in Lincoln, I went to a concert with Jeanne Maltby, whom I had met the year before, in Riseholme Park given by *Pete Upton* & *The Sultans*, which was a huge success and showed just how talented my old schoolmate was on the piano and vocals.

I began to put a few feelers out with prospective employers. I met with Roger Neat on 27th February in his office to discuss joining his Production Management Company on either a freelance or permanent basis. I also began to look seriously at other non-theatre work to pay the bills. I had suddenly lost what was by now a comfortable salary, which with the emoluments usually came to around £525 per week, to living off my savings.

I had never signed on with Job Seekers before, apart from the odd week between jobs in 1973, but did not dismiss the possibility, as I had now been contributing funds via my NI & Taxes for thirty-five years.

I had been looking weekly through *The Stage* for anything that caught my eye and contacted Swiftcall Couriers in Rivington Street (near Old Street in the square mile) about some work. I was invited to see Bruce Madge, the Operations Manager at 10am on Monday 18th March for an interview. After a few basic questions, such as what road would I use to take a package to Heathrow Airport for a flight, or where is Mount Pleasant Sorting Office, I was given a Swiftcall name board, a radio and the call sign Alpha 37. I was now a freelance courier, back on Schedule 'D' Tax status, and would be paid by the job whether it was in London or elsewhere.

I was told that the Swiftcall Name Board was intended to indicate that I was a working courier and would give me some immunity from Traffic Wardens. I soon found out this was not the case, and if I got just five minutes to load in a restricted area, I was lucky. The firm specialised in moving documents and files between firms of solicitors and their clients, as well as having the concession for courier delivery at Selfridges. I chose to work the late morning shift from 10am and not finish until given the last job of the day. This very often involved taking a parcel from Selfridges to someone in the suburbs, who had forgotten it, or needed it urgently.

This was before the days of satellite navigation, so once I had been given the last job of the day, the office closed, and I was left to my own devices to find 'Honey Tree Cottage' near Marlow in Buckinghamshire for example. If I had been given a contact number, I would stop at a coin box en route, and ask for directions from say the M40, but if not a visit to the local Police Station was required. I had a good collection of maps and a London A-Z large scale atlas in the Volvo with me, but inevitably I did not have a map of where I had to deliver, which was most time consuming, and all for a fixed price however long it took to find in the dark. I always made sure I had a bagful of coins with me which a working call box would take (if you could find one that had not been vandalised) and two torches with spare batteries as well. One was a head torch similar to those that cave divers use, as it left my hands free to make directional notes, in an unlit coin box in the middle of nowhere. Jeanne would often visit me in London and act as my navigator for the day, which made the job bearable.

It was quite often 10pm before I located many venues to deliver my parcel, or even on occasion just an envelope. I then had to retrace my route and head for home, where a stiff drink was the order of the day with my main meal. If trying to find a location out of London at night was not bad enough, then finding somewhere in The City to park within walking distance of the pick up point during the day, was another nightmare, as I had to pay for any parking fines out of the money I made. I naturally had to change the car insurance from leisure use to 'Hire and Reward' which was not cheap. Also the Volvo 240 was not the most economical car in which to plod around the City with the constant stopping and starting at lights and sitting in traffic jams. If one also took into account the constant waiting around for jobs to be allocated to you by the radio controller, who may not have liked you, then this was to become a nightmare job that I hated, with a passion, and wanted out of as soon as possible.

The boredom of grabbing a catnap in the car whilst waiting for the call "Alpha 37 – Job for You at Noon….. pick up at so and so in Grays's Inn Road….deliver to Lincoln Inns Fields, wait and return" soon got very irksome. Very often a motor cycle or push bike courier could have done the job just as well and probably quicker if it was small. I was only paid the same as they were, which with my overheads made the job a complete joke. I would see cycle couriers jumping lights, turning right into no entry streets, and even taking their cycles into the foyers of buildings to save time finding somewhere to lock them to, and thought how lucky they were. The only time they were slightly worse off than me was when it was pouring with rain all day, but as they were also freelance, many did not work in the wet and I would get their job, for what it was worth, after expenses, parking, fines etc. had been deducted.

Weekends were quiet at Swiftcall, and I was usually the only car working. I tried to finish early to catch up with friends and went out to a few pubs and clubs where I knew people, mainly sticking to SE London, but occasionally going Up West for the night. Up the Creek was still a good night out where you could catch some up and coming comedy acts performing. On 23rd March I was lucky enough to catch Jenny Eclair top the bill there, and I thought that this 1989 Time Out Cabaret Award winner's act was very original and told her so afterwards. I went to dinner with my friend Jackie Kennedy on her 37th birthday on the same day, 13th April, as Julian was celebrating his 19th, and first as a student at Sheffield. I had met Jackie at an NCP garage party in the City one weekend when it had been turned into a rave venue for the night, a few years before, and we used to meet up after work as often as we could. At her party she introduced me to Steve & Linda Uzelac who were owners of *Satin & Lace Lingerie* of New York, where Jackie used to get much of her own items from. Steve and Linda had clients in show business, and were keen to open an exclusive boutique in Soho to rival *Agent Provocateur*, who had proved there was a market for luxury lingerie, at a price. I told them I knew Paul Raymond and that if anyone had a shop in his portfolio that was suitable, it was he, and offered to help find them a vacant shop, if I could. In return, I was invited to choose any item that I wanted from their range for any of my girlfriends. They also invited me over to stay with them in Suwanee in Georgia, which was most kind of them. In the end a suitable location for an upmarket lingerie boutique could not be found at a realistic price and the deal fell through, but we remained friends.

One of the (very) few joys about working for Swiftcall, especially on a Saturday, was that I was soon known to the Selfridges security staff who operated the barrier to their loading bay under the huge store, and whilst waiting for my next job I could park there and go around the store. I loved the Food Hall, where I could shop with my eyes, but not with my wallet as on most weeks I was struggling to make the rent money needed for the flat at Harrison's Court. On one occasion I saw the biggest lobster I have ever seen on the fish counter, and asked for it to be weighed. "It's £55, Sir." was the price, which was just *slightly* out of my reach that weekend for dinner for Jeanne and me at home. We found a raw Horseradish root in the fresh vegetable section however, which was a good buy for £2.50 and made many jars of delicious creamy, snowflake sauce that must be served with rare bloody beef in my book. My Grandfather, George Henry Toogood, used to make his own special Horseradish Sauce in the 1950s when I was a child, and to combat the noxious tear making fumes given off when grated, used to wear his old WW2 gas mask. He taught me that the best creamy sauce was made by using a tin of Carnation milk as the mixing agent, and I have always used that since. The sauce can make or break a Roast Beef dinner, or can be used cold in a beef sandwich.

On one occasion I had to take a parcel from Selfridges Gift Department to a Mrs. Gibb in Little Venice, where the Grand Union and Regents Canal meet. The house I was delivering to was well appointed and obviously large, and I had the surprise of my life when Lulu opened the front door and before I could say: "Delivery for Mrs. Gibb" she said: "What are you doing here?" She invited me in and I explained that I had just finished working as GM at the PET and was between jobs. "Well Good Luck and I hope that you find what you deserve." she said as I walked back to the car.

Some of my best paid jobs were the ones I picked up last thing at night, as I was the only vehicle still working. One night I got the radio call: "Alpha 37, do you want a run to the Clifton area in Bristol?"

"Yeah I'll take that one please." I radioed back, as I would have no problem in finding the drop in Clifton as I had lived in Bristol for 3 years between 1963-66, and since those days there was the M4 and M32 to use, so I thought it would be an easy trip, once out of London. If all my work had been long distance like this one, which would earn me over £100, I would have been far happier, but this was a rare opportunity and not to be missed. Once I knew that the delivery address was BBC Bristol in Whiteladies Roan, I knew exactly where to head when I reached Bristol, and had a trouble free and lucrative round trip, getting back home about 2am.

On 10th July 1996, some four months after I had left The PET, their new show *Martin Guerre* opened to brutal reviews and closed on 28th October for major re-writes. The piece had been presented in operatic style by the same creative team that had conceived Les Miserables and Miss Saigon, but failed to match the box office success of its predecessors.

I tried to plan something different to do each weekend with regular girlfriend Jeanne. On 20th July we went to Whitstable on the Kent coast for the night after work. After a picnic, we went out to a pub to meet the locals. The following morning we took a walk along the coast before we went to visit one of my favourite restaurants in the world. Wheelers Oyster Bar on Whitstable High Street of has been serving the finest and freshest seafood in the town since 1856 and is a Gourmet's Delight once you enter the small bar area and perch on one of the high stools. We could not resist ordering half a dozen Native Oysters to consume while the £20 Mixed Seafood Platter was prepared. To our delight when it arrived it contained both white & brown Dressed Crabmeat, King Prawns, Brown

Shrimps, Whelks, Mussels, Winkles, Roll Mops, Anchovies and, as a rare treat, freshly picked salt marsh Samphire Grass. With a nice bottle of Hock, we were in seventh heaven for an hour or so, and wished we could dine like that more often.

Another long trip was called for one Friday evening when I was asked if I wanted an urgent job to take a package from IBM in London and drop off at a works near Liverpool. I quickly calculated that this was a round trip of over 400 miles and asked the controller: "How much?" "Sorry 37, can't tell you that over the air, but worth your while" was the reply. "OK then, I'll take it, please." I collected the package to find that it was a letter that someone had forgotten to post to the ICI Chemical Works at Ellesmere Port on the Wirral.

I filled the Volvo up and expected this to be an 8 hour trip to drive there, find the factory, get a signature for the delivery in the early hours and drive back home. I wasn't far out with my estimate as the ICI Factory was quite well signposted, but finding a way into the secure building at 1am was a nightmare. After driving round the site perimeter fence for half an hour, a security patrol in a Land Rover blocked me in at a gate to find out what I was up to. This was the opportunity that I had wanted and explained that I was a courier up from London with a special delivery that had to be signed for. "We can do that for you, Mate." was their reply, so I handed the envelope over to them and got a signature on my job sheet, with a printed name and works number, should it go missing once I had left.

It was pedal to the metal for the return trip, and I went to bed at 5am only to be woken by the controller five hours later, with the call: "Job for you Alpha 37. Are you ready to receive?" I received £200 for that trip, so what Swiftcall charged IBM to take this one letter up to Ellesmere Port, which someone had forgotten to post, is frightening to contemplate.

I also managed to put the sleeping arrangements in the back of the Volvo to good use when I went to Grass Track meetings. With a barbeque on board and a cool box full of food I could survive quite happily for most weekends in the dry. As the August Bank Holiday weekend would predictably be a quiet one for Swiftcall, I headed north to The Lincolnshire Poacher meeting, which was growing in reputation and stature. The meeting was at Thorpe St. Peter, which was close enough to Skegness to make it a viable and fun weekend. By now I was regarded as a bit of a character and was usually the first up dancing in the beer barn on the Saturday night. The racing was close with Kevin Tatum (son of the legendary 'Spud' Tatum) taking the Solo crown whilst father & son Alan & John Blewitt won in the sidecar class.

I was quite happy in my new flat in Harrison's Court off Myers Lane, but became worried that mail I was expecting, failed to be delivered. I was even more alarmed when I received a phone call from my bank about a loan that I had allegedly requested. I hadn't made such a request but someone had obtained all my banking details and pretended to be me. I knew I had never given such details to anyone, and suspected that my mail had been intercepted. As it was a communal entrance, all the mail was just pushed through the main entrance door letterbox, and left on the stairs for residents to collect.

As my flat was on the ground floor and next to the main entrance, I had a clear view of what was about to happen after the postman had left. A few moments later a young man, who was not a resident, let himself into the block with a key. I watched him riffle through the mail looking for anything of interest, which he then put into the rucksack over his shoulder. Once he had left, I followed him at a discrete distance as he went from block of flats to block of flats doing the same thing, then going into one of the communal bin rooms. Again I waited until he moved on, and then went in to it to find out what he was up to. In one of the almost full bins were opened envelopes he had discarded, with addresses of people at a multitude of different flats.

I came to the conclusion that he was getting peoples banking details by this method and reported what I had seen to the local Police. I was never informed if he had been arrested or charged, but felt that I had done my public duty by acting in this way.

In November I applied for a teaching job at The Guildhall School of Music & Drama, and went for an interview in Silk Street. I felt the interview went well, supported by my experience of part time teaching at RADA in previous years. Before I left I was asked if there was anything else, so I asked if they would like to see my portfolio. "Yes" was the reply and they were most impressed with its contents, but I failed to get the job. Naturally I was disappointed and rang them to find out why I had been unsuccessful to be told: "You are far too experienced for such a position. You should be teaching us."

My plan for Christmas that year was to finish work as early as I could on Christmas Eve and drive up to Pershore to spend Christmas with Sue and the girls, but fate stepped in again. As usual I was the last vehicle working when at about 6pm I got the call for an urgent pick up at Selfridges. It turned out that someone who lived in Southampton had not received a Christmas Gift that had been ordered and it had to be delivered that night. I did not relish a drive down to Southampton and then up to the Cotswolds, but I was the only one working and I had little option but to take it, albeit reluctantly.

Fearful that I could not do the whole trip on one tank of petrol I bought a spare can en route and filled it up. I stopped on the outskirts of Southampton and phoned the person expecting the delivery for directions, which thankfully were not too difficult to follow.

The recipient was most grateful to me for the delivery and wished me a Happy Christmas as I departed for the long drive up to Sue's. On the journey north *Driving Home For Christmas* by Chris Rea was on the radio, and whenever I hear that song I recall that 110 mile journey on a Christmas Day morning. The joys of being a courier.

In February the following year, 1997, I had a falling out with the controller about the number of envelope jobs I was getting and left, with a reference that said that I had "proved to be a very capable and willing driver and my diligence, commitment and overall efforts could not be faulted." This was very nice to hear, but I wanted out, and signing on was more appealing than working as a parcel car driver, thank you.

Act 8 Scene 1
THE GREEN ROOM CABARET
(1997)

When I left Swiftcall as a parcel car courier on 17th February 1997, although I was delighted to have left, my final pay came to only £392.23, which would not last me very long. I got very depressed, which is most unlike me, and began to drink to excess to drown my sorrows, which on reflection years later, was the wrong thing to do, and I regret it now.

As I had been employed on a freelance basis, there was no holiday pay to help see me over, and signing on was not an option as I had left of my own accord. Life was tough, living off my limited savings for a while until I reluctantly went back to being a courier again. I first worked for Herald Couriers, with whom I only stayed a week as the work they put my way was very little, but the expenses were the same as before. I then tried Direct Couriers, but hated this firm even more. Part of the reason was they expected you to be on call and ready to roll at 7am, a time of day that is alien to me. I would have stuck it out longer had there been jobs to do at that hour, but my regular routine was to get up and drive to the local Tesco car park, sleep in the car and await my first job call over the radio, often not until 10am. There was little or no night work with this firm and I moved again over Easter. This time the lucky firm was Mach 1 Couriers and things began to pick up with them for six weeks, until my old mate Jon Swain came to the rescue. Jon had been working for Bill Kenwright for many years either as a touring Company Manager, or in The West End, but was now not too well and knew that I was desperate to get back into showbiz again. Bill's brother Tom Kenwright was now running the Green Room Cabaret Restaurant on the first floor of The Café Royal in Regent Street, and Jon offered to get me an interview with them for The General Manager position.

I met Tom, had a look round, discussed what he was looking for, who was going to be appearing and a deal was done for me to start as soon as possible with a salary of £500 per week, which suited me fine. I finished with Mach 1 on Monday 19th May and started my new job as General Manager the following day.

I could not have wished for a better act to begin with than the fabulous Cleo Lane singing with *The John Dankworth Band,* classic jazz at its very best, and they had two more weeks of their engagement to fulfil. On the kit for the cabaret, was that old friend of John Dankworth's Allan Ganley who was a player I much admired and had enjoyed listening to in the past. Allan was self-taught and, in addition to playing, was a composer and arranger of some note. He had begun his career with Bert Ambrose when he left the RAF, and had teamed up with Dankworth in 1953 before being part of The Tubby Hays Band during the swinging sixties. As the House Drummer at Ronnie Scott's Club in Frith Street, he had worked with all the great American Jazz Musicians during his residency.

Part of the deal with the Artistes was they were entitled to partake of a staff meal in their Dressing Room before the show. On one occasion Allan was not hungry and offered me his meal when I did my nightly check that everything was in order and that they were happy. It was Sirloin Steak and Chips, which was a nice start before the show began. Playing the piano was the very underrated John D. Horler, who had accompanied amongst others Maynard Ferguson, Tommy Whittle, Tony

Coe and Ronnie Ross, and was highly respected by fellow musicians on the British Jazz Scene, but not very well known to the general public, as his playing style was quite calm on the surface but with many surprises underneath.

The whole evening oozed quality and the magnificent venue in Regent Street was perfect for this late night Cabaret show as one dined to culinary delights from the menu of Master Chef Marco Pierre White.

One of my duties was to cross check and tally all the table bills for the night, and keep a running total as each bill was paid, and then brought to me by the Receptionist who was also compère for the evening. To log this accurately I devised a master sheet with payments divided into cash, cheque or the increasingly popular credit card. As the bills were paid, and the master sheet filled up, I was able to add both vertically and horizontally to finish (one hoped) with a gross figure in the bottom right hand corner. If this did not tally it was back to cross checking them all again, to locate the discrepancy. Any mistake was often not found until the final bill was paid at around 2am, and quite often took much cross checking to locate, before I could cycle home.

If Gillian, the compère, was unavailable (she had a very relaxed attitude to being there or going out to dinner somewhere, which the higher management did not object to), I would cover and make the introduction and sign offs / good nights onstage after encouraging an encore. This was part of the job I enjoyed, as was the meeting and greeting on arrival. The bookkeeping was new to me and not what I had been taught or enjoyed doing and would have quite happily delegated it, if I could.

After the incoming and when the show was on, before any of the bills were paid, I was free to explore the labyrinth of rooms that were used for various functions in the building and made a startling discovery one night. Way down in the bowels of the venue I came across a room that was set out and contained various objects that at the time were a complete mystery to me. I had found, quite by accident, as it was not behind any locked or closed doors, a Freemason's Masonic Temple set out with all its ritual paraphernalia. I was on my own and had a similar feeling to that which I had when investigating the burglary at the PET, very vulnerable, and quickly retraced my steps up to the safety of my office in The Green Room.

I asked Cleo and John, along with the other members of the band, to sign a memento flyer on the last night, which I had mounted and they were good enough to write some most kind remarks on it that included: "Thanks for treating us so well." "Thanks for Everything." And from Cleo & John: "Such a pleasure to work with you, here's to the next time."

I felt that I was back and doing something I enjoyed most of the time and looked forward to working with the next Guest Artiste Rita Coolidge, who began her three-week run on 2nd June 1997.

I did not know much about Ms. Coolidge at the time. In my research I found out some interesting facts, which I thought would be useful topics of conversation for when we first met for her rehearsals. I knew she was an American recording artiste / songwriter, in the Country, Jazz, Contemporary fields, and had been married to fellow musician Kris Kristofferson for seven years in the seventies. I did not know though, that she was born in Tennessee with Scottish and Cherokee ancestry, which accounted for her striking good looks and long black hair. She had recorded four consecutive hits in 1977-78 and perhaps her most memorable was *We're All Alone*.

(L-R) JT, Lynn Keller, John Canning and Rita Coolidge 1997

On this occasion she would be leading a trio of highly acclaimed American musicians, one of whom, Lynn Keller, was the bass player. She had played with all the great American stars such as Diana Ross, Dionne Warwick, Donna Summer and Mel Torme. Originally a flute player, she had switched to the electric bass whilst at University in Illinois, and the Gibson EB-3 became her new voice.

As soon as we all met up for the first rehearsal, I got good vibes that this was going to be a happy three weeks, as we all got on so well with each other from the very start. This time the meal provided was arranged differently. Tom was now running a restaurant in Soho which was the designated venue for their pre-show meal, which they were not very happy about. I tried to revert to the previous arrangement, but without success.

The show was slick, well received by all, and Rita was a joy to work with. She was so easy going, but performed nightly to the highest standards, which was all a management could wish for. The final performance came too soon on Saturday 21st June and we toasted the success of the run with a bottle of Champagne. Lynn was booked next to play on The European Tour with Diana Ross, and invited me and a guest along to see the show at Wembley, and meet the Superstar for drinks post show, which I gratefully accepted. I took along Jeanne, who had come to stay with me in London and of whom I was very fond, and we had a memorable night. I still treasure the kind remarks the trio wrote on the mounted flyer I asked them to sign on the last night, which include: "You're a Gem.", "You will be lovingly remembered" and "You are definitely too good - the best."

Gerry Marsden was the next top line act booked in on 7th July. The night before Jeanne and I went to see a group I had been longing to see for ages, *Earth, Wind and Fire*, who were performing at The Royal Albert Hall. On arrival, I asked to see the Duty Manager, introduced myself and asked if there were any House Seats available. "I can do better than that for you, John." he replied and showed us into a Private Box with an unrestricted view of the stage. "Be my guest," he said "Enjoy the show" which we did.

E.W.F. was formed in Chicago in 1969, and effortlessly mix R & B, Soul, Jazz, Pop and Funk music to critical acclaim, which had made them one of the most successful bands of the twentieth century. To hear a band of this quality sing and perform such everlasting classics as *September*, *Fantasy*, and *Boogie Wonderland* live is awesome and they are one of the most exciting bands I have ever seen perform, second only to seeing 'The Godfather of Soul' Mr. James Brown strut his stuff.

I knew a lot about *Gerry and The Pacemakers* from my days working in Liverpool, as Norman Hurst, who I employed to run the Green Room Canteen at the Playhouse, had been one of his roadies in the early days of their career. Susan had also appeared with him in the musical *Pull Both Ends* at The Piccadilly Theatre in July 1972. The show was set in a Christmas Cracker Factory (hence the title of the show) and was really a vehicle for *The Young Generation* dance group to appear live in a musical, not just be seen on Saturday night television. Sadly the show was a box office flop and ran for only 36 performances.

Gerry had previously had more success in musical theatre when he took over the role of Joe Studholme in *Charlie Girl* from Joe Brown at The Adelphi Theatre in 1968. Also in that cast were Anna Neagle, Derek Nimmo and Hy Hazel, and the show was conceived by Ross Taylor, with whom I had worked as Production Manager when he co-produced *The King & I* at The Palladium in 1979. Small world this theatre lark.

Gerry and the Pacemakers were the second group to be signed by Brian Epstein, and their first number one hit was *How Do You Do It* followed in quick succession by *I Like It* and the song that has become forever associated with Liverpool Football Club *You'll Never Walk Alone*. All of the aforementioned songs were included in the show along with other favourites *Don't Let The Sun Catch You Crying* and of course *Ferry Cross The Mersey*.

Gerry was by now rather more rotund than when he first sang the songs back in the sixties, but still had charisma and that boyish charm that had made him such a huge success from the start. I had always wanted to ask him a question, which had troubled me for years. One evening when we were chatting in his Dressing Room I had the opportunity I had been waiting for. "Gerry, what made you choose to sing a song from the 1954 Rogers and Hammerstein musical *Carousel* for your third hit?" I asked. "Well it was like this John" he began."I was walkin' down Lime Street one day when it started to pour down, so I popped into the ABC Cinema to keep dry and Carousel was de film dat was showin' dat afternoon, and when they sung *You'll Never Walk Alone* I thought that would be a good song to sing, and recorded it." "So how did the Liverpool fans adopt it as their anthem?" I asked him. "John, before de kick off all the fans in de Kop used to av a sing along, and once the song was in de charts, they raised their red scarves above their 'eads, and began to sway from side to side in time with the music" Great story and answer.

People did not bring their scarves with them to the show, but every evening when Gerry began singing "When you walk through a storm, hold your head up high and don't be afraid of the dark" people would pick up their table napkins, and perform the time honoured ritual that is now synonymous with the song and Gerry's rendition of it.

Gerry and the band were kind enough again to sign the mounted show flyer for me and make complimentary remarks about the way I had run the show, which I had thoroughly enjoyed working on for three weeks, which had passed without a problem.

The next group booked in to open on 29th July was *10CC* featuring Graham Gouldman and Rick Fenn, best known for *I'm Not In Love*, *The Things We Do For Love*, *Dreadlock Holiday* and *Life is a Minestrone* which they had recorded and made their own. Because of prior commitments, they would only be playing at The Green Room for two weeks and not the usual three, finishing on Saturday 9th August. The group originated from Stockport and had begun working as *10CC* in 1972 with the original line up of Graham Gouldman (Bass & Vocals), Eric Stewart (Guitar & Keyboard), Lol Creme (Guitar & Keyboard), and Kevin Godley on the drums. There were two song-writing teams from within the band, one commercial, the other more artistic. Stewart & Gouldman wrote the pop songs whilst Godley & Crème were more experimental. The band played sublimely for the eleven performances. The play list naturally included all the well-known hits from their heyday in the seventies, which the Green Room diners expected to hear. The band inscribed my now customary mounted flyer, with remarks such as "Five minutes please, Gentlemen."; "Thanks for your kindness and help" and "Absolutely Bang On."

After their show closed, and I had finished doing all my paperwork for the week, I set off to drive to Wainfleet in Lincolnshire for the first Leg of the Grasstrack Masters Championships at Irby-in-the Marsh. The roads were very quiet that Sunday morning and I arrived tired, but in plenty of time for the racing at 1300 hrs. I managed to sleep for a few hours in the back of the Volvo, which was proving invaluable for such occasions, and saw some fast and furious racing. The sidecars were red-hot that day with Gary Jackson & Mick Stace emerging as winners from a hard riding John Halsey & Jason Glenie. The defending solo champion, Kelvin Tatum, rode the meeting without being beaten, but chasing him hard in second place was the up and coming Paul Hurry, who was desperate to clinch his first Masters Title.

British singer, songwriter, musician and entertainer Leo Sayer was the next artiste to be booked in for the now customary three weeks starting on 11th August 1997. Leo had begun his career in 1973 with critical acclaim singing *The Show Must Go On* dressed in a Pierrot style costume and make up, which bemused many. He had two golden years 1975-77 when he had a US number one with *You Make Me Feel Like Dancing* and the stylish romantic *When I Need You* which topped the charts at number one in both countries.

I knew that he was a Formula One fanatic as he was one of the few people to have been given a lifetime pass to F1 by Bernie Ecclestone. When we used to chat quite regularly about the recent races he had attended all over the world, he astounded me with his depth of knowledge about the sport, the people he knew, and it was obvious that he knew his subject. One of his first memories was witnessing Stirling Moss's near fatal crash whilst racing in the Glover Trophy race at Goodwood in 1962 when he was only fourteen years old. To help promote the show it was arranged that the diminutive Leo, who was only five feet four inches tall, would be photographed with a bevy of elegant, stunningly beautiful show girls, all of whom would be over six feet tall. They arrived and looked the part, with Leo's head and face only at boob level with les girls in their high heels, which was the shot that all the photographers present wanted. Leo's remarks at the end of a hugely successful three weeks were: "Thanks for the wonderful, wonderful engagement. It's been a real thrill to work here. Let's do it again."

When Jeanne and I arrived back at the flat in the early hours of Sunday 31st August, I turned the television on as usual to find that normal programmes had been taken off the air and replaced with news flashes and updates from Paris, where a car with Princess Diana and her boyfriend Dodi Fayed had been involved in an accident in an underpass. To our distress the news was not good. Dodi and driver Henri Paul were pronounced dead at the scene while The Princess succumbed to her injuries and was pronounced dead at 0400 hrs in a Paris hospital. Her bodyguard Trevor Rees-Jones was the only survivor of the crash, which had happened when the car in which they were travelling hit the 13th pillar in the Alma Tunnel, allegedly being pursued by members of the Paparazzi. The following day, like so many others, we went to pay our respects at Kensington Palace, where the floral tributes could only be described as a sea of flowers dedicated to The Queen of Hearts.

The mood in the whole country was sombre as the chill autumn evenings began to bite. I tried to look forward to working with one of America's top Motown legends, the great Jimmy Ruffin, who was booked in for three weeks from 2nd September. R & B, Pop and Soul singer Jimmy was five years older than me, and his brother David Ruffin was a member of the hugely successful *Temptations* group, who were part of Berry Gordy's Empire on the Tamia Motown label, based in the then US motor capital Detroit. Jimmy's hits were numerous, but amongst the most outstanding were: *What Becomes of the Broken Hearted, Farewell Is A Lonely Sound, Hold On*, and *This Guy's In Love With You*. In 1980 he decided to concentrate on promoting himself in the UK and moved here. Following David's untimely death in 1991 as a result of a drugs overdose, he had become an active Anti Drugs advocate, and spoke passionately about the subject which was affecting so many people's lives, especially in the music industry.

The National Public (not State) Funeral for Princess Diana was held on Saturday 6th September, and after joining thousands of others lining the funeral route, I watched the most moving service and her final journey to Althorp on television. I thought it was a marvellous idea to ask Elton John to sing *Candle in the Wind* and the eulogy given by her younger brother Earl Spencer touched the hearts of all who heard it. His opening address representing a family in grief, a country in mourning and a world in shock, set the right tone for his most truthful speech. His reference to the fact that having been given the name Diana (The Goddess of Hunting) she herself had become the most hunted person of the modern age, and I knew from my own experiences when entertaining her, that this was true. The listening crowds outside Westminster Abbey agreed and burst into spontaneous applause, as did most of the congregation present.

Naturally business at The Green Room was down as one would expect, but Jimmy being the professional he is still gave a spellbinding show. I was able to invite my friend of many years Darcy to see the show one night.

I had got on very well with Jimmy during his run, and found him to be a gentleman, and he thought the same about me as his last night inscription said: "It has been fun and a pleasure to be here, thanks to your good self, from one gentleman to another gentleman."

It had been the Green Room policy for one night specials to be played on a Monday night when the star artiste did not perform. This was usually Alan Price who was the original keyboard player for The Animals and helped make *House of the Rising Sun* the big hit it had been in 1964. Now, in 1997, he either worked as a solo artiste or with The Alan Price Set, with many of his songs dedicated to County Durham where he was born. Most notable of these was the *Jarrow Song* retelling the 300 mile march by 207 men from the town, to protest over the lack of work during The Great Depression in 1936. Other memorable songs from his repertoire included *Simon Smith And His Amazing Dancing Bear, The House That Jack Built* and *I Put A Spell On You*. I did not see eye to eye with Alan over some professional matters, like starting on time, and the band's habit of drinking alcoholic beverage onstage during the show. I did not have a problem with them drinking to their hearts content before or after the show, either in the Dressing Room or in the local, just when they were onstage with their pints of whatever. It wasn't the image I thought The Green Room at The Café Royal should present to the public, which I believe was reported back to Tom.

The delightful Maggie Moone was the guest artiste on Monday 22nd September, the day before the next big name act was booked in. Maggie was perhaps best remembered for her role in Thames Television's *Name That Tune* compèred by Lionel Blair. She sang *Happy Everything* in A Song for Europe in 1980, hoping to represent the UK in Eurovision, but after a voting fiasco, was runner up. She was still a fine performer, and gave a great show before *The Manfred's* opened for their run.

Formed in 1991, as a reunion band of former members of Manfred Mann, but now without their founder, the line up still consisted of the greats of British R & B music. Included in the lineup were Paul Jones, Mike Hugg, Tom McGuinness, Marcus Cliffe and arguably the best R & B Drummer in the whole country Rob Townsend, who was heavily influenced by Jazz greats Buddy Rich and Gene Krupa. Their play set during the excellent show included many of their well known and loved songs, for example *Just Like a Woman, Semi Detached Suburban Mr Jones, Ha! Ha! Said the Clown* and, of course, *The Mighty Quinn*.

On the Thursday evening of their second week, things came to a sudden head with Tom, and he raised several matters pertaining to my performance, as he saw it. As I was not under formal contract, he relieved me of my duties with immediate effect. I protested and asked for a meeting the following day, when he had calmed down and was more rational, but he would not reverse his decision and after six months of putting my stamp on The Green Room, I found myself out of work again.

This time, as I had been relieved of my duties and not resigned, I was able to sign for Job Seekers Allowance, and thus began eighteen months in the wilderness, when I resorted to the demon drink too much, and found it hard to find work again being in my mid-fifties. Managements did not want to pay for my experience, when someone younger would do the job for less money.

Act 9 Scene 1
THE OLD VIC
(1999)

After my departure from The Green Room at The Café Royal, I wondered if my standards had been too high. I had enjoyed much of the work, with the many International artists who had played the venue, loathed the paperwork, and satisfied my gourmet palate with some outstanding staff meals. On one occasion I had bought a lobster at a Food Fair in Hay's Wharf, and asked the Duty Chef for his special recipe for Lobster Mornay. I was now reduced to buying food at Tesco's in Surrey Quays from the offer shelf.

This I found was not a big problem, as I enjoyed the challenge of making a palatable meal out of different ingredients. I came to the conclusion that had I not gone into showbiz then I would have made a decent chef. The bigger problem was financial, and trying to make ends meet. I found I could just about exist on £50 per week for my basic needs, if I was very careful, but paying the rent of the flat was crippling me. I also still had to pay off my Barclaycard debts, run up on petrol whilst being a courier. In October '97 alone, this came to £272, which had to come out of savings.

A typical day consisted of getting up at lunchtime, unless I had to sign on or meet someone, laze around, contact people for information about possible work, go shopping, buy some cheap cider and a bottle of sherry, settle down about 7pm to watch the usual rubbish on television, until the early hours when I was blotto, and fall asleep. Not a healthy life style at all, but one I fell into with so much time on my hands.

Occasionally I would go out, usually on my trusty cycle, as it was cheap to run, to see shows when I was a guest and did not have to pay for my seat. On 20th November I went to see comedian Lee Hurst perform his Stand Up Comedy Show at Lewisham Town Hall, and thought he was a very funny man, with lots of talent and original patter. I don't recall doing anything special on my birthday and was invited to spend Christmas with Sue and her girls, Joanna and Katy in Pershore. This was most convenient because Dad, who was about to celebrate his 84th birthday, was now wheelchair bound and required full time nursing care. After much searching, Sue had found a Residential Home which was prepared to take him, close to her in Norton, near Worcester. Whenever I could, I stayed with Sue and took Raymond George out for visits to places of local interest. We also always tried to visit him at suppertime to check that he was being well cared for, which for the most part he was. However on one occasion, when we went to visit him the nurse who was supposed to be feeding him was reading a book, and not giving RGT her full attention.

We were also having real problems with the financial arrangement for his care as the Lincolnshire Health Authority were not happy we had moved him from the Lincoln area to Worcestershire. They imposed a legal charge on our family home on Steep Hill, which we had planned to convert into a London Style Sandwich Bar. Under the circumstances we now found ourselves in, we abandoned the plan, having run up a bill of £8,000 with a firm of Architects, and were forced to put the Grade Two Listed property, containing part of the Roman South Gate of Lincoln, on the market for a pittance.

I continued to see as much as I could of Julian, who was now 22 and still at Sheffield University. Rachel, now 20, was studying Spanish at Bristol University, and Becky was almost 16. At weekends when they were all in London, they would come round for supper on a Sunday at the flat, as taking them to a restaurant, which I would have loved to have done, was out of the question. I did provide the services of Dad's Taxi Service to take them to and from University still, and was in dispute with Maris over maintenance which resulted in a few visits to the local Magistrates Court to plead my case.

Friday was signing on day at the Job Seekers office in Greenwich, but they frequently had nothing to offer, and I had to take the initiative to find work. In March my old friend Bill Denis offered me work, which I gladly accepted. He was the Production Manager for a Summer Season of shows at holiday camps in Kessingland, near to Lowestoft in Suffolk, and he wanted a Scenic Carpenter to build the sets on site for him. The deal was that I could stay with him and his new partner (who he had met whilst working at The Open Air Theatre in Regents Park as The F.O.H. Manager, and she was in the Box Office) and her son. They would feed and water me, and Bill would pay my out of pocket expenses to get to Kessingland and back to London.

This would be the first time for over thirty-five years that I had been asked to build scenery, and I looked forward to the challenge as I drove up the A12, with the Volvo Estate packed with my tools, trestles, portable work bench and a hundred and one other items I thought I might need. Not only did I enjoy the work, I found I had lost none of the skills I had learnt during my apprenticeship in Lincoln. I was also able to present a well finished job for the Scenic Artist to paint, complete with chamfered edges and French Braces for ease of setting onstage quickly in a blackout. The highlight of the time I spent there that Spring however, was the evenings I spent chatting to Bill, as he quaffed his Whiskey. I enjoyed a bottle of good red wine, whilst he enthralled me with his tales and anecdotes about touring the old Variety Theatres as one of the *Denis Brothers Dancing Act*. It was fascinating to hear about the customs that were the norm then, and I felt that this was an area of The Business that had sadly passed when I started in the late 1950s, which I would have been happy to work in.

I told him I remembered going over to the old Sheffield Hippodrome in 1963 to remove a four section lighting baton from the building in Cambridge Street before the building was demolished to make way for development of the area and the building of the Grosvenor House Hotel. I remembered it as a huge auditorium with in excess of 2,500 seats, which made it the largest auditorium in Sheffield. It had been built in 1907 as direct opposition to Moss Empires Empire just down the road. In its later years it had been used as a cinema, but those old theatre smells and feel still existed.

I had thoroughly enjoyed my time with Bill in Kessingland, and it was a rather unhappy person who made the return journey to solitude in my humble flat in South East London. I continued to seek work again, either from adverts in *The Stage*, or from the SMA Free List (the organisation of which I had been Chairman between 1984 – 93) which was published to Managements monthly. On 16th April, I went for an interview for the Manager's position at The Richmond Theatre.

Richmond was a hugely successful touring date and an ideal venue for pre West End try-outs. Despite giving a good interview, and them being very impressed with the glowing testimonials in my portfolio, they did not offer me the post because: "I was much too experienced". I seriously considered changing my CV and omitting the more senior positions I had held, but knew that someone, somewhere would know the truth about what I had achieved. I felt I was in a position when people with less experience than me were worried that I would prove to be a threat to them and their position, should they choose to offer me a post, and felt that I was being discriminated against because of my age and vast experience. What could I do, but keep trying? I did make it a policy however to omit my date of birth when asked for it on a pro-forma application sheet, or accidentally put the wrong year in the box.

Despite my reluctance to go computerised I now had time on my hands to be taught how to use a computer properly, and not just play around with it as I had done at the PET five years earlier. It was not something I enjoyed, I must confess, but thought that it was now becoming a necessity to have these basic skills. I was constantly being told not to bang the keys so hard, as previously I had always used a manual typewriter and had broken a hammer key on one occasion (which I was able to mend myself). The problem I found with the new set up was that when it worked, I was able to follow the hand written notes I had made as to what to press for this or that, but when it all went wrong I was at a loss. Being a practical person, and being able to master most jobs, I was at a loss what to do when I got the back off the computer and had a good fiddle around. Someone told me to boot it when it went wrong and would not do what I wanted it to, but after several good kicks, it was sometimes worse. Somehow by August I was sufficiently experienced to be awarded a certificate from the RSA to say that I was now computer literate and able to use word processing facilities to enter and load text, and use a spreadsheet, but never have since then, a bit like being taught Algebra at School.

My fight with Lewisham Council over the amount of money they were paying me came to a head on 19th June when I was granted the right to appeal against their ruling at a meeting of the Housing Benefit Board in the Town Hall. I had sought legal advice from several sympathetic solicitors, who thought that I had a good case provided I presented it properly and had evidence to back my claims. As they all naturally wanted a fee to present my case and do the necessary research, I decided that I had no option but to represent myself, knowing full well that the Council would be legally represented on the day.

Having previously won a Small Claims Court case whilst working at the PET (and being referred to as Rumpole of Old Compton Street) along with the court procedures I had seen in action during my lunch breaks visiting Bow Street Magistrates Court, I felt confident that Rumpole could do it again.

The crux of my case was that the money being paid by the Council was not sufficient to rent a one bed roomed flat in the SE 14 postcode of South East London. With my new computer skills, I drew up a pro-forma letter which I took to all the local Estate Agents for them to simply fill in the current going rate to rent a flat in that postcode and then certify the letter to prove it was not fictitious. I had to use all my charm and guile to convince many of the Agents of what I was doing, but in the end obtained a dozen statements, which all confirmed what I knew was the case, that you could not rent a property for what the Council was offering.

It was a baking hot Summer's day when I turned up at the hearing, dressed to impress and determined not to be put off by the occasion. Like all good lawyers have done over the years, I gave a performance to sell my case to the assembled Board Members. I was cross-examined by the solicitor for the Council, who attempted to discredit me, but after an hour or so the Board retired to consider the case and give a ruling that would not only affect me, but others in a similar position to myself.

My throat was parched when they returned and the Chairman began by congratulating me on the concise way that I had presented my case, and the overwhelming evidence from Estate Agents that I had presented to back up my claim. He continued that no one had ever challenged the Council before, and that from the evidence that they had seen, I was correct. I had set a precedent, and had won the case. I began to think that if I had not gone into showbiz or become a chef, then joining the ranks of George Carmen, who had represented Ken Dodd in his tax evasion case in 1989, would have been another job I would have enjoyed.

One evening when I was having dinner with Darcy at a local restaurant, I was finding it hard to read the smaller print on the menu. "Try these," she said offering me her spectacles. I decided I needed a pair of glasses, and with the expected use of the computer screen on my eyesight, it could not be put off any longer, and I went for an eye test on 5th August. I have used glasses to read and wear when on the computer ever since. I have recently had a successful cataract operation.

My next interview was with The English National Opera Company in mid September, but I went to the interview unsure if I wanted to work in Opera, even if I was offered the job. I wasn't.

In November, between signing on days, I went to Pershore to lay a new tongue and groove floor for my sister, but the unexpected events of bonfire night 1998 meant it never got laid. At 0210 hrs Sue got a phone call from the Residential Home to tell us that Dad had passed away in his sleep and could we attend the Home as soon as possible. Sue picked a red rose from the garden and we set off for the short, sad journey to Norton, where we found the Police waiting for us. They informed us that as it was an unexpected death there would have to be a post mortem. Ray looked at peace as my sister placed the single red rose in his hands. We took away his clothes and personal belongings, and began thinking what to do about the funeral.

It had always been planned that Raymond would be laid to rest with Joan, and space had been allocated in a joint plot in Newport Cemetery in Lincoln, but how were we to get the coffin there? I knew what I wanted to do but was it legal, I asked the Undertakers? My plan was to take Ray on his last journey to Lincoln in the back of the Volvo. I was told if that was what we wanted then they would hand the coffin over to me on Saturday 7th November, with all the necessary paperwork, for the trip back to the City he loved.

We loaded the car with the coffin. We had made arrangements with Undertakers in Portland Street, who had handled Mum's funeral, to receive it that afternoon. My plan was to drive past as many places he had known en route and announce: "Dad we are now passing Arthur and Gertie's house in North Hykeham" or "Just Passing the so and so pub" which I hoped made him happy to be back home in Lincoln. The changeover went according to plan with the Undertakers. We planned a service similar to Mum's at our family Church, St. Mary Magdalene, on the corner of Exchequergate and Bailgate, on the Tuesday following.

Family and a few close friends attended the church service. We again played Peggy Lee's definitive version of Jerome Kern's *The Folks Who Live On The Hill* from the 1937 film *High, Wide and Handsome* (which could have been his epitaph) as the coffin left the church. Ray's final journey was to Newport Cemetery to be laid to rest, as we had planned.

I had to be back in London to sign on again on Friday 13th, and in early December returned to Lincoln to close bank accounts and tie up loose ends, before again spending Christmas with Sue and the girls. New Year's Eve was a sad day as it would have been Raymond's 85th birthday, and I had little to be joyous about, as 1998 had proved to be an Annus Horribilis for me, and I was glad to see the back of it.

The New Year started off in much the same vein as 1998 with me hitting the bottle far too much, generally feeling worthless and thinking I would never get theatre work again. In March I heard that a new Management Company had taken over running FOH at the Old Vic Theatre in Waterloo. I knew little about *The Entertainment Team* but Phil Course, who had been my Corps of Commissionaires doorman at the PET between 1986-93, was now employed there, and had put in a good word for me.

On Thursday 25th March I went for an interview at the theatre, where I met one of the Entertainments Team's Directors. I could not believe how quickly things moved from that moment. I was offered the job of General Manager almost immediately, and they insisted on telling me how lucky they were to have someone with my experience joining them. I began work holding interviews for possible staff on the Saturday morning. The money was what I wanted - £500 per week - and I started officially on Monday 29th March.

No references were taken up, and no contracts were signed, as I was just happy to be in theatre work again. I knew that the famous old theatre, built in 1818, had been saved from being turned into a themed public house, or bingo hall. Sally Greene, now the Chief Executive, had set up The Old Vic Theatre Trust. The previous owner was Ed Mirvish who had out-bid Andrew Lloyd-Webber to buy the building in 1982 before spending £2.5 million on major refurbishments to restore it to its previous elegance.

The current show, which had been playing there since October 1989, was Peter Hall's production of *Amadeus* starring David Suchet, and was doing good business. I was to be working alongside the Entertainment Team's Director, who shadowed me for the first few weeks until I knew the procedures which were in place, and then would be on my own. I inquired about employing an Assistant to cover me on days off, and was told that would be possible if the right person became available.

I was not that happy with some of the procedures, as amongst other things the banking was way behind and the safe was crammed full with money. I asked what the limit for cash held on the premises in the office safe was, and was told what I expected: "I don't know." I asked for it to be found out from the Insurance Company, and then placed a notice on the inside of the safe door indicating the maximum amount covered by them. We were four times over the limit by then, and I began to organise bank runs in a taxi with two people on each run, as I correctly assumed the cash in transit limit for a single person (me!) was not known either.

Other procedures for the issue of stock to the three bars was very lax as was the paperwork for the sale of ice creams, confectionery and programmes. If there were any fiddles going on it would be impossible to find them on the systems I inherited. New ones had to be introduced. It was also not unknown for the Usherettes to run out of change during the incoming, and I began a new system of having two persons per selling station, with one to act as a runner for change, in exchange for a banknote given to me, whilst the other continued to sell. All this took time, and some staff were reluctant to change the old system, and again some feathers were ruffled. It had to be done, so I could account to my superiors what sales and banking were being done.

There was no record kept of when or if any emergency drills had been held, which was required to satisfy the conditions of licence, and I did not dare ask about COSHH. I began to introduce weekly drills for both the FOH Staff and the visiting Company that related to a fire, bomb or general emergency, and established Assembly Points for them to report to. One of these was at The Young Vic Theatre just down The Cut, and a reciprocal arrangement was established should they ever need to vacate their building in an emergency. I introduced a signing in sheet to know who was on duty and at what station, which I changed every week so that staff were sometimes on busy stations and then on a less busy point of sale or bar, for the following week, which they liked.

I had proof that my systems worked because on the evening of 30th April an incident occurred in Soho which had a devastating effect on many people. That evening I was entertaining Jonathon Pryce in the Stalls bar at the Old Vic, south of the river, during the interval. We discovered we had both worked in Liverpool although at different times and at different venues: me at the Playhouse and he at The Everyman. I told him I had rented a bed-sitter in Canning Street, and he said: "So did I, what number?" When I told him, it turned out that we had both rented the same room in the same house, he in 1972 the year after I vacated it. Whilst we were chatting I asked him where he was going for supper after the show, and was told Soho. I advised him not to as Soho was a prohibited area as a result of a bomb being detonated at The Admiral Duncan public house in Old Compton Street, just yards away from the PET. Many of the injured were people who were planning to see the show, and the PET Staff had swung into action to assist the casualties. I made PA announcements during the outgoing that patrons should avoid Soho "because of an incident earlier" and several patrons asked for details, as they had friends in Soho then.

Amadeus ended its run on 5th June, and I then had just two weeks to prepare for a new and exciting show that was to be staged in an unusual manner at the Old Vic. The world renowned Magician Ricky Jay and his 52 Assistants (a pack of playing cards) were booked for a short run of four weeks. As many of his illusions were sleight of hand or Prestidigitation in the business, it was decided that the audience would be onstage with him to create a more intimate atmosphere.

This idea was fine but the logistics were a nightmare. A temporary raked seating block was to be built onstage, with the audience having their backs to the Safety Curtain and facing upstage where Mr. Jay would work. They would enter via the main Foyer entrance, and then be directed through the auditorium and onto the stage, via the Pass Door. Temporary signage needed to be in place, and new emergency exit routes signposted as it is a well-known fact that the majority of people will reverse their entrance route to exit in an emergency. This is fine if that route is the safest one to use, and does not go into an area where, for example, a suspect device may have been found.

Because of the limited number of seats we could safely erect on stage for the show, prices had to be sky high, and at £75 each were the most expensive in London at that time. We also had a problem with where the Usherettes would sit on stage during the performance, as two were required to be on duty. Ricky's efficient Assistant rejected my suggestion for their seating, as they would have been able to see how some of the spectacular illusions were done. The only compromise was to give them both a stool to sit on at either end of the front row, which all parties agreed.

The next unforeseen problem came when the rows of seats were installed and fixed down by the seating contractor. On checking that the numbering was correct as per the Box Office Plan, I discovered to my horror that the seat numbering was all over the place and not consecutive. Furthermore the row letterings from A upwards were not visible as you went up the centre aisle to find your allocated seat. I contacted the Contractor who informed me that the person who booked the seating had not stipulated row lettering or consecutive seat numbering and he had assumed it was unreserved seating. As luck would have it, I had sheets of large Letraset letters in my Emergency Box, which I could use to mark the rows of numbers to indicate the seat in that row, having first removed the wrong seat number. All this was very time consuming, but had to be done, as I did not relish the thought of our patrons fighting over the same £75 seat.

Ricky Jay was a master craftsman and part of the act was to throw one of his 52 assistants into a watermelon. This had somehow been timed and the card was found to be travelling at 90mph on impact. I now realized why he had been reluctant to have the Usherettes seated where I had originally suggested. The show was directed by Pulitzer Prize winning playwright David Mamet and was warmly received at each sell out performance.

I had a very pleasant surprise one evening when I was on stage, and a lady came up to me and asked: "How are you John. It is nice to see you again after 35 years!" I vaguely recognised her face, but could not put a name to it, so had to say that I could not remember her name. It turned out to be Suzanne Billings who had been a scenic designer in Lincoln Rep in 1963. She had spotted my name in the programme and decided to make herself known to me after all these years. Ricky Jay took his 52 Assistants back to the USA after the final show of a most successful run on Saturday 17th July.

The following Tuesday I met an old friend, Production Manager Paddy Wilson. I liked Paddy as he was a bit of a character, many would say like me. We got on well together as we had a similar attitude to work, which was, work is there to provide funds for 'fun' and he, like me, liked having fun.

I knew already that he had secured the rights to present Keith Waterhouse's super play *Jeffrey Barnard is Unwell* and that it was to open at The Old Vic in early August. The great Peter O'Toole was again to play the title role of Jeff. He said he was delighted that I would be looking after the FOH, as General Manager, and told me that the Director was Ned Sherrin (who I already knew from our days working on *Side by Side by Sondheim*) and wanted to sound me out about an idea he had about the sale of drinks during the run. His idea was that as the play was about Jeff being locked in Norman Balon's Soho hostelry The Coach & Horses overnight, that it might be a good idea to sell spirits as doubles only during the run, and what did I think?

I told him that when I was at The PET, the Doubles Bar had been very successful. Also, at The Revuebar Paul Raymond only sold doubles. I said I thought it was entirely appropriate to limit sales to doubles only bearing in mind most people who came to see the show would be drinkers themselves, and the bar sales figures would be fantastic. "Let's go for it" I concluded, so we did just that. During the eight weeks run of *JB is Unwell* I had very few complaints to deal with, and most people were happy.

Expecting full houses for the whole of the run, I increased staff numbers, trained them to be polite and efficient, and am delighted to say that many of the drama students who came to work FOH were very good and in the end were up to the standard that the staff at the PET had been when we opened with *Crazy for You*.

The show was a tour de force for Peter who was ably supported by a cast of four, who played a multitude of roles that were flashbacks of episodes of JB's life in Soho. Most notable of the supporting cast was Royce Mills who managed to capture the real spirit of what went on at The Coach, including events such as the betting on the indoor Cat Racing, when all the National Hunt meetings were abandoned because of the foul weather.

I often used to pop into the Auditorium during the show to see if the egg trick that Peter did nightly worked. We frequently had VIPs in to see the show. One night I met up with Mel Smith and Richard Curtis who had both been involved with The Rowan Atkinson Revue which I had managed for Michael Codron at The Globe in 1981. Elaine Paige who I had worked with at The PET on two of her big shows also came in one night and we had a long chat at the bar. On another occasion Kevin Spacey, who was the new Artistic Director of the Vic, hid his identity and asked to use the pass door to visit Mr. O'Toole. As he was wearing a baseball cap pulled down to hide his face I did not recognise him, and said that I was sorry but he would have to go round to the Stage Door.

During the run of *JB is Unwell*, Norman Balon, The Rudest Landlord in London and proud of it, would hold court in the Foyer of the Vic and tell endless stories about Jeff and his fifty-six years being the landlord of the *Coach and Horses*. The pub had been in the Balon family since 1943, and was the only establishment that I have ever found that opened 365 days a year, without fail. Seventy-two years old Norman always refers to *JB is Unwell* as 'my play' and should you ever have found yourself drinking in The Coach on Christmas Day lunchtime, his Yuletide gift for you was a mug with 'You're Barred' on it, which was a real collector's item.

During the run, which came to an end on 25th September, I had enjoyed going out after the show with friends for dinner at a couple of smashing restaurants in the Waterloo area. I was very fond of Livebait, and had come to an agreement with them that I would recommend it to patrons who sought my advice about a good place to eat after the show and they gave me a number of discount vouchers to hand out.

La Barca in Lower Marsh Street serves the finest Italian food from Tuscany in London. I went there with Jeanne, who by now used to visit me regularly, and Jackie & Peter from Cornwall, whom I had met at my Uncle Bill's 80th birthday in July. They came to see the show, and insisted on taking us out for dinner afterwards as they had enjoyed the show so much. I suggested a few places to them, and their choice was La Barca, because it sounded nice. Jeanne and I ordered modestly, because I knew that it was not the cheapest place in the area, but Jackie went for it big time and ordered Lobster as a starter. We drank a nice bottle of wine with each course and the final bill was close to £200, which Jackie and Peter did not object to as they were on holiday in London. It was a fitting end to a great night out at the theatre.

Following the closure of the hugely successful run of *JB is Unwell* the Entertainment Team was restructured and the post of General Manager was dispensed with. I was made redundant, with a termination date of 7th October 1999. Yet again, I had done all the hard work and sorted the place out, putting my individual stamp on yet another theatre, only for it not to be recognized. I began to wonder yet again, what was I doing wrong?

Act 9 Scene 2
ATLANTA BALLET
(1999)

As I had been made redundant at The Old Vic, I was able to sign on again the following day at Greenwich Job Centre. As Christmas and the Millennium celebrations were only a couple of months away, I felt confident that something would turn up. I have always believed that if you are not working over Christmas and The New Year, then you must be doing something very wrong.

I hated going back to the old lifestyle, and was soon relying too much again on a bottle of sherry and cider for my health and wellbeing. It was not until November that my old friend from Liverpool, Jon Swain contacted me again with details of a job he thought would suit me. The *Atlanta Ballet Company* was booked to play the Christmas and Millennium New Year season at The Royal Festival Hall and wanted a General Manager to look after their needs and requirements. He suggested I contact them via email, using my new skills, to give details of my experience, and mention that I had been ballet trained. The show was to be their ballet version of J.M. Barrie's 'Play for Children' *Peter Pan*, first seen in 1904. I enlisted help from my IT Tutor, wrote to their headquarters in Atlanta, Georgia, and was offered the job, which was paying the going rate of £500 per week.

Peter Pan was a show I knew intimately, having managed three productions of it in the past. However this would be a new experience for me, as I hadn't managed a Ballet Company before, despite having worked in the business for over forty years. Ballet Dancers are well known for being the most professional and dedicated performers around, and I expected their demands to be high, which would be a challenge.

The first thing they asked me for was my mobile telephone number, in addition to my landline number. Now I had managed very well in the past with just home and office phone numbers. I valued my time away from these as quite precious, and to be able to get away from work to do my own thing. Having said that, as I had now moved into the world of computers, the need to have a mobile became inevitable.

I went to Surrey Quays shopping centre to buy a mobile telephone, saw one in a window for £15 and as it was quite small, went in to buy it. Knowing nothing about them, but having seen my sister walking around with one, I assumed that it would be compatible with my landline number, but a mobile version of it. Wrong. I was asked about this tariff and that tariff, pay as you go, a year or two year contract and so on. "I just want a mobile phone" I persisted, "and to keep my existing eleven digit number, please". "Can't be done" I was told. "You have to buy a SIM card as well." Eventually I got a new mobile, on Pay as you Go, and a new eleven digit number that I had to write down to remember. Would it be worth it, I wondered?

On 16th November, I went to the Royal Festival Hall to meet the Production Manager and the Staff who would be working on the show. They knew far more about the show than I did, showed me the ground plans, Fit Up schedule, props list, and general requirements which had been sent to them. As Property Master, I was delighted to be working with old friend Paul Murphy, who was an experienced Touring Company Manager, but wanted to work in London over the Millennium. I was more than happy he would be on the show with me. The ballet was due to open on Tuesday 21st December and have a limited run of 28 performances to 8th January 2000. The basic Company of twenty dancers and five apprentices would be augmented with students from The Central School of Ballet, which I knew had been founded in 1982 by Christopher Gable.

Following the meeting I thought it prudent to find out a little more about *The Atlanta Ballet* and the show I was going to be working on. The Company had been founded in 1929 and been a fully professional ballet company since 1967, with John McFall as Artistic Director, who would direct and choreograph the show. Cameron DeLeone (Musical Director of the Cincinnati Ballet Company) had composed the score for Pan, and the Maestro himself would come to London to conduct the 47-piece Royal Philharmonic Orchestra for the first six performances. The Designs for the show were by Peter Cazalet, and from enquiries I made at the Box Office, business looked good. There was a great deal of interest as this production was the centrepiece of the Royal Festival Hall's Millennium Celebrations. The auditorium sat 2,500 people and had been built as part of the Festival of Britain in 1951. It was therefore about to celebrate its own Golden Jubilee in 2001.

Accommodation for the Company and Staff (who would be arriving in waves from Georgia from 15th December) was at The Strand Palace Hotel just over Waterloo Bridge. I made myself known to the General Manager and Concierge there to check details and tweak arrangements. It was agreed I would be their only point of contact, and that all drop offs and pick ups would be at their Exeter Street side entrance, thus avoiding blocking The Strand at peak times. The trips to and from Heathrow would be in Luxury Coaches, which had already been booked, whilst I arranged for minibuses to run a shuttle service before and after the shows from the Hotel and RFH. They were also kind enough to offer me a room any night I needed it, as part of the deal. I foresaw that Central London would be in shut down on Millennium Night as the planned *River of Fire* on the Thames was directly in front of the Festival Hall, so we would have a fantastic view from the balcony. I planned to take them up on their offer that night.

I also made myself known to the Principals at The Central School of Ballet as this was to be used as our rehearsal space before moving to the Festival Hall for a Dress Rehearsal on Monday 20th December. I made sure there were enough portable Ballet Rails for the Company to use, and enquired about Physiotherapists they knew who specialised in ballet and dance injuries. I wanted to have a list of such professionals who were prepared to be on Emergency Call should a member of the Ballet Company be injured. I rang round and was able to do this for the whole run, apart from 31st December when it appeared everyone had plans, and it was estimated there would be 3 million people in Central London that night, a nightmare scenario for the emergency services. My first meeting with the advance party was arranged via emails and I would meet David Tatu and the other senior members of the technical team at Heathrow where Flight 1347 was due to land at 2220 hrs on 15th December. I was again thankful of having my Volvo Estate as I imagined that they would have plenty of luggage, and parked up in plenty of time.

I was waiting at the Exit Gate from the Customs Hall, with my Letraset sign 'Meeting Atlanta Ballet' when the Fire Alarm sounded and the Terminal had to be evacuated immediately. Once the All Clear was given, about an hour later, I returned to my meeting point but was unsure whether these people, whom I had never met, had gone through during the time I had been outside. I looked around madly waving my sign, but to no avail, and decided that all I could do was have them paged over the Terminal PA system to meet me at a central point, where I waited until I was approached. "You John Toogood?" they asked, "Sure am." I replied and led them to where I was parked. With careful loading, all their bags went in to the back and we set off for their hotel in The Strand, arranging to meet the following day.

I was next at Heathrow at 0620 hrs on Friday 17th, my 55th birthday, to meet American Airlines flight 086 on which the main Company was arriving. I had prepared a Welcome Pack for each member of the Company (again using my new computer skills) and gave the coach driver a nice tip to drive past as many London landmarks as he could en route to The Strand Palace Hotel. I acted as the tour guide pointing out things such as: "Next on your right you will see Buckingham Palace, and as the Royal Standard is not flying, Her Majesty is not in at home this morning" which they all loved to know about.

I waited at the Hotel Reception until everyone had registered, and were all happy with their rooms, before going over to my office in one of the Dressing Rooms at the RFH. I had wisely chosen to use a room that had a couch in it, and so was able to catch up on my sleep for a couple of hours. I had been up since 0430 to get to the airport on time, and it just wasn't worth going home.

The following two days were spent at The Central Ballet School where the pupils were integrated into the show as required. On the Saturday evening I was invited to attend an event in The Queen Elizabeth Hall, which is the second largest venue at the Southbank Centre, after the main Royal Festival Hall. I bumped into Carole Collins and her husband Bob, quite by chance. I had not seen her since we had had a drink in a pub in Victoria, when she was working on Ross Taylor's revival of *The Sound of Music* in 1981, but she was still the delightful person I had worked with on *The King and I*. We chatted, and I told her I was now working on *Peter Pan*, with The Atlanta Ballet, and she wished me good luck as I departed.

We all heard the score for the first time at the Dress Rehearsal on the Sunday evening, and I realised I was working on a quality show. It not only looked and sounded good, but had some real dancers of note onstage. All four of the main characters, Peter, Wendy, Michael and John Darling were expert flyers and for once the black, piano flying wire was almost invisible to the eye. I arranged with the FOH Manager and the Corner that I would personally give the Maestro his clearance to make his entrance, with the inevitable round of applause. The first night was well received by both public and press, and attracted remarks such as 'Peter Pan captivates both young and old at the Royal Festival Hall, which is the main attraction of their Millennium celebrations.' Performers who caught the eye were John Walker (Pan), Marjorie Hardwick (Tiger Lilly), Wei Dongsheng (Hook), and Steven Salter (Crocodile).

The burning question the visiting company wanted to know was: 'What is planned to see the old Millennium out and the new one in?' The RFH staff I knew intended to stay put, and see *The River of Fire,* which was to stretch from Tower Bridge to Vauxhall Bridge, from the top balcony which overlooked the River. It was suggested that The Atlanta Ballet Company do the same. With this idea in mind I approached the Atlanta Ballet top brass and told them I would be prepared to organise a party for this very special night, if they would fund it. "How much will it cost, John?" they asked. Not having the faintest idea I replied: "No more than £500." which they approved. What had I let myself in for?

I ordered wine from a local wine shop on a sale or return basis and drew up a shopping list of items to buy for a buffet that we could prepare on site after the Matinée, as there was not an evening show. I planned things like Asparagus Spears wrapped in Palma Ham, Smoked Salmon Bagels, precooked Chicken legs, whole Stilton & Camembert Cheeses, Crudites, assorted dips and Fruit. My plan was to buy it at the 24 hr Tesco store in Surrey Quays, and deliver it straight to the RFH, where I could park up in their private car park.

The first problem happened when I checked the £30 worth of Parma Ham I had asked to be sliced whilst I bought the other things. Instead of it being sliced on the thinnest of settings, it had been cut at the same thickness as Wiltshire Ham, which was no good for wrapping round Asparagus. I told the Deli Manager it was not what I had ordered, and thankfully another ham was sliced correctly. What they did with the other, I have no idea.

There was a huge upright fridge in the Company Green Room, which I emptied of all the soft drinks and stored them in my office, before filling it up with bottles of sparkling wine (Champagne was beyond the budget) and locked it with the chain I used to secure my cycle to railings. I kept one key and Property Master Paul Murphy kept the other. We planned to use a shopping trolley to transport the chilled bottles up to the Balcony Bar as and when required.

Security had to be ultra rigid for this night, and unless you had a pass or were on the Visitor's List, it was 'Sorry No Entry.' As none of the Company had any guests to bring, I invited Jeanne to come and spend the night with me, having taken advantage of the room at The Strand Palace. We were very fond of each other by now, and she was my ideal partner for this once in a lifetime celebration. The party went well and I soon discovered that female American Ballet Dancers are partial to Vodka and Cranberry juice as their tipple of choice. I have never seen so many empty Champagne bottles in the street as I did that night as we made our way over Waterloo Bridge to the hotel.

By some miracle, and lots of hard work, Westminster Council managed to clear things up by the following day. When I went to collect my car, I found that people who had been desperate to catch a glimpse of the non-event that was the River of Fire, had climbed up onto the bonnet and roof, which were all bent inward. Thanks a lot.

So we were now in a brand new Century. The show was due to close at the end of the week on Saturday 8th January, with the Company flying home the following day. I would be out of work again. Two coaches were planned from the hotel to the airport, one at 0800 and another at 1030 and it was a sad time for me to say goodbye to the many friends I had made during their stay in London, as I saw them all safely onto the coach for the last time.

Act 9 Scene 3
SHEFFIELD CITY HALL
(2000)

The Millennium Night *River of Fire* was a fiasco, and had been a huge disappointment to the three million people who were estimated to have been in central London that night. As the dust settled I read what was supposed to have happened at midnight on 31st December. Thirty-nine tons of fireworks were distributed between sixteen barges moored between Tower and Vauxhall Bridges and from a shore based control the display of rockets was supposed to be ignited and travel between the two in 10.8 seconds at a speed of 775mph.

This was very ambitious in hindsight, and as it was impossible to have a Dress Rehearsal of such a once in a lifetime spectacle, it did not work on the night, much to everyone's disappointment.

I signed on again on the Monday after we had closed. I also had a court hearing on the same day, as a final financial divorce settlement was near to completion. My weekly income was now £51.46 per week, and I had to cut my cloth accordingly. I was getting thoroughly disillusioned with life in London, as it is a place that you need more than £50 per week to exist, let alone live on. I discussed my situation with Jeanne, who had recently bought a two bed roomed house in Lincoln for £19,000, and as we got on very well, she invited me to come and live with her. At the back of both our minds, we both thought we had found a soul partner to spend the rest of our lives with. In late January she found a job she liked, and began full time employment. I therefore began to make regular runs from London with as many of my worldly goods as I could pack into my replacement Volvo (I had clipped a low metal bollard in the previous car one night, and the insurance said it was not worth repairing the front axle) as it was cheaper than using a removal firm, and I had time on my hands. I organised these runs between signing on days in Greenwich and attending interviews for new opportunities elsewhere, when I could use Lincoln as a base.

On Monday 13th March, I found myself in Nottingham for an interview for a Management role at The Arts Theatre in the old lace making area, which must be Nottingham's best kept secret. The 300 seat little theatre was run by the Co-Op. Its claim to fame was that the outrageous Sue Pollard had started her career there, prior to getting her big break on Opportunity Knocks. I say outrageous because once I had been out shopping in Lincoln, and met her in the Hat Department of the Co-Op in Silver Street. She must have tried on every hat on display, asking each time: "What about this one then, it's much better i'nt it?" It was quite a strange interview, as my technique was to slowly switch the conversation and answers round, until in the end I was interviewing them. They asked what changes I could suggest to increase their annual turnover, and I asked if they had a late club licence, which would enable the venue to operate as a night club. The looks on their faces at this suggestion clearly showed my fate had been sealed. I was not invited back for a second interview, or offered the post.

I packed my bags for the last time at Harrison Court on Friday 31st March, and headed back to Lincoln for a new life in the City that I had been born in, although I had of late visited only for weekends or short periods of time. As I drove up the A1, I wondered what it was going to be like being a big fish in a small pool again, instead of being a small fish in the large pool that is our capital city.

I had done a deal with a 'man with a van' to bring the bulk of what remained in the flat up to Lincolnshire, and put these items into storage in the garage of a friend of Jeanne's. The 'man with a van' obviously had no idea how far Lincoln was from London, as soon as we were on the A1 he was asking: "How much further then?" He had not filled up and soon wanted to stop for a meal break. It became a nightmare as he grumbled and moaned about how far it was, and that had he known, he would have charged me more than the £35 he had quoted me. In the end we came to a compromise. I paid him extra for his miscalculation, he did the drop as requested, and drove me back to the London flat, where I slept on the floor for the last four nights. Some months later I went to the garage to collect the items I had bought up in that van, and discovered all my framed posters of the shows I had worked on in London were missing. Had the man with the van purloined them? I still wonder to this day, as I have never seen them since that night.

The first job I had to do was to re-sign on, but now at the Lincoln Job Centre. I was surprised when they told me that something had just come in which would suit me. I was flabbergasted and asked for details of the job. "It's for a Theatre Technician" they told me. "Great," I said "Where?" She went to get the card and told me that it was a Monday to Friday job as a Technician at The County Hospital. "Wrong sort of Theatre" I told her.

Bill Denis had invited me to go and stay with him in Kessingland, and Jeanne and I visited him in mid April for a long weekend, which was fun for all of us, as we enjoyed each other's company and copious amounts of wine.

The Newark & Sherwood District Council owned the Palace Theatre Newark, which was the next place I went for an interview on Friday 5th May. Again it was a strange experience with mountains of paperwork to fill in before the face to face interview began. Despite the fact that all the information they were requesting was contained in my CV, on my personal information sheet, or in my Portfolio, you were not permitted to write on the forms 'See details on CV' or 'See Portfolio for Information requested'. To my mind it was an utter waste of time, but that was how Councils work, I discovered. The actual interview went well, I thought, and I liked the set up and change of programme on a regular basis. I was told if I had been successful I would be invited back for a final second stage interview, but I never heard from them again.

I went regularly to see my old friend Art Walker, who had spent the whole of his career working at Lincoln Theatre Royal, most weeks when there was a show on that I wanted to see. I considered working there again as the days of it being a Repertory Theatre had long passed and it was now run by Chris Moreno, as a receiving house for touring shows and one night stands. I began to slip effortlessly into the Lincolnshire social scene going to events like Market Rasen Races on Ladies Day, or visiting the Gainsborough Model Railway Society's layout of the East Coast Main Line from Kings Cross to Leeds. This is generally recognised as being one of the best '0' gauge layouts in the country and is run just like a real railway, with a timetable, signals to indicate a clear line, and semaphore bell signals, between the many operators on duty at an time, and is a real treat to visit for any 'Train Spotter' like I had been in the '50s.

Another theatre I applied for work was the New Theatre Hull, which was, and still is, a Regional Touring House. I went there for an interview on 19th May. Much to my dismay the two people interviewing me were not impressed with what I had worked on, both in London and the provinces over the past forty years. Yet again I got the impression that I was far too experienced for them, and could be a threat to their positions.

As I had evenings free, I made the most of being able to go out and attend whatever event took my fancy. On the last evening in May I went to a lecture on 'Night Bombing during WW2' at the old Metheringham RAF Station, which was well attended and fascinating to listen to. I was finding that if I did not go out and do something I would just stay at home, cook supper for Jeanne and I, and then drink far too much wine, cider, sherry or whatever I could lay my hands on. It was beginning to become a problem for others, but I thought that I could handle it, no problem.

In mid June I read in the local daily paper, The Lincolnshire Echo, that my old Ballet Teacher Christine Orange had passed away, which was a great sadness to me, as she had been instrumental in teaching me the high standards that I had always strived for in my career, to be the very best at whatever you do. This had manifested itself when I danced in competitions in the early '60s. Being the only male dancer competing, I had set my stall out to not only beat all the other female dancers from her Dance School, but from elsewhere as well. She had lived for as long as I had known her in a charming cottage on the High Street in Nettleham. The funeral at the local church on 20th June was packed with ex pupils, with a wake in the garden of the Sub Deanery, where I had played as a boy.

Saturday 15th July was a busy day for me. During the afternoon there was an open air fair in the local Boultham Park, which had many attractions, and in the evening we went to see my old school pal Pete Upton play a gig with his band *The Sultans* at The Drill Hall. This would turn out to be their final concert together as Pete died after a long illness in December 2005. He was a sad loss to the local music scene, as he was such a talented musician, and had been a friend of mine for over forty years.

By July the financial settlement from my divorce had at last been agreed. *Jeanne* and I had found a semi-detached house we both liked. It was on the market as a 'Four bed roomed property', one of which was so small you would be hard pressed to squeeze a cot in. It had a nice sized garden, a conservatory and a large workshop with power. This was large enough for me to store all the tools I had inherited from Dad, and others which I had collected and amassed over the years. The two main bedrooms had fully fitted wardrobes. I hoped that as we didn't have a chain we would be able to negotiate a deal with the current owners who were anxious for a quick sale. A deal was struck and I paid a 10% deposit on 19th July.

Before completion however, I was invited to attend an interview for a job at the prestigious Sheffield City Hall on 24th July. I attended and was offered the post of Production and Customer Services Manager, which was in effect The General Manager. Sheffield International Venues (SIV) had taken over the operation of the Hall in March with the task of restoring its fortunes. The Chief Executive was Steve Brailey who knew me from my time working for Lord Delfont's FLC from 1986-96 at The PET. The SIV Portfolio also included The Don Valley Stadium, Ponds Forge International Swimming Pool, The Beach Leisure Centre at Hillsborough and the Beauchief Golf Course.

In addition to overseeing the main house at City Hall, my brief also included responsibility for the smaller Memorial Hall and the weekend City Hall Nightclub in the basement under the building, which attracted many regulars each week to boogie the night away until 3am. The hours were 'as required' and the remuneration, without emoluments, was £538 per week. Horror of horrors, I was given a works mobile, so I was virtually on call 24/7, which I did not relish, and used to let it go uncharged at times.

My official starting date was set for Monday 18th September. Meanwhile the house purchase was completed and I set about having work done, such as timber treatment and DPC. I collected all my worldly goods in a trailer, with the help of cousin Steve, who also gave me a sofa for the living room. I next had to decide whether to commute the forty odd miles to and from my new place of work, or to find a small apartment to rent for the nights when I finished work at 4am and had an early start the following day.

I went for the latter option and found a single en-suite flatlet on the top floor of a large house in Kenwood Park Road, not far from the City Centre. The owners, Jack & Kay, were sympathetic to the hours that us thespians keep. It had off street parking and several other theatre folk who were playing The Lyceum used to stay there as well. On one occasion I recognised someone getting out of a car. I opened my window and shouted down: "Hello Ian, and welcome to Sheffield" for it was Ian Talbot I had spotted three floors down. We had known each other since Liverpool in the late '60s and during his reign as Artistic Director of the Regents Park Open Air Theatre. I had been for an interview once when I was resting in London. "Come on down and have a bowl of soup" he shouted back, and it was nice to find out what he was up to.

I was looking forward to the varied programme of shows booked in for the three months up to Christmas, when the traditional Amateur Pantomime was presented for Christmas and the New Year. There were Classical shows, Pop Shows, Big Bands, and Comedy Acts to keep me on my toes, and each attracted a different style of audience. I had an overlap period with the staff I had been appointed to replace for two weeks, which was hard work as they were not very forthcoming or helpful. They were very taken aback when I changed into my dinner suit for my first night on duty. "You won't wear that when you're unblocking a sink of sick in the ladies" was one of the printable remarks my appearance attracted.

During the first weeks I kept a note of the hours I worked and found that during week one I was on duty for 39 hrs, and was able to travel back to my new home in Lincoln over the weekend. The following week was 62 hours with no day off, which I was not happy about. The first big name to appear was flautist James Galway, on Saturday 30th September. He was very good, and I enjoyed what I saw of the show.

Comedy duo French & Saunders were booked into the main hall on 4th October. I was astounded when I was expected by the Directors to join them for a round of golf during the afternoon to bond with the other senior managers employed within the SIV Organisation, when my priority should have been to look after Dawn and Jennifer back at the venue.

On another occasion, having finished work, and cashed up at the City Hall Nightclub at 4am, I was expected to be bright and cheerful for a working breakfast at The Don Valley Stadium some four hours later. Most of the other senior managers had finished the previous evening at 6pm. This arrangement did not go down well with me, unlike the bacon sandwich we were offered.

Jack & Kay were kind enough to invite me to their traditional Friday curry nights at the house, if I was not working. On one occasion Jeanne phoned to tell me that she had been made redundant at work, and asked me to return to Lincoln immediately, which I couldn't because of work. This upset her very much and signalled the beginning of the end of our relationship, she told me years later.

The Memorial Hall attracted some of the best of the up and coming comedy acts around at the time. I was fortunate to work with Scottish Comedian Rhona Cameron who wasn't happy about the Feng Shui in her Dressing Room, but still managed to give a very funny show. Multi instrumentalist, comedian and Labour Party supporter Bill Bailey from Bath on the other hand, who also played the small Hall later in mid October, couldn't have cared less about such things and just got on with the show. His performance not only showed him to be a funny man, but also a talented musician.

Ronan Keating filled the building with his army of fans for a sell out performance on 26th October, with a well-balanced show that of course included songs from his time with the boy band Boyzone. Whilst organising the queue waiting at the Stage Door for his autograph, I met Tracey, who was a big fan, and invited her in to meet the Star. She was grateful enough to give me her phone number, which I naturally followed up and arranged to meet her for dinner.

By now my weekly hours were regularly 60+, and I enjoyed getting away when I could to rest up in Lincoln. I was at home on my own on Sunday 29th October. Carrying my television upstairs, after a bit of a bender, I lost my balance and fell backwards downstairs. I was knocked out when my head hit the square corner of the newel post at the bottom. I came to in a pool of blood with a violent headache, but showered and went to bed. Waking in the morning my pillow was soaking in blood and it was by luck that Jeanne came round and arranged for me to go to hospital, where the deep skull wound was stitched. As a precaution I had a scan, and luckily nothing serious was found. However, it was a wake up call for me. It was also the end of my relationship with Jeanne, who phoned Susan and expressed her concern about my excessive drinking. I was forced to have a couple of days off work for the first time in my career. Thankfully I suffered no long term effects, other than a scar on my head and a big dent to my pride.

I was finding it hard to get the staff at the City Hall to work the way I wanted, and up to West End standards, as they were reluctant to change their ways. The emergency procedures were very lax and devoid of any record in the office files.

For example, in every toilet I wanted the sink plug to be hung around the right hand tap, with the soap on the left hand side of the sink in a small soap dish. I marked the disposable towel container with the minimum level that was acceptable to try and ensure that we did not run out during a show, along with additional loo paper. This was all basic stuff, and I thought added a touch of finesse to each loo, but the staff were reluctant to do it, saying: "But we have never done it like that in the past."

In the Nightclub on a weekend I was constantly at loggerheads with the Security Staff whom, I have found over the years, are not the sharpest pencils in the box. They were under the impression that it was they and not the Management, i.e. ME, who ran the club and is ultimately responsible as the Licensee. They admitted who they liked, and refused entry to those they didn't. They lounged around, were not in uniform, sat aggressively on chairs the wrong way round, and did not take criticism at all well. No wonder that some nights we had a rough crowd.

Harry Hill was a big hit when he came and played the venue for a Saturday night in early November. When I met him to say "Hello" in his Dressing Room before the show, as was my custom, we spoke about his early days playing Up The Creek in Greenwich. Malcolm Hardee was generally known as the father of British Alternative Comedy, with his never ending supply of cigarettes and regular rendition of *The Deptford Blues* on his Harmonica, which was always in his top pocket. I had seen Harry work that intimate room to perfection and now he was playing venues that seated 2,270 fans in a purpose built Concert Hall.

I had regular meetings with Jonathan Day, to whom I reported, about how things were going and what he wanted done next. He wasn't a Theatre Man, and what I and he wanted were sometimes miles apart.

A rare treat for me came on 11th November when The BBC Big Band played the Hall with compère Sheila Tracey introducing the band. I knew she played trombone herself (sometimes with the BBC Big Band on Radio Two) and had been a part of the Ivy Benson all girls band from 1956-58, like my friend drummer Crissy Lee. We spoke at length during the sound check about Big Band Jazz and she said to me how rewarding it was for her and the Band to be playing in a venue where the Manager had such a vast knowledge of this type of music. The show was terrific and I longed to find a venue in Sheffield that regularly played this type of music.

One thing I could not change, or would have wanted to change, was the tradition on Remembrance Sunday for the Lord Mayor to take refreshments in the City Hall before and after the march past. This was an occasion for all the pomp the staff and I could muster to impress our VIP Visitors.

I had enjoyed the visit of *The Hollies* a couple of days before this, as Carl Wayne (original lead singer with The Move) had now replaced Allan Clarke on lead vocals with them. Carl and I had been at loggerheads over his punctuality when we worked on *Emu in Pantoland* in 1976. When we met again, he said on reflection I had been correct in reporting him to his agent back then and thanked me. This was the last time I ever met Carl as he later died in Norway. He had been a great lead singer in his day.

One artiste whose reputation preceded him was the Irish singer Daniel O'Donnell or 'Wee Daniel' as he is known to his many fans. The close relationship he had with his adoring fans, and his charismatic, engaging presence on stage left me cold, and perplexed. I had discovered he was a cultural icon in his native Ireland and the ambassador for Donegal. I had been warned that most of the audience would wait patiently after the show to say "Hello" to Wee Daniel. On previous visits this had taken until 1am for them all to be seen and spoken to, so I came prepared with a flask and sandwiches. What all these nuns and others saw in him I do not know for I found his performance to be so bland as to be tasteless. I much preferred the performance of Daniel's regular singing partner Mary Duff, who was also on the bill with him.

In early December the mighty *Status Quo* played a sell out gig to a full house. We had endless trouble with most of their fans who had front row seats, as they would not stay seated, preferring to stand. This was not only against the licensing regulations, but of course meant that fans sitting behind them could not see, and had to stand as well. I went along the front row several times and asked them to be seated, only to be told 'But we always stand at a Quo Concert' which is all well and good at a standing rock venue or open air concert but not permitted in a Concert Hall with rows of seats. I asked The Tour Manager to announce that the concert would not start before everyone was seated, which happened, but soon the front row stood up again and there was little I could do to protect the licence apart from stop the show, which would have caused a riot.

The events of that evening and other matters pertaining to the way I was attempting to change and improve the image of the City Hall came to a head on 6th December at a meeting I had with Mr. Day. It soon became apparent there were a number of issues he was unhappy with, and he cited the fact that it had been reported to him that I summoned some staff with a blast on the whistle. I explained it was not the case, but was a tradition in the West End to indicate that the house was open to the public, and that is what I had been doing. However as I was still in my trial period I was given the opportunity to resign or be sacked.

Not wishing to be unable to sign on yet again, I argued the case that I should leave by mutual consent, which was agreed. The local Sheffield Telegraph got wind of (or were tipped off about) my sudden departure, and ran a story about my leaving the following week. I paid the rent due on the flat, packed the car and left Sheffield, only having partially achieved what I had hoped for, and headed back over Dunham Bridge to Lincoln for the last time.

Act 10 Scene 1
BACK TO LINCOLN
(2001-2007)

As I made my way back to Lincoln, I reflected on my time in the City of Steel. Although it may be that all things in life happen for one reason or another, this time I could not be sure why I had failed. I had worked hard to try and re-establish the City Hall with my own style of Management, but it wasn't the SIV's style and I reluctantly had to accept that. I had not had a great deal of time to go out, because of the hours I had been working, but I had been out clubbin' a bit and made some new acquaintances.

I recall the advice someone had given me before I went to work there, which was: "John, it's the birds that drink the pints in Sheffield and the fellas that drink the shorts." This may have been the case but I still had some good times at The Palais, Leadmill and especially at La-Chambre in Attercliffe.

I had met some old theatre friends in Sheffield when they came to play a week or two at The Lyceum Touring date. In addition to Ian Talbot at the flat, I had a delightful supper in the Stage Door Pub with Ned Sherrin, when *Jeffrey Barnard is Unwell* paid a fleeting visit. Now all I could look forward to was meeting friends when they came on tour to The Theatre Royal in Lincoln, and wondered if I could get a job there.

On my return to my new home in Lincoln, which I had spent very little time in while working at The City Hall, my priority was to sign on again, as I would be relying on what savings I had made whilst in Sheffield. Feeling very low and sorry for myself, I was soon seeking solace with the contents of a bottle again, and tried to overcome the self-loathing that causes people in a similar position to gravitate to each other for alcoholic company, but it was hard. I again arranged to go and spend Christmas with Susan, but before my departure I went to a concert that featured a band I had heard a great deal about. *Soultime* played a great cross section of Soul and Blues to a standard that many professional bands fail to achieve.

I was immediately completely blown away with the sound from this eleven-piece combo, and they did not have to ask you to get up and dance, you could not stop yourself. Fronting the band were hairdresser Keith Reeve and Jenny Colclough on vocals, with a four-piece sax and brass section at their side. Their repertoire included evergreen classics from the likes of Al Green, James Brown, Smokey Robinson, Arthur Conley, Otis Reading and Aretha Franklin. I found out the band had been formed in 1998, and their renditions of *Sweet Soul Music, Jimmy Mac, My Guy, Peter Gunn, Mr. Pitiful, Soul Man* and *Midnight Hour* were hard to fault and so full of raw energy. This was a band I liked and saw them as often as I could from then onwards.

I decided that as the Theatre Royal was looking for FOH Staff for the Pantomime Season, I would offer my services on my return from Pershore to help them out in an unpaid capacity, and started on 27th December. First there was a briefing outlining duties, which I was well aware of anyway, before we were given positions, to check tickets, sell programmes, and ice cream at the interval.

I was astounded how lax the system was, as there was no means of accounting for collection of goods and return of cash. I wondered whether I wanted to be part of this FOH team because of my reputation, but matters were taken out of my hands on 10th January, when Director Chris Colby rang me at home to say that he had been unaware that I was working at the theatre, and that my voluntary services were no longer required. Nice start to 2001.

I had to find a new social outlet to meet new friends, and found out that a local Big Swing Band played a monthly gig at Grafton House on Newland. The first time I heard The *Sounds Easy Band* was on Friday 2nd February. I was most impressed. It was a full 17 piece Swing Band made up of local amateur and semi-pro players, led on Saxophone by Sid Snell. The play list included many of the more familiar numbers that one associates with the era when every ballroom in the country had a live big band to dance to. People were able to dance at this venue, as it had a good-sized dance floor, but many of the forty or so present just came to listen to the music and wallow in nostalgia. On the door collecting the small admission money was a man that I now know to be Roy Coppin, and in addition to that duty Roy also set up and took down all of the music stands that were used. I liked what I heard that night, and have been a regular attender ever since.

Having made a few contacts that night, I was now able to broaden my social network. I was told there was another Big Band Night, but this time out of town at The Four Seasons at Dunholme, just off the A46 road to Grimsby. In its heyday The Seasons had attracted many of the top name stars to play there, where quality, not quantity was the byword. I know that my late parents had been there to dine and dance in the '60s, before the top of the bill came on at 11pm. The names of those who had graced the stage read like a Who's Who of performers Les Dawson, Frankie Howard, Sacha Distel and many others have appeared there. It was, by now, rather past its prime, but still a venue for live music. As it was my custom by now to consume a bottle of wine before I went out, to lose my inhibitions, I was compelled to travel there and back by taxi, which all added to the expense of the evening, which I could ill afford. I surmised however that I was not going to meet female company or socialise sitting at home watching television.

Being a resident again in Lincoln, I was surprised and delighted to find out that in addition to Big Bands appearing in Lincoln, if I was prepared to travel a little I could see Big Name Bands at nearby theatres. *The Syd Lawrence Band*, which I had not seen live for many years, was booked into The Palace Theatre Newark on Saturday 17th March, and I went along of course. Following Syd's death in 1998, the band had continued to perform, and was now led by Brian Pendleton, and presented by Chris Dean. I had forgotten what a fine Band trumpet player Syd had founded. I recalled first hearing him play as a member of *The Trad Lads* from within the ranks of the Manchester based BBC Northern Dance Orchestra on the radio.

The tribute band led by Todd Miller was the next I went to see, this time at Lincoln Theatre Royal, on 22nd April. Todd had taken over the running of the hugely successful *Joe Loss Band* following Joe's death in 1990 and so continued its uninterrupted run of entertaining people since 1930. Hearing the band's signature tune *In the Mood* reminded me of something I had been told when working at the Café Royal in 1997. On VE night (8th May 1945) a wealthy Jewish business man from the East End, who was out celebrating, had paid a deposit of £250 (worth £10,000 based on average earnings in 1999) to book a ballroom there for Joe Loss to play at a Millennium Ball. Unfortunately I was not working there on Millennium night to see if the deal was honoured, but it just shows the high esteem the band was held in.

I was meeting up with a few female friends again since splitting up with Jeanne, and in mid May celebrated knowing Louise for nine years. However life in general was becoming boring as I was frequently short of cash, and spent most evenings drinking, eating and watching television. This was not the lifestyle I wanted, but I slipped quite easily into it and wondered what would happen to me to break this downward spiral and, more important, when it might happen.

I continued to sign on, but any work in the entertainment business never came to the attention of the Lincoln office and I went about using my own initiative and known contacts for something, but luck was not on my side. The Employment Service sent me for interviews for several non theatre jobs but nothing came from them. For the last 43 years I had only worked in the entertainment business, and knew nothing about retail sales, which they thought I would be good at.

In the Autumn my youngest daughter Becky (19), who had been travelling during a gap year after finishing her schooling, went to University in Cardiff to study Politics & Philosophy for three years. I was immensely proud that she had followed both her elder brother and sister to University.

Priorities in life were brought sharply into focus for me, and the whole world, on Tuesday 11th September, when I received a phone call from Jeanne: "Are you watching the television?" she asked, "No, why what's on?" I queried. "New York is being attacked by terrorists" came the reply. Naturally I immediately put the TV on and was shocked to see the carnage as the second of the twin towers imploded, and fell into a pile of rubble. Having known many Firemen in the past, during my time in London, one could not help but be saddened to see many of 'New York's Bravest' walking into a building that was likely to collapse, to try and save as many of the thousands of people in the building as they could, only for 300 of them to perish themselves.

The famous *Squadronaires Band,* formed during the Second World War, originally as *The Royal Air Force Dance Orchestra*, was the next band I had the pleasure of hearing, when they played The Palace Theatre Newark on Friday 28th September to a full house. Newark, unlike Lincoln, appeared to be a real hotbed of Jazz and it was always a real pleasure to spend time there. How I wished my job application to be the Manager of the venue had been successful.

Post WW2 *The Squads* had become a civilian band led by pianist and arranger Ronnie Aldwich, and used to play regular Summer Seasons at The Palace Ballroom in Douglas on the Isle of Man. The highlight of their concerts was to hear them play their signature tune, the slow foxtrot *Something in The Air* which had first been recorded on the Decca label 'by Permission of the Air Council'.

Being very much a night owl I was kept awake during the day by the neighbour's huge Alsatian dog barking most of the time. 'Buster', as I found he was called, used to be let out to roam the back garden, which my bedroom window overlooked, by the owners when they went to work at 8am, and was left unattended all day. In the end this was such a distraction to my sleep pattern that I moved rooms, and now sleep at the front of the house.

In November I joined a Singles Club as my sister had found a new partner Brian Parker that way and we thought I might be as lucky. I went speed dating, which I quite liked as you had just five minutes to impress your lady before you moved on to the next table. What I did not like was the fact that any future contact had to be made via the organiser, and used to get round this by presenting the lady with my business card when I introduced myself to her. Several contacted me again, and we went out, but nothing serious ever became of any of them.

I spent Christmas in the now traditional way at Pershore and a new year began. Darcy visited from London and stayed over the New Year, and as we were both down on our heels, we discussed different ways we might be able to make a bob or two as work for me was not forthcoming. It was impossible to exist let alone live on job seekers allowance. We came up with several ideas for each other, but nothing came of it, and I was soon back in my old lifestyle.

In my heart of hearts, I knew I was overdoing the drinking to drown my sorrows. It was a way of life I could not rid myself of and continued to cope with things in my own way. I managed to have a few good nights out, visiting Sheffield on 25th January, where I was surprised and delighted to unexpectedly bump into my friend Paul Murphy who had been my Property Master and right-hand man at the RFH.

He was on tour with a show that week playing at The Lyceum, and asked me where the best night out was to be found. As it was a Friday, which I knew would be a busy night at La-Chambre, where I was a member, I suggested that we go there. As I was driving and therefore could not drink, he suggested I dump the car at his digs, where there was room for me to stay. We got a cab into Attercliffe where he came into The Club as my guest for the night.

The year dragged on with me signing on, going to regular Big Band Concerts, and supporting *Soultime* as often as I could. I had met a rather shady character called Arthur, who planned to open the first Pole Dancing Bar in the City and offered to help him get it off the ground, with my contacts in London. My plan was to get the un-named club up and running and then manage it for Arthur, and we had several on-site meetings. Arthur knew nothing about recruitment, advertising, club membership and the like, so I suggested to him that we advertise for experienced local dancers in The Stage. On the Thursday following this, I went into WH Smith as usual to collect my copy of The Stage to find Arthur buying his copy as well: "I've put an advert in it, John" he told me, but we got few replies and Arthur lost interest and moved on. Another prospective opening for employment had been lost, and I began to despair of ever finding work again.

On Saturday 30th March, I turned on the television expecting to hear the latest sports news, only to find solemn music and tributes being paid to HM Queen Elizabeth The Queen Mother, whose death had been announced. I, with the rest of the nation, watched her funeral on television, and recalled that I had been asked to escort her twice at the PET, on her 89th and 93rd birthdays. What happy memories came flooding back.

With all the children now living busy lives of their own, it was a rare treat for me to entertain them for the weekend on 20th April in my new home. Julian (26) now had a good job in the City, spending much time abroad overseeing various projects. Rachel (24) was contemplating a move to work for The British Council in Madrid, as she was fluent in Spanish, whilst Becky (19) was still studying at Cardiff University. They enjoyed visiting Up-Hill Lincoln again and seeing the family home that Sue and I had to sell for a pittance in 1999 to pay-off Dad's Nursing Care Bills, which had been re-opened as a souvenir shop.

During the Summer months, as I had much free time to kill, in addition to working in the garden, where I was attempting to grow as many vegetables in large plant pots as I could, I paid my first visits to the highlights of any Lincolnshire Summer, both The Lincolnshire Show at The Showground and the International Air Show at RAF Waddington**.** To save on expensive travel and parking fees, I travelled to both events by bicycle, as I was putting on weight with the couch potato lifestyle I found myself living, and cycling was good exercise.

In July, The Job Centre appointed a 'New Deal Personal Adviser' to try and help me get work and Lynn Taylor was to look after me. One of the things she suggested was that for a nominal sum I could have a computer of my own to work from at home, which would assist me in my search for work. I was reluctant to begin with, as I had had a bad time with them at the PET, because I hadn't been formally trained. Training, I was assured, would be provided, and so on the 23rd August 2002, I received my very own system, courtesy of George Johnson at Everyman Computers.

I was soon using it for more than just work. I had been told that I could 'Google' questions such as 'Who arranged *April in Paris* for the *Count Basie Band* in 1957?' and get the answer, Wild Bill Davis. I was happy to play with the machine and was quite enjoying what I was doing, until the screen would suddenly go blank, usually at 4am, because I had pressed something I shouldn't have and deleted an application letter. A phone call to George the following day usually sorted it out, and he is still my advisor and main trouble shooter some twelve years later.

It was also a tradition to hold live open air concerts in the grounds of Lincoln Castle and Darcy, who was a friend of Jules Holland, arranged a guest pass for me to see Jules play with his big band on Sunday 21st July. When I went to the Box Office to collect the pass, there was nothing there for me, and despite much arguing and pleading my case, I could not get in to the concert and had a nightmare round the houses bus journey home. I had better luck the following weekend however when I visited Heckington Show for the first time. What a glorious setting this is for a traditional village Summer Show that has something for everyone. As an ex-allotment vegetable grower, I was naturally drawn towards the best in show specimens which had been grown locally with such loving care.

I was delighted to be able to see The National Cycle Grass Track Championships being contested so near to home, and stayed on for the fireworks and concert that traditionally end the first day. This again is part of a Lincolnshire Summer to me, and one that I try not to miss each year.

Rachel got the job with the British Council in Madrid and moved there to start a new chapter in her career on 19th August 2002. Her father continued his quest for that elusive lucky break which surely was just around the corner, if only I could find which corner to turn.

Maris had now moved to France, I presume with her money from the divorce settlement. The three children spent Christmas over there with her and her new partner, returning for the New Year on 27th December.

Could 2003 bring me a change of luck I wondered? I soon found myself pretty much in the same routine as before, with the occasional highlights to bring me some joy and happiness.

In early May Rachel invited several of us over to stay with her for a week in Madrid which sounded fun until we saw the size of the small apartment she was living in. The kitchenette was minute and hidden away behind what appeared to be wardrobe doors, and I was sleeping on a blow up bed in the living room. We toured the City, ate out, sampled the nightlife and went to a bullfight, which I found fascinating with all the associated ritual. We went to an open-air restaurant that I liked very much as it only served Spit Roasted Chicken, very smelly and ripe local cheese, with a flagon of the local Cider. I was in heaven.

The highlight however was the day that Julian and I went sent to see Real Madrid play a home match at the huge 80,000 seater Bernabeu Stadium, where the atmosphere was electric and like nothing I had experienced at a match in the UK, even Anfield. We mixed with the home fans before that game and one even went out of his way to take us to the correct entrance for our seats. Post match we mixed with the fans again in the bars on the way back to the underground and found them to be real fans and not hooligans. We shared our flight back home to Birmingham with Ron Atkinson and his wife (who were in first class) along with the press pack and ITV commentators like Clive Tyldesley who weren't.

My old school mate and lead singer with *The Sultans*, Pete Upton, had by now ceased performing with the band and invited many of his closest friends to a house party on Saturday 12th July, in the village of Scothern, where he had a charming house. I got a taxi there, not wishing to drive and not drink, and had a great night, where Pete played some Boogie Woogie, sang some Jerry Lee Lewis numbers along with some of his own compositions. Some friend of his offered me a lift back to Lincoln, which I accepted but was so full of Red Wine that I could not remember where I lived. They kindly drove me round for twenty minutes to see if I recognised any landmarks, and eventually gave up leaving me to find my own way home, which I did somehow, only to find that I had lost my house keys somewhere or other. Luckily I always kept a spare set of keys for the Volvo hidden, and was able to find them, before collapsing in the back of the car, where I slept, until I sobered up. I rang Pete on the Sunday to apologise and asked him to thank his friends for their kindness in attempting to take me home, and accepted that I was well out of order on this occasion.

Over the August Bank Holiday weekend, I missed my annual pilgrimage to Wainfleet to watch the Grass Track Poacher meeting, as Rachel was back home for a short while. She had been at The Edinburgh Festival for a few days and was travelling back to London on the Sunday, and had suggested stopping off en route to stay with me. I arranged to pick her up at Retford, as the train did not stop at the more convenient Newark Northgate, but no sooner was she in the car than bless her, she fell asleep for the whole journey back to Lincoln. We had a smashing time together and really bonded as father and daughter for the first time since I had left the family home, after the divorce.

Another venture I thought worthy of pursuing came to my attention when a new Nightclub opened in the City, near South Park. The idea was that a resident comic would introduce the acts to what was a mixed audience looking for a different night out from the only other recognised Nightspot in Town, Ritz in Silver Street. The idea of Burlesque however was way ahead of its time for Lincoln, despite the growing youth culture following the opening of The University six years earlier. I never got the opportunity to manage it, because it did not last for very long.

Entertainment highlights for me that Autumn were *Songs from the Shows* on 11th October, an evening of the *Rocky Horror Show* on the stage behind the bar at The Chicago Rock Club, *Soultime* performing at The Hospital Social Club on 18th October, and a revival of *Crazy for You* at The Theatre Royal in November. I had made enquiries about touring with the show as the Company Manager, but Keith 'Paddington' Richards got the job. Christmas was spent in Pershore, and another new year dawned.

The pattern of my existence was very much the same for the next three years as it had been since moving back to Lincoln. Work was apparently non existent for me now in my sixtieth year, and I began to hit the bottle for real now, with just the occasional event to resurrect my spirits.

I continued to go and see *Soultime* play as often as I could, be it a Gig in Lincoln, out at RAF Scampton, or any other venue. Over time I got to know lead singer Keith very well, and when I could afford it I had my hair razor-cut by him at The Talking Heads Salon, where he was the proprietor. I was still looking for the right lady to spend time with. I joined many of the singles clubs that were flourishing in the City, and met up with people in the same position as me at The Bentley Hotel, The Eastgate Hotel, The Lion & Snake Pub, and the new Pride of Lincoln. One glimmer of hope for employment came with the announcement The Drill Hall, was about to re-open as a multi-purpose entertainment venue. I applied for the post of General Manager, attended interviews, looked at plans, made observations and pointed out the problems of a Get In door opening onto the busy Broadgate main road. I was short listed, but did not get an offer, as Simon Hollingworth was more the type of person they were looking for, and over the last ten years he has proved that point.

I was by now seeing my GP on a fairly regular basis to have blood tests and for her to monitor my blood pressure, which at times was erratic. Over the internet I had met Rose who from her picture looked a fun loving girl, but it was a problem meeting up for a date as she lived in Essex. We exchanged presents on a regular basis, and still keep in touch, but haven't yet managed a date.

A new Lincolnshire event was added to my social diary, after I visited The Carrington Steam Rally, near Boston. Just the smell of these leviathans, once an everyday sight in the fields and roads of the county, was enough to bring childhood memories flooding back. I was fascinated to see a huge saw-wheel being driven by a belt from a traction engine slice effortlessly along the trunk of a mature tree, and marvelled at the techniques used to ensure a clean cut by the use of wedges to keep the cut open and not bind the saw-wheel.

I also began to take someone special each year to The Bailgate Ball, which traditionally was held in a huge marquee in the castle grounds. It was a dress to impress evening, a sit down dinner and dancing to usually a 'name' band. One year I teamed up with a group of other singles to make up a table of ten, and we all met for Pimms at a nice house at the bottom of Steep Hill. These were grand evenings, and fun to attend.

The Drill Hall was attracting some 'name acts' and in July 2004 I saw Jamie Cullum play live for the first time. What a revelation and talented artiste this multi–instrumental composer, vocalist and pianist is, with his roots firmly set in Jazz. Another venue that appeared on the scene, and catered for us singles, was the Black Horse Chambers in Eastgate, which used to be a rather run down local prior to being tastefully restored. I got to know several of the girls whom I knew would be there, and used to change names around on the seating plan, so the girls I knew and liked were sitting next to me.

Having had my appetite whetted again for the intoxicating aroma of sulphur from the Carrington Steam Rally, I also added The Lincolnshire Showground Steam Rally held each August to my growing social diary. I made contact with Colin Reed again, another of my old friends from yesteryear, who was now a successful business man and managed the works Moto Cross Team for the mighty Honda factory. I helped him celebrate his sixtieth birthday on 11th October and met his wife Val who had known my late mother, along with others from the days when we tried to emulate our motorcycle scramble heroes on our converted push bikes.

Having completed her University training, I was delighted when Becky got her first proper job working in a Theatrical Agency in London. I offered to help her as much as I could with the many contacts I had made in the business. She told me that when she phoned clients to introduce herself, on many occasions she was asked: "Are you related to John Toogood, as it is such a memorable name?"

I went to Browns Pie Shop on Steep Hill with close friends to celebrate my own sixtieth birthday on Friday 17th December 2004, and had a Seafood Banquet on the Sunday evening at home. Pete Upton celebrated his big '60' on 8th January 2005, but sadly never saw the year out as he died in the December. What a tragic loss that was to his army of fans from *The Sultans* days. I miss a true friend I knew for fifty years.

A new quality restaurant opened in Burton Road around this time on the site of the bakery that used to bake bread for the Lunatic Asylum, just round the corner in Union Road, now the site of The Lawn Complex. It was appropriately named The Old Bakery, and I frequented it as often as I could afford, when trying to impress a new lady friend.

By now Julian had met a nice girl, Lindsay Cuthill, who was then one of only two female BA pilots. It appeared from what he told me that she was the one for him, as they shared many interests. In the Autumn of 2005, I went down with a full tool box to help Julian with a few jobs at his flat in Streatham and met Lindsay for the first time, when we went out for dinner at a local Italian Restaurant. I liked her and thought they were well suited.

On the evening of 13th September I went to see a revival of *Guys and Dolls* at the Piccadilly Theatre where my old doorman friend from the PET and Old Vic Theatres, Phil Course, was now working. For the first time ever I was late for Curtain Up as I could not get a mini-cab and felt most embarrassed on my late arrival. The show starred Ewan McGregor as Sky Masterson. The only people I knew in the show were Musical Director Jae Alexander and Gaye Brown whom I had not seen since we did Liberty Ranch at Greenwich.

I had a new neighbour move in next door in November, and at last I was able to sleep without 'Buster' barking all day. Tracey was a keen runner and looked the part, when I saw her out training for a 10K or whatever, and she was pleasant enough to me after I introduced myself to her.

Susan joined the ranks of us sixty year olds, with a surprise party that was organised by daughters Joanna (29) and Katy (28) on the weekend before 10th January 2006, at a select venue near Evesham. Most of the family and guests stayed the weekend at a nearby public house, and some of her old dancing friends from *The Young Generation* came along as well. I managed to get hold of a rare copy of their LP, which I gave to her as a special 60th present. As usual I over indulged and could not face eating the lunch with everyone else on the Sunday, leaving mid afternoon to drive back home.

Rachel had also met the man of her dreams, Sean Gregory, while they were both working in Madrid, and he celebrated his fortieth on Valentine's Day 2006. When I first met them at Julian's flat, it was quite obvious that they were hopelessly in love, and I was delighted to give them my blessing later in the year when he rang me from South America, where they were on holiday, to ask for my approval, as he had just slipped an engagement ring onto her finger.

A new local Big Band came to my attention in February when I first saw and heard *The RAF Swing Wing* Band play. Having been formed in 1989, and following the tradition of past RAF Swing Bands ever since the end of hostilities, the band came from within the ranks of a bigger ensemble, in this case *The RAF College Band* based at Cranwell. Their rivals, the *Shades of Blue Orchestra*, was formed a year later when the *RAF Regimental Band* transferred to Cranwell. I liked what I saw and heard, and have been a big fan of theirs ever since.

Despite making every effort to find work, and attending many interviews for jobs that were just not for me at all, I had a change of luck with my personal life on 6th March, when I met Catherine at a singles evening at The Lion and Snake. We chatted and stayed on after everyone else had gone home, and arranged to meet again later that week. The date went well and by the end of the month we had been out together five times. We continued to see each other and as she was a horsey type she invited me as her guest to The Lincolnshire Show, where we received VIP treatment.

Clan Toogood had spoken for some time about tracing our family roots further than any of us could remember. What better place to start than Norfolk, where we knew my Great Grandfather had lived in the Fakenham area? This quaint market town is situated north east of Kings Lynn and south west of Cromer, so we decided to rent a big cottage for the weekend of 29th July and explore the area and old churchyards for clues. Cousin Steve had already been to the area and reclaimed a huge tombstone from un-consecrated land, so we had a good idea that my Great Grandfather, who was also called John Toogood, must have had other relations there. We spent all Saturday, which was a baking hot day, searching churchyard after churchyard, all to no avail. We returned exhausted in the evening to our rented accommodation for a barbeque. As I was half way to Kessingland, I travelled over to see my theatre pal Bill Denis and his daughter Jody on the Sunday night, before making my way back home on Monday afternoon.

I was still not in work, but at least my social life was better than it had been for a long time. I was getting on well with Catherine, who also liked a drink or two, and occasionally like me went too far, but she was a good friend and lover. We celebrated her fifty-fourth birthday in style. When Rachel announced that she and Sean were to marry in 2007, I had no hesitation in inviting her along as partner to the Father of The Bride.

We travelled down to London on the train on Saturday 26th May. I wore a new suit to travel in, as I did not want to pack and crease it. This was a bad decision however as someone had kindly left a used piece of chewing gum stuck to the train table leg, and yes, you've guessed it, the gum transferred itself to my trouser leg. I asked for ice to freeze it, and picked off as much as I could, but it was a job for a specialist dry cleaner.

Once we arrived at Julian and Lindsay's new flat, I went to the local dry cleaners and asked if they could do an 'Express' clean. "Leave the trousers now and collect them 9am on Monday" they said, which of course was no good as the wedding was the following day. I explained the situation and begged them to help me, which they did. I took the trousers off, wrapped myself in a sheet, and they kindly worked their magic to remove the gum within half an hour. They would not accept any payment for what they had done, and wished the family a happy wedding day. I was very touched by their gesture, and such small kindnesses always stay large in the memory. That night all four of us went out for a meal, and I read my speech out loud to Catherine to make sure it sounded OK.

On Sunday I went to Rachel's flat off the Severn Sisters Road, and waited patiently for her and her bridesmaids to get ready before driving with her to Camden Town Hall for the ceremony. I was so proud that day, and Rachel looked radiant and so happy as I escorted her up the impressive stairs to the first floor chamber, where the congregation was waiting. The service went without a hitch as Rachel Gregory, as she was now to be known, had planned it like a military operation. The reception was to be held at The Almeida Theatre, just off Upper Street in Islington, and a fleet of mini cabs had been booked to transfer us.

Following a delightful buffet meal, I was first in to bat with my speech which I had memorised, but kept bullet points on cards held discreetly in my hand as reminders. I thanked everyone for coming, told an anecdote about Rachel, kept it short, sweet and to the point, with a bit of humour, but was sincere with what I had to say. The speech was well received and I handed over to Sean for his speech. As is the tradition, it is the Best Man who gets the final say and Sean's brother Dominic made a most humorous speech before the dancing began and people let their hair down.

I had promised everyone not to get drunk for once, and kept my word. With all my official duties complete I was able at last to spend some time with Catherine, who had been a bit neglected all day. We stayed the night in the Travelodge in Kings Cross, which was handy for the train home on the Bank Holiday Monday, after a most joyous and memorable weekend with family and friends.

Sad news came in mid August when Jody Chapman rang me to tell me that Bill Denis had died, but I was unable to travel to Kessingland for his funeral. I was still drinking far too much for my own good. Over Christmas my sister said I did not look well, and it was as though I had yellow jaundice. I thought nothing of it and said I was able to cope on my own. Catherine and I spent a boozy New Year's Eve in one of the many new nightclubs that were opening up in the City.

On Friday 11th January 2008 I went for a routine blood test in the morning. While I was out shopping in the late afternoon, the doctor came round to my house because she was so concerned with the results of the blood test. She had left a note telling me that I must go to Accident and Emergency at once, and gave me a number to call straight away.

I did not know what all the fuss was about, as I felt as fit as a butcher's dog, and said so to the hospital Doctor when I rang him. "But you don't understand the seriousness of the situation, John" he said. "What's the problem then?" I asked. "Your bilirubin reading, which should be between zero and 21, is currently over 500. You need to be admitted for tests, and immediate treatment. We have found you a bed, and an ambulance will be there soon. You are lucky to be alive. Pack a bag."

This was it. I had been half-expecting to hear this for years, as I knew in my heart of hearts that something would happen one day, but I never imagined it would be like this.

Act 10 Scene 2
A CLOSE SHAVE
(2008-10)

Following my admission to Lincoln County Hospital, I spent a fretful first night in the Emergency Admissions Ward. I could not sleep for the shouting of some poor girl who sounded as if she had O.D.'d on drugs. In the morning a Consultant, who I now know to be Dr. G.M. Spencer, came to see me. He came straight to the point. "Mr. Toogood, if you want to see your next birthday, you have had your last drink. Any more could kill you." I asked what was wrong with me, to be told I had decompensated liver disease and that my bilirubin was thirty-five times higher than it should be. I soon realised the solution was total abstinence from that day or it would be curtains.

I was taken to a ward where I was given a bed and had more blood tests. Not knowing how long I would be in I hadn't told any of my family about going into hospital for the first time in my life. When I was told I would be a patient for 'weeks rather than days' I told them what had happened. Naturally they were most concerned and, thankfully, supportive, as I now realised they had all spotted tell-tale signs in the lead up to my admission.

As they all lived a long way from Lincoln and visiting would not be easy for them, I relied heavily on my cousin Steve and his wife Lynn to visit as often as they could, and check that the house and car were OK. I am eternally grateful for what they did at this difficult time.

Very soon I was bored stiff with the daily routine of the ward, having been an active person all my life, from the 7am "Morning – a nice cup of tea for you" right through to the "What biscuit would you like with your cocoa tonight?" I soon found out that meal times were something to look forward to. However, I found that 'Cottage' Pie tasted the same as 'Shepherd's' Pie, and I was soon using the public cafeteria on the top floor.

When I had visitors from out of town such as Sue, Julian, Rachel or Becky, it was a treat to be brought some Smoked Salmon or Parma Ham, and my house was theirs for as long as they wanted to stay. When I was eventually given permission to leave some five weeks later, I found they had spring cleaned the whole house for me.

I will be forever grateful to Dr. Spencer and the medical staff at Lincoln County Hospital for all they did for me in those painful five weeks. As I would soon discover, my enforced sobriety was the best thing that could have happened, and I became re-born as a new and much better person.

Steve kindly took me home from the hospital on 13th February. I began to settle into an alcohol free life as all the bottles of booze had been poured down the sink. Having always been a disciplined person, and not having had a drink while I had been in hospital, I was not tempted to buy booze and found that I did not miss it at all. I was, and still am, determined to be on the wagon. I have learnt my lesson.

Sue came to stay with me for the first weekend following my discharge and Rachel the following week. I felt so grateful to Steve & Lynn for all they had done for me that I took us all out for a slap up meal at The Old Bakery Restaurant and, as I wasn't drinking, drove there and back.

I tried to pick up my social life from where I had left it. I went to see shows at the local theatres, and started going to Big Band Concerts, but I just wasn't up to it and often used to leave before the end. I was on medication, and my feet were swollen and puffy. I had been warned they would be the last parts of my body to get back to normal. Although my weight was constant, with the lack of regular exercise, both before and during my time in Hospital, I was something like four stones overweight, and this had to be addressed as soon as I felt fit enough.

I was finding my new life difficult, as it was a complete change from my former lifestyle. By the Summer I felt up to going to a Speed Dating Club to try my luck again, as Catherine had not been in touch all the time I had been indisposed. Rachel, God bless her, was the most concerned that I should not go back to my old ways, and despite now being a married woman used to come up from London and stay as often as she could. On one of these visits she told me she was pregnant, and I would be a Grandfather by Christmas. This was wonderful news, as had things continued the way they were, it is more than likely that I would never have seen my first grandchild.

Before this event there was another family celebration, as Julian & Lindsay were to marry on Friday 12th September. They had chosen a nice hotel, where everything would take place under the same roof. The hotel complex was situated off the M3 motorway and close to a local airfield as the plan was for Lindsay and her Father to arrive in the grounds of the hotel, by helicopter. This was an appropriate arrival on her special day, bearing in mind her profession as a pilot. I travelled down the day before, staying in London overnight, before going on to the hotel with the rest of the family. I was looking forward to an event where I did not have to make a speech. The ceremony went well, the party was great and I was sober for once. On Saturday at breakfast I bumped into Maris, and we exchanged a few pleasantries. Some of us decided to make a weekend of it and set off to explore Winchester, a city I had not visited before. We went to Stockbridge to eat that night, why I don't know, as I am sure there are nice places in Winchester. I was impressed with the Cathedral and wanted to know more about it, but time was of the essence and there were other pressing things to do.

As Summer gave way to Autumn, my feet were still a problem. I had bought new shoes to wear at the wedding which were two sizes bigger than I normally wore. Socially I felt more comfortable mixing with people and found I did not need to be inebriated to have a good time. I went for a scan in October and found that everything was progressing OK. I began to look forward to being a Grandfather in early November.

At 0630 hrs on 10th November 2008, Rachel gave birth to a baby girl, which happened to be ten years to the day since we had buried Dad. God works in mysterious ways. As it was Remembrance Day the following day, baby was called Poppy, which suits her down to the ground, and she has brought me tremendous joy as I have watched her grow up over the years. There was a change of plan for Christmas, as I went to London to stay with my extended family for the first time, rather than Pershore.

I had found a new Jazz Band to support, *Andrew Hall's Memories of New Orleans*, and Andrew came from Newark. They had a residency at The Green Dragon public house on Sundays and, as I knew the landlord, I was invited to a private party on New Year's Eve. Unfortunately this turned out to be a bit of a non event, so as Steve & Lynn had invited me to their house in Nettleham, I saw New Year 2009 in with them, as a good night was always assured. As I was on soft drinks an added bonus was I did not have to pay triple time for a taxi home that night. I did not stay long after the New Year chimes, as this was the first occasion in almost a year that I fancied having a drink with all the other revellers. Thankfully, I resisted temptation.

On 8th January, almost a year to the day since I had been admitted to The County, I went for a check up with Dr. Spencer, who was pleased with my progress and for remaining completely abstinent. Along with ultrasound scans every six months, and regular blood tests, this has been my way of life now for the past five years.

I was by now following Jazz of all kinds in the City and surrounding areas on a regular basis, and could usually find at least one concert to attend every week. In February Andrew Hall moved residency to The Dog & Bone pub in John Street, off Monks Road, as the landlord there was a Jazz fan and had liked what he had heard at The Green Dragon. The gigs at The Grafton House Ballroom moved to the second Friday of the month, and later in the year the *Sounds Easy Band* switched from playing every month, to playing every other month, alternating with The *Monsonaires Band*.

As well as attending live concerts I was in the habit of listening to Jazz twice weekly on BBC Radio Lincolnshire. On a Thursday night I could listen to *Jazz Incorporated* from Radio Nottingham, which was presented by Tommy Saville, whilst on a Sunday afternoon, Howard Leader presented his Big Band and Swing Show for two glorious hours. I knew of Howard as he and I had both worked on shows for the same Producer in London. As he was an accomplished accordion player he was a natural to join the cast of *'Allo 'Allo*. I began to start sending him a list of who was on and where on a weekly basis for him to broadcast, and this has now developed into the local definitive Gig Guide for Lincolnshire and the surrounding area.

On 11th July, Uncle Bill celebrated his ninetieth birthday at Nettleham, with most of the family present. On 22nd August I went to London to celebrate Peter Russell's 80th birthday. Peter had been a most loyal FOH Duty Manager during my time at the PET, and had given me advice and his support during the more difficult times. It was to be a surprise lunch party for him in The Grand Salon of the TRDL, hosted by Rupert Bielby. Rupert had worked with Peter and me as Catering Manager at The PET but was now General Manager of the TRDL. He had laid on a superb luncheon for Peter's friends, and work colleagues, many of whom I had not seen for sixteen years. Naturally I stayed with Rachel, Sean and Poppy, who was a joy to see develop.

There was another family celebration in September, when Susan's elder daughter Joanna married Craig in Stow-on-the-Wold. This is a delightful market town in Gloucestershire, on top of an 800 foot high hill and has the Fosse Way (A46) running through it from Lincoln. The last time I had been there was in the Spring of 1962 when Dad drove through there to Bristol for my audition at The Bristol Old Vic Theatre School. I had forgotten what a charming place it was and the array of lovely houses that make the place a joy to visit. Joanna & Craig had refurbished a house there as a family home and the family all had a fantastic weekend.

I had seen Jeanne a couple of times for dinner since my time in hospital, as we were by now very close friends, but not lovers. I continued my quest to find that special someone who I could cuddle up to. I had heard about a band called *Swingtime* that used to play at the Horse & Jockey in Waddington, but had not heard play yet. Previously, when I was drinking, it would have cost me a taxi there and back. This was a nine-piece band, which had been around for about five years, had a good overall sound, and played the music I enjoyed. The room was not ideal by any means, and on occasions I dined there with friends during the gig. I got to know alto player Bill Clark quite well. He told me he thought his parents had inherited the perambulator I had used. I became a regular after my first visit on 1st October 2009. When a new landlord decided to terminate the Band's residency a few years later, it was a sad day for live music in Linconshire.

Family events were coming thick and fast by now, and thank God I was now sober enough to enjoy them. I went to London for Poppy's first birthday celebration, and Julian & Lindsay had a son Zachary born at 0330 hrs on Sunday 22nd November. We now had a male heir to the Toogood dynasty and I was delighted with the news that Mum and Grandson were doing well.

Later that month I went to see *The Shades of Blue Orchestra* play for the first time at Lincoln Drill Hall. This was another fine band with its members coming from within the *RAF Regimental Band*, which had been re-located to RAF College Cranwell in 1999. This band became another one that I made every effort to support as often as I could. 14th December was a sad day as Liz Best had died and was being buried on that day. She had been a pupil with me at The Christine Orange School of Dance in the early '60s and was a regular Pippin in Pantomimes and dancer in the CAODS shows at the Theatre Royal. Sue came over to pay her last respects to *Ularniva* as Liz was known, and many of the friends we had made in our formative years, when we were both starting out in our theatrical careers, were there as well.

I naturally wanted to spend Christmas with my extended family in London now and found a much better way to travel down there than driving. I drove over to Newark, parked up near Northgate Station on the Main East Coast line, and caught the 1606 train, which started there and was virtually empty.

This arrived in Kings Cross by 1730 where I was picked up by one of the family. The plan that year was for me to stay at Rachel's the first night, then go with them to spend Christmas Day with Sean's brother at his house, spend Boxing Day at Julian's, where I first met my Grandson Zac, before going back to Rachel's for the Sunday. As a treat for me Sean, who was a season ticket holder at Arsenal FC, took me to the new Emirates Stadium for a match. I was most impressed with the new concept of an all seated stadium, which had been introduced following the Hillsborough disaster, but found it rather soulless compared to what I had been used to at Anfield. I was back in Lincoln to see in 2010, sober for once.

I went to see Dr. Spencer in early January for my second annual liver MOT and celebrated 730 days of being abstinent on the 11th. With her growing family Rachel, Sean and Poppy moved into a much larger house four days later. I was beginning to improve my skills on the computer by now, and found a site dedicated to Motor Cycle Grass Track Racing with a Grass Forum where you could contribute. I started by making comments, before writing regular items reflecting on the heyday of the sport using the byline *Old Timer*. I began a series of interviews with the riders of today and yesteryear, which I called *Ask The Rider*, and it proved to be very popular and was well received by the majority of readers. It soon became apparent however, that some so called fans were posting negative comments, using nom de plumes and were therefore untraceable. From reading the GT Forum, I discovered there were other like-minded people in Lincoln and met up with Chris Hogarth and David Mayfield for chats at The Duke William Pub near Newport Arch. Both of them turned out to have had varied experiences in Track Racing, as Chris had at one time been the spanner man for multi-national Champion Brian Maxted, who also lived in Lincolnshire at Brant Broughton.

Dave on the other hand had been an official with The Navenby Club, but of late had been organising trips abroad to premier meetings on the Continent. These had been christened, by those who had been on them, as Shite Tours and Dave relished being Herr Organiser. I made friendships as well with two other people who were if anything more knowledgeable than I on the history of Grasstrack Racing. Carl Croucher from Maidstone had not only a fantastic memory of riders and meetings, but a vast collection of memorabilia to which he could refer. Noel Clark was a real character from near Kidderminster, and was so passionate about the sport that we both enjoyed, that he had opened a Museum with priceless Racing Bikes, Speedway Racing Bibs, Helmets, and Press Cuttings that were all filed away for reference.

My interest in listening to live music, be it Jazz, Blues, or a Musical, was never far away. I was delighted, and a little surprised, to learn of a new venue, The Sands, which had recently opened in Gainsborough. It was a conversion of the Old Town Hall in Lord Street, and I paid my first visit there in mid March, but regrettably it did not last long as a music venue.

I was beginning to get used to an alcohol free life style, and was going to more and more Jazz concerts and shows in Lincolnshire. The highlight of the Autumn Season at the Theatre Royal was a show called *The History of The Big Bands*. It starred Darius Campbell who had made a name for himself on Pop Idol, and featured a new band (to me) *The Barisons*. An added attraction was Nova Novelle from the USA, who performed Burlesque Dance Routines to many of the numbers in the show. As Nova was on her own in the UK, I naturally offered to show her the nightlife of Lincoln, but as it was a Sunday, there wasn't much to show her.

The next highlight was a very personal one when Rachel gave birth to her second child on 30th September. During her pregnancy I had teased her that if it were a boy he should be named Gregory, as his full name would then be Gregory Gregory. However in the end he was called Laurence Joseph or Laurie for short.

The year ended with my customary visit to spend Christmas in London, but as Maris was going to be staying with Rachel I was billeted out to stay with Becky at her flat nearby, as both her flatmates were away. I went to South London to stay with Julian and his family on Boxing Day before heading back to Lincoln to hear Great Tom usher in what would turn out to be a most memorable year in 2011, for all the right reasons for a change.

Act 10 Scene 3
THE LINCOLN LEGEND
(2011-12)

I should have had a premonition that 2011 would be a vintage year as The Cathedral's 'Great Tom' Bell announced its arrival to the assembled crowd of revellers in Castle Square. Number eleven is a lucky number for me, and was the number I used to race under years ago.

I was given an ideal opportunity to lose some weight early in the New Year when I joined The Shape Up & Slim Course at The David Lloyd Gym at Burton Waters. This was a scheme set up by The St. Barnabas Hospice to raise much-needed funds. I met the organiser Becky Otter on 3rd February, and discovered I was the only male who would be taking part, just like being back at Ballet School. We were weighed and photographed, and I was just under sixteen stones, which was far too heavy for me. My aim was to lose four stones and return to my best 'fighting weight' of 12 stones. At the end of the twelve weeks, thanks to a change in diet, and lots of hard dedicated work, I tipped the scales at just over 14 stones. I was half way there, and determined to continue at another Gym, as the annual fees to stay at David Lloyd's were prohibitive for a person on a limited income. I did a deal with Yarborough Leisure Centre, for a third of the price and continued to train there until early 2014.

The previous autumn Graham Gent, who knew of me from my articles and contributions to The Grass Track Forum, had contacted me. He was organising a riders' reunion on 19th March at The Sixhills Hotel, and asked me to help him. I had the time, agreed, and approached the project with the same professionalism I would have used on an event for MMA. Attention to detail and pre planning was vital to the success of the event, and I worked hard going on-site to discuss the hundred and one things that had to be agreed. I also got in touch with many of the riders in my contact book, who all pledged their support. The event was a huge success, and I was asked to organise one the next year, but was of the opinion that it should remain a one off.

I continued to follow Jazz avidly, writing reviews for many, and enjoyed listening to many new multi-talented artistes. I particularly liked the charismatic Nicola Farnon, a most talented and gifted vocalist and bass player, *The Rat Pack Tribute Show*, featuring songs made famous by Sinatra, 'Deano' and Mr. Sammy Davis. *Paula Baldwin's Big Swing Band*, with vocalists Gary Grace, Sara Blair Manning & Christine Scott, also became firm favourites.

Katy, my goddaughter, was selling Gertie, a small camper van. In mid March I went up to Barnard Castle where she was now living, to collect it, as I had agreed to buy it from her. I planned to use Gertie to sleep in when away from home. As it had a cooker, fridge, loo, sink and running water, I could be self-sufficient. During the Summer months that followed, I put it to good use, making several away trips to events and generally touring round the country visiting areas I had not been to before.

I continued to attend shows on a regular basis at Lincoln Theatre Royal, and support the venue where my career began 53 years ago, writing reviews of the shows I saw there. Ian Dickens was the new Chief Executive Officer and Artistic Director but sadly we had a falling out and Mr Dickens emailed me to say he did not wish me to come to the Theatre. His decision upset me greatly at the time, but I have observed his wishes for four years now, preferring to see shows at other local theatres, where I am made welcome.

The first long weekend away in Gertie occurred when I was invited to attend the wedding of Graham Phoenix at Ely on 3rd June. Graham was to marry Cheta in Ely Cathedral, for which he had recently designed the interior and exterior lighting. I parked up in a local caravan park close to the City Centre the night before and met up with the family at a pub. Being dry I was able to give Graham a lift back to his hotel, as he had enjoyed a good night. The day of the wedding was perfect and at the open-air reception following the service in the Cathedral, Pimms, Strawberries & Cream were the order of the day.

I was by now firmly established as a nightly regular at Yarborough Leisure Centre. I managed to knock myself out there on 9th June, when I slipped on the wet floor going into the sauna and steam room area. An emergency ambulance was called, as I lay motionless on the wet floor covered in a survival blanket. I was advised to go into hospital overnight, but I declined the offer as I still had memories of my last visit there. I knew that I would not be given any food before breakfast, and I hadn't eaten so far that day. As a precaution I rang Julian and left a message for him to phone me at 8am, and if I did not answer, to call the Police to break in. I did answer the call and asked on my return to Yarborough a few days later, for an entry to be made in their accident book, should I ever have any side effects from the incident.

It was a great shock to me, when I learnt about the sad passing of Cyril Ornadel on 22nd June, as we had remained close friends ever since working together at The Palladium. He had given me good advice, and advised me as any fellow Sagittarian would. We would remain 'ever the best of friends' which he would write on the birthday card he always sent me. RIP Cyril, you were the best Musical Director I ever worked with.

Since getting to know him better at The Riders Reunion, I had become close friends with Brian Maxted and his wife Sheila. As a 70th birthday 'surprise surprise' for him on 26th June I phoned the six times World Speedway Champion Ivan Mauger in New Zealand. Brian and Ivan had contested what many consider to be the best six lap final ever seen in the UK at The Lydden Speedtrack in Kent in September 1969, when they were both at the height of their careers. I asked Ivan to call Brian at home on the morning of his birthday, which he willingly agreed to do for a fellow rider. That evening when I proposed the toast "Happy Birthday number 37" (Brian's regular racing number) he told me that the phone call had made his day. Much as our respective lifestyles are as different as chalk and cheese, Brian and I are good friends, and respect what each other has achieved in life.

Brian Maxted at Lydden Speedtrack September 1969

I had heard so much about the reputation of Shite Tours, that when I was invited by *The East Midlands Mafia* to join them on a trip to Holland to see round five of the 2011 World Long Track Championships on 23rd July I could not resist the opportunity. There would be four of us in the party: 'Herr Organiser' Dave Mayfield, 'Official Photographer' Ken Smith, 'Driver Major Metcalf' and me. The plan was to fly from Liverpool to Amsterdam, pick up a hire car and drive north to Groningen where the meeting was to be held. I had arranged for us to meet up with Bennie Ludolphy, who lived in the town and whom I had contacted via The Grass Track Forum. The weekend turned out to be great fun, and full of incidents that began at John Lennon Airport, when I remembered that I had left my jacket where we had eaten our breakfast. I had to talk my way out of the Passport and Customs Hall to return and collect it. Incident number two came when the hire car turned out to be only a two-door and not a four-door, but 'Herr Organiser' soon sorted that out and we were on our way. Bennie met us at the hotel and showed us round the town, but I was the only one who tried the local delicacy of brined raw herrings from the market. We visited a local Motor Cycle Museum, which is not open to the public. We naturally took Bennie out for dinner that night, and following the meal the third incident of the trip happened. We had parked the hire car, courtesy of Bennie, in one of the University car parks, the entry and exit to which was controlled by a hydraulic bollard set into the road. Once the control button was pressed there was a time delay of a few seconds to permit the vehicle to pass over the bollard, before it rose up again. Now the Major was not used to the hire car yet, and managed to stall it as he drove over the bollard when "Bang" the pillar rose up and shattered the front spoiler. We waited to see the tell-tale signs of water which would indicate whether the radiator had been damaged, but thankfully it hadn't. In the mayhem that ensued, I somehow managed to get part of my foot caught under one of the wheels, but thankfully it wasn't broken. What an eventful first day in the Netherlands. Would we have any more incidents?

We got the answer the following morning when we arrived bright and early at the track to get a good spot to watch the racing from. I could not see over the safety fence very easily, and found an empty Pepsi crate to stand on. Unbeknown to me this crate was the pride and joy of a German who demanded it back in no uncertain terms. I took a white handkerchief out of my pocket and said "Peace In Our Time" as Mr. Chamberlain had said in 1938 to pacify my Germanic 'friend'. World War 3 was averted when he retired with his Pepsi crate.

By now I had given up hope of ever working again for anyone other than myself, and decided to enjoy the freedom that this new lifestyle presented. I could work as and when I wanted, doing what I wanted with my life. My reputation as a knowledgeable Track Racing Historian was further enhanced two days after my return from Holland when I was asked to write and read an eulogy to the rider Arthur Pell. Arthur was a boyhood idol of mine, and I was honoured to be asked by his daughter to speak at his funeral in the south of the county. As it was an early funeral, and not wanting to be late, I put Gertie to good use again as a mobile B & B. The eulogy was well received, and many came up to me afterwards at the wake to congratulate me.

Not wanting to miss any opportunity to get out and around the country in Gertie, I planned to make as much of August as I could. The GT Masters was to be held at The Astra Club's Swingfield venue, so I planned to make a weekend of it, meeting up with *The East Midlands Mafia*. I reserved a prime spot for us all to see some of the best racing for years with the sidecars being outstanding. This arrangement was also in place for The International Poacher over the August Bank Holiday weekend, before I set out on an extended tour of the Lincolnshire and North Norfolk Coasts.

My plan was to visit as many seaside shows as I could between Cleethorpes and Cromer, staying in camp sites along the way. I started with *Cannon and Ball* in Skegness, then moved on to the South Holland Centre, before going to Norfolk stopping at the King's Lynn Corn Exchange. I arrived in Hunstanton on the last day in August where Martyn Lucas was presenting his *One Night in Vegas* show. As parking Gertie overnight was a nightmare there, I waited until the parking restrictions finished and parked outside the stage door of the Princess Theatre where the show was on. It was a tight slick show, which I enjoyed, and I met the cast afterwards for a chat and a drink. I went back to Gertie after the show and had a huge fresh crab supper. The following day it was on to Sheringham to the intimate Little Theatre, before parking up for the night on a campsite in Cromer.

I had a soft spot for the Pavilion Theatre in Cromer as it was not only the last traditional Summer Show in the country still being produced, but it was the theatre I had visited when I was seeing Yvonne Lloyd in the '60s. It too was an excellent show and comedy ventriloquist Steve Hewlett used some most original material during the show. I felt very much at home in the venue and resort, and was saddened to leave the following day.

At the end of September, I went to a concert at Lincoln Drill Hall to hear a new big band, *The Good Guys Orchestra*, play their debut. The date is etched on my mind as 30th September 2011 as it was such a memorable concert. From the moment leader Guy Garrett stepped forward and said to an expectant audience: "Good evening Ladies and Gentlemen, Hello, Hello, we're going to Strike Up The Band", we all knew that this big band was something very special. The concert was recorded, and for the first time my review appeared on the sleeve of a CD. The band was so dynamic that I wrote that it was reminiscent of hearing *Stan Kenton's Wall of Sound* for the first time. Not only did this band play numbers by Cole Porter, The Gershwins, and Harold Arlem, but many of their musical arrangements were by the great Sammy Nestico and Lennie Niehaus. As if that were not enough the band also tackled numbers by Gordon Goodwin, which most professional bands won't touch because of their complexity. Goodwin's own *Big Phat Band* had made a name for itself on the West Coast of America, but numbers such as The Jazz Police, Count Bubba and Back Line Politics were new to many of the audience present that night. Many were used to hearing Louis Prima's tune *Sing Sing Sing* played in the style made famous by Gene Krupa with the Benny Goodman Orchestra in 1938, but were in raptures when Good Guys drummer, the dynamic Ade Gardner, took centre stage to play Goodwin's version, renamed *Sing Sang Sung*. Of course for all this to work, some fine soloists were required, and in Tony Giles, Daz Carter, Dave Taylor, Pete Storey and Dave Stansfield, they had pure quality in the saxophone section. The evening had been an outstanding success and remains one of my most memorable nights out for a long, long time.

A new influx of University Freshers hit Lincoln during September, and I was in town after my nightly workout and swim at the Gym, when it began to rain. I kept a cowboy style hat in the camper van for such eventualities, and was greeted by an attractive student sheltering under the House of Fraser canopy who shouted: "Nice hat. Can I try it on?" I naturally agreed and we introduced ourselves to each other. Her name was Robyn Smith, and she asked what I was doing in town that night. I told her and she said: "Why don't you join us?" The 'us' was three fellow students and I took them to a few of the clubs where I was known. We had a good laugh that night and they were fun. They lived uphill off Burton Road and as I was sober, which they found strange, I drove them all home in Gertie. At the end of the evening, by now the early hours, as I departed their flat, I was referred to as *The Hugh Hefner of Lincoln* which I took as a compliment. I thought 'If this can happen just because of wearing a cowboy hat, then I am going to continue to wear it.' and it became my trademark around the nightclubs of Lincoln.

The nightlife of the City was expanding and the old Conservative Club in Silver Street had undergone a major refurbishment to become Tokyo. As anywhere new in Lincoln was the place to be, I introduced myself to the General Manager Rob Halliday and was made most welcome whenever I went there. On one visit I met up with Alicia, who was a dance student at the Uni. She was very petite, and had a twin sister called Georgina, who was also a dance student, but not quite as wild as Alicia. We chatted in the exclusive VIP bar on the first floor, had a couple of drinks, danced a bit. She and her friends were fun and obviously liked to let their hair down and enjoy life, like me. I gave Alicia my card at the end of the evening, and we remained friends throughout the rest of her time in Lincoln. I gave her a lift home many times, as she trusted me, stopping en route for a take-away. On one occasion, after we had pulled up outside The Charcoal Grill, where I was known, I went inside and told them I had a 'Princess' outside in the car, who did not want to be recognised, so could they please bring the order out to her? This they agreed to and came out with the meal on a tray, with folded napkins etc. On another occasion after she had enjoyed a good night out at Superbull, she sent me a text message that simply said: 'Drunk and broke, please take me home Jayjay". As I was still in town, I was happy to help a friend out.

I had become known by my nickname of *JAYJAY*, rather than John, which I used for all my professional work. I soon began to go out every night of the week, which many of the students I was mixing with (there was/is no nightlife in Lincoln aimed at the over 25's), who thought that it was amazing and began calling me the *Legend of Lincoln*. "But how can you afford to go out every night?" was a frequently asked question. My reply was always the same: "By not drinking, or having to pay for a cab home." I replied truthfully. That was not to say that when out in a crowd, I would not pay when it was my round - quite the opposite. I am often accused of being too generous when buying drinks for friends.

A new weekly Jazz venture came to my attention in the Autumn of 2011, when I discovered Commuter Jazz for the first time. The idea was simple, and had been proved to be a winning formula in other cities. Based in The Zing Bar of the Lincoln Performing Arts Centre (LPAC) on The University Campus, small exciting Jazz bands were booked for a two-hour spot, between 5-7 pm on a Friday evening, to catch the commuter on the way home. It was run by Drummer Stevie Smith and ex Theatre Lighting Designer Graham McLusky. I soon became a regular there and over the years have seen some new bands and artistes that in normal circumstances I would not have seen or heard. I have been asked to compère the gig on several occasions, and although I found it difficult to start with, have been told that my style is informative, to the point and that I am a natural for such a role, and I enjoy doing it.

In keeping with my new look, achieved by a regular nightly work out, followed by a good swim and a session in the steam room and sauna, I began to go to The Tanning Shop in town to get that healthy look. I was by now feeling on top of the world and enjoying life like I hadn't done since before getting married and settling down. The staff at the Tanning Shop were super, and advised me how long a session my skin tone could take without any damage. I knew Becky quite well, as I had seen her when out clubbing, and she advised me to buy the special offer rate of a set number of minutes for a set price, which was a better deal than paying every time I went. After a few visits people began to ask if I had been on holiday, so it was obviously working.

During November, I was having a glass of water (my usual tipple, as I find 'fizzy drinks' are not only fattening but make me feel bloated after a few), when a girl I now know to be Sarah Raymond, said: "You look interesting (cowboy hat again) sit down and join us." It transpired that she was a final year student studying photography, but told me she had no idea what to do for her end of year project. As the evening progressed we discussed various options, and as I was 'interesting' and quite at ease with a camera being pointed at me, I agreed to be her 'end of year project' and to help her as much as I could, over the next few months. Photo sessions were planned and soon a theme began to develop that would ultimately lead to her gaining a First Class Honours Degree when she left Lincoln in 2012 to start her career in London. We remain good friends to this day.

The major event in Lincoln that November was the opening of HOME on 11th November (11.11.11) - my lucky number three times. A small fortune had been spent converting what had been the Navy, Army, Airforce Institute building in Park Street into a venue that would be open all day, serving food, and at night become a club on six levels with different music at each level. The décor was the best in Lincoln I discovered, when Promotions Manager Mark Smith showed my guest and me round on the opening night. I had been looking forward to a club of this quality opening in Lincoln for ages. It was well run, with standards as high as any club I had attended in London.

I was soon given a VIP card that gave me fast track entry and permitted me to take my guests into the VIP bar, where it was possible to chat without having to shout over the music. At weekends the strictly enforced dress code was Dress To Impress which again made a visit there special. I gave the new club a glowing review following my first visit. I took many of my theatrical friends there when they were playing the City, and it became my home from home for five nights a week and my venue of choice.

Life was good. I was meeting lots of new friends on my nights out at HOME, where I went for a night of dancing, and also at Jazz events in other local towns.

On Saturday 3rd December *Paula Baldwin's Big Swing Band* played a gig at The Cocked Hat Hotel in Scunthorpe with a full Christmas dinner provided in the inclusive price. During the evening their new Musical Director, retired Major Paul Murrell, came over to me at my table and introduced me to the other diners. Following some banter about me being there to review the concert, he handed me the words to *Chattanooga Choo Choo*, the 1941 song composed by Harry Warren and immortalised by Glenn Miller in the film *Sun Valley Serenade*. I was led forward to front the band and sing a song I had heard many times before. It was all in good fun and added to the Christmas spirit of the evening, which was superb value for money.

The next opportunity I had to hear the Big Band that had knocked me off my feet at the Drill Hall in September, *The Good Guys*, was when they were playing at Melton Mowbray on my birthday. This time, in addition to vocals by Guy Garrett, Cherie Gears was making her debut singing with a big Jazz Band. I took Art Walker along as my birthday guest because I knew he would enjoy hearing the band and this would be a rare evening out for him. The surprise highlight was when the band played Happy Birthday for me, but in the style of Gordon Goodwin.

On my return from Christmas with the family in London, I was delighted to find that the new Double Tree by Hilton Hotel on the Brayford was to open on 30th December. It would prove to be a great asset to Lincoln's growing reputation, and would become a venue I used frequently. There was a Fancy Dress theme to the New Year's Eve event at HOME and I hired a *Phantom of the Opera* costume from 1 2 1 Disguises in Waddington for the occasion. My date for the evening was CJ, a hairdresser that I had met, but somehow during the evening we were separated. Around 2am I got a phone call from her to say she was drunk and money-less in a doorway in Silver Street and could I please come and find her and drive her home? I left the celebrations, found her, and took her home, but that was my last date with her.

2012 continued in the same great way as 2011, with me having lots of fun, making new friends whenever I went out and burning the candle not only at both ends but in the middle. I got to know many dancers at clubs, and made friendships with those who could hold a decent conversation like Chelsea, Natalie, Jenny, Candy and Charlie. I was also a regular at Sukura, Walkabout, Trebles, Jumping Jacks, Dogma and Kind Bar, but they did not compare to the ambiance of HOME for a good night out with other nice people.

On 16th February I had my own life story published in The Lincolnshire Echo under the by-line *In his own Words – John Toogood*. Thereafter I became a freelance reviewer of Jazz, Plays, Concerts, Events and the Nightlife of Lincoln, with a regular column, which I still enjoy writing. I was also interviewed on Radio Lincolnshire to talk about my 50 years in show business, which was broadcast on a Sunday afternoon.

My fourth grandchild Auraya was born to Julian and Lindsay on 24th February, much to my delight. Following the success of the Buble & Friends Champagne & Canapés evening on 21st December, in early March HOME began to present monthly Comedy Nights. I attended the first one and invited Sarah along as my guest for the evening.

In May I was invited to give my second talk to The Lincoln Ladies Theatre Lunch Club at The Green Room Club, which went very well with an unexpected fee to boot. I felt I was not getting as much use and fun out of Gertie now, despite an amusing incident that happened one night in town. I had been out to a black tie event at the Epic Centre and had driven into town to go out clubbin'. I had parked in Silver Street, when I was spotted by a number of student clubbers I knew. They all wanted to have their photo taken in the back of Gertie and as it was harmless fun, I did not object. Now I am not sure if someone who was jealous of the attention Gertie was attracting told the Police, or if it was just coincidence that a passing WPC stopped to find out what was going on. I explained, and she said: "But there are beds in the back" to which I reminded her that it was a camper van with built in beds as standard. "I'm going to breathalyse you" She told me, but being on foot patrol she didn't have a test kit with her. I offered to drive her to the Police Station in West Parade to take the test there, but was told that wasn't permitted. We got to chat to each other until a patrol car arrived with the test kit, and left as friends when the test came up negative.

Deciding to sell Gertie was difficult, as she had served me well, but one evening when driving home down Dixon Street, I saw a yellow MG ZR for sale which looked quite snazzy. I thought it would be more than I could afford, but did a deal and bought her for a good price, as an investment. I christened her Yvonne after one of my first girlfriends. When some of my clubbing friends saw me in Yvonne and not Gertie, they gave me a sticker to put on the windscreen which proclaimed *Jayjay - The Legend*.

Most weekends there would be a regular crowd of us at HOME, and although I frequently arrived there on my own, there was always someone I knew to dance with for most of the night. I could always spot another trained dancer and soon got to know Lizzie, Taryn and Chloe who knew how to enjoy themselves, were good company, attractive, and became good friends, who respected and trusted me.

Having enjoyed my trip abroad with Shite Tours so much the previous year, when the opportunity arose to join them and go behind the iron curtain to Tetrow in East Germany, I jumped at the chance. The track there is unique, with both left and right hand corners, gradients and jumps for good measure. I had read about the venue, and had wanted to visit at least once in my life, before the circuit closed. It was to be the same gang of four going again. If we were to have as much fun on this trip as we had in Holland, then it would be another memorable event in my life. The plan was to fly from East Midlands to Berlin on 25th May, pick up a hire car again, drive north through Germany, stay in a local B & B for two nights, and return on Monday 28th May.

The incidents this time were few. One was my having a wardrobe malfunction with my shorts, and another trying to pick up a pretty girl when we went to the local speedway on the Saturday night, which was difficult as I could only communicate with gestures.

The new Hilton Hotel soon became a regular haunt, especially on Saturday nights when many clubbers called in there for cocktails before going into town. The bar staff soon knew my usual order of a Chateau de Brayford served in a Champagne flute with a slice of lemon, and a Martini for the lady please. It was a delightful venue to start the evening off. Being a regular I was invited by The Food and Beverages Manager to a Gala Evening on 22nd June, and had a delicious dinner, before dancing until the early hours to a very good soul band from Manchester. At about 2am the lead singer asked for a round of applause for the guy in the hat (me) as I had been dancing to all their numbers, for an hour and a half.

As part of the celebrations for the Olympics that summer, I volunteered to be part of a dance ensemble that would follow the Olympic torch as it made its way through the streets of Lincoln. I went to register at the Urban Dance Studios in Clifton Street, to find out details of what we were going to wear, contingency plans in the event of inclement weather, and a schedule of rehearsals, which I expected them to know about. This was all basic information, which had I been organising the celebrations, I would have known. However they didn't and from what I soon gathered, no one was in charge of the overall concept, and I thought about quitting. I then found out that Stagecoach, for whom my dance friend Lizzie worked, was involved as well, which changed my mind.

The torch arrived in Lincoln on 27th June. It was a hot sunny Summer day, and we all met up at the University, only to be bussed the few hundred yards to Morrison's car park where we waited to join the parade. We were then fitted with costumes, which were badly made, and given huge headdresses to wear, which we had never seen or rehearsed in before and were ultra difficult to control. Dehydration became an issue for many of us, and when eventually we did move off, the

JT & Britt dinner at The Hilton 2012

music was inaudible and inevitably the rehearsed dance was forgotten, in favour of "Just do what you want." The people lining the route around the Brayford appeared to like what they saw, and I was recognised by many people, but in my professional opinion it was a disorganised disaster from start to finish.

I met Britt early in June who was over here from Canada and visiting the UK for a while. She was most attractive and we arranged to go for dinner at the Hilton on 10th June. She then told me she didn't have anything suitable to wear for such an occasion. I agreed to buy her a dress, and we went out to shop arm in arm, which caused a few raised eyebrows. Then of course there was underwear, and shoes to match. She borrowed jewellery from the friend she was staying with in Gresham Street, and looked stunning when I picked her up in the MG.

We had our photographs taken whilst eating, but at the end of the night, when I added up what the date had cost me, I questioned my sanity. But I had enjoyed the evening, and as I was beginning to realize, as more and more friends died, life is for living, and we are only here the once.

As a freelance Jazz critic I was regularly invited to go and see new bands perform in the area. Even when I was critical, as I can't be expected to like everything, I tried to be polite and constructive with my comments. The concert on 29th June was to be performed at the New Life Christian Centre in Newland and feature a new band I had not come across previously, *Jazz Vehicle*. That concert was quite outstanding, and was the most exciting and exhilarating evening of Big Band Jazz I had experienced for a very long time. All 30 or so members were still at school, and the sound they produced was unforgettable. I was full of admiration for the quality of musicianship in the band and for its Musical Director John Crouch. They played numbers and arrangements that many professional bands won't touch because of their complexity, and they even had the audacity to play the notoriously challenging Back Line Politics by Gordon Goodwin. As I left the concert that night I felt the future of Big Band music, which I loved, was safe in the hands of these most talented youngsters, and have continued to support them as often as I can, since that unforgettable night.

Earlier in the year I had been invited to cousin Steve's big 60th birthday in Greece. I made an executive decision not just to go to the Island of Aegina for the event itself on 29th August, but to go away for 35 days and escape the Olympics. As a prelude to this, and following a chat one night with Jenny, one of the staff at the Hilton, I made an appointment to see a clairvoyant called Michelle whom Jenny had visited a few days before. Michelle had told Jenny things about her past life that only she knew, and also told her what she might expect to happen in the future. I had never been a believer in such things, but I thought it was worth a try. Michelle was accurate with what she told me about my past life, and told me that there was a blonde lady with a black dog hovering over my shoulder. What was that all about, I wondered?

I left Lincoln on 1st August to go to London, before flying to Athens, and would not sleep in my own bed again until 4th September. It turned out to be my best holiday since my trip to Spain with Beatles Manager Alun Williams in the late sixties, when I made so many friends and had such a laugh. A typical day would consist of getting up and walking to the open-air swimming pool by 11am, where I would swim and sunbathe until the sun went down behind the mountains. Then a walk to the beach, meet up with friends at one of the many beach bars, home to shower and then go out to eat at one of the nice restaurants in the main street or down by the harbour. At the Akrogiali Beach Bar Restaurant there was Jazz, or Karaoke at another bar or on some nights a party back at the pool. The company was fantastic, the fish fresh and seafood delicious, the weather hot and sunny. Life was idyllic, but where was the blonde with the dog on my shoulder?

I was socialising in one of the bars in the main street one night when I spotted an attractive girl I now know to be Zara sitting alone with a bottle of lager on a bar stool. We chatted, and she told me, in broken English, that she lived in Athens and was working on the island during the Summer as it was too claustrophobic and hot at home. She was most attractive with a nice tan, good company, and dressed well, so I invited her to join me for dinner the next night, which she accepted. I chose a nice restaurant, where I knew we would be well looked after, and during the meal I asked her if she had any pets? "Yes a dog" she replied. "It's black isn't it?" I suggested. "You have been speaking to my friends, haven't you?" was the reply. "No" I said to her, "I have been expecting to meet you since I came to Greece." Which was the truth. I had discovered the blonde with the dog, which Michelle had predicted. How weird is that?

JT & Zara on holiday in Aegina 2012

We shared many happy hours together before the holiday ended, and she invited me to visit her in Athens, but I just wanted to keep it as a holiday fling.

Before going to Greece I had agreed to take part in the next fund raising event for St. Barnabas Hospice, and this time it was to be a Strictly Ballroom competition. The dances selected were The Jive and The Tango, with lessons every Sunday as soon as I returned from holiday, up to the big night on 11th November. I had been doing my version of The Jive for years, but the Tango was new to me. I asked Sue Jones, who I had known since chatting her up during my dinner breaks at the Lincoln School, to be my partner, as we had jived together at Grafton House in the past and we knew each other's moves. Getting friends and family to pledge amounts for the fundraising was easy compared to learning the Tango from scratch. I soon discovered that Sue picked up the intricate foot and head movements far quicker than I did, and at times I struggled. She was very patient with me and we felt confident we could get a good score in the Jive, dancing to *In The Mood*, and would be happy with a "Seven" (as Len Goodman would say) in the Tango. I hired a Zoot Suit from the same Costumiers in Waddington I had used for the Phantom costume on New Year's Eve and looked the part. Sue made her own costumes and we began confidently, with the Tango being the first dance. However the scores we received were not as high as we hoped they would be, and as one couple, the reigning Champions, scored a maximum, we stood no chance of winning, so we just went for it in the jive, which was well received by the fans. We had both had a good time, and raised much needed funds for a worthy Charity.

After visiting my dentist in late September, she prescribed some Penicillin for me as she had found a small abscess in my mouth. Over the following weekend my legs began to swell and became itchy, growing to balloon size. I took myself to the new Walk In Clinic in Monks Road, where they said: "Hospital for you, you have had an allergic reaction to something." I was kept in for a week, whilst they did tests to establish the cause. I had never had a problem with Penicillin in the past, but that was what they discovered was the root cause of the inflammation. It had manifested itself late in life and I was unaware of the reaction that it would cause. This latest hospital stay prevented my attending a *Good Guys* concert at the Embassy Theatre in Skegness on Sunday 7th October, but hearing Nestico's fine arrangement of *Strike Up The Band* played on the radio lifted my spirits no end.

For my birthday I invited friends to join me for drinks in the VIP bar at HOME. Kim got rather the worse for wear on red wine, whilst I had a great time dancing most of the night with many of my girlfriends. New Year's Eve was again a Dress to Impress Hollywood Oscars night at HOME, which ended a good 2012.

Act 10 Scene 4
IDENTITY FRAUD
(2013)

The last two years had been two of the best in my life. Unbeknown to me that was about to come crashing down around me because I had become a victim of Identity Fraud, and what was worse, I found it had been going on for almost a year.

I have never been a keen fan of Facebook, Twitter and the other social networking sites, but had been persuaded one night to join them by a couple of girlfriends, who said it was the way forward. One of them had set them up for me, as I had no idea how to go about it. Soon afterwards, I later discovered, someone had set up a Facebook account, stalked me, and taken photographs of Yvonne when parked in a supermarket car park. They had stolen my identity using the mug shot photo that is printed every week with my column in The Echo.

With the help of friends, whom I trusted, I traced the first fraudulent posting back to 17th February 2012, and as I had not responded to these postings, Facebook readers believed they were from me and the contents true. I noted that they got more brazen as time progressed, with one posting which read "Just won £500 on the Grand National" when it is well known to those who know me that I never bet. Others read "I won't be out tonight lads, put my back out last night dancing." All were false and malicious from someone who obviously knew my lifestyle, and I suspect was jealous of the fun that I was having, and the many girlfriends I had got to know. Things came to a head on the night of Saturday 9th March when the Manager of a well known club in the city took me to one side. He showed me a Facebook posting on his mobile that claimed I was the owner of his club and had invited readers to come as my guest. Naturally they, like me, did not find it amusing, and I was refused entry to the club for a period of two months, 'to let the negativity go away' and the perpetrator(s) to be traced.

These inappropriate, misleading and false postings on Facebook naturally caused me much distress. They had created a totally wrong and inaccurate impression of me that people who did not know me believed to be true. I contacted the Police at the first opportunity on Monday 11th, and was given a case reference number. The following day I was interviewed by Police at home and wrote to the club to apologise for the distress and upset that this incident, albeit not of my doing, had caused.

The Identity Fraud was now in the hands of the authorities who set about tracking down the person(s) concerned via details that were unknown to me on the Facebook page. On 4th May I was advised to close the false account forthwith, as postings were still apparently being made. For someone like me, with only a limited knowledge of the workings of these social networking sites, this was another nightmare. All I wanted to do was ring someone, tell them what had happened, and get this false account deleted as soon as possible, but I couldn't find a number to call.

The repercussions of my Persona non Grata status in the City were far-reaching and unexpected. Some Management and their door staff at other establishments had obviously read the malicious Facebook postings and assumed, wrongly, that they were genuine and posted by me. Chinese whispers and gossip were soon rife about me. I knew I did not have any skeletons in the cupboard, and female friends, who actually knew and trusted me, such as Sarah, Lizzie, Charlie, Hannah, Helen, Taryn, Alicia and Chloe, were prepared to come forward and say so.

People found it hard to comprehend that unwittingly I had gained a reputation as a charismatic character around Lincoln and had a circle of friends and acquaintances in the age group 20-50. By socialising with these people, I was dancing all night, keeping fit, was young at heart and active. I knew that if I sat at home watching television or doing a crossword, as many in my age group did, I would probably be in a box within a month. I had no intention of that happening.

Despite these setbacks, life went on. I began a new venture as a Jazz and Club Promoter, and worked hard with the club and restaurant owners who knew the real me. I began to represent *Andrew Hall and his Memories of New Orleans*, a band I liked to listen to, and were good value for money. I negotiated a residency at the new Strait & Narrow Bar with co-owner Olly Davis, and at The Lincolnshire Red Steakhouse in Newland, with owners Chris Regan and Mark Cumming.

I teamed up with a DJ friend Ian Anderson to co-promote an over 25's Singles Night on a Sunday, along the same lines as the International Club which we both remembered as being such a success. The venture failed, however, as the venue, in a club close to The Brayford, and the night, were both wrong. We were forced to abandon the idea after a few months anyway, when the venue suddenly went bankrupt.

For years I had wanted to go and see the show at The Crazy Horse in Paris, as I had met some of the beautiful dancers who had worked there when working for Paul Raymond, but the opportunity had never come my way. This all changed however, when *Forever Crazy* came to England, and was presented in a purpose built temporary structure on the South Bank in London. One of the attractions about the show, in addition to the stunning dance numbers by identical looking dancers wearing identical bob cut wigs, was the imaginative use of projections. The idea of presenting the show away from its home in Paris would only work if the exact stage size were recreated for the pre-programmed projections to be shown. As there wasn't a venue in the UK that met these criteria, one was built. As an added attraction, for those who were unaware of the show outside Paris, ex model Kelly Brook was booked as a special guest artiste. The Belgian Tent, made by Spiegler, was an ideal venue for this spectacular show, which was not at all sleazy, and had attracted as many females as males on the night I went. I wore my tuxedo and made myself known to the Maitre d' on arrival. He showed me to a front row table, from where I had an unrestricted view of the show, which was even better than I had imagined, and showed why Le Crazy Horse has such a worldwide reputation for quality. I met some of the girls post-show and they were all utterly charming. It was such a great night out that when my friend Lindsey asked me to recommend a show for her and a girlfriend to see when they were in London, I suggested *Forever Crazy*. That was the show they went to see and on their return they told me they had enjoyed it.

Kay Darbyshire, who had been such a driving force for over sixty years, both with CAODS, and Lincoln Theatre Association, died in January and I went to pay her my last respects on 12th February at The Lincoln Crematorium. Many of us there that day had no doubt whatsoever that without her tireless work over the years The Lincoln Theatre Royal would no longer exist.

The next fundraising event I supported for St. Barnabas Hospice, was a Take Me Out evening based on the popular television show of the same name. I shot a pre-recorded video with voice over, which formed part of my spot in the show, and planned to come on to the Sam & Dave tune *Soul Man* with chocolates for each of the twenty or so girls I was attempting to impress. This went down well and I was through to the next round, which was pre-recorded. This also went well and I was into the final section. Selecting a tune I thought was most appropriate, Michael Buble's *Haven't Met You Yet*, my intention was to bring the girls that had most caught my eye forward and dance with them one at a time. However this all went wrong because of the way the stage had been set up. I could only dance with the two girls either side of the opening, and was popped off by the girls, who I had failed to impress, one by one.

Dr. Spencer was again delighted with the fact that it had now been 1825 days since I had consumed an alcoholic beverage when I went to see him for my fifth annual MOT on 15th March. At the same time a new lady Danni came into my life. She was older and more mature than many of my other female friends, and was great company.

In the Spring, as a result of my slightly curtailed visits to some of the clubs, some of whom had come up with unsubstantiated reasons for refusing me entry, such as 'taking photographs without the Managers permission', and 'you're a bad insurance risk,' I looked elsewhere for company. I met Lorna, who was also more mature than many of my other female friends, and I would see her on a regular basis. We would chat for hours, as she found me interesting with my many anecdotes, and we had a good time together.

I pledged my support to help Jazz et Vin in May, run by Peter and Ann Duncan, in Newark, as there were always interesting artistes to hear during their annual festival in a converted bus garage in Castlegate. The lineup was as varied as ever, and I especially liked Dave O'Higgins, TJ Johnson and the utterly charming and talented Nicola Farnon.

Earlier in the year, nominations had been requested for the National Stage Management Awards. I put Art Walker forward for consideration in The *Outstanding Lifetime Contribution* category. Art had now retired after an illustrious career that had spanned 55 years as Stage Manager at *Lincoln Theatre Royal*. He was well respected in the business by fellow technicians and performers, and had helped to train many youngsters who were forever grateful for his kindness in giving them that vital first big break. The nomination was accepted, and we were both invited to The Awards Ceremony on 12th June, at The Old Truman Brewery in the East End. Louise Dancy from The Salisbury Playhouse had also been nominated for the prestigious Golden Headset Award.

I asked Graham McLusky to join us at Newark, on the only direct train from Lincoln to London, and we all arrived in plenty of time at The ABTT Show, where the Stage Management Awards were to be presented. The award for *Outstanding Lifetime Contribution* was the last to be presented and Art won. His acceptance speech was delivered in a gracious, humourous way that had the assembled audience in stitches, and was dotted with many anecdotes that broke down any perceived barriers between the modern Stage Manager and his predecessors. The whole event had been a huge success from start to finish, and Art was as proud as punch on the train journey back home to Lincoln.

It was up to Durham Dales for the weekend of 21st July to visit the historic market town of Barnard Castle where my Goddaughter Katy was having a reception to celebrate her marriage to Elliot Smith. She had asked me to be the Master of Ceremonies for the event. I was naturally very thrilled and delighted to be asked to undertake the role, as Katy and I have always been very close. The formal wedding ceremony had taken place earlier in the year and was a very private affair, but this reception was planned to be a joyous occasion with family and friends. We took over a hotel close to The Wine Bar, where the reception was to be held. On the Saturday night, after dinner, I thought it my duty to visit the venue and make myself known to the landlord and his staff. They were most welcoming and I found it hard to imagine how my sister planned to transform the garden into an attractive reception area. I knew that Katy's garage was full to overflowing with white flowerpots and bunches of flowers, because I had seen them, but that was all I knew. The Wine Bar is Barnard Castle's late night club but did not fill up until about 1.30am, and closed at 4am. The staff planned to clear up once the revellers had gone home, so that we could move in and transform the place as Sue had planned, from first thing after breakfast on the Sunday morning.

When Sue had finished, the Reception area looked like something you would see in an upmarket magazine. It looked sensational, and was a perfect setting for the speeches that started the day. We had trouble getting the trailer with the pig roast down the narrow passageway from the street, and Brian had to remove the trailer wheels to enable this to happen. As Elliot is a Music Teacher and plays in a local band we naturally had a live band to die for, which was augmented when my son-in-law Sean joined them on piano for part of the set.

The event was a huge success, and I was asked by two separate people if I would act as MC for their forthcoming events. They were astounded and very complimentary when I told them that I didn't MC for a living, but had been honoured to do it for Katy and Elliot.

My continued Persona non Grata status at some of the nightspots led me to change the way I went out to enjoy myself. People I met for the first time asked me why I was not out in a big gang like they were. I explained that because of my work and pastimes, I was quite happy to come into town on my own, as I would always meet up with someone I knew. I could do what I wanted, and when, without having to discuss it with loads of others, who invariably wanted to do their own thing anyway. I had always been quite happy with my own company, and as my charismatic personality developed, I had become somewhat of a Lincoln celebrity who people wanted to have their photo taken with, and to dance with at clubs and late night bars. I was told by many that I am as well known in Lincoln now as the Cathedral.

When Moka & Shack clubs opened on 13th August, after major refurbishment and alterations, I went there, was made most welcome by the management, and felt that a review was in order. My weekly column in The Lincolnshire Echo was well received by those who read it every Thursday. I had always included the nightlife of Lincoln in an honest and open way, in addition to my coverage of Jazz and other live shows, and this was a golden opportunity to help spread the word that there was a new kid on the block.

A further opportunity to report on Lincoln's ever-expanding nightlife came when The Cotton Club held its second evening at The Collection Gallery on Friday 6th September. The idea of a glam evening was conceived by Nick Peel from Stokes Café who had the concession to run the onsite café bar. His quite original idea was to have an inclusive evening of entertainment starting with a glass of sparkling wine on arrival before having an hours' Lindy Hop dance tuition with professional dancers. This was followed by a most acceptable two course supper before listening to a Jazz Band play music from the era of the original Cotton Club. Karl Hird, who I knew from his days playing saxophone and clarinet with Andrew Hall, led the band, and the whole evening was a huge success. This was in no small part due to the most informative introductions and background information given to us by trombonist Michael Pointon, whose company and banter was a delight to share. I felt then, and still do, that events of this nature should be encouraged and supported in our City, as many people are fed up with listening to the same old music at other establishments, night after night.

I continued to see Lorna and Danni as often as I could during the Autumn. On the Jazz front a sensational new singer came onto the radar. I had first seen and heard Shannon Reilly sing in the Café Bar at The Drill Hall during Lincoln Jazz week and thought, like many other aficionados, that she was just sensational. This is a much-used word by the pundits on the numerous TV talent shows, but in her case was spot on. Accompanied by one of England's most talented guitarists, Pat McCarthy and ace Bassist Warren Jolly, they made a formidable trio, and I still go to see as many of their local gigs as I can.

As long as I had been a fan of the Golden Era of Steam, and Sir Nigel Gresley's magnificent A4 locomotives in particular, which used to run up and down the East Coast main line when I was a 'Spotter' in the late '50s, I had wanted to go on to the footplate of one of these leviathans. A once in a lifetime opportunity presented itself when all six of the still running and preserved members of the Class came together for The Great Gathering.

The event was to celebrate the 75th anniversary of the world steam speed record, which had been achieved by Mallard at Stoke Bank, near Grantham, on 3rd July 1938. Kevin Gillingham, a friend of Art Walker, arranged a lads outing to the National Railway Museum in York on 7th November to see the Gathering. This was a dream come true for me, as not only did I get the opportunity to climb on to the footplate of (using BR numbers as I fondly remembered them) 60007 Sir Nigel Gresley, but 60008 Dwight D. Eisenhower, 60009 Union of South Africa, 60010 Dominion of Canada, 60019 Bittern, and 60022 Mallard. Two of the locos had been brought over to this country for the anniversary, and given paint jobs. Three were shown in their original LNER Garter Blue, two in BR Brunswick Green, and Sir Nigel in the BR Dark Blue livery of the period 1950-52. This was without a doubt a day to remember, and is up there to treasure and remember with my most happy moments.

After the success of the last Grass Track Riders Reunion Evening, I was approached by Trevor Diggle to help organise a similar event on 23rd November at Woody's Bar near Ancaster. I again set about the organisation with the same professionalism that I had done previously, to help make it a success. I met up with the owner of the bar Malc Corradine, who was an ex-rider himself. He was most helpful and did a special deal for Trevor. Using the good points from the last time, and forgetting the bad points, we all hoped that it would be another night to remember. At Sixhills, Paul Hurry had been the Guest of Honour, and for this event we asked a rider who was fondly known as *The Welsh Wizard*. I had first seen Cyril Jones, whose usual racing number was 79, race at The Lydden Speedtrack in the late sixties, but he had suffered a nasty fall of late and was now in a wheelchair. Cyril was a real character in the sport, and was renowned for being the lead singer and front man with his band *The Turnip Tops*. We decided to ask him to perform a song or two for us that night, which wasn't hard to do, and we had also booked another wheelchair bound rider to perform the cabaret spot.

Graham Miles, who had the nickname *The Red Devil*, was also by coincidence wheelchair bound, following a racing accident at Hackney Speedway. He had courageously re-invented himself as a Comic. He had performed at many events similar to ours in the Kent area where he was based, but Lincolnshire and the crowd there that night were not quite ready for his style of humour. After a lukewarm reception to his early gags, he wisely cut the rest of his act before anyone was offended too much. Following the cabaret spot there was dancing to a local DJ, but the only partners I could find to dance with me were the female carers and nurses who were there to look after Cyril, and we danced together for the rest of the night.

I had by now developed a stand up spot myself, based on observational humour, and began performing at clubs in the City. I based the act on what I had learnt from the numerous comics I had seen work over the years. Whoever said that being a solo stand up comedian is the loneliest job in the world is right. On some occasions the act went down well but on others it was a disaster and the audience was at a loss to know what I was on about. One of the best-received spots I performed was based on a fictitious letter I had allegedly received from Gordon Brown. It outlined a policy that was to be introduced to Retire Aged People Early. Another spot I enjoyed presenting was based on the morning roll call at a public school for the sons of gentlemen. In it I used the most bizarre names I could think of, such as Rancid, Elgar Major, Elgar Minor, Flatulence and others, covering most letters of the alphabet. The more outrageous they were the better as they got the bigger laugh that just saying a word out of context got. Those who remembered having their names read out at school could relate to it. Mike the organiser liked what he saw. He also ran a successful night on Tuesday at a city centre club, which I enjoyed attending, door staff permitting.

As December approached, I realised that the 17th, my birthday, fell on a Tuesday. I asked him and the Club Management about pre-ordering drinks and having one of the VIP booths reserved for my personal use, which was agreed. Mike then told me that the theme for the evening would be Jayjay's Birthday, and my mug shot appeared on all the flyers and publicity for the night. The bar did quite well out of it as well, because my tab in the end was over £60, but I and my many friends had a night to remember.

Whilst I was in London for Christmas I informed the family that from 1st January 2014, I would be taking six months out to write the book that people had pestered me to write for such a long time. That was good bye, thank goodness, to 2013.

ENCORE

Here we are then, six months down the line and at the end of June 2014. I have managed (just) to keep to the schedule I set myself. It has been hard work, and I am thankful that since 1970 I have saved all of my wall chart diaries, and have been able to refer back to what happened on a certain day in a certain year. Don't ask me why I have moved them from flat to flat and house to house over the years, but they have proved invaluable as an aide memoire for this book.

There have been a few highlights in the past six months, and my social activities have naturally had to change whilst I have had my nose to the grindstone working often until 6am from home. I have still managed go to a few concerts and shows, but have had to be more selective than before in what I see and review for my weekly column in the Echo. That has been frustrating because I like to show my support for the many talented musicians and artistes that come to Lincoln and the surrounding area.

On the music front, I have continued to support Nicola Farnon, *The Good Guys Orchestra*, and *Paula Baldwin's Big Swing Band*, as well as the much-improved *Sounds Easy Band*, and *The Monsonaires*, at their bi-monthly gigs at the Grafton House Ballroom. Two new female singers I have recently heard and liked are Jenny Smith and Julie Edwards. I have also become friends with Chris Saunders, the legendary Bass & Piano Player.

My continued status with some of the clubs in the City has still not been resolved to my satisfaction, but a more permanent change of lifestyle may be on the horizon. I say this after I met Lilly Rose on Saturday 8th March and since then we have become close friends. I think another visit to see the lady who predicted I would meet a blonde with a dog before I went to Greece is called for.

For the first four months I religiously set my stall out to write a minimum of two pages a day, and kept on target. I took a weekend off in late April to meet up with The East Midlands Mafia members of Shite Tours for a weekend in Kent. It was nice to meet up with the lads again. While there I managed to find time to check out the nightlife of Folkestone, which was a good night of fun and frolics. I met many new friends who were not accustomed to *The Legend of Lincoln*.

I can trace the discipline, which has been the cornerstone throughout my career, back to the dance training I received at *The Christine Orange School of Dance*. It has also helped my social life. If I say that I am going to do something for a friend, I will do it to the best of my ability come what may. As a result of my willingness to help friends this has, I am told, made me an easy touch, but that's me.

When I am taking a lady out, I am still old-fashioned enough to open doors, buy the meal and most of the drinks, even though I still abstain myself, and usually provide a taxi service, to and from her home. I know that some acquaintances take advantage of me, but if they eventually become a true friend whom I can rely on, then I feel that it has been worthwhile.

Three other people in the business have made the greatest impression on me, and helped me shape the way that I work and live. They are Chris Bullock, Cyril Ornadel, and John Avery. When I went to spend six happy years at The Liverpool Playhouse, I was so damn lucky to have Chris as my Production Manager, because he had such high standards and principles. He taught me the importance of pre-planning for a production weekend Fit Up, which was to become the hallmark of my future success. I soon realised that an hour spent on pre-planning and preparation was worth three hours on the Fit Up.

Cyril was the most competent Musical Director I ever worked with, and we became life-long friends for over thirty years. He taught me how to deal with difficult stars, to get on with the job with charm, and understanding. If you work with someone who is on the way up you will inevitably meet them later in your career, when they are on the way down.

John ran The London Palladium like a Cunard Liner ploughing its way across the Atlantic. I had vowed that if I ever had the opportunity to be General Manager of a West End Theatre, I would run it as efficiently as he ran The Palladium. Always immaculately dressed and with as much time for the humble cleaner, American super-star or member of Royalty, I realised that although The General Manager sets the standard and is the figurehead, it is teamwork that makes it all happen.

I found it is important to delegate, because as hard as one tried, you are only human and can't be everywhere, doing everything, every day. I recall a visit to my office once by Jeffrey Campbell, who expressed surprise that my office desk was not overflowing with paperwork. "How do you do it John?" he asked. "By delegating, but retaining an overall view of things, like a bird flying high in the sky" I replied.

I am often asked if I have a favourite show, artiste, song or band. The answer is: "Yes, several." *The King and I* ranks highly, partly because of the local fame and reputation that I attracted when I played the King's son and heir to the throne in Lincoln, and then was the Production Manager for the show at The Palladium. As a Christmas show, *Peter Pan* has to be up there, as I worked on four different productions over the years. But as someone who was not a big fan of his to start with, the work of Stephen Sondheim, and the show *Follies* has to be an all-time favourite.

It would be churlish to pick one individual out and name them as my favourite, but John Inman was not only very talented, and a great professional, but also a friend. Lulu was a dream to work with, and how lucky was I to be Company Manager for Rowan Atkinson in 1981, before he became the super-star that he now is? Readers may find it strange that I also include Yul Brynner in the list, but despite our mutual dislike, he always gave 110 per cent at every performance and you cannot ask for more than that.

One song sticks out head and shoulders above the thousands I have heard over the years. It is not from a show, but the 1937 film *High Wide and Handsome*. Whenever I listen to the 3 min 35 seconds of Peggy Lee singing Jerome Kern and Oscar Hammerstein's wonderfully emotive *The Folks Who Live On The Hill*, I feel a tear coming into my eye as it was my parents' anthem, and this is the definitive version.

On the big band list it would have to be *The Count Basie Band* playing an arrangement by Sammy Nestico, and the version of *Strike Up The Band* played by *The Good Guys Orchestra*. It would be hard to beat and certainly one of my Desert Island Discs.

On a lighter note, a song that became our song when I was seeing Darcy regularly, and years before it became a hit in the show Spamalot, was *Always Look on the Bright Side of Life*, which is something I have always tried to do.

The first time I heard the Act One Finale to *Les Miserables*, in The Palace Theatre, *One Day More*, it sent shivers down my spine and still does, almost 30 years later. I don't think there is a better ensemble number to compare with it, in any other show. I feel fortunate I was in the right place at the right time and made the right choice of which show to join, when I started with Cameron Mackintosh on *Side by Side by Sondheim* in 1977 when he was virtually unknown, and then at The Prince Edward Theatre in 1991, when it became a Delfont Mackintosh Theatre.

If I had to choose two songs that best sum me up, both as a professional and a person, they would have to be *My Way* and *I Am What I Am*. I believe passionately that life is for living, provided that you don't hurt anyone on the way, and never to dismiss any experience in life, until you have tried it at least once.

Someone I hold in high esteem recently told me: "There is no one who has so much right as you have, to be where they are today, who can deliver dividends and ensure success, than you, John." which coupled with the phrase 'He was firm but fair' on my gravestone, just about sums me up I suppose.

In conclusion, I wish all of you who have read the book and come to your own conclusions about me, 12 months of happiness, 52 weeks of joy, 365 days of success, 8,760 hours of good health, 525,600 minutes of good luck, 31,536,000 seconds of love, and peace forever in your lifetime.

This has been my story of *The Life that I Loved*.

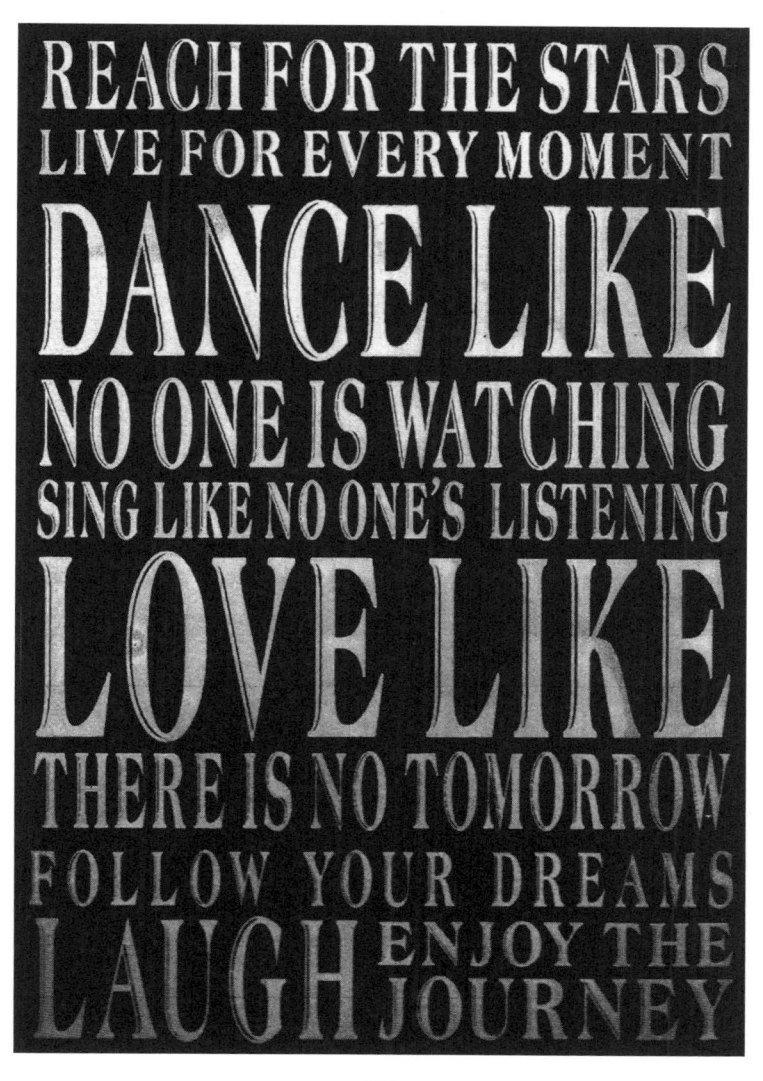

REACH FOR THE STARS
LIVE FOR EVERY MOMENT
DANCE LIKE
NO ONE IS WATCHING
SING LIKE NO ONE'S LISTENING
LOVE LIKE
THERE IS NO TOMORROW
FOLLOW YOUR DREAMS
LAUGH ENJOY THE JOURNEY

ACKNOWLEDGEMENTS & THANKS

My most sincere thanks go to the many people who originally encouraged me to put pen to paper and reminisce about my life in The Entertainment Business, and of late those who have guided me through the many pitfalls of being a virgin author.

I am forever grateful to Henry Ruddock, who has patiently and most professionally, overseen the project during the past year. Without his advice, guidance, and understanding I am quite certain that I would not have been able to complete the task, on time and within budget. His attention to detail would make him an ideal Stage Manager, and I sincerely hope that we remain friends for a long time to come.

John Exton, who kindly read, commented and advised me on my original prose.

Howard Leader for his kind remarks in The Foreword to the book.

Ned Seago, Stage Door Manager at The Old Vic.

Michael Halstead, Everyman Theatre Cheltenham.

Sarah Raymond for the Cover photograph.

Roger Hendry, Tricia Martin, Billy Meal, Dafydd ap Rees, and John Fitzsimmons for their invaluable contributions.

Last and most important my entire extended family for the support and love that they have given me, and the many friends that I have made over the years.

All photographs used are from the author's personal collection. Efforts have been made to trace copyright holders but this has not been possible in every instance.

The picture of JT as Prince Chulalongkorn on page 17 printed by kind permission of CAODS (Lincolnshire County Amateur Operatic and Dramatic Society).

The picture of HM the Queen Mother on page 179 printed by kind permission of the Press Association.

Primary Professional Development

The Spelling Teacher's Handbook

Strategies for the Classroom

Jo Phenix

Folens Publishers

Folens books are protected by international copyright laws. All rights are reserved. The copyright of all materials in this book, except where otherwise stated, remains the property of the publisher and author. No part of this publication may be reproduced, stored in a retrieval system, or transmitted, in any form or by any means, for whatever purpose, without the written permission of Folens Limited.

Jo Phenix hereby asserts her moral right to be identified as the author of this work in accordance with the Copyright, Designs and Patents Act 1988. Additional material by Sue Peet.

First published in 2000 by Folens Limited.
United Kingdom: Folens Publishers, Albert House, Apex Business Centre, Boscombe Road, Dunstable, LU5 4RL
Email: Folens@folens.com

Ireland: Folens Publishers, Greenhills Road, Tallaght, Dublin 24
Email: Info@folens.ie

Poland: JUKA, ul. Renesansowa 38, Warsaw 01-905

Editor: Karen Westall
Illustrations: Debbie Riviere
Layout artist: Suzanne Ward
Cover design: Martin Cross
Cover image: 'The Four Evangelists', Vyserad Gospel Book, Prague

© 2000 Folens Limited, on behalf of the author.

Every effort has been made to contact copyright holders of material used in this book. If any have been overlooked, we will be pleased to make any necessary arrangements.

British Library Cataloguing in Publication Data. A catalogue record for this book is available from the British Library.

ISBN 1 86202 914–8

Contents

Chapter 1:
UNDERSTANDING SPELLING   **4**
The skills of spelling   4
A sequence of spelling development   7
What skills should we teach?   11

Chapter 2:
ORGANISING A SPELLING CLASSROOM   **12**
Creating a climate for spelling learning   12
The reading – writing connection   14
Risk-taking   15
Planning instruction   16
Purpose   17
Information   19
Practice   21
Spelling across the curriculum   22

Chapter 3:
PLANNING SPELLING LESSONS   **23**
Objectives   23
A four-step model for instruction   23
Grouping   24
Teaching spelling through children's writing   26
Responding to spelling errors   27

Chapter 4:
TEACHING SPELLING PATTERNS   **31**
Why teach spelling patterns?   31
Four kinds of spelling patterns   32

Chapter 5:
SPELLING ACTIVITIES   **42**
Repertoire of activities   42
Word-collecting   42
Word-building   46
Pattern matching   50
Spelling investigations   51

Chapter 6:
USING SPELLING LISTS   **54**
Using lists of words   54
Word family lists   54
Reference lists   57
Prompt lists   59
Core vocabulary lists   60

Chapter 7:
GETTING SPELLING RIGHT   **65**
When does spelling count?   65
Proofreading   66
Using a dictionary   67

Chapter 8:
DEVELOPING A SPELLING CURRICULUM   **69**
The need to plan   69
Lifelong learning   71

Appendix: References   **72**

Chapter 1

Understanding spelling

The skills of spelling

English spelling reflects the history of the British Isles. A succession of invasions by different language speakers created a hybrid that many linguists classify as a pidgin tongue. The language that the printing press fixed on the page for us contains elements of many languages, predominantly Latin (although this influence largely disappeared in the post-Roman period and is now evident in English-from-French words), Anglo-Saxon, Norse and French. Moreover, English speakers have never been slow to adopt words from any language they have come into contact with.

Because of this chequered background, we have come to think of English as a language devoid of logic and pattern, and its spelling as often random and confusing. Even what we call 'spelling rules' always seem to have exceptions.

Order out of chaos

To unravel the maze of spelling for children, we need to show them that there is far more logic than they might at first recognise. Our spelling is, in fact, full of patterns that we can identify and use to become proficient spellers.

Learning the real skills of spelling has little to do with memorising lists of words. A good speller is not necessarily a person with a good memory, but one who understands the patterns of English and can use them to construct words as they are needed.

Effective spelling instruction must focus on patterns and word-building strategies that children can use in their own writing. The teaching of spelling should also be closely linked to the teaching of handwriting since the experienced writer often 'feels' he or she may have made an error before seeing it. We can learn much by looking at the five stages which children go through on the road to becoming effective at spelling.

Stages of development in learning to spell

Pre-phonetic
Children attempt a message which may be a mixture of pictures, letter shapes or signs. The meaning can very often only be interpreted by the writer.

Characteristics
- ✔ Random use of both conventional and invented symbols.
- ✔ Repetition and perseveration of symbols.
- ✔ Mixture of upper and lower case symbols.
- ✔ Translatable only by the writer.

Moving the child forward
- ✔ Develop an interest and attention to print.
- ✔ Encourage the child to 'hold' the message.
- ✔ Provide a translation *after* the child has written.
- ✔ Draw attention to and demonstrate written messages, vocalising sounds, rhymes and patterns.
- ✔ Introduce alphabetic names and initial sounds.

Semi-phonetic
The picture begins to be separated from the message. The message often contains pictograms and letter-like shapes. Children will often use upper case letters, especially from their own name. One symbol often symbolises a whole sentence.

Characteristics
- ✔ Attempts to match letters or symbols to sounds.
- ✔ Often uses letter names to represent sounds.
- ✔ Begins to orientate letters and words left and right.
- ✔ Begins to distinguish strong consonant sounds; not many vowels.

Moving the child forward
- ✔ Encourage the 'have-a-go' approach and the use of 'invented' or 'temporary' spelling.
- ✔ Reinforce knowledge of letter sounds, names and alphabetical order.
- ✔ Vocalise sounds when demonstrating spelling and encourage children to listen for sounds and vocalise as they spell.
- ✔ Begin to split words into beginning, middle and end.
- ✔ Direct attention to common words in the classroom and environment for copying.
- ✔ Begin banks of high-frequency and 'key' words.

Phonetic
The message contains some symbols which represent sounds. The sounds are usually very familiar, such as letters from a name or from a word which the child uses frequently. Familiar letters are often included as capitals.

Characteristics
- ✔ Uses known sounds to write words.
- ✔ Writing becomes readable by others.
- ✔ Becomes aware of word boundaries and leaves spaces (not always in the conventional place!).
- ✔ Pronunciation plays a large part in the spelling of words.
- ✔ Nasal consonants often omitted.
- ✔ If in doubt, often puts extra letters in to cover gaps in knowledge.

Moving the child forward
- ✔ Begin to record words in alphabetical lists.
- ✔ Encourage syllabification of words.
- ✔ Focus on the visual features, onsets, rime patterns, letter strings, etc.
- ✔ Encourage children to make analogies when spelling.
- ✔ Introduce a 'look, cover, say, write and check' approach.
- ✔ Encourage children to practise words with their eyes shut.
- ✔ Work on the different ways of representing sounds, e.g. long vowels.
- ✔ Build lists of words with similar spelling patterns.

Transitional to visual
Children may stay in this stage for some time; indeed it is where many 'stick'. They should be moving from a phonic to a visual approach, starting to recognise if a word 'looks right'. This can often be helped by proofreading the work of others. They should show evidence of an increasing bank of known words and some spelling should now be 'automatic'. Many children may need to practise words to the point of 'overlearning'. They may still use an inappropriate but logical pattern or revert to phonic strategies.

Characteristics
- ✔ Uses strategies other than phonic and able to make analogies.
- ✔ Majority of letters in words correct if not in correct sequence.
- ✔ Includes a vowel in every syllable.
- ✔ May over-generalise on a rule, e.g. final e (*biye* for *buy*).
- ✔ More frequently used words spelled correctly.
- ✔ May develop word 'blocks' for specific words, e.g. *sentance*.
- ✔ Begins to use unvoiced or silent letters, e.g. *finking* instead of *fickig* for *thinking*.

Moving the child forward
- ✔ Emphasise the role of 'drafting' in writing and spelling.
- ✔ Extend children's 'automatic' spelling vocabulary by 'look, say, cover, write and check' strategies.
- ✔ Encourage children to proofread and check each other's work.
- ✔ Extend children's range of vocabulary.
- ✔ Focus on the meaning of words to examine root words and derivatives.
- ✔ Develop children's research strategies and use of dictionaries, thesauruses, word lists and spellcheckers.
- ✔ Encourage children to discuss the strategies they use when spelling with others.

Conventional or mature

If children have been encouraged to observe print around them and to build up their visual memory of words encountered in their reading, sentence and word work, these should begin to appear in their writing. There will be some reliance on phonetic spelling and children should be praised for what they get nearly right and encouraged to check spellings (perhaps with a partner) before presenting their work. Class and group work should be aimed at both building a spelling vocabulary of 'key words' and learning the patterns and letter strings common to English. At this stage, children should be able to 'invent' a word using conventional spelling patterns, e.g. *dracularess* or *pedophobia*.

Characteristics
- ✔ Uses a full range of strategies – phonic, visual, morphemic, conventional – to spell words.
- ✔ Ability to make analogies from known spelling patterns.
- ✔ A large bank of words known 'automatically'.
- ✔ Tries alternatives to see which 'look and feel right'.
- ✔ Effective use of spelling resources and reference books.
- ✔ Ability to recognise incorrect spelling.
- ✔ Confidence not to settle for the 'easy' option.

Moving the child forward
- ✔ Further develop use of drafting, proofreading and editing skills.
- ✔ Explore and examine the functions and meanings of words and how this affects their spelling.
- ✔ Investigate the origins of words and the history of spelling systems.
- ✔ Develop the ability to spell correctly when writing at speed.
- ✔ Extend knowledge and use of appropriate reference sources.
- ✔ Foster an interest and enjoyment in word play and word collection and exploration.

(This material is based on the stages originally identified by R. Gentry in An analysis of developmental spelling, *The Reading Teacher*, 36(2), 1982.)

A sequence of spelling development

A child's first encounter with written language is usually in picture books. Children's first realisation that the language they are hearing someone read aloud is represented by the print, rather than by the pictures, is one of the intellectual breakthroughs of literacy. In early writing, children often use pictograms such as smiley or sad faces, hearts to say 'I Love You!' and xxx for kisses. This demonstrates that they understand the importance of writing as a means of sending a message.

Once children recognise the function of print, they can move on to learning the alphabet and naming the letters. It is useful to remember this natural pattern for learning: if children first understand what something means, and what it is for, they can more easily learn how to use it. To teach spelling effectively, we must put meaning first.

Spelling development usually follows a sequence like the following:

1. Letter names

Can you relate the names of these letters to the following sentence?
O   I C U   F N   N E N R G
Oh, I see you haven't any energy.

Children can use the similarity of letter names to actual words in order to write down much of their own language. When children try to write using strings of apparently random letters, it is a sign that they have learned the connection between letters and language.

Translation: hedgehog, cucumbers, wire netting.

2. Phonics

Consonants

The next step in literacy comes when children learn that letters represent sounds. This is the time when phonics instruction is vitally important. They learn consonant sounds first, because they are easier to hear and distinguish from one another. Writing may still appear to be strings of letters, but the children will be attempting to represent the sounds they hear.

This child wrote frequent shopping lists to help his Mum. Items on the list are: Bread, Potatoes, Eggs, Rice Crispies, Marge, Baked Beans.
(Reproduced with the permission of Nelson Thornes from *Responding to and Assessing Writing, National Writing Project 1989*.)

Vowels
As the children learn more about phonics, they learn to listen also for vowel sounds. At first, they will use vowel names; then they will learn rhyming patterns for writing vowel syllables.

Daddy Bear, Goldilocks, Tiny Bear.

(Reproduced with the permission of Nelson Thornes from *Responding to and Assessing Writing*, National Writing Project 1989.)

As we look at the children's writing at this phonetic stage, we can assess what they know and what they have not yet learned.

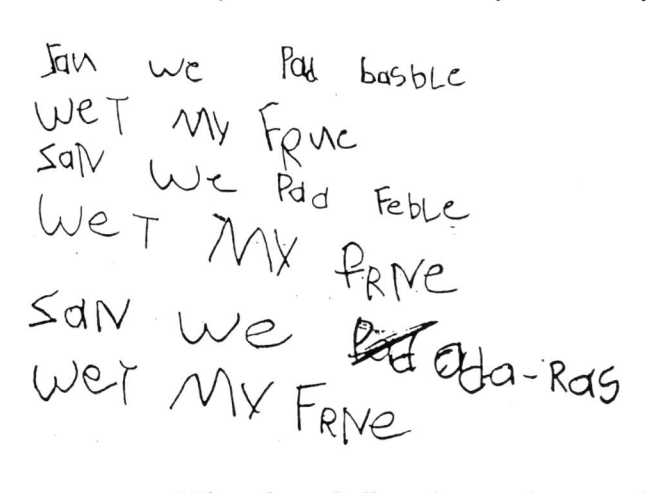

Then we played baseball
with my friend
Then we played football
with my friend
Then we had a race
with my friend

Colleen, age 5

What does Colleen know about spelling?
- ✔ She uses consonant sounds correctly most of the time.
- ✔ She represents every syllable of every word.
- ✔ She knows some sight words: *my, we*.
- ✔ She may have recognised *le* as a typical word ending.
- ✔ She uses spaces between words, therefore understands what a word is.

What does Colleen not yet know?
- ✔ Long-vowel patterns. She uses vowel names to represent vowel sounds: *pad, basble, ras*.
- ✔ Short-vowel patterns. She uses the closest vowel name she can find to represent short-vowel sounds: *a* in *then*, *e* in *with*.
- ✔ Consonant combination *th*. She uses a reversed *z*, which is the closest letter-name match she can find.

The next step in learning for Colleen will be short-vowel rhyming patterns, followed by long-vowel patterns.

3. Spelling patterns

To progress from phonetic spelling to standard spelling, the children need to learn spelling patterns. These fall into three main groups:

- ✔ Sound patterns, in which similar sounds are represented by the same groups of letters:
  splat, splash, splinter
  rough, tough, enough.

- ✔ Function patterns, in which spelling is influenced by the way a word is used:
  parted, danced
  Although pronunciation may change, the spelling of the past-tense marker remains the same.
  dogs, cats
  Although pronunciation changes, the regular plural ending is always *s*.

- ✔ Meaning patterns, which connect words according to their meaning and origin.
  please, pleasant, displease, pleasure
  Although pronunciation changes, the spelling of the root remains the same.
  In words derived from French, *ch* sounds like *sh*.
  chandelier, chemise, chamois, chef
  In words derived from Greek, *ch* sounds like *k*.
  chorus, choir, chemist.

4. Spelling by analogy

Because English spelling reflects patterns from many different languages, there is a large number of patterns to learn. As our vocabularies grow, we can fit new words into the patterns we know. To spell a word we have never written before, or perhaps never seen before, we think of other words with which it might match. This spelling-by-analogy is a strategy successful spellers use throughout their lives. It will not eliminate spelling errors, but it does give a writer a reasonable chance of logically figuring out how a word is most likely to be spelled.

---

medicine or medisine?

Think of other words in this pattern: medical   medication
                                      medicate   paramedic.
Now you can predict that *c* will be the right choice.
If in addition you know that the word comes from French, you will predict that *cine* is the more likely spelling.

What skills should we teach?

Teaching the patterns that will enable children to construct the words they need will demonstrate that spelling is not a guessing game. It is a problem-solving activity with its own logic and predictability. Letter combinations, roots, prefixes and suffixes form the building blocks of words. The more children know about the parts of words, and what they mean and how they join together, the better spellers they will be.

Even more important, once children know that they have strategies to use and a reasonable chance of success, they can become more confident to try new words.

> The most severe spelling problem children can have does not concern the number of spelling errors they make. The greatest problem comes when a child draws the conclusion that being a poor speller is the same as being a poor writer.

Writing is the only purpose for spelling. When spelling forms a barrier between children and their writing, this is a spelling disability.

Three aspects of spelling learning

We can see spelling instruction as a three-part focus:

Attitude

Spelling is not boring slug-work. Nor is it a necessary evil of the writing process. Words are interesting and worthy of study. We want children to have a positive attitude towards spelling and understand its place in the writing process.

Knowledge

Facts and information about words will provide the raw materials with which to build words. Throughout their lives, children will continue to add to this store of knowledge.

Skills

Through frequency of use, children will develop an ability to use the information they have in order to construct words as they are needed.

Chapter 2

Organising a spelling classroom

Creating a climate for spelling learning

Most people make spelling mistakes, and it is in the nature of our society to regard errors as signs of carelessness, illiteracy and poor teaching methods. Even adults who are themselves poor spellers often define 'good teaching' as 'the way it was done when I went to school'. As spelling is one of the more visible aspects of writing, it may be a first focus for comment. Parents often expect their young children to be able to write without making errors, not recognising that, with such a complex spelling system, it will take many years for their children to learn enough even to come close to standard spelling.

Many children are afraid of making spelling mistakes. This fear may be the result of criticism, poor test results, losing marks for spelling, laborious corrections or frustration in trying and failing to remember words. Fear of making spelling mistakes can lead children to use strategies that work very successfully to cut down errors but restrict writing.

Confident versus safe

The confident speller	The 'safe' speller
Has a try at any word within his or her vocabulary.	Uses 'easy option' words – writes about a 'wood', never a 'forest' or a 'copse'.
Is happy that making mistakes is part of learning to write.	Often spells all words correctly because he or she won't use a word that cannot be spelled.
Makes a close attempt and then checks later.	Finds proofreading and checking a traumatic task.
Understands the link between letter and sound patterns, even before he or she has totally mastered them.	Often spells the same word differently within the same piece of writing – hasn't made the link between sound and letter patterns.
Writes as much or as little as time and interest allows, not as much as his or her spelling allows.	Writes as little as possible; often indulges in time-filling or time-wasting to cover lack of confidence.
Makes analogies and generalisations from words he or she knows.	Is unable to make analogies and generalisations.
Is prepared to 'play' with words.	Is less likely to 'play' or invent words.
Has a range of different strategies, using clues from phonic, visual and word knowledge.	Tends to rely on one strategy all the time. Often 'sounds out' words which should be known on sight.

If we look at the writing of Katie, we can see that as early as 6 years old she is a confident writer:

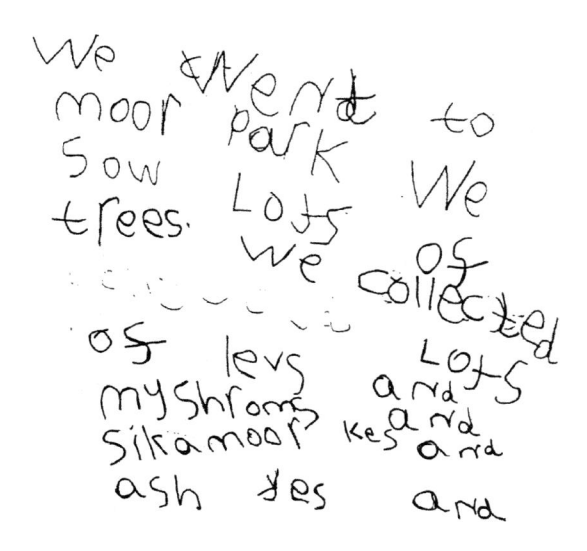

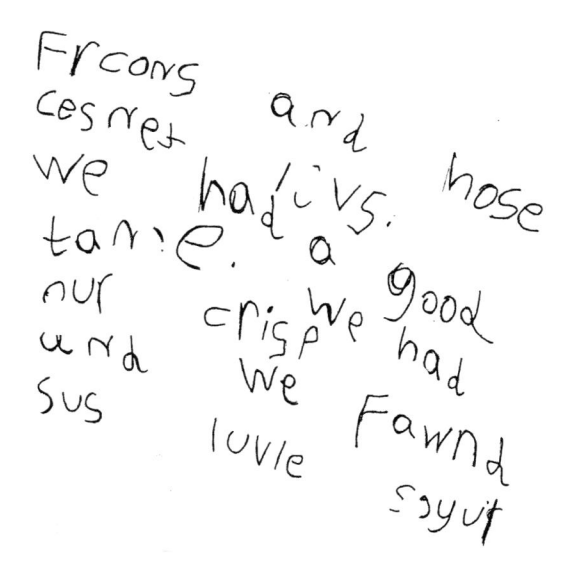

[Handwritten sample by Katie:]

We went to moor park to sow lots of trees. We collected lots of levs and myshroms and sikamoor kes and ash yes and Frcons ces rret and we had ivs. hose tame. our and sus crispe we had good we luvle Fawnd soyut

Katie: English Martyrs RC School, Preston, Lancashire. Year 2, aged 6 years old, August 1994. With thanks to the school for granting permission to reproduce this writing.

- ✔ She writes about what she sees, not what she can spell.
- ✔ She is not frightened to attempt *sikamoor* and uses her phonic knowledge to make a very logical attempt.
- ✔ She is able to split words into segments and attempt each part: *collected ... myshroms*.
- ✔ She has vocalised the word *soil* and her attempt reflects her pronunciation.
- ✔ She is beginning to experiment with long-vowel sounds and although she has not yet learned all the rules, this does not put her off attempting a word.
- ✔ She is confident in her writing and spelling.

Key points to encourage confidence in spelling

- ✔ Demonstrate the strategies you use as an adult when spelling words.
- ✔ Know what stage of spelling development the children are at and what will be necessary to move them forward.
- ✔ In SHARED sessions, encourage all the children to volunteer help in spelling and praise attempts, however unconventional.
- ✔ In GUIDED sessions, work closely with groups to attempt words that they will need to use or which will extend their vocabulary.
- ✔ Encourage children to use all their senses – eye, ear, hand, mind – and their knowledge about language.
- ✔ Encourage children to vocalise their spelling strategies as they write.

- ✔ Allow strategies to cover a 'draft' or 'temporary' spelling: clxxd, croc-d–l, etc.; examining these attempts can often reveal a rule imperfectly understood.
- ✔ Encourage children to use the symbol 'sp' in their own writing to indicate a word they wish to check later.
- ✔ Encourage children to discuss their spelling with a partner or their group and to use as many alternative strategies as they can before approaching you.
- ✔ Allow them to copy words or phrases that they see around them in the classroom and in the environment, but always with a 'look, say, cover, write, check' approach (for further details, see p.60).
- ✔ Teach each stage of the above approach and explain why it is important. (They need to hold the correct spelling in their mind for long enough for it to be stored correctly in long-term memory.)
- ✔ Encourage them to practise key and high-frequency words with their eyes closed. This helps them to feel the movements involved in forming the letters.
- ✔ As soon as is practicable, teach children to practise spellings in a joined hand so that the movement is continuous.
- ✔ Emphasise and re-emphasise that spelling is part of editing and that incorrect spelling in initial drafts is perfectly acceptable.
- ✔ When marking spelling tests, praise what has been spelled correctly, rather than counting errors; encourage children to perform against their own 'personal best' rather than competing with others in the class.

The reading – writing connection

The first step towards teaching children how to produce writing of their own is to demonstrate the purposes reading and writing serve. Children need to know not only that literacy is important to participate fully in life, but that it can fulfil personal purposes for them too.

The best atmosphere in which to learn any of the skills of literacy is one in which reading and writing are valued, used for real purposes, studied and practised.

Some people have believed that if children do enough reading and writing, the learning of skills will take care of itself; that children will pick up all the information they need during reading and writing activities. In some cases, this does happen; some children seem to learn about spelling and grammar spontaneously without much direct teaching. For many children, though, this kind of learning does not happen, and in most cases we can help in the learning. In a complete and balanced classroom programme, regular practice and planned instruction will operate side by side.

The same model for teaching holds true in both reading and writing:

- ✔ Engage the children in daily reading and writing for real purposes. This will create a need for learning the skills in order that the job is done well.
- ✔ Teach the children the skills they need to help them to become more proficient. This in turn will make reading and writing tasks more successful and more satisfying. There is nothing more motivating for further learning than success.

Risk-taking

Children cannot learn to spell before they start to write; throughout their lives, their ability to spell will always lag behind their vocabulary. If we want improvement in both spelling and in composition, we must establish a risk-free environment in which children can use the best knowledge they have to write using every word in their speaking vocabulary.

Strategies to encourage risk-taking

- ✔ Establish a 'writers' workshop' atmosphere. This will help children to learn that writing is moulded into shape, rather than springing full-blown into a finished form. Working towards correct spellings is one part of this process.

- ✔ Allow plenty of time for children to proofread and correct, before they are held accountable for spelling errors. Final draft is the time to assess spelling competence. It is often helpful if children are encouraged to work with a partner when editing their writing before presentation or marking. Children find it much easier to proofread the work of others and this helps to train them to spot errors.

- ✔ Reward failed attempts to spell difficult words. You want children to keep trying, not be afraid to use new words.

- ✔ Do not regard spelling errors as signs of carelessness or laziness. They are more likely to be signs that a child has not yet internalised a pattern. Many good spellers make errors in first-draft writing because they are concentrating on what they have to say, or writing very quickly.

- ✔ Use spelling errors as opportunities to assess what children know and do not know. Explain to the children why their words are wrong and which spelling concept they did not know.

✔ Respond to what children do correctly, as well as to what they do wrong. No one can get a word completely wrong; if you have every letter wrong, you have written a different word. An error is usually one letter or syllable, a word ending, a vowel combination, a doubled letter, and represents a spelling concept or pattern. Point out which parts are correct before explaining the error.

✔ Do not expect children to be able to proofread for patterns they have not yet learned. Their speaking vocabulary will always exceed their ability to spell.

✔ Provide all the help children need to bring their writing to final-draft stage. Even poor spellers deserve to have their writing displayed and published.

✔ Encourage children to use tape-recorders to compose orally. This will enable them to use the best language they can, without considering whether or not they can spell the words. They can then transcribe their own language, or have a scribe to do it for them. Once children know how well and how much they can compose, few of them are satisfied with lesser efforts. It will also give you a chance to assess their composing ability separately from their skill in transcription.

✔ Encourage even older children to compose by drawing a series of pictures. They can then write accompanying text for each picture, or use a tape-recorder as in the example above. This will break down the task of composing and writing into smaller units and allow children to focus on composing and spelling one at a time.

✔ Make a record, keeping a list of patterns and concepts each child knows and uses. Whatever the level of achievement, each child can have a growing list.

Planning instruction

If we are to help our children to become more proficient in spelling, we must plan our instruction around the three prerequisites for learning anything:

✔ Purpose
✔ Information
✔ Practice.

Purpose

Writing provides the only valid purpose for learning to spell. A classroom that provides opportunities for many different kinds of writing will create a need for learning to spell. (For more details, see *The Writing Teacher's Handbook*.)

In order to write effectively and efficiently, children need two different kinds of spelling skill. They will learn which one is appropriate as they use the drafting process in their writing (see *The Writing Teacher's Handbook*).

- ✔ Have-a-go spelling
- ✔ Correct spelling.

Have-a-go spelling

Children need to be able to write quickly and freely without giving spelling undue thought. Although this may result in many spelling mistakes, it is intended for first-draft writing and for quick, personal jottings, not for public scrutiny. A reasonable spelling facility enables children to get their ideas and language down on paper quickly and to focus on the composing aspects of writing first.

Strategies to encourage have-a-go spelling

- ✔ Teach the 'have-a-go' strategy. If children are not sure of a spelling, they should have a go, make their best attempt and mark the word to check later. You can establish a 'have-a-go' symbol, such as the acronym HAG. Establish the principle that if the children write this beside a word, they will not be penalised or criticised for a misspelling, as long as they check it at the appropriate time. HAG can be a licence to experiment, a 'get out of jail free' card. As you look at their attempts, you can get information about the kinds of thinking children do as they try to form words. Do they sound it out phonetically? Are they trying to use a spelling pattern? Do they represent all the syllables? Is their attempt a possible or an impossible spelling?

- ✔ Avoid comments, either verbal or written, on spelling during first-draft writing. Whenever you mention spelling, even to praise, you are sending the message that spelling is something that the child should be thinking about at this time.

- ✔ From time to time, give children a speed-writing task. Assign a topic and ask them to write for three minutes. At the end of the three minutes, they are to count how many words they have written. The children can record their own score and try to beat it next time. Do not read this writing; it is only to give the children practice in writing quickly without thinking about spelling or neatness.

- ✔ Encourage children to cross out, rather than trying to erase spelling errors. Do this yourself when you write on the board and need to change a word or phrase. This will foster the notion that at this time speed is important, rather than neatness.

- ✔ Model these strategies when you write on the board, or while the children are watching. They should see that when you write it is not always right first time.

- ✔ Provide scrap paper, or an exercise book in which no marks or comments are recorded, for first-draft writing and quick notes. This can then become a risk-free workplace in which children can focus on getting their thoughts and language down on paper. Children will not be so anxious about messing up writing that will remain totally private.

Correct spelling

Children need to know how to produce correct spellings, and when and why this is important. For this, it is not enough just to write. It is of little importance if we misspell words on a shopping list, or when writing the first draft of a story. To provide real purpose for correct spelling, the writing must be intended for another person to read. Then we learn that if our spelling is incorrect, we will make a poor impression. For writing to be a significant factor in learning to spell, the writer must be writing for a real audience. No one wants to look silly in print.

Strategies to encourage correct spelling

- ✔ Provide many opportunities for children to write for audiences both within and outside the classroom (see Chapter 6 in *The Writing Teacher's Handbook*).

- ✔ Teach children that correct spelling, neat handwriting and an attractive presentation are courtesies you pay to your reader. You want to make reading your writing an easy and pleasant experience. If their work is too messy and untidy for you to want to read, say so. Real audience feedback is a good way to learn what is important.

- ✔ Teach children that correcting their spelling is like combing their hair when they are going to have their photograph taken, cleaning the house when visitors are coming, or putting on their best clothes for a special occasion. Sometimes writing has a public face, and there are times when we all want to look our best. Analogies like these may help children to understand how much time and effort they should put into making their writing correct and attractive.

- ✔ Do not display or publish work with spelling mistakes. Children should know that the final draft is the public face of writing and should be as correct and attractive as they can make it.

- ✔ Do not expect children to proofread and correct every piece of writing. This will foster the notion that spelling is equally important in every writing task, and will work against them learning when spelling really matters.

- ✔ Give children all the help that they need to proofread and correct spellings for final-draft writing.

✔ Make good use of short dictation practice as an aid to checking how well children are progressing with high-frequency words or with particular spelling patterns or rules. A dictation should be given in the same 'have-a-go' manner as normal writing and should be pitched at or slightly above the children's level. This might make it more suitable for a group GUIDED activity than a whole class activity. At first, the children should be given as much time as they need, although as children approach end-of-stage assessments, it might be administered as a speed test. The children should mark and correct their own attempts, perhaps working with a partner, and should only be graded against their own progress. You, however, will find that these first attempts reveal very useful diagnostic information about the main strategies that the children use and any persistent errors. They can be particularly helpful in stretching 'safe' spellers to attempt words that they might avoid in their personal writing, thus revealing gaps in their knowledge. It is particularly important that dictation be delivered in sentence or paragraph form rather than the isolated words of a spelling test, so that children can use their knowledge of context to help them. Young children might begin with three or four short sentences of regular phonic or high-frequency words. Dictation, if it focuses on high-frequency or taught vocabulary, can teach children that spelling 'sight words' correctly at the first attempt saves time in the long term and makes writing much easier.

Children need to know which kind of spelling is appropriate to any writing task. To help them to learn this, we must be very consistent in the way we set expectations and respond to spelling errors, not only from lesson to lesson, and from teacher to teacher, but throughout the children's school career. If children understand the purpose of spelling, and of the drafting process, they should never need to ask, 'Does spelling count?'

Information

The information that children need is two-fold:

✔ Spelling is a thinking activity.
✔ Specific information about words can be given.

A thinking activity

They need to know that spelling is a thinking, not a memorising, activity. 'Why?' is often as important a question in spelling as 'how?' Understanding why words are spelled the way they are can help children to find patterns, make logical connections and develop strategies for making reasonable predictions about words. The more children know about the usage, history and derivations of words, the better spelling choices they will make.

> Why does *debt* have a *b* although it is silent? It comes from the Latin *debitum*.
>
> debt   debit   debenture
>
> It is very difficult to pronounce the *b* in *debt*, and in Old English it disappeared from the word. It was later put back in to show the link with its origin. Other words that English has absorbed from other languages show similar patterns (see p.10).

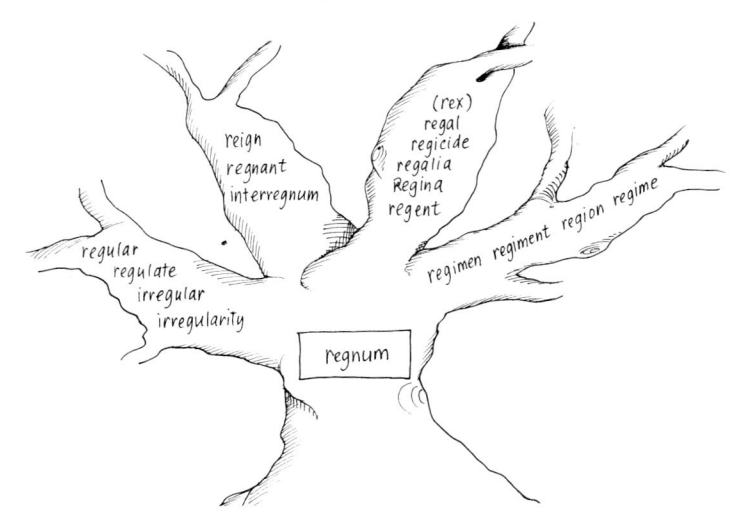

Why does *reign* have a silent *g*? From the Latin *regnum*, meaning rule or govern.

Tree diagram showing words derived from regnum: *regular, regulate, irregular, irregularity; reign, regnant, interregnum; (rex) regal, regicide, regalia, Regina, regent; regimen, regiment, region, regime.*

Strategies to encourage thinking

✔ Point out the logic in words that the children are writing. This will demonstrate for them how they can 'spell by analogy', and work out possible spellings.
  'The first sound is the same as in your name. Which letter should you use?'
  'Can you think of another word that rhymes with dog? How would you spell it?'
  '*Revise* and *revision* have the same root; it means 'to see'. Notice that even though the pronunciation is different, the spelling is the same. Which other words have the same root as these?'

✔ Explain the origins of words.
  Because is a short form for three words (*be the cause*). This can help children to spell the second syllable correctly.
  Tomorrow used to be *on the morrow*. This can help children to remember which letter is doubled and which is not.

When children are fascinated by words and their origins, when they become engaged in the task of generating spellings as children learning to talk are engaged in generating language, then we will know that they understand spelling as a cognitive process.

Specific information At the same time as children are learning to think logically about words, we can give them specific information about words.

Strategies for gaining information

- ✔ Collect and categorise words. Sorting words according to spelling patterns will not only help children to recognise patterns, but will teach them to expect and look for patterns.

- ✔ Investigate words. Find out their language of origin, their meanings, their usages, their abbreviations, their synonyms, antonyms and rhymes. This will not only raise children's interest in words, but demonstrate how words are linked.

- ✔ Analyse words. Find a word's root, prefixes and suffixes. Note how these parts are joined together.

- ✔ Help children to build a store of sight words. These might be high-frequency words, or words personal to each child. Frequency of use is the best way for children to learn these words.

- ✔ Teach children to use reference materials, so that they can find the words they need.

Practice

Learning to spell is largely a matter of pattern recognition. Once we have identified a pattern, we make a generalisation: this kind of word is built in this kind of way. It is these generalisations that allow us to make reasonable predictions about how a word is most likely to be spelled.

Some people recognise and use patterns easily, often without being aware that they are doing so. These people learn to spell early, subconsciously assimilating information about words as they read, and are reasonably good spellers all their lives. Other people see words as individual entities, and do not recognise how they are linked to one another.

Seeing words grouped according to spelling patterns will help children to recognise the patterns. Building words according to these patterns will show children how to use them to spell. Using words frequently will help to make the patterns, and hence the words, automatic.

Some children will need many repetitions of patterns to be able to make the generalisations necessary for them to become competent spellers.

Strategies for providing practice

- ✔ Build words. Using the same pattern to build many words will help children to internalise the pattern and show them how they can use the pattern to spell new words for their writing.

- ✔ Play with words. Use crosswords, word searches and word games. Investigate palindromes and acronyms. Use alliteration. These all draw attention to ways in which words are constructed.

✔ Proofread regularly. It is a learned skill.

✔ Write many times a day for different purposes. Frequency of use is the best way to learn patterns, sight words and strategies.

Spelling across the curriculum

It is a truism that every teacher is a teacher of English. This also means that every teacher is a teacher of spelling. While some principles apply in every subject, different subject disciplines can also make different contributions to a child's spelling learning. Children and their parents should receive a consistent message about what is important, and about how they should be thinking about spelling.

It is primarily the English teacher's task to build up children's knowledge of spelling patterns and concepts and to provide the practice time necessary for children to become skilled at using this information. The methodology used in English time should be carried through in other subject areas. It is very confusing for children to learn a drafting approach to writing in English, then lose marks for spelling in a first-draft history report. Similarly, when children are learning spelling as a word-constructing activity, they should not at other times be expected to memorise lists of words for a test.

It is a good idea to establish some guidelines for teaching spelling and for responding to spelling errors in children's writing. These can be used in different subjects and by different teachers.

Sample guidelines

✔ A risk-taking atmosphere should be present at all times. Doing your best is all we expect if you run a race or paint a picture; it should be acceptable in spelling too.

✔ The drafting process should be used for all writing. If writing stays in first-draft form, it should be evaluated as such.

✔ Children should not be penalised for spelling errors unless they have had ample time for proofreading and correcting, and been given all the help they need.

✔ Each subject teacher can teach subject-specific vocabulary and spellings. These should be taught by grouping words into patterns and word families, and through investigation of their origins, roots, meanings, derivations and so on, not by rote memorisation.

✔ Children can keep personal reference lists of theme words, subject-specific words, words they have difficulty with, high-frequency words, and so on. They could do this in a spelling journal they keep with them throughout the day.

Chapter 3

Planning spelling lessons

Objectives

The prime objective of a spelling lesson is to enable children to understand words, think about them logically and make connections among them so that they can build the words they need for their writing. It is essential to focus on long-term learning, rather than short-term memory. This long-term learning will result when children gain an understanding of the way in which words are constructed, and the way they link with one another.

All the words used in a spelling lesson should have a logical spelling connection. Focus on only one pattern at a time. It does not matter how many or how few words go together; a spelling pattern may have five words or a hundred words. Remember, the children are not learning the words, but the patterns.

Lists of words play an important part in spelling lessons. However, they are not lists of words to learn, but lists of words to illustrate patterns. If children internalise a pattern, they do not need to remember the words – they can reconstruct them whenever they need them. Not only that, they can use the pattern to spell similar words they meet in the future correctly. A pattern that they learn in class today can help them to spell words not yet in their speaking vocabularies. A spelling pattern lasts forever.

A four-step model for instruction

A spelling lesson can be a four-step process:

Step 1 Select appropriate patterns or rules from the scheme of work and collect example words.

Step 2 Sort the words according to the spelling patterns involved.

Step 3 Examine the lists of words and make generalisations about why they are different.

Step 4 Use the pattern to build new words.

Sample spelling lesson

Spelling focus: Plural patterns

Time span: 3–4 days

Whole class work (10 minutes)
On an overhead transparency, list plural words from the first three pages of Chapter 1 of *Alice in Wonderland*:

    pictures   *daisies*   *bookshelves*   *conversations.*

Children contribute other plural words. Start with objects around the room. Then suggest themes – animals, fruit.

Group work – groups of four (10 minutes)
Duplicate copies of the transparency list, one for each group.
Children cut apart the words and sort them according to plural endings.
Children read aloud each list, listening for similar endings.

Individual work (ongoing for 1 or 2 days)
Children list other plural words from Chapter 1.
Children jot down any plurals from their current reading and writing.
Children add their words to the transparency list.

Whole class feedback (10 minutes)
Discuss what makes each list different.
Help the children to write some rules for making plurals:

    To make a plural, add *s*.
    When you hear an extra syllable, add *es*.
    When the singular word ends in a consonant then *y*, change the *y* to *ies*.
    (Continue, depending on the lists that the children have.)

Children write the appropriate rule at the head of each of their lists.

Assessment
Ask the children to write words representing the different patterns that they found to make the plural:

    watch   *country*   *cat*   *peach*   *baby*   *elf*

Grouping

The four-step spelling lesson is suitable for a whole class, for small groups, or for individual help. It is a good idea to make the small groups mixed-ability. A group of children all of whom have a limited vocabulary will not produce much worthwhile learning.

Benefits for the whole class

✔ Spelling patterns are the same for everyone. Whatever the children's level of vocabulary and language use, each will use the same patterns and concepts every time they write. The difference is in the words that they will use. Whole class learning becomes individual when children use the patterns that they have learned to enable them to construct the particular words they need for their own writing.

✔ In a large group, there are more children to contribute words and ideas. This will enable you to collect a useful number of words more quickly and move on to the next part of the activity.

✔ When you write down the children's words and ideas as they suggest them, you can collect information quickly. The 'meat' of the lesson is not the list of words, but the discoveries that children will make from it.

✔ Working with the whole class does not single out poor spellers. Children can learn in a mixed-ability setting, and recognise that everyone needs to learn the same concepts.

✔ Non-native English speakers and children whose vocabularies are not large will have an opportunity to benefit from the words suggested by other children.

✔ You can demonstrate word-collecting and categorising. With a little experience of working with you, children will be able to work in small groups to do similar activities.

✔ You can take a few minutes at any time of the day and in any subject to pick out a subject-oriented word and make a list of related words. These might be *ology* words in science, *metre* words in mathematics, or *geo* words in geography. There will be many opportunities for a five-minute spelling lesson with the whole class.

Benefits for small groups

✔ Some children are more willing to contribute in small groups than in front of the whole class.

✔ Small groups can work physically with words, to cut them apart, sort and categorise them, discuss them.

✔ Whenever children work in small groups, talk is built into the process. Through negotiation, children can put forward their ideas, try out theories and justify their thinking. This will help them to think logically about spellings and see spelling as a problem-solving task.

Benefits for individuals

✔ When you are talking about spelling errors in a child's writing, you can focus on the specific words the child is using at the time they are needed.

✔ Work with individuals is private.

✔ As you work with individuals, you can assess each child's knowledge, attitudes, confidence and ways of thinking about words.

Teaching spelling through children's writing

Teaching opportunities

Writing provides not only the best motivation for spelling, but also the ideal place to practise building words. It also gives some excellent opportunities for teaching.

- ✔ When you talk with children about their writing, take some time to focus on words they are using.

- ✔ Make sure that you focus on spelling at the editing stage, rather than in the first flush of composition.

- ✔ Give children spellings that they need but which they have not yet learned. This will help them to keep the flow of their writing going and give them confidence to use more difficult vocabulary. Encourage them to use a 'look, say, cover, write, check' approach (see p.60) to transfer the word to their own writing.

- ✔ When you give a spelling, point out one or two other words that fit the same pattern. Then ask the child to add more words. In this way, the child can place the new spelling in its own context and learn a spelling pattern.

- ✔ Make a note of patterns in the errors that children make. For example, they may add endings incorrectly, fail to use double letters, or misspell a suffix. You can point out these kinds of errors and demonstrate how the child can correct them.

- ✔ Assess children's attitude towards spelling and writing. Are they confident or nervous? Do they take risks? Are they trying to use all the words in their speaking vocabulary, or do they stick to words that are easy to spell? Can they add words to a spelling pattern? Can they find their errors? Do they see themselves as good or as poor spellers? Does this affect their composition?

Drawbacks

While working through their own writing gives unique opportunities to help children on an individual basis, there are some drawbacks.

- ✔ Individual writing conferences and spelling conferences are very time-consuming. It is unlikely in a regular classroom that you will be able to give each child enough personal attention to consider this a major part of spelling instruction. Work with children on spellings in their own writing as much as possible, but supplement this with whole class and group instruction on a regular basis.

- ✔ Language is not a solitary activity. Working in groups with other children provides opportunities to engage in many word-collecting and word-building activities that children cannot do alone.

Responding to spelling errors

The way in which we respond to spelling errors will influence what the children feel is important, as well as their confidence and attitude towards spelling and writing.

In the past, teachers red-pencilled every error and returned the writing for the child to make corrections. More recently we have considered this to be discouraging for children and a negative influence on composition. This has often led to errors being ignored in favour of creativity. Neither of these approaches reflects an understanding of writing or of spelling. Rather than picking sides, we can take a more pragmatic approach.

We know that mistakes can lead to learning in every kind of endeavour, from cooking to carpentry. It would be ideal if this could also be the case in spelling. In order to bring this condition about, we must go back to the question of purpose. When and why do we mark spelling errors in children's writing?

There are three purposes for responding to errors:

- ✔ Editing function
- ✔ Instructional function
- ✔ Assessment function.

As what we do is quite different in each case, it is vitally important that children know which of these is in effect.

Editing function Editing is for the purpose of writing a final draft that has no errors, omissions, or spelling mistakes. If we write a final draft that still has errors, it is not final and must be redone before going on public view.

In order to eliminate all spelling errors, writing must be proofread, every error located and the correct spelling substituted. If children see this kind of marking as a positive strategy, one that helps them at the next draft stage, they will be grateful for the help, not discouraged by the number of words you mark.

- ✔ When you have a piece of writing in front of you, whether the child is present or not, first consider the stage of the writing and what will happen to it next. If the child is preparing to write a final draft to be read by someone else, find and signal every error. Develop a code, perhaps underline the word, put an asterisk beside it, or write the correct spelling above.

- ✔ Establish yourself as a classroom editor, whose job it is to help to prepare manuscripts for final draft. Put up a sign, advertising your position, and listing what you will do to help.

> **PHENIX**
> EDITORIAL SERVICES
>
> - Help with final-draft manuscript
> - Spelling errors found
> - Punctuation added
> - Grammar tips free
>
> YOU NEED IT.. WE PROVIDE IT!

- ✔ Ensure that children see you making use of a range of dictionaries and reference sources as you edit. Make sure that the children have access to these materials as they proofread and that they use them to check their work. (See 'Using a dictionary', p.67.)

- ✔ Mark spellings with a colour other than red. Red has pejorative overtones.

- ✔ Teach children to recognise and use some editing shortcuts and symbols, e.g. symbols for omissions, reversals or a new paragraph. These can make editing quick and easy.

- ✔ It is ideal if you can proofread and edit while the child is present. Then you can 'talk through' the corrections you are making: 'This is a question. What punctuation mark do you need?' 'You have the *ie* the wrong way round here. Do you remember that rhyme for putting *i* before *e*?'

✔ If you edit when the child is not present, make sure it is clear that editing is what you are doing. Encourage children to ask when they need a final edit. They can write a note at the end of the writing: 'Please help me to edit.'

✔ Do not mark a large number of errors and ask the child to make all the corrections. If there are many spelling errors, the task is probably too great for the child to contemplate without discouragement. This will work against positive attitudes towards using a dictionary that you are trying to establish. Choose one or two words that you think the child can correct, suggest one or two to look up in a dictionary and indicate which these are.

✔ Establish the principle that children must do all the editing they can for themselves before asking for your help. You can set up a system of editing partners, so that each child can have someone to help with the proofreading. Children who are good spellers and good proofreaders can volunteer to have their names on an 'Editing Partners' list, and help when they are asked.

✔ Children may be able to enlist editorial help at home, and ask for it only when they are preparing for a final draft. This will help families to understand when spellings need to be corrected and when they do not.

Instructional function

This kind of response is for the purpose of helping the child to learn something about spelling. For this, it is a waste of time trying to deal with a large number of errors. It is better to have real learning of one or two spelling concepts than to try for too much and have the child forget or be discouraged.

✔ Choose only one or two words for a spelling-instruction focus.

✔ When you focus on a word, give the correct spelling and help the child to fit it into its own spelling pattern. 'This is how you spell *sock*. There is a *ck* at the end. It goes with *rock*. Can you think of another rhyming word?' In this way, you can help the child to learn a spelling pattern.

✔ Choose a misspelled word and help the child to think logically about the spelling. '*Mechanic* uses the same root as *machine*. That's why they both have *ch* inside. Can you add another word to this pattern?' In this way you can demonstrate the kind of reasoning that will help the child to work out spellings in the future.

✔ You can respond in these ways either verbally, as you talk to a child about the writing, or in writing, as you highlight a spelling error and comment on the child's page. If you respond in writing, invite the child to add more spellings to the pattern you have mentioned.

Assessment function

Deducting marks from a score because of spelling mistakes does not fit in with either of the above response functions and is not likely to help a child to become a better speller or writer. This does not mean that there is no place for making a judgement of a child's spelling. It does mean that you and the child must be quite clear about when assessment is taking place and what the criteria are.

✔ The most regular form of assessment will be for diagnostic purposes to determine what progress a child has made against his or her former attainment and what steps will be necessary to move him or her forward.

✔ Sometimes you will want to assess a child's spelling in relation to a norm for the child's age group.

✔ Sometimes you will be assessing the child's spelling according to the level you feel that child is capable of.

✔ Spelling and composition are totally different skills within the writing process. If you need to assign a numerical mark or a grade to writing, separate the different categories of writing skill and give the child a true value judgement for each one: composition, language usage, organising information, spelling, handwriting. Spelling problems should not detract from a child's sense of achievement in other areas of writing.

✔ When you assess spelling in children's writing, be aware of whether it is first-draft writing, or whether the child has had an opportunity to proofread and edit. Assessment at all stages of writing is appropriate and useful, but will give you different kinds of information. In first-draft writing you will be able to see which words and patterns are automatic for the children. After editing, you will see which words and patterns the child can proofread for and correct.

✔ Use the assessment function sparingly. The prospect of assessment changes the character of a writing task. It discourages risk-taking and can lead to simple words and short sentences. The 'what does the teacher expect me to write?' syndrome may take over and detract from the real purpose. The most revealing assessment takes place without the child's knowledge and is an ongoing record of concepts and skills that the child knows and is able to use in writing.

You can use all three methods of responding to spelling errors. If children understand the function of editing and final draft, they will not be confused when sometimes you focus on all the errors and sometimes you don't.

Make sure families also understand that you will sometimes mark all the spelling errors and sometimes ignore them. Children should be able to explain to their families why some writing has spellings corrected and some does not. If they cannot, it is a sign that the child does not understand the writing process.

Chapter 4

Teaching spelling patterns

Why teach spelling patterns?

Think of a spelling pattern as a group of words that share the same element of spelling for the same reason, either sound, function or meaning. Spelling patterns are very useful when we are trying to work out the spelling of a new word. We need to teach children first that spelling is not random, but largely logical and highly predictable. Then we can help them to build up their knowledge of spelling patterns.

Perhaps the most important thing children can learn from studying spelling patterns is that knowing how to spell one word can help you to spell many other words. All you have to do is make the right connections. It is many-for-the-price-of-one learning.

Roots, prefixes and suffixes form the building blocks of words. We use them to build words just as young children use alphabet blocks to sound out words. Just like the alphabet blocks, word-parts can be taken apart and combined in different ways to make many different words.

Understanding word-parts and how to use them together is one of the most important skills of spelling. This knowledge will also help children to decode and understand new words that they meet in their reading.

A word of warning about spelling patterns

Sharing the same grouping of letters does not necessarily make words members of the same spelling pattern.

Although they share an ending that looks the same, these words do not belong to the same spelling pattern: *farmer, wiser.*

This is a better way to group them:
   List *farmer* with *baker, potter, builder*   (the *er* ending denotes one who does a certain job).
   List *wiser* with *bigger, wetter, greater*   (the *er* denotes a comparative ending).

When you group words together for study, look for logical connections whenever possible. Try to answer the questions, 'Why are these words spelled this way? What makes them similar?'

Four kinds of spelling patterns

There are four kinds of spelling patterns that can be helpful for children to learn about:

- ✔ Sound patterns
- ✔ Function patterns
- ✔ Meaning patterns
- ✔ Word-building patterns.

Fitting a word into its 'family', based on sound, function or meaning, can help children to make connections; the more connections they can make, the more predictable spelling becomes and the fewer spelling errors they will make.

Sound patterns

Sound patterns are those in which what we hear influences the letters we choose. For the beginning speller, this means listening to the sounds in each word and trying to match letters to the sounds; in other words, spelling by phonics. If we know the sounds represented by consonants, vowels and their various combinations, we can make reasonable predictions about how words are likely to be spelled.

Sound-pattern knowledge starts with phonics, as children learn about consonant sounds, consonant combinations, short- and long-vowel rhyming patterns, silent letters, and so on. At first, children will over-generalise and use a pattern where it does not belong. They will learn a pattern but need to be told that there will be exceptions. (Some exceptions to recognisable patterns, such as *have, give, said, was*, are better treated as 'sight vocabulary' and practised as separate items.) The more experience children have of reading and writing, and the more help in recognising and building sound patterns, the more likely they are to choose the correct spelling. This process, however, is not automatic and even fluent readers need explicit teaching about spelling patterns both within and out of context. Children can build up their knowledge of sound patterns by collecting words that share the same sound and spelling.

Once they have learned a few basics about letter sounds, beginning writers spell almost entirely according to the sounds they hear, as these are the only patterns they have so far had a chance to learn. This is sometimes called 'invented spelling' or 'developmental spelling'. Spelling phonetically gives children the opportunity to write using every word in their speaking vocabulary; they are not limited by their lack of spelling knowledge. As a result, the writing of young children is often as interesting and varied as their talk.

A beneficial side-effect of spelling-by-sound is that children become phonics experts and can apply this knowledge when they read. Phonics is far more useful and far more thoroughly learned and practised through spelling and writing than through reading.

> ## Dialect note
>
> As you work with sounds, be aware that vowel sounds are greatly affected by dialect. Words that rhyme in some dialects do not rhyme in others. In North American English, *ball* and *doll* rhyme. In the rest of the world, they do not. In the south of England, *bath* and *hearth* rhyme; in the north they do not. *Day* and *die* sound the same in several accents, including Australian.
>
> Although vowel rhymes may vary from dialect to dialect, they remain constant within each person's speech. We can all build rhyming patterns that are meaningful for each one of us.

Strategies for teaching sound patterns

A study of sound patterns involves investigating the many ways in English in which we represent sounds with consonants and vowels. (For 99 ways to spell consonant sounds, 46 ways to spell short-vowel sounds, and 74 ways to spell long-vowel sounds, see *The Spelling Teacher's Book of Lists*.) This begins with basic letter sounds, or phonics, and progresses to ways in which these are combined to represent sounds.

- ✔ With beginning spellers, start with consonants, then move on to vowels. It is easier for children to hear and distinguish consonant sounds. Also, knowing a few consonant sounds will make it possible for children to start writing, and this is the purpose for it all.

- ✔ The best way to learn vowel sounds is by finding and building words with the same vowel rhyming pattern, and it is easier to do this if children already know some consonant sounds.

- ✔ Start with single letters, then progress to letter combinations.

- ✔ When you work with consonant combinations, ask children to listen for first one sound (*cat*), then two sounds together (*scat*), then three sounds together (*scrap*).

- ✔ The nasal *m* and *n* (*m* and *n* followed by a consonant: *ju<u>m</u>p*, *se<u>n</u>d*) are difficult for young children to hear. Do not try teaching these patterns to beginning spellers. There are many other sounds that are easier for them to learn at an early stage.

- ✔ Start with short vowels, then progress to long vowels. Most short-vowel sounds are made with one letter, while most long-vowel sounds need two letters. (Exceptions include the frequently used words *he, me, she, go, so, to*, as well as words ending in a final *o* – *tomato*.)

- ✔ It is not necessary to work through every letter and letter combination one at a time. Once children understand the general principle of listening for letter sounds and combinations, they will work many of them out for themselves.

- ✔ Encourage children to write, whether they know enough letter sounds or not. They will be able to fill in more letters as they continue to learn more about sounds. Do not worry if you cannot read their spelling; the learning is not a result of our reading it, but in the child's continuing efforts to listen for sounds and match them with letters.

✔ Syllables represent one kind of sound pattern. While beginning spellers build words sound by sound, more experienced spellers build words syllable by syllable. Syllables often match up with prefixes, roots and suffixes, and being able to separate them can help to spell each part of a word correctly.

✔ It is not vital that children know how to divide syllables the way a dictionary does. It is helpful if they can identify how many syllables, or beats, there are, and build and proofread them one by one.

Raw materials for building sound patterns

Sound patterns are made with word-parts called 'onsets' and 'rimes'. (It is not necessary, and can be confusing, for children to know these terms.) Children can use onsets and rimes to build many words.

An onset may be a single consonant or a combination of two or three consonants.

These onsets each combine another letter with *l*
 bl, cl, fl, gl, pl, sl

These onsets each combine another letter with *r*
 br, cr, dr, fr, gr, pr, tr

These onsets each combine another letter with *s*
 sc, sk, sm, sn, sp, st

These onsets each combine another letter with *w*
 sw, tw

This onset sounds as if it is made with *w*, but it never is
 qu

These onsets have two letters, but only one sound
 ch, ph, sh, th, wh

These onsets have three sounds you can hear
 scr, spr, str, spl

These onsets have three letters, but only two sounds you can hear
 shr, thr

These rimes build words having a final, silent *e*:
 ace, ade, age, ake, ale, ame, ate, ave
 eme, ese, eve
 ice, ide, ife, ike, ile, ime, ine, ipe, ise, ite, ive
 obe, ode, oke, ole, ome, one, ope, ose, ote, ove
 ube, ule, use, ute

These rimes use vowel combinations:
 aid, ail, ain, air
 ead, eal, eam, ean, ear, eat
 ie
 oar, oat, oe, oil, ood (wood), ook, oot (foot), ood (food), oof, oom, oon, oop, oot (shoot), ool, oor, owl, own, oy
 ue

This is not a complete list of onsets and rimes. It illustrates the kinds of patterns that children will need to use in their writing.

For each sound that you investigate you can use the four-step spelling lesson described on p.23.

This lesson focuses on the sound of *f*.

1. **Collect words**	3. **Sort the words**
List words with the sound *f* on an overhead projector. *Safe, chief, phone, graph, elephant, laugh, tough, half, calf* Choose a vowel sound, and ask the children to suggest words that have the same sound.	Give a copy of the list to children in small groups. The children are to cut apart the words, and sort them according to their spelling of the vowel sound. *Safe, chief* *Laugh, tough* *Elephant, phone, graph* *Calf, half*
2. **Investigate the patterns**	4. **Build more words**
Pointing to the list on the board, ask the class to arrange the words under each of the following letters: *f, gh, ph, ff, lf* Ask questions to help children to make discoveries about the words. How many patterns have we found? Which is common? Which is rare? Which words do we find hard to spell? Which letters can come at the beginning of words? Which can never come at the beginning of words? Which vowel never follows *ph*?	Children use a dictionary and build a *ph* list for each vowel: A: *Phantom, pharaoh, pharmacy, phase, phrase* E: *Pheasant, phenomenon* I: *Philadelphia, philately, Philip, philosophy* O: *Phobia, phonics, phoney, phosphate* Y: *Physics, physical*

Function patterns   Function refers to the way that a word is used in a sentence. Typically in English we add different endings to words to change their function. For example:

adjective	noun	adverb	verb
sad	*sadness*	*sadly*	*sadden*

Most suffixes are function patterns because they change singular to plural, verb tense or part of speech. The spelling of a suffix remains the same, no matter which word it is added to; if you can spell it in one word, you can spell it in all words. Knowing function endings can make spelling at least part of a word highly predictable.

Strategies for teaching function patterns

The best way for children to learn function patterns is to collect and build words that share the same function and ending. As they work with word endings, children will also gain an awareness of how words are used, and the different kinds of words that make up our grammar and syntax.

- ✔ Perform 'function magic' to change the part of speech.
  Add *y* to change a noun into an adjective
    funny, rainy, smelly, snowy.
  Add *ly* to change an adjective into an adverb
    wisely, swiftly, greatly, cunningly.
  Add *ment* to change a verb into a noun
    judgement, adjustment, argument, placement.
  Add *en* to change an adjective or noun into a verb
    widen, sharpen, lengthen, frighten.

- ✔ Perform similar 'function magic' to change a word's application.
  Add *ist* to turn an object into a person
    harpist, typist, artist, balloonist.
  Add *y* to turn a person into a place
    pottery, bakery, grocery, ironmongery.

- ✔ When the children are used to building words in this way, they can make endings 'disappear' to change a part of speech. This will teach children to look for the different parts of words. Being able to recognise a prefix, root and suffix, and to separate them from one another, is very helpful in spelling.

- ✔ Collect different ways to make plurals. Most plurals are highly predictable; for example, the *s* ending that marks plural nouns is often pronounced like *z* (*dogs*) but is never spelled with *z*. It is a safe bet that, except for a few irregular plurals, *s* will be the final letter. Children will readily find examples of the three most common plural endings: *s, es, ies*. They may not so readily identify plurals such as *people, children* and *media*. Start a classroom list that the children can add to as they find more plural patterns. Although the vast majority of plurals that we use belong to the three regular patterns, there are a great many other plural patterns. Because these represent many different languages, they provide a good opportunity to teach the children about word origins.

| *dogs* | *churches* | *babies* | *children* | *people* | *geese* | *mice* |
| *sheep* | *wolves* | *men* | | | | |

Latin:	*formulae*	*cacti*	*media*	*indices*
Greek:	*hypotheses*	*criteria*		
French:	*gateaux*			
Hebrew:	*cherubim*			

Children may be able to recognise some patterns-within-patterns in these plurals. For example, words with Latin origins tend to be used in science contexts, while words that do not change in the plural form are animals.

✔ In order to add endings to words correctly, children need to know the word-building patterns described below. To avoid the confusion of trying to teach more than one concept at a time, you can start off by giving children examples that do not require any change of the ending.

✔ Children will understand grammar more readily and be able to name parts of speech if they understand the functions of words. Looking at endings and how they change the way in which a word can be used will contribute to this understanding.

Meaning patterns

Dr Johnson, author of the first great English dictionary, believed that English spelling owes more to meaning than to sound. This is why he maintained the different spellings of homophones; they may sound the same, but when you meet them in reading they look different.

'What is written without effort is in general read without pleasure.'

The meaning of a word is often centred in its root, the spelling of which tends to remain the same even when a variety of prefixes and suffixes is added to it. Prefixes which alter meaning also maintain their spelling on all words, and do not change the words to which they are added.

Understanding a word's meaning and origin is helpful in spelling. If you know a word is medical, and that our science of medicine came from the Greeks, you will be able to predict that an *f* sound will be spelled with Greek *ph* (*physician*). If you are writing about Italian food, you will know that many words end in *i* rather than the *y* your ear would lead you to expect (*fusilli*).

Children can build word-families of words that share the same root or prefix and learn how the meanings and the spelling remain constant.

Strategies for teaching meaning patterns

Meaning patterns involve roots and prefixes. When children understand the meaning of a root or prefix, they can use this knowledge to build words. Teach children to use meaning links to help them to spell words they are not sure of.

✔ Help children to understand that words are built up of different parts, each with its own meaning and function. With beginning spellers, start out with whole words to which prefixes and suffixes can be added.

Farm er	*paint er*	*teach er*
Free ly	*calm ly*	*foolish ly*
Snow y	*smell y*	*munch y*
Kind est	*cool est*	*hard est*
Re use	*re model*	*re form*
Un do	*un mask*	*un fasten*
Pre cut	*pre form*	*pre mature*

✔ As you build lists of words that share the same root, children will come to expect the spelling of a root to remain the same in all the words. Point this out particularly in words in which pronunciation of the root changes, but the spelling does not.

please/pleasant   revise/revision

✔ Pay particular attention to prefixes that end with the first letter of the root to which they are added. These often cause one of the letters to be omitted.

mis spell, un natural, re elect

Children will avoid such misspellings if they know that all the letters of both prefix and root must still be included.

✔ Teach children to work out the spelling of new words by writing down one or two other words that may be connected in meaning. For example, listing *signature* and *signal* may help you to remember the silent *g* in *sign*.

LISTEN FOR THE SILENT LETTERS

Now You Hear it	Now You Don't
signal	sign
condemnation	condemn
muscular	muscle
columnist	column
autumnal	autumn
phlegmatic	phlegm
solemnity	solemn
agnostic	gnostic

✔ Compound words form a special kind of meaning pattern. Children need to know that all the letters of both words must still be present. This is particularly important when joining the two words results in repeating a letter in the middle (*bookkeeper, granddaughter*). In the United Kingdom, the compound word *granddad* has been misspelled as *grandad* for so long that this usage is now accepted as being correct.

✔ Many prefixes fall into meaning groups that are helpful for a teaching focus. Some larger dictionaries list these prefixes.

Numbers: *uni, bi, kilo*
Size: *micro, poly*
Where: *circ, tele*
Negation: *un, mis*
Opposites: *pro/anti, bene/mal*

✔ Meaning is particularly important for spelling homophones. These are words that sound the same, but have different spellings and different meanings. In order to learn homophones, children must know the meaning of each word. It is more productive to teach each one in its own meaning context than to group them together into one lesson. These homophones do not form a spelling pattern: *there   their   they're*. Grouping them together is what makes them difficult to distinguish. It is better to put each word in its own pattern:

There	*Their*	*They're*
Thereabouts	*His*	*We're*
Here	*Her*	*You're*
Where	*My*	*I'm*
Everywhere	*Our*	
Therefore	*Your*	
Nowhere		
Somewhere		

It is only by making the right meaning connection that children can choose the correct homophone spelling.

Word-building patterns

These are sometimes called 'spelling rules', but this is a misnomer. There are no rules in English spelling, because there is no recognised authority to make them. Even the dictionaries reflect usage; they do not mandate it. Dictionaries recognise the evolutionary nature of spelling by listing alternative spellings that are in use in different dialects of English. However, there are some regular patterns in the ways in which we construct words, and knowing these can help children to make more correct choices about spellings.

The best way for children to learn one of these word-building patterns is to collect many examples and to look for the similarities. Once they make a generalisation about a pattern, they can use it to construct other words.

Adding endings

There are four patterns for adding endings to words.

1. Double the final consonant
It is a common pattern in English that double consonants follow short-vowel syllables.
   grabbed, messy, kitten, coffee, butter

When adding a suffix to a short-vowel syllable, double the final consonant.
   Can   canned   slip   slipping   fun   funny

Children can learn this pattern by listing words using each vowel. You can also draw their attention to the change in meaning that a mistake can create:
   Canning or caning?   Pinning or pining?   Ridding or riding?

2. Change y to i

Some children find this confusing because it does not apply to all words ending in *y*. There are two ways to explain these patterns to them:

✔ When a word ends in a consonant + *y*, change *y* to *i*: *baby babies*.
When a word ends in a vowel + *y*, just add the ending: *bay bays*.
This is a linguistic definition and is sometimes hard for young children to understand and remember.

✔ When the last vowel sound that you hear is *y* all by itself, change *y* to *i*: *pon y pon ies*.
When *y* is only part of the last vowel sound you hear, just add the ending: *monk ey monk eys*.

Whichever way you explain it, many children will find it confusing. The best way for children to internalise the pattern is to collect many words that illustrate the two ways of adding endings to words ending in *y*. Children can then both see and hear the difference. They will probably respond to the notion that it is important not to make the words look funny.
ponys   monkeies

3. Drop the final e

We drop the final *e* because if we did not, some words would look very strange and 'un-English'. Show the children some examples of the kind of words we would make if we just added endings to these words:
use + ed = useed   rise + ing = riseing   wide + en = wideen

These strange-looking spellings occur when two vowels come together. This is why we do not drop the final *e* when adding suffixes beginning with consonants; the problem just does not arise.
safety   useless   strangeness   vengeful

If they see enough examples of both kinds of patterns, children will come to see their logic. When spelling is logical, children have a much better chance of remembering and using the patterns.

Recognising when words look right and when they look strange is an important sense to develop. If children understand why to drop the *e*, it becomes a matter of common sense, rather than just another spelling rule that they have to remember.

4. Just add the endings

This one applies to all words in which one of the special cases described above does not apply.

i before e

There is a common rhyme we have all used to help to remember the order for these two vowels:
i before *e*
when it sounds like *e*
except after *c*

It is important to remember that this pattern applies only to the long *e* sound.
   field   *believe*   *brief*
   receive *deceit*   *ceiling*

Other vowel sounds will not follow the pattern.
   sleigh   *height*   *forfeit*

This makes it a series of relatively simple rhyming patterns, with few exceptions. Perhaps the most often misspelled of these is *seize*. (Names seem to be exceptions to this pattern: *Sheila, Reid, Keith, Neil, Madeira*. Any child with one of these names is likely to remember this pattern.)

Soft c and g

c and *g* are much influenced by the vowels that follow them in words. Here is a rhyme that will help to teach these patterns:
  i, y and *e*
  soften *c* and *g*

This means that *c* or *g* followed by *i, y* or *e* will have a soft sound:
  civil   *cedar*   *cygnet*   *gender*   *ginger*   *gymnast*

c or *g* followed by *a* or *u* will have a hard sound:
  cat   *cup*   *gap*   *gust*

Children can take each pair of letters and build as many words as they can. Initially they will use the letters to start words, but older children can try to place the letters within the word.

  ca   *ce*   *ci*   *co*   *cu*   *cy*   *ga*   *ge*   *gi*   *go*   *gu*   *gy*

Reading each list vertically will emphasise the sound caused by each vowel. It will also show up any exceptions that the children may find.
  Celtic (e.g. Celtic cross)   *get*   *tiger*   *gills*   *girl*   *girder*   *girdle*

Knowing this pattern will also help children to see why they need to use *gu* for some hard *g* words:
  guest   *guess*   *Guernsey*   *guild*   *guide*

Chapter 5

spelling activities

Repertoire of activities

You will need a repertoire of activities for three kinds of spelling investigation:

- ✔ Word-collecting
- ✔ Word-building
- ✔ Pattern matching.

You can then select an activity to suit each kind of spelling pattern that you are working with. The more variety in the activities, the more interesting spelling will be for the children and the greater the potential for learning.

Word-collecting

A large number of activities lend themselves to this sort of investigation.

Spontaneous list

Use a starter-word or idea and ask the children to suggest words that fit the pattern. You can list the words as the children call them out, or ask them to work in small groups, each with a scribe. When you do this, children will often suggest a word that sounds as if it fits, but does not. You can list this to the side, explaining that it belongs in a different pattern that the children will learn about later.

Two ways to say ow

cow	brown	know	window
now	clown	blow	fellow
chow	drown	crow	below
how	howl	low	callow
allow	cowl	snow	tallow
scow	jowl	show	wallow
	fowl		follow
	scowl		tomorrow
	owl		sparrow
	prowl		
	down		
	town		

Some words can be pronounced both ways

bow	bow
sow	sow

Researched lists

When you introduce a word or pattern in class, you can ask children to look out for other examples as they read, write and go about their daily activities. They may go to specific sources, such as a dictionary, telephone directory or expert, to find words. Sometimes they may ask family members to help. When the children find a new word, they can add it to the list. After two or three days, or when there are enough words on the list, you can revisit it and help the children to learn about the patterns.

Example

If you are looking at words that end with a long e sound, ask the children to take along a notebook when they go to a supermarket, and note down food words that spell this final sound with *i*. Back in class, they can set this list beside a list of words that spell this final sound with *y*, then you can draw their attention to the fact that those ending in *i* are Italian.

Display

Set up a display of objects representing the same spelling pattern. You can start it off with one or two items, and ask the children to add other objects over the next day or two. Print a card to label each object as it is added. When the display is over, make the name cards available for children to sort, categorise, or put in alphabetical order. This is a basic skill needed for finding words in a dictionary.

Collages

Children can build letter collages by cutting out pictures of objects starting with the same letter. They can paste these on a large shape of the letter they are using. If children work in groups of three or four, the class can build a whole alphabet in a very short time. You can post these on the wall where the children can refer to them for letter sounds and shapes. Children will learn not only by finding pictures for their own collage, but by identifying objects in the other pictures. Catalogues are good for cutting out pictures of objects.

You can extend this activity by asking the children to cut out words starting with the designated letter to make a word collage. They can build word collages for such groups as proper nouns, titles, different words meaning street, place names.

Rhymes

When you are working with a vowel pattern, children can often come up with a list of words by thinking of rhyming words. One way you can extend a list is by asking the children to try different consonants before and after the vowel sound in question. Use each consonant in turn through the alphabet and see what words it triggers.

Example

An alphabetical list of words rhyming with *air* might produce a list such as this:

air, bear, bare, care, dare, fair, fare, glare, hair, hare, lair, mare, pear, pair, pare, rare, share, spare, stair, tear, there, their, wear, ware, where

When listed according to spelling pattern, it would look like this:

Words that rhyme with air

air	bear	bare	there	their
fair	pear	care	where	
hair	tear	dare		
lair	wear	fare		
pair		glare		
stair		hare		
		mare		
		pare		
		rare		
		share		
		spare		
		ware		

This will not only show children how many different patterns there are, but will help them to see which are the most common and which are rarely used.

Homework

Involve families in word collecting. After starting a collection in class, the children can ask their families to contribute other words. This is not only a way to increase the length and variety of your word lists, but also a good way to show families how their children are studying spelling.

Group themes

When children work in groups to collect words, give each group a different focus or theme. For example, if you are collecting adverbs ending in *ly*, groups could list words for ways to move in water, ways insects move, ways gymnasts move, and so on. In this way, different groups are likely to come up with different words, and they can pool them to make a common list.

Observation post

Place the children in spots where they can observe action taking place, perhaps on the playground, in the gym, in the school office, at a street corner, or on a family shopping trip. They can take a notepad, and list words in a particular category, perhaps adjectives ending in *y*, or past-tense verbs.

What are they doing?

In the gym	In the office	In the library	On the playground
jumping	typing	reading	throwing
vaulting	writing	viewing	shouting
climbing	talking	searching	playing
tumbling	sorting	asking	skipping
tossing	photocopying	whispering	chanting

Personal dictionaries

Spelling instruction becomes personal when it helps the children with words that they need for their own writing. With a personal dictionary, children can keep words that they have trouble spelling, new words that they would like to use, words that they need for a particular task, and words that they find interesting. They can list family names, street names, birthdays and words personal to their own lives. Children can select a few words that they think they might need from the word lists made in class and add them to their own dictionaries.

Beginning spellers who will be learning many new words might have an exercise book with a page for each letter. When they ask you for a spelling, you can print it on the correct page so they can find it again. Each time they add or look for a word, they will be practising finding information by using alphabetical order.

Theme words

When the children are working on a particular topic, it is often helpful to have a reference of words that they may need to use. These words are likely to be subject-related and can be difficult to spell. At the beginning of the theme, children can brainstorm a list of words which you can print on a chart to remain on the wall for the duration of the study. Add any words you want the children to be able to use. As the theme progresses, you and they can add more words.

Children may be more willing to use difficult words if they are readily available. It is less time consuming to find the words on a theme list than to look them up in a dictionary each time they are needed.

At the end of the theme, take the list down to make room for a new one. Keep the lists so they are accessible for the rest of the year. Store them on a chart stand, or list them to fit in a ring-binder. Before filing them away, ask one of the children to alphabetise the list.

Make sure the children do not see this list as words they have to memorise. It is not appropriate to test them on the words, except as they use them in their writing. You can, however, expect children to use the list when they are proofreading and editing their writing for a final draft.

You can use words from the list for spelling instruction by picking out one word at a time, and using it to build its own spelling pattern, to investigate its meaning and origin, and to build derivations (words built from a single root). If children continue to use some of the words in their writing, they may come to remember the spellings. If they do not continue to use them, they will be able to find them again in the future.

Word-building

Again, a variety of activities of this sort is available.

Word wheels

This is ideal for building words based on the same prefix, root or suffix. Draw a wheel with the key word-part in the hub and different prefixes and suffixes in the outer rings. Children print words they have built in a list.

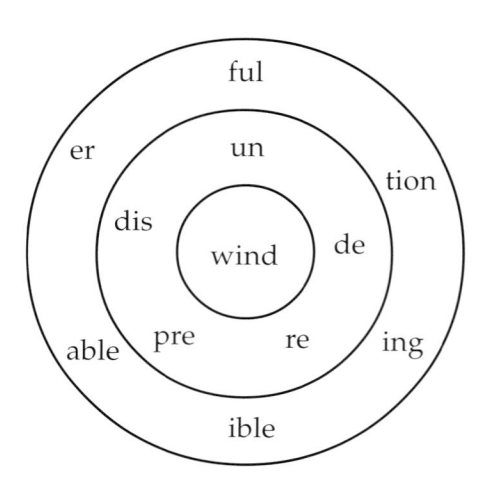

unwind
rewind
winding
winder

Word trees A word tree is rather like a flow-chart, and can grow branches or roots, or both (see p.20). You can use a word tree to show derivations.

Letter cards Beginning spellers can use cards with individual letters on them, then onsets and rimes to build words. Older children can use cards with roots, prefixes and suffixes on them to build longer words. Any time that children are manipulating letters to build words, they are learning about how letters work together.

If you keep a number of blank cards, children can add their own words and word-parts. They will enjoy making up their own games using the cards. As they make up the games, they will be finding ways to sort and to match the words.

Word frames A word frame gives the beginning and end of a word, leaving the middle blank. Children can see how many different letters or letter combinations that they can use to fill in the 'picture'. Beginning spellers may fill in one vowel between two consonants: p__n, b__t. Older children may fill in letter combinations: m__ __l, p__ __t.

You can reverse this activity by giving children the 'picture' and asking them to frame it: __ea__, __oa__.

Extend the activity by not limiting the number of letters that children can use to make a word.

Child's list

___ ___ ___ ___ *ea* ___ ___ ___ ___

beast	*bread*
bleat	*breadth*
bean	*thread*
creature	*treasure*
least	*pleasant*

Word webs To start a word web, print a word in the centre of the board or a large piece of paper. You will want your web to branch off in more than one direction, so ideal words to start with are compound words, or words with a prefix and suffix. Take each part of the word in turn, and beside it list derivations. Then choose individual words from these new lists from which to build more derivations. Each list that you make will give you more words to start new lists. Word webs tend to go on forever, being limited only by the available space.

Word web

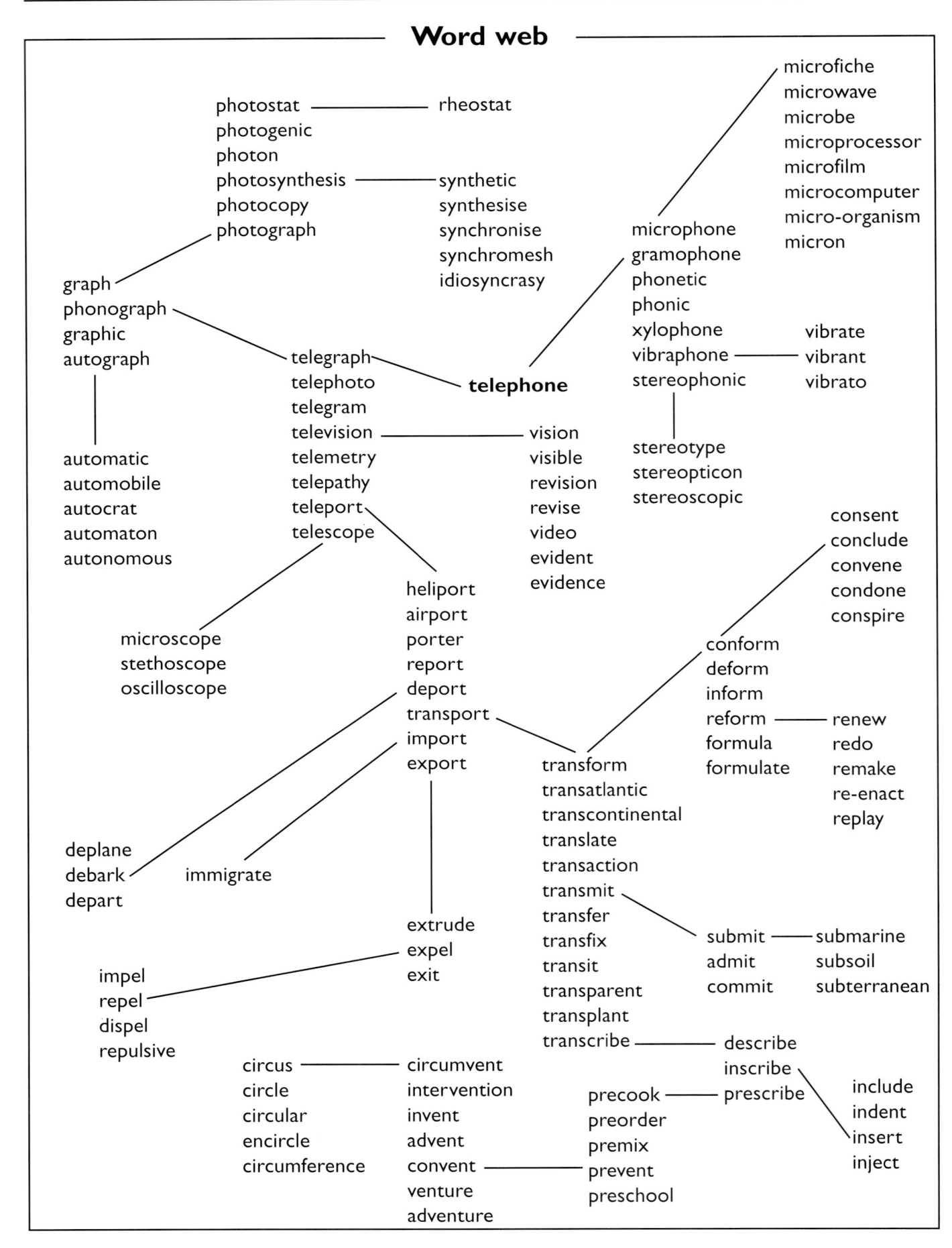

photostat — rheostat
photogenic
photon
photosynthesis — synthetic
photocopy   synthesise
photograph   synchronise
               synchromesh
               idiosyncrasy

graph
phonograph
graphic
autograph
                telegraph
                telephoto
                telegram   **telephone**
                television — vision
automatic   telemetry   visible
automobile   telepathy   revision
autocrat   teleport   revise
automaton   telescope   video
autonomous   evident
                                  evidence

microfiche
microwave
microbe
microprocessor
microfilm
microcomputer
micro-organism
micron

microphone
gramophone
phonetic
phonic
xylophone — vibrate
vibraphone — vibrant
stereophonic   vibrato

stereotype
stereopticon
stereoscopic

                heliport
                airport
microscope   porter
stethoscope   report
oscilloscope   deport
                transport
                import
                export   transform
                              transatlantic
                              transcontinental
                              translate
                              transaction
deplane   transmit
debark   transfer
depart   immigrate   transfix   submit — submarine
                              transit   admit   subsoil
                              transparent   commit   subterranean
                              transplant
               extrude   transcribe — describe
               expel   inscribe
impel   exit   prescribe   include
repel   precook   indent
dispel   preorder   insert
repulsive   premix   inject
                              prevent
                              preschool

consent
conclude
convene
condone
conspire

conform
deform
inform
reform — renew
formula   redo
formulate remake
          re-enact
          replay

circus — circumvent
circle   intervention
circular invent
encircle advent
circumference
         convent
         venture
         adventure

Once children know how to build a web, they can work individually or in small groups to make their own. This is an ideal activity for children to do in groups, or to take for homework to involve the whole family.

Word searches

Finding words in a word search involves looking for letters that work in combination with one another. This will help children to distinguish between possible and impossible letter combinations. It can also help them to recognise theme words, high-frequency words, or any words you want them to be able to read and use. You can introduce two levels of difficulty: provide the words, so the children have to find their match, or do not provide the words, and let the children discover them for themselves.

It is relatively easy to construct a word search. First make a list of the words you want to include. Take a grid of squares, and fill in a word across the top. Then try to fit in as many of your words as you can. Fill in the blanks with random letters. A well-constructed word search fills as many squares as possible with real words.

For young children, stick to words written horizontally. Do not expect them to find words written from right to left. For older children you can add words written vertically and, later still, diagonally.

Word mobiles

A mobile is one way to display words that are connected. After collecting words, the children can sort them into subcategories, and hang them from different strings on a wire coat-hanger. While most of the learning will be in finding the words and preparing the mobile, children will enjoy having their words on display.

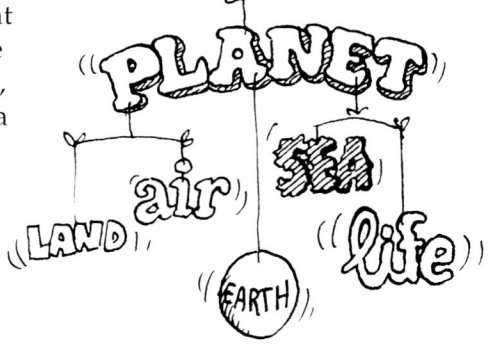

Word chains

Build a word chain with a string of derivations. Start with a root, and add prefixes and suffixes one at a time to see how long it can grow. Print each word on a card and link the cards with paper clips.

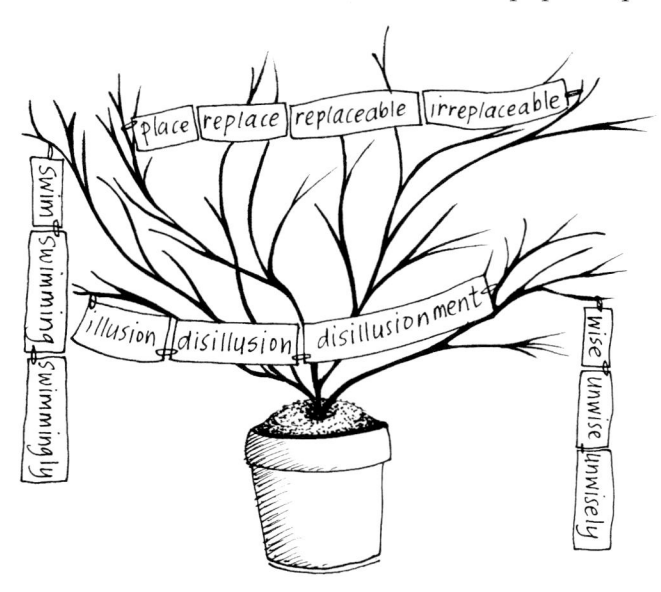

Word games Give the children opportunities to play word games, such as crossword puzzles and Scrabble. Let them solve anagrams, and play Hangman. Any time children are building and manipulating words and letters, there is a potential for spelling learning.

Pattern matching

Here are a few activities that involve pattern matching.

Venn diagrams Venn diagrams are ideal for sorting words, and sorting involves finding similarities among groups of words. For young children, start out with one circle, and ask them to put words that fit a pattern inside the circle, leaving the other words outside. Later, they can use multiple circles to sort words into different groups. When the children have learned how to sort using crossed circles in mathematics, they can apply this also to sorting words.

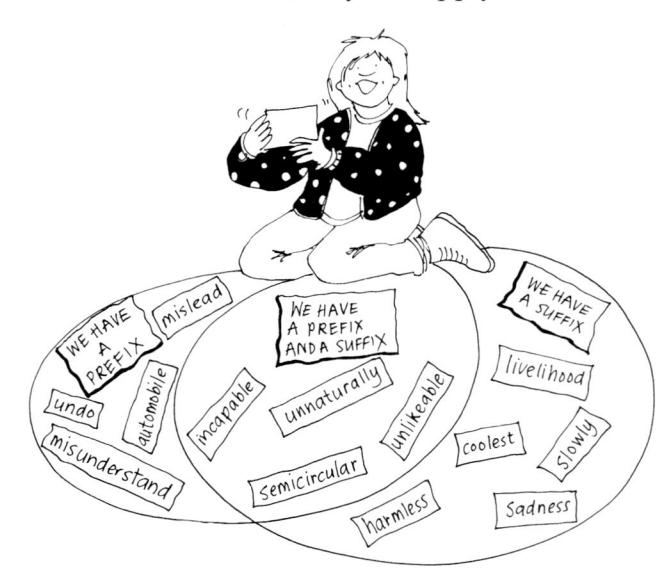

Concentration Use any pairs of words to make a concentration game: upper and lower case letters, rhyming words, onsets, rimes, verb tenses, prefixes, suffixes, and so on. The players place all the cards face down, and take turns to turn over two cards. If they make a match, they keep the cards and have another turn. When all the cards are picked up, the game is over.

Sorting Cut apart words from a list, and ask the children to sort them in as many ways as they can. In order to do this, they will need to find ways in which the words are similar and ways in which they are different. This will help to teach them how to look for patterns and connections. They may sort according to rhyme, number of syllables, letter combinations, root, prefix, or suffix, or even such personal categories as words they use or do not use. After the sorting activity they should be able to explain and justify their choices either to you, to another child, or by labelling the categories. Children's justification for grouping words together is often the basis for a generalisation that will allow them to use the same logic when trying to spell similar words in the future. This is the learning you want them to take away from a spelling lesson and is far more useful than a memory of the actual words.

Spelling investigations

Whenever possible, make spelling a 'let's find out' kind of activity. You can use the four-step spelling lesson for this:

Ask a question, give a piece of information, or form a hypothesis. Then:

1. Collect words
2. Sort out the words
3. Look for the pattern and logic
4. Use the patterns to build more words.

When to use investigations

You can use these kinds of activities as:

✔ individual or group investigations
✔ homework assignments
✔ challenges for the whole family
✔ quiz-of-the-day on your bulletin board
✔ a follow-up to reading, using an example word from the text
✔ a starting-point for a spelling lesson
✔ activities for children who have misspelled similar patterns in their writing.

Ideas for investigations

Here are some examples of the kind of questions you can ask to start such an investigation:

✔ In how many different ways can two vowels be combined? Write example words for each combination.

✔ In how many different ways can three vowels be combined? Write example words for each combination.

✔ Find words in which a long-vowel sound is made with only one letter. (Children should include *y* as one of the vowels that make a long sound – *y* and *w* are considered vowels when they come at the end of a syllable but consonants when they begin a syllable.)

✔ Find words in which two vowels together make a short-vowel sound. (*head, forfeit*)

✔ What is the longest word you can write with only one vowel? (*strengths* is probably the longest they will find. Attempting to build long words will involve trying out combinations of three consonants.)

✔ Find words that have *y* as their only vowel.

✔ Which vowel combinations can have more than one pronunciation? List examples of each. (*ea, ou, oo, oe*)

✔ The pattern *a_e* makes a long *a* sound. Which consonants can fill the space? Write words for each. (Repeat with each vowel.)

✔ *ow* can have two pronunciations, as in *snow* and *cow*. Write examples for each sound. (Repeat for *ea* – *bread/bead* and *oo* – *foot/food*.)

✔ Which consonants can follow *s* in a word? Write example words for each combination. (Follow up with consonants that can follow *m*, or *n* at the end of a word.)

✔ Which consonants can come before *r*? Write example words for each combination. (Follow up with consonants that can follow *r* at the end of a word.)

✔ Which consonants can come before *l*? Write an example word for each combination. (Follow up with consonants that can follow *l* at the end of a word.)

✔ Which consonants can double at the end of words? Write three example words for each pair. Which are common? Which are rare?

✔ Are there any words that begin with a double consonant?

✔ Which consonants can pair with *h*? Write example words for each combination. Which can come at the beginning of words? Which can come at the end of words?

✔ Which is more common at the end of words: *c* or *ck*?

✔ Which letters can be silent at the beginning of words?

✔ List adjectives that end with a long *e* sound. How is this ending most often spelled? What other spellings are possible?

✔ What different suffixes can denote a person who does a certain job? (Start with examples, such as act*or*, art*ist*, electri*cian*.)

✔ Which words are spelled differently in American and British English?

✔ Which words are spelled exactly the same as French words? (Extend the list by adding other languages.)

✔ What abbreviations can you find for titles and jobs? (Start with *Mr, Mrs, Dr*. The telephone directory will provide many more examples.)

✔ Which words can be abbreviated to form a contraction?

✔ In how many different ways can we make a word plural? (This is an excellent activity for children to take home. With the help of adults, they may find close to 20 ways.)

✔ Find words with four, five, or six syllables. What is the largest number of syllables you can write in a single word? (Finding a few words will involve a lot of syllable counting along the way.)

✔ The double letters found most often at the end of words are *ll*, *ss* and *ff*. Which vowels can come immediately before these endings? Write example words for each.

✔ When *ch* makes a hard *c* sound, the word is most likely of Greek origin. Write musical examples. Write scientific examples.

✔ Words ending in *eau* are of French origin. Write examples. Write the plurals of these words.

✔ When *ph* makes the sound of *f*, the word is probably of Greek origin. Find examples in which the *ph* comes at the beginning of the word, and examples in which the *ph* comes at the end of the word.

✔ The ending *ery* often denotes a place where a certain job is carried out. Write as many examples as you can.

✔ In compound words, all the letters of both words must be written. Write examples of compound words in which the last letter of the first word is the same as the first letter of the second word, as in *gran**d** **d**aughter*.

✔ In consonant combinations in which both letter sounds are heard, the most common letters are *l*, *r* +and *s*. Which consonants can combine with these? Write example words for each.

✔ *ology* is a Greek suffix meaning the *science of* or *study of*. Write as many *ology* words as you can. Illustrate/mime/explain the meaning of each. Turn each one into a person by changing the suffix to *ist*.

Chapter 6

Using spelling lists

Using lists of words

Lists of words have always played a part in spelling instruction. Typically, children have spent a week memorising a list ready for a test. Activities have been designed to allow the children to read and write the words many times, in the hope that this would imprint the word indelibly on their memories. Most teachers have seen children spell words correctly on the test, then misspell them in their own writing. Many children failed every week to get all their words right.

Lists of words play an important part in spelling learning. However, they should be lists that illustrate spelling patterns, not lists to memorise. When we understand the logical nature of spelling, we can use lists of words more effectively to help children to learn to spell.

Children can make use of three kinds of lists:

- ✔ Word family lists
- ✔ Reference lists
- ✔ Prompt lists.

Word family lists

The hardest and most short-lived way to learn a spelling is to try to remember a word in isolation. As most words fit into spelling patterns, learning to spell one word can contribute to our learning of all the other words in the same pattern.

A word family list is designed to help children to recognise the similarities among words. Then when they want to spell a new word, they can try to match it to other similar words.

Spelling instruction is most effective when we can help children to think of words in 'families', words that share the same spelling pattern. A large part of the learning takes place in the construction of the list, as children recognise the pattern and find words that fit. It is not necessary for children to try to memorise all the words. All they need to remember is the pattern; they can then reconstruct the words when they need them, as well as make reasonable predictions about the spelling of new words as they learn them.

Suggestions for word family lists

Any two or more words that have some connection with one another can form a word family. Your lists will represent three kinds of spelling patterns. The following is not a complete list of spelling patterns; it represents the kind of patterns children need to use in their writing.

Sound patterns

Consonant	Single	b, d, f, g
	Double	bb, cc, dd, ff
	Combinations of 2	br, cr, dr, fr, sc, sk, sl (two sounds)
		sh, th, ch, ph, gh (one sound)
		th, sh, ph, gh (new sound)
	Combinations of 3	spr, str (three sounds)
		thr, chr, shr (two sounds)
		tch, ght (one sound)
Vowels	Short	a, e, i, o, u
	Long	silent e, igh(t)
	Double	ee, oo
	Combinations	ai, ea, ie, oa, ui
	r controlled	eer, ear, or, are
	l controlled	eel, eal, ail
	Diphthongs	oi, ow, oy
Silent letters	Beginning	kn, gn, pn, ps, mn
	End	lf, lm

Function patterns

Verb tense	Regular	d, ed, ing
	Irregular	was, flew, meant
Plurals	Common	s, es, ies
	Foreign origin	Latin, Greek, French
	Rare	en, ice, ren
Suffixes	Derivations	tion, ly, ful, ness, ment, able
	How to add	plain, drop final e
		double final letter, change y to i
Contractions	Words contracted	not, will, am, are, is, has, have, us
Abbreviations	Titles	Mr, Mrs, Dr
	Addresses	St., Ave., Blvd., Cres., Dr., Rd.
	Days	Mon., Tues., Wed.
	Months	Jan., Feb., Mar.
	Measurements	m, km, ft, in, kg, l
	Acronyms	RADAR, SONAR, SCUBA
	Words	Fax, mini, phone
Punctuation	End	full stop, exclamation, question
	Medial	comma, quotation
	Possessives	's, s'
Capitalisation	Proper nouns	people, places
	Sentences	

Meaning patterns

Compound words	Building All letters of both words	snow, ball, light granddaughter, withhold, bookkeeper
Roots	Latin	port, sign, dict, fact, flect, ject, circ, cap, script, urb
	Greek	graph, geo, photo, therm, hyd, mech, scop, chem, aero
Prefixes	Negation Number Size When Where Again Judgement Latin Greek	un, dis, mis, in, im, il, non uni, bi, tri, milli, dec, kilo, multi micro, mega, mini, maxi pre, post, ante sub, super, tele, in, ex, trans, mid re pro, anti, con, contra mono, pre, aqua phono, psych, phys, cycl, therm
Sight words	Commonly used Pronouns Theme words	the, because, they, who my, his, her, our, their

Here is an illustration of a silent letter family:

The silent *h* family

whack	wheat	which	whither	whoa	why
whale	wheedle	whichever	whiting	whorl	
wham	wheel	whiff	whittle		
wharf	whelk	Whig	whiz		
what	whelp	while			
whatever	when	whilst			
	whenever	whim			
	where	whimper			
	whereabouts	whimsical			
	wherry	whinny			
	whet	whip			
	whether	whippet			
	whey	whirl			
		whisk			
		whisker			
		whisper			
		whist			
		whistle			
		Whitby			
		white			

Reference lists

A reference list takes the place of a dictionary. It is intended for temporary use, to give children words they need for a particular topic or project. Looking up words on a list takes less time than using a dictionary, yet can get children used to using such a reference to find out about words. A reference list is particularly useful in content-area subjects, where specialised and technical vocabulary may be too difficult for children to learn.

You can build such a list by first asking the children to brainstorm words that they think they might need for the topic. They can do this as a class while you record the words, or they can work in small groups first listing the words, then exchanging with another group for proofreading and finally checking the spellings with a dictionary or spellchecker. As the theme progresses, you or the children can add new words as you meet them in reading, or need them for writing.

Encourage children to list their words in alphabetical order, then each time they use the list they are practising the skills they need for using dictionaries and other reference books. If children build their own lists, they will learn the value of correct spelling, accurate copying and neat handwriting.

A reference list can be quite long, as its function is to be a mini-dictionary. When the theme is over, the list could be stored either in a file box or a ring-binder to be consulted when children write about this theme in the future. Children would then be able to refer to these lists during independent research or writing. A useful strategy is to select a certain number of these words for groups of children to rewrite as a glossary to be kept at the back of a file containing information on particular topics or subjects. A short dictation exercise using some of the words in context could be used as a check or assessment at the end of the topic.

Children can use the word lists when they are writing or editing. You can make them responsible for proofreading for list words before their writing goes to final draft. Proofreading is generally more successful when children know what they are looking for.

Revisiting words from lists

Make sure that children do not see the reference list as a list of words to be memorised by rote. Using words frequently in context is the best way to learn new spellings and vocabulary. If children continue to use some of the words after the theme is over, they will more likely remember the spellings. You will find that frequency of use will help the words to pass into children's speaking and writing vocabularies.

Take every opportunity to revisit the words and use them in the classroom, even when the theme is over.

✔ Point out a list word when you meet it in a reading activity.
✔ Draw the children's attention to a list word in the news, for example a newspaper article about space exploration could allow you to revisit space words.

✔ Help children to understand and internalise new vocabulary by using it in class discussion and general conversation.
✔ Have a word-of-the-day. Print a word from a previous list on the board and encourage children to use it in speech and in writing.

Word-play activities

In addition to using their words for writing, children can also use them in word-play activities such as the following:

✔ Print each word on a card. The children can alphabetise the cards to the first, second or subsequent letters.

✔ Take a closer look at some of the individual words. You might investigate a Latin or Greek root, or explore a word's origins.

✔ The children can sort the words in a variety of ways: meaning connections, number of syllables, prefixes, suffixes, parts of speech, or any category that they can devise for themselves.

✔ Use the words to build an illustrated alphabet book. This could also double as a glossary to help children to learn new vocabulary.

✔ Make a collage of the words. The children can use fancy script to print each word, or experiment with fonts from a computer.

✔ The children can test each other informally and in private to find out which of the list words they know already. They could then make shorter, personal lists of words that they cannot spell and need as a reference.

✔ The children can devise a spelling test for their family. They can choose what they think are the most difficult words on the list, and take them home to administer the test. In doing this, they will be raising their own awareness of words with which they have the most trouble, and will be rereading and checking them. It can also give you insights into which words children find difficult.

✔ The children can use list words to make a chant or rap. Pay attention to syllable count, and arrange the words to fit a particular rhythm. For example:

Countdown, blast-off, galaxy, moon.
Meteor, telescope, satellite, sun.

Several small groups can each develop a chant, then repeat them in turn while the whole group claps the rhythm. You can even sing them to an appropriate tune such as 'Twinkle, twinkle, little star'.

Prompt lists

A prompt list is for learning new spellings that do not fit a pattern that the children know.

Children all learned to spell their own names through frequency of use. They managed it because learning it was important to them, and because they saw and wrote their name many times. The best way to learn words in which the spelling is not predictable is through frequency of use, both in reading and in writing.

Frequency of use is only helpful if the children spell the words correctly each time they write them; otherwise, they may just become accustomed to using a misspelling.

Young writers need many 'sight' words as soon as they begin to write. Service words, like *the, said, why, because,* are hard to sound out correctly, and belong to patterns that the children will not learn until much later. Older children will also need to learn some words by sight, either because they belong to no recognisable pattern, or because they are exceptions to familiar patterns, or because the children have not yet learned enough about words to recognise the patterns.

Hints on prompt lists   Trying to memorise these words in isolation on a list is not effective; they may pass into short-term memory long enough for children to pass a test, but if they are not used regularly, many children will soon forget them. However, children can print a few at a time on a reference list and have it beside them when they write or edit.

- ✔ List high-frequency words that the children need but have not yet learned. You can make common lists for beginning writers, containing the most frequently used words. As children learn words at different rates, the lists will soon become more individual.

- ✔ Children can make their own lists of words that they misspell frequently in their writing. They can add new words as they discover them in their writing, and delete those they no longer need.

- ✔ Keep the list short, perhaps five words at a time.

- ✔ When children need one of the words in their writing, they should look for it on their list and write it correctly; when they become more confident, they can try to write it then check the spelling with the list afterwards.

- ✔ Make children responsible for checking their prompt-list words every time they write; they will only learn the spellings if they write them correctly. Looking for specific words is also the best way to learn the skill of proofreading.

- ✔ As children find they can write a word correctly without looking on the list first, they can cross it off. Every crossed-out word is a visible sign of learning. When all the words are no longer needed, children can have another group of words to use and learn.

Core vocabulary lists

Many schools have a list of words that children are expected to be able to spell by a certain age. They are usually high-frequency words that the children will need in their daily writing, or words that are frequently misspelled. As these come in lists, perhaps one for each year of school, it is tempting to slip back into old ways of expecting children to memorise the list.

How to use these lists

Listing words together does not make them into a spelling pattern. Unrelated words cannot effectively be learned as a group. Regard these lists as guidelines for planning the content of your spelling curriculum. Then children can learn these words in the same way that they are learning all the other words they need.

- ✔ Place each word in the list in its own spelling context, and teach it in the same way that you are teaching all the other words the children are studying.

- ✔ Look for the significant features of a word; what makes it predictable and what could make it difficult to spell. It is usually possible to predict the kind of error that children are likely to make, perhaps omitting a silent letter, or incorrectly adding an ending. This will help you to find a suitable context for teaching the word.

- ✔ Use the list as an assessment checklist for each child. Note whether the children can spell the words in their daily writing.

- ✔ For those words that do not seem to fit with any others, put a few of them at a time on a prompt list, so the children can keep them handy when they write. After looking them up on the list a number of times, and using them regularly, the children may spontaneously remember them. Frequency of use in writing is one of the best ways to learn this kind of word.

- ✔ Make children responsible for words they have studied or that they have on their personal prompt lists. They can keep their own checklists to show which of the words they know and can proofread for.

Look, say, cover, write, check

By their very nature, the high-frequency vocabulary words will need to be used almost every day in children's writing. Many will be covered through the same patterning approaches already discussed. Through regular practice, children will learn even those which may seem to be exceptions to rules or follow no predictable pattern. One means of helping children to hold these words in their short-term memory is to use a 'look, say, cover, write, check' method. This method has many variants. Although many classrooms will declare that they use it, it can become little more than a mantra for children if not properly taught. One child in a Lancashire nursery knew it as the 'look, cover, write, cheat' method!

Look

- ✔ Look carefully for patterns, analogies with known words and any 'tricky' conventions.
- ✔ Try to 'hold' the word in the mind.

	✔ If the word has syllables, break it up into parts and try each part before attempting the whole word. ✔ Look particularly for vowel combinations.
Say	✔ Vocalise each syllable. ✔ Sound the beginning and final sounds; remember particularly any silent or unvoiced sounds. ✔ Say the sounds and word again as you write it – this helps to fix it in the mind. ✔ If the word is practised on a separate notepad or word-book, it is particularly important to 'say it again' as it is written into the piece of writing. (Some children, especially those with SpLD [Dyslexia], find it easier to <u>name</u> letters than to use their sounds when spelling.)
Cover	✔ This is particularly important as it helps to transfer the word into the memory. ✔ Some children need training to 'hold' a picture in their imagination. Train them using a TV screen in their heads which they must switch on and picture a topical advertisement containing letters or words, e.g. Cereal adverts, Beefburger restaurants and designer fashion. ✔ It sometimes helps if they visualise the words in colour. ✔ Once they can create this picture, they should 'hold' it as long as they can. Asking them to copy words at a 'word table' and hold them while walking back to their own desk aids this.
Write	✔ This is where mistakes are often made in copying. If necessary, break the word up into sensible units or syllables. ✔ Copying from a classroom black/white board is particularly hazardous for many children who have to look up and down again constantly. If possible, provide them with a photocopied sheet of any large amounts of copied text so that they can place it nearer to themselves. ✔ Write, if possible, in joined writing – this helps the children to 'feel' the correct movements. ✔ It is even better if the children write <u>with their eyes closed</u> to place the emphasis on feeling – we often 'feel' that we have misspelled a word before we see the error. If we can write a word with our eyes closed, it has become 'automatically' learned. Practising this again to make absolutely sure is called 'overlearning'.
Check	✔ It is always easier to check someone else's work – encourage children to check each other's practice words as well as proofreading their writing. ✔ Hold lessons in proofreading skills at each stage; as children progress as writers, the practice in this helps them to become more skilled at spotting errors including their own. ✔ Appoint a group, including less able spellers, as 'Official Spellcheckers' for a day and provide them with a range of references. Encourage the other children to take their work to this group to be checked. This could become a standard *independent* activity when writing is in progress.

Strategies for specific words

A lot
Regard each of the words as the subject of its own spelling investigation, along with other words that share a pattern. Here are some examples:

The mistake people make is to write *alot*. (My spellchecker corrects this to *allot*.) Teach this with *a little*, which no one would ever want to write as one word. Teach children to say 'a little' whenever they want to write 'a lot'. Sing the song, 'Little Things Mean a Lot'. You never know what kind of trigger will help children to remember spellings.

Their
Put this in a list with other personal possessive pronouns: *my, our, his, her*. Then give children plenty of practice using these pronouns in sentences. They must understand the meaning in order to choose the correct homophone. It might help to point out that *he* and *I* are both in this word, and *her* is not hard to find. Never link it with *there* or *they're*; this will only add confusion.

Every
Children may omit the central *e*, as they do not pronounce it. Link this with compound words using *ever: evergreen, everlasting, forever*. The children can then build a pattern using *every: everyone, everywhere, everyday*.

They're
Teach this along with other contractions. Recognising that this is really two words is essential to choosing the correct homophone spelling. Children will often misspell this word in first-draft writing. See if they are able to find and correct it when they proofread.

Too/Two
Too is one of the most misspelled words throughout school. Like most homophones, the word itself is not difficult to spell. The mistake is in choosing the wrong spelling, or in not being aware that there are alternatives. Children will often write *to*, no matter which homophone they need. Always teach *two* along with the other words related to the number *two: twins, twice, twelve, twenty*. The story of the Three Bears is ideal for teaching *too: too* hot, *too* cold, *too* hard, and so on. Exaggerate the sound; encourage children to write *tooooooo*, adding as many *o*s as they like. Tell them that *too* has too many *o*s. Do anything that will draw attention to what makes this word different from *to*. One of the keys to teaching homophones is to make children aware of them, so they stop and think which one to write and can proofread for them.

Tomorrow
Children often put *mm* instead of, or as well as, *rr*. Teach them that this used to be two words: *to* and *morrow*. *Morrow* was a noun, as in 'on the morrow'. If children think of *morrow* as a separate word, and write it as such, they are unlikely to prefix it with *tom*. The more children understand about a word's meanings and origins, the more likely they are to spell it correctly.

Because
This word is also best learned by looking at its history. It is a short form for *be the cause*. When they say *cause*, children are more likely to be guided by the pronunciation and less inclined to write *becos*.

Before
The challenge here is to get children to add the final *e*. Teach them the meaning of *in front of* or *ahead of*, and build this spelling pattern of compounds: *forehead, forecast, foreground, forefront, foremost, foremast*. Children can ask at home to find out the meaning and significance of shouting *'fore!'* It might come in handy in the classroom or playground.

Once Link this with other words with a connection to *one*: *unit, unify, unicorn, unicycle*. Its best partner is *only*. Children can use the mnemonic *only once*. (A mnemonic is a memory trigger. The word comes from Mnemosyne, the Greek goddess of memory and mother of the Muses. Older children will enjoy linking this with *amnesia*, in which they will be able to hear the silent *m*.) Reading and writing the word in stories starting 'Once upon a time ...' is also a good way to encourage children to use the word frequently.

Knew Children can first learn about the silent *k* by building a word tree or word wheel with these words: *know, knowledge, knowing, knowledgeable, unknown*. They can then link *knew* with this past-tense pattern: *know/knew; blow/blew; grow/grew*. Children can then have some fun by noting that *flow* and *flew* are not part of the same verb. Perhaps they can find more silly examples, like *crow* and *crew*. Noting the anomalies of spelling and playing with words adds interest and can also lead to learning.

Which This fits with a group of question words, all starting with *wh*. They are listed nicely in the Kipling poem:
>I keep six honest serving men.
>They taught me all I knew.
>Their names are Who and What and Why
>And When and Where and Who.

This is a good list of question words for children to keep beside them when they are doing research or conducting an interview. It could form a specialised prompt list for the classroom wall.

Sure/Sugar *Sure* and *sugar* are the only words in which an initial *s* is pronounced like *sh*. They form their own spelling pattern, along with derivatives like *surely, ensure* and *sugary*. Put the words on the board for a few days. Children can challenge their families to think of words in which an initial *s* sounds like *sh*. This will give children a chance to be the spelling experts at home. To give them practice in using the words, they could use a dictionary to find compounds and phrases using *sure* and *sugar*: *sugar beet, sugar cane, sugar-coated, sugar loaf, sugar-maple; sure-fire, sure-footed, for sure, sure enough, make sure*.

Enough	This belongs in two spelling patterns. Children can collect words in which *gh* sounds like *f*. If they know about words in which *ph* sounds like *f*, they will note that while *ph* can come at the beginning or at the end of a word, no word or even syllable starts with *gh*. They can also collect words that have the letter string *ough*, and list them according to their different pronunciations: *enough, tough, rough; cough, trough; bough, slough; dough, doughnut*.
Really	This word also can be looked at in two patterns. First, the *real* pattern: *realistic, realism, unreal, reality*. In many of these words, children will be able to hear both vowels and know with certainty what they are. It can also form part of a look at how to add the adverb ending *ly: nicely, quickly, wisely, coolly*. The usual patterns for adding endings apply: add the *ly* to the whole word, drop a final *e*, change *y* to *i*. An offshoot of this pattern is words ending in *ic*, to which we add *ally: electrically, politically*. Follow this up by looking at words ending in *ic* or *ick* and see if the children can work out what makes the two groups different. One spelling investigation often leads to another. Be prepared to be spontaneous and follow up any interesting or puzzling phenomena.
Girl/First/Birthday	Children often reverse letters to write *gril*. A vowel + *r* combination is difficult to sound out and can produce reversal errors in words like *park* and *first*. Beginning spellers often omit the vowel completely and need to learn that every syllable must have a vowel. Group together words with this '*r* controlled vowel' to form rhyming patterns. Find words ending in *ar, er, ir, or, ur*, and ask the children to add other letters at the end to make new words: *fir – firm, for – form, fir – first*.
Opened/Called/ Turned/Walked/ Followed	Look for words with similar prefixes, roots or suffixes, and group them together. These all belong in a past-tense verb pattern. Looking at past tenses will also generate a list of irregular past tenses which you can put on a reference list for the classroom.
Happy/Swimming	Many errors are caused by an inability to add endings to words correctly. Group these together and ask the children to categorise them according to the four ways to add endings (see pp.39–40).
They're/Don't/Didn't	Group contractions together and make sure the children can read them correctly. Practice in writing the complete words along with their contraction may reinforce this pattern.
Together	Children will be interested in seeing the three little words that make up this word. Often finding a word interesting is enough to help them to remember the spelling.
Children	Once children learn how to spell the sound of *ch*, this is not a difficult word. Until they learn it, they can put it on a prompt list.

Chapter 7

Getting spelling right

Demonstrating strategies

Children often link poor spelling with lack of intelligence. They can also see adults as being infallible.

It is extremely important for children to see their teachers using the same strategies as they do. Putting some 'deliberate mistakes' on a board or flip-chart can help to train them to spot errors.

Many teachers keep a dictionary handy on their desk to demonstrate the need for all of us to refer to particular words to check their spelling. It may take longer in the initial stages to help children to find a word that they wish to spell rather than writing it out for them, but in the longer term it helps them to develop independent strategies.

When does spelling count?

Children often ask this question when they are asked to write. Children need to know when they should have their spellings correct and when spelling should not be a primary focus of attention. When writing is to be read by another person, correct spelling is far more important than if the writing is for the writer's eyes only. Even when writing is for a public audience, a focus on spelling belongs at the editing stage, not during the composition of the first draft.

There are two questions any writer must ask before embarking on a piece of writing:

✔ What is it for?
✔ Who is it for?

Whether we are writing a shopping list or a party invitation, a story or a business letter, answering these two questions will let us know exactly what the task entails. The importance of spelling is directly linked to purpose and audience. The more we want to make a good impression, the more trouble we take with spelling and neatness.

If children focus on spelling at appropriate times in the writing process, they will be able to give it their undivided attention at the editing stage.

Strategies to link to the writing process

✔ Make sure that every writing activity in the classroom reinforces the writing process. (For specific teaching strategies, see *The Writing Teacher's Handbook*.)

✔ Provide many opportunities for children to write for audiences both inside and outside the classroom.

Proofreading

Proofreading is not an innate ability; it is a learned skill. It is quite different from reading a story or finding a name in a telephone book. Children need instruction in how to go about it and regular practice in proofreading their own and other people's writing. It is not enough to say, 'Read through your writing and see if you can find any spelling mistakes.' Many children, and adults, do not find their errors, even when they know how to spell the words.

When we teach children to read, we try as soon as possible to stop them finger-pointing and reading word by word, and instead teach them to absorb larger chunks of meaning. Fluent reading demands that the reader predicts what will come next and only looks at enough of the text to confirm these predictions. Most of the time we actually decode only parts of words and often skip over words completely. This is a strength in reading, as it increases speed and understanding. However, this kind of reading is not productive for proofreading.

Proofreading is not a skill of looking 'at'; it is more a skill of looking 'for'. If we know what we are looking for, we are much more likely to find it. (For proofreading checklists that children can use, see *Words at Work* and *Words at Work Teachers' Guides*.)

Strategies for teaching proofreading

✔ When children have had little experience, ask them to proofread for one concept only: capital letters at the beginning of sentences; speech marks when someone is talking on the page; two or three high-frequency words.

✔ Encourage children to point to each word as they proofread. This will slow down the reading and remind them to look at every word. It can also be helpful to move a finger or pencil down the left-hand margin, or move a ruler down line by line.

✔ Put a symbol in the margin against lines with a spelling error. Then ask the child to find the mistakes in those lines. You need not always mark every error; limit the task to the words and the amount you feel the child has the experience and knowledge to handle.

✔ Point to misspelled words and ask the child to find the error. 'You have left a letter out of this word. Can you put it back in?'

✔ Children can make their own lists of words that they have trouble spelling. They can use this as a reference for proofreading.

✔ Children can work together to proofread for each other. It is often easier to find someone else's mistakes, as you do not get so caught up in the meaning.

✔ Encourage children to proofread several times, looking for different kinds of errors each time. One read-through can be for punctuation, another for specific words, another for capital letters, and so on. Even professional proofreaders do not expect to find all the errors in one reading.

✔ Reading aloud is often helpful. When children stumble over the meaning, it can be a signal that something is wrong with the sentence, perhaps an omitted word or punctuation mark. When children cannot see that words have been omitted, it can be helpful for someone else to read their writing aloud to them.

✔ Help children to see words in their component parts: onsets, rimes, syllables, prefix, root, suffix. This can help them to proofread each part to make sure the spelling is correct.

✔ It is still important to read for meaning while proofreading. You cannot tell if a verb has the wrong ending, or if subject and verb do not agree, or if the punctuation is wrong, if you read each word as a separate entity.

✔ You can only expect children to proofread for words and spelling patterns they know. Make sure they get all the help they need to find and correct words they have not yet had a chance to learn.

✔ Remember that extensive proofreading is only purposeful when it is in preparation for a final draft. Laborious correcting can discourage children from writing. Little and often is a good rule for teaching the skill of proofreading.

✔ Sometimes children think that being a good writer means getting everything right the first time around. If they hold this belief, they may regard errors as a sign of weakness or inadequacy. Ask someone at your local newspaper or a publishing company to provide marked-up copy for the children to look at. Show them that everyone needs to proofread and make corrections, even the teacher.

Using a dictionary

For many children, a dictionary is not a friendly object. This may be because they cannot find the information they need quickly enough. It may be because looking up all their spelling mistakes takes too long and distracts them from more interesting aspects of writing.

A dictionary is such a basic tool for a writer that it is worth taking time to help children to make friends with their dictionary.

Strategies for teaching dictionary skills

✔ The basic dictionary skill is using alphabetical order. Anything that makes children familiar with using the alphabet is a dictionary skill. Alphabetise anything you can in the classroom: coat hooks, books, storage boxes, art equipment. The more often children find things using alphabetical order, the more it will become automatic for them.

✔ Teach children to distinguish among the different kinds of information in a dictionary: word, origin, derivations, definitions, examples. Sorting out the relevant piece of information and ignoring the rest is one of the skills of using a dictionary.

✔ Many dictionaries have more information than is necessary for spelling. When all you need is to find a spelling quickly, definitions, origins, examples and grammar tips get in the way and slow down the task. Direct the children to a Spelling Dictionary when all they need is to check a word.

✔ Keep a large-print dictionary, even for older children. Anything that makes finding a word quick and easy is helpful.

✔ Try to have a dictionary for each child. Then you can play dictionary games and give children daily practice in finding words.

✔ Any reference book that uses alphabetical order will teach children how to use a dictionary. Copies of your local Yellow Pages are often available free at the end of the year and will give you a resource for search games and puzzles. If you take two or three minutes a day and ask the children to find one or two pieces of information, dictionary searching will become a game and children will learn to find their way around a reference book quickly and easily.

✔ Gear the time children spend looking up their errors in a dictionary to the total time they spend writing. Using a dictionary should be a regular task, but should not become an overwhelming part of writing time.

✔ Be alert for the children who over-use a dictionary. If they try to look up too many words during the course of first-draft writing, they will find composition next to impossible. Encourage children to place a mark beside words they are not sure of, and to check them at the end of the writing time, or when the first draft is finished. A child who will not write without having all the correct spellings first is not a risk-taker. Direct this child to the have-a-go strategy (see p.17), and offer proofreading help at a later stage in the writing process.

✔ Make sure children do not see looking up their errors in a dictionary as some kind of punishment or penalty. You can make it a positive activity by keeping the task to a manageable size and by providing help when needed.

Chapter 8

Developing a spelling curriculum

The need to plan

A spelling curriculum tells a school and a teacher what to teach and how to teach it. Some objectives are mandated by government and society; others we plan according to the needs of the children and the subjects we teach. If we do not articulate the desired outcomes for education, we cannot effectively plan to make sure they are achieved.

The curriculum will act as a framework on which we can build our year's work. While the basic structure and content will be the same for everyone, each teacher can develop short- and long-term plans to integrate word-level work into the classroom programme.

You can base such a school curriculum on the three prerequisites for learning described earlier (see p.16):

- ✔ Purpose: why we bother to learn
- ✔ Information: what we need to know to be successful
- ✔ Practice: repetition to make skills automatic.

Objective	Implementation
Purpose Writing is the only purpose for learning to spell. It is fundamental to spelling instruction that its prime objective is to help children to construct words they need for their own writing. This presupposes that children will have writing that they want and need to do. Children should have many opportunities to set their own purposes for writing. Then they will need to learn about spelling to fulfil their own goals. There is nothing as motivating as self-interest. Writing gives spelling meaning. Meaning is what makes it possible to learn. It is also what makes it worthwhile to bother.	Establish a writers' workshop (see *The Writing Teacher's Handbook*) atmosphere in the classroom, in which children are encouraged to take risks, and not be penalised for making mistakes. Teach the drafting process, in which spelling has its own focus at the appropriate time. Make writing a part of every subject throughout the day. Engage children in the fun of playing with words and finding out about their history and origins. Words are interesting for their own sake and worthy of study. Children should look forward to and enjoy a spelling lesson.

Objective	Implementation
Information This is the content of the curriculum, the topics for our spelling lessons. Once we have decided on the significant patterns and concepts to teach, we can make a sequence for instruction. This will be just a general guideline, as spelling is not a sequential subject. However, it can be helpful for each teacher to have an idea of what children have learned before, and what can be left until later years. The list will also provide continuity throughout the child's school life. Each teacher can use the relevant list to plan spelling lessons for the year. The list can also become an assessment checklist for each child, a growing list of what each child knows and is able to do.	List spelling patterns that children need. Categorise the patterns according to sound, function, meaning and word-building. Sequence each category in order of difficulty and suggested sequence of teaching. Divide the list according to what will be taught each year. This will provide a scope-and-sequence chart that each teacher can use as a starting-point for planning. Be prepared to adapt the scope and sequence to the abilities of individual children. Use children's own writing to gauge where they fit and what level of instruction is appropriate.
Practice There are two kinds of practice that children need in order to become familiar with spelling patterns and adept at using them. – First, they need enough examples to be able to recognise a pattern, and enough repetitions of using it to be able to construct their own words as needed. – Second, they need to engage in many different kinds of writing on a daily basis, in order to make using the patterns automatic for them. This will bring them full circle back to writing as the major motivation for learning more about words and spellings.	Teach a concept using the four-step lesson plan. Provide practice exercises, to help children to become familiar with using the pattern for constructing words. Provide time daily for personal writing, at which time children write on topics and in modes and styles of their own choice. Plan for teacher-directed writing activities throughout the day. Through these, you can make sure children learn about and engage in many different kinds of writing for different purposes and audiences.

Lifelong learning

When these three conditions, purpose, information and practice, are present, children have their best chance of learning to spell. Not only that, they will see spelling as a tool for writing and a way of learning more about our language and how it can be used. This in turn will contribute to their growth as readers and writers.

A teaching methodology that focuses on pattern recognition and word-building will also give children problem-solving strategies that will enable them to continue their spelling learning throughout their lives. This lifelong learning is the most valuable outcome we can aim for in school.

Appendix: References

Words at Work by Jo Phenix (Folens, 1999)
Word-level and sentence-level work for excellence in spelling and grammar
- ✔ Textbooks for children ages 5–11
- ✔ Activities and games to give children practice in learning spelling patterns, building words, writing sentences, using punctuation, understanding grammar

Words at Work Teachers' Guides by Jo Phenix (Folens, 1999)
- ✔ Specific information about what children need to know about spelling
- ✔ Help in using the *Words at Work* pupil books
- ✔ Extra activities for class and home

The Spelling Teacher's Book of Lists by Jo Phenix (Pembroke Publishers/Drake Educational, Cardiff)
- ✔ Facts, examples, and over 140 lists of words illustrating spelling patterns
- ✔ Teaching suggestions

Spelling Instruction that Makes Sense by Jo Phenix and Doreen Scott Dunne (Pembroke Publishers/Drake Educational, Cardiff)
- ✔ The history and evolution of English spelling
- ✔ Interesting facts and trivia about words
- ✔ Spelling development observed through children's writing
- ✔ The Las Vegas Rules of Spelling – learn to play the odds
- ✔ Teaching strategies, games, puzzles, study skills
- ✔ Evaluation and record-keeping

Spelling for Parents by Jo Phenix and Doreen Scott Dunne (Piccadilly Press, 1994)
- ✔ A companion book to the above
- ✔ A help for parents to understand how we teach spelling through patterns

The Reading Teacher's Handbook by Jo Phenix (Folens, 2000)

The Writing Teacher's Handbook by Jo Phenix (Folens, 2000)